국제비즈니스 용어 사전

월드사이언스
worldscience.co.kr

국제비즈니스
용어 사전

월드사이언스
worldscience.co.kr

最新國際ビジネス 用語 辭典

Copyright © 株式會社 アイ・エス・エス
Originally published by WAVE出版

국제비즈니스 용어 사전

(The Dictionary of Newest International Business Terms)

| 인 쇄 | | 2013년 4월 1일 |
| 발 행 | | 2013년 4월 10일 |

원저자		주식회사 アイ・エス・エス
역 자		정혜진
발행인		박선진
발행처		도서출판 월드사이언스

주 소		서울특별시 서초구 방배4동 864-31 월드빌딩 1층
등록일자		1988년 2월 12일
등록번호		제 16-1601호
대표전화		(02) 581-5811~3
팩스		(02) 521-6418

| E-mail | | worldscience@hanmail.net |
| URL | | http://www.worldscience.co.kr |

| 정가 | | 20,000원 |
| ISBN | | 978-89-5881-214-2 |

이 도서의 국립중앙도서관 출판시도서목록(CIP)은 e-CIP홈페이지(http://seoji.nl.go.kr)와
국가자료공동목록시스템(http://www.nl.go.kr/kolisnet)에서 이용하실 수 있습니다.
(CIP제어번호: CIP2013001813)

「증보·개정판」 간행의 인사말

비즈니스 거래의 국제화는 멈출 줄을 모르며 자유화, 다양화에 따라 많은 새로운 상품이 생겨나고 거래방법도 나날이 새로워지고 있다.

따라서 비즈니스 분야의 전문용어도 대폭 증가하여 영어와 우리말 사이의 확인과 통일이 불가피한 상황에 이르렀다.

본 사전은 이러한 인식하에 기업의 최전선에서 일하는 국제비즈니스맨 여러분은 물론 변호사, 공인회계사, 세무사, 대학관계자, 통역사, 번역사 등을 위한 간편한 전문용어사전으로 편찬되었다.

본 사전은 편자가 오랫동안 통, 번역 업무에 종사하는 과정에서 축적한 영한 두 언어의 정보를 데이터베이스화하고 중요한 용어를 엄선하여 수록하였다. 그러나 새로운 용어는 매일같이 생겨나므로 본 사전의 출간 이후에도 신어의 정보는 끊임없이 축적되었다.

그리하여 이번 개정판에서는 중요한 부분을 개정함과 동시에 최신 인터넷용어를 수록하여 더욱 독자의 수요에 부응하고자 노력하였다.

마지막으로 인터넷용어의 수록은 미와 요시오(三輪芳夫) 씨와 나일 미나이 씨의 도움을 받았다. 이 자리를 빌려 깊이 감사를 드리는 바이다.

1999년 8월

편저자

목차

ENGLISH-KOREAN ·· 9

KOREAN-ENGLISH ·· 325

최신약어 ·· 615

계약용어 ·· 647

멀티미디어용어 ·· 659

인터넷용어 ·· 669

[범례]

Ⅰ (이 사전은 국제비즈니스 분야에서 날로 증가하는 새로운 전문용어에 중점을 두고 편집하였다. 또 영어에 대한 기초지식을 갖춘 이용자를 대상으로 하였으므로 일반적인 영한사전의 품조와 발음기호는 생략하였다.)

Ⅱ (용어의 배열은 영한의 경우에는 알파벳순으로 배열하고 복수를 나타내는 **s**, 또는 **es**는 무시하였다. 한영의 경우는 가나다순으로 배열하였다.)

Ⅲ (동일한 용어라 할지라도 사용방법이 다르면 두 종류의 번역어를 모두 게재하였다)

[ENGLISH-KOREAN]

영한편

ab initio 처음부터
abandonment of action 소송방기
abandonment of right 권리방기
abatement 감액
abbreviation 약어
ABC inventory management ABC재고관리
abide by 따르다; ~을 지키다
abiding conviction 결정적인 확신
ability 능력
ability to pay 지불능력
ability to pay basis 지불능력기준
ability to pay dividend 배당능력
ability to pay principle 응능원칙
abishering 벌금면제
abnormal growth model 이상성장모델
abnormal item 이상항목
abnormal returns 이상수익
abolition 폐지
above par 평가이상
above the line 표준 이상으로; 경상수지계산의
above the market strategy 고가격시장전략
abridged life table 간이생명표
abridgment 적요
abrogation 폐지
absence 부재
absence of demand 부재수요
absentee ownership 부재소유권
absolute 무조건의; 절대로
absolute advantage 절대우위
absolute beneficiary 변경불능보험금수취인
absolute conveyance 절대양도
absolute cost 절대원가

absolute delivery 무조건인도
absolute fixed capital 절대고정자본
absolute frequency 절대빈도
absolute income hypothesis 절대소득가설
absolute liability 결과책임
absolute profit 순익
absolute sales 무조건판매
absolute total loss 절대전손
absolute value 절대치
absolutism 절대주의
absorbed bond 완매채권
absorbed burden 배부필 제조간접비
absorbed corporation 흡수된 회사
absorbed cost 회수된 원가
absorption 완매; 흡수합병
absorption account 배부계정
absorption approach 총지출접근방법
absorption cost 전부원가
absorption costing 전부원가계산
abstention 회피
abstract 초본
abstract of account 발췌계산서
abstract of financial statements
    재무제표적요
abstract of register 초본
abstract of title 권리서
absurdity 불합리
abuse 남용
abuse of confidence 배신
abut 인접하다
accelerated benefits 전불(前仏) 전불사망
    보험금

accelerated depreciation 특별상각
accelerated method 가속법
acceleration 기한이익상실
acceleration claims 촉진클레임
acceleration clause
　변제기일을 앞당기는 약관
acceleration coefficient 가속도계수
acceleration of registration 등록을 앞당김
acceleration principle 가속도원리
acceptable price 지불가능가격
acceptance 승낙; 인수
acceptance commission 인수수수료
acceptance credit 인수조건부 신용공여
acceptance criteria 합격기준
acceptance line 인수한도
acceptance notice 인수통지
acceptance on security 담보부 인수
acceptance payable 지불어음
acceptance price of net assets
　순자산 인수액
acceptance process 수용과정
acceptance rate 수입어음결제상장
acceptance receivable 인수된 어음 수취어음
acceptance slip 인수슬립
acceptance system 인수방식
acceptance theory 권한수용설
accepting bank 어음인수은행
accepting house 어음인수상사
accepting rate of exchange 환인수율
acceptor 인수인
access 교환
access card 액세스카드
access charge 액세스차지
access point 액세스포인트
access to books 장부열람
access to counsel 변호사의뢰권
access to courts 재판을 받을 권리
access to market 마켓액세스
accessibility of store 접근용이성
accession 취득; 근접
accessorial service 부가서비스

accessories 부속품
accessory building 부속건물
accessory contract 부수계약
accessory obligation 부수채무
accessory product 부산물
accessory to tax evasion 탈세방조범
accessory use 부속용도
accident 사고
accident and health insurance
　상해건강 보험
accident and indemnity insurance
　상해보상보험
accident and sickness insurance
　상해질병보험
accident at work 취업중의 사고
accident compensation 재해보장
accident insurance 상해보험
Accident Offices' Association
　재해보험회사해외협회
accident prevention 방재
accidental cost 우발경비
accidental death benefit 사고사급부금
accidental grounding 우발적인 좌초
accomenda 적하매각위탁계약
accommodation 융통
accommodation area 특설서비스장소
accommodation bill 융통어음
accommodation lands 증가토지
accommodation line
　영업정책상 무리하게 맺은 계약
accommodation maker 융통어음발행인
accommodation works 편익공작물
accompanying document 첨부서류
accord 동의
accord and satisfaction 대물변제
accordance 일치
accordant 동의시킴; 일치하는; 조화된
accordion fold 주름지게 접기
account 계산서; 고객
account analysis 계정분석
account book 출납부

account chart 계정과목일람표
account closing procedure 결산수속
account current 당좌계정
account day 결산일
account debtor 외상채권채무자
account due from sales on approval
　시용판매미수금
account due on consignment-out
　위탁판매미수입금
account executive 광고기획자
account form 계정식
account form income statement
　계정식 손익계산서
account form profit and loss statement
　계정식 손익계산서
account headings 계정과목
account in arrears 잔업수당계정
account in transit 미달계정
account method 장부방식
account number 계정과목번호
account number plan 계정과목번호표시법
account of business 영업보고서
account of credit sales 외상계정
account of sales 매상계산서
account opener
　신규고객을 확보하기 위한 경품
account owed to employees
　종업원에 대한 채무
account paid 지불필 계정
account payable 외상채무
account planner 광고전략가
account receivable
　수취계정; 외상매출금; 미수금계정
account receivable discounted
　할인수취계정
account receivable due from affiliated
　company 관계회사외상매출금
account receivable insurance 외상보험
account receivable ledger 고객원장
account reconcilement 계정대조표
account record 보고서

account rendered 확정계정
account report service
　어카운트레포트 서비스
account sales 매상계산서
account stated 확정계정
account statement 계정서
account system 계정시스템
account title 계정과목
account transfer 계좌대체
accountability 책임
accountability unit 책임단위
accountable condition 회계사상
accountable officer 회계담당자
accountable person 책임자
accountable receipt 수령증
accountable warrant 회계워런트
accountancy 회계학
accountancy service 회계감사업무
accountant's inspection 회계감사
accountant's office 회계사사무소
accountant's responsibility 회계사책임
accountant 회계사
accountant in bankruptcy 파산청산인
accountant in charge 주임회계사
accountant liability policy
　회계사배상책임보험
accountant report 감사보고서
accountbook 장부
accountee 신용장발행의뢰인
accounting beta value 회계베타수치
accounting book 회계장부
accounting by month 월할계산
accounting control 회계관리
accounting convention 회계원칙
accounting data process 회계사무처리
accounting department 경리과
accounting division 회계과
accounting earnings 회계이익
accounting entity 회계실체
accounting evidence 회계증거
accounting firm 회계사무소

accounting for branch office 지점회계

accounting for business combinations
기업결합회계

accounting for changing prices
화폐가치변동회계

accounting for compensated absences
유급휴가회계

accounting for income tax allocation
세금배포회계

accounting for income taxes 세효과회계

accounting for internal reporting
내부보고회계

accounting for inventories 재고자산회계

accounting for leases 리스회계

accounting for pension plan 연금회계

accounting for price-level change
가격수준변동회계

accounting for tax allocation 세금배분회계

accounting function 회계직능

accounting identity 회계등식

accounting information system 회계조직

accounting manual 회계매뉴얼

accounting organization 회계조직

accounting period 사업연도

accounting period in case of merger
합병사업연도

accounting policy 회계방침

accounting postulate 회계공준

accounting practice 회계실무

accounting principle 회계원칙

Accounting Principles Board
회계원칙심의회

accounting principles for business enterprise
기업회계원칙

accounting procedures 회계절차

accounting profession 회계사업

accounting ratio of profits to net worth
회계자기자본이익률

accounting records 회계기록

accounting regulation 회계규정

accounting report 회계보고

Accounting Research Bulletin
회계연구공보

accounting rules 회계통칙

accounting section 회계과

Accounting Series Release 회계연속통첩

accounting sheet of collected amount
징수액계산서

accounting standards 회계기준

accounting system 회계제도

accounting terminology 회계용어

accounting transactions 회계거래

accounting treatment 회계처리

accounting unit 회계단위

accounting valuation 회계평가

accounting year 회계연도

accounts due 미수금

accounts of the Bank of Japan
일본은행계정

accounts receivable insurance
인수계정보험

accounts to receive 인수계정

accredit 신임장부호

accredited investor 적격투자가

accredited party 신용장발행의뢰인

accreditee 신용수령자

accrediting party 신용장개설자

accreting swap 원금증가형 스와프

accretion 재산증가

accrual 발생

accrual account 자연증식(이자)계정

accrual accounting 발생주의회계

accrual basis 발생주의

accrual item 자연증식계정

accrual of cause of action
소송원인이 발생함

accrual of discount 할인액기간 대응할부

accruals 미수지계정

accrued account 자연증식계정

accrued assets 자연증식자산

accrued basis 발생주의

accrued bonuses 상여수당금

accrued charge 미불비용
accrued commission 미불수수료
accrued depreciation 감가상각발생액
accrued dividend 미불배당액
accrued donation 미불기부금
accrued employees retirement benefit
　퇴직급여준비금
accrued expenses payable 미불비용
accrued income 미수이익
accrued income taxes 미불수입세
accrued interest 경과이자
accrued interest on loan 대부미수이자
accrued liabilities 미불금
accrued payroll 미불급여
accrued premium 계상보험료
accrued rent 미수임차금
accrued revenue 미수이익
accrued salaries 미수급료
accrued severance indemnities
　퇴직급여예비금
accrued taxes on income 납세예비금
accrued wages 미불공임
accruing costs 추가비용
acculturation 문화적응
accumulated investment 누적투자
accumulated amount 누적액
accumulated assets 적립자산
accumulated benefit obligation 누적급부채무
accumulated depreciation 감가상각누적액
accumulated dividend 누적배당
accumulated dividend deposit 배당예탁
accumulated earning tax 유보수익률
accumulated earnings 이익잉여금
accumulated fund 적립금
accumulated income 누적이익
accumulated preferred stock
　누적배당우선주식
accumulated surplus 이익잉여금
accumulation 누적
accumulation clause 보상액누증약관
accumulation of capital 자본축적

accumulation process 집적과정
accumulation system
　어큐뮬레이션 방식 누적시스템
accumulation trust
　수익을 원본에 편입하는 형태의 투자신탁
accumulations 이자적립
accumulative 누적적인
accumulative investment period
　누적투자기간
accumulative investment plan
　누적투자플랜
accumulative investment unit 누적투자유니트
accumulative judgment 누적판결
accumulative risk 누적위험
accumulative stock 누적배당형 주식
accusation 고발
accusatory body 기소결정기관
accusatory instrument 기소서류
accusatory part 기소부분
accused 피고인
accuser 기소자
achievement 업적
achievement level 달성수준
achieving need 달성동기
acid ratio 당좌비율
acid test ratio 산성시험비율
acknowledgement of declaration 보험인수증
acknowledgment 승인
acknowledgment of order 응낙
acquest 취득재산
acquiescence 묵인
acquired needs 후천적인 수요
acquired right 기득권
acquired surplus 취득잉여금
acquirement of properties 자산취득
acquisition 취득
acquisition agent 계약모집대리점
acquisition commission 계약모집수수료
acquisition cost 계약모집비
acquisition cost adjustment 취득원가조정
acquisition cost method 취득원가법

acquisition cost of depreciable assets
　감가상각자산취득가액
acquisition cost of inventory
　재고자산취득가액
acquisition cost of leasehold　차지권취득원가
acquisition cost of securities
　유가증권취득가액
acquisition cost price　조달가격
acquisition for value　유상취득
acquisition of concessions　이권획득
acquisition of debenture　사채취득
acquisition of right　권리수록
acquisition of stock　주식취득
acquisition of the application right
　출원권 취득
acquisition value　취득가격
acquisitive prescription　취득시효
acquittal　채무면제
acquittance　채무완제
acreage　지적
across the board
　모든 종류를 포함하는; 일괄의
act　행위; 제정법
act of bankruptcy　파산행위
act of God　불가항력
act of grace　은사법(恩赦法)
act of honor　참가인수
act of incorporation　설립법
act of indemnity　면책법
act of insolvency　지불불능행위
act of law　법의 행위
act of parliament　국회제정법
act of sale　매매기록
act of state　국가의 행위
act of stealing　절도행위
act of war　전쟁행위
act tax　행위세
action　상장의 움직임
action for accounting　계산소송
action for damages　손해배상청구소송
action in personam　대인소송

action in rem　대물소송
action of detinue　동산인도청구소송
action program　액션프로그램
action quasi in rem　준대물소송
actionable fraud　사기
actionable negligence　기소할 수 있는 과실
actionable words　명예훼손이 될 만한 표시
active account　활동계정
active bond　이자부채권
active bond management　적극적인 운용
active buying　적극적인 매입
active conduct of business　사업활동
active dealer　적극적인 딜러
active debt　채권
active employee　현재종업원
active investment management theory
　적극투자이론
active life fund　현직자기금
active management　적극적인 운용
active market　호황시장
active method　액티브방식
active portfolio　액티브포트폴리오
active return　액티브리턴
active risk　액티브리스크
active risk aversion　액티브리스크 회피도
active stock　인기주
active trust　적극신탁
activity accounting　활동회계
activity analysis　업무분석
activity rates　활동율
actual acquisition cost basis
　실제취득원가주의
actual annual percentage rate　실질연리
actual assets　실가자산
actual basis　발생주의
actual basis accounting　실제주의회계
actual burden rate　실제배부율
actual cash value　현금환가가치
actual cost　실제원가
actual cost accounting system
　실제원가계산제도

actual costing 실제원가계산
actual deaths 실제사망수
actual delivery 현물수도
actual delivery of stock sold 현물인도
actual demand rule 실수원칙
actual expenses 실비
actual instruction 실효명령
actual inventory 실지재고
actual life 실제내용연수
actual loss 실제손해
actual market 현재시장
actual position 액추얼포지션
actual price 실제가격
actual product 실제제품
actual production 생산실적
actual purchase price 실제구입가액
actual quantity of mining 실제채굴량
actual rate of growth 현실성장율
actual receipt of stock purchased 현실거래
actual results of recent stock transactions
    주식거래실적
actual return on plan assets
    연금자산실제운용수익
actual total loss 현실전손
actual trading behavior 실제거래행위
actual transfer price 실제양도가액
actual useful life 실제내용연수
actual value 실가
actual value method 실가법
actually expected standard cost
    현실표준원가
actuals 원자산
actuarial contribution 수리보험료
actuarial cost method 연금수리비용계산방식
actuarial expectation 보험수리상의 기대치
actuarial gains or losses 수리손익
actuarial hours 평균실제노동시간
actuarial mathematics 액추얼수학
actuarial method 연금이회법
actuarial relationship 액추얼관계
Actuarial Society of America 미국액추얼협회

actuarial soundness 보험수리건전성
actuary 보험계리인; 액추어리
ad damnum 손해배상청구문서
ad hoc 임시의
ad hoc arbitration 개별중재
ad interim 임시의
ad litem 소송을 위한
ad opus (…의) 때문에
ad valorem storage 종가보관료
ad valorem tariff 종가세율
ad valorem tax 종가세
adaptation level 적응수준
adaptive behavior 적응행동
adaptive planning and control sequence
    신상품 마케팅모델
adaptive product 시장적응제품
adaptive strategy 적응전략
add-back method 가감법
added discount 추가할인
added value 부가가치
addenda 추가문서
adding to holdings 추가소유
addition 부가
addition to reserve 준비금이월
addition to retained earnings
    이익잉여금으로 대체함
additional amount to a refund of national tax
    국세환부가산액
additional arrearage charge 연체가산금
additional benefit 부가급부
additional budget 보정예산
additional call 추가분담금
additional capital 증가자본
additional charge 추가비용
additional charge for deficient return
    과소신고가산금
additional charges 운송료할증
additional collateral 증가담보
additional conditions 추가조항
additional depreciation deduction 할증상각
additional establishment 추가설정

additional expenses 추가비용
additional expenses clause 추가비용약관
additional extended coverage endorsement
　확장담보이서
additional freight 할증운임
additional interest 추가이해관계자
additional investment 추가출자
additional issue 추가설정
additional living expense insurance
　임시생계비보험
additional margin 추가이익
additional markup 추가가격인상
additional paid-in capital 추가 자본준비금
additional premium 추가보험료
additional security 추가보증
additional tax 가산세
additional tax due to failure to file a return
　무신고가산세
additional tax for deficient returns
　과소신고가산세
additional tax on nonpayment 불납부가산세
additions and omissions 추가 및 생략
additions to plant and equipment
　설비신규구입액
additions to reserves 적립금편입
additions to tax 부대세
additive substruction 가법감산
add-on charge 추가요금
add-on markup 추가마크업
add-on rate 애드온금리
add-on system 애드온방식
addressee 수신인
adduce 인증하다; 제시하다
adequate 상당한
adequate liquidity 적정유동성
adequate protection 충분한 보호
adjacent 인근의
adjacent experience 인접경험
adjective law 절차법
adjoining 근접의
adjourned sale 발매연기

adjournment 연기
adjudge 사법적인 판단을 내리다
adjudication 재판
adjudication of bankruptcy 파산선고
adjudication order 파산명령
adjunct account 부가계정
adjuration 서약
adjust 조정하다
adjustable basket technique
　비대칭바스켓방식
adjustable fire policy 조정화재보험증권
adjustable life policy 조정가능생명보험
adjustable peg system 조정가능고정상장
adjustable policy 조정보험
adjustable rate 변동이율
adjustable rate mortgage 변동금리모기지
adjustable rate mortgage loan
　조정금리저당론
adjustable rate preferred stock
　변동이율우선주
adjusted 조정필
adjusted basis 수정기초액
adjusted beta value 수정베타수치
adjusted capital gain 조정후 양도소득
adjusted central bank money stock
　조정후 중앙은행통화스톡
adjusted death rate 증정사망율
adjusted debit balance 신용거래융자잔고
adjusted dividend increase
　조정후 배당증가율
adjusted gross income 수정총소득
adjusted historical cost 수정취득원가
adjusted income 조정소득금액
adjusted net profit 수정후 순이익
adjusted premium 조정보험료
adjusted regression analysis 수정회귀분석
adjusted to seasonal variations
　계절변동조정필
adjusted trial balance 정리후 시산표
adjuster 손해사정인
adjusting entry 수정기입

adjusting journal entry 수정분개
adjustment 손해사정
adjustment account 조회계정
adjustment at term-end 기말정리
adjustment bond 정리사채
adjustment bureau 손해사정국
adjustment costs 손해사정비
adjustment entry 정리기입
adjustment for price fluctuations
　가격변동수정
adjustment for taxable income 세무조정
adjustment in filing a Final tax return
　신고조정
adjustment in settling accounts 결산조정
adjustment inflation 조정인플레이션
adjustment item 조정항목
adjustment of accounts 장부정리
adjustment of business income 기업이익조정
adjustment of capital 자본수정
adjustment of cost variance 원가차액조정
adjustment of debts 채무조정
adjustment of supply to demand 수급조정
adjustment of surplus 잉여금조정
adjustment of the carrying amount 부가수정
adjustment premium 조정보험료
adjustment process of balance of payments
　국제수지조정과정
adjustment securities 조정증권
admeasurement 배분
administered price 관리가격
administered-price inflation 관리가격
　인플레이션
administration 사무관리
administration estate 유산관리
administration in bankruptcy 파산관리
administration of insurance contract
　계약보전
administration suit 유산관리소송
administrative 행정입법
administrative accounting 관리회계
administrative act 행정행위

administrative and maintenance expenses
　유지관리비용
administrative appellate law 행정불복심사법
administrative audit 관리감사
administrative discretion 행정재량
administrative disposition 행정처분
administrative dispute 행정쟁소
administrative expense 일반관리비
administrative expenses budget
　일반관리비예산
administrative expenses variance
　일반관리비예산
administrative fit 관리적합
administrative guidance 행정지도
administrative interpretation 행정해석
administrative law 행정법
administrative litigation 행정소송
administrative officer 행정직원
administrative order 행정명령
administrative power 행정권
administrative protest 불복신청
administrative reform 행정개혁
administrative remedy 행정구제
administrative review 불복심사
administrative uncertainty 관리상의 불확실성
administrator 관재인
administrator cum testamento annexo
　유언부 유산관리인
administrator de bonis non 후임유산관리인
administrator in bankruptcy 파산관재인
administrator of bequest 유산관리인
administrator of tax payment 납세관리인
admiralty bond 해사사건보증증권
admiralty court 해사재판소
admissible 마땅히 허용해야 하는
admission 보석허가명령
admission tax law 입장세법
admissions 입장자수
admitted assets 허용자산
admonition 훈계; 권고
adopted concept 차용개념

adoption curve 채용곡선
adoption model 채용모델
adoption order 양자결정
adoption process 채용단계
adoptive act 임의법
adoptive provisions 임의규정
adult 성년자
adulteration 조악화
advance 대부금
advance account 대부계정
advance by customers 고객전수금
advance call 전불분담금
advance collection 사전징수
advance demand 사전청구
advance dividend 사전계약자배당
advance for purchase 구매대전도금
advance freight 선불운임
advance from controlled companies
  자회사선수금
advance funding method 사전적립방식
advance made for purchase of material
  원료구입대전도금
advance made on contract 계약전도금
advance made to salesmen 판매원전도금
advance money 입체금
advance of salary 급료선불
advance on a promissory note 어음대부
advance on account of sellers 구입선불대금
advance on consignment-in 수탁판매입체금
advance on construction 건설공사전도금
advance on indent 매부위탁입체금
advance on subscription 신청증거금
advance payment 선금
advance payment bond 선불금반환보증증권
advance premium 선납보험료
advance preservative seizure 이월보전차압
advance pricing agreement 사전가격확인제도
advance received 선수금
advance received on contract 계약선수금
advance received on indents 수탁매부전도금
advance received profit 선수수익

advance refunding 사전조달
advance salary 선불급여
advance sale 선매
advance seizure 사전차압
advance to subcontractor 하청선불금
advance to vendor 거래처선불금
advance wages 전불임금
advanced accounting 상급회계학
advanced collection on sale contracts
  매매계약선수금
advanced countries 선진국
advanced depreciation 압축기록
advanced depreciation deduction 압축손
advanced depreciation limit 압축한도액
advanced money 전도금
advanced processed 고도가공품
advanced redemption 사전상환
advanced television 고도화텔레비전
advance-decline line 등락선
advancement barrier 진입장벽
advances received on consignment out
  적송품선수금
adventure 모험
adversary party 상대방당사자
adversary proceeding 대심수속
adversary system 당사자과실책임제도
adverse claim 이의신청
adverse effects 악영향
adverse element 마이너스요인
adverse financial selection 금융상의 역선택
adverse interest 상대이익
adverse opinion 부정적인 의견
adverse physical conditions claims
  지하조건클레임
adverse possession 취득시효
adverse selection 역선택
advertised price 광고표시가격
advertisement 광고
advertisement agency 광고대리점
advertisement exposure 광고노출
advertisement for bid 입찰공고

advertisement media 광고매체
advertisement mix 광고활동을 통합함
advertisement source 광고소스
advertisement tax 광고세
advertisement theme 광고주제
advertising sales ratio 광고비비율
advertising allowance 광고지원금
advertising and general publicity expenses 광고선전비
advertising appeals 광고소구
advertising appropriation 광고예산
advertising budgeting 광고예산편성
advertising campaign 광고캠페인
advertising copy 광고원고
advertising criticism 광고비판
advertising decision 광고결정
advertising differentiation 광고차별화
advertising effect 광고효과
advertising evaluation 광고평가
advertising expenses 광고비
advertising fantasy 광고의 환상
advertising group 광고집단
advertising media 광고매체
advertising message 광고메시지
advertising network 광고대리점망
advertising objectives 광고목표
advertising opportunity 광고기회
advertising psychology 광고심리학
advertising regulation 광고규제
advertising research 광고조사
advertising society 광고사회
advertising specialty 애드버타이징스페셜티
advertising strategy 광고전략
advertising technology 광고기술
advertising testing 광고효과테스트
advertising theme 광고주제
advertising unexpired 미경과광고료
advice of credit 입금통지
advice of shipment 선적통과
advice of subrogation 대위통지서
advice slip 통지전표

advising bank 통지은행
advisory 조언적
advisory committee 자문위원회
advisory opinion 조언의견
advisory organization 요율자문기관
advisory rates 권고요율
advisory service 투자고문업
advisory tax board 세무자문위원회
advocacy advertisement
   애드보커시광고; 자기를 옹호하는 광고
advocate 변호사; 옹호자
Advocate General 법무관
aerial transport 항공수송
affairs 업무
affect 영향을 주다
affection 담보설정
affectional drives 감정적인 동기
affectivity 감성
affidatio 충성선서
affidavit 선서공술서
affiliate 관계자
affiliated company 관계회사
affiliated family corporations 동족관계회사
affiliated financial institute 계열금융기관
affiliated loan 제휴론
affiliated middleman 가맹중간업자
affiliated store 가맹점
affiliation 계열화
affine transformation 어필변환
affirmance 시인
affirmant 확약증언자
affirmation 확약
affirmation of fact 사실확인
affirmative 긍정적인
affirmative charge 긍정표시
affirmative covenants 긍정적인 약인
affirmative defense 적극적인 항변
affirmative statute 명령적인 법률
affix 서명하다
affluent economy 윤택한 경제
affordable growth 여유 있는 성장

affranchise 개방하다
affreightment 해상운송계약
affreightment contract 해상대물운송계약
afiency fund 대리인자금
African Development Bank
　아프리카개발은행
Afro-Asian Common Market
　아시아아프리카공동시장
after cost 후비용
after effective tax 실효세공제후
after image lag 잔상
after loss 애프터로스
after market 신규발행 후 시장
after maturity endorsement 만기 후 이서
after recording 애프터리코딩
after tax 세금공제 후
after tax profit rate 세금공제 후 이익률
after-acquired clause 사후취득조항
after-acquired property 사후취득재산
afternoon session 후장
after-session undertone 공제후의 상황
aftershock 여진
after-tax income 세금공제 후 이익
after-tax yield 세금공제 후 이익
against all risks 전위험담보
against the will 뜻에 반하여
age at entry 가입연령
age at expiry 만기 시 연령
age distribution 연령분포
age limit 연령제한
age of discretion 분별연수
age of retirement 퇴직연령
age of vessel 선박
age setback 연령의 후퇴조정
aged account 연체보험료
aged dependent 노인공양친족
aged person 노령자
agency 대리점
agency account receivable 대리점대여
agency accounts 대리점계정
agency activity 대리점활동

agency agreement 대리점계약자
agency backed securities
　정부기관증권담보증권
agency bookkeeping 대리인부기
agency commission 대리점수수료
agency contract 대리점계약
agency cost 대리점경비
agency department 외무부
agency fee 대리점수수료
agency filing 회원사의 대리요율신청
agency ledger 대리점원장
agency loan 대리대부
agency market 에이전시마켓
agency network 광고대리점망
agency note 정부기관채
agency system 대리점제도
agency theory 에이전시이론
agency to receive tax 수납기관
agency transaction 위탁거래
agency work 보험모집활동
agenda 협의사항
agent 대리인
agent account 대리점계정
agent bank 대행은행
agent commission 대리수수료
agent development era 외무원개발시대
aggravation 가중사유
aggregate 총계
aggregate active risk 총액티브리스크
aggregate average 총평균
aggregate corporation 사단법인
aggregate face amount 액면통액
aggregate gross margin 조이익총계
aggregate liability index
　총인수액누적조사카드
aggregate limit 총보상한도액
aggregate managed portfolio
　총운용 포트폴리오
aggregate market value 시가총액
aggregate net sales 순매상고총계
aggregate normal 총 노말 포트폴리오

aggregate of depreciation deduction
　감가상각비누계

aggregate response curve 총반응곡선

aggregate supply 총공급량

aggregate supply function 총공급함수

aggregate table 종합표

aggregate theory 집합이론

aggregated shipment 일괄운송

aggregatio mentium 의사일치

aggregation 합산

aggregation of income amount 소득금액합산

aggregation of profit and loss 손익통산

aggregation problem 집계의 문제

aggressive investment 공격적인 투자

aggressive portfolio 적극적인 운용

aggressive securities 공격적인 증권

aggressively held up 다소 높은 유도

aggrieved party 불복당사자

aging 노화; 숙성

agio 프리미엄; 환전

agrarium 지조; 토지수익에 부과하는 조세

agreed case 합의사건

agreed insured value 협정보험가액

agreed interest rate 약정금리

agreed statement of facts 합의사실진술서

agreed value 보험평가액

agreed yield to maturity 약정만기이익

agreement 계약; 약정

agreement among underwriters
　인수업자간계약

agreement for overdraft 당좌이월약정서

agreement jurisdictional court
　합의관할재판소

Agreement of the International Bank for
　Reconstruction and Development
　국제개발부흥은행협정

Agreement of the International Monetary
　Fund 국제통화기금협정

agribusiness 기업농업

agricultural adjustment act 농업조정법

agricultural bank 농업은행

agricultural bookkeeping 농업부기

agricultural credit 농업금융

agricultural goods markets 농산물시장

agricultural income 농업소득

agricultural insurance 농업보험

agricultural lien 농업선취특권

agricultural machinery and equipment floater
　농기구포괄보험

agricultural machinery insurance
　농업기계보험

agricultural production corporation
　농업생산법인

agricultural society 농업조합

Ahlers model 어레즈주가모델

aid 상납금

aid and abet 범행을 방조하다

aid and comfort 도움

aid bond 보조공채

aid prayer 원조청원

aid societies 공제조합

aids 원조금

ailing 업적부진의

air carrier 항공화물운송업자

air fare 항공요금

air right 상공권

air transport insurance 항공운송보험

air transportation 공수

air waybill 항공화물운송장

air-borne cargo insurance 항공운송보험

aircraft financial responsibility act
　항공기배상자력법

aircraft hull insurance 항공기체보험

aircraft liability insurance 항공기책임보험

aircraft passenger insurance 항공상해보험

aircraft third party liability insurance
　항공책임보험

airport owner's or operator's liability
　insurance 공항관리자 배상책임보험

airway 항공로

airway freight 항공운임

alba firma 백지대

alcohol bond 주정보증증권
alcoholic beverage 주류
aleatory contract 사행계약
ale-silver 주류판매세
alias 별명
alien 외국인
alien corporation 외국법인
alien insurer 외국보험회사
alien juris 타주권자
alien property 외국인재산
alien tax 입국세
alien taxpayer 외국인납세자
alienable 이전가능한
alienation 이전
alienation clause 양도무효조항
alienator 양도인
alienee 양수인
alieni juris 사람의 감독하에 있는
alignment 일렬; 정렬; 배열
alimony und separate maintenance payment
　부조료 및 별거수당
all amounts invested in capital 총출자금액
all and singular 예외없이 모두
all buyers 모든 소비자
all gone 품절
all issued stocks 발행필 주식총수
All Japan Fire & Marine Insurance Agency
　Association (일본)전국손해보험대리업협회
all lines insurance 생손보상호보험
all lines insurer 전보험종목인수회사
all lines organization 전보험종목인수기구
all purpose card 범용카드
all risks clause 올리스크담보약관
all risks coverage 올리스크담보
all risks dwelling house insurance
　주택종합보험
all risks insurance 올리스크담보보험
all sold 품절
all status endorsement 전미담보특약
all totaled 총계로
allegation 주장

allege 주장하다
allegiance 충성의무
alleging diminution 기록결손주장
allergist 알러지전문의
alliance 동맹
allied company 동맹회사
allied line cover 계열위험담보계약
allied line risks 계열위험
allied members 증권거래소 준회원
all-inclusive basis 포괄주의
all-inclusive income concept
　포괄주의이익개념
all-inclusive income statement
　포괄손익계산서
allocated benefit 표정급부
allocated funding instrument 할당적립방식
allocating function 배분기능
allocation and execution of budget
　예산배부와 집행
allocation by market potential
　시장잠재능력별 할당
allocation of cost 원가배당
allocation of new shares to a third party
　제3자 할당
allocation on bases 배분기준
allocatur 비용사정증
alloction procedure 배부절차
allodial 자유보유토지의
allodium 사유지
allograph 대필; 대서
all-or-none order 일괄매매주문
allot 분할하다
allotment 증권할당
allotment certificate 할당증
allotment ledger 할당예산원장
allotment letter 할당서
allotment note 선원급료수취지도서
allotment of sharps 주식할당
allotment system 토지배분제도
allotment to shareholders 주주할당
allotment warden 배분지관리인

allotted amount in constructing public facility
　공공시설건설부담액
allow 허용하다
allowable limit for depreciation amount
　상각한도액
allowable maximum amount 허용한도액
allowance 협정손해율; 준비금
allowance for bad debt 대손예비금
allowance for bad loan 대손준비금
allowance for dependent 부양공제
allowance for depreciation 감가상각예비금
allowance for dismissal without notice in
　advance 해고수당
allowance for doubtful accounts
　대손 준비금
allowance for old person 노령자공제
allowance for promotion of employment
　취직촉진수당
allowance for spouse 배우자공제
allowance for uncollectable accounts
　대손예비금
allowance for undistributed profits
　유보공제액
allowance for widow 미망인공제
allowance for working student 근로학생공제
allowance in kind 현물지급
allowed amortizable limit 상각한도액
allowed cost 허용원가
allowed depreciation 상각범위
allowed limit of accumulation 적립한도액
allowed retirement income deduction
　퇴직소득공제
allowlince for repairs 수선수당금
all-purpose 만능의
all-purpose financial statement
　다목적대무재표
all-time high 신고치
alms 의손금
alongside delivery 자가배달; 자가인도
alpha value 알파수치
alphabet fund 알파벳펀드

already-issued bond 이미 발행한 채권
alter ego doctrine 분신이론
alteration 변조
alteration bordereau 변경비망록
alteration of species 성질이 상실됨
alternate preference beneficiaries
　순차우선수취인
alternate product 대체제품
alternation 교체
alternative accounting principles
　대체회계원칙
alternative contract 선택계약
alternative costs 대체비용
alternative duties 선택세
alternative health care delivery system
　대체의료서비스공급시스템
alternative mixes 대체믹스
alternative obligation 선택채무
alternative order 선택주문
alternative plan 대체안
alternative price change 대체가격변동
alternative pricing 선택형 가격결정
alternative remedy 선택적인 구제
alternative sources 대체구입처
alternative withholding tax on dividends
　배당원천선택과세
alternatives 대체안
altogether 통계로
altruistic 이타주의
always open basis 상시유효
amalgamation 합병
amalgamation on an equal basis 대등합병
amalgamation procedures 합병절차
amalgamation surplus 합병잉여금
ambience 분위기
ambient light 빛 주위의 밝기
ambiguity 모호; 불명료함
ambit 권한범위
ambulatory 변경할 수 있는
amelioration 개선
amend 수정하다

amended budget 수정예산
amended return 수정신고
amendment 수정
amendment of articles of corporation
  정관변경
amendment to a contract 계약내용수정
amercement 벌금
American Academy of Actuaries
  미국액추어리협회
American Accounting Association
  미국회계학회
American Annuitants Mortality Table
  미국연금가입자사망표
American Arbitration Association
  미국중재협회
American Association of Medical Social
  Workers 미국의료사회사업자협회
American Association of Social Workers
  미국사회사업가협회
American Bar Association 미국법조협회
American Bar Endowment 미국법조기금
American clause 중복보험의 순위주의약
American Council of Life Insurance
  미국생명보험협회
American Depositary Receipts 미국예탁증권
American Federation of Labor
  미국노동총동맹
American Institute Cargo Clauses
  미국협회화물약관
American Institute of Accountants
  미국회계사협회
American Institute of Certified Public
  Accountants 미국공인회계사협회
American Institute of Marine Underwriters
  미국해상보험업자협회
American Intellectual Property Law
  Association 미국지적소유권법협회
American Judicature Socidty 미국사법협회
American Law Institute 미국법률협회
American Life Insurance Association
  미국생명보험협회

American Management Association
  미국경영자협회
American Mutual Insurance Alliance
  미국상호보험회사협회
American National Standards Institute
  미국규격협회
American option 미국형 옵션
American Risk and Insurance Association
  미국보험학회
American Standards Code for Information
  Interchange
  아스키; 미국정보교환표준코드
American Stock Exchange 미국증권거래소
American type 미국형
Americus Trust 아메리카트러스트
Amex Commodity Echange
  아메리카증권거래소
AMEX Index 아메리카증권거래소 주가지수
amicable action 우호적인 소송
amicus curiae 법정조언자
Amnesty International 국제사면위원회
amortization 채무상환; 정액상각
amortization cost 상각비용
amortization fund 부채상각준비금
amortization loan 분할반제형 대부
amortization of bond premium
  사채발행차금상각
amortization of deferred assets 이월자산상각
amortization of goodwill 영업권상각
amortization of initial expenses 창업비상각
amortization of intangibles 무형자산감가상각
amortization of prior service cost
  과거근로채무의 상각액
amortization of taxes 세금환원
amortization schedule 채무상환계획
amortize 상각하다
amortized balance 미상각잔고
amortized cost 상각원가
amortizing diffusion model 절대확산모델
amortizing swap 약정반제부 스와프
amotion 박탈

amount added to capital 증자
amount advanced 대부금액
amount assessed 평가액
amount billed 청구액
amount carried forward 차기이월고
amount claimed 청구액
amount covered 보험금액
amount deducted 공제액
amount due 만기지불고
amount financed 대출액
amount imposed 부과액
amount in arrears 미불금
amount in hand 현재수량, 재고
amount insured 보험금액
amount invested 출자액
amount issued 발행고
amount of annuity certain 확정연금종가
amount of claim 구상액
amount of clearing 어음교환고
amount of the first payment 초회금
amount on hand 현재고
amount on hand goods in stock
　재고; 현재의 수량
amount outstanding 잔고
amount overbought 과잉구매고
amount oversold 과잉매출고
amount paid 지불고
amount paid out lo the outside distribution of
　net profit 이익처분에 따른 사외 유출액
amount paid per new stock paid per new
　stock 신주1주당 불입가액
amount receivable 수취금
amount received 수입금액
amount subscribed 응모금액
amount withhold 원천징수
amoveas manus 재산반환영장
amplitude 음량
amusement 오락설비
amusement and restaurant tax 유흥음식세
amusement expenses 접대비
anagraph 기록

analog method 아날로그방식
analog to digital conversion
　아날로그를 디지털로 변환함
analogy 유사
analysis 분석
analysis of budget variance 예산차이분석
analysis of cost variances 원가차이분석
analysis of credit 신용분석
analysis of lender's preference
　대출자의 우선권 분석
analysis of problem 문제해석
analysis of routes 루트분석
analysis of securities 증권분석
analysis of the affairs of a business
　경영 분석
analyst 분석가
analytic system 위험비율분석방식
analytical data 분석데이터
analytical forecast 분석적 예측
analytical jurisprudence 분석법학
analytical model 분석모델
analytical tools 분석수단
anamnesis 기왕증, 병력
anchorage 정박세
ancient lights 채광권
ancient rent 임료
ancient watercourse 고대수로
ancient writing 고문서
ancients 고참변호사
ancillary 보조의
ancillary attachment 가차압
ancillary bill or suit 부수소송
ancillary product 보조제품
Andean Common Market 안데스공동시장
angle of view 사각
anglers' insurance 낚시보험
Anicrican Association of University Teachers
　of Insurance 미국보험교수연맹
animal insurance 동물보험
animus et factum 의사와 행위
animus furandi 절도의사

animus manendi 영주의사
animus revocandi 철회의사
annates 초년도수익
annex 부속서류
annexation 병합
annexed letter 부속서류
annexed structure 부속설비
annire 소환
anniversary date 계약해당일
annotation 주석
announcement 공시
announcement effect 고지효과
annoyance 골칫거리; 곤란한 것(사람)
annual accounting 연차결산
annual audit 연도감사
annual audited financial statement
　　감사필 연차재무보고서
annual basis 연환산
annual bonus agreement 임시급여협정
annual closing 연도마감
annual club due 연회비
annual compounding 유럽식 복리이율
annual coupon 연불쿠폰
annual dues 연회비
annual earnings 연간소득
annual economic review 경제연보
annual expenditure 세출
annual financial statements 연차재무제표
annual income 연간수입
annual installment 연간할부
annual interest rate 연이율
annual meeting 연차총회
annual member 연회원
annual payment 연 1회후불
annual payment budget facilities
　　연간할부방식
annual percentage rate 연율의 퍼센테이지
annual premium adjustment 보험료조정정산
annual profit disposition amount
　　연간이익처분액
annual rate of returns 연수익률

annual report 연차보고서
annual revenue 세입
annuitant 연금수취인
annuity 확정연금
annuity bond 원리균등불채
annuity certain 확정연금
annuity certain due 기시불연금
annuity consideration 연금의 대가
annuity insurance 연금보험
annuity purchase rates 연금구입요율
annuity refund 상환식 연금
annuity repayment method 원리균등상환방식
annuity unit 연금유닛
annul 취소하다
annulment 무효화
annulment of a contract 계약해제
annulment right 취소권
anomaly 변칙; 편차
anony mous association 익명조합
another debt 기존채무
answering time 응답시간
antedated 전일부
antedated check 전일부수표
antenna shop 안테나숍
ante-nuptial 혼인전의
anthropological jurisprudence
　　문화인류학법학
anticipated acceptance 만기전 인수
anticipated cost 예상원가
anticipated profit 예상수익
anticipation 기한전 처분
anticipation discount 기한전 지불할인
anticipation of falling market 염가예상
anticipation of low interest rate 저금리예상
anticipatory breach of contract
　　기한 전의 계약위반
anticipatory demand 가수요
anti-dilution clause 희박화 방지조항
anti-dumping code 안티덤핑코드
anti-monopoly law 독점금지법
anti-positivism 반실증주의

antiqua statuta 구법률
antique customa 구관세
antique customs 구관습세
anti-rebate law 리베이트금지법
antiselection 역선택
antithetic variable 대칭변수
anti-trust acts 독점금지법
apartment dwellers' comprehensive insurance
   단지보험
aperture grille 애퍼처그릴
aperture grille pitch 애퍼처그릴피치
apology 사죄
apparatus 기기
apparel industry 어패럴산업
apparent 명백한; 외견의
apparent agency 표면상의 대리
apparent danger 명백한 위험
apparent easement 명시지역권
apparent heir 법정추정상속인
appeal 공소
appeal bond 상허보증증권
appeal of felony 중죄소추
appeal power 소구력
appeals 국세심판관
appear 법정에 출두하다
appearance 응소
appellant 상소인
appellate court 상소법원
appellate jurisdiction 상소관할
appellee 피상소인
appendix 첨부서류
appetite 흥미
appliance 설비
applicable 적용할 수 있는
applicable law 준거법
applicable statutory useful life 적용법
applicable useful life 적용법정내용연수
applicant 신청인
application 채무변제충당; 보험계약자의 사실
   고지; 신청요항
application for approval 승인신청

application form for stock 주신신청서
application ion for listing 상장신청서
application money 신청금
application money for stock 주식신청금
application of funds statement 자금운용표
application of working capital
   운전자금을 적용함
application program 응용프로그램
application rate of overhead cost
   간접비할부율
application right 출원권
application to list 상장신청서
applied cost 적용원가
applied manufacturing expenses account
   제조간접비배부계정
applied research 응용조사
appointed day 기일
appointed goods 지정상품
appointee 피임명자
appointing authority 중재인선정기관
appointment 지정
appointment of depreciation 상각비배부
appointment sales 어포인트상법
appointor 지정권자
apportion 분할
apportionable part 보험가액할당가능부분
apportioned tax 배부세
apportionment 분할(계약의)
apportionment of cost variance
   원가차액 조정
apportionment of loss 손해분담
apportionment valuation 보험가액할당
appraisal 감정
appraisal loss 평가손
appraisal method 평가법
appraisal of assets 자산감정
appraisal profit 평가익
appraisal profit or loss 평가손익
appraisal report 감정서
appraisal rights of shareholder
   주식매취청구권

appraisal securities 유가증권평가
appraisal standard 평가기준
appraisal surplus 재평가적립금
appraisal system 업적평가제도
appraisal value 평가액
appraised price 산정가격
appraisement 재산평가
appraisement method of securities
　유가증권평가방법
appraiser 평가인
appreciated market price 시가상승
appreciation 등귀
appreciation duty 증가세
appreciation surplus 재평가잉여금
appreciation swap 어프리시에이션스와프
apprehension 체포
approach 수법
appropriate 계상하다
appropriate cash supply for economic growth
　성장통화
appropriated earned surplus
　처분필 이익잉여금
appropriation 공용징수
appropriation account 이익처분계정
appropriation of profit 이익처분
appropriation of refund 환부금충당
appropriation section 이익처분부문
appropriation surplus 목적적립금
approval 승인
approval of special liquidation
　특별청산 승인
approval sales 시용판매
approved bidder 지정입찰자
approved investment 투자승인리스트
approved pension contract
　적격퇴직연금 계약
approved pension funds 적격퇴직연금적립금
approved person 승인임원
approved retirement annuity 적격퇴직연금
approved society 인가조합
approved superannuation fund 적격퇴직연금

approved tender 지정입찰
approvement 개량지수익
approximate cost 개산원가
approximate market price 시가개산액
approximate price 개산가격
approximate value 개산가격
appurtenance 재산에 부속하는 권리
appurtenant 타물부속
apt time 적기
aptitude test 적성검사
aquatic rights 용수권
aquisition opportunity 매수기회
aquit 면소를 언도하다
Arab League 아랍연맹
Arab Maghreb Union 아랍마그레브연합
arbiter 중재인
arbitrage 중재; 재정거래; 차익매매
arbitrage business 재정거래
arbitrage house 중재소
arbitrage margin 재정마진
arbitrage operation 재정거래
arbitrage opportunity 재정기회
arbitrage position 재정포지션
arbitrage trader 중재업자
arbitrage transaction 재정거래
arbitrageur 재정거래자
arbitral tribunal 중재판정부
arbitrament 중재판단
arbitrament and award 중재판단항변
arbitrate pricing theory 재정가격결정이론
arbitrated rate of exchange 재정환율
arbitration 중재
arbitration clause 중재조건
arbitration Commission 중재조정위원회
arbitration of exchange 환재정
arbitration proceeding 중재절차
arbitrator 중재인
architect's liability policy 건축가배상책임
　보험
archives 공문서
area of normal curve 정규곡선의 범위

area of welcome enterprise 기업유치지역
area polluted with soot and smoke
　대기오염지구
area selection 지역선정
arena 입회장
arguendo 가령 ~라 해도
argument 변론
arithmetic average 산술평균
arithmetic dividend yield average
　단순평균이율
arithmetic stock price average 단순평균주가
arm's length price 독립기업간가격
arm's length principle 독립기업원칙
armchair theory 탁상공론
arpentator 토지측량자
arranged total loss 협정전손
arrangement 채무정리
arranger 알선인
arrearage 연체금
arrears 체납
arrears coupon 연체금거치쿠폰
arrears of local tax 지방세연체금
arrears swap 어리어스와프
arrest of inquest 배심심문저지신청
arrest of judgment 판결저지
arrestment 저지
arrival 착선
arrival draft 도착후 일람불어음
arrival of shipment 착하
arrived damaged value 총손품가액
art director 아트디렉터
article 조항
article in custody 보관품
article of confederation 연합규약
article of the peace 안전보증신청
article on the free list 관세면제품
article subject to taxation 과세품
articled clerk 실무수습생
articles 정관
articles of agreement 계약각서
articles of association 통상정관

articles of confederation 연합규약
articles of impeachment 탄핵조항
articles of incorporation 회사정관
articles of partnership 조합정관
articles of union 연합개조(箇条)
artificer 명의
artificial 법
artificial environment 인공환경
artificial intelligence 인공지능
artificial life 인공생명
artificial person 법인
artificial presumptions 법률적인 추정
artificial statement 다행식 시산서
artificially 전문적으로
as at ~일 현재
as spent project cost 지불한 프로젝트비용
ascendants 직계존속
ascending 상승
ascending curve 상승커브
ascending tops 어센딩톱스
Asia Pacific Economic Cooperation
　아시아태평양경제협력회의
Asian Clearing Union 아시아결제동맹
Asian Currency Unit 아시아통화단위
Asian Development Bank 아시아개발은행
Asian Development Fund 아시아개발기금
Asian dollar bond 아시아달러채
Asian Insurance Commissioners Association
　아시아보험감독관협회
Asian Monetary Unit 아시아통화단위
Asian Payment Union 아시아지불동맹
Asian Reinsurance Pool 아시아재보험
Asian Reserve Bank 아시아준비은행
Asian-dollar market 아시아달러시장
asked rate 매호치
aspect ratio translation 편평비변환
aspiration 원망 열망
aspiration level 요구수준
aspirin theory 아스피린이론
assart 삼림개척
assay office 순분검정소

assecurator 보험자
assemble editing 어셈블편집
assemblv order sheet 조립순위표
assembly cost system 조립원가계산
assembly department 조립부문
assembly industry 조립공업
assembly order 조립명령서
assembly process 조립공정
assembly production order 조립명령서
assembly service 집하서비스
assent 수락
assertory covenant 확인약속
assess 견적하다
assessable income 과세소득
assessed amount 사정액
assessed income 사정소득액
assessed tax 과세금
assessed valuation 평가가치
assessed value 사정가액
assessing organ 사정기관
assessment 세액사정액
assessment and collection 부과징수
assessment and decision 부과결정
assessment insurance 부과식 보험
assessment mutual association
　부과식 상호보험조합
assessment of income tax 신고소득세
assessment of market timing 시장타이밍평가
assessment plan 부과식 보험
assessment rate of collateral 담보물건의 가격
　보다 낮게 평가할 때의 비율
assessment roll 과세원부
assessment system accumulation
　부과식 적립제
assessor 감정인; 평가인
assessor cadere 소송이 각하될 만한
asset accounting 자산회계
asset acquisition 자산매입
asset allocation technique 자산분배법
asset and liability management
　자산부채종합관리

asset approach 어셋어프로치
asset backed securities 자산담보증권
asset base swap 어셋베이스스와프
asset class target 어셋클래스타겟
asset coverage 자산담보율
asset income 자산소득
asset out of books 장부외자산
asset pool segment 자산세그먼트
asset position 자산상태
asset preference 자산선호
asset reserves 자산준비금
asset reshuffling 자산이체
asset revaluation 자산재평가
asset revaluation tax 자산재평가세
asset sales 자산매각
asset settlement 자산결제
asset swap transaction 어셋스와프거래
asset turnover ratio 자산회전율
asset utilization 자산활용
asset valuation reserve 자산평가준비금
asset value 자산가치
asset-pass-through certificate
　어셋패스스루증권
assets 자산
assets and equities 자산과 지분
assets differentials 자산격차
assets effect 자산효과
assets money 자산화폐
assets not admitted 비공인자산
assets producing interest 운용자산
assets revaluation law 자산재평가법
assets share method 자산할당방법
assets subject to lien 담보차입자산
assets turnover 자산회전율
asset-utilization ratios 자산활용율
asseveration 엄숙한 선언
assign 양도하다
assigned accounts 양도채권
assigned counsel 국선변호인
assigned risk plans 불량물건할당계획
assigned surplus 특별적립잉여금

assignee 수탁자
assignment 양도
assignment and transfer 양도 및 이전
assignment clause 양도조건
assignment fee 양도수수료
assignment in blank 백지양도
assignment of business 영업권양도
assignment of claim 채권양도
assignment of responsibility 책임할당
assignment of sales contract
　매매계약상의 양도
assignment of stock 주식양도
assignor 양도자
assigns 양수인
assimilation theory 동화이론
assistance 원조
assistant certified public accountant
　회계사보조
assisted acquisition 구제합병방식
assize of mort d'ancestor
　상속부동산점유회복소송
associate 연합시키다
Associated Aviation Underwriters
　항공보험협회
associated gas 부수가스(천연가스의)
associated person 특수관계인
association 협회
association behavior 단체행동
Association Cambiste Internationale
　상공회의소
association captive 자가보험취급기관
association group insurance 협회단체보험
Association of Average Adjusters
　해손정산인보험
Association of Casualty and Surety
　Companies 재해 및 보증보험회사협회
Association of Insurance and Financial
　Analysts 보험재무분석가협회
Association of South-East Asian Nations
　동남아시아국가연합
association test 연상테스트

assoile 사면하다
assorting 분류
assortment 상품구성
assortment breadth 상품구색폭
assortment structure 상품구색구조
assortment utility 상품구색효용
assume 인계
assumed bond 보증사채
assumed liability 인계부채
assumed rate of interest 예정이율
assumed settling day 가결산일
assumption 채무인수
assumption of risk 위험부담인수
assumption reinsurance 계약이전재보험
assumptions 가정
assurance 보험
assured 피보험자
at cost 원가로
at issue 쟁점에 달한
at low ebb 몹시 차가와지다
at par 액면대로
at risk 앳리스크
at sight bill 일람불어음
at sight buying rate 일람불어음매입률
at sight buying rate with credit
　신용장부 일람불어음매입률
at the close of the market 종장무렵
at the market 시장동향
at-home nursing service 재택간호서비스
at-market 앳마켓
atomic power plant construction reserve
　원자력발전공사상각준비금
attached document 첨부서류
attached goods 차압물건
attachment 차압
attachment of privilege 소환절차
attainder 사권박탈
attained age 현재연령
attendance 입회
attendant term 연기임차권
attest 증명하다

attestation 진정한 증명
attestation clause 증명문서
attestation witness 본드증서의 증인
attested copy 인증등본
attested witness 증명증인
attitude change 태도변용
attitude change research 태도용이조사
attitude measurement 태도측정
attitude study 태도연구
attitude survey 태도조사
attorney 변호사
attorney at law 변호사
Attorney General 법무장관
attornment 토지양도승인
attraction of factory 공장유치
attractive nuisance 유인적인 방해물
attractive trading opportunity 절호의 매장
attributable income principle 귀속주의
attribute 속성
attribute listing 속성열거법
attribution 직권
attribution analysis 요인분석
attrition rate 감소율
auction 경쟁매장
auction market 경매시장
auction sale 경매
auction system 옥션시스템
auctioneer 경매인
audience analysis 시청자분석
audio-visual display 시청각기기
audio-visual education 시청각교육
audit 감사
audit adjustment 감사결정
audit after the contract 계약체결후 감사
audit and criminal investigation 세무조사
audit certificate 감사증명
audit corporation 감사법인
audit fee 감사보수
audit frequency 감사빈도
audit objective 감사목적
audit on bank account 은행조사

audit on property 재산조사
audit opinion 감사의견
audit policy 감사결정에 따른 보험계약
audit premium 감사결제보험료차액
audit procedure 감사절차
audit program 감사계획
audit report 감사보고서
audit year 감사연도
auditee 피감사자
auditing 회계감사
auditing organization 감사기관
auditing standards 감사기준
auditor's opinion 감사인의 의견
auditor 감사역
augmentation 수입증가
augmentation of earnings 수익증가
augmented product 확장제품
austere budget 긴축예산
austere fiscal policy 긴축재정
Australian National Bond
   오스트레일리아국채
authentic 진정한
authentic act 인증행위
authentication 인증
authorities 당국
authority 권한
authority bond 공사공단채
authority of correction or determination
   개정이나 결정을 담당하는 관청
authority to inquire and inspect 질문검사권
authority to purchase 어음매입수권서
authorization 승인
authorization by law 법률위임
authorization number 승인번호
authorization test 확인테스트
authorize 권한을 수여하다
authorized capital 수권자본
authorized dealer 공인딜러; 지정판매점
authorized deferred payment 연납
authorized foreign exchange bank
   외국환공인은행

authorized insurer 면허보험자
authorized investment list 투자허가리스트
authorized shares 수권주식
auto sales 자동차판매대수
auto tax 자동차세
automated clearinghouse 자동결제기구
automated customer account transfer
  자동고객계정대체
automated reservation service
  자동예약서비스
automated teller machine 자동예금수납기
automatic approval system 자동인가방식
automatic call distributor
  외선전화집중접수부
automatic collection service
  자동집금(集金)서비스
automatic fund transfer 계좌자동대체
automatic increase in tax revenue 자연증수
automatic increased value clause
  자동가치증가보험약관
automatic increasing annuity 자동증액연금
automatic markdown 자동치하락
automatic premium loan 보험료자동대체대부
automatic reinstatement clause
  보험금액자동복원조항
automatic renewal system 자동계속제도
automatic renewal time deposit
  자동계속정기예금
automatic settlement 자동결제
automatic stay 자동정지
automatic transfer account 자동대체계좌
automatic transfer service 자동대체서비스
automaticity 자동성
automobile acquisition tax 자동차취득세
Automobile Association 자동차연맹
automobile bodily injury liability insurance
  대인배상보험
automobile comprehensive liability policy
  자동차포괄손해배상책임보험
automobile drivers' liability insurance 자동차
  운전자 손해배상책임보험; 드라이버보험

automobile insurance 자동차보험
**Automobile Insurance Rating Association of
  Japan** (일본)자동차보험요율산정회
automobile liability insurance
  자동차손해배상책임보험
automobile liability insurance certificate
  자동차손해배상책임보험증명서
**automobile passengers' personal accident
  insurance** 탑승자상해보험
automobile physical damage insurance
  차량보향
**automobile property damage liability
  insurance** 대물배상보험
automobile repair costs index
  자동차수리비지수
automobile sales finance 자동차판매금융
automobile tax 자동차세
automobile tonnage tax 자동차중량세
autonomic decision 자주결정
autonomous investment 독립투자
autonomous item 자발적 항목
autonomous tariff 자주관세
autonomously strong 자율반등
autonomy 자율성
autoregressive model 자기회귀모델
autre action pendant 소송계속의 항변
auxiliary 보조의; 부(副)의
auxiliary book 보조부
auxiliary journal 보조장부
auxiliary ledger 보조원장
availability 이용도
availability clause 가능성 조항
availability of bank 은행의 어베이러빌러티
availability risk 어베이러빌러티리스크
available 환금성이 높은
available assets 이용가능자산
available bond 이용가능채권
available profit 가처분이익
avails 수익
average 비례증보
average absolute deviation 평균절대편차

average adjuster 해손정산인
average balance outstanding 평균발행잔고
average bond 공동해손맹약서
average claim 분손손해
average collection 평균회수기간
average collection period 매상채권회수기간
average condition 비례보상조항
average contracted rates on loans and
　discounts 대출약정평균금리
average cost 평균원가
average cost method 평균원가법
average cost of claims 평균손해가액
average current cost method 평균시가법
average earnings 평균수익
average future lifetime 평균여명
average growth rate 평균신장률
average income 평균소득
average index monthly earnings
　평균표준보수월액
average interest rate cap 평균금리캡
average inventory 평균재고
average life 평균잔존연수
average loss settlement 분손계산
average markup percentage 평균이익가산율
average maturity of debts 평균부채기간
average period of production 평균생산기간
average policy 비례보상계약
average premium 평균보험료

average premium system 평균보험료방식
average rate 평균요율
average rate of dividend 평균배당률
average return on investment 평균투자수익
average risk 표준체
average tax rate 평균세율
average taxation 평균과세
average term to maturity 평균상환연한
average unless general 공동해손이 아닌 해손
average volatility 평균변동율
average warranty 분손약관
average yield 평균이율
averaged type forward contract
　애버리지타입 선물환 예약
averaging 애버리징
averaging clause 비례보상조항
aviation cargo insurance 항공운송보험
aviation fuel tax 항공기 연료세
aviation hull insurance 항공기체보험
Aviation Insurance Offices' Association
　항공보험회사협회
avoidable cost 회피가능원가
avoidable risk 배제가능리스크
avoidance of recurrence 재발방지
avoidance of sections 과제폐지
avowry 정당점유신청
avulsion 갑작스럽게 떼어놓음
award 재정

BA rate BA 레이트
Babbage's Table 바베지의 생명표
baby bond 소액채권
baby fund 베이비펀드
back away 후퇴하다
back bond 손실보상증서
back dating 실제보다 전날일자로 하다
back dividend 파급불배당금
back door listing 정규가 아닌 상장
back money 연체금
back office 백오피스; 배후부문; 비영업부문
back pay 파급급여
back rent 체납임차금
back spread 시중은행의 할인율상회
back tax 체납세
back to back credit 동일개설신용장
back-door selling 정규가 아닌 판매
back-end load 이연판매수수료
back-end rights 백엔드라이트
back-haul allowance 상품거래할인
back-to-back loan 백투백론
back-up facility 백업퍼실리티
back-up inventory 예비재고
back-up merchandise 예비상품
backbond 처분제한증서
background information 배경사항
backing 이서
backlighting 역광
backlog of orders 주문잔액
backup line 백업라인
backward channel 후방유통경로

backward countries 후진국
backward difference 후방차이근사치
backward integration 후방통합
backward needs 과거의 수요
backward vertical integration 후방수직통합
backwardation 수도연기금; 연전
bad 부적법한
bad account 대손계정
bad debt 불량채권
bad debt loss 대손금
bad debt provision 대손준비금
bad debt ratio 불량 채권율
bad debt reserve 대손준비금
bad debt written-off 대손상각
bad delivery 불완전인도
bad faith 악의
bad loan 대손
bad member 불량회원
bad news 악재료
bad risk 불량물건
bad standing 하자가 없는 자격
badger 행상인
bail 보석금
bail bond 보석보증증권
bail-piece 보석계약서
bailbond 보석보증
bailee 수탁자
bailee clause 수탁자약관
bailees' customers floater
　　　　수탁자고객포괄보험
bailees' liability policy 수탁자배상책임보험

bailment 수탁
bailor 수탁자
bailout 구제조치
bait advertising 미끼광고
bait ad 미끼광고
bait pricing 미끼광고
balance account 잔고계정
balance at the bank 은행예금잔고
balance book 잔고장
balance due 부족액
balance form 잔고식
balance in hand 생계잔고
balance of accounts 수지계정
balance of clearing 결제수지
balance of current account 경상계정수지
balance of international indebtedness
　국제대차
balance of international payments 국제수지
balance of loans 융자잔고
balance of monetary movements 금융계정
balance of payments statistics 국제수지통계
balance of stock loans 차주(借主)잔고
balance of the amount charged to special
　account 특별계정잔고
balance of trade 무역수지
balance on current account 경상수지계정
balance on invisible trade 무역외수지
balance on ledger 원장잔고
balance on nonmonetary transactions
　비금융적 거래수지
balance order 주금불입명령
balance renewal 론갱신
balance sheet 대차대조표
balance sheet analysis 대차대조표분석
balance sheet reserve system annuity
　적립방식연금
balanced budget 균형예산
balanced budget theorem 균형예산정리
balanced finance 균형재정
balanced form 계정식
balanced fund 밸런스펀드

balanced fund portfolio
　밸런스 펀드 포트폴리오
balanced growth 균형성장
balanced manager 밸런스형 매니저
balanced power 균형세력
balanced stock 균형재고
balances 잔채
ballast 바닥짐(배의)
balloon payment 차입잔고를 일괄 지불함
ban 공고
ban call 밴콜
band and crawl 밴드 앤드 크롤
band wagon effect 밴드 왜건 효과
bandwidth compression 대역압축
banishment 추방
bank account 은행계좌
bank act 은행법
bank balance 은행예금잔고
bank bill 은행어음
bank bookkeeping 은행부기
bank check 은행수표
bank clearing 어음교환결제
bank credit card 은행계신용카드
bank crisis 은행공황
bank dealer 은행딜러
bank debenture 금융채
bank deposit 은행예금
bank discount method 은행할인방법
bank discount rate 은행할인료
bank examination 은행검사
Bank for International Settlements
　국제결제은행
bank full dealing 은행풀딜링
bank guarantee 은행보증
bank holding company 은행주주회사
bank holiday 은행휴업일
bank interest 은행이자
bank line 뱅크라인
bank liquidity 은행유동성
bank loan-deposit ratio 예대율
bank loans 단기차입금

bank loans payable 은행차입금
bank loans secured by mortgage
　담보를 통한 은행차입
bank note 은행권
bank of issue 발권은행
Bank of Japan Act 일본은행법
Bank of Japan credit 일은신용
Bank of Japan note issue tax
　일본은행권발행세
bank point-of-sales 은행 POS
bank rate 은행이율
bank reference 은행조회
bank reserve 은행준비
bank's automatic accounts transfer system
　은행자동납부시스템
banker's acceptances 은행인수어음
banker's blanket bond 은행포괄보증
banker's credit 은행신용장
bankers forgery bond 은행위조보증증권
banking accounts of all banks 전국은행계정
banking business 은행업무
banking day 은행거래일
banking facilities 금융기관
banking principle 은행주의
banking syndicate 은행단
banking transaction contract 은행거래약정서
bankrupt 파산자
bankrupt law 파산법
bankrupt's estate 파산재단
bankruptcy 파산
bankruptcy administrator 파산관재인
bankruptcy and composition 화의
bankruptcy court 파산법원
bankruptcy debtor 파산채무자
bankruptcy law 파산법
bankruptcy notice 파산고지
bankruptcy proceedings 파산절차
bankruptcy rules 파산규칙
bankwire 뱅크와이어
bar 소송
bar association 법조협회

bar chart 막대그래프
bare body 드러난 본문
bare trustee 수동적인 수탁자
bargain 매매
bargain counter
　본래의 가격을 밑돌다가 매각된 증권
bargain purchase option 염가구입권
bargain stock 할인주
bargainee 사는 쪽
bargaining agreement 노동협약
bargaining cost 계약비용
bargaining power 교섭력
bargainor 파는 쪽
barometer stock 표준주
barratry 소송교사
barrier free 배리어프리
barrier trade 무역장벽
barriers to entry 진입장벽
barter 물물교환
base case 규범사례
base cost estimate 기초비용견적
base courts 하급법원
base currency 기준통화
base date for assessment 부과기일
base earnings 기초수익
base free 제한부동산권
base money 베이스머니
base of taxation 과세표준
base pay 기본급
base period 기준기간
base premium 기준보험료
base price 기준가격
base rate 기준레이트
base series 기준계열
base standard cost 기준표준원가
base year 기준연도
base-stock method 기준재고법
basement merchandise 특매상품
basic allowance 기초공제
basic assortment 기본요구구성
basic automobile policy 일반자동차보험

basic balance 기초수지
basic deduction 기초공제
basic deduction for bequest
　유산에 관계된 기초공제
basic discount rate 기준할인레이트
basic exemption 기초공제
basic period 기본기간
basic rate 기준상장; 기본요율
basic retirement funds 기초퇴직연금기금
basic salary 기본급
basic service 기본서비스
basic stockholder 판정의 기초가 되는 주주
basic taxable year 기준연도
basing-point pricing 기점가격제
basis 베이시스
basis for conclusions 결론의 근거
basis for recording sales 매상계산기준
basis gap 베이시스 갭
basis of calculation 계산기초
basis on the amount of salary 급여기준
basis point 1/100퍼센트
basis risk 베이시스 리스크
basis swap 베이시스 스와프
basis to prorate local tax 분할기준
basis trading 베이시스거래
basket 바스켓
basket purchase 일괄구입
basket system 바스켓방식
Basel Agreement 바젤협정
batch file 일괄파일
batch processing 묶음처리(자료)
batch production 연속생산
batch trading system 배치거래시스템
battle of the brands 브랜드경쟁
bear 낳다
bear bond 베어본드
bear call spread 베어콜스프레드
bear hug 베어허그(강한 포옹)
bear index bond 베어인덱스채
bear market 하락시세
bear raiding 시장을 어지럽히다

bear spread trading 베어 스프레드거래
bear the market 마구 팔기
bear-squeeze 금융규제
bearer 지참인
bearer bond 무기명채권
Bearer Depositary Receipts 무기명예탁증권
bearer form 무기명식
bearer instrument 지참인지불식 증권
bearer share 무기명주식
bearing date 일정 기일이 있는
bearish 약세의; 내림시세의
bearish channel 약한 채널
bearish consolidation patterns
　약세 콘솔리데이션 패턴
bearish market 약세시장
bearish resistance line 약세저항선
bearish reversal patterns 하락전환패턴
bearish sentiment 약세의 감정(정서)
bearish support line 약세지지선
bearish tone 약세시세
become due 기한이 오다
before due endorsement 만기전이서
before tax 세금포함
beggar-my-neighbor policy 근린궁지화 정책
beginning balance 기초잔고
beginning day of the taxable year
　사업연도개시일
beginning inventories 기초재고자산
beginning of period 기초(期初)
behavior approach 행동적인 어프로치
behavior criteria 행동기준
behavior science 행동과학
behavior-primacy theory 행동우선이론
behavioral modification 행동수정
behavioral theory 행동이론
belated claims 청구지체손해
bell and whistle 증권의 특권
bell-shaped curve 벨형 곡선
bellwether issue 지표상표
belly up 무가치증권
belongings 재산

below cost 원가이하로
below par 액면이하; 평가이하
below the market 벨로우 더 마켓
below-cost sale 원가이하판매
benchmark 표준
benchmark portfolio 벤치마크포트폴리오
benchmark rate 표준가격권
benchmark securities 지표증권
bending 곡손
beneficial association 상호부조단체
beneficial duty 편익관세
beneficial interest 수익권
beneficial owner 실질소유자
beneficiary 신탁수익자; 보험금수취인
beneficiary certificate 수익증권
beneficiary company 수익기업
beneficiary of the retirement annuity
　　퇴직연금수취인
beneficiary right 수익권
beneficiary securities 수익증권
benefit 급부
benefit association 공제단체
benefit formula 연금급부액산정방식
benefit of insurance clause
　　보험이익향수(享受)약관
benefit principle 응익부담원칙
benefit segmentation 효익세분화
benefit society 공제조합
benefit taxation 부조료과세
benefits for survivor 유족급부금
benevolent association 상호부조조합
benign failure 고장영향완화
benting 밑진 손해
bequest 동산유증
besoin 예비지불인
best evidence 최량증거
best-efforts basis 최선노력원칙
best-efforts selling 위탁판매
beta 베타
beta coefficient 베타계수
beta value 베타수치

betterment 개선
betterment expense 개장비(改裝費)
bid 입찰; 매긴 값
bid and offer 호가
bid ask spread 매매치 폭
bid bond 입찰보증증권
bid by advertising 경쟁 입찰
bid price 판매가; 입찰가격
bid rate 매수율
bid-offer spread 호가 스프레드
bidder 입찰자
bidding 입찰
bidding for public offering 공모입찰
bidding up 값을 끌어올림
Big Bang 대폭발
Big Board 뉴욕증권거래소
big jump 대폭 반등
big push in the downward move 하락촉진
big shareholder 대주주
big ticket merchandise 고가상품
bilateral contract 쌍무계약
bilateral monopoly 쌍방독점
bilateral trade 쌍무무역
bilateral trade agreement 상호무역협정
bilged 선저침수
bill 청구서; 법안
bill accepted 인수필 환어음
bill bearer 어음소지자
bill bought 환매입
bill broker 어음브로커
bill buying and selling rate 어음매매레이트
bill buying system 어음매입제도
bill clearing 어음교환
bill collection 외상매출금회수
bill discounted account 할인어음계정
bill drawn for sale 매출어음
bill for foreclosure 권리상실소장
bill foreign currency 외화어음
bill in domestic currency 방화어음
bill obligatory 강제채무증서
bill of advocation 재심리신청서

bill of certiorari 이송영장청구소장
bill of complain 소장
bill of credit 채무증권
bill of debt 채무증서
bill of exceptions 항소취의서
bill of exchange 수출어음
bill of lading 선하증권
bill of mortality 사망기록
bill of others 타행인수
bill of particulars 청구명세서
bill of quantities 수량표
bill of rights 권리장전
bill of sale 양도담보증서
bill pass 빌패스
bill payable 지불어음
bill payable at a fixed date 확정일지불어음
bill payable to bearer 지참인지불어음
bill payable to order 지정인지불어음
bill receivable 수금환; 역환
bill sent 발송송금환
bill sold 환매출
bill-book 어음계정
bills bought 환매입
bimetallism 복본위제
binary file 바이너리파일
binder 각서
binding 구속력이 있는
binding clause 구속조항
binomial coefficient 이항계수
binomial expansion 이항전개
binomial model 이항분포모델
bio computer 바이오컴퓨터
biorhythm 바이오리듬
birth rate 출산율
bit guarantee insurance 입찰보증보험
bit-ask spread 매매폭
black box 블랙박스
black box au box auction 블랙박스옥션
black check 납치방지
black knight 블랙나이트
black market 암시장

black market dealing 암딜링
Black Monday 블랙먼데이
"black out" period 공백기간
Black-Scholes model
　블랙숄즈 모형(옵션 이론의 한 가지)
blacklist 블랙리스트
blank 백지어서
blank acceptance 백지인수
blank book 미기입장부
blank endorsement 백지이서
blank stock 백지주식
blanket bond 포괄저당권부 채권
blanket brand 통일상표
blanket clause 포괄조항
blanket mortgage 포괄저당권
blanket order 일괄주문
blanket policy 포괄보험계약
blanket pricing agreement 포괄 가격 계약
blanket system 포괄담보설정방식
blazing a trail 신기원을 열다
blind 익명의
blind advertisement 익명광고
blind bidding 익명입찰
blind check 표본검사
blind pool 위임기업동맹
blind test 피시험자가 내용을 모르고 실시하는
　화학검사
bloc economy 블록경제
block copy
　블록카피; 제판에 적합하게 정서한 원고
block exemption 집단적용면제
block flow 블록플로
block offer 일괄매출; 블록오퍼
block policy 일괄담보보험계약
block positioner 블록포지셔너
block registration system 일괄등록제도
block sales 대량매매거래
block trading 블록거래
block transaction 대량거래
blockade 봉쇄
blood relationship 혈연

blotter 일계표
blotting book 거래일계표
blue chips 우량주
blue form return 청색신고
blue return system 청색신고제도
blue sky law 창공법; 부정증권거래금지법
blue-collar 블루칼라
Board of Audit 회계검사원
board of directors 이사회
Board of Governors of the Federal Reserve
　System 연방준비제도이사회
board of pardons 사면위원회
Board of Review 과세평가심사위원회
board of supervisors 감리위원회
board of trade 상공회의소
board room 중역실, 입회장
board trading 보드거래
bodily injury 신체상해
bodily injury liability cover
　인적배상책임담보
body copy 본문
body of an instrument 문서의 본문
bogus dividend 배당이익이 없는데도 배당함
bogus stock 위조주
boilerplate 공통기사; 틀에 박힌 문구
bona fide contracts 선의계약
bona fide cost 진정한 원가
bona fide creditor 선의채권자
bona fide holder 선의소지자
bona fide purchaser 선의취득자
bona fides 성실
bona vacantia 무생물
bonanza 노다지; 대성공
bond 채권
bond account 채권계정
bond and debenture 채권
bond anticipation notes 장기채차환예정증권
bond authorized 사채최고발행한도
bond broker 채권브로커
bond call provision 채권의 임의상환조항
bond certificate 사채권

bond collateral loans 공사채담보금융
bond credit rating 채권의 등급을 매김
bond creditor 채권권리자
bond dealer 채권딜러
bond demand 채권수요
bond discount 채권할인
bond dividend 사채배당
bond flotation 기채
bond flotation market 기채시장
bond for distrain of rent 지대차압보증증권
bond form 보증증권주식
bond fund 채권펀드
bond futures 채권선물
bond futures option 채권선물옵션
bond held 보유채권
bond holder 사채권자
bond holding 채권보유
bond in a pipeline 발행예정채권
bond in portfolio 수중에 있는 채권
bond interest 사채이자
bond inventory 재고채권
bond investment business 증권투자사업
bond investment trust 공사채투자신탁
bond issue 채권발행
bond issue costs 사채발행비용
bond issued 발행필 채권
bond issued by government related agency
　정부계 기간채권
bond issuing bank 채권발행은행
bond market 채권시장
bond market equilibrium 채권시장균형
bond of affiliated company 관계회사사채
bond of international agency 국제기관채권
bond of petitioning creditors
　파산신립채권자보증증권
bond on tap 탭채
bond option 채권옵션
bond option at over-the-counter
　채권장 외 옵션
bond outstanding 미상환채권
bond premium 채권상승액

bond price 채권가격
bond purchase 채권구입
bond rating 채권등급을 매김
bond refunding 채권차환
bond register 사채원부
bond return 채권이율
bond selection option 채권선택옵션
bond subscription 채권응모
bond swap 채권스와프
bond switching 채권입체거래
bond trader 본드 트레이더
bond trust indenture 채권신탁증서
bond underwriting 채권인수
bond unissued 사채미발행고
bond unit trust 단위형 채권투자신탁
bond valuation 사채평가
bond washing 윤리에 반하는 거래
bond with debt warrant 데트워런트채
bond with stock purchase warrant
　　주식매취권부 사채
bond with subscription warrant
　　신주인수권부 사채
bond with voting right 의결권부 사채
bond with warrant 워런트채
bond yield 채권이율
bond-equivalent yield 채권환산이율
bond-stock mixes 채권주식조합
bonded area 보세지역
bonded debt 채권발행차입금
bonded goods 보세항고내 화물
bonds and mortgage 사채
bonus nausea 특별배당
bonus paid per employee 일인당 상여
bonus paid to director 임원상여
bonus payment entered into expenses
　　손금산입상여
bonus payment reserve 상여준비금
bonus reserve 이익배당준비금
bonus scheme 이익분배계획
bonus stock 특별배당주
book 장부

book account 당좌계정
book balance 장부잔고
book binding 제본
book credit 외상매출금
book entry 장부기입
book inventory 장부재고
book keeper 부기계
book money 장부화폐
book of final entry 최종기입부
book of original entry 원시기입부
book runner 사무간사회사
book value 장부가격
book-entry securities 등록정부증권
book-entry system for bond
　　채권대체결제제도
book-keeper 장부계
book-keeping machine 기장기
booking 장부기입
booking center 기장장소
bookkeeping 부기
bookkeeping by double entry 복식기장법
bookkeeping by single entry 단식부기
boom 호황
boom and bust 어지러운 상황(商況)
boom town 신흥도시
boomerang effect 부메랑효과
boost 경기증대
boosting 자극하다
booth 부스
bootstrap acquisition 부트스트랩매수
borax goods 싸구려상품
border tax adjustment 국경세조정
bordereau 재보험계약명세서
borderless economy 국경없는 경제
borderline risk 경계체
borough courts 시재판소
borrowed capital 차입자본
borrowed money 차입금
borrowed reserves 대출준비금
borrowed securities 차입유가증권
borrowed share 차입주식

A
B

borrowing 차입금
borrowing account 차입금계정
borrowing cost 차입코스트
borrowing demand 차입수요
borrowing in advance 가불
borrowing rate 조달금리
borrowing requirements 차입필요액
borrowing short 단기차입
bottle-neck inflation 애로인플레이션
bottom 바닥
bottom line 당기이익
bottom price 바닥값
bottom straddle 하향제한스트래들
bottom vertical combination 수직컴비네이션
bottom-up approach 버텀업어프로치
bottom-up forecasting 버텀업형 예측
bottom-up process 버텀업형
bottoming out 최저시세까지 내려감
bottomry bond 모험대차증권
bought and sold note 매매보고서
bought deal 매입인수
bought for cash 현금구입
bounce 부도반각
boundary 경계선
boundary representation 경계표현
boundary strategy 경계전략
bounds 경계
bounty 교부금
bourse 환거래소
bourse tax 거래소거래세
bourse transaction tax 거래소세
boutique 전문적인 증권회사
box-Jenkins 박스젠킨스모형
bracket 서열
bracket creep 요율단계를 변경함
brag and boast commercial 과장광고
branch 지점
branch accounting 지점회계
branch banking system 지점은행제도
branch handling foreign exchange business
    외국환취급지점

branch ledger 지점원장
branch line 지선
branch office 지점
branch system 지사제도
brand acceptance 브랜드 수용
brand advertising 브랜드 광고
brand awareness 브랜드 인지
brand comparison 브랜드 비교
brand equity 브랜드 에퀴티
brand image 브랜드 이미지
brand label 브랜드 라벨
brand loyalty 브랜드 로얄티
brand management 상표관리
brand merchandising 브랜드 상품화 계획
brand naming 브랜드 이름 짓기
brand policy 상표정책
brand preference 상표선호
brand recognition 브랜드 인식
brand strategy 상표전략
brand switch 브랜드 변경
brand switching 브랜드 이행
brand-extension strategy 브랜드 확장 전략
brand-named item 브랜드 상품
branding 날인; 브랜드 설정
brass-plate office 간판만 걸어둔 가게
breach 위반
breach of confidence 신뢰위반
breach of contract 계약위반
breach of covenant 날인증서계약위반
breach of duty 의무위반
breach of law 법률위반
breach of privilege 특권남용
breach of warranty 담보위반
breadth 넓이
breadth of assortment 상품구비폭
break-down 내역
break-even analysis 손익분기분석
break-even chart 손익분기도표
break-even line 채산수준
break-even point 손익분기점
break-even yield 투자 수익률이 같음

break-up value 청산가치
breakage 파손
breakdown 붕괴
breaking bulk 세분화
breakthrough 브레이크스루; 돌파구
breakup value 해산가치
Bretton Woods 브레턴우즈협정
brewery-tax 주조세
bribery 뇌물; 증회
bridal market 혼례시장
bridge finance 입금예정의 공백을 메우기 위해
　받는 융자
bridge loan 브리지론; 연결융자
bridging exchange 브리지환
brief 준비서면
brief rally 일시적인 반등
bring forward 이월하다
bring over 인도하다
brisk market 활황시장
brisk recovery 순조로운 회복
British Banker's Association 영국은행협회
British Export Trade Research Organization
　영국무역진흥회
British Insurance Association 영국보험협회
British Stock Exchange 영국증권거래소
broad based stock index 종합주가지수
broad form 종합보험증권
broad market 대상; 큰장사
broad market index 광범위한 시장지표
broad tape 전광정보판
broadcast advertising 방송광고
broadcast commercials 방송광고
broadcast media 방송매체
broadcaster 방송업자
broadcasting satellite 방송위성
broadened marketing concept
　확장마케팅개념
broken term 특정기간인도
broker 중개업자
broker agent 주식거래원
broker's business 브로커업무

broker's loan 브로커즈론
broker's market 업자에 의한 투기상장
brokerage 브로커업무
brokerage commission 위탁수수료
brokered market 브로커시장
brokers blanket bond 브로커포괄보증증권
broking business 중개업무
brought-in capital 지입자본
brown goods 브라운상품
bucket shop 장외거래점
bucketeer 거래소, 경마장에서 부당이익을 얻는
　사람
budget 예산
budget allotment 예산배분
Budget Committee 예산위원회
budget deficit 재정적자
budget draft by Ministry of Finance
　재무부원안
budget principle 예산원칙
budget system 예산제도
budget variance 예산차이
budgetary account 예산계정
budgetary control 예산통제
budgetary process 예산편성
budgeted balance sheet 견적대차대조표
budgeted cost 예산원가
buffer stock 완충재고
buffer stock financing facility 완충재고융자
builders' risks insurance 선박건조보험
building account 건축계정
building and loan association 건축대부조합
building and loan blanket bond
　건물 및 대부금포괄보증증권
building block 구성부분
building expenses 건축비
building lease 건축대차권
building lot 건물용 부지
building lots for sale 분양지
building societies 건축조합
building tax 건축세
building under construction 건설중인 건물

built-in flexibility 빌트인플렉서빌리티
built-in stabilizer 자동안정장치
bulk buying 생산전량구입
bulk discount 대량광고할인
bulk marking 대량가격매김
bulk order 일괄주문
bulk purchase 대량구입
bull 사는 쪽
bull and bear index 강약지수
bull bear bond 불베어채
bull buying 강세매입
bull clique 강세근성
bull market 강세시장
bull speculation 투기매입
bull spread transaction 강세스프레드거래
bull the market 시세에 파동을 일으키다
bulldog bond 불독본드; 외국기업이 런던시장
　에서 발행하는 파운드표시 채권
bullet 일시불형
bullet bond 만기일괄상환채
bullet maturity 만기일괄상환
bullet swap 불릿스와프
bulletin board system 게시판체계
bulletin report 보고서
bullish 희망적; 낙관적
bullish channel 강한 채널
bullish factor 강한 재료
bullish resistance line 강한 저항선
bullish support line 강한 지지선
bullish tone 강세
bunched cost 일괄원가
buoyant market 급상승상장
burden 부담
burden charge 부담금
burden of paying tax 납세부담
burden of proof 입증책임
burden on cost 간접비(원재료와 노무비 이외)
bureau 국(局)
bureau adjuster 손해검사인
bureau company 요율산정회가맹회사
bureau filing 요율신청

bureau rates 산정회요율
burglary insurance 도난보험
burning ratio 재보험지불액
bus 버스
business 사업
business accountability 독립채산제
business accounting 기업회계
Business Accounting Deliberation Council
　기업회계심의회
business accounting principle 기업회계원칙
business adjustment 경기조정
business analysis 경상분석
Business and Industry Advisory Committee
　경제산업자문위원회
business annuity 기업연금
business attitude 기업태도
business audit 업무감사
business automation 비즈니스오토메이션
business barometer 경기지수
business buying 기업의 구매활동
business canvasser 보험판매원
business circle 업계
business climate 경기
business combinations 기업결합
business commencement expenses 간접비
business concern 기업
business conditions 경기
business consumer 기업소비자
business continuation insurance
　사업계속보험
business corporation 사업회사
business cycle 경기순환
business cyclical company 경기순환형 기업
business cyclical stock 경기순환주
business day 영업일
business environment risk index
　사업환경리스크지수
business establishment 사업소
business expansion 사업확장
business expenses 영업비
business finance 기업금융

business finance company 사업금융회사
business finder 사업아이디어를 발견하는 사람
business forecast 경기예측
business fund 사업자금
business game 비즈니스게임
business growth 기업성장
business hours 영업시간
business income 사업소득
business indicator 경기지표
business information 경제정보
business information service 경제정보서비스
business insurance 사업보험
business interception 사업방해
business interruption insurance
　영업중단보험
business inventory 기업재고
business investment 기업투자
business judgment principle 경상판단의 원칙
business law 사업법
business liability insurance 영업책임보험
business life insurance 사업생명보험
business line 영업과목
business loan 사업금융
business meeting 영업회의
business name 상호
business of renting property 부동산대부업
business of underwriting 인수업무
business office tax 사업소세
business operations audit 업무감사
business opportunity 상기(商機)
business place 사업소
business plan 경상계획
business portfolio 포트폴리오
business practice 상습관
business profit 영업이익
business profit tax 영업수익세
business proprietor 사업주
business report 영업보고
business responsibility 기업책임
business results 영업성적
business risk 경영위험

business round table 비즈니스 라운드 테이블
　(미국 내 대기업협의체)
business statistics 경상통계
business stimulating measure 경기자극책
business structure 기업구조
business survey 경기동향조사
business tax 사업세
business terms 거래조건
business transaction 기업거래
business trust 사업신탁
business unit 사업단위
business year 사업연도
businessman's orientation 경상자지향
bust-up proposal 회사청산요구
but-for income 가정이익
butterfly spread trading
　버터플라이 스프레드 거래
butting 버팅
buy and hold strategy 장기보유전략
buy back 되사다
buy high 비싸게 사다
buy on close 싸게 사다
buy on opening 오전장의 최초 가격으로 매입
　하다
buy on reaction 시세가 내릴 때 매입하다
buy on scale 세분화하여 매입하다
buy out 매수하다
buy signal 매신호
buy-back 되사다
buy-down loan 보조부 융자
buy-out arrangement 지주매입협정
buyer 구매자
buyer behavior 구매자행동
buyer segmentation 구매자세분화
buyer's credit 바이어즈크레디트
buyer's guide 구매자차관
buyer's market 매수시장
buyer's risk 매수부담
buyer's surplus 매수여잉
buying 매입; 처분매입
buying ability 구입능력

buying agent 구입대리점
buying and selling 매매
buying at top price 비싼 값으로 구입
buying by institutional investors 기관구입
buying calendar 구입캘린더
buying commission 매입수수료
buying cost 구입원가
buying criteria 구입기준
buying energy 구입에너지
buying error 구입실패
buying exchange 환구입
buying for resale 재판(再版)구입
buying habit 구매습관
buying hedge 연계구입
buying information 구매정보
buying offer 구매신청
buying on an yield basis 이익구매
buying on commission 위탁매입
buying on credit 외상구입
buying operation 구매오퍼레이션
buying opportunity 구매장
buying order 구입주문
buying over 매수

buying period 구입기간
buying power 구매력
buying power index 구매력지수
buying price 구입가격
buying procedure 구입절차
buying process 구입과정
buying psychology 구매심리학
buying rate without credit
　　신용장 없는 어음 매입률
buying side 구입측
buying support 구입지원
buying terms 구입조건
buying title 권원(權原)구입
buying trip 매부(買付)여행
buying up 매점
buzz session 버즈세션; 버즈학습
buzz word 현학적인 전문용어
by deed 증언에 따라
by judgment 판결에 따라
by-laws 정관세칙
by-product 부차적인 결과
bystander 방관자
byte 바이트

cabinet offer 캐비넷오퍼
cabinet order 여행령
cabinet security 값싼 증권
cable 펀드 대 미달러율
cable address 해외전보수신인
cable credit 전신신용장
cable television 유선방송
cable transfer 전신송금
cadaster 토지대장의
calculate 계산하다
calculated tax amount 산출세액
calculation 산정
calculator 계산조견표
calendar day 역일
　(자정에서 자정까지의 24시간)
calendar month 역월(1년의 12분의 1)
calendar spread 캘린더 스프레드
calendar spread transaction
　캘린더 스프레드 거래
calendar year 역년(曆年)
calender month delivery 역월(曆月) 인도
calender month delivery rate
　역월제(曆月制) 선물율
calender month delivery rates with option
　역월(曆月)인도율
calibration 눈금, 교정
calibration data 공정데이터
call 조기상환; 콜
call and bill market 콜어음시장
call loan 콜론; 단자; 당좌차입금
call loan broker 단자업자

call loan dealer 단자회사
call loan market 단자시장
call market 콜시장
call money 콜머니
call money and discount market 단자시장
call money discount markets
　콜어음매시장자금
call money rate 콜레이트
call option 콜옵션
call option valuation and dividend
　콜옵션 평가와 배당
call premium 콜옵션의 옵션료
call price 상환가격
call provision 임의상환조항
call rate 콜레이트
call ratio back spread transaction
　콜레이쇼 백스프레드거래
call spread 콜스프레드
call swaption 콜스왑션
call-sales merchant 방문판매업자
callable bond 임의상환채권
callable debt 즉시상환가능한 채권
callable loan 콜러블론
callable preferred stock 상환가능주식
callable shares 상환주식
callable swap 콜러블스와프
callable swaption 콜러블스왑션
calling the jury 배심원호출
calling the plaintiff 원고호출
cambist 어음취급업자
campaign advertising 캠페인 광고

campaign concept 캠페인컨셉

Canadian'dollar long-term bond
캐나다달러장기국채

cancel money 위약금

cancel order 취소주문

cancelable swap 캔슬러블스와프

canceled order 캔슬드오더

canceling date 해약기일

cancellation 해약

cancellation before maturity 중도해약

cancellation card 캔슬카드

cancellation clause 계약해제약관

cancellation money 해약금

cancellation of a contract 중도해약

cancellation of approval of filing a blue
return 청색신고승인을 취소함

cancellation of contract 계약을 해약함

cancellation of debts of directors
임원채무면제

cancellation of shares 주식소각

cancellation request 해약청구

cancellation return 해약반환금

cancer insurance 암보험

cannibalization 자기잠식현상

canons of descent 부동산상속순위법칙

canvasser 보험판매원

cap 캡; 상한

cap and floor 캡&플로어

cap interest rate 상한금리

capacity 계약인수능력; 행위능력

capacity to contract 계약능력

cape 토지회복영장

capias ad audiendum judicium
판결언도를 위한 출정명령

capital 자본

capital account 자본계정

capital account balance 자본수지

capital adequacy requirements
자기자본비율규제

capital adjustment 자본수정

capital and liabilities ratio 자본부담비율

capital appreciation 값이 오른 이익

capital arrangement 고정성 배열법

capital asset pricing model
자본자산가격 모델

capital assets 자본자산

capital balance 자본계정

capital budget 자본예산

capital budgeting 설비투자계획

capital coefficient 자본계수

capital composition 자본구성

capital consumption 자본소비

capital consumption adjustment
자본소비를 조정함

capital consumption allowance 자본감모준비

capital contribution 자본거출

capital cost 자본비용

capital decrease 감자

capital disposition 자본지출

capital duty 자본세

capital equipment 자본설비

capital equipment ratio 자본장비율

capital expenditure 자본지출

capital export 자본수출

capital flight 자본도피

capital flow 캐피탈플로

capital formation 자본형성

capital formation account 자본형성계정

capital formula 자본등식

capital gain 캐피탈게인; 매매이익

capital gain free of taxation 비과세양도소득

capital gain fund 캐피탈게인펀드

capital gain taxation 캐피탈게인과세

capital gearing 캐피탈기어링

capital goods 자본재

capital import 자본수입

capital improvement
자본지출로 처리하는 개선

capital in excess of par or stated value
자본준비금

capital in excess of par value 액면초과금

capital income 자본소득
capital increase 증자
capital increase by new shares at market price
시가발행증자
capital inflow 자본유입
capital interest 자본이자
capital interest tax 자본이자세
capital investment 설비투자
capital investment intention 설비투자의욕
capital lease 캐피탈리스
capital levy 자본과세
capital liabilities 자본부채
capital liberalization 자본자유화
capital loan 캐피탈론
capital loss 캐피탈로스
capital market 자본시장
capital market line 자본시장선
capital meeting for merger
합병을 위한 주주총회
capital outflow 자본유출
capital outlay 자본지출
capital paid-up 불입자본
capital participation 자본참가
capital productivity 자본생산성
capital profit 자본이윤
capital ratio 자기자본비율
capital receipt 자본수입
capital redemption 자금상환업무
capital redemption business
원금상각보험사업
capital reduction 감자
capital requirement 자기자본규제
capital reserve 자본준비금
capital risk 캐피탈리스크
capital saving technical progress
자본절약을 위한 기술진보
capital spending 자본투자
capital stock 발행필 주식총수
capital stock account 자본계정
capital stock adjustment 자본스톡조정
capital stock adjustment principle

자본스톡조정원리
capital stock issued 발행필 자본금
capital stock preferred 우선주자본금
capital stock registered 공칭자본금
capital stock subscribed 인수필 자본금
capital stock tax 자본세
capital stock unpaid 미불입액
capital structure 자본구성
capital subscription 출자
capital sum 최고급부금; 자본액
capital supplier nation 자본공급국
capital surplus 자본준비금
capital surplus reserve 자본준비금
capital tax 자본세
capital transaction 자본거래
capital transfer 자본이전
capital turnover 자본회전율
capital utilization 설비가동률
capital working rate 자본가동률
capital-intensive merchandise
자본집약적인 상품
capital-output ratio 자본 대 산출고비율
capital-reconciliation statement 자본설정표
capitalism 자본주의
capitalist 자본가
capitalist bracket 자본가계급
capitalization 자본편입
capitalization issue 신주발행
capitalization of accumulated earnings
이익적립금을 자본편입함
capitalization of interest cost
차입이자를 자산계상함
capitalization of market price 시가총액
capitalization rate 자본환원율
capitalization unit 자산화 단위
capitalization weighted 시장가치가중
capitalization weighted indices
시가총액 가중 인덱스
capitalized surplus 자본금구성 잉여금
capitalized value of stock 배당환원가액
capitation tax 인두세

capped floating rate note 캡부채
capped loan 캡부론
capped swap 캡스와프
capping 캐핑
capsized 배가 뒤집힌; 전복된
capsule shop 캡슐점포
caption 제목; 머리말
captive audience 붙잡힌 청중
captive finance company 금융자회사
captive market 전속시장
card counterfeiting 카드위조
card criminal fraud 카드범죄
card discrimination code 카드식별코드
card issuer 카드회사
card loan 카드론
card member 카드회원
card of accounts 계정과목표
card renewal 카드갱신
card replacement 카드재발행
card standardization 카드표준화
card system 카드시스템
card system of bookkeeping 카드식 기장법
card-holic 다중채무
care and custody 관리책임; 재물관리
care of works 공사관리
career agency system 전속외무원제도
career average 전기간평균
career development program
  경력개발프로그램
career plateau 경력정체
cargo capacity 화물적재능력
cargo damage survey 화물손해검사
cargo insurance 화물해상보험
Cargo Loss Prevention Committee
  화물손해방지위원회
cargoworthiness 재화(載貨)적성
Caribbean Community and Common Market
  카리브공동체 공동시장
Carlisle Mortality Table 카라일생명표
Carpenter cover 카펜터식 재보험
carriage 운송비

carriage and insurance paid to
  운송비·보험료 포함
carriage paid to 운송비 포함
carried forward 이월
carried interest 이월지분
carrier's risk 상업과실
carriers liability insurance 운송인책임보험
carry forward 이월
carry income 캐리인컴
carry on 경영하다
carryback of deficit 결손금환급
carryback of loss 손실환급
carryback of net loss 순손실환급
carrying broker 고객계정을 보유한 브로커
carrying charge 이월이자; 재산보유비용
carrying cost 운송비
carrying firm 증거금취급업자
carrying value 이월가액
carrying-in expenses 반입비
carrying-over contract 이연계약
carryover of casualty loss
  잡손실을 이월 공제함
carryover of deficit 결손금이월
carryover of expense 이월사용
carryover of foreign tax credit
  외국세액을 이월 공제함
carryover of loss 손실이월
cartage 운임
carte blanche 백지위임
cartel 카르텔
cartel tariffs 카르텔관세
carucate 지조(地租) 기준 면적
cascade process 폭포이론
cascade tax 누적세
cascade-type turnover tax 누적형 거래고세
case 준비서면; 소송
case administration 파산관리
case law 판례법
case method 사례연구법
case of first impression 선례가 없는 소송사건
case on appeal 상소사실기재서

case reserved 합의를 위한 사실기재서
case stated 사실기재서
cash account 금융계정
cash advance 현금선지급
cash and carry 현금지불
cash and carry system 현금지불방식
cash and carry trade 현금지불거래
cash and carry wholesaler
　현금판매를 전문으로 하는 재고업자
cash and deposits banks accounts
　현금예금계정
cash and deposits with banks 현금예금
cash asset value 현금자산가치
cash assets 현금자산
cash at bank 당좌예금
cash audit 현금감사
cash balance 현금잔고
cash basis 현금주의
cash basis accounting 현금주의회계
cash before delivery 선불로
cash book 현금출납장
cash break-even point 수지분기점
cash buying rate 현금매상장
cash credit 당좌대출
cash currency 현금통화
cash delivery 즉일인도
cash deposit 현금예금
cash deposited for bond interest
　사채이자 지불자금
cash disbursed 지출
cash disbursement 현금지불
cash disbursement book 지불장
cash discount 현금할인
cash dispenser 현금지불기
cash dividend 현금배당
cash dividend declared 현금배당결의액
cash earnings 현금수입
cash equivalent 현예금
cash flow 캐시플로
cash flow analysis 수지분석
cash flow coverage ratio 캐시플로부담배율

cash flow interest 캐시플로이율
cash flow projection 캐시플로예측
cash flow ratio 캐시플로비율
cash flow ratio to capital expenditures
　설비투자 캐시플로비율
cash flow ratio to long-term liabilities
　장기부채 캐시플로비율
cash flow return 캐시플로리턴
cash flow statement 자금운용표
cash flow to current liabilities
　캐시플로 대 유동부채
cash flow-back 현금회수
cash forecasts 수지예측
cash forward contract 캐시플로계약
cash forward transaction 현물선도거래
cash immediate market
　패스 스루 증권 청산 시장
cash in advance 선불로
cash in bank 은행예금
cash in banks and hand 예금현금
cash in hand 생계현금보유고
cash in transit 미달현금
cash income 현금수입
cash items 현금항목
cash journal 현금분개장
cash letters 현금송장
cash liabilities 현금부채
cash loan 현금대부
cash loss 즉시지불 재보험금
cash management bill 재무부 단기어음
cash management service
　캐시 매니지먼트 서비스
cash market 캐시마켓
cash on delivery 대금교환인도
cash on hand 생계현금
cash on shipment 선적지불
cash option 현물옵션
cash outlays 현금지출
cash over and short account 현금과부족계정
cash payment 현금지불
cash payment journal 현금지불장

cash position 현금상태
cash price 현금가격
cash purchase 현금구매
cash ratio 현금비율
cash receipt 현금수령
cash receipt book 현금수납장
cash receipt journal 현금수납장
cash received 수입현금
cash records 현금기록
cash redemption 현금상환
cash remittance 현금반송
cash reserve ratio 예금지불준비율
cash reserves 현금준비고
cash sale 현금매매
cash selling rate 현금매상장
cash settlement 현금결제
cash slips 출납전표
cash statement 현금계산서
cash surrender value 해약반환금
cash take 현금거래
cash to current liabilities ratio
　현금유동부채비율
cash transactions 당일결제거래
cash value 운용부분
cash with order 현금주문
cash-book 출납부
cash-disbursement journal 지불분개장
cash-matching 캐시매칭
cash-matching techniques 캐시매칭기술
cash-receipts journal 수입분개장
cash-sale 현금매매
cashability goods 환금성 상품
cashier 현금출납계
cashier's check 은행수표
cashier's department 현금출납과
cashing 현금화
casset execution 집행정지명령
casseteur breve 소송종료판결
casting vote 결정표
casual expenses 임시지출
casual loss 우발손실

casual profit 우발이익
casualty 재해
casualty and surety insurance
　신종보험; 손해보증보험
casualty insurance 재해보험
casualty loss 잡손
casualty loss deduction 잡손공제
casualty losses carried over 이월재해손실
casus fortuitus 우연한 재해
casus major 재해
casus omissus 관련 법규정이 미비한 사항
catastrophe reinsurance 이상손해재보험
catastrophe reserve 이상손해준비금
catch-up adjustments 파급수정
catching bargain 부당계약
category killer 카테고리킬러
category of business 업종
category width 카테고리폭
cats and dogs stock 투기주
causa causans 직접원인
causa inducement 동기
causa remota 간접원인
causa sine qua non 필요조건
causal analysis 인과분석
causal credit 원인채권
causal path analysis 인과 패스 분석
causal relationship 인과관계
causality 인과관계
cause 원인
cause list 사건목록
cause of action 소송원인
cause of bankruptcy 파산원인
cause proximate 근인주의
cause-books 사건부
caution 등기변경예고
caution money 보증금
cautionary 보증채무의
cautious stance 경계자세
caveat 절차중지신청자
caveat emptor 매주(買主)의 위험부담
caveat venditor 매주(賣主)의 위험부담

CD market CD 시장
cease orders 정지명령
cedant 출재보험자
cede back 인도재보험
ceded reinsurance 매출재보험
cedel 세델
ceding commission 출재(出再) 수수료
ceding company 출재(出再) 회사
ceding reinsurer 재보험자
ceding 상한
ceiling price 최고액
ceiling system 실링방식
celebration of the beginning of operation
　조업개시기념축연
cellular approach 셀룰러 어프로치
cellular communication system 셀룰러 방식
census of commerce 상업통계
census register 호적
center of demand 수요중심점
center spread 중앙의 마주보는 양면
Central American Common Market
　중미공동시장
central bank 중앙은행
central bank intervention 평형개입
central bank rate 중앙은행할인율
central buying 본부집중구입
central death rate 중앙사망율
Central European Free Trade Association
　중부유럽자유무역연합
central market 중앙시장
central rate 센트럴레이트
central tendency 중심경향
centralized management 집권관리
centralized organization 집권조직
centrifugal market 원심적인 시장
centripetal market 구심적인 시장
cepi corpus 체포보고서
cepit 탈취
certain assets 확실성 자산
certainty 명백성
certificate 증명서

certificate of analysis 분석증명서
certificate of automobile receivables
　자동차론 저당증서
certificate of bank balances
　은행예금잔고증명서
certificate of beneficial interest 부분수익증권
certificate of compliance 납세필 증서
certificate of deposit 양도가능정기예금증서
certificate of financial security
　손해배상자력증명서
certificate of incorporation 회사설립면허
certificate of indebtedness 채무증서
certificate of insurance 보험인수증
certificate of origin 원산지증명
certificate of registry 선박증명서
certificate of seal impression 인감증명서
certificate of share 주권
certificate of tax payment 납세증명서
certificate of time deposit 정기예금증서
certificate of weight and measurement
　중량용적증명서
certificated financial statement
　감사필 재무제표
certificated share 주권이 있는 주식
certification body 인증기관
certification market 인증마크
certification of audit 감사증명
certification of payment 지불보증
certified check 지불인수수표
certified copy 인증등본
certified copy of commercial registration
　상업등기부등본
certified copy of real estate register
　부동산등기부등본
certified equipment 인정장치
certified public accountant 공인회계사
certified public accountant Law
　공인회계사법
certified tax accountant 세무사
certified tax accountant association 세무사회
certified tax accountant law 세무사법

certifying bank 지불보증은행
certiorari 이송명령
cessation of payment of premium
　보험료지불정지
cesser 태만
cesset execution 집행정지명령
cession 재산인도
cession of an obligation 채권양도
cession of portfolio 포트폴리오양도
cestui que trust 신탁수익자
chafing 마찰; 마찰손
chain banking 체인뱅킹
chain break 체인브레이크
chain of command 명령계통
challenge 기피
chamber of commerce 상공회의소
chambers 사실(私室)
champerty 소송원조
chance to sell 매장
chancellor of a university 대학총장
Chancellor of the Exchequer 재무부장관
change 환산
change claims 변경클레임
change in employment 전적
change in growth rate 성장률변화
change in par value 액면변경
change in valuation method 평가방법 변경
change in work 변경공사
change of business 사업전환
change of category of land 지목변환
change of depreciation method 상각방법 변경
change of risk 위험 변동
cnange of tax computation basis
　세액 계산 기준 변경
change of taxable year 사업연도 변경
change of the place of tax payment
　납세지 변경
change of valuation method 평가방법 변동
change of venue 관할이전
change over 체인지오버
changes in accounting principles

회계원칙변경
changes in estimates 견적금액변경
changes in gross margin 이익이 증감함
changes of owners of the principal
　원본소유자이동
channel control 경로통제
channel cost analysis 경로비용분석
channel development 경로개발
channel efficiency 경로효율
channel environment 경로환경
channel line 채널라인
channel of distribution 유통경로
channel system 경로시스템
channeling back 환류
channeling of liability 배상책임집중
chaos 카오스
characteristic line 특성선
characteristic of goods theory 상품특성론
characteristics 특징
charge 수수료
charge account 외상매출금계정
charge against revenues 손금
charge back 입금취소
charge coupled device 차지커플디바이스
charge extra 부대비용
charge for call 독촉료
charge for collection 수금수수료
charge for collection of bill 어음수금수수료
charge for demand for tax in arrears
　체납독촉수수료
charge for development 개발부담금
charge for installment payment 할부수수료
charge on the declining balances 잔채방식
charge-off 대손금상각
charges for custody 보관료
charges for remittance 환수수료
charges forward 입체지불
charitable trust 공익신탁
charities and donations 자선기부금
chart 차트
chart of accounts 계정과목표

chart pattern 차트패턴
chart reading 차트분석
charta 날인증서
charter 기본정관
charter party B/L 차터파티 B/L
charter provision 회사설립허가서
charter-land 특허보유지
charterage 용선계약; 용선료
chartered 공인의
chartered accountant 칙령으로 허가된 회계사
chartered financial analyst
　공인증권분석전문가
Chartered Life Underwriters in Japan (일본)
　인정생명보험사회
chartered property casualty underwriter
　공인재산재해보험사
chartered public accountant 공인회계사
chartering broker 부정기화물 중개업자
charterparty 용선계약
chartist 차티스트
chat 차트
chattel 동산
chattel loan 동산대부
chattel mortgage 동산저당
cheapest-to-deliver 최염가저당
cheat 사기
check 조합
check act 수표법
check book 수표장
check drawee 수표지불인
check drawer 수표발행지
check guarantee card 체크개런티카드
check holder 수표지정인
check mark 조회필 기호
check register 수표기입장
check to bearer 지참인지불수표
check to order 지정수표
check-off 공제
check-out counter 계정구
checkable deposit 결제성 예금
checkbook stub 수표장원부

checking 조회
checking account 당좌계정
checking deposits 당좌예금
checking inventory 재고조회
checking system 수표제도
Chicago Board of Trade 시카고상품거래소
Chicago Board Options Exchange
　시카고옵션거래소
Chicago Mercantile Exchange
　시카고상공회의소
chicken market 치킨마켓
chief 주석
chief accountant 회계주임
chief actuary 보험계리인
chief examiner 통괄국세조사관
chief executive officer 최고경영책임자
chief financial officer 재무담당임원
chief investigator 통괄국세사찰관
chief justice 수석판사
chief of the taxation office 세무서장
chief operating officer 최고업무책임자
chief revenue officer 통괄국세징수관
child's deferred insurance 유아거치보험
children's insurance 유아보험
chilling effect 냉각효과
china eggs 물건을 사지 않고 눈요기하는 사람
Chinese wall 만리장성; 큰 방해물
chirograph 자필증서
chit 전표
chit system 전표지불제도
chitbook 송달부
chose 물산(物産)
chose in action 무체동산
chose in possession 유체동산
chroma 채도
chroma key 크로마키
chrominance signal 색차신호
chronic 만성적
chronic absenteeism 만성적인 태업
chronic deflation 만성적인 디플레이션
chronic inflation 만성적인 인플레이션

chumming 가장매매
churning 과도한 매매권유
CIF price 원가·보험료·운임포함 가격
circuit breaker 동시거래정지
circuit court 순회재판소
circuitswitching 서킷교환
circular flow of economic system 경제순환
circular note 신용장
circulating assets 유동자산
circulating capital 유동자본
circulating fund 운임자금
circulation 발행부수; 유통
circulation of cost 원가배부
circulation of national income 국민소득순환
circulation tax 유통세
circumstantial evidence 정황증거
circus swap 서커스스와프
citation 소환
citizen 공민
citizen bond 시민채권
City 시티; 도시
city bank 도시은행
city planning tax 도시계획세
civil 민사의
civil action 민사소송
civil code 민법
civil death 법률상의 사망
civil engineering 토목
civil engineering works 토목공사
civil law 민법
civil rights 공민권
civil servant 공무원
civil service 공무원
civilian demand 민수
civilian enterprise 민간사업
claim 채권; 청구
claim adjustment 손해정산
claim and delivery 동산회복소송
claim expenses 손해사정비용
claim for a refund 환부청구
claim for compensation 구상

claim for correction 갱정청구
claim for damage 손해배상청구
claim for examination 심사청구
claim for guarantee 미수보증금
claim for reimbursement 상환청구
claim for tax refunds 조세환부청구권
claim frequency analysis 손해빈도분석
claim in bankruptcy 파산채권
claim in foreign currency 외화기준채권
claim note 보험금청구자
claim notice clause 손해통지조항
claim of prepayment of income tax
　　예정납세액독촉
claim of recourse 상환청구
claim of redemption 상환청구권
claim paid 지불필 보험금
claim paid or payable 보상액; 보험금
claim payable abroad clause
　　보험금해외지불약관
claim payable to a specific person 지명채권
claim period 구상기간
claim probability 손해발생확률
claim ratio 손해율
claim reserve 지불비금
claim right insurance 청구권보험
claim settlement 보험금지불
claim settlement analysis 손해결제분석
claim settlement fund 보험금지불자금
claim settling fee 보험금지불수수료
claimant 보험금청구자
claiming bank 구상은행
claims 배상금
clamor 신청
clandestine theft 비밀절도
clarification 설명
class action 집단소송
class cost 조별원가
class cost system 조별원가계산
class media 특정 층을 대상으로 한 매체
class mutual 직업별 상호보험
class of insurance 보험의 종류

class of risk 위험의 종류
class-product production 급별생산물생산
classes of stocks 주식의 종류
classical school of economics 고전파경제학
classification of a taxpayer 납세의무자분류
classification of account 계정과목일람표
classification of goods 상품분류
classification of item of accounts
　계정과목분류표
classification of lan 지목(地目)
classification of media 매체분류
classification of motives 동기분류
classification of securities 유가증권분류
classification of shares 주식분류
classification of tax 세금분류
classified advertising 안내광고
classified income 각종소득
classified income tax 분류소득세
classified stock 분류된 주식
classified trial balance 구분식 시산표
clause 조항
clausum fregit 부동산점유침해
clean bill of lading 클린B/L
clean credit 무담보신용장
clean cut system 클린컷시스템
clean float 클린플로트; 자유변동시세제도
clean letter of credit 클린신용장
clean loan 클린론; 무담보론
clean opinion 클린오피니언
clear band 클리어밴드
clear days 순일수
clear space clause 공지조항
clearance 어음교환
clearance fee 출항수수료
clearance goods 재고품
clearing 청산
clearing account 어음교환계정
clearing agency 청산기관
clearing agreement 청산협정
clearing balance 어음교환차액
clearing bank 어음교환소가맹은행

clearing contract 청산거래
clearing corporation 청산회사
clearing for nonmember 대리교환
clearing function 청산기능
clearing fund 클리어링펀드; 결제기금
clearing house 어음교환소
clearing member 청산회원
clearing organization 청산기관
clearing price 청산가격
clearing procedure 청산절차
clearing system 어음교환제도
clearing time 결제시
clearing transaction 청산거래
clearinghouse 어음교환소
clearing-house balance 교환 잔고표
clearinghouse for commodity futures
　상품선물거래청산소
clearinghouse proof 어음교환결산표
clerical mistake 오기
client and server 클라이언트와 서버
clientele effect 고객효과
clients 거래처
climbing angle 상승각
climbing power 상승력
clique 파벌
clock frequency 클록주파수
clone fund 복제펀드
close 장부를 마감하다
close down 종가가 전일의 종가보다 값이 낮음
close of the session 인출
close one's position 거래관계를 청산하다
close up 종가가 전일의 종가보다 값이 높음
close-out 재고품을 싸게 처분함
closed account 마감필 계정
closed corporation 동족회사
closed door membership store 회원제 점포
closed economy 봉쇄경제
closed market 폐쇄시장
closed out method 거래관계를 해소하다
closed period 클로즈드기
closed-circuit system 폐쇄회로시스템

closed-end dual fund 폐쇄형 듀얼펀드
closed-end fund 폐쇄형 펀드
closed-end mortgage 폐쇄식 담보
closed-end mortgage bond
  폐쇄식 담보부 사채
closed-end trust 폐쇄식 신탁
closed-end type 폐쇄식
closely-held company 비공개회사
closing 계약내용을 실행함; 인출
closing account 결산
closing adjustment 결산정리
closing all accounts in the ledger
  원장의 각 계정을 마감
closing balance 기말잔고
closing business 사업폐쇄
closing date 결산일
closing entries 결산분개
closing high 시세가 높을 때 물러남
closing inventories 기말재고
closing lower 시세가 낮을 때 물러남
closing meeting 최종회의
closing of the ledger 원장체결
closing price (거래소의)종가(終價)
closing quotation
  (거래소에서의) 입회죄종가격
closing sale 마감세일
closing the ledger 원장마감
closing tone (거래소의) 최종분위기
closing transaction 반대매매
closing trial balance 마감시산표
closing-out 결제
clothing and shelter expenses 의식주의 비용
club deal 공동인수
club dues 회비
cluster analysis 클러스터분석
cluster marketing 클러스터마케팅
clutter position 클러터포지션
co-branded card 제휴카드
co-existing cover clause 중복보험약관
co-finance 공동융자
co-heir 공동법정상속인

co-lead-manager 공동주간사
co-maker 공동발행인
co-manager 부간사
co-movement of earnings 이익이 같이 변동함
co-ownership 공유
coal stock 저탄(貯炭)
coast-to-coast 미국횡단의; 전미의
coastwise cargo insurance
  내항화물해상 보험
coaxial cable 동축케이블
Cobb-Douglas production function
  코브-더블러스 생산 함수
cobweb cycle 거미집순환
cocket 관세서
cocktail swap 칵테일스와프; 복합스와프
code 법전
code division multiple access
  부호분할다원접속
code of civil procedure 민사소송법전
code of ethics 윤리규정
code of legal procedure 소송법
code of liberalization 자유화규약
Code of Procedure for Handling Trade
  Practice Complain
  전미증권업협회 분쟁처리규칙
codicil 추가조항
coefficient 계수
coefficient of correlation 상관계수
coefficient of determination 결정계수
coefficient of elasticity 탄력성계수
coefficient of income sensitivity
  소득감응계수
coefficient of multiple correlation
  중상관계수
coefficient of variation 변동계수
coercive power 강제력
cogeneration 열병합발전
cognitive judgment 인지적인 판단
cognitive science 인지과학
cognizance 승인
cognovit actionern 채무승낙

cognovit note 원고청구승낙서

cohort analysis 동세대분석

coincident indicator 일치지수

coincident series 일치계열

coinsurance 공동보험

coinsurance account payable
공동보험지불계정

coinsurance account receivable
공동보험수취계정

coinsurance limit 공동보험인수한도

coinsurance share 공동보험인수비율

coinsurer 공동보험자

cold call 전화로 거래를 권유함

cold canvassing 돌연한 방문판매

cold chain 저온유통조직

collaboration 제휴

collapse 폭락

collapse in oil prices 유가하락

collar 칼라

collared swap 칼라스와프

collateral 담보

collateral bond 부대증서

collateral commodity 상품담보

collateral condition 부대조건

collateral consanguinity 방계혈족

collateral deposit 담보부 예금

collateral estoppel 부수적인 금반언

collateral import 담보부 수입

collateral issue 방계쟁점

collateral loan 담보대부

collateral note 담보부 약속어음

collateral on loans on bills 어음대부담보

collateral on property 물적담보

collateral promise 부대약속

collateral security 대용증권

collateral source rule 배상금중복회수의 원칙

collateral trust bond 담보부 신탁채권

collateral value 담보가치

collateral value of substitute security
대용증권담보율

collateralized mortgage obligations
저당부 모기지증서

collation 대조

collation of seals 날인의 인장조회

collect 징수하다

collected amount 징수액

collectible 회수가능한

collecting agent 징수의무자

collecting commission 징수수수료

collecting tax 징수

collection 회수

collection agency 회수업자

collection bank 징수은행

collection basis 회수기준

collection bill 징수어음

collection charge 징수경비

collection cycle 회수순환

collection expenses 징수비용

collection fee 징수료

collection floater 수집물포괄보험

collection letter 독촉장

collection management technique 회수기술

collection of bad debts
상각필 대손금을 회수함

collection of bill 외상매출금회수

collection of claim 채권회수

collection of loans 대부금회수

collection of premiums 보험료집금

collection of securities by purchase
유가증권매출집금

collection of taxes 조세징수

collection period 회수기간

collection practices 회수업무

collective accident insurance 단체상해보험

collective accumulation 집단적립제

collective agreement 노동협약

collective bargaining 단체교섭

collective bargaining agreement 단체협약

collective insurance 단체보험

collective investment fund 합동운용형 펀드

collective leadership 집단지도

collective mark 단체마크

collective name schedule policy
단체기명식 보험
collective personal accident insurance
단체상해보험
College Retirement Equities Fund
미국대학교직원퇴직변액연금기금
collision 충돌
collusion 공모; 통모(通謀)
color 시황; 표견
color chart 컬러차트
color dynamics 색채조절
color lookup table 색참조표
color naming system 색상명명법
color of office 표면상의 직권
color of title 표면상의 권원
color proof 색교정
color separation 색분해
color system 표색계
color temperature 색온도
color video signal 컬러비디오신호
colorable alteration 외견상의 변경
column measure 칼럼폭
column number 칼럼수
combination of causes 연계원인
combination plan reinsurance
조합방식재보험
combination policy 조합보험
combination sale 공동판매
combine 합동
combined 총계의
combined balance sheet 결합대차대조표
combined depreciation 결합상각법
combined financial statement 결합재무제표
combined house 주거겸용주택
combined income statement 합병손익계산서
combined marine surcharges 종합할증보험료
combined policy 복합보험증권
combined profit and loss statement
결합손익계산서
combined single limit 사고 1건당 보상한도액
combined transport documents 복합운송서류

come to terms 마주침
comfort letter (비공식)감사의견서; 각서
commanding 지휘명령
commemorative dividend 기념배당
commerce and industry finance company
상공업금융회사
commerce clause 통상조항
commercial accounting 상업회계
commercial agent 대리점
commercial arbitration 상사중재
commercial automobile policy
상업용 자동차보험
commercial bank 시중은행; 상업은행
commercial bank credit 시중대출
commercial banker 상업은행가
commercial bill 상업어음
commercial blanket primary bond
상업포괄신원보증증권
commercial block policy 판매업자일괄보험
commercial bookkeeping 상업부기
commercial business 영리사업
commercial code 상법
commercial company 영리회사
commercial court 상업재판소
commercial credit 상업신용
commercial credit insurance 상업신용보험
commercial discount 상업할인
commercial enterprise 영리사업
commercial expenses 영업비
commercial finance 상업금융
commercial forgery policy 상업용위조보험
commercial guarantee 상업보증
commercial insurance 영리보험
commercial invoice 상업송장
commercial letter of credit 상업신용장
commercial law 상법
commercial loan 상업대출
commercial mortgage 상업용 모기지
commercial paper 상업어음
commercial registration 상업등기
commercial risk 신용위험

commercial statistics 상업통계
commercial trader 상업트레이더
commercial transaction 상행위
commingled fund 합동운영펀드
commingled investment account
　혼합투자계정
commission 위탁매매인
commission account 수수료계정
commission agent 위탁매매인
commission broker 거래소중매인
commission del credere 보증부 위임
commission earned 수취수수료
commission for purchase 매입수수료
commission income 수수료수입
commission of authority 위탁계약서
commission on consignment 위탁수수료
commission payable 미불수수료
commission receivable 미수수수료
commission sale 수수료매매
commission system 커미션제
commission to consignee 위탁판매수수료
commission to examine witnesses
　증인심문위탁서
commissioners for oaths 선서관리관
commissioning 시운전
commitment 계약채무; 계약의무
commitment fee 약정수수료
committee 위원회
committee bond 후견인보증증권
committee of inspection 검사위원회
Committee of Lloy's 로이즈위원회
Committee on Accounting Procedure
　회계절차위원회
committee on auditing procedure
　감사절차위원회
commodities investment trust 상품투자신탁
commodity 상품
commodity account 상품거래계좌
commodity approach 상품연구
commodity backed bond 상품담보채권
commodity customers agreement
　상품고객계약
commodity demand 상품수요
commodity exchange 상품거래소
commodity exchange act 상품거래법
commodity exchange responsibility reserve
　상품거래책임준비금
commodity excise 물품세
commodity flow method 커머디티플로방법
commodity futures 상품선물
commodity futures index 상품선물지수
commodity futures price 상품선물거래가격
commodity futures trading adviser
　상품 선물 어드바이저
Commodity Futures Trading Commission
　미국상품선물거래위원회
commodity market 상품시장
commodity money 물품화폐
commodity option 상품옵션
commodity pool 커머디티 풀
commodity pool operator 상품 풀 운영자
commodity price 물가
commodity rate 상품운임
commodity statistics 상품통계
commodity swap 커머디티스와프
commodity tax 물품세
commodity tax law 물품세법
commodity trading adviser 상품거래고문
commodity transaction 상품거래
commodity transaction responsibility reserve
　상품거래책임준비금
common account 공동계정
common assurance 양도증서
common background 공통기반
common carrier
　일반운송업; 공중전기통신사업자
common carriers liability insurance
　운송업자책임보험
common collateral 공통담보
common cost 공통원가
common counts 일반항목
common dividend 보통배당

C
D

common dollar statements
안정가치로 수정한 재무제표
common employment 공동작업
common external tariff 대외공통관세
common factor risk 공통요인리스크
common fund 공통기금
common gap 커먼갭
common informer 정보제공자
common injunction 보통금지명령
common law 관습법
common liquidation 통상해산
common market 공동시장
common nuisance 공적불법방해
common property 공유자산
common recovery 공모한 부동산회복소송
common signaling channel 공통선신호방식
common stock 보통주식
common stock book value 보통주의 장부가격
common stock equivalents 준보통주
common stock for treasury 자기주식
common stock outstanding 사외발행보통주식
common stock preemptive right 신주인수권
common vouchee 권리담보자
common-law action 민사소송
common-law corporation 관습법주식회사
common-law trust 관습법신탁
common-size balance sheet
백분율 대차대조표
common-size financial statements
백분율 재무제표
commons 입회지
commorancy 가주소
commorientes 동일사고 사망자
communication analysis 커뮤니케이션분석
communication barrier 커뮤니케이션장애
communication channel 커뮤니케이션채널
communication charges 통신비
communication control procedure
통신제어절차
communication control unit
통신제어장치

communication gap 커뮤니케이션 갭
communication satellite 통신위성
communication strategy 커뮤니케이션전략
communicator 전달자; 발신기
community 공동체
community involvement 지역활동참가
community paper 지역사회신문
community reinvestment
그 지방에 대한 재투자
community trust 지역공익신탁
commutation 환산
commutation function 계산기수
compact disk 콤팩트디스크
compact disk read only memory CD-ROM
company demand 자사수요
company law 회사법
company limited 주식회사
company limited by guarantee
유한책임보증회사
company limited by shares 주식회사
company organization 회사조직
company rehabilitation law 회사갱생법
company representative 회사대리인
company union 어용조합
company with reduced capital 감자회사
company's own stock 자사주
company-administered annuity 순수자가연금
company-specific 개별기업고유의
comparability 비교가능성
comparative advantage 비교우위
comparative advantage theory 비교우위이론
comparative advertising 비교광고
comparative analysis 비교분석
comparative balance sheet 비교대차대조표
comparative cost 비교원가
comparative cost studies 비교원가조사
comparative financial statement
비교재무제표
comparative income statement
비교손익계산서
comparative influence 비교작용

comparative marketing 비교마케팅
comparative profit and loss statement
　비교손익계산서
comparative statement 비교계산서
comparative statement of cash flows
　비교수지계산서
comparative statistics 비교통계학
comparison 조회
comparison of beta values of funds
　펀드베타수치를 비교함
comparison slip 조회표
comparison table 비교표
compatibility 양립성
compensated absence 유급휴가
compensating balance 구속잔고
compensating error 상쇄오차
compensating interest 상쇄이자
compensating trade or transactions 구상무역
compensatio criminum 죄의 상쇄
compensation 보수
compensation culpae 과실상쇄
compensation for damage 손해배상
compensation for eviction 입퇴료
compensation for expense and loss 경비보상금
compensation for expropriation
　수용에 의한 보상금
compensation for injuries and deaths
　부상사망보상금
compensation for residual land
　잔지(殘地) 보상금
compensation for revenue 수익보상금
compensation paid to directors 임원보수
compensation plan 보수방식
compensation plans based on assets
　운용자산액비례보수방식
compensation principle of taxation
　조세의 수익자부담원칙
compensation system 보상제도
compensation trade 구상무역
compensatory budget policy 보정예산정책
compensatory deposit 보상예금

compensatory effect 보정효과
compensatory financing facility 보상융자
compensatory fiscal policy 보정재정정책
compensatory item 보정항목
compensatory model 보정모델
compensatory surplus 보정여잉
compete 경합하다
competence 직권
competency 능력이 있음
competent 자격이 있는; 관할권이 있는
competent authority 권한이 있는 당국
competent parties 능력이 있는 당사자
competent taxation office 관할세무서
competent witness 증인능력이 있는 증인
competition strategy 경쟁전략
competitive access provider 시내경쟁사업자
competitive advertising 경쟁광고
competitive depreciation 경쟁적인 평가절하
competitive intelligence 경합타사정보
competitive market maker system
　투자기관경합시스템
competitive pattern 경합패턴
competitive pressure 경쟁압력
competitive price 경쟁가격
competitive sale 경쟁판매
competitive tender 경쟁입찰
competitor analysis 경쟁자분석
compilation 조제
complainant 원고
complaint 고정(苦情); 고소
complementary color 보색
complementary demand 보완수요
complementary goods 보완재
complete annuity 완전연금
complete audit 완전감사
complete competition 완전경쟁
complete life table 완전생명표
complete specialization 완전특화
complete stripping between interest and
　principal 원본금리를 완전 분리함
completed audit 기말감사

completed contract method 완성기준

completed operations hazard 완성작업위험

completely adaptive strategy 완전적합전략

completeness fund 보완펀드

completion basis 공사완성기준

completion bonus 완공보너스

completion guarantee 완성보증

complex instruction set computer
시스크; 중앙처리장치의 한 종류

complex salvage operation 복잡한 구조작업

complex transportation 복합수송

compliance 준수

compliance program 수출관리규정

component analysis 구성비율분석

component percentages 구성비율

component ratio 구성비

component signal 컴퍼넌트신호

components of cost 원가구성요소

composing 조판

composite depreciation 종합감가상각

composite depreciation assets 종합상각자산

composite index 종합경기지수

composite insurer 복수보험자

composite office 종합보험회사

composite price 컴포지트프라이스

composite quotation system
종합거래정보시스템

composite signal 컴포지트시그널

composite stock price index 종합주가지수

composite stock price tables 종합주가표

composite useful life 종합내용연수

composition 화의

composition law 화의법

composition of inventory 재고자산의 범위

composition of working capital
운전 자본 구성

compound annual rate 복리연율

compound annual return 연복리 수익률

compound discount 복리할인

compound entry 복합기입

compound interest 복리

compound interest bonds 할인지방채

compound interest method 복리방식

compound interest yield 복리이율

compound transaction 복합거래

comprador 매판

comprehensive 포괄적인

comprehensive bonded area 종합보세지역

comprehensive dwelling policy 주택종합보험

comprehensive general liability policy
종합배상책임보험

comprehensive income taxation 종합과세

comprehensive insurance 종합보험

comprehensive major medical insurance
종합고액의료비보험

comprehensive marketing system
포괄마케팅시스템

comprehensive personal liability insurance
종합개인배상책임보험

comprehensive system model 코스모 모델

comprehensive trade bill 포괄통상법안

compromise 타협

compromise method 절충방식

compromised total loss 협정전손

comptroller 감사역

comptroller in bankruptcy 파산감사관

compulsory 강제적

compulsory accident insurance 강제상해보험

compulsory audit 강제감사

Compulsory Automobile Liability Insurance
Council 자동차손해배상책임보험심의회

compulsory bond 강제재판보증증권

compulsory cancellation 강제해약

compulsory composition 강제화의

compulsory conversion into money 강제환가

compulsory deposit as a condition for loans
상환준비예금

compulsory execution 강제집행

compulsory insurance 강제보험

compulsory liability insurance 강제배상보험

compulsory or involuntary transfer of
property 강제적인 자산양도

C
D

compulsory sale by auction 강제경매
compulsory surplus 강제잉여금
compulsory third party liability insurance
　제3자 강제배상책임보험
compulsory winding-up 강제청산
compurgation 면책선서
CompuServe 컴퓨서브
computation 산정
computation of business income
　사업소득계산
computation of tax amount 세액계산
computation of useful years 내용연수계산
computation period 산정기간
computation procedure 계산절차
computed price 계산가격
computer aided design 캐드
computer assisted animation
　컴퓨터애니메이션
computer assisted execution system
　딜링거래시스템
computer personnel 컴퓨터요원
computer supported cooperation work
　컴퓨터지원협조작업
computerization 컴퓨터화
conative judgment 능동적인 판단
concealment 고지의무위반
concentrated investment 집중투자
concentrated marketing strategy
　집중마케팅전략
concentrated merchandising 집중머천다이징
concentration effect 집중효과
concentration of enterprise 기업집중
concentric diversification 동심원적인 다각화
concept formation 개념형성
concept of conservatism 보수주의회계
concept of historical cost 원가주의회계
concept statement 컨셉설명서
concept testing 컨셉테스팅
conceptual framework 개념틀짜기
concern 이해관계
concerned 해당의

concerns interested 관계회사
concerted activity 공동행위
concerted intervention 협조개입
concession 수수료
concession contract 양허계약
concession hunter 중개인
concessionaire 영업권소유자
concessions for nonresident
　비거주제에 대한 감면
conciliation 조정
conclusion 결론
conclusion drawing 결론을 내는 법
conclusion of a contract 계약체결
conclusive presumption 결정적인 추정
concord 화해
concurrent cause 병존원인
concurrent insurance 동위보험
concurrent jurisdiction 경쟁관할권
concurrent lease 변존임차권
concurrent liens 동순위선취특권
concurrent negligence 경합과실
concurrent policies 동위계약
concurrent promises 동시이행약속
concurrent test 동시조사테스트
concurrent writs 복수영장
condemn 공용수용하다
condemnation 유죄선고
condemnation of land 토지수용
condensed account form 요약계정식
condensed balance sheet 요약대차대조표
condensed income statement 요약손익계산서
condensed report form 요약보고식
condition 조건
condition collateral 부대조건
condition express 명시조건
condition implied 묵시조건
condition of average 비례증보조항
condition precedent 정지조건
conditional 조건부
conditional acceptance 조건부 인수
conditional approval 조건부 승인

conditional contract 조건부 계약
conditional distribution 조건부 분포
conditional liquidity 조건부 유동성
conditional loan 조건부 융자
conditional regression analysis
　조건부 회귀분석
conditional sales 조건부 매매
conditional sales agreement
　정형적으로 규정된 약관
conditional sales floater
　대금미불상품포괄보험
conditional subsidy from the national
　treasury 조건부 국고보조금
conditions for payment 지불조건
conditions of issuance 발행조건
conditions of sale 경매조건
condolence money 조위금, 부조금
condor type spread transaction
　콘도르 스프레드 거래
confederacy 공모
conference 협의
Conference of Ministers and Governors
　선진국상장 중앙은행총재회의
Conference of Non-Aligned Nations
　비동맹국회의; 중립국회의
Conference on International Economic
　Cooperation 국제경제협력회의
Conference on Security and Cooperation in
　Europe 유럽안보협력회의
confession 자백
confession of judgment 판결승인
confidence 신임
confidence coefficient 신뢰계수
confidence game 대금을 치를 생각 없이 물품
　을 대량으로 구매하여 사취함
confidence interval confidence coefficient
　신뢰구간신뢰계
confidence value 신뢰수치
confidential operation 은밀오퍼
confidential relation 신뢰관계
confidentiality 기밀성

confidentiality agreement 비밀유지계약
confidentiality of information 비밀유지의무
configuration management 구성관리
confirmation 확인
confirmation letter 확인장
confirmation note 확인통지서
confirmation request 확인청구
confirmed letter of credit 확인필 신용장
confirming bank 확인은행
confirming charge 신용장확인인수수료
confirming house 컨퍼밍하우스
confiscation 몰수
conflict of interest 이해가 충돌함
conflict of laws 법률에 저촉됨
conformity 적합성
confounded variable 변화무쌍함
confrontation 대심(對審)
confusion 혼동
conglomerate 콘글로머리트; 거대복합기업
conglomerate merchandising
　콘글로머리트머천다이징
conjunctive model 지배 모델
connivance 묵인
consecutive dividend 안정배당
consecutive quarters 연속사반기
consensual contract 낙성계약
consensus 일치
consensus on earnings estimate
　수익 예측 컨센서스
consent 동의
consent dividend 간주배당
consent judgment 동의판결
consequential damage 간접손해
consequential loss insurance 사업중단보험
conservatism 보수성
conservator 후견인
conservator bond 재산관리보증
considerable rise 급증
consideration 대가; 약인
consideration clause 약인조항
consignee 수탁자

consignment 위탁판매적송품
consignment contract 위탁계약
consignment fee 위탁수수료
consignment goods 위탁품
consignment guarantee money 위탁증거금
consignment invoice 위탁품송장
consignment ledger 납세위탁
consignment of tax liability 납세위탁
consignment of tax payment 납부위탁
consignment sale 위탁판매
consignment sales and purchases 위탁매매
consignment sales contract 위탁판매계약
consignor 위탁인
consilium 변론기일
consistency 일관성
consistency of auditor 감사원의 일관성
consolation money 위로금
console 조종대, 제어탁자
consolidate 경합하다
consolidated 연결의
consolidated account 연결계정
consolidated annuities 콘솔공채
consolidated balance sheet 연결대차대조표
consolidated delivery system 혼재배송시스템
consolidated financial statements
　　연결재무제표
consolidated financial statistics
　　연결재무통계
consolidated goodwill 연결된 선의
consolidated income 연결이익
consolidated income statement
　　연결손익계산표
consolidated income tax 종합소득세
consolidated net loss 연결순손실
consolidated profit and loss statement
　　연결손익계산서
consolidated quotation system
　　통합시황정보시스템
consolidated sales 연결매상
consolidated stock ticker 종합주식티커
consolidated surplus 연결잉여금

consolidated tape 종합테이프
consolidated tax return system 그룹과세
consolidated working capital 연결운전자금
consolidation 신설합병
consolidation excess 연결초과액
consolidation group 연결집단
consolidation ledger 연결원장
consolidation loan 콘솔리데이션론
consolidation of corporations
　　기업의 신규합병
consolidation of mortgages
　　양도저당이 병합됨
consolidation of public loans 공채정리
consolidation of stocks 주식병합
consolidation pattern 조정패턴
consolidation policy 연결방침
consolidation take-over 흡수합병
Consols 콘솔공채
consortium 국채모집인수단컨소시엄
consortium bank 컨소시엄뱅크
conspiracy 공동모의
constant capital 불변자본
constant claims amount distribution
　　항상손해액분포
constant continuously compounded
　　일정한 연속복리
constant cost 고정비
constant divisor 항상제수(恒常除數)
constant dollar net income
　　안정가치로 수정한 순이익
constant dollar plan 정액법
constant dollars 안정가치
constant elasticity of variance model
　　정탄성 분산모델
constant expenses 고정비
constant model 일정형 모델
constant percentage method 고정비율법
constant power purchasing accounting
　　안정구매력회계
constant purchasing power 안정구매력
constant risk 항상위험

constant risk tolerance 불변리스크

constant sum scale 고정수치를 각 항목에 분배해서 선호도를 나타냄

constant-dollar accounting 안정가치회계

constant-dollar profit 안정가치이익

constant-growth rate model
고정비율성장 모델

constant-growth rate valuation model
고정비율성장평가 모델

constituent 선거권자

constitutional right 헌법상의 권리

construction 해석

construction account 건설비계정

construction bond 건설국채

construction claim 건설클레임

construction contracts 청부계약

construction cost 건축비

construction expenditure 건설지출

construction in process account 건설가계정

construction of completion 완성공사고

construction revenue 공사수입

Construction Standard Law 건축기준법

construction subsidy 건설조성금

construction work 건설공사

construction work account receivable
공사미수금

construction work revenue 건설공사수입

constructive 추정의

constructive bonus 인정상여

constructive conversion 법정횡령

constructive delivery 의제인도

constructive dividends 간주배당

constructive eviction 의제퇴거

constructive notice 추정악의

constructive receipt 인정수입

constructive service 간접송달

constructive taxable year 인정사업연도

constructive total loss
해석전손(全損); 추정전손(全損)

constructive trust 법정신탁

consuetude 관습

consul 영사

consular courts 영사재판소

consular invoice 영사송장

consulting sales 컨설팅세일즈

consumables 소모품

consumer advertisement 소비자광고

consumer behavior 소비자행동

consumer behavior analysis 소비자행동분석

consumer choice 소비자선택

consumer credit 소비자신용

consumer credit company 소비자금융회사

consumer credit control law
소비자금융규제법

consumer credit life insurance
소비자금융생명보험

consumer credit rate 소비자금융의 금리

consumer demand 실수요

consumer education 소비자교육

consumer electronics 가전(家電)

consumer expenditure 소비자지출

consumer exploitation 소비자개척

consumer finance company 소비자금융회사

consumer leasing 소비자리스

consumer loan 소비자금융

consumer movement 소비자운동

consumer perception 소비자지각

consumer premises equipment 고객단말

consumer price index 소비자물가지수

consumer relations 컨슈머릴레이션

consumer sector stock 소비자관련주

consumer spending 소비자지출

consumer testing 소비자테스트

consumer thought variable 소비자사고변수

consumer's behavior 소비자행동

consumer's cooperative society
소비생활협동조합

consumer's credit 개인신용정보

consumer's union 소비자단체

consumerism 소비자주의

consumers' durables 내구소비재

consumers group insurance 소비자단체생명

보험
consumption demand 소비수요
consumption entry 소비세 신고
consumption function 소비함수
consumption lag 소비 래그
consumption multiplier 소비승수
consumption quota 소비할당
consumption tax 소비세
consumption transfer tax 소비양여세
consumption trend 소비동향
consumption values 소비가치
containerization 컨테이너 수송
contamination damages 오염손해
contango 주식결제연기이식
contemplation of bankruptcy 파산예기
contemporaneous reserve accounting
　동시적립방식
contempt 모욕
content provider 정보제공자; 정보제공기업
content-certified mail 내용증명우편
contentious 서로 다투는
contestable period 논쟁기간
Continental Depositary Receipts
　유럽주식예탁증서
continental form of closing the ledger
　대륙식 원장마감수속
contingency 우발사상
contingency freight 불확정운송임
contingency fund 위험준비금
contingency insurance 우연손실보험
contingency loading 안전할증
contingency reserve 이상위험준비금
contingency risk 우발적인 위험
contingency theory 상황적합이론
contingent 파생적인
contingent annuity 부정연금
contingent assets 우발자산
contingent beneficiary 차순위보험금수취인
contingent business interruption insurance
　미필영업중단보험
contingent charge 우발비용

contingent claim 파생상품
contingent commission 이익수수료
contingent estate 불확정재산권
contingent fee 성공보수
contingent fund 우발자금
contingent interest 불확정이자
contingent liabilities 우발채무
contingent liability policy 미필배상책임보험
contingent loss 우발손실
contingent order 일정 가격차에 따른 조합주문
contingent outlay 임시비
contingent profit 우발이익
contingent reserve 우발채무적립금
contingent transaction 우발거래
continuance 재판을 속행함
continuation 지속
continuation clause 지속약관
continuation pattern 지속패턴
continued expenses 지속비
continuing account 지속계정
continuing contract 지속계약
continuing education 지속교육
continuing expenditure 지속비
continuing guaranty 무기한보증
continuing operations 지속사업
continuous annuity 연속생명연금
continuous audit 지속회계감사
continuous buying and selling 지속적인 매매
continuous compound interest rate 연속복리
continuous compounding calculation
　연속복리 계산
continuous disclosure 계속개시
continuous dividend 연속배당
continuous inventory 지속재고
continuous manufacturing 연속생산
continuous market 계속시장; 연속거래
continuous policy 지속적인 예정보험계약
continuous probability distribution
　연속확률분포
continuous reinsurance cover 재보험특약
continuous sampling 연속발췌

continuous session 연속회기
continuous time 연속시간
continuous trading 연속매매
continuous variable 연속변수
contra 상대
contra account 대조계정
contra broker 상수브로커
contra entry 상대기입
contra-cyclical 반순환적인
contraband 수입금지품
contraband of export 수출금지품
contraband of import 수입금지품
contract 계약
contract balance 계약잔고
contract bond 계약보증
contract charge 계약수수료
contract curve 계약곡선
contract deposit paid 계약전도금
contract deposit received 계약전수금
contract entered into by mutual consensus
  낙성계약
contract for service 역무계약
contract in bulk 일괄계약
contract in kind 요물(要物)계약
contract market 계약시장
contract money 계약금
contract month 한월(限月)
contract notice 약정통지
contract of merger 합병계약서
contract position 계약포지션
contract price 협정가격
contract rate system 계약운임제
contract ratio 계약률
contract review 계약내용확인
contract salvage 계약구조
contract salvage charges 계약구조료
contract size 계약규모
contract slip 매매확인서
contract specification 계약사양서
contract system 청부제도
contract term 계약기간

contract terms 계약조건
contract type 계약형
contract type accumulative investment plan
  계약형 계속투자플랜
contract type investment trust
  계약형 투자신탁
contract uberrimae fldei theory 선의계약설
contract work 청부공사
contract work account receivable
  청부공사미수금
contract work system 청부제도
contracted interest rate 약정금리
contracted out 적용제외
contracted price 약정가격
contracted rate 약정이율
contracting out 하청하다; 연금적용제외
contracting party 계약당사자
contractor 공사청부인
contractors' all risks insurance 건설공사보험
contractors' contingent liability insurance
  건설청부업자 미필배상책임보험
contractors' equipment floater
  건설청부업자 기계기구포괄보험
contractors' insurance policy
  공사청부인 보험증권
contractors' liability insurance
  건설청부업자 책임보험
contractual accumulation plan
  이익누적형 투신
contractual documents 계약서
contractual liability 계약책임
contractual liability policy 계약배상책임보험
contractual vertical marketing
  계약형 수직적 마케팅
contractual wage 협정임금
contrarian 역발상에 능한 주식투자가
contrary opinion 반대의견
contravention 위반하다
contributed stock 거출자금
contributed surplus 거출잉여금
contribution 거출금; 분담금

contribution deduction 기부금공제
contribution in aid of construction
공사부담금
contribution margin 공헌이익
contribution margin form 공헌이익식
contribution plan 거출제도
contribution system 보험료분담제
contribution to welfare facilities
복리시설부담액
contributions to affiliated company
관계회사출자금
contributories 출자의무자
contributory annuity 거출제연금
contributory infringement 기여침해
contributory margin 공헌이익
contributory negligence 조성과실
contributory plan 보험료분담제
contributory shares of estate 기여분
contributory sickness fund 거출식 질병보험
contributory value 공동해손부담가액
control account 통괄계정
control limit 관리한계
control market 지배시장
control measure 억제조치
control mechanism 관리기구
control of inflation 인플레억제
control procedure 관리절차
control stock 지배주
controllable expenses 관리가능원가
controlled account 피통괄계정
controlled company 피지배회사
controlled currency 관리통화
controlled discretion 법규재량
controlled preferred stock 보증우선주
controller 회계검사관
controlling account 통괄계정
controlling company 지배회사
controlling inflation 인플레억제
controlling interest 경영지배권
contumacy 명령불복종
convenience 편의

convenience goods 일용잡화, 식료품
convenience of tax collection 징세상의 편의
convenience shelf registration 편의일괄등록
convenience yield 편의수익
conveniences 설비
convention expense 회의비
convention for the avoidance of double
taxation 이중과세방지조약
Convention on International Civil Aviation
국제민간항공조약
Convention on International Combined
Transport 국제복합운송조약
conventional commodity market
전통적인 상품시장
conventional loan 일반대출
conventional marketing channel
전통적인 마케팅경로
conventional mortgage loan 통상형 모기지론
conventional tariff 협정관세
conventional undamaged value
협정무손상가액
converge 수렴하다
convergence analysis 집중분석
convergent fluctuation 수검성변동
convergent marketing 수검형 마켓팅
converse preference 역특혜
conversion 횡령; 환산
conversion at market price 시가전환
conversion at par 액면전환
conversion conditions 전환조건
conversion cost 가공비
conversion cost system 공정별 종합원가계산
conversion discount 전환 디스카운트
conversion factor 변환계수
conversion into cash 환가처분
conversion into cash of seized property
차압재산환가
conversion issue 차환발행
conversion of items in foreign currencies
외화 기준 계정 항목을 환산함
conversion parity 전환비율

conversion period 전환청구기간
conversion premium 전환프리미엄
conversion price 전환가격
conversion price formula 전환가격방식
conversion privilege 보험종류변경청구권
conversion ratio 전환비율
conversion to gold 금태환
conversion value 전환가치
convertible 가변보험
convertible bond 전환사채
convertible bonds with option
　옵션부 전환사채
convertible contract 중도전환계약
convertible currency 태환통화
convertible mortgage 전환모기지
convertible note 태환지폐
convertible preferred stock 전환우선주
convertible ratio 교환비율
convertible reserve 태환준비
convertible securities 전환증권
convertible stock 전환주식
convertible term insurance 가변정기보험
convexity 볼록한 모양
conveyance of estate 재산양도
conveyancer 부동산양도취급인
conveyer system 컨베이어시스템
conviction 유죄결정
convincing proof 확신적인 입증
cooking of a book 장부위조
cooling time 냉각기간
cooling-off 냉각시키기 위한
cooperation between industry and academic
　organizations 산학협동
cooperative association 협동조합
cooperative association on indirect taxes
　간접세협력단체
cooperative bank 신용조합
cooperative business association
　사업협동조합
Cooperative Credit Purchase Corporation
　공동채권매입기구

Cooperative Financing Facility
　수출변동보상융자제도
cooperative marketing 공동판매
cooperative society 협동조합
coordinate system 좌표계
coordinated cut 협조가격하락
coordinated intervention 협조개입
coordination of bond issues 기채조정
coparcenary 상속재산공유
copyright 저작권
core 중핵
core business division 주력부문
core competence 핵심역량
core holding 코어홀딩
core market 핵심시장
core stock 핵심주
core-fringe model 코어프린지모델
corn hog cycle 콘허그순환
corner lot 길모퉁이땅
cornering 매점
corporate accounting 기업회계
corporate accounting principles
　기업회계원칙
corporate action 회사행위
corporate alliance 기업연합
corporate average tax rate 평균법인세율
corporate banking 기업금융
corporate board of directors 이사회
corporate body 법인단체
corporate bond 사채
corporate card 법인카드
corporate charter 인가장
corporate citizenship 기업시민성
corporate color 코퍼레이트 컬러
corporate communication 기업홍보
corporate culture 기업문화
corporate customer 법인고객
corporate debenture 사채
corporate deposit 법인예금
corporate domain 기업도메인
corporate equivalent yield 사채환산이율

corporate executive 회사중역
corporate finance 사업금융
corporate franchise 회사특권
corporate identity 기업이미지통합전략
corporate image 기업이미지
corporate income 법인소득
corporate income tax rate 법인소득세율
corporate income taxes expenses
　法人소득세비용
corporate juridical person 사단법인
corporate management 기업경영
corporate mission 기업의 사명
corporate name 상호
corporate pension 기업연금
corporate profile 기업프로필
corporate raider 기업매수자
corporate reorganization 회사갱생
corporate resolution 이사회 결의
corporate right 법인권
corporate ripoff 기업사취
corporate savings 법인저축
corporate seal 법인인감
corporate securities 사채
corporate's separation 회사분할
corporate settlement 기업안정
corporate shareholder 법인주주
corporate strategy 기업전략
corporate suretyship 법인보증인
corporate tax 법인세
corporate treasurer 기업재무담당자
corporate trust 법인신탁
corporate vitality 기업활력
corporation 법인
corporation aggregate 집합법인
corporation amalgamated 피합병법인
corporation bond 사채
corporation card 법인카드
corporation ceased to exist after merger
　합병으로 소멸한 회사
corporation filing a blue return
　청색신고법인

corporation finance 기업금융
corporation for profit 영리법인
corporation free from taxation 비과세법인
corporation in need of reorganization
　갱생회사
corporation in public interest 공익법인
corporation in the course of liquidation
　청산중인 법인
corporation levy 법인세할주민세
corporation liable to taxation
　납세의무가 있는 법인
Corporation of Lloyd's 로이즈조합
corporation of public utility 공익법인
corporation profit tax 법인이득세
corporation reorganization law 회사갱생법
corporation report 회사레포트
corporation sector 기업부문
corporation tax credit 법인세공제
corporation type 기업형
corporation type investment trust
　기업형 투자신탁
corporation under liquidation
　청산 절차 중인 법인
corporation's own stock 자사주
corporeal hereditament 유체 상속 부동산
corpus 원본
corpus delicti 죄의 주체
corrected probability 수정된 확률
correction 갱정; 조정
correction of errors 오진을 정정함
correction of prior periods 전기수정항목
corrective action 시정처치
corrective advertising 사죄광고
corrective market 정정상장
corrective selling 정정매출
correlation 상관관계
correlation analysis 상관분석
correlation coefficient 상관계수
correlation diagram 상관도
correlation matrix 상관행렬
correlation of return 수익률의 상관관계

correlation table 상관표
correlative adjustment 대응조정
correlative industry 관련산업
correspondent account 코레스계정
correspondent agreement 코레스계약
correspondent bank 코레스은행
correspondent financial institution
    코레스거래금융기관
correspondent relation 코레스관계
corresponding account 상대계좌
corresponding deposit 상대예금
corresponding period of last year 전년 동기
corroborate 보강하다
corroborating evidence 보강증거
corruption 뇌물수수, 부패
corruption of blood 혈통이 탁해짐
cost 원가
cost absorption 원가흡수
cost account 원가계정
cost accounting 원가계산
cost accounting by department 부문별 원가계산
cost accounting by product 제품별 원가계산
cost accounting period 원가계산기간
cost accounting standards 원가계산기준
cost accounting system 원가계산제도
cost analysis 원가분석
cost and expenses 원가 및 비용
cost and freight 운임포함
cost at the margin 한계비용
cost basis 원가주의
cost behavior 비용동향
cost card 원가계산서
cost classification 비용분류
cost consciousness 원가의식
cost control 원가관리
cost depletion 감모상각비
cost depletion method 취득잔고비례법
cost distribution 원가배분
cost effective 비용효율이 좋은
cost effectiveness analysis 비용대비효과분석
cost element 원가요소

cost finding 원가산정
cost flow assumption 재고자산평가방법
cost for development 개발비
cost for judicial proceedings 소송절차비용
cost function 비용함수
cost improvement cost 경비개선비용
cost insurance and freight 운임 · 보험료포함
cost ledger 원가원장
cost matching income principle 비용수익대
    응의 원칙
cost method 원가법
cost method of depletion 감모상각원가법
cost of arbitration 중재비용
cost of assets 자산취득원가
cost of capital 자본코스트
cost of carry 자산소유비용
cost of conformity 적정비용
cost of construction 공사비
cost of disposal 처분비용
cost of finished goods 제품원가
cost of goods purchased 구입원가
cost of goods sold 매상원가
cost of issuing stocks 주식발행비용
cost of living index 생활비지수
cost of maintenance 유지비
cost of manufactured goods 제조원가
cost of processing 가공비
cost of product 제품원가
cost of production budget 제조비예산
cost of products sold 매각원가
cost of raising funds 자금조달코스트
cost of repairs 수선비
cost of reproduction 재생산원가
cost of sales 판매원가
cost of short-term funds 단기자금조달비용
cost of tax collection 징세비용
cost of temporary repair 가수선비
cost of transferred properties
    양도자신취득비용
cost of work performed 생산고원가
cost or market whichever is lower basis

분리저가법
cost overrun 예산초과
cost per thousand 시청자 천 명당 광고비
cost performance 가격대비성능비
cost plus 원가(이윤)가산방식
cost plus fixed fee contract
　정액보수실비지불계약
cost plus method 원가기준법
cost price 구입가격
cost principle 원가주의
cost rate 원가율
cost recovery 원가회수
cost reduction 코스트삭감
cost report 원가보고서
cost savings 원가삭감
cost sheet 원가계산표
cost standard 원가기준
cost statement 원가계산서
cost system 원가시스템
cost trade-off 코스트트레이드오프
cost unit 원가단위
cost value 원가가치
cost variance 원가차액
cost-benefit analysis 비용·편익분석
cost-of-living index 생활비지수
cost-or-less principle 원가이하주의
cost-plus contract 실비정산계약
cost-push inflation 코스트푸시인플레이션
cost-reduction programs 원가저감계획
cost-volume-profit analysis
　비용·조업도·이익분석
costing 원가계산
costing period 원가계산기간
costing unit 원가계산단위
costs bond 소송비용보증증권
cosurety 공동보증인
cotenancy 부동산공동보유
council 평의회
Council of Europe 유럽회의
council of managing directors 상무회
Council of the Bar 법정변호사평의회

council on alcoholic beverages 주류심의회
counselor 법률고문
count 항목; 총계
count out 정족수를 채우지 못했다고 인정하여
　유회하다
counter cyclical 반순환적
counter cyclical policy 반순환정책
counter deed 반대증서
counter guarantee 역보증
counter purchase 대응구매
counter value 대가
counter-affidavit 반대선서진술서
counter-plea 반대항(답)변
counter-security 역담보
counterclaim 반소(反訴)
countercyclical advertising 역주기 광고
counterdeed 반대증서
counterfeit 위조
counterfeit card 위조카드
countermand 취소하다
countermeasure 대책
counteroffer 반대오퍼
counterpart 상대방
counterparty (계약의)한쪽 당사자
counterrolls 공동장부
countersign 부서
countersignature 연서(連署)
countervailing duty 상쇄관세
countervailing power 대항력
counting 계정; 계좌
country damage 원산지손해
country exposure 컨트리익스포저
country having deficit in cap transaction
　자본수출국
country limit 국별한도
country risk 국가신용도
county borough 특별시
coupon 이자표
coupon advertisement 쿠폰광고
coupon bank debenture 이부금융채
coupon bond 이표채; 이자부채권

coupon income 쿠폰수입
coupon off 이자표가 떨어진
coupon on 이자표가 붙은
coupon pass 쿠폰패스
coupon payment 이자지불
coupon payment date 이불기일
coupon plan 쿠폰방식
coupon rate 채권의 표면이자율
coupon sale 쿠폰세일
coupon swap 쿠폰스와프
coupon-only currency swap
　쿠폰 만의 통화스와프
courier service 쿠리어서비스
court 법원
court above 상소법원
court below 원법원
court clerk 법원소기관
court for the trial of impeachments 탄핵재판
court in bank 대법정
Court of Admiralty 해사재판소
court of appeal 공소재판소
court of bankruptcy 파산재판소
court of equity 에퀴티재판소
court of first instance 제일심재판소
court of general sessions 형사제일심
court of justiciary 형사상급재판소
court of nisi prius 민사제일심재판소
court of probate 검인재판소
court of request 소액채권재판소
court-hand 법정서체
covariance 공분산
covariance analysis 공분산분석
covenance 관용
covenant 특약조항; 약인
covenant for title 권한담보조항
covenant of seisin 권리담보조항
cover 보험을 통한 담보
cover bid 커버비드
cover dealing 커버딜링
cover note 가증서, 보험인수증
cover the loss 손실을 메꾸다

coverage 담보범위
covered call 커버드 콜
covered call option 커버드 콜 옵션
covered option 커버드 옵션
covered position 커버드 포지션
covered quarter 피보험기
covered warrant 커버드 워런트
covering entry 분개기입
covering of a deficit 적자보전
craft 동업조합
crash 붕락
crawling peg 크롤링페그; 단계적인 평가변동
　방식
crawling peg system 단계적인 평가변동방식
craze for speculation 투기열
cream skimming 크림스키밍
creaming merchandise 가장 유망한 상품
creation 창립
creation of utility 효용을 창조함
creative strategy 크리에이티브전략
credibility 신용도
credit 대변공제; 채권; 신용
credit accommodation 신용공여
credit account 외상거래계정
credit against corporation tax 법인세공제
credit against tax 세액공제
credit agreement 여신계약
credit among corporations 기업간 신용
credit analysis 여신분석
credit and suretyship insurance
　신용 및 보증보험
credit association 신용조합
credit authorization terminal 신용조합단말
credit availability 여신공여량
credit balance 대변잔고
credit bill 신용어음
credit business 여신업무
credit buying 기한부 어음을 매입함
credit capability 신용력
credit card 신용카드
credit card burglary insurance 카드도난보험

credit card business 신용카드업무
credit card company 신용카드회사
credit cards issued by the agent 대행카드
credit ceiling 신용한도
credit ceiling application system
　대출한도액 적용제도
credit control 여신관리
credit conversion factor 신용환산계수
credit creation 신용창조
credit crisis 신용공황
credit crunch 신용제한
credit customer 신용외상거래처
credit ease 신용완화
credit economy 신용경제
credit exposure management 여신관리
credit facility 크레디트퍼실리티; 신용편의
credit for dividend 배당공제
credit for foreign taxes 외국세액공제
credit for handicapped person 장애자공제
credit for income tax 소득세액공제
credit guarantee 신용보증
credit guarantee corporation 신용보증협회
credit history 크레디트히스토리
credit inquiry 신용조회
credit insurance 신용보험
credit investigation 신용조사
credit life insurance 신용생명보험
credit limit 신용한도
credit line 대출한도액; 신용한도
credit line system 신용한도제도
credit loan 신용대출
credit losses 대손
credit margin 신용증거금
credit memorandum 대출메모
credit money 신용화폐
credit note 대변전표
credit past due date 기일도래원본
credit policy 신용정책
credit price 외상거래가격
credit purchase 외상구입
credit quality 신용도

credit rating 신용등급부여
credit ratio 신용비율
credit rationing 신용제한
credit records 신용정보
credit reference 신용조회
credit risk 여신리스크
credit sales 외상거래
credit sales accounts 신용판매계정
credit slip 입금표
credit spread 신용격차
credit squeeze 금융긴축
credit standing 신용상태
credit standing condition 신용상태
credit structure 신용구조
credit system 신용제도
credit terms 신용조건
credit tranche 크레디트트란시
credit union 신용조합
credit union exchange 신용조합환
credit watch system 신용감시시스템
credit worthiness 신용력
creditable amount of foreign taxes
　외국세액공제한도액
creditor 채권자
creditor account 대출계정
creditor bank 대출은행
creditor country 채권국
creditor group insurance 단체신용생명보험
creditor side 대출란
creditor's equity to total assets 부채비율
creditor's meeting 채권자회의
creditor's voluntary winding-up
　채권자에 의한 임의청산
creditors ledger 구입처원장
creditworthy 신용력이 있는
creep back upwards
　시세가 조금씩 오르는 경향
creeping 신고없이
creeping inflation 크리핑 인플레이션;
　잠행성 인플레이션
creeping nationalization 점진적인 국유화

crime bond 범죄보증증권
crime insurance 범죄보험
crime of interference with execution of
   official duty 공무집행방해죄
crimen falsi 위조죄
criminal action 형사소송
criminal information 약식기소장
criminal investigation 강제조사
criminal investigation system 사찰제도
criminal of tax evasion 탈세범
criminal proceedings 형사소송절차
criminal record 범죄력
crisis 공황
crisis at maturity 일괄반제리스크
crisis rate 위기 레이트
criteria 표준
criteria rights 기준설정권
critical function 비판기능
critical mass 임계질량
critical mass of reward 보수한계량
critical path method 크리티컬 패스 메소드
critical point 임계치
critical-path accounting 크리티컬 패스 회계
criticality hazard 임계위험
crop 생산고
crop basis 수확기준
crop insurance 수확물보험
cross 크로스매매
cross action 반대소송
cross arbitration 크로스재정
cross claim 강제소송참가
cross correlation 상호상관
cross culture 비교문화
cross currency swap 통화간 채무교환거래
cross debt 상대채무
cross default 크로스디폴트
cross default clause 크로스디폴트조항
cross elasticity 교차탄력성
cross entry 대체기입
cross examination 반대심문
cross hedge 크로스 헤지

cross impact analysis 크로스 임팩트 분석
cross liabilities basis 교차책임주의
cross license 특허권 교환
cross license contract 특허권교환계약
cross margin 크로스 마진
cross offer 교차 신청
cross order 크로스 오더
cross rate 크로스 레이트
cross reference list 상호참조표
cross sectional analysis 타기업비교
cross slip 대체전표
cross subsidization 내부상호보조
cross tabulation 크로스 집계표
cross trading 크로스 거래
cross-appeal 반대상소
cross-cultural analysis 이문화비교분석
cross-currency interest rate swap
   교차통화금리스와프
cross-demand 반대청구
cross-examination 반대심문
cross-holding 복수기업이 주식을 소유함
cross-sectional analysis 횡단분석
cross-sectional data 횡단데이터
cross-sectional valuation approach
   크로스섹셔널 평가법
crossed check 횡선수표
crossed market 역전된 시장
crossing for the purpose of financing
   금융크로스
crowd 군중; 대중; 동아리
crowd trading 크라우드 거래
crowding out 크라우딩 아웃; 구축
crowding out effect 크라우딩 아웃 효과; 구축
   효과
crown event 관 이벤트
crown jewel 중요 부문
crown law 형법
CRT projection display
   CRT 투사 디스플레이
crude oil futures 원유선물옵션
crunch 재정제한

crystallization 유동담보를 결정함
cuff quote 양을 가늠하여 값을 부름
culpa 과실
culpa concurrens 경합과실
culpability 유죄
culpable 과실을 범하다
cultural assimilation 문화융합
cultural change 문화변용
cultural influence 문화경향
cultural synergy 문화시너지
cultural values 문화적인 가치관
cum call 불입부
cum coupon 이자표부
cum dividend 배당부
cum new 신주부
cum right 신주인수권부
cum warrant 컴워런트
cumulative amount of depreciation
　감가상각누계액
cumulative deficit 누적적자
cumulative dividend 누적배당
cumulative experience 누적경험
cumulative fiscal deficit 국가예산누적적자
cumulative index 누적지수
cumulative legacy 누적유증
cumulative liability 누적책임
cumulative limit 누적한도액기준
cumulative limitation 누적제한
cumulative method 누가법
cumulative of offenses 반복범죄
cumulative preferred stock 누적우선주
cumulative surplus 누적흑자
cumulative taxation 누적과세
cumulative voting 누적투표
Curacao Depositary Receipts 유럽예탁증서
curator 후견인
curb dealings 장외거래
curb market 장외시장
curia 재판소
currency 통화
currency alignment 통화조정

currency and demand deposits
　현금 및 예금통화
currency appreciation 통화등귀
currency basket 통화바스켓
currency commodity 통화상품
currency conversion 통화환산
currency conversion bond 커런시컨버전채
currency convertible in fact
　사실상 교환 가능한 통화
currency crisis 통화위기
currency deflation 통화디플레이션
currency deposit 통화성 예금
currency depreciation 통화가치하락
currency devaluation 통화절하
currency fluctuation 통화변동
currency futures 통화선물
currency futures price movement
　통화선물가격동향
currency futures trading 통화선물거래
currency hedging 환 헤지
currency in circulation 통화유통고
currency indemnity 통화보상
currency inflation 통화 인플레
currency movement 환 동향
currency note 정부통화
currency option trading 통화 옵션 거래
currency principle 통화주의
currency swap 통화 스와프
currency swap bond 통화 스와프 채
currency system 통화체계
currency translation adjustments 외화환산조
　정액
currency unit 통화단위
currency upvaluation 통화절상
currency value 통화가치
current 경상(經常); 당좌의
current account 당좌계정
current account balance 경상수지
current account cheek 당좌수표
current annuity 현재 유효한 연금
current arrangement 유동성 배열법

current assets 유동자산
current balance 경상수지
current budget 경상예산
current cost 현재 원가
current cost accounting 취득원가주의회계
current cost method 시가방식
current cost/constant dollar accounting
  시가주의 안정가치회계
current cost/nominal dollar accounting
  시가주의 명목가치회계
current coupon 기간지표
current credit accounts with agencies
  대리점대출
current deposit 당좌예금
current disbursement approach 부과방식
current dollar 경상달러
current expenditure 경상지출
current expenses 경상비용
current fiscal year 현회계연도
current fund 당좌자금
current income 당기이익
current insurance 현재 유효한 보험
current insured status 당좌수급자격
current interest rate 현행이자율
current investment 단기투자
current level of stock price 현재의 주가수준
current liabilities 유동부채
current market value 현행시장가액
current market yield spread 실제시장이율폭
current maturities of long-term debt
  장기부채반제액
current maturity 당기만기부분
current money 유통화폐
current operating performance basis
  당기업적주의
current operating performance income
  statement 당기업적주의에 따른 손익계산서
current operating performance theory
  당기업적주의
current payment 경상지불
current period 당기

current premium value 현행 프리미엄
current price 시가
current ratio 유동비율
current replacement cost 재취득가격
current risks 책임보유리스크
current service pension 현재근무연금
current taxable year 당기
current taxes 당기세액
current term net income 당기순익
current term net loss 당기순손실
current term net profit 당기순이익
current term net profit or loss 당기순손익
current term settlement 당기결산
current transaction 경상거래
current transfer 경상이전
current value 현재가치
current value accounting 시가회계
current year 당기
current yield 직접이익
current-asset cycle 유동자산회전기간
current-assumption whole life insurance
  커런트 어섬션 종신보험
current-first order 유동성 배열
current-outlay cost 당기지출원가
curtailment of expenditure 경비삭감
curtailment of operation 조업단축
curtate expectation of life 단순평균여명
curve steepening 커브를 가파르게 함
curving trend line 비선형 추세선
cushion bond 쿠션채
custodial account 보관계정
custodian 주식보관인
custodian bank 보관은행
custodian's agent 행사명의대리인
custody 보관
custody fee 보관료
custom 관습법
custom free 세관수수료
custom index 커스텀인덱스
custom of merchant 상습관
custom-house 세관

customary losses 통상손해
customary practice 관행
customary tenure 관습상의 보유
customary tenure estates 관습상의 보유권
customer holdover effect 고객이월효과
customer market 고객시장
customer mix 고객믹스
customer oriented 고객지향
customer preference 고객을 엄선함
customer rationalization 고객을 합리화함
customer relations 고객관계
customer repos 고객보고
customer research 고객조사
customer transaction 고객단가
customer's account 거래처계정
customer's agreement and consent
　거래약정서
customer's loan 신용거래대출
customer's order 고객주문
customer's satisfaction 고객만족도
customers 거래처
customers' deposits 예금보증금
customers' ledger 외상매출금원장
customers' liabilities on guaranties
　보증채무담보

customers mobilizing power 고객동원력
customized performance standards
　커스텀 퍼포먼스 스탠더드
customs autonomy 관세자주권
customs debenture 세환급증명서
customs duty refund system 관세환부제도
customs duty tariff 관세
customs house 세관
customs invoice 통관용 송장
customs of merchant 상관습법
customs procedures 통관수속
customs tariff table 관세율표
customs union 관세동맹
cutoff date 마감일
cuttings 이자표
cyan magenta yellow black
　인쇄 프로세스 컬러
cybernetics 사이버네틱스
cycle 주기
cycle of fashion 유행주기
cycle stock 운전재고
cyclical depression 순환불황
cyclical fluctuation 순환변동
cyclical growth 성장 순환성장
cyclical stock 순환주

daily account 일계표

daily balance 일일잔고

daily bordereau 계약일보

daily chart 일일차트

daily diminishing clause 일차체감약관

daily interest for arrearage 연체이자

daily pro-rata return of premium
　일할반환보험료

daily rate 하루이자

daily trial balance 일계표

daily workers insurance
　일일고용노무자건강보험

daimyo bond 다이묘 본드

damage 손해

damage insurance 손해보험

damageability 손상성

damaged property 피해자산

damaged value 손상가액

damages 손해배상액

damnum sine injuria
　배상청구를 인정받지 못하는 손해

dangers of navigation 해상위험

data broadcasting 데이터방송

data processing business 데이터가공업무

data reduction 데이터정리

data retrieval 데이터검색

data transmission 데이터통신; 데이터전송

date 기일

date of enforcement 시행일

date of execution 집행기일

date of record 기준일

date proved by notary 확정일부

dated date 이자기산일

dating backward 후일부의

dating forward 선일부의

daughter company 자회사

dawn raid 긴급구입

day duty allowance 일직수당

day for paying taxes 납세기일

day loan 당일상환대출

day order 당일만 유효한 주문

day trading 일계매매

daylight trading 일계매매

days after sight 일람후 지불

days in arrears 연체일수

days of grace 지불유예기간

days to run 할인일수

day-to-day management 항상 운영함

day-to-day trader 단기투자가

de bone esse 잠정적인 효력을 지니다

de bonis asportatis 동산의 불법수법

de bonis non 승계유산관리

de facto 사실상

de jure 법률상

de novo 새로이; 다시

de son tort 권한이 없는

dead corner 사각

dead cross 데드크로스

dead freight 공하(空荷)운임

dead loan 대손금

dead stock 불량재고

dead weight loss of customs duty
관세가 사중 손실됨

deadline for filing 신고마감기일

deal between speculators 투기 전

dealer's bond 소매업자 보증증권

dealer's fee 딜러수수료

dealer's option 딜러옵션

dealer's position 딜러포지션

dealer's turn 중앙은행의 공정할인율상회

dealer 딜러

dealer financing 딜러금융

dealer loan 딜러론

dealer market 딜러시장

dealer paper 딜러어음

dealers' market 업자간 상장

dealing 자기매매

dealing for money 현금거래

dealing market 업자간 상장

dealing risk 딜링 리스크

dealings 거래고

dean 학부장

dear money policy 고금리정책

death duty 상속세

death from natural causes 자연사

death rate 사망률

debenture 채권

debenture assignment 사채권양도

debenture bond 사채권

debenture convertible at par 액면전환사채

debenture interest 사채이자

debenture redemption 사채상환

debenture stock 무상환사채

debenture trust 사채권신탁

debenture with lump-sum payment at
maturity 이자일괄불 이자부금융채

debenture-issuing expenses 사채발행비

debentures account 채권계정

debit 차변

debit account 차변계정

debit advice 차기(借記)통지서

debit authorization 차변승인

debit balance 차변잔고

debit card 지불카드

debit memorandum 차변메모

debit note 차변표

debit note for premium 보험금청구서

debit side 차변

debit slip 지불전표

debit system 데빗시스템

debt 채무; 부채

debt account 차금계정

debt accumulation 누적채무

debt assumption 채무인수

debt bond swap 채무의 채권화

debt ceiling 차입한도액

debt collection 채권회수

debt collector 회수업자

debt cross 데트 크로스

debt discount and expenses 사채발행차금

debt exposure 대출리스크

debt finance 차입으로 자금을 조달함

debt for collection 수금채무

debt in foreign currency 외화기준채무

debt in U.S. dollar 달러기준채무

debt instrument 채무수단

debt leverage 채무레버레지

debt loan 차입금

debt management policy 공채관리정책

debt maturity 부채기간

debt pooling 채무일괄조정

debt ratio 부채비율

debt reduction 채무삭감

debt relief 채무면제

debt retirement 채무반제

debt securities 채무증권

debt service 미불금

debt service ratio 채무반제비율

debt servicing 원리지불

debt warrant 데트 워런트 채

debt-credit transaction 대차거래

debt-equity ratio 부채자본비율

C
D

debt-equity swap 대외채무의 주식화
debtor's bond 채무자보증증권
debtor's deposit 채무자예금
debtor 채무자
debtor account 차변계정
debtor and creditor accounts 대차계정
debtor and estate 채무자 및 파산재단
debtor balance 차변잔고
debtor bank 대차은행
debtor country 채무국
debtor in possession 점유채무자
debtor side 대차란
debts and credits 채권채무
debugging 디버깅
decay rate 고객상실률
decelerating trend 감속경향
deceleration 둔화
decentralization 집중배제; 분권
decentralized buying 분산구매
decentralized channel 분산경로
decentralized management 분권관리
decentralized responsibility 분산책임
decision 결정
decision effectiveness 결정의 유효성
decision making 의사결정
decision making unit 의사결정단위
decision of a general meeting of
    stockholders 주주총회결의
decision of a reorganization scheme
    재건계획결정
decision of the general meeting 총회의 결정
decision on request for reinvestigation
    이의결정
decision room 디시전룸; 특별회의실
decision support system 의사결정지원시스템
decision technology 결정기술
decision variable 결정변수
deckholder 덱홀더
declaration 신고; 배당발표
declaration against interest
    이익에 반하는 공술

declaration form 신고용지
declaration of bankruptcy 파산선고
declaration of change of land category
    지목변환계
declaration of import 수입신고
declaration of income 소득신고
declaration of nonpayment 지불거절선언
declaration policy 통지보험
declaratory 확인하다
declaratory decree 확인결정
declaratory judgment 선언적인 판결
declaratory part of law 법률의 선언적인 부분
declaratory statute 선언적인 법률
declaratory stipulation 선언규정
declared back reinsurance 되돌림재보험
declared capital 공시자본
declared profit 계상이익
declination 인수사절
decline 하락하다
decline in prices of inventories
    재고자산평가하락
declining balance depreciation
    정율감가상각법
declining balance method 정율법
declining industry 쇠퇴산업
decode 해독; 해독하다
decrease in book value 장부가격감소
decrease of capital 감자
decrease of income tax 소득세감액
decreased receipts 감수
decreasing rate 저하율
decreasing term insurance 체감정기보험
decree 판결
decree of distribution 배분판결
decree of insolvency 지불불능판결
decree of nullity 무효판결
decrement 저감; 감소
dedi et concessi 권원담보문서
dedicated bond portfolio 채권에 대한 데디케
    이트 포트폴리오
deductible 공제면책금액

deductible amount for donation
기부금의 손금산입한도액
deductible clause 공제조항
deductible coverage
공제면책조건부 담보방식
deductible expenses 손금
deductible franchise 공제면책보합
deductible liabilities 공제해야 하는 채무
deductible reserve 손금산입할 수 있는 준비금
deduction 공제
deduction for casualty losses 잡손공제
deduction for contributions 기부금공제
deduction for damage insurance
손해보험공제
deduction for dependents 부양공제
deduction for dividends 배당공제
deduction for donation 기부금공제
deduction for employment income
급여소득공제
deduction for family employees
가족고용공제
deduction for foreign taxes
외국세액손금산입
deduction for housing savings 주택저축공제
deduction for insurance proceeds 보험금공제
deduction for life insurance premiums
생명보험료공제
deduction for medical expenses 의료비공제
deduction for old-age person 노령자공제
deduction for physically handicapped person
장애인공제
deduction for public pension 공적연금공제
deduction for retirement income
퇴직소득공제
deduction for small enterprise mutual aid
premiums 소규모기업공제 외상금공제
deduction for social insurance premiums
사회보험료공제
deduction for spouse 배우자공제
deduction for tax reduction 감면세액공제
deduction for widow 미망인공제

deduction for working student 근로학생공제
deduction from property
유형고정자산에서 공제함
deduction limit applicable to donation
기부금 손금산입한도액
deduction of entertainment expenses
교제비공제
deduction of estimated expenses
개산경비공제
deduction of interest on borrowed fund
부채이자공제
deduction of liabilities 채무공제
deductions from income 소득공제
deductions from working capital
운전자본감소
deductive method 연역법
deed 날인증서
deed of arrangement 채무정리증서
deed of conveyance 양도증서
deed of incorporation 주식회사설립증서
deed of title 권리증서
deed of trust 신탁증서
deed poll 평형날인계약서
deemed accounting period 간주사업연도
deemed bounty 간주교부금
deemed dividend 간주배당
deemed donations 간주기부금
deemed inherited property 간주상속재산
deemed request for reconsideration
간주심사청구
deemed transfer 간주양도
deemer clause 간주인가규정
deep bid 디프비드
deep discount 대폭의 할인 대폭할인
deep discount bond 디프디스카운트채
deep earth natural 심층천연가스
deep in the money 디프인더머니
deep pocket 유복한
deep rock doctrine 디프록주의
deep-rooted inflation 만성적인 인플레
defalcation 위탁금착복

defamation 명예훼손

default 디폴트

default interest 연체이자

default loss compensation reserve
위약손실보상준비금

default of obligation 채무불이행

default risk 채무불이행리스크

default risk premium 채무불이행 프리미엄

defaulter 불이행자

defcased 기한전

defeasance 채무계약해제

defeasance clause 해제조항

defease 해제하다

defeasible 무효로 할 수 있는

defeasible fee 소멸조건부 소유권

defeasible interest
소멸시킬 수 있는 피보험이익

defeasible title 취소할 수 있는 권원

defective 불완전한

defective check 부정수표

defective goods 결함품; 하자품

defective random variables 불완전확률변수

defective title 하자가 있는 권원

defective work 결함품; 하자품

defendant 피고

defendant bond 피고보증증권

defendemus 하자담보문서

defense 항변

defense association 소송비용상호보험

defense bond 방위채

defense insurance 응소보험

defense of the dollar 달러방위

defense right of attachment 검색항변권

defensive allegation 응소주장

defensive investment 방위투자

defensive purchase 방위매입

defensive securities 방위증권

defensive stock 방위주

deferment 연기, 거치

deferment of investment 투자연기

deferment of payment 연납

deferment of taxation 과세연기

deferred 거치; 미수

deferred account 이연계정

deferred and accrued accounts 경과계정

deferred annuity 이연연금

deferred assets 이연자산

deferred bond 이연채권

deferred charge 이연비용

deferred charge account 이연비용계정

deferred charge before amortization
상각전의 이연자산

deferred charges 이연비용

deferred compensation 이연보수비용

deferred debit 이연대변항목

deferred delivery 이연

deferred depreciation 이연상각

deferred expenditure 이연지출

deferred expenses 이연비용

deferred income 이연수익

deferred income tax liability 이연법인채무

deferred income taxes 연체세

deferred interest 연체이자

deferred item 이연계정

deferred liabilities 이연부채

deferred life annuity 거치종신연금

deferred payment 후불; 연납

deferred payment basis 연불기준

deferred payment conditional sales
연불조건부 판매

deferred payment credit 후일불신용장

deferred payment note 이연불입채권

deferred payment of income tax 소득세연납

deferred payment sales 연불조건부 판매

deferred premium 미수보험료

deferred rebate 보험료환불

deferred rebate system 운임환불제

deferred repairs 이연수선비

deferred revenue 이연수익

deferred savings 거치저금

deferred share 후배주

deferred swap 디퍼드스와프

C
D

deferred tax 연납세
deficiency 결손
deficiency account 결손계정
deficiency bill 일시차입어음
deficiency guarantee 부족액보증
deficit 적자
deficit account 결손금계정
deficit disposition statement
　결손금처리계산서
deficit finance 적자재정
deficit financing 적자융자
deficit for the current term 당기손실금
deficit of fiscal balance 재정적자
deficit reconciliation statement
　결손금처리계산서
deficit statement 결손금계산서
deficit-covering bond 적자국채
deficit-covering finance 적자금융
defined benefit plan 확정급부형 연금플랜
defined contribution plan
　확정거출형 연금 플랜
definite bordereau 확정보르드로
definite declaration 확정통지
definite policy 확정보험증권
definite premium 확정보험료
definite settlement of accounts 확정결산
definition 정의
definitive bond 정식본권
definitive policy 확정보험증권
definitive sentence 종국판결
deflation 디플레이션
deflation caused by won appreciation
　원고 디플레
deflation expectation 디플레 기대
deflation gap 디플레이션 갭
deflation policy 디플레 정책
deflationary effect 디플레 효과
deflationary gap 디플레 갭
deflationary period 디플레 기간
deflationary pressure 디플레 압력
deflator 디플레이터; 가격수정인자

deforceor 불법점유자
deforciant 화해양도인
defrayal 지불
defunct company 말소회사
degree 등급
degree of accuracy 정확도
degree of concentration 집중도
degree of concentration of control
　지배집중도
degree of confidence 신뢰도
degree of consanguinity 촌수
degree of dependence 의존도
degree of dependence upon exports
　수출의존도
degree of dependence upon imports
　수입의존도
degree of financial leverage
　재무면의 증익효과도
degree of freedom 자유도
degree of monopoly 독점도
degree of operating leverage
　영업면의 증익효과도
degressive cost 체감원가
deindustrialization 산업공동화
del credere agent 매주지불보증대리인
del credere commission 지불수수료
delay 지체
delay claims 지체클레임
delay of evacuation 철수지체
delayed interest 연체이자
delayed payment 연납
delaying settlement 지연결제
delegate 위임하다
delegation 권한부여
delegation of authority 권한위임
deletion of exclusion 면책조항삭제
delict 불법행위
delictum 유책성
delinquency 체납
delinquency tax 연체세
delinquent charge 지연손해금

delinquent tax 체납세
delinquent taxpayer 체납자
delisting 상장폐지
deliverable issue 인도적격상표
deliverance 발표
delivered 인도필
delivered at frontier 국경인도
delivered at frontier price 국경인도가격
delivered duty paid 발송지지입인도(관세입)
delivered duty unpaid
　발송지지입인도(관세 제외)
delivered ex quay 부두지입인도
delivered ex ship 본선(本船)지입인도
delivered money due to merger 합병교부금
delivered price 인도가격
delivered stock due to merger 합병교부주식
delivery 인도
delivery against payment 지불인도
delivery basis 인도기준
delivery bond 교부국채
delivery date 결제일
delivery expenses 발송비
delivery month 한월(限月)
delivery of articles 물품납부
delivery of dividends 배당금지불
delivery of government bond 교부국채
delivery of long-term contract work
　장기공사를 인도함
delivery of subsidies 보조금교부
delivery of substitute property
　장거리 이동에 따른 재산처분
delivery order 하도지시서
delivery price 인도가격
delivery settlement 인도결제
delivery system by calendar month 역월도제
delivery versus payment 지불인도
delivery with option 옵션인도
delivery-certified mail 배달증명우편
Delphi method 델피법
Delphi process 델피과정
delta 델타

delta hedge 델타 헤지
delta neutral hedge 델타 뉴트럴 헤지
delta value 델타수치
demand 수요; 독촉
demand account 요구불계정
demand analysis 수요분석
demand and supply 수급
demand bill 일람불어음
demand changes 수요변화
demand creation 수요창조
demand curve 수요곡선
demand debt 요구불채무
demand deficiency 수요부족
demand deposits 통지예금
demand draft 일람불어음; 송금수표
demand elasticity 수요탄력성
demand for capital 자본수요
demand for fund 자금수요
demand for money 화폐수요
demand for tax payment 납부독촉
demand forecast 수요예측
demand function 수요함수
demand function for money 화폐수요함수
demand in reconvention 반소(反訴)
demand index 수요지수
demand line 신용화
demand loan 당좌대부
demand note 요구불어음
demand pull inflation 디맨드 풀 인플레;
　초과수요인플레
demand season 수요기
demand stimulation 수요자극
demand to hold securities 증권보유수요
demand-and-supply balance 수급밸런스
demandant 원고
demesne 점유
demises 지소(地所)
demographic factors 인구통계적인 요인
demographic statistics 인구통계
demolition 해체; 분쇄
demolition expenses 해체비

demonetization of gold 금폐화(金廢貨)
demonstration 실증
demonstration effect 데몬스트레이션효과
demonstrative legacy 지시유증
demotion 강등
demurrage 체선료; 하차유치료
demurrer 방소항변
demurrer book 쟁점기록
demurrer to evidence 이의
denial 부인
denization 국적부여
denominated in each currency 각국통화단위
denominated in foreign currency 외화기준
denominated in U.S. dollar 달러기준
denominated in won 원기준
denomination 권면; 디노미네이션
denomination related stocks
　디노미네이션 관련주
denotative meanings 외연적인 의미
dental insurance 치과치료보험
Department of Commerce 미국상무부
Department of State 미국국무부
Department of Trade and Industry
　무역산업부
Department of Treasury 재무부
department store floater 백화점포괄보험
department store sales 백화점매상고
department variance on overhead
　부문간접비차이
departmental burden 부문부담비
departmental charge 부문비
departmental cost 부문원가
departmental cost accounting
　부문별 원가계산
departmental costing 부문별 원가계산
departmental expenses 부문비
departmental expenses budget 부문비 예산
departmental overhead 부문간접비
departmental process cost system
　공정별 종합원가계산
departmental profit 부문별 이익

departure 이탈
dependence 의존
dependence effect 의존효과
dependency 종속
dependent 부양가족
dependent allowance 가족수당
dependent family member 부양가족
dependent variable 종속변수
depletable 감모가능한
depleted cost 상각후 원가
depletion 감모상각
depletion allowance 감가수당금
depletion assets 감모자산
deponent 선서공술자
depose 공술하다
deposit 예탁금
deposit account 예탁계정
deposit administration 예탁관리
deposit administration fund 예탁관리기금
deposit and saving 예저금
deposit at financial institutions 금융기관예금
deposit at notice 통지예금
deposit by the Ministry of Finance
　MOF 예탁금
deposit certificate 예금증서
deposit company 기탁회사
deposit diary 예금기입장
deposit due to bank 은행예금
deposit for public auction 공매보증금
deposit for tax 납세준비예금
deposit from employees 종업원예금
deposit in a fictitious name 비실명예금
deposit in trust 신탁예금
deposit insurance system 예금보험제도
deposit interest rate 예금금리
deposit law 공탁법
deposit ledger 예금원장
deposit loan 예금대부
deposit minus checks and bills on hand
　실세 예금
deposit money 예금통화

deposit of nondebtor 비채무자 예금
deposit of public money 예금통화
deposit of title-deeds 권리서기탁
deposit office 공탁소
deposit on a net basis 실세예금
deposit payoff 예금정산불방식
deposit premium 예탁보험료
deposit rate 예금이율
deposit received 보증금
deposit share 예금쉐어
deposit slip 예금전표
deposit taking business 수신업무
deposit through deduction from monthly pay 공제저금
deposit to be relet to a third party 도입예금
deposit transfer 예금대체방식
deposit window 예금창구
deposit with landlord 전세보증금; 거래보증금
deposit with other bank 예금
depositary 예탁인
depositary assets 예탁자산
depositary bank 예탁은행
depositary institution 예금수입금융기관
depositary receipts 예탁증서
Depositary Receipts of Singapore 싱가포르 예탁증서
depositary shares 예탁주식
depositary trust company 주권대체기관
deposited article 공탁물
deposited money 예탁금
deposited securities 예탁유가증권
deposition 증언기록
depositor's forgery bond 예금자위조보증증권
depositor 공탁자
depositor protection 예금자보호
depository correspondent 디포지터리 코러스폰던트; 예치환거래은행
depository preferred stock 예탁우선주
deposits and savings 예저금
deposits in current account 당좌예금
deposits of securities on contracts 보증차입유가증권
deposits on contract 예탁보증금
deposits on long-term leases 장기임대계약예금
deposits paid on construction work 공사전도금
deposits paid to trade creditors 구입전불대금
deposits received for guarantees 예탁보증금
deposits with public utility corporations 공익사업회사예금
deposit-to-loan ratio 예금율
depot theory 데포이론
depreciable 감가상각가능한
depreciable assets 감가상각자산
depreciable cost 감사상각원가
depreciable limit 상각한도액
depreciable property 상각자산
depreciable property for nonbusiness 비영업용 상각자산
depreciated cost 감가상각후 원가
depreciated original cost 감가상각후 원시원가
depreciated value 감가상각후 가액
depreciation 감가상각
depreciation account 상각계정
depreciation accounting 감가상각회계
depreciation adequacy 감가상각타당성
depreciation allowance 감가상각수당금
depreciation and amortization 상각
depreciation assets 상각자산
depreciation base 감가상각기초액
depreciation burden 감가상각부담
depreciation by depreciation rate 감가율에 따른 상각
depreciation expense 감가상각비
depreciation fund 감가상각기금
depreciation in excess of the limit 초과상각
depreciation insurance 신가(新價)보험
depreciation method 감가상각법
depreciation of building 건물감가상각
depreciation of currency 통화가치저하**

depreciation of deposit by inflation 예금감소
depreciation of ship costs 선가(船價)상각
depreciation of time value 시간가치감가
depreciation on obsolete assets
　진부화자산상각
depreciation on property 자산감가상각
depreciation period 감가상각연수
depreciation rate 감가상각율
depreciation reserve 감가상각준비금
depreciation reserve ratio
　감가상각준비금비율
depreciation unit 감가상각단위
depression 불황
depression of business 불경기
depth interview 심도면접
depth of exposure 노출강도
deputy 대리
deputy governor 부총재
depyramidding 디프라이미딩과정
derailment 탈선
derecognition 인식종료
deregulated interest rate 자유금리
deregulated interest rate product
　자유금리상품
deregulation 규제완화
deregulation of financial and capital market
　금융자본시장자유화
dereliction 유기
derivative deposit 파생예금
derivative income 파생취득
derivative pass-through securities market
　파생 패스 스루 증권시장
derivative product 파생상품
derivative security 파생증권
derivative suit 파생소송
derivative transaction 파생거래
derived demand 간접수요; 파생수요
derived function 도함수
derived income 파생소득
derogatory-clause 실효약관
descendant 직계존속

descending 하강
descending curve 하강곡선
descending tops 최저점
descending triangle 하락삼각형
descending triangle pattern 하락삼각형
description of business 영업과목
descriptive data 기술데이터
descriptive financial statement
　설명부 재무제표
descriptive function 설명기능
descriptive labeling sea 설명표시
descriptive statistics 설명을 위한 통계
desertion 방기
design change 설계변경
design control 설계관리
design fee 의장료
design law 의장법
design qualification 설계인정
design review 설계심사
design right 의장권
design verification 설계검증
designated account 지정계좌
designated city 지정도시
designated currency 지정통화
designated deposit 지정예금
designated exchange 지정거래소
designated net 지명네트
designated nominee 지정명의인
designated statistics 지정통계
designated stock 지정상표
designation for transfer 불입지정
designation of accounting period
　사업연도지정
designation of place for tax payment
　납세지 지정
designs 의장
desired profit 목표이익
desk top music 데스크톱뮤직
desk top publishing 데스크톱퍼블리싱
desk top video 데스크톱비디오
desperate debt 대손금

destination 발송지
destocking 재고를 줄임
destruction of environment 환경파괴
destructive disposition 파괴처분
detachable warrant 분리가능워런트
detached employees 파견사원
detailed account form 세목계정식
detailed audit report 장문식감사보고서
detailed check 자세히 조사함
detailed enforcement regulations 시행세칙
detailed statement 내역서
deteriorate 저하시키다
deteriorated assets 열화자산
deterioration 악화
determination 부동산권 만료
determination by estimate 추계를 통한 결정
determination coefficient 결정함수
determination of dividend 배당결정
determining the necessary adjustments
　수정사항결정
deterministic model 확정모델
deterred credit 이연대변항목
detinue 동산반환청구소송
devaluation 절하
develop and import scheme 개발수입
developer 개발업자
development assistance 해외원조
development cost 개발비
development cost of residential site
　택지조성비
development expenses 개발비
development fund 개발자금
development gap 개발격차
development of route 루트개발
deviating company 요율산정기관불참가회사
deviation 특별요율적용; 편차
deviation permit 규격외허가
device 장치, 설비
devise 유증(부동산의)
devisee 수유자(受遺者)
devisor 유증자(遺贈者)

diagnostic process 진단과정
diagonal spread 대각스프레드
dial telephone line 다이얼회선
diamond formation 다이아몬드포메이션
diamond semiconductor 다이아몬드반도체
DIC color 딕 컬러
dichotomous question 이분질문법
dichotomous variable 이분변수
dichotomy 이분법
dichroic mirror 색상선별 거울
difference 차액
difference among issues 상표 간 격차
difference by renewal 갱신차금
difference from exchange of property
　교환차금
difference in yield 이익격차
differences 차금
different account 다른 계좌
differential cost 차액원가
differential of return 수익률교차
differential payoff 차별이득
differential rate 차별요율
differentiation 차별화
differentiation strategy 차별화전략
diffusion 보급
diffusion index 경기동향지표
diffusion model 보급모델
diffusion of risks 위험분산
diffusion process 보급과정
diffusion rate 보급률
digest 소화하다; 요약하다; 침지하다
diggings 채굴료
digital audio workstation
　디지털 오디오 워크스테이션
digital compact cassette 디지털 콤팩트 카세트
digital picking 디지털 피킹
digital picture effect 디지털 영상효과
digital signal processor
　디지털 시그널 프로세서
digital video interactive
　디지털 비디오 인터랙티브

dilapidations 손모료
dilatory 연기하는
dilatory plea 지연을 위한 항변
diligence 주의
dilution 희석화
dimension 차원
dimensionality 차원성
diminishing balance depreciation 정율상각
diminishing balance method 체감원가법
diorama 디오라마
dip 침하; 후퇴
direct financing lease 직접금융형 리스
direct issue paper 직접매출페이퍼
direct method 직접법
direct participation program
　　직접 참가 프로그램
direct attack 직접공격
direct broadcasting 위성방송
direct capital 직접자본
direct channel 직판경로
direct claim of claimant 피해자 직접 청구
direct costing 직접원가계산
direct deal 직거래
direct dealing 직접환거래
direct department 직접부문
direct department cost 부문개별비
direct deposit 직접예금
direct evidence 직접증거
direct examination 직접심문
direct exchange arbitrage 직접환재정
direct expense 직접경비
direct financing 직접금융
direct foreign tax credit 외국세액직접공제
direct insurance 원수(元受)보험
direct insurer 원수(元受)회사
direct interest 직접이해관계
direct investment 직접투자
direct inward investment 대내직접투자
direct labor 직접노동
direct labor cost 직접노무비
direct liabilities 확정부채

direct loan 직접금융
direct material cost 직접재료비
direct method of depreciation 직접상각
direct national tax 직접국세
direct or equity investment 직접투자
direct overhead 직접경비
direct paper 다이렉트어음
direct payment 완전변제
direct placement 직접모집
direct premium 원수(元受)보험료
direct premium tax 원수(元受)보험료세
direct presentation 직접표시
direct pricing 직접정산법
direct rated deposit administration contract
　　직접 참가 예탁 관리 계약
direct tax 직접세
direct tax credit 세액 직접공제
direct valuation 직접평가
direct writing premium 원수(元受) 보험료
direct writing system 직접모집제도
direct yield 직접이익
directed verdict 지도평결
direction 지도
directional index 방향성지수
directional movement 방향성
directive 통달
director's retirement allowance
　　임원퇴직급여금
director's salaries and remuneration 임원보수
director 이사, 임원
directors and officers liability insurance
　　임원배상책임보험
directory statute 지시적인 법률
directory trust 지시신탁
dirty float 더티플로트; 관리변동환율제도
dirty shares 오염주식
disability 고도장애
disability annuity 고도장애연금
disability benefits 고도장애급부
disability benefits insurance
　　고도장애급부보험

disability income insurance
　취업불능소득보상보험
disability insurance 소득보상보험
disablement benefit 장해보상
disabling statutes 재산이전금지법
disagreement 동의하지 않음
disappointing 낙담
disappointing export 수출부조
disbar 박탈하다
disbursement 지불
disbursement book 현금지불장
disbursement cycle 지불순환
disbursement slip 출금전표
disbursements 직무집행비용
disbursements insurance 선비(船費) 보험
disbursing agent 지불대리인
discarded equipment 폐잔설비
discharge 방출; 면책
discharge in bankruptcy 파산취소
discharge of debts 채무면제
discharge of delinquent tax 연체세면제
discharge of repayment 상환면제
disclaim report 의견거절보고서(재무제표에
　대한 감사의견 중 하나)
disclaimer 면책문서
disclaimer clause 발주자면책조항
disclaims 의견거절
disclosing function 공시기능
disclosure 개시
disclosure of terms and conditions of loans
　대출조건명시
disclosure philosophy 개시원칙
disclosure system 공시제도
disconfirmation of expectations
　기대불일치효과
discontinuance 취하
discontinuance of business 폐업
discontinued operations 폐지부문
discount 현재가치로 환원하다; 디스카운트
discount bank 할인은행
discount bank debenture 할인금융채

discount bond 할인채
discount broker 어음할인중개인
discount charge 할인율
discount commission 할인수수료
discount earned 수취할인료
discount factor 할인계수
discount function 할인함수
discount government bond 할인국채
discount house 할인상사
discount issue 할인발행
discount ledger 할인어음원장
discount market 할인시장
discount on banker's acceptances
　은행인수어음할인
discount on bill 어음할인
discount on bills sold on condition of
　repurchase 환매조건부 매각어음
discount on bond premium 사채발행차금
discount on note 어음할인료
discount policy 할인정책
discount rate 할인율
discount rate cut 공정할인율인하
discount rate policy 공정율할인율조작
discount register 할인어음기입장
discount structure 할인구조
discount window 할인창구
discount yield 할인이익
discounted bill 할인어음
discounted cash flow 할인수익
discounters 수수료할인업자
discounting 할인
discounting of a bill 어음할인
discounts on bills bought 매입어음할인료
discounts on bonds payable
　사채할인발행차금
discovery 개시
discovery basis 디스커버리베이시스
discovery bond 디스커버리본드
discovery period 발견기간
discredit 신용하지 않다
discrepancy 차이

discrepancy of assortment 제품구비불일치
discrepant information 어긋난 정보
discrete time 이산(離散)시간형
discrete variable 이산변수
discretion 자유재량
discretional act 재량행위
discretionary account 매매일임계정
discretionary account transaction
　매매일임계정거래
discretionary expenses 임의비용
discretionary loan 재량대출
discretionary order 일임주문
discretionary trust 일임신탁
discriminating duty 차별관세
discrimination 차별대우
discrimination test 식별테스트
discriminative price 차별가격
discriminative tariff 차별세율
diseconomies of scale 규모의 불경제성
disequilibrating capital flows
　교란적인 자본이동
disequilibrium 불균형
disequilibrium growth 불균형성장
disfranchise 공권을 박탈하다
disguised act 가장행위
dishonesty loss 불성실 손해
dishonor 인수거절
dishonored bill 부도어음
dishonored check 부도수표
disinflation 디스인플레이션
disinterested 이해관계가 없는
disinterested party 이해관계가 없는 사람
disinterested witness 이해관계가 없는 증인
disintermediation 비중개
disjunctive allegation 흑백논리
dismissal 각하(却下)
dismissal notice 해고통지
dismissal without prejudice 각하(却下)
disorderly conduct 치안문란행위
disparity 불균형
dispatch 급파하다; 급파

dispatch money 급송료
dispensation 적용면제
displaced diffusion model 확산변환모델
display advertising 디스플레이광고
disposable income 가처분소득
disposable personal income 개인가처분소득
disposable profit 가처분이익
disposal 처분
disposal of fixed assets 고정자산처분
disposal price 처분가격
disposal value 처분가치
disposing capacity 재산처분능력
disposition 처분
disposition by public sale 공매처분
disposition by suspension of bank credit
　은행거래정지
disposition by suspension of business
　거래정지처분
disposition for failure to pay 체납처분
disposition of assets 자산처분
disposition of cost variance 원가차액조정
disposition of failure to pay income tax in
　advance 예정납세액체납처분
disposition of net income 순익처분
dispossession 불법점유
dispute 분쟁
disqualify 자격을 빼앗다
disregard of tax rule 세법을 무시함
disruption claims 방해클레임
disseise 부동산의 점유를 뺏다
disseisin 점유침탈
dissent 반대하다
dissenting opinion 반대의견
dissolution 해산
dissolution of corporation 법인 해산
dissolve 녹이다; 해산하다
distance clause 공지조항
distance concept 거리개념
distance learning 원격교육
distrain 유치하다
distrainor 차압인

distress 무기한 차압
distress 차압
distress carrier 인수전문보험회사
distress merchandise 덤핑상품
distress sale 차압물건매각
distress selling 투매; 출혈판매
distribution 분배
distribution channel 유통경로
distribution channel selection 유통경로선택
distribution cost 판매비
distribution cost analysis 유통비분석
distribution industry 유통업계
distribution logistics 유통로지스틱스
distribution mix 유통믹스
distribution of local allocation tax
　　지방교부세교부금
distribution of net profit 이익처분
distribution of overhead cost 간접비 분배
distribution of profits 이익배당
distribution of property 재산분여
distribution of residual property
　　잔여재산분배
distribution of stocks 주식분포
distribution of surplus 잉금처분
distribution productivity 물류생산성
distribution rate of overhead cost
　　간접비 배분율
distribution ratio 구성비율
distribution revolution 유통혁명
distribution structure 유통기구
distribution tax 배부세
district attorney 지방검사
district registry 지방등록소
districts 관할구
disutility 역효과
divasa 판정
divergence 괴리
divergence indicator 괴리지표
divergence threshold 괴리한도
divergent marketing 분산형 마케팅
diverse exercise of voting right

의결권불통일행사
diversification 분산화
diversification of risks 리스크분산
diversification strategy 다각화전략
diversified company 다각화기업
diversified investment 분산투자
diversified management 다각경영
diversified portfolio on stock investment
　　분산 주식 투자 포트폴리오
diversified type common stock fund
　　분산형 보통주 펀드
diversified type investment company
　　분산형 투자회사
diversified type portfolio 분산형 포트폴리오
diversify 분산하다
diversion charge 양륙지변경료
diversion of water 용수
diversionary pricing 양동적인 가격설정
diversity antenna 다이버시티 안테나
divestiture barrier 철수장벽
divided account 분할계좌
dividend 배당
dividend account 배당계정
dividend addition 보험금액증가
dividend credit 배당공제
dividend cut 감배
dividend declared 이익잉여금
dividend decrease age 감배
dividend discount method 배당환원방식
dividend discount model 배당환원모델
dividend discount rate 배당할인율
dividend distribution 배당
dividend earned 수취배당금
dividend equalization fund 배당평균준비금
dividend equalization reserve
　　배당평균적립금
dividend excluded from income
　　수취배당금익금불산입
dividend exclusion 배당공제
dividend extra 특별배당
dividend flow 배당플로

dividend for the second half 후기배당
dividend from capital 자본배당
dividend from stocks owned
　주식소유와 관련 있는 배당
dividend in arrears 연체배당금
dividend income 배당소득
dividend increase 증배
dividend off 배당락
dividend on 배당부
dividend on common stock 보통주 배당금
dividend on dummy stock 명의주 배당
dividend on interest 이자배당
dividend on preferred stock 우선주배당금
dividend on stock 주식배당
dividend option 우선주배당금
dividend payable 미불배당금
dividend payment 배당지불
dividend payout ratio 배당성향
dividend per share 일주당 배당금
dividend preferred stock 배당우선주식
dividend rate 배당율
dividend receivable 미수배당
dividend received 수취배당금
dividend reinvestment plan 배당재투자계획
dividend reserve 배당준비적립금
dividend stock 배당주
dividend to policyholders 계약자배당
dividend yield 배당이익
dividend-paid deduction method 배당손금법
dividend-paying stock 유배주
divisible claim 가분채권
divisible contract 가분계약
divisible obligation 가분채무
divisible surplus 배당가능잉여금
division of markets 시장분할
division of succession 분할상속제
division system 사업부문제도
divisional breakdown 부문별 손익
divisional management 부문경영진
divisional sales 부문매상
divisional sales breakdown 부문별 매상내역

divisional structure 부문구조
divisionalized company 사업부문제회사
dockage 부두사용료
docket 심리예정표
doctrine of discovered peril 발견위험의 원칙
doctrine of immunity 면책주의
doctrine of liability without fault
　부과실책임주의
document 서류
document against acceptance 인수도
document control 문서관리
document of seizure 차압서
document of title 권리증권
documentary bill 화환어음
documentary clean credit 무담보신용장
documentary credit 화환신용장
documentary evidence 증거서류
documentary stamp tax 인지세
documentation 문서화
documented discount note
　신용장보증부 할인어음
documented procedure 절차서류
documents for opening a U.S. dollar account
　달러계좌개설서류
Dodge Line 다지라인
dog and pony show 신상품설명회
doing business 영업행위
doli capax 책임능력
doli incapax 책임무능력
dollar account 달러계정
dollar average method 달러평균법
dollar bloc 달러블록
dollar call option 달러콜옵션
dollar convertible bond 달러기준전환사채
dollar cost averaging 코스트평균투자법
dollar crisis 달러위기
dollar merchandise budgeting 상품예산편성
dollar overhung 과잉달러
dollar parity 달러평가
dollar preference 달러선호
dollar price 채권가격

dollar put option 달러풋옵션
dollar sales volume quota 판매할당
dollar shift 달러시프트
dollar support 달러방위
dollar-weighted rate of return
　달러가중수익률
dollar-weighted return 금액가중수익율
domain 활동영역
domestic corporation 내국법인
domestic currency 자국통화
domestic demand 내수
domestic demand expansion 내수확대
domestic demand oriented industry 내수산업
domestic demand related stock 내수관련주
domestic demand stimulation 내수진흥
domestic equilibrium 국내균형
domestic expenditure 국내지출
domestic goods 국산품
domestic institutional investor
　국내기관투자가
domestic investment 국내투자
domestic loan system 국내론방식
domestic operations 국내사업
domestic satellite communication
　국내위성통신
domestic source 국내원천
domestic source income 국내원천소득
domicile 어음지불장소
domiciled bill 지불지정어음
dominant estate 요역지(要役地)
dominant firm 지배적인 기업
dominate the market
　시장의 대부분을 점유하다
dominated strategy 우위적인 전략
domino effect 도미노효과
donated property 증여재산
donated stock 증여주
donated surplus 증여잉여금
donation 증여
donation due to death 사인(死因)증여
donation tax 증여세

donation to designated organization
　지정기부금
donator 기증자
done 계약성립
donee 수증자
donor 증여자
door-to-door sales 방문판매
dormant account 휴지계정
dormant balance 휴지잔고
dormant motive 수면동기
dormant partnership 익명조합
dots per inch 화면 1인치당 도트수
double account interests 이중이자
double accounting 복식부기
double attachment 이중차압
double barreled 이중보증의
double bottom 이중바닥
double check 재확인
double counting 이중계산
double crossover 더블크로스오버
double dated 이중만기
double declining balance method 배액정율법
double decremental table 이중탈퇴잔존표
double dipping 이중이익의
double distribution 이중분배
double endowment insurance
　만기배액지불양로보험
double exemption bond 이중면제채
double indemnity 보험금을 두배로 지불함
double insurance 중복보험
double jeopardy 이중의 위험
double liability 이중부채
double name paper 복명(複名)어음
double option 옵션 더블옵션
double peak 이중천장
double price 이중가격
double sampling 이중추출법
double seizure 이중차압
double settlement 영업일도
double tariff 이중세율제
double taxation 이중과세

double truck 좌우양면기사광고
double-digit recurring profit growth
　두 자리 수 성장기조
double-entry bookkeeping 복식부기
double-up 더블업
doubtful account 불량채권
doubtful loan 불량대출
Dow Jones Average 다우평균
Dow Theory 다우이론
Dow-Jones Commodity Index
　다우식 상품지수
down payment 전도금
down spread 매매차익금
down trend 하강기조
down under bond 호주달러유러채
down-and-out option 다운 앤드 아웃 옵션;
　하향 실격 옵션
downfall 하락
downhill course 하강선
download 다운로드
downside potential 하향탄력성
downside risk 가격인하여지
downsizing 가격인하불안
downstairs merger 역흡수합병
downswing phase 하강국면
downtick 전날 종가보다 싼 거래
downturn 악화; 하강
downward movement 시세가 내리는 상태
downward phase of the business cycle
　하강국면
downward revision 하향수정
downward revision on business results
　실적을 예상한 하향수정
downward rigidity of price 가격하향경직성
draft 환어음; 어음
draft at sight 일람불어음
draft authority 소손해를 사정, 지불할 권한
draft bill of exchange 환어음
dragon curve 드래곤곡선
drainage district 배수사업지구
dramatic surge 대상(大商)

draw 작성하다; 발행하다
draw down 자금인출
drawback 관세환불
drawback allowance 환불세급부
drawee 어음수신인
drawer 발행인
drawer of bill 어음발행인
drawing 작성; 발행
drawing bank 발행은행
drawing of bill 어음발행
drawing right 발행권
drawn bill 발행어음
drifting management 성행관리
drifting mix 표류믹스
driver's liability policy 운전자배상책임보험
drop 하강
drop below par 액면이 하락
drop-lock bond 드롭록채
dry weight 건조중량
dual banking system 이중은행제도
dual capacity 이중용량
dual character of investment
　투자의 이중성 이중적인 투자
dual closed-end fund
　듀얼 클로즈드 엔드형 펀드
dual convertible bonds 듀얼전환사채
dual currency 이중통화기준
dual currency bond 이중통화기준채
dual economy 이중경제
dual exchange market 이중환시장
dual fund 듀얼펀드
dual interest policy 이중금리정책
dual listing 이중상장
dual merchandising 복합머천다이징
dual option 이중옵션
dual pricing 이중가격표시
dual purpose 이중목적
dual rate system 이중운임제
dual structure 이중구조
dual tariff 복관세
dual trading 이중계정거래

duality 이중성
dubbing 더빙
due and deferred premiums 미수보험료
due bill 금전채무인증서
due bill check 신용증서수표
due date 만기일
due date coming basis 회수기한도래기준
due date for payment 지불기한
due date for tax payment 납기한
due date of bills 어음만기
due date of filing return 신고기한
due date of payment 불입일
due date of property tax payment
　고정자산납세기한
due date of the tax return 신고기한
due diligence 자세히 조사함
due from foreign banks 외국지점예금
due on sale 매각시반제
due process of law 적법절차
due to foreign banks 외국타점예금
dues 요금
dull 별로 마음이 내키지 않음
dum bene se gesserit 죄악이 없는 한
dumbbell portfolio 덤벨 포트폴리오
dummy company 더미회사
dummy stock 명의주
dump 손해를 각오하고 처분하다
dumping 덤핑
duopoly 두 회사의 독점
duplex system 이중계약주의
duplicate 부(副)의
duplicate policy 보증증권의 부본
duplicate taxation 이중과세
duplicate tenor 등본
duplicity 범죄복합
durable consumer goods 내구소비재
durable years 내용연수
duration 계속기간
duration method 듀레이션법

duration of bond 채권평균만기
duration of guaranty 보증기간
duration of insurance 보험기간
duration of risk 위험기간
duration of risk clause 보험기간조항
duration-matching 듀레이션매칭
duration-weighted yield 듀레이션가중이익
Durbin-Watson ratio 더빈-왓슨비
Dutch auction 값을 깎아 내려가는 경매
dutiable goods 세금이 붙는 물품
dutiable value 과세가격
duties 공과
duty contingency 미필수입세
duty exemption 면세
duty free 면세의
duty free imports 면세수입품
duty of care 주의의무
duty of disclosure 고지의무
duty of support 부양의무
duty to sue and labor 손해방지의무
duty-paid 납세제
dwelling house 주거
dwelling risk 주택물건
dyad customer 고객 한 쌍
dyadic communication 쌍방향 커뮤니케이션
dynamic analysis 동태분석
dynamic data exchange 다이내믹 데이터 교환
dynamic hedge scheme 다이내믹 헤지
dynamic input-output analysis 동학적인 산업
　연관분석
dynamic marketing 동태적 마케팅
dynamic model 동태모델
dynamic multiplier 동학(動學)승수
dynamic programming 다이내믹 프로그램
dynamic random access memory 디램; DRAM
dynamic range 다이내믹 영역
dynamic risk 동태적인 위험
dynamic strategies 다이내믹 전략
dysfunction 역기능

each way 수수료 각자지불
early adopters 초기채용자
early exercise 기한전 행사
early majority 초기추종자
early ownership mortgage loan
　초기반제 모기지론
early redemption option 조기상환옵션
early redemption 조기상환
early repayment 조기반제
early warning system 조기경보시스템
earmarked tax 목적세
earmuff problem 일방적인 상황설명
earn out 여잉이익을 분배하다
earn-out right 여잉수익수취권
earned basis 실수(實需)기준
earned income 가득(稼得)기준
earned income allowance 근로소득공제
earned income tax 근로소득세
earned premium 경과보험료
earned reinsurance premium 경과재보험료
earned surplus 이익잉여금
earned surplus reserve 이익준비금
earned surplus statement 이익잉여금계산금
earnest money 계약증거금
earnest money received 예금수부금
earning assets 수익자산
earning per share 일주당 순익
earning power 수익력
earning rate 수익률
earning statement 손익계산서
earning tax 수익세

earnings 수익
earnings before extraordinary items
　특별손익전 이익
earnings before interest and taxes
　금리세금공제전 이익
earnings before tax 세금공제전 이익
earnings coverage ratios 부담이익배율
earnings forecast 수익예상
earnings from continuing operations
　계속사업부문이익
earnings growth 수익증가
earnings growth rate 수익성장률
earnings growth ratio per share
　일주당 수익성장률
earnings model 수익모델
earnings on 자기자본이익률
earnings per share of common stock
　보통주식일주당 순이익
earnings performance 업적
earnings retained in business 이익잉여금
earnings retention rate 수익유보율
earnings stability 수익안정성
earnings yield 이율
earthquake clause 지진위험담보특별약관
earthquake insurance 지진보험
ease 반락(反落)
ease off 시세가 떨어지다
easement 지역권
easement appurtenant 부속지역권
easement holder 지역권자
easement in gross 대인지역권

easier 수월함
easing 완화
East African Community 동아프리카공동체
East Asia Economic Caucus
　동아시아경제협의체
eastern account 분할인수
easy 완만한 약세인(물가)
easy payment 분할불
eat inde sine die 즉시방면
eavesdropping 도청
EC joint floating system EC공동플로팅
echo effect 반향효과
echo principle 반향원리
eco-system 생태계
ecological factor 생태적인 요인
ecology 생태학
econometric analysis 계량분석
econometric model 계량경제모델
economic activity 경제활동
economic activity stimulating measure
　경제활동자극책
economic aid 경제원조
Economic and Development Review
　Committee 경제개발검토위원회
Economic and Social Commission for Asia
　and the Pacific
　아시아태평양경제사회위원회
Economic and Social Council of the United
　Nations 국제연합경제사회이사회
economic assistance 경제협력
economic barometer 경제지표
economic benefits 경제적인 편익
economic big power 경제대국
economic bloc 경제권
economic blockade 경제봉쇄
economic center 경제센터
economic channeling 경제집중
economic channeling of liability
　경제적인 책임이 집중됨
economic circles 경제계
Economic Commission for Africa

국제연합아프리카경제위원회
Economic Commission for Asia and the Far
　East 아시아극동경제위원회
Economic Commission for Europe
　유럽경제위원회
economic conditions 경제상황
economic consequence 경제의 귀결
economic continuity 경제의 연속성
economic cooperation 경제협력
economic cost 경제원가
economic crisis 경제공황
economic cycle 경기순환
Economic Deliberation Council 경제심의회
economic dualism 이중경제구조
economic earnings 경제적 이익
economic earnings beta
　경제적 이익의 베타수치
economic emulation stage 경제적 모방단계
economic engineering 경제성 공학
economic ethics 경제윤리
economic figure 경제지표
economic fluctuation 경기변동
economic forecast 경제예측
economic friction 경제마찰
economic function 경제기능
economic goods 경제재(經濟財)
economic growth 경제성장
economic growth model 경제성장모델
economic growth policy 경제성장정책
economic growth rate 경제성장률
economic index 경제지수
economic indicator 경제지표
economic integration 경제통합
economic interaction 경제상호작용
economic interpretation 경제해석
economic life 경제생활
economic malaise 경제질병
economic man 경제인
economic maturity 경제적인 성숙
economic model 경제모델
economic number effect 경제지표효과

economic obsolescence 경제적인 진부화
economic order 경제질서
economic organization 경제조직
economic outlook 경제예측
economic philosophy 경제철학
economic plan 경제계획
economic policy 경제정책
economic prediction 경제예측
economic priority 경제우선
economic progress 경제진보
economic prospect 경제전망
economic quality 경제품질
economic recession 경기후퇴
economic recovery 경기회복
economic reform 경제개혁
economic regime 경제체제
economic risk 경제리스크
economic sanction 경제제재
economic science 경제학과
economic security 경제안전보장
economic slump 경기후퇴
economic statistics 경제통계
economic structural adjustment
　경제구조조정
Economic Summit 선진국수뇌회의
economic system 경제체제
economic table 경제표
economic tide 경제의 흐름
economic union 경제동맹
economic unit 경제주체
economic utility 경제효용
economic viability 경제활력
economic war 경제전쟁
economic waste 경제적인 낭비
economic white paper 경제백서
economies of scale 규모의 경제성
economies of scope 다각화의 경제성
edge down 소폭하락
edge up 소폭상승
edict 포고
education expense 교육비

educational endowment 학자보험
educational level 교육수준
edutainment 에듀테인먼트;
　교육적이고 흥미 있는 프로그램
effect 효과
effect of correction 개정 등의 효력
effect of discount 할인효과
effect of exchange rate changes 환 환산수정
effect of limiting risk 위험한정 효과
effect of message 메시지 효과
effect of rescission 계약해제 효과
effective address 실효어드레스
effective aggregate tax rate 종합효과세율
effective buying income 실질구매소득
effective competition 유효경쟁
effective date 발효일
effective demand 유효수요
effective exchange rate 실효환상장
effective interest rate 실효금리
effective life 유효기간
effective price 실효가격
effective rate 실세레이트
effective rate of discount 어음할인율
effective rate of protection 실효보호율
effective tariff 실효세율
effective volatility 실제가격변동율
effective yield 실효이율
effectiveness of diversified investment 분산
　투자의 유효성
effects 인적재산
efficiency audit 능률감사
efficiency management 능률관리
efficiency of measuring 측정효율
efficiency variance 능률차이
efficient cause 주요원인
efficient frontier 유효프론티어
efficient market 효율적인 시장
efficient market hypothesis
　효율적인 시장 가설
efficient portfolio 효율적인 포트폴리오
efficient statistics 유효통계

efficient-scale facility 효율적인 규모
effluxion of time 기간만료
either way market 쌍방향시장
ejectment 부동산회복소송
"ejusdem generis" doctrine 동종제한의 원칙
elapsed years 경과연수
elastic demand 탄력적인 수요
elastic limit system 굴신(屈伸) 제한제도
elastic tariff 탄력관세
elasticities approach 탄력성 어프로치
elasticity index 탄력성지수
elasticity of advertising 광고탄력성
elasticity of demand 수요탄성치
elasticity of distribution 유통탄력성
elasticity of expectations 기대탄력성
elasticity of price 가격탄력성
elasticity of substitution 대체탄력성
elasticity of supply 공급탄성치
elasticity of the balance of payments
　　국제수지탄력성
elasticity optimism 탄력성 낙관
elasticity pessimism 탄력성 비관
elbow 경사도가 심한 이율곡선
elder title 선권원(先權原)
electric access member
　　시스템으로 입회장에 액세스할 수 있는 회원
electric power expense 전력비
electricity and gas tax 전기가스세
electricity tax 전기세
electronic banking 전자금융
electronic book 전자북
electronic data gathering analysis and
　　retrieval system EDGAR 시스템
electronic Filing system 전자파일링시스템
electronic fund transfer 전신송금
electronic library 전자도서관
electronic mail 전자메일
electronic media 전자매체
electronic money 전자화폐
electronic order transfer system
　　전자주문전달시스템

electronic publishing 전자출판
electronic video recording 녹화
elegit 토지강제관리영장
element of control 관리요소
element of cost 원가요소
elementary cost accounting 요소별 원가계산
elementary unit 기본단위
eligibility 적격성
eligibility requirements 적격조건
eligible 유자격
eligible bill 할인적격어음
eligible investment 적격투자
eligible security 적격담보
elimination of cause 원인제거
elimination of intercompany indebtedness
　　회사상호간 대차소법
elimination of intercompany ownership
　　회사상호간 지분소법
elimination of intercompany profits
　　회사상호간 이익소법
elisors 배심선정관
elite card 엘리트 카드
Elliot Wave Theory 엘리엇 파동이론
emancipation 해방
embargo 수출금지
embezzlement 횡령
emergency amortization 긴급상각
emergency duty 긴급관세
emergency funds 임시비
emergency legislation 긴급입법
emergency loan 긴급융자
emergency 긴급관세
emergency warning system 긴급경보방송
emergent financial disposition
　　재정상 긴급처분
emerging industry 첨단업계
emerging market 신흥경제지역
emerging technology 첨단기술
Emigration and Immigration Central Order
　　출입국관리령
eminent domain 재산권수용권

empirical analysis 실증분석
empirical approach 경험적 어프로치
empirical demand curve 경제적 수요곡선
empirical study 실증연구
employed assets 운용자산
employee 종업원
employee bonus 상여
employee compensation 미불급여
employee deposits 사원예금
employee discount 종업원할인
employee evaluation 인사고과
employee pension benefit plan
　종업원연금제도
Employee Retirement Income Security Act
　엘리사법
employee stock ownership plan
　종업원지주제도
employee stock purchase plan
　종업원주식구입계획
employee welfare benefit plan
　종업원복지급여제도
employee-director 종업원 겸 임원
employees bonus and allowance
　종업원급여수당
employees' deposits 종업원예금
employees' own conveniences
　종업원의 자기사정
employees' pension fund
　종업원연금기금적립금
employees' relief fund 부조기금
employees' retirement allowance
　고용자퇴직급여금
employees' retirement benefit 퇴직급여이익
employees union 종업원조합
employer 사용자
employer's liability insurance
　사용자배상책임보험
employment 고용
employment adjustment 고용조정
employment 기간이 정해지지 않은 고용 계약
employment cost 인건비

employment income 급여소득
employment income deduction 급여소득공제
employment income earner 급여소득자
employment income exemption
　급여소득공제
employment index 고용지수
employment market 고용시장
employment multiplier 고용승수
employment producers 고용절차
employment service 직업안정소
emptor 매주
empty nest 빈가족; 빈집
empty set 공집합
emulation 대항
emulative product 경쟁제품
enabling statute 수권법
enacting clause 제정조항
enactment 판정
encashment 환가
enclosure 담; 울타리
encode 암호화하다
encroachment 불법적인 권리확장
encumbrance 토지부담
encumbrancer
　토지부담의 권리자 토지부담권리자
end of the fiscal year 연말
end of the month 월말
end of the year 기한
end run 교묘하게 회피함
end-user 최종수요자
ending balance 기말잔고
endogenous change 내생변화
endogenous variable 내생변수
endorsed 이서된
endorsed bill 이서어음
endorsed bills exchanged between two parties
　회전어음
endorsed bond 이서채권
endorsed note 이서어음
endorsee 피이서인
endorsement 이서

endorsement fee 이서수수료

endorsement for option contract
옵션계약의 이서

endorsement for transfer 이서양도

endorsement in blank 백지식 이서

endorsement to order 지도식 이서

endorsement to transfer 양도이서

endorsers 이서인

endowment insurance 양로보험

endowments 기금

energy risk 에너지리스크

energy sector stock 에너지주

enforce 강제하다

enforceable 강행가능

enforced vacation 강제사임

enforcement 시행

enforcement law 시행법

enforcement order 시행령

enforcement regulations 시행규칙

enforcement right 실시권

enfranchisement 특허부여

engagement 약정; 채무

English auction 영국식 경매

English form of balance sheet
영국식 대차대조표

engrossing 마음을 사로잡는

enhance 가치를 높이다

enhanced graphics adapter
인핸스드 그래픽 어댑터; EGA

enjoin 명령하다

enlarged European Communities 확대 EC

enquiry 조회; 조사; 연구

enrollment 등기

ensuing account 차기계정

ensure 확실히 하다

enter 기입하다

enter in an account-book 기재하다

enter wrongly 오기하다

entering short 어음수금기입

enterprise 사업

enterprise accounting 기업회계

enterprise approach
기업 전체의 리스크를 평가함

enterprise cost 기업원가

enterprise economy 기업경제

enterprise mortgage 기업담보권

enterprise tax 사업세

enterprise tax on corporation 법인사업세

entertainment 오락

entertainment and social expenses 교제비

**entertainment expenses not qualifying for
deduction** 손금불산입교제비

entire agreement clause 완전합의조항

entire day 만기계산

entire tenancy 단독보유

entitle 권리를 부여하다

entitlement 권리확보

entity 실체

entity accounting 실체회계

entity theory 법인이론

entrance fee 입회금

entrance to korea 입국

entrant 신규참가업자

entrepreneurial orientation 기업가지향

entrepreneurship 기업가정신

entropy 엔트로피

entrust of collection 징수촉탁

entrusted business commission
위탁업무수수료

entry 기입

entry age cost method 가입연령방식

entry market 참가시장

entry of judgment 판결등록

entry under homestead laws 등기

entry value 입장가액

enumerate 열거하다

envelope curve 포괄곡선

environment assessment 환경평가

environmental change 환경변화

environmental diagnosis 환경진단

environmental impairment liability insurance
환경오염배상책임보험

E
F

environmental refugee 환경난민
environmental variable 환경변수
epistemological criteria 인식론적인 기준
equal annual premium 평균연불보험료
equal credit opportunity 신용기회균등
equal employment opportunities
　고용기회균등
equal footing 공정한 경쟁
equal installment repayment method
　원본균등불방식
equal interval sampling method
　등간격추출법
equal monthly payments with interest
　원리균등반제
equal payment method 원리균등불방식
equal protection of the laws 법의 평등한 보호
equal weighted portfolio 등금액 포트폴리오
equal-annual-payment method
　연간정액지불법
equal-weighted average 균등가중평균
equaled time of payment 평균지불기일
equalization fund 평형준비금
equalization of tax burden 세부담의 평준화
equalization of tax collection 공평한 징수
equalization of tax payment 공평한 납세
equalization reserve 평준화준비금
equalizer 이퀄라이저
equalizing divergences 격차균등화
equalizing dividends 배당평균준비금
equally divided 균분
equation of exchange 교환방정식
equilibrium basis 적정베이시스
equilibrium economies 균형경제학
equilibrium price 균형가격
equilibrium rate of exchange 균형환상장
equilibrium rate of interest 균형이자율
equipment 설비
equipment control 설비관리
equipment fund 설비자금
equipment trust 설비신탁
equipment trust certificate 동산신탁증서

equitable mortgage 형평법상의 모기지
equities insurance 변액보험
equity 주식; 형평법; 지분
equity at book value 자기자본부가
equity at market value 자기자본시가
equity capital 자기자본
equity capital ratio to fixed assets
　고정자산자기자본율
equity capital ratio to long-term capital
　장기부채자기자본율
equity capital ratio to long-term liabilities
　장기부채자기자본비율
equity capital ratio to total debt
　총부채자기자본율
equity financing 주식을 통한 자금조달
equity fund 출자금
equity growth rate 자기자본성장률
equity in earnings 순이익에 대한 지분
equity instruments 출자계약
equity investment 주식투자
equity investor 주식투자가
equity kicker 주식구입권부
equity margin 공정한 이익
equity method 지분법
equity note 주식채
equity participant 출자자
equity participation 자본참가
equity products 공정상품
equity purchase accounting 지분법
equity purchases by institutions 기관구매
equity ratio 자기자본비율
equity receiver 회사갱생절차관재인
equity risk premium 주식위험프리미엄
equity securities 소유주식
equity securities dealer 주식딜러
equity share 지분주식
equity stake 주식지분
equity warrant 주식워런트
equity weighting 주식편입률
equivalence 등가
equivalence relationship 등가관계

equivalent bond yield 채권상응이율
equivalent coefficient 등가계수
equivalent exchangee 등가교환
equivalent level annual dividend
　균등평준연차배당
era of high interest rate 고금리시대
erasure 삭제
erection insurance 조립보험
erection work 설치공사
ergonomics 엘고노믹스; 인간공학
erode 저감하다
erosion in purchasing power 구매력침식
erosion rate 침식률
erratic 불안정한
erratic fluctuation 불안정한 동요
error of prediction 예측오차
errors and omissions excepted 오차탈루제외
errors in calculation 계산차이
errors in posting 전달 과정에서 발생한 차이
errors or omissions 오차탈루
escalator clause 에스컬레이터조항
escapable cost 회피가능원가
escape clause 면책조항
escape sequence 에스케이프시퀀스
escheat 부동산복귀
escrow 조건부 날인증서
escrow account 에스크로계정
escrow agreement 에스크로계약
escrow and trust agreement
　에스크로신탁계약
escrow credit 에스크로신용장
escrow receipt depository
　에스크로보관증서예탁
essential condition 필수조건
established surplus 확정잉여금
establishing a lease 차지권설정
establishment 사업소; 설정
establishment expenses 사업소비(事業所費)
establishment of corporation 법인설립
establishment of hypothec 저당권설정
establishment of leasehold 차지권설정

establishment of tax liability 납세의무확정
establishment of the right of pledge
　질권 설정
estate 재산
estate accounting 유산회계
estate agent 부동산업자
estate contract 부동산계약
estate duty 상속세
estate income 유산소득
estate planning 자산계획
estate upon condition 조건부 부동산권
estate upon limitation 제한부 부동산권
estimate 추계
estimate of budget requests 개산요구
estimate of sales 예상매상고
estimated appropriation 경비예산
estimated balance sheet 견적대차대조표
estimated cost 개산원가
estimated cost accounting 견적원가계산
estimated cost accounting system
　견적원가계산제도
estimated cost of construction work
　견적공사원가
estimated expenses 견적비용
estimated future income taxes
　이연소득세채무
estimated holding period return
　예상보유기간수익률
estimated liabilities 견적채무
estimated mining period 채굴예정연수
estimated profit 견적이익
estimated profit and loss statement
　견적손익계산서
estimated tax 견적세액
estimated tax prepayment 예정납세
estimated uncollectable amount
　수금불능예상액
estimated usable period 사용가능기간
estimated useful life 견적내용연수
estimated value 평가가격
estimating-cost system 견적원가제도

estimation 견적
estoppel 금반언(禁反言)
estovers 필요물
ethernet 이더넷
ethics 윤리
ethnocentrism 국내지향
etiquette of the profession 변호사 도덕
Eurobond 유러채
Eurobond market 유러채시장
Euroclear 유럽시장의 어음교환소
Eurocommercial paper 유러기업어음
Eurocredit market 유러대부시장
Eurocurrency banking market 유러금융시장
Eurocurrency market 유러통화시장
Eurocurrency syndicated loan market
　　유러통화신디케이트론시장
Eurodollar 유러달러
Eurodollar deposit 유러달러예금
Eurodollar depositary interest futures
　　유러달러예금금리선물
Eurodollar futures option 유러달러선물옵션
Eurodollar market 유러달러자금시장
Eurodollar time deposit 유러달러정기예금
Euroline 유러라인
Euromark futures 유러마크선물
Euromarket 유러시장
Euromoney 유러머니
Euronote 중기유러채
Euronote facility 유러노트퍼실리티
European Atomic Energy Community
　　유럽원자력공동체
European Central Bank 유럽중앙은행
European Coal and Steel Community
　　유럽석탄철강공동체
European Communities 유럽공동체
European Currency Unit 유럽통화단위
European Depositary Receipts 유럽예탁증권
European Economic Area 유럽경제지역
European Economic Community
　　유럽경제공동체
European Free Trade Association

　　유럽자유무역연합
European Investment Bank 유럽투자은행
European Investment Trust
　　유럽투자신탁기관
European Monetary Agreement
　　유럽통화협정
European Monetary Cooperation Fund
　　유럽통화협력기금
European Monetary Fund 유럽통화기금
European Monetary System 유럽통화제도
European option 유러피언옵션
European Options Exchange
　　유러피언옵션거래소
European Parliament 유럽의회
European Payment Union 유럽지불동맹
European term 유럽방식
European type 유럽타입
European Union 유럽연합
European unit of account 유럽계산단위
Europound bond 유러펀드채
Eurosyndicate loan 유러신디케이트론
Eurotrack 유러트랙
Euroyen 유러엔
Euroyen bond for resident 거주자유러엔채
Euroyen bond issue 유러엔채 발행
Euroyen interest rate 유러엔 금리
Euroyen market 유러엔시장
evacuation 철수
evade 회피하다
evaluation of importance 중요성을 평가함
evaluation of market mechanism 시장기구를
　　평가함
evaluation of solvency 지불능력평가
evasion of tax 탈세
even bails swap 이븐 베일스 스와프
even keel 금융정책에 변경이 없는 상태
even lot 단위주
evening up (신용거래나 선물거래에서) 전매
　　환매를 마치고 거래관계를 청산함
event insured against 보험사고
event of default 기한이익의 상실사유

event subsequent to balance sheet date
대차대조표일 후의 발생사항
events 사상(事象)
evergreen credit 계속적인 신용공여
evergreen prospectus 운용설명서
eviction 퇴거시킴
eviction order 퇴거명령
evidence 증거
evidenced document 증거서류
evidences of indebtedness 채무증서
evidentiary facts 증거사실
evil practice 악용
ex contractu 계약상의
executive judgment 경영자판단
ex facto 행위에 바탕을 둔
ex gratia 은혜로서
ex gratia payment 임의급여
ex post facto 사후(事後)의
ex proprio motu 임의로
ex works 공장인도
ex-allotment 신주분매, 할당
ex-ante analysis 사전분석
ex-coupon 이표락
ex-dividend 배당락
ex-dividend date 배당락일
ex-interest 이자락
ex-interest bond 이락채권
ex-interest period 이락기간
ex-new 권리락; 신주락으로(의)
ex-post alpha value 사후수치
ex-post analysis 사후분석
ex-post assessment 사후평가
ex-post characteristic line 사후특성선
ex-post investment 사후투자
ex-post saving 사후저축
ex-rights of capital increase 증자권리락
ex-warrant bond 순수채권
exaction 불법보수청구죄
exaggerated advertisement 과장광고
exaggerated final return 과대신고
examination 심사

examination and decision 심사재결
examination by reference 조사
examination in chief 주심문
examination of entrance qualification
입회심사
examination of loan application 대출심사
examination of witness 증인심문
examined copy 대조한 등본
examiner 국세조사관
except for ~을 제외하고는
excepted perils 면책위험
excepted risks 제외위험
exception 제외사항
exception clause 면책조항
exception principle 예외의 원칙
exception rate 예외운임
exception to amortization of deferred charge
이연자산상각특례
exception to depreciation deduction
감가상각특례
exceptional rates of tax 예외세율
exceptional tax treatment 세무상의 특례
exceptions clause 면책약관
excess 소손해면책
excess and deficiency 과부족
excess capacity 과잉설비; 과잉능력
excess cash 여유자금
excess demand 초과수요
excess disbursement 초과지불
excess franchise 공제면책보합
excess general average 초과공동해손
excess income 초과소득
excess insurance 이차보험
excess legal liability policy
법정책임액 초과배상책임보험
excess liabilities clause 초과책임담보약관
excess line 초과액
excess line reinsurance 초과액재보험
excess liquidity 과잉유동성
excess margin 초과증거금
excess margin account 여잉마진계정

excess mortality 초과사망율
excess of loss 초과손해액
excess of loss ratio reinsurance
　초과손해율재보험
excess of loss reinsurance 초과손해재보험
excess of loss treaty reinsurance
　초과손해액특약재보험
excess payment 초과지불
excess profitability 초과이윤
excess profits 초과이윤
excess profits credit 초과이윤공제
excess profits tax 초과이윤
excess receipt over contract price
　계약초과금액
excess reinsurance 초과액재보험
excess reserves 초과준비
excess supply 초과공급
excessive competition 과당경쟁
excessive consumption 과잉소비
excessive depreciation deduction
　초과상각
excessive lending 과잉융자
excessive liquidity 과잉유동성
excessive profit 부당이득
excessive savings 과잉저축
excessive seizure 초과차압
excessive stocks 과잉주
excessive trading 과잉거래
exchange 환; 거래소
exchange acquisition 거래소매입
exchange arbitrage 환재정거래
exchange arbitrage transaction 환재정거래
exchange at night 야간교환
exchange bank 환은행
exchange bill payable 병위채
exchange bought 매환
exchange broker 환브로커
exchange business 환업무
exchange cambiste 환딜러
exchange check for money 금전의 인환권
exchange clause 환율문언

exchange clearing 환결제청산
exchange clearing agreement 환청산협정
exchange contract 환예약
exchange contract with option
　선택권부 환예약
exchange control 환관리
exchange cover 카버거래 커버거래
exchange cover rate 환은행이 환보유고를
　조정하기 위해 다른 은행과 조건이 일치할
　때 하는 거래
exchange dealer 환딜러
exchange dealing 환거래
exchange distribution 거래소분배
exchange dumping 환덤핑
exchange efficiency 교환효율
exchange equalization account 환평형계정
exchange equalization fund 환평형기금
exchange equalization operation 환평형조작
exchange fluctuation 환변동
exchange for collection 수금환
exchange for means of foreign payment
　대외지불을 위한 환
exchange for physical program
　프로그램매매
exchange forward contract 선물환예약
exchange fund cover 자금조정거래
exchange fund cover or operation
　환자금조정거래
exchange funds operation 자금조작
exchange gain 환차익
exchange gain from the won appreciation
　원고차익
exchange gain or loss 환환산차손익
exchange intervention 환개입
exchange law 거래소법
exchange link 외국환의 링크
exchange loss 환차손
exchange loss and profit 환차손익
exchange manipulation 환조작
exchange market 거래소시장
exchange marriage profit 환매리이익

exchange marry 환매리
exchange member 거래소회원
exchange of equivalents 등가교환
exchange of notes 교환공문
exchange of property 자산교환
exchange offer 주식취득신고
exchange operation 환조작
exchange parity 환평가
exchange position 환지고(持高)
exchange premium 환프리미엄
exchange profit 환차익
exchange quotation 대고객환상장
exchange rate 환율
exchange rate at break-even point
　손익분기환상장
exchange rate in favor of won 원고
exchange rate in foreign currency
　외화기준상장
exchange reservation 환예약
exchange risk 환리스크
exchange risk cover 환보유고조정조작
exchange risk insurance 환변동보험
exchange settlement 환결제
exchange sold 매환
exchange speculation 환투기
exchange stabilization fund 환안정기금
exchange tax 거래소별세
exchange ticket 주문집행확인서
exchange traded option 상장옵션
exchange transactions 거래소거래
exchequer bills 영국재무부증권
excise duty 물품세
exclude 제외한; 면책으로 하다
excluded perils 면책위험
exclusion 제외; 면책
exclusion from expenses 손금불산입
exclusion from expenses of corporation tax
　법인세액손금불산입
exclusion from gross revenue 익금불산입
exclusion from taxation 비과세
exclusion of loss 손실제외

exclusion of profit accrued from valuation
　profit 평가익의 익금불산입
exclusion of refund from gross revenue
　환부금의 익금불산입
exclusion of subrogation 대위구상권행사폐지
exclusive agent 독점대리점
exclusive channel 폐쇄형 채널
exclusive dealing 경쟁품취급금지계약
exclusive distributorship 독점판매권
exclusive jurisdiction 전속관할권
exclusive privilege/right 독점권
exclusive selling agency 독점판매대리점
exclusive use 전용
exclusive-occupation house 전용주택
exculpatory clause 면책조항
excusable 면책되는
excuse 변명; 면책사유
executed 이미 이행한
executed contract of sale 완성매매계약
execution 체결; 이행
execution creditor 집행채권자
execution of order 주문집행
execution organ 실행기관
executive committee 집행위원회
executive compensation option
　임원보장을 위한 옵션
executive measure 집행처분
executive officer 집행관리
Executive pension 경상관리자연금
executive power 집행권
executive proceedings 집행절차
executive salaries 임원보수
executor 집행자
executor be son tort 권한이 없는 임원집행자
executory contract 미확정계약
executory interest 장래권
exemplification 인증등본
exempt corporation 비과세법인
exempt from taxation 면세의
exempt gift 비과세증여
exempt income 비과세소득

exempt private company 면제사회사(私會社)
exempt property 비과세재산
exempt securities 면제증권
exempt stock exchange 등록면제거래소
exempted securities 적용제외증권
exemption 비과세
exemption agreement 면책 약관
exemption and deduction from income
　소득공제
exemption clause 면책조항
exemption for aged person 노령자공제
exemption for dependents 부양공제
exemption for handicapped person
　장애자공제
exemption for spouse 배우자공제
exemption for working student
　근로학생공제
exemption from payment of premium
　보험료지불면제
exemption from return of subsidy
　보조금반환면제
exemption from taxation 면세
exemption method 외국소득면제방식
exemption point 면세점
exemptions 차입금지채권
exercise 권리행사
exercise date 만기일
exercise limit 권리행사가 인정된 거래량
exercise of security right 담보권행사
exercise price 행사가격
exhaustion 소모
exhibit 증거서류; 첨부서류
existential proposition 존재명제
existing assets 기존자산
existing debt 기존채무
existing preferential duties 기존특혜
exit barrier 철수장벽
exit bond 졸업채
exit value 퇴장가액
exogenous change 외생변화
exogenous demand 외생수요

exogenous variables 외생변수
exoneration 면책
exorbitant profit 법외이익
exotic bond 엑조틱 본드
exotic derivatives 엑조틱파생상품
expand mode 확장모드
expansion of a new market 신시장 개척
expansion of currency 통화팽창
expansionary budget 적극예산
expansive economy 확대경제
expectancy theory 기대이론
expectancy-value model 예측모델
expectant heir 기대상속인
expectation 예상
expectation function 예상함수
expectation gap 기대갭
expectation hypothesis 기대가설
expectation of life 평균여명
expectation theory 기대이론
expected demand 기대수요
expected earnings 기대수익
expected earnings growth rate
　기대이익성장률
expected holding-period rate of return
　기대보유기간수익률
expected income 예정수입
expected life 견적내용연수
expected mortality rate 예정사망률
expected profit 기대이윤
expected return ratio of loan trust
　대부신탁예상배당률
expected satisfaction 기대만족
expected total rate of return 기대총수익률
expected value 기대치
expected value theory 기대치이론
expected volatility 예상변동률
expected yield-to-maturity 기대만기이율
expendable fund 지출가능자금
expenditure 지출
expenditure curtailment 지출삭감
expenditure for public bond 공채비

expenditure for public works 공공사업비

expenditure on capital accounts
자본계정지출

expenditure on unemployment benefit
실업보험지출

expenditure rate 지출율

expenditure tax 지출세

expenditure unaccounted for
사용용도불명금

expense analysis book 경비내역장

expense arising from outside manufacture
외주가공비

expense distribution 비용배부

expense item 비목

expense ledger 경비원장

expenses 비용

expenses budget 경비예산

expenses for education and culture 교양비

expenses incurred for having the user remove
이전료

expenses incurred for maintaining household
가사관련비

expenses incurred for opening of business
개업비

expenses incurred for the transfer 양도비용

expenses of bringing up children 양육비

expenses of entering port 입항비용

expenses paid-in advance 미경과비용

expenses quota 경비할당

experience assumptions 기초율

experience curve 경험곡선

experience effects 경험효과

experience grading and rating schedule
경험분류요율표

experience rating 경험요율

experience table 경험표

experimental and research expense
시험연구비

experimental and research expense tax credit
시험연구비세액공제

experimental effect 실험효과

experimental manufacturing cost 시작비

expiration 만료

expiration date 만기일

expiration date of the credit card
카드유효기한

expiration file 만기파일

expiration notice 만기통지

expiration of obligation 채무소멸

expired card 기한이 끝난 카드

expired cost 소멸원가

expiry 기한만료

explanatory note 주

explanatory variable 설명변수

explicit cost 명시적 비용

exploitation 착취

exploitation of new resources 신자원개발

exponential distribution 지수분포

exponential function 지수함수

exponential growth 지수성장

export account 환당좌대

export advance 수출전도금

export advance loan 수출전대금융

export advanced account 수출전대계정

export and import price index
수출입물가지수

export and import statistics 외국무역통계

export bill 수출어음

export bounty 수출장려금

export credit 수출신용

export credit insurance 수출신용보험

export declaration 수출신고

export dependence 수출의존도

export drive 수출드라이브

export duties 수출세

export exemption 수출면세

export factoring 수출채권매입

export financing 수출금융

export function 수출함수

export in terms of won 원기준수출

export insurance 수출보험

export license 수출승인증

E
F

export on consignment 위탁판매수출
export price index 수출물가지수
export profitability 수출의 수익성
export supplier credit 수출업자신용
export tax 수출세
export to an overseas territory 이출(移出)
export-import bank 수출입은행
exposure 익스포저
exposure draft 공개초안
exposure frequency 노출빈도
exposure hazard 연소위험
exposure to risk 리스크부담
express 명시된
express condition 명시조건
express contract 명시계약
express trust 명시신탁
express warranty 명시담보
expropriation 공용징수
expropriation loss 접수로 인한 손실
expropriation of land 토지수용
extel card 익스텔 카드
extended benefit 확장급부
extended bill 연기어음
extended coupon 이연이자표
extended cover clause 연장담보약관
extended coverage 확장담보특약
extended definition television 클리어비전방송
extended fund facility 확대신용공여제도
extended insurance 연장보험
extended slot 확장슬롯
extended term insurance 연장정기보험
extendible debt security 익스텐더블채권
extendible maturity 연장가능만기
extensible swap 연장가능형 스와프
extension 확장
extension effect 기간효과
extension of due date 납기연장
extension of loan 융자실행
extension of the maturity 상환연장
extension of time claims 연장클레임

extension of time for completion 공기연장
extension of time to file 제출연기
extensive channel 해방형 채널
extent 재산평가
extent of audit 감사범위
extenuation 경감
external audit 외부감사
external auditor 외부감사인
external bond 외채
external consistency 외부정합성
external economy 외부경제
external equilibrium 대외균형
external evidence 외적인 증거
external failure 외부실패
external financing 외부금융
external forces 외압
external hazard 외부위험
external information 외부정보
external intangible loss 외부의 무형손실
external liabilities 외부부채
external loan 외채
external purchasing power of money
　화폐의 대외가치
external quality assurance 외부품질보증
external quality audit 외부품질감사
external reserves 외화준비
external resources 외부자원
external restraint 외부적인 제약
external transaction 외부거래
external transactions account 해외계정거래
external user 사외이용자
externality 외부성
extinction 소멸
extinctive prescription 소멸시효
extinguishment of hypothec 저당권소멸
extinguishment of property 자산의 소실
extinguishment of the right of rescission
　해제권 소멸
extortion 강요
extra 별도계정지불
extra charges 부대비용

extra cost 추가비용
extra depreciation 할증상각
extra dividend 특별배당
extra expenditure 임시비
extra expense insurance 임시비용보험
extra item 이상항목
extra premium 할증보험료
extra risk 추가위험
extra wage 할증임금
extra work claims 여분공사클레임
extra-judicial 재판외의
extradition 본국송환
extramural 구역외의
extraneous evidence 외부증거
extraneous risk 부가위험
extraordinary average 비상해손(海損)

extraordinary depreciation 특별상각
extraordinary expenses 임시비
extraordinary gain 특별이익
extraordinary income 임시소득
extraordinary items 특별손익항목
extraordinary loss 특별손실
extraordinary profit and loss 특별손익
extraordinary repairs 임시수선비
extraordinary resolution 임시결의
extrapolation 외삽법
extraterritoriality 치외법권
extraterritoriality on tax laws 면세특권
extrinsic evidence 외부증거
eye camera 아이카메라
eye catcher 아이캐처

E
F

fabless 제조부문이 없는 개발 메이커
fabricating cost 제조원가
face 액면
face amount 액면금액
face amount certificate company
　액면증서회사
face of instrument 증서의 문면
face of note 할부가격
face value 액면가액
facilitating functions 보조기능
facilitation order 퍼실리테이션오더
facilities 설비
facility of payment clause 지불편의조항
Fackler's formula 패클러공식
fact book 팩트북
fact finding 사실조사
fact in issue 주요사실
factor 재료; 팩터; 요인
factor analysis 인자분석
factor beta 팩터베타
factor comparison system 요소비교법
factor loadings matrix 인자부하행렬
factor return 요소수익률
factor risk 팩터리스크
factor's lien 도매상 리엔
factorage 팩터수수료
factoring 외상채권매입업무; 팩터링
factors of production 생산요소
factory 공장
factory account 공장계정
factory accounting 공장회계

factory bookkeeping 공업부기
factory burden 공장간접비
factory cost 공장원가
factory cost report 제조원가보고서
factory expenses 제조간접비
factory expenses variance 경비차액
factory furniture 공장용 집기
factory furnitures and fixtures 공장비품
factory ledger 공장원장
factory ledger account 공장원계정
factory mutual insurance 공장주상호보험
factory overhead 제조간접비
factory preset 팩토리프리셋
factory risk 공장물건
factory supplies 공장용 소모품
facultative reinsurance 임의재보험
facultative reinsurance agreement
　임의재보험협정
faculty theory of taxation 지불능력과세설
fade 패드
fade in 페이드인
fade out 페이드아웃
fade-out formula 페이드아웃방식
fade-out policy 외자비율소멸정책
faded 하향수정된
fail 파산하다
fail position 불이행포지션
failing company 파탄기업
failing of record 기록미제출
failure 불이행
failure mode 고장모드

failure of consideration 약인멸실

faint action 무력(無力)소송

fair 적정

fair and equitable 공정과 형평

fair average quality 평균품질

fair leasehold value 차지권가격

fair market value 공정시장가격; 시가

fair price 공정가격

fair trade bureau 공정거래국

Fair Trade Commission 공정거래위원회

fair value 공정가치

fair value accounting 시가주의회계

fair wage 적정임금

fairness 공평성

fairness doctrine 공정원칙

fairy and impartially 공평하게

fall 하강

fall due 지불기일이 되는

fall of building clause 건물파괴약관

fall of gold standard 금본위제도붕괴

falling in price 가격하락

falling in stock price 주가하락

falling interest rate 금리하락

falling market 하락기조상장

false declaration 부정신고

false demonstration 오류표시

false imprisonment 불법감금

false missing 위장분실

false personation 성명사기

false pretense 사기죄

false representation 허위표시

false return 허위신고

false statement 허위진술

false trade description 상품허위표시

false verdict 부당평결

family allowance 가족수당

family bookkeeping 가계부

family brand 통일브랜드

family characteristics 가족특성

family corporation 동족회사

family estate 그 집의 상속인; 호주상속

family fund 모자형 투자신탁

family income and expenditure survey
    가계조사(家計調査)

family insurance 가족보험

family medical expense policy
    가정의료비보험

family member 친족

family partnership 동족조합

family persona accident policy 가족상해보험

family saving survey 저축동향조사

family taxation of assets income
    자산소득의 세대합산과세

family-register 호적

fan line 팬라인

Fan theory 팬이론

fancy stocks 저가주

Fannie Mae 패니메이; 저당증권

fare 운임

farm accounting 농업회계

farming of taxes 조세수금청부

fashion forecasting 유행예측

fault 과실

fault tree analysis 고장트리해석

favorable 순조

favorable balance of overall 종합수지흑자

favorable balance of payments 국제수지흑자

favorable balance of trade 무역수지흑자

favorable balance on current account
    경상수지흑자

favorable cash flows 바람직한 현금의 흐름

favorable factor 호재

favorable leverage effect 긍정적인 증익효과

favorable news 호재

fear 경계

feasance 행위

feasibility study 타당성조사

Fed watcher FRB전문가

Federal Advisory Committee 연방자문위원회

Federal Bankruptcy Act 연방파산법

Federal Communication Commission
    연방통신위원회

federal credit agency 연방금융기관
federal decentralization 연방분권제도
Federal Deposit Insurance Corporation
　연방예금보험공사
federal fund market 연방자금시장
federal fund rate 연방자금금리
Federal Home Loan Bank 연방주택대부은행
Federal Home Loan Bank Board
　연방주택대부은행이사회
Federal Home Loan Bank System
　연방주택대부은행제도
Federal Home Loan Mortgage Corporation
　연방주택금융저당금고
federal income tax 연방소득세
Federal Intermediate Credit Bank
　연방중개신용은행
Federal Land Bank 연방토지은행
Federal National Mortgage Association
　연방저당금고
Federal Open Market Commission
　연방공개시장위원회
Federal Reserve Bank 연방준비은행
Federal Reserve Bank of New York
　뉴욕연방준비은행
Federal Reserve Board 연방준비제도이사회
Federal Reserve District 연방준비지구
fee 보수
fee basis 수수료원칙
fee business 수수료사업
fee for legal advice 법률상담료
fee simple 단순부동산권
feed 원재료를 보내다
feed consumption 원료소비량
feedback 피드백
feedback information 피드백정보
feemail 피메일
fees and permits 면허료
fellow 정회원
fellowship grant 연구보조금
fence sitter 투자판단을 내릴 수 없는 사람
feneration 고리대

fertility rate 출생률
feverish market 과열장세
fiber to the home 파이버 투 더 홈방식
Fibonacci sequence 피보나치수열
fiction 법률상의 의제
fictional theory of corporation 법인의제설
fictitious 가공
fictitious assets 의제자산
fictitious capital 의제자본
fictitious demand 가수요
fictitious dividend
　회사의 신용을 유지하기 위한 배당
fictitious name deposit 가공명의예금
fictitious price 에누리
fictitious profit 가공이익
fictitious sales slip 가공매상전표
fidelity guarantee insurance 신원신용보험
fidelity insurance 신용보험
fidelity rebate system 운임할인제
fiduciary 수탁자
fiduciary accounting 신탁회계
fiduciary bond 수탁자보증증권
fiduciary contract 신탁계약
fiduciary duty 신탁의무
fiduciary estate 신탁재산
fiduciary issue 보증발행
fiduciary power 신탁권한
fiduciary relation 신뢰관계
fiduciary responsibility 수탁자책임
field 매초상수
field audit 실지감사
field examinations 임점검사
field inspection 현장감사
field inspector 현장감사인
field test 시운전
field underwriter 외무직원
field-work audit standards 감사실시기준
file allocation table 파일앨로케이션테이블
file and use 계출후 사용제
File and use system 보험요율계출제
file compression 파일압축

file income tax return 소득액을 신고하다
filiation 인지
filing 파일링
filing final return of merger 합병확정신고
filing of claims 채권계출
filing return 신고
Fill-ins 보충발주
fill-or-kill order 즉시 또는 취소주문
filing up of a deficit 적자보전
film sensitivity 필름감도
final 종국의
final audit 기말감사
final balance 기말잔고; 최종잔고
final balance method 최종잔고방식
final beneficiary 최종수익자
final call 최종분담금
final claim 본클레임
final declaration 확정신
final demand 최종수요
Final depreciable limit 상각가능한도액
Final maturity 만기
final notice of claim 확정손해배상청구통지서
final pay type 최종급료형
final payment 확정신고에 따른 납부
final products 최종생산물
final prospectus 최종설립취지서
final rate of return 최종수익률
final return 확정신고
final return in the case of loss 손실신고서
Final return of liquidation 청산확정신고서
final return of merger 합병확정신고서
final settlement of accounts 확정한 결산
final tax return 확정신고
final transaction date 최종거래일
Final value 종가
final verification 최종검증
Final yield 최종이익
Final yield on investment 최종투자이익
finally settled financial statements
　최종적으로 확정한 재무제표
finance 금융

finance bill 정부단기증권
finance capital 금융자본
finance charge 금융비용
finance company 금융회사
finance for deficit 적자금융
finance for prepaid installment sales
　전불식 할부판매금융
finance law 재정법
finance lease 파이낸스리스
Finance Ministry note 재무부증권
Finance Ministry Ordinance 재무부령
finance paper 금융어음
finance receivable 대출채권
finance receivables as collateral 채권담보
Finance System Council 재정제도심의회
financial accounting 재무회계
Financial Accounting Deliberation Council
　기업회계심의회
Financial Accounting Standards Advisory
　Council 재무회계기준자문위원회
Financial Accounting Standards Board
　재무회계기준심의회
financial accounting standards for business
　enterprise 기업회계원칙
financial accounts 금융계정
financial activities 금융활동
financial advisor 재무고문
financial affairs 재무
financial agreement 금융협정
financial aid 금융원조
financial analysis 재무분석
Financial Analysts Federation
　전미증권분석가연합회
financial appraisal 재무평가
financial assets 금융자산
financial assets and liabilities account
　금융자산부채잔고표
financial audit 재무감사
financial balance 재무밸런스
financial books 회계장부
financial capital 금융자본

financial center 금융중심지
financial charges 금융비용
financial claim 금융채권
financial clique 재벌
financial collapse 금융붕괴
financial condition 재무내용
financial considerations 재무상의 배려
financial cost 재무코스트
financial crisis 금융공황
financial damages 금전상의 손실
financial decision 금융면의 결단
financial deficit 자금부족
financial democracy 재정민주주의
financial difficulty 금융난
financial documents 계산서류
financial engineering 재테크
financial environment 금융환경
financial expenses 금융비용
financial facilities 금융서비스
financial forward contract 금융선도계약
financial futures 금융선물
financial futures contract 금융선물계약
financial futures instrument 금융선물상품
financial futures market 금융선물시장
financial futures option 금융선물옵션
financial futures transaction 금융선물거래
financial guarantee 자력보증
Financial Guaranty Insurance Company
　금융보증보험회사
financial highlights 경리의 하이라이트
financial innovation 금융혁신
financial institution 금융기관
financial institution for agriculture forestry
　and fisheries 농림어업금융기관
financial institution for foreign exchange
　외국환금융기관
financial institutions for long-term credit
　장기신용금융기관
financial institutions for small business
　중소기업금융기관
financial instrument 금융상품

financial intermediaries or brokers
　금융중개기관
financial item 금융항목
financial lease 금융리스
financial leverage 재무레버리지
financial leverage effect 재무면의 증익효과
financial leverage ratio 재무레버리지비율
financial liability 금융부채
financial liberalization 금융자유화
financial liberalization policy
　금융자유화정책
financial management 재무관리
financial market 금융시장
financial market analysis 금융시장분석
financial model 금융모델
Financial News index option
　파이낸셜 뉴스 지수 옵션
financial obligation 금융채무
financial operations 금융업
financial option contract 금융옵션
financial option market 금융옵션시장
financial panic 금융공황
financial planner 생보FP
financial planning 재무계획
financial policy 금융정책
financial position 재정상태
financial position statement 대차대조표
financial product 금융상품
financial profit 금융수익
financial ratio 재무비율
financial regulation 금융규제
financial report 유가증권보고서
financial reporting accounting 재무보고회계
financial research center 금융연구소
financial resources 재원
financial retrenchment 경비절감
financial revenue 재무수익
financial review 재무개황
financial revolution 금융혁명
financial sector stocks 금융주
financial service 금융서비스

financial slack 재무상의 슬랙
financial standing 재정상태
financial statement analysis 재무제표분석
financial statement audit 재무제표감사
financial statements 재무제표
financial statistics 금융통계
financial status 재정상태
financial strain and stress 금융긴박
financial strength 재무건전성
financial structure 재무체질
financial surplus or deficit 자금과부족
financial system 금융제도
financial transaction 금융거래
financial year 회계연도
financier 출자자
financing 자금조달
financing activities 재무활동
financing adjustment law 자금조정법
financing bill 금융어음
financing burden 금융부담
financing charge 금융비용
financing corporation 금융회사
financing for carrying unsold inventories
　체화금융
financing for deficit-covering 적자융자
financing for sales by installment payment
　월부판매금융
financing for stocks 주식자금조달
financing from brokers' own capital
　자기융자
financing method 자금조달방법
financing regulation 융자준칙
financing regulation law 자금조정법
financing vehicle 금융수단
finder 파인더
finding of fact 사실인정
fine 벌금
finished artwork 완전원고
finished goods 완성품
finished goods on hand 소유제품
finished product verification 완성품검사

finished products 완성품
finished products account 제품계정
finished products inventory 제품재고액
finished products on hand 제품소지액
finite difference 유한차분
finiteness 유한성
Fire and Marine Insurance Rating
　Association of Japan
　일본손해보험요율산정회
fire and other casualty insurance premiums
　deduction 손해보험공제
fire clause 화재보험약관
fire company 화재손해
fire damage 화재보험
fire insurance 화재보험
fire insurance on dwelling houses
　주택화재보험
fire insurance policy 화재보험증권
fire insurance premium 화재보험료
fire insurance proceeds 화재보험금
fire loss 화재손실
fire loss suspense account
　화재손실미결산계정
fire mutual insurance 화재상호보험
fire peril 화재위험
fire wall 방화벽
fire-insurance for mortgagee interest
　채권보전화재보험
firm 견조(堅調); 사업법인
firm banking 펌뱅킹
firm bid 확정매호수치
firm commitment 확약; 전액인수
firm commitment underwriting 매입인수
firm contract 확정계약
firm offer 확정가격제시
firm order 확정주문
firm price 확정가격
firm quote 확약가격
firm tone of the U.S. dollar 달러고기조
firmer 강보합
firmer tone 시세가 오를듯한 기세

E
F

first blush 일견하여
first board 전장입회
first call date 첫 도중산환일
first check 초감
first cost 구입원가
first coupon date 첫 이자지불일
first demand bond 퍼스트디맨드본드
first exchange 제1권
first generation on-line system 제1차온라인
first instance 제일심
first mortgage 제일저당
first mortgage bond 제일순위 저당권부사채
first preferred stock 제일우선주식
first purchaser 최초취득자
first risk policy 일차손해보험
first section market 일부상장
first session of the month 발회
first surplus treaty 일차초과액특약
first year commission 초년도수수료
first-dollar coverage 무공제담보방식
first-in first-out method 선입선출법
first-loss insurance 실손전보
fisc 국고
fiscal agent 재무대리인
fiscal agent agreement 재무대리인계약
fiscal agent for treasury fund 국고재무대리인
fiscal and monetary policy 재정금융정책
fiscal balance 재정수지
fiscal drug 재정팽창억제
fiscal expenditure 재정지출
fiscal illusion 재정착각
fiscal inflation 재정인플레이션
fiscal inflexibility 재정경직화
fiscal investment 재정투자
fiscal investment and loan 재정투융자
fiscal outlook 재정예견
fiscal period 회계기간
fiscal policy 재정정책
fiscal privileges of diplomat 외교관과세특권
fiscal reform 재정개혁
fiscal target 재정목표

fiscal tightness 재정핍박
fiscal year 회계연도
Fisher effect 피셔효과
fishing right 어업권
fit 적성정도
fitness for purpose 목적적합성
fitness for use 사양적합성
fittings 부속품
five-and-dime store 균일가격점
fixed amount method 정액법
fixed amount minimum payment 최저한도지불의무액
fixed amount taxation 정액과세
fixed annuity 정액연금
fixed arrangement 고정성 배열법
fixed asset ledger 고정자산대장
fixed asset ratio 고정자산비율
fixed asset tax 고정자산세
fixed asset to net worth ratio 고정비율
fixed asset turnover ratio 고정자산회전율
fixed assets 고정자산
fixed capital 고정자본
fixed capital investment 고정자본투자
fixed charge 특정담보
fixed collateral 근저당
fixed costs and expenses 고정비
fixed coupon bond 확정이부채
fixed date 확정일부
fixed date delivery 확정일인도
fixed debt 고정차입금
fixed deposit 정기예금
fixed difference 확정차액
fixed dollar security 고정달러증권
fixed exchange rate 고정환율
fixed exchange rate system 고정환율제도
fixed expenses 고정비
fixed fee 정율보수
fixed gain 확정이익
fixed general tariff 고정세율
fixed income 고정수입
fixed income market 고정채시장; 채권시장

fixed income security 고정금리증권
fixed installment 정액상각
fixed installment method 정액법
fixed interest 확정이자
fixed interest security 확정이자부 증권
fixed interest-bearing bond 확정이자부 채권
fixed investment 고정자본투자
fixed liabilities 고정부채
fixed liquidity reserve requirements 고정유
　동비율제도
fixed loan 고정대부금
fixed mortgage 근저당권
fixed obligations 확정채무
fixed overhead 고정비
fixed parity system 고정평가제
fixed penalty bond 정액책임보증증권
fixed percentage depreciation
　정율감가상각법
fixed percentage method 감가정율법
fixed percentage on unexpired cost method
　정율법
fixed position 정위치
fixed price 고정가격
fixed property 부동산
fixed rate 고정금리
fixed ratio 고정비율
fixed return securities 고정이율증권
fixed salary 고정급
fixed tax rate 일정세율
fixed term policies 확정일지불보험
fixed trust 확정신탁
fixed unit trust 고정단위형 투자신탁
fixed wages 고정급
fixed-asset schedule 고정자산명세표
fixed-charge coverage ratio
　고정비용부담배율
fixed-date delivery 확정일인도
fixed-first type 고정성 배열
fixed-income benchmark
　확정이자부 증권 벤치마크
fixed-income target 확정이자부 타깃

fixed-percentage on declining balance
　method 정율법
fixed-rate assets 고정금리자산
fixed-rate bond 확정이자부 채권
fixed-rate liability 고정금리부채
fixed-rate payer 고정금리지불인
fixing 고정
fixtures 비품
flag 깃발
flag of convenience vessel 편의치적선
flat 균일의; 배당락의
flat commission 균일수수료
flat curve 플랫거브
flat deductible 정액공제면책율
flat exchange contract 균일환예약
flat growth 동일한 성장률
flat loan 플랫론
flat market 플랫마켓
flat rate 균일요율; 균일레이트
flat yield 균일이자배당
flattening of the yield curve 이율곡선평준화
flea market 도떼기(고물, 벼룩)시장
fleet insured 플리트계약자
fleet retention 보험그룹의 보유액
flexform 플렉스폼
flexible forward contract
　플렉서블 포워드 거래
flexible mortgage 근저당
flexible tariff 신축세율
flexible time 플렉서블 타임
flexible-premium variable life insurance
　변액유니버설보험
flier 광고쪽지; 등귀
flight to quality 질로 도피함
flip-flop 플립플롭채권
flip-over clause 플립오버조항
float 미결제수표
floater 유동증권; 포괄보험증권
floating assets 유동자산
floating basis 플로팅베이시스
floating capital 유동자본

floating charge 유동담보
floating debt 유동채무
floating exchange rate 변동환율
floating exchange rate system 변동환율제
floating interest rate 변동이율
floating interest rate account with ceiling
　변동상한금리부 계정
floating liability 유동부채
floating lien 유동리엔
floating policy 포괄예정보험계약
floating prime rate 시장연동형 우대금리
floating property 포괄재산
floating rate 변동금리
floating rate bond 변동이자부 채권
floating rate certificate of deposit
　변동금리 CD
floating rate index 변동금리지표
floating rate lending 변동금리대출
floating rate mortgage 변동이자부 모기지
floating rate note 변동이자부 채권
floating rate of interest 가변금리
floating rate payer 변동금리지불인
floating stock 유동주
floating supply 매매수요
floating system 변동상장
floor 하한; 입회장
floor broker 중매인
floor issue 입회장상표
floor of the court 당사자석
floor price 바닥시세
floor rate 하한금리
floor representative 증권업자의 대리인으로서
　거래소에 나와 거래하는 점원
floor trader 플로어트레이더; 룸트레이더
floored swap 플로어드스와프
flooring debt 일시차입금
flotation 증권발행
flotation of external loan 외채모집
flotation of government bond 공채발행
flotation of loan 기채
flow chart 플로차트

flow of fund account 자금순환계정
flow of funds analysis 자금순환분석
flower bond 플라워본드
fluctuate 변동하다
fluctuating and extraordinary income
　변동소득 및 임시소득
fluctuating income 변동소득
fluctuation clause 변동조항
fluctuation limit 변동폭제한
fluctuation of stock prices 주가동향
fluctuations in prices of raw materials
　원료가격변동
flyer 광고쪽지
focus strategy 집중전략
follow-up advertisement 사후광고
follow-up selling 권유장을 내어 판매함
following underwriter 추수(追隨)보험자
font 폰트
food bill 식량증권
foot 합계하다
foot note 각주
footing 계산다툼
for sale 매물
force majeure 불가항력
force majeure clause 불가항력조항
force of discount 할인력
force of interest 이자력
forced auction 강제경매
forced conversion 강제전환
forced liquidation 강제청산
forced sale 강제매각
forced saving 강제저축
forced transfer 강제이전
forced-sale value 강제처분가치
forcible disposition 강제처분
forcible entry 불법침입
forcible execution 강제집행
forcible provisions 강행규정
forcing methods 촉성법
forecast by the econometric model
　계량모델예측

forecast for market tendency 상장관
forecast of sales 예상매상고
forecasting model 예측모델
foreclosure 저당권집행; 포어클로저
foreclosure under power of sale
　사법처분과 관계없는 매각
foregift 권리금
forehand rent 전불지대
foreign 외국의; 예외적의
foreign access zone 수입촉진지역
foreign adjustment clause 외국정산약관
foreign affiliate 외자계기업
foreign agents accounts 외국대리점계정
foreign attachment 채권차압
foreign banks in Japan 재일외은
foreign bill 외국어음
foreign bill of exchange 외국환어음
foreign bond 외국채권
foreign branch-our account
　외국지점발송계정
foreign branch-their account
　외국지점피발송계정
foreign buying 외국인구매
foreign capital 외자
foreign capital consumer finance company
　외자계 소비자금융
foreign capital inducement 외자흡수
foreign capital intake 외자수입
foreign competition 국제경쟁
foreign corporation 외국법인
foreign corporation company 외국기업
foreign corporation tax 외국법인세
foreign corporation tax credit
　외국법인세액공제
Foreign Credit Insurance Association
　외국신용보험협회
foreign currency 외화
foreign currency account 외화계정
foreign currency bill receivable
　외화징수외국환
foreign currency bond 외화채

foreign currency deposit 외화예금
foreign currency deposit account
　외화예금계정
foreign currency deposit with exchange bank
　외화예탁
foreign currency futures 외국통화선물
foreign currency futures contracts
　외국통화선물계약
foreign currency holdings 외화보유고
foreign currency inflow 외화유입
foreign currency reserves 외화준비
foreign currency securities 외화증권
foreign currency series securities
　외화기준증권
foreign currency statements
　외화표시재무제표
foreign currency transactions 외화거래
foreign currency translation gain or loss
　환차손
foreign currency-denominated bond
　외화기준채권
foreign debt 외채
foreign direct investment 해외직접투자
foreign environment 국제환경
foreign exchange 외국환
foreign exchange accounts 외국환계정
foreign exchange allocation system
　외화할당제
foreign exchange bank 외국환은행
foreign exchange bill 외국환어음
foreign exchange bills bought 매입외국환
foreign exchange broker 외국환브로커
foreign exchange budget 외화예산
foreign exchange centralization system
　외화집중제도
foreign exchange contract 외국환예약
foreign exchange control 외국환관리
foreign exchange conversion rate
　외국환환산율
foreign exchange conversion table
　외국환환산표**

foreign exchange fund bill 외국환자금증권
foreign exchange futures 외국환선물
foreign exchange gains and losses
　외국환차손익
foreign exchange law 외환법
foreign exchange market 외국환시장
foreign exchange market intervention
　외국환시장개입
foreign exchange market operation
　외국환시장조작
foreign exchange operation 외국환조작
foreign exchange position 외국환포지션
foreign exchange position sheet
　외국환 포지션 표
foreign exchange rate 외국환율
foreign exchange reserves 외화준비고
foreign exchange speculation 외국환투기
foreign geographic areas 해외지역별
foreign income tax 외국소득세
foreign insurer 외국보험자
foreign investment 해외투자
Foreign Investment Law 외자법
foreign investors 외국인투자가
foreign judgment 외국의 판결
foreign juridical person 외국법인
foreign jurisdiction 영토외관할권
foreign loan 외채
foreign means of payment 대외지불수단
foreign money bill 외화어음
foreign operations 해외사업
foreign reserves 외화준비
foreign securities company 외국증권회사
foreign service allowance 해외근무수당
foreign source income 해외원천소득
foreign stock holding ratio 외국인지주비율
foreign stocks unlisted 외국비상장주
foreign subsidiary corporation 외국자회사
foreign tax 외국세액
foreign tax credit 외국세액공제
foreign tax credit method 외국세액공제방식
foreign tax credit system 외국세액공제제도

foreign tax deductible as expenses
　손금산입외국세
foreign tax exemption method
　외국세액면제방식
foreign trade finance 무역금융
foreign trade multiplier 외국무역승수
foreign trade policy 무역정책
foreign trade statistics 무역통계
foreign transactions 외국거래
foreigner's investment 외국인투자
forejudge 권리를 박탈하다
foreman 감독자
forensic medicine 법의학
forerunner stock 선구주
forest fire insurance 삼림화재보험
forestall 통행방해
forestalling the market 시장방해
forestry income 산림소득
forestry income deduction 산림소득특별공제
forex club 포렉스 클럽
forfeit 위약금
forfeited share 실권주
forfeiture 몰수
forfeiture clause 실권약관
forfeiture of bail 보석금상실
forged bill 위조어음
forged cards 변조카드
forged check 위조수표
forged note 위조지폐
forged securities policy 유가증권위조보험
forged stock 위조주권
forgery 문서위조
forgery insurance 위조보험
forgery insuring clause 위조담보약관
forgiveness of debt 채무면제
forgiveness of repayment 상환면제
form 형식
form of action 소송방식
form of bid 입찰서
form required by law 법률에서 요구하는 형식
formal 형식적인

formal capitalization of reserves 자본구성
formal contract 정식계약
formal lawsuits 본소(本訴)
formal model 형식모델
formal plan annuity 공식연금
formalities of incorporation 설립절차
formation expenses 창업비
formation of concept 개념형성
former adjudication 전(前)판결
forms control 장표관리
forms of enterprise 기업형태
formula 공식
formula additions 정식편입액
formula fund 포뮬러펀드
formula investing 포뮬러투자
formula plan 포뮬러플랜
formula timing 포뮬러타이밍
forswear 강하게 부인하다
forthwith 신속하게
fortuitous event 우연한 사고
fortuity 우연성
forum 법원
forum origins 출생지법원
forward agreement 선도거래
forward bargain 선물환매매
forward calendar 포워드캘린더
forward commitment 대부예약
forward contract 선도계약
forward delivery 선도
forward deposit 선도예금
forward difference 전방차분
forward discount 선물디스카운트
forward discount of U.S. dollar 달러화약세
forward exchange 선물환
forward exchange contract 선물환예약
forward exchange rate 선물환상장
forward exchange transaction 선도환거래
forward integration 전방통합
forward interest rate 장래이자율
forward margin 선물마진
forward market 선물시장

forward operation 선물환거래
forward position 선물환포지션
forward premium 선물환프리미엄
forward price 선도가격
forward quotation 선물환상장
forward rate 선도금리
forward rate agreement 금리선도거래
forward rate spread 선물환스프레드
forward settlement 선도결제
forward swap 선스타트스와프
forward transaction 선도거래
forward vertical integration 전방수직통합
forward-backward integration 전후방통합
forward-forward rate 선-선레이트
forwarder 촉진자; 운송업자
forwarding charges 운송료
forwarding merchant 운송취급인
fossil fuel 화석연료
foul B/L 파울B/L
foul bill 고장어음
foundation 재단; 창설
foundation collateral 재단저당
founder 창립자
founder's profit 창업자이익
four nine 포나인
fourth market 기관투자가간 시장
fractal 프랙탈
fraction of a day 하루의 일부
fractional figure 단수
fractional interest 단수이자
fractional order 단주주문
fractional year 일년이 안 되는 해
fragmentation 세분화
fragmented industry 다수난전(亂戰)업계
frame editing 프레임에디팅
frame relay 프레임릴레이
frame translation 프레임수 변환
franchise 소손해면책율
franchise clause 면책율조항
franchise group insurance 개별계약단체보험
franchise selling 특약판매

E
F

franchise tax 특허세
franchised retail store 프랜차이즈가맹점
franco 반입인도
frank 무료배달우편
fraternal benefit society 공제조합
fraternal insurance 공제보험
fraud 부정수단
fraudulent act 부정행위
fraudulent bankruptcy 사기파산
fraudulent cards 부정카드
fraudulent conveyance 사기양도
fraudulent creditor 사기채권자
fraudulent gains 부정이득
fraudulent misrepresentation 사기표시
fraudulent transfer 사기양도
Freddie Mac 프레디맥
free alongside ship 선측(船側) 인도 선측인도
free article 면세품
free carrier 운송인인도
free dial 수신자요금부담통화; 프리다이얼
free economy 자유경제
free enterprise system 자유기업제도
free financial fund 프리파이낸셜펀드
free floating exchange rates system 자유변동
　　상장제
free flow system 프리플로시스템
free form deformation 자유형상변형법
free form modeling 자유형상모델링
free from all averages but to cover salvage
　　charges 전손 및 구조비담보
free from capture and seizure clause 포획나
　　포부담보조항
free from particular average 단독해손부담보;
　　분손부담보
free goods 면세품
free list 무세품표
free of damage absolutely
　　물적분손절대부담보
free of premium 보험료지불면제
free of taxation 무세
free offer 자유오퍼

free on board 본선인도
free paper 무료신문
free payment 임의인도
free payment system 자유반제시스템
free rate 자유요율
free reserves 자유준비
free riding 달러로 신주를 일부 유지함
free share 자유주
free surplus 자유잉여금
free trade zone 자유무역지대
free won account 자유원계정
free won deposit 자유원예금
free-price 자유가격
free-ride period 우대조치기간
free-standing store 독립점포
freedom from incumbrance 무부담
freedom of association 결사의 자유
freedom of expression 표현의 자유
freedom of movement 이전의 자유
freedom of speech 언론의 자유
freedom of the press 출판의 자유
freedom of the sea 해양의 자유
freehold 자유토지보유권
freight 화물
freight and cartage outward 발송운임
freight collect 착불
freight contingency 미필운송임
freight earnings 화물수입
freight insurance 운임보험
freight inward 구입운임
freight out 판매운임
freight prepaid 운임전불
freight pro-rata 할부운송임
freight rates 화물운임
freight receipts 운임수입
freight tariff 화물운임
freight to collect 운임후불
freight usance 운임유전스
freight-in 구입운임
freight-out 판매운임
frequency curve 도수곡선

frequency distribution 도수분포
frequency modulation 에프엠
frequency modulation oscillator 에프엠음원
frequency of risk 위험발생률
fresh pursuit 즉시속행
fresh water damage 담수에 젖음
frictional unemployment 마찰로 인한 실업
friendly society 우애조합
fringe banking 프린지뱅킹
fringe benefits 부가급부
fringe market 주변시장
frivolity 낭비함
frivolous answer 불성실한 답변
front end computer 전위컴퓨터
front end processor 전위프로세서
front loaded 예정, 예산 따위를 앞당겨 씀
front running 앞서감; 프런트러닝
front-end fee 프런트엔드피
front-foot rule 전회규칙
frontage 개구; 인접지
frontier tax 국경세
fronting 프런팅
fronting business 프런팅비즈니스
frozen account 동결계정
frozen assets 동결자산
frozen credit 회수불능
frozen stock 잔품; 팔다 남은 물건
fruit 수익
frustration 계약의 목적을 달성하지 못함
fuel account 연료계정
fuel and light prices 광열비
fuel expenses 연료비
fugitive from justice 도주범
fulfillment of a contract 계약이행
full age 성년
full capacity output 완전이용산출량
full cash refund annuity 완전즉시상환식 연금
full compensation 충분한 보상
full cost 전부원가
full cost principle 풀코스트원칙
full costing 전부원가계산

full coupon bond 풀쿠폰본드
full disclosure 완전개시
full employment 완전고용
full employment policy 완전고용정책
full hedge 풀헤지
full insurance 전액보험
full legal tender 완전법정통화
full payment 전액지불
full pension 완전연금
full preliminary term reserve
　　초년정기식 책임준비금
full proof 완전증명
full repayment before maturity 조기완제
full service middlemen
　　완전 서비스형 중간업자
full value insurance 전부보험
full year 평년도
full year business result 본결산
full-banking service 풀뱅킹서비스
full-bodied money 완전화폐
full-faith-and-credit debt 신의신용-채무
full-paid capital stock 전액지불필 주식
full-scale local production 현지일관생산
fully depreciated 감가상각필
fully diluted 희석필
fully insured status 완전수급자격
fully owned subsidiary 전액출자한 자회사
fully paid-up 전액불입
function 기능
function of group 집단기능
functional accounting 기능별 회계
functional analysis 기능분석
functional approach 기능적인 어프로치
functional currency method 기능통화법
functional depreciation 기능적인 감가
functional effect 기능적인 효과
functional organization 기능별 조직
functional pricing 기능적산법
functional responsibility 직무상의 책임
functional specialization 기능적인 전문화
functional statement 기능별 계산서

E
F

functionalized organization 직능별 조직
functions of marketing 마케팅기능
functus officio 임무완료
fund 기금; 자금; 펀드
fund absorption 자금흡수력
fund account 자금계정
fund accounting 자금회계
fund and trust 펀드앤드트러스트
fund balance sheet 자금대차대조표
fund cost 자금조달코스트
fund for operation of foreign exchange
　외국환운영자금
fund management 자금운영
fund management method 자금운용수단
fund manager 펀드매니저
fund obligation 자금부채
fund of funds 자금 중의 자금
fund position 자금포지션
fund raising business 자금조달업무
fund raising capacity 자금조달력
fund settlement 자금결제
fund shortage 자금부족
fund statement 자금운용표
fund surplus 자금잉여금
fund swap 자금관련스와프
fund transfer 자금이전
fund transfer service 자금대체서비스
fund's mission 연금기금의 역할
fundamental analysis 펀드멘털분석
fundamental directives of income tax
　소득세기본통달
fundamental disequilibrium 기초불균형
fundamental financial approach
　기초금융상품 어프로치
fundamental rights 기본권리
fundamental rules 기본규제
fundamental scientific research 기초연구
fundamental tax 기간세
fundamental theorem 기초정리
fundamentalist 경제기초조건 중시파
fundamentals 경제기초조건; 펀드멘털즈

fundamentals deterioration 펀드멘털즈악화
funded debt 1년 이상의 채권을 발행해서 확보
　한 차입금
funding 자금조달
funding agency 연금기금적립기관
funding cost 조달코스트
funding 자금부족
funding instrument 연금기금적립계약
funding method 적립방식
funding policy 차환정책
funds for purchase 매입자금
funds from operations 영업수입
fungibility 대체가능성
fungible 대용할 수 있는
fungible goods 대체가능성
fungible securities 대체가능증권
funnel 집중시키는
furnishings 비품
furniture and fixture 가구집기
furniture and household goods 가재도구
further advance 재대부(再貸付)
further consideration 심리속행
further directions 속행
further maintenance of the action 소송속행
fusion process 융합과정
future cash flows 자금의 장래흐름
future cost 미래원가
future service benefits 장래근무연금
future service credits 장래의 근속실적
future service pension 장래근무수당
future specific risk 장래의 고유리스크
future value 장래가치
futures 선물(先物)
futures commission merchant 선물중개업자
futures contract 선물계약
futures dealer 선물딜러
futures margin 선물마진
futures market 선물시장
futures option 선물옵션
futures option market 선물옵션시장
futures price 선물가격

futures product 선물상품
futures quotation 선물상장
futures rate 선물레이트

futures trading 선물거래
fuzzy theory 퍼지이론

gag order 함구령

gage 담보

gain 수익

gain from forfeiture 해약익(解約益)

gain opportunity 이득기회

gaining 강보합

gains 상승폭

gains from appreciation of securities 유가증
권평가익

gains from exchange of properties 교환차익

gains from forgiveness of debt 채무면제익

gains from revaluation off fixed assets 고정
자산평가익

gains from sale of fixed assets
고정자산매각익

gains from stock retirement 감자차익

gains from the transfer of property
자산양도익

gains of sales 매상증가

gains on bond retirement 사채상환차금

gains on insurance claim 보험차익

galley proof 교정쇄

galloping inflation 악성인플레이션

game plan 게·플랜

gamma correction 감마보정

gamma exposure 감마익스포저

Gantt chart 갠트차트

gap 차액

gap analysis 갭분석

gap management technology 갭법

garnishee 제3채무자

garnisher 채권차압인

garnishment 채권차압통지

gas and water expenses 가스수도세

gas tax 가스세

gasoline tax 휘발유세

gather steam 활황

gavel 지대; 조세; 연공(年貢)

gazette 관보

gearing 기어전동장치; 기어링

gearing effect 기어링효과

gearing ratio 기어링비율

general account 일반회계

general account expenditure 일반회계세출

General Accounting Office 회계검사원

general accounting principles 일반회계원칙

general administrative and selling expenses
일반관리비 및 판매비

general administrative expenses budget
일반관리비예산

general advertising 전국광고

general agency system 총대리점제도

general agent 총대리점

general agreement 일반협정

General Agreement on Tariffs and Trade
가트; 관세와 무역에 관한 일반협정

General Agreement to Borrow 일반차입결정

general and administrative expenses
일반관리비

general audit 일반감사

general audit standards 감사기준

general authority 포괄적인 권한

general average 공동해손
general average balance 공동해손정산고
general average bond 공동해손맹약서
general average contribution 공동해손분담액
general average expenditure 공동해손비용
general average sacrifice 공동해손희생손해
general balance sheet 일반대차대조표
general binded-debt fund 일반공채자금
general building scheme 일반주택지 분양계획
general business 일반사업
genera cargo 일반화물
general cash 일반현금
general closing 통상결산
general condition of contract 보통계약약관
general conditions and terms of the contract
일반조건서
general corporate assets 전반자산
general corporate bond 일반사업채
general corporate revenues and expenses
일반 손익
general credit 제너럴 크레딧
general crossed check 일반횡선수표
general election 총선거
general expenses 일반경비
general fixed-assets fund 일반고정자산자금
genera fund 일반자금
general government section 일반정부부문
general index 종합지수
general indirect cost 일반간접비
general insurance 손해전종목보험
general insurance clause 보통보험약관
general insurance law 보험법
general inventory 재산목록
general journal 보통분개장
general ledger 총계정원장
general ledger account 총계정원장계정
general letter of credit 매입은행무지정신용장
general liability insurance 일반배상책임보험
general management 총괄경영층
general market 일반시장
general means of payment 일반적인 지불수단

general meeting of shareholders
주주총회
general meeting of substitutional members
사원총대회
general merchandise 잡비
general mortgage 제너럴모기지
general mortgage bond 제너럴모기지사채
general obligation bond 일반재원채
general operating expenses 일반영업활동비
general overhead 일반간접비
general partner 무한책임사원
general partnership 무한책임파트너십
general place of tax payment
원칙적인 납세지
general price level 일반물가수준
general price-level accounting
일반물가수준회계
general profit and loss account 손익계정
general property tax 일반재산세
genera provisions 총칙
general provisions of budget 예산총칙
general reserve 별도물건
general risk 별도적립금
general security agreement 일반담보계약
general staff 제너럴스태프
general survey 전반검사
general tax 보통세
general tax reduction 일반감세
general taxation 종합과세
general terms and conditions of trade
일반무역조건
general words 일반문언
general-obligation bonds 일반공채
general-purpose financial statements
일반목적재무제표
generally accepted accounting principle
일반적으로 공정타당하다고 인정하는 회계
기준
generate favorable cash flows
바람직한 자금의 흐름을 산출하다
generating function 생성함수

generic market 제너릭 시장
generic strategy 포괄적인 전략
genetic algorithm 유전적인 알고리즘
genre 장르
Gensaki 겐사키 시장
geocentrism 세계지향
geographical price different
    지역적인 가격 차이
geographical pricing 지역별 가격제
geometric average 기하평균
geometric model 형상모델
German Bearer Certificate 독일무기명증서
getting ashore 싸게 매입한 주를 시세가 올랐
    을 때 매각함
ghosting 고스트
Gibson paradox 깁슨의 역설
gift 증여
gift advertisement 기프트광고
gift causa mortis 사인증여
gift during life 생전증여
gift enterprise 경품부 대매출
gift in kind 물품을 통한 증여
gift tax 증여세
gift tax credit 상속세공제
gift tickets account 상품권계정
giga byte 기가바이트
giga chip 가가칩
gilt-edged bond 길트에지채
gilt-edged securities 길트에지채; 금연증권
Ginnie Mae 지니메이
giving quotation 지불계정기준상장
glamor stock 매력주
global bearer certificate
    글로벌 무기명 예탁증서
global bond 글로벌본드
global chess 글로벌체스
global corporation 세계기업
global industry 지구규모산업
global market 세계적인 시장
global marketing 글로벌마케팅
global note facilities 글로벌노트퍼실리티

global portfolio 글로벌포트폴리오
global trading 글로벌트레이딩
globalization 세계화
GNMA debenture 미국정부주택저당
gnome 금언
gnomes of Zurich 취리히의 난쟁이;
    스위스 금융계의 실력자
GNP deflator GNP 디플레이터
go on selling 주가가 일정 수준 이하로 떨어질
    때까지 지속적으로 매각함
go to protest 부도가 나다
goal conflict 목표 갈등
goal congruence 목표일치
goal variable 목표변수
going concern 지속기업
going concern value 지속기업가치
going long 시세가 오를 것을 예상하고 증권을
    매입함
going private 기업의 비공개화
going public 주식공개화
going short 시세가 내릴 것을 예상하고 증권을
    매각함
going value 지속기업가치
sold and foreign exchange reserves
    외화준비고
gold and silver bimetallism 금은복본위제도
gold bond 금채권
gold bullion futures contract 금선물계약
gold bullion standard 금지금본위제
gold center 골드센터
gold clause 금약관
gold coin standard 금화본위제
gold exchange reserve 금환준비
gold exchange standard 금환본위제
gold fixing 금기준치결정
gold futures option 금선물옵션
gold holdings 금보유고
gold parity 금평가
gold points 금현송점(金現送點)
gold pool 금풀
gold purchase warrant 금구입와런트

gold rush 골드러시
gold standard 금본위제
gold sterilization policy 금불태화정책
gold tranche 골드트란시
golden cross 골든크로스
golden hand cuffs 골든핸드커프스
golden parachute 골든패러슈트
golden rule 황금률
golden section 황금분할
golfers' insurance 골퍼보험
good 유효한
good and collectible 확실히 회수할 수 있는
good and lawful men 유자격자
good behavior 선행
good consideration 선량약인
good debt 확실히 회수할 수 있는 자금
good delivery 적격인도
good faith 성실
good merchantable quality 판매적성품질
good money 사용가능자금
good news 호재
good offices of banking facilities
　금융기관의 알선
good result return 호성적 되돌림
good risk 우량물건
good this month order
　당월에 한해 유효한 주문
good value 자금화 자금
good yield 호이율
good-until-canceled orders
　취소할 때까지 유효한 주문
goods 재(財)
goods account 상품계정
goods and chattels 인적재산
goods and products 상품 또는 제품
goods carried over 보유품
goods earnings 화물수입
goods for sale 판매용 상품
goods in process 제작중인 물건
goods in process ledger 제작중인 물건원장
goods in transit 미착품

goods left 잔품
goods on approval 시송품
goods on consignment-in 수탁품
goods on hands 소유재고품
goods returned to vendor 반품
goods sold on credit 외상으로 판 상품
goods to arrive 미착품
goodwill 영업권
governing clause 준거법(準據法)조항
governing law 준거법(準據法)
government account 정부계정
government accounting 관청회계
government agency 정부계 기관
government agency bond 정부계 기관채권
government agency securities 정부기관증권
government bond 국채
government bond book-entry system
　국채대체결제제도
government bond for tax 감세국채
government bond for the purpose of public
　works 건설국채
government bond in foreign currency
　외화국채
government bonds and corporate debentures
　공사채
government bonds in domestic currency
　국내국채
government bookkeeping 관청부기
government broker 정부브로커
government compensation bond 교부공채
government credit 정부차관
government current surplus 정부경상여잉
government debt 공채
government enterprise 정부기업
government expenditure 정부지출
government financial agency 정부금융기관
government financial corporation 공고
government fund transactions 국고수지
government fund transactions with the public
　국고 대 민간수지
government guaranteed bond 정부보증채

G
H

Government National Mortgage Association
정부저당금고
Government National Mortgage Association
debenture 지니메이채
government note 정부지폐
government obligation 정부보증채
government ordinance 정령(政令)
government purchases 정부구입
government related deposit 정부관계예금
government saving 정부저축
government securities 정부증권
government subsidy for capital expenditure
건설조성금
government to government trade 정부간 무역
government trade 정부무역
government transaction 정부거래
government transfers 정부이전수지
governor 총재
grab 불법으로 손에 넣다
grace of payment 지불유예
grace period 거치기간
gradation 단계적인 변화
grade 등급
grade description system 분류법
graded commission 등급별 수수료
graded expense 단계적인 경비
graded tariff 차등세율
grading function 등급기능
grading transaction 등급거래
gradual devaluation 서서히 절하
graduated payment mortgage
고정금리기준모기지
graduated tax 누진세
graduated taxation 누진과세
graduation clause 졸업조항
grain market 곡물시장
grand bill of sale 선박양도증서
grand distress 전부차압
grand jury 대배심
grand strategy 종합전략
grand total 총계

grandfather clause 상부조항
grandfather provision 기득권조항
grant 허가, 인가
grant element 그랜트엘리먼트
grant in aid 조성금
granting credit 신용공여
grantor 양여자
graphic accelerator 그래픽액셀러레이터
graphical user interface (GUI)
그래픽을 통한 사용자 중심의 인터페이스
gratis appearance 임의출두
gratis dictum 임의진술
gratuitous bailment 무상기탁
gratuitous contract 무상계약
gratuitous use of property
재산을 무상으로 사용함
gravure printing 그라비아 인쇄
gray market 발행전 유통시장
great depression 대공황
greater fool theory 그레이터풀이론
green buck 미달러지폐
green card 소액저축 등 이용자카드
green card system 그린카드제도
green field 그린필드
green goods 위조지폐
green mail 그린메일
green marketing 그린마케팅
green shoe clause 그린슈조항
Gresham's law 그레샴의 법칙
grid 그리드
grievance committee 고충처리위원회
grievance machinery 고충처리기관
gripsack general agent 출장총대리점
gross amount 총액
gross amount principle 총액주의
gross assets 총자산
gross base 총액베이스
gross billing 광고회사의 총매상
gross book value 총장부가격
gross capital 총자본
gross cost 총원가

gross cost of merchandise sold 총매상원가
gross demand 총수요
gross domestic capital formation
　국내총자본 형성
gross domestic product 국내총생산
gross earnings 총수익
gross error 과실
gross expenditure 총지출
gross fund position 그로스펀드포지션
gross gain 총수익
gross income 총소득
gross income of corporation 법인이익금
gross investment 총투자
gross loss 총과실
gross loss on sales 매상총손실
gross margin 매상총이익
gross margin ratio 조이율
gross merchandise margin 총상품매매차익
gross national expenditure 국민총지출
gross national product 국민총생산
gross national wealth 국민총자산
gross negligence 중과실
gross operating spread 총영업이익폭
gross profit 총이익
gross profit analysis 총이익분석
gross profit margin rate 조이익률
gross profit method 총이익
gross profit on sales 매상총이익
gross profit percentage 총이익률
gross profit ratio 총익률
gross profit test 총이익테스트
gross profits 총익금
gross purchase 구입총액
gross rating point 그로스레이팅포인트; GRP
gross revenue 총수익
gross sales 총매상고
gross sound value 총정품가액
gross spread 인수모집수수료
gross trading volume 그로스거래고
gross transaction 총거래
gross up method 그로스업 방식

gross-profit ratio 매상총익률
ground coverage 지상위험담보
ground of action 소송원인
ground price 공장원가
ground-making expenses 토지조성비
groundage 정박료
grounded 기초를 둔; 근거있는
grounding clause 근거있는 조항
grounds for disbarment 변호사자격박탈이유
group accident insurance 단체상해보험
group annuity 단체연금
group annuity insurance 단체연금보험
group annuity insurance contract
　단체연금보험계약
group auction 격탁매매
group behavior 집단행동
group buying 공동구입
group conformity 집단적합
group cost system 등급별 원가계산
group credit insurance 단체신용보험
group credit life insurance
　단체신용생명 보험
group deferred annuity contract
　단체거치연금계약
group deposit administration contract
　단체예탁관리계약
group depreciation 조별상각
group dynamics 집단역학
group endowment insurance 단체양로보험
group financial statement 기업집단재무제표
group health insurance 단체건강보험
group insurance 단체보험
group interview 집단면접
group life insurance 단체생명보험
group marketing 균일가격설정
group medical expense insurance
　단체의료비보험
group method 조별법
group mortgage insurance
　단체모기지보상생명보험
group norm 집단규범

group pension 단체연금
group permanent insurance 단체종신보험
group permanent insurance contract
　단체장기보험계약
group pressure 집단압력
group representative 보험담당자
group retention 단체보유액
group special mobile communication
　이동체 통신
group term insurance 단체정기보험
group variable annuity 단체변액연금
groupe speciale mobile
　범유럽디지털전화 방식
groupware 그룹웨어
growing at a moderate speed
　적절하게 성장하는
growing currency 성장통화
growth of industrial structure 산업구조고도화
growth potential 성장성
growth rate 성장률
growth stock 성장주
growth strategy 성장전략
growth vector matrix 성장벡터매트릭스
guarantee 보증
guarantee by endorsement 이서보증
guarantee capital 보증자본
guarantee charge 보증료
guarantee deposits 보증금
guarantee in favor of the primary guarantor
　이보증(裏保證)
guarantee insurance 보증보험
guarantee loan 보증론
guarantee money 보증금
guarantee of repayment 차입반제보증
guaranteed bond 보증사채
guaranteed continuous policy 지속보증계약

guaranteed cost contract 비용보증계약
guaranteed deferred annuity 보증거치연금
guaranteed dividend 확정배당
guaranteed freight 보증운임
guaranteed immediate annuity 보증즉시연금
guaranteed income contract 보증부투자계약
guaranteed insurability rider
　무진단증액권특약
guaranteed insurance trust 보증보험신탁
guaranteed interest contract 이율보증계약
guaranteed investment contract
　보증투자계약
guaranteed minimum life annuity
　최저보증부 종신연금
guaranteed securities 보증증권
guaranteed spread 보증스프레드
guaranteed stock 보증주
guarantor 보증인
guarantor bank 보증은행
guarantor's right of indemnity 구상권
guaranty 보증계약
guaranty insurance 손해담보계약
guaranty money 보증금
guaranty money deposited 차입보증금
guaranty of liabilities 채무보증
guardian ad litem 후견인
guardianship 후견
guessed mean 가평균
guessing 억측
guidance 지침
guideline 가이드라인
guild 동업조합
guilty 유죄
Gulf Cooperation Council
　페르시아만협력회의
gun jumping 정보공개전의 증권거래

habeas corpus 출정영장
habit 관행
habit persistence hypothesis 관습가설
haggling price 할인가격
Hague Protocol 헤이그의정서
hair cut 헤어컷
halation 헐레이션
half tax 1/2 후생보험
half tone 망판(網版)
half-finished goods 반제품
half-yearly 반년마다(의)
hammering the market 해머링 마켓;
　값을 몹시 깎는 시장
hand-to-mouth buying
　꼭 필요한 만큼만 구입함
handle 접수총액
handling expenses 취급비
happening subsequent to balance sheet date
　대차대조표일후의 발생사항
harakiri swap 하리키리스와프
harbor 감추다
harbor dues 입항세
hard currency 교환가능통화
hard disk 하드디스크
hard labor 중노동
hard landing 하드랜딩
harden 굳히다; 경화하다
harmless error 무해한 오진
harmless warrant 할리스 워런트채
harvesting strategy 수확전략
haulage 운반비
hazard 위험

head 주석
head and shoulder 헤드 앤드 숄더
head book 주요장부
head hunter 인재스카우트담당자
head money 인두세
head mount display 헤드 마운트 디스플레이
head office 본점
head office account 본사계정
head tax 인두세
heading 항목
health care obligation 의료급부채무
health examination 건강진단
health insurance 건강보험
health insurance premium 건강보험료
healthy revenue growth 순조로운 매상신장
healthy trend 고수준
hearsay evidence 소문증거
heating 가열하는; 가열
heavy 연조(軟調)
heavy additional charge imposed 중가산금
heavy additional tax 중가산세
heavy electrical stocks 중전(重電)스톡
heavy market 둔조(鈍調)시장
heavy penalty tax 중가산세
heavy taxation 중세
heavy users 헤비유저
hedge 헤지
hedge account representation letter
　헤지계산대행서
hedge clause 면책조항
hedge fund 헤지펀드
hedge operation 헤지조작

hedge ratio 헤지비율
hedge selling 시세하락을 예상하고 매각함
hedge trading 헤지거래
hedge transaction 헤지거래
hedged bond 헤지채
hedger 헤저
hedging 헤징; 연계매매
hedging against inflation 인플레이션헤징
hedging cost 헤지코스트
hedging function 헤지기능
hedging on commodity futures
　　상품선물거래헤징
hedging on option 옵션헤징
hedging scheme 헤지스킴
hegemony 주도권; 헤게모니
heir 상속인
heir apparent 법정상속인
heir collateral 방계상속인
heir general 통상상속인
heir of the body 직계상속인
heir presumptive 추정상속인
heir-looms 법정상속동산
held to maturity 상환기간까지 보유함
hell or high water clause
　　헬오어하이워터조항
hello effect 헬로 효과
help 보조
hereditaments 재산부동산
heritage 상속부동산
heterogeneous competition 이질적인 경쟁
heterogeneous demand 이질수요
heterogeneous market 이질시장
heterogeneous oligopoly 이질적인 과점
hidden assets stock 비밀적립자산주
hidden line elimination 은선(隱線)처리
hidden profit distributions 감춘 이익을 처분함
hidden reserve 은닉한 적립금
hierarchical theory 계층이론
high 고가
high assay model 하이에세이모델
high context 고맥락

high cost 원가고
high definition television 고화질텔레비전;
　　HDTV
high degree of positive correlation
　　고도로 긍정적인 상관관계
high density 고밀도
high grade investment 유리한 투자
high income brackets 고액납세자
high income trust security 고액신탁증권
high interest rate 고금리
high interest rate policy 고금리정책
high justice 재판할 수 있는 권한
high level of business activity 고수준의 경기
high mortality 높은 사망률
high possibility 높은 공산
high powered money 하이파워드머니
high price 고가
high rise 급등
high seas 공해(公海)
high taxpayers 고액납세자
high yield bond 고이율채
high-coupon bond 하이쿠폰
high-interest-bearing debenture 고리부 사채
high-leveraged 효과가 높은
high-low method 고저법
high-priced stock 고가주
high-risk high-return 하이리스크하이리턴
high-tech stock 하이테크주식
higher in quotation 고가
higher interest rates application system
　　고율적용제도
higher order goods 고차재(高次財)
higher quotation 고가
higher quotation at the close 마감장의 고가
highly traded stock 집중적으로 거래되는 주
highway 공수로
highway by prescription 시료로 인한 공도
highway by user 영년사용으로 인한 공도
hire purchase 분할불구입
hire purchase agreement
　　매입선택권부 물품사용계약

histogram method 히스토그램법
historical cost 취득원가
historical cost basis 취득원가기준
historical cost/constant dollar accounting
　취득원가주의 안정가치회계
historical cost/nominal dollar accounting
　취득원가주의 명목가치회계
historical earnings 과거의 실적
historical trading range 과거의 수치폭
historical volatility 누적변동성
historical yield 누적이율
historical-cost financial statements
　취득원가주의 재무제표
history-dependent derivative
　경로의존형 파생상품
hit 확정된 손실
hit the bottom 최저수준까지 하락하다
hitting the ceiling 최고시세에 달하다
hive off 하청으로 돌리
hoarding 매점
hold 보유하다
hold harmless agreement 면책특약
hold off buying 매입을 미루다
hold point 홀드포인트
holder 소지인
holder for value 유상소지인
holder in bad faith 악의의 제삼자
holder in due course 선의의 제삼자
holder in good faith 선의의 소지인
holder of record 주주명부 상의 주주
holding company 지주회사
holding gain or loss 보유손익
holding high 고보합
holding of assets 자산보유
holding period return 보유기간수익률
holding period value-relative
　보유기간상대가치
holding ratio for a company's stock
　주식보유율
holding the market 매입을 촉진하여 급격한
　시세 변동을 막다

holdings 지분
hole sort card 홀소트 카드
holism 전체론
hologram 홀로그램
holograph 자필증서
holography 홀로그래피
home banking 홈뱅킹
home country control
　원적국주의; 본점감독주의
home currency 자국통화
home currency bill bought 자국환매입외국환
home equity loan 홈에퀴티론
home improvement loan 증개축론
home made inflation 홈메이드인플레
home mortgage 주택모기지
home port 선적항
home production 국내생산
home rule 자치
home service 내지근무
home service agent 지구외무원
home service life insurance 간이생명보험
home state 출신주
homestead 농장이 딸린 농가
homogeneity 동질성
homogeneous competition 동질적인 경쟁
homogeneous market 동질시장
homogeneous security group 동류증권그룹
homologation 확인
honor 인수
honor policy 명예보험증권
honorable agreement 명예계약
honorarium 사례금
hook damage 갈고리손
hooked 갈고리모양의
horizon analysis 투자계획기간분석
horizon return 소유기간이율
horizontal 수평적
horizontal acquisition 수평적인 매입
horizontal analysis 수평분석
horizontal angle of view 수평화각
horizontal audit 수평적인 감사

horizontal buy 수평구입
horizontal competition 수평적인 경쟁
horizontal concurrence 수평적인 협력
horizontal integration 수평형 통합
horizontal international specialization
  수평적인 국제 분업
horizontal market 수평시장
horizontal merger 수평합병
horizontal organization 횡단조직
horizontal specialization 수평분업
horizontal split 수평분단
horizontal spread 수평스프레드
horizontal trade 수평무역
hospital expense insurance 입원비 보험
hostage 인질
hostile possession 자주점유
hot 막 훔쳐낸
hot issue 인기증권
hot money 국제단기부동자금; 핫마니
hot money market 핫머니시장
hot pursuit 긴급추적
hours worked 가동시간
hours-of-service method 사용시간비례법
house agency 하우스에이전시
house bill 하우스빌
house breaking 주거침입죄
house duty 건물세
house farmer 건물전대인
house margin rule 증거금내부규제
house media 자가매체
house organ 사내보
house rent received 수취가임(受取家賃)
house-rent income 임대료
house-rent law 임대법
household 가계
household consumption expenditure
  가계소비지출
household expenses 가계비
household goods 가재도구
household sector 가계부문
household taxation 세대과세

householders' comprehensive insurance
  주택종합보험
housekeeping expenses 가계비
housing allowance 주거수당
housing credit 주택신용
housing expenses 주거비
housing loan 주택금융
housing loan corporation 주택금융회사
housing permits 주택착공허가건수
housing renewal program
  하우징리뉴얼프로그램
housing savings tax credit 주택저축공제
housing starts 주택건축착공수
hub 허브
hull insurance 선박보험
human assessment 휴먼어세스먼트
human engineering 인간공학
human interface 휴먼인터페이스
human life value 인간의 생명가치
human relations 인간관계
human resources accounting 인적자원회계
human resources development 인재개발
humped 혹이 있는
humped curve 험프드커브
hung up 정서가 불안정한; 걱정하는
hunters' insurance 헌터보험
hurdle rate 최저목표수익률
hush-money 입막음돈, 무마비
hybrid 혼합
hybrid cap 혼합캡
hybrid model 혼합형
hybrid securities 복합증권
hybrid stocks 혼합주식
hybrid trust 혼합신탁
hygiene factor 위생요인
hyper inflation 초인플레이션
hyphenation 하이프네이션
hypothecate 저당권을 설정하다
hypothecated assets 담보자산
hypothecation agreement 담보차입동의서

I-S curve · L-M curve IS곡선 · LM곡선
icon 아이콘
ID code 아이디코드
idea advertising 의견광고
ideal standard cost 이상표준원가
identifiable assets 인식할 수 있는
identification 식별
identification card 신분증명서
identified cost method 개별법
identity 동일성
identity matrix 단위행렬
idle assets 유휴자산
idle balance 이상적인 밸런스
idle capacity cost 저조업도원가
idle cash 여잉현금
idle cost 부동비
idle equipment 유휴설비
idle facilities 유휴시설
idle money 행방이 정해지지 않은
idle plant 유휴설비
idle properties 유휴자산
idle time 한가한 시간
ignorance 알지 못함
ignore 각하하다
illegal 불법의
illegal 위법행위
illegality 불법
illiquid 비유동적
image advertising 이미지광고
image board 이미지보드
image formation 이미지형식

image maker 이미지메이커
image profile 이미지프로필
image research 이미지조사
image setter 이미지셋터
image strategy 이미지전략
imaginary demand 가수요
imbalance 불균형
imbalance of orders 주문의 불균형
imbedded 끼워 넣어진
IMF loan IMF 차관
IMF par value IMF 평가
imitation 유사물제작
imitative price 추수(追隨)가격
immaterial 무형자본
immaterial evidence 중요하지 않은 증거
immaterial issue 중요하지 않은 쟁점
immaterial property 무형재산
immediacy 즉시유동성
immediate annuity 즉시개시연금
immediate cause 직근원인
immediate descent 직접상속
immediate liquidity 당면의 유동성
immediate order 지급주문
immediate participation guarantee contract
      직접참가방식단체연금계약
immediately available fund
      즉시 이용가능한 자금
immovable property 부동산
immovables account 부동산계정
immunity 면제
immunity of witness 증언의무면제특권

immunization 면역화
immunization fund 이뮤니제이션펀드
impact claims 파급효과클레임
impact loan 임팩트론
impact printer 임팩트프린터
impairment of contract 계약상의 권리침해
impartial taxation 공평한 과세
impeachment 탄핵
impeachment of witness 증인탄핵
imperfect competition 불완전경쟁
imperfect competition market
　불완전경쟁시장
imperfect obligation 불안전의무
imperfect trust 불완전신탁
impersonal deduction 물적공제
impersonal exclusion from taxation
　물적과세제외
impersonal security 대물담보
impersonal tax 물세
impertinent 무관계한
impignoration 저당잡힘
impignorative contract 저당계약
implead 소추하다
implication 추단(推斷)
implicit call price 내재적인 콜가격
implicit cost 명시하지 않은 비용
implicit deflator 암묵적인 디플레이터
implicit interest 내포금리
implied 암묵적인
implied condition 묵시조건
implied contract 준계약
implied forward rates 임플라이드선도금리
implied license 묵시허용
implied need 암묵적인 니드
implied repo rate 이론상의 환매수익률
implied trust 묵시신탁
implied undertaking 묵시적인 약속
implied volatility 내재변동성
implied warranty 묵시담보
import bill 수입어음
import control 수입무역관리

import duties tariff 수입세표
import duty 수입세
import finance 수입금융
import financing system 수입자금대부제도
import for manufacturing 이입(移入)
import function 수입함수
import license 수입승인증
import on consignment 위탁판매수입
import permit 수입허가
import price index 수입물가지수
import quota 수입할당
import restriction 수입규제
import settlement bill system
　수입결제어음제도
import substitute 수입대체
import surcharge 수입과징금
import tax 수입세
import usance 수입유전스
important factor 중요한 요소
importation of foreign capital 외자수입
imported inflation 수입인플레
imposition 과세
imposition of income tax 소득세과세
impossibility of performance 이행불능
impossible contract 불능한 계약
impost 수입세
impound 몰수된
impressment 징발
imprest 전불금
imprest cash 전도자금
imprest cash fund 소액전불준비금
imprest fund 정액전도자금
imprest money 징발보상금
imprest system 정액전도제
imprimatur 간행허가
imprisonment 구금
iniproveiiient 개량
improvement expense 개량비
improvement of the property 자산을 개량함
improvement patent 개량특허
improvidence 재산관리상의 태만

impulse buying 충동구매
impulse goods 충동구매
impunity 충동구매상품
imputation 면제
imputation method 임퓨테이션방식
impute 귀속시키는
imputed cost 귀속원가; 부가원가
imputed income 귀속소득
imputed interest 귀속이자
imputed negligence 귀책과실
imputed price 귀속가격
imputed value 귀속가치
in concert 공동으로
in extenso 완전히
in fee 단손부동산권으로
in good faith 성실히
in good standing 우량인
in gross 인적
in kind 동종의
in lieu 대신
in line with 운동하여
in number 숫자상으로
in pais 법적절차를 밟지 않고
in person 스스로
in real terms 실질베이스로
in rem 대물적
in return 그 자체
in se 그 자체
in session 개정중
ill specie 정화의; 특정의
in terms of revenue 수익면에서
in the near term 목전
in uptrend 상승경향에 있는
in-and-out trading 단기로 매매하는
in-and-put dealer 인앤드풋딜러
in-basket method 인바스켓방법
in-charge accountant 주임회계사
in-cycle work 기계운전시작업
in-house exchange 행 내 교환
in-house product 자사제품
in-house training 기업 내 교육

in-port duty 항만세
in-process inspection 공정 내 관리
in-sourcing 인소싱
inactive 한산한; 활발하지 않은
inactive account 미활동계정
inactive bond 비인기채권
inactive market 한산시장
inadequate capital 과소자본
inadmissible 허용할 수 없는
inadmitted assets 승인되지 않은 자산
inalienable rights 양도할 수 없는 권리
inaugural meeting 창립총회
incentive 장려
incentive effect 장려효과
incentive fee 성공보수
incentive stock option 자사주저가격구입권
incentive wage system 능률급
incidence of taxation 조세부담
incidental 부수적인
incidental appeal 부대소송
incidental condition 부대조건
incidental expenses 부대비용
incidental gains 부수적인 수입
incidental increase payment 일부증액반제
incidental suit 부대소송
including tax 세포함
inclusion in expenses 손금산입
inclusion in gross revenue 익금산입
income 이익
income account 손익계정
income accrued from domestic sources
　　국내원천소득
income accrued from foreign sources
　　외국원천소득
income after tax audit 조사후 소득
income and expenditure liquidation
　　수지방정식
income and expenses 손익
income approach 소득접근법
income at liquidation 청산소득
income before employee bonus 상여전 소득

income before income taxes 세금공제전 이익
income bond 배당사채
income bracket 소득층
income by coupon re-investment
　쿠폰재투자수입
income deposit 소득예금
income derived from business
　사업에서 생기는 소득
income distribution 소득분포
income earned 가동이익
income effect 소득효과
income effect of exchange adjustments
　환조정의 소득효과
income elasticity 소득탄력성
income endowment 연금부 보험
income enhancer 인컴인헨서
income from appreciation of assets
　재산평가익
income from assets 자산소득
income from continuing operations
　지속사업부문의 이익
income from discharge of indebtedness
　채무면제익
income from discontinued operations
　폐지부문의 이익
income from real estate 부동산수입
income from transfer of securities
　유가증권양도소득
income from trust deposits 금전신탁이익
income fund 인컴펀드
income gain 인컴게인; 배당소득
income in advance 전수(前受)수익
income indemnity insurance 소득보상보험
income inflation 소득인플레이션
income leveling 이익평준화
income leveling off 소득평준화
income policy 소득정책
income realization 이익실현
income received but unearned 이연수익
income redistribution effect 소득재분배효과
income return 소득신고

income return blank 소득신고용지
income share 채산주
income share note 이익분배채
income statement 손익계산서
income statement account 손익계산서 계정
income statement approach
　손익계산서 어프로치
income statement audit 손익계산서 감사
income statement principles 손익계산서 원칙
income statement ratio 손익계산서 비율
income stock 자산주
income summary 손익
income tax 소득세
income tax allocations 소득과세배분
income tax credit 소득세공제
income tax law 소득세법
income tax prepayment system 예정납세제도
income tax rapid calculation table
　소득세 속산표
income tax rate 소득세율
income tax return 소득세신고
income tax return form 소득세신고서
income tax self-assessed 신고납세액
income tax withheld at source
　원천공제소득세
income taxes payable 미불법인세
income terms of trade 소득교역조건
income-consumption curve 소득소비곡선
income-generating effect 소득창출효과
incompetency 금치산(禁治産)
incomplete transaction 미완료거래
inconvertible bank note 불환은행권
inconvertible paper money 불환지폐
incorporated company 회사
incorporated school 학교법인
incorporation 법인설립
incorporation procedures 회사설립수속
incorporator 발기인
incorporeal chattel 무휴동산
incorporeal property 무체재산
incoterms 인코텀스

increase and decrease method 증감법
increase in capital at the market price
  주식을 시가 발행함
increase in capital stock 증자
increase in cost of working insurance
  임시비용보험
increase of revenue 수입증가
increase of sales 매상증가
increased income tax 증가소득세
increased tax 증세
increased value insurance 증식보험
increasing annuity 체증연금
increasing domestic demand 내수확대
increasing term life insurance 체증정기보험
increasing whole life insurance 체증종신보험
increasing working capital 증가운전자본
increment card 인크리먼트 카드
incremental analysis 증분분석
incremental cost 증분원가
incremental rate of return 증분수익률
incremental return 증가수익
incumbrance 토지에 대한 부담
indebtedness 채무
indebtedness of affiliates 관계회사채권
indefeasible 무효라 할 수 없는
indemnification 변상
indemnify 보상의 약속을 하다
indemnities 배상금
indemnity 면책
indemnity agreement 보증위탁계약
indemnity allowance 보상금
indemnity reinsurance 보상재보험
indent 매부위탁서 주문서; 매입위탁서
indenture 계약서
indenture trustee 인덴처 수탁인
independence of auditor 감사원의 독립성
independent accountant 독립회계사
independent agency 독립기관
independent audit 독립계약
independent contract 청부인
independent contractor 독립중개자

independent intermediary
  독립책임액 비례주의
independent liability method 독립판매조직
independent marketing organization
  독립판매조직
independent tax 독립세
independent variable 독립변수
index 지수
index arbitrager 지수재정거래자
index bond 인덱스채권
index clause 지수약관
index clause insurance 지수보험
index fund 인덱스펀드
index holding 지수보유
index linked bond 인덱스채
index new value insurance 지수신가보험
index number by aggregative method
  총화법지수
index number of production 생산지수
index number technique 지수법
index of financial condition 재정력지수
index of net terms of trade 순교역조건지수
index of productivity 생산성지수
index of retail price 소매물가지수
index of trade 무역지수
index option 인덱스옵션
index participation 인덱스파티시페이션
index risk 지수리스크
index-number trend series 경향지수
indexation 지수화
indexes of producers' shipments
  생산자 출하지수
indicated market 참고상장시장
indication 시세수치; 표시
indication method 인디케이션방식
indicative price 시세수치
indicator 지표
indices of urban land prices
  전국시가지 가격지수
indictment 기소
indifference curve 무차별 곡선

indirect deposit 간접예금
indirect evidence 간접증거
indirect exchange arbitrage 간접재정
indirect expenses 간접비
indirect financing 간접금융
indirect foreign tax credit 간접외국세액공제
indirect guarantee 간접보증
indirect incidental expenses 간접부수비용
indirect investment 간접투자
indirect inward investment 대내간접투자
indirect issue 간접발행
indirect labor cost 간접노무비
indirect liability 간접부채
indirect material cost 간접재료비
indirect method 간접법
indirect method of depreciation 간접상각
indirect presentation 간접표시
indirect production 간접생산
indirect sales 간접매매
indirect securities 간접증권
indirect tax 간접세
indirect trade 간접무역
indirect wage 간접임금
indirect yield 간접이익
individual annuity 개인연금
individual bond 개별보증증권
individual dealing system 개별매매방식
individual depreciation 개별상각
individual exclusion 개인공제
individual Fidelity bond 개별신원보증증권
individual firm 개별기업
individual health insurance 개인건강보험
individual income tax 개인소득세
individual inhabitant tax 개인주민세
individual insurance 개별보험
individual investor 일반투자가
individual policy pension trust
　개별보험연금계획
individual production 개별생산
individual proprietor 자영업자
individual retirement account 개인퇴직계정

individual separate account
　단일고객 분리계정
individual stockholder 개인주주
individual taxation 개별과세
individual underwriter 개인보험업자
individual useful life 개별내용연수
individual variable annuity 개인변액연금
indivisible credit 불가분채권
indorsed note 이서어음
indorsement 이서
indoser 이서인
induced investment 유발투자
inducement 유인
inducement to invest 투자유인
induciae 적하처분기간
inductive statistical model
　귀납적인 통계 모델
inductive statistics 귀납적인 통계
indulgence 지불유예
industrial accounting 공업회계
industrial advertisement 산업광고
industrial bank 노동자나 소매상의 저축,
　융자를 담당하는 금융기관
industrial bond 사업채
industrial bookkeeping 공업부기
industrial cap 산업자본
industrial classification 산업분류
industrial complex 콤비나트
industrial composition 산업구조
industrial cooperation method 산업협력방식
industrial corporation 사업법인
industrial debenture 사업채
industrial design 공업디자인
industrial development bond 상업개발채권
industrial dispute 노동쟁의
industrial distribution 산업재유통
industrial dynamics 인더스트리얼 다이내믹스
industrial engineering 생산공학
industrial espionage 산업스파이
industrial estate 공업단지
industrial factory foundation 공장재단

industrial foundation 공업재단
industrial fund 산업자금
industrial insurance 간이보험
industrial law 노동법
industrial life insurance 간이생명보험
industrial loan 사업대부
industrial new design 실용신안
industrial organization 산업조직
industrial origin of net national product
　산업별 국민순생산
industrial pension 기업연금
industrial policy 산업정책
industrial production 공업생산
industrial production index 광공업생산지수
industrial proprietorship 공업소유권
industrial publication 산업출판물
industrial rationalization 산업합리화
industrial revenue bond 특정재원채
industrial right 공업소유권
industrial risk 공장물건
industrial stock 공업주
industrial structure 산업구조
industrial structure policy 산업구조정책
industrial-accident reserve 산업사고준비금
industrialized countries 공업국
industry 사업
industry association 업계단체
industry average 업계평균
industry beta value 산업의 베타수치
industry concentration 산업집중
industry effect 산업효과
industry information 산업정보
industry protection 산업보호
industry segments 업계
industry specialist 업계스페셜리스트
industry standard 업계기준
industry weighting ratio 업종별 편입률
ineligible 적합하지 않은
ineligible bill 비적격채
inescapable cost 회피불능비
inevitable accident 불가피한 사고

infamous crime 파렴치죄
infamous punishment 불명예로운 형벌
infamy 명예박탈
infant 미성년자
inference 추리
inference engine 추론엔진
inferior character 하부문자
infirmative 경감하는
inflation 인플레이션
inflation accounting 인플레회계
inflation caused by won depreciation
　원저인플레
inflation differential 인플레격차
inflation gap 인플레갭
inflation led by import 수입인플레
inflation-sensitivity factor 인플레감응도
inflationary demand curve 인플레수요곡선
inflationary expectation 인플레기대
inflationary money supply 인플레머니
inflationary supply curve 인플레공급곡선
inflow of foreign capital 외자유입
influence the market trend
　시장동향을 좌우하다
influx 유입
influx of foreign capital 외자유입
informal group 비공식집단
informal investigation 약식조사
informal organization 비공식조직
informal plan annuity 비공식연금
informal proceeding 간이수속
informal sector 비공식부문
information disclosure 정보공개
information home electronics 정보가전
information input 정보입력
information network system
　고도정보통신시스템
information output 정보출력
information processing facility 정보처리설비
information provider 정보제공자
information ratio 정보지수
information revolution 정보혁명

J

information society 정보화사회
information sources on beta value
　베타수치에 기반을 둔 정보원
information system 정보시스템
information system business 정보시스템사업
information utility 정보효용
information value 정보가치
information vendors 정보벤더
information-motivated trader
　정보동기로 인한 거래자
information-motivated transaction
　정보동기에 따른 매매
informed consent 설명에 기반을 둔 승낙
informercial 인포머셜
infostructure 인포스트럭처
infringement 권리침해
infringement of copyright 판권침해
infringement of ownership 소유권침해
infringement of patent 특허권침해
infringement of trade-mark 상표권침해
ingredient labeling 성분표시
ingress 진입
inhabitant tax 주민세
inherent defect 고유하자
inherent hazard 고유위험
inherit 법정상속하다
inheritance 상속
inheritance of bequest 유산상속
inheritance tax 상속세
inheritance tax on undivided bequest
　미분할 유산에 대한 상속세
inheritance tax paid in kind 상속세물납
inherited property 상속재산
inheritor 상속인
initial 기초
initial balance 기초잔고
initial capital 기초자본
initial cost 원가
initial cost of business 개업비
initial date in reckoning 기산일
initial delivery 최초인도

initial depreciation 초기상각
initial down payment 내입금
initial establishment 초기설정
initial expenses 창업비
initial goods in process 기초제작 중인 물건
initial installment 내입금
initial inventories 기초재고자산
initial listing requirement 상장기준
initial margin 기본증거금
initial margin requirement 초기증거금율
initial measurements 초기측정
initial par value 일차평가
initial payment 내입금
initial public offering 신규주식공모
initial reserve 초회준비금
initial special depreciation 초연도특별상각
initial work in process account 기초제작품계정
initiation fee 입회금
injunction 보전처분
ink jet printer 잉크젯프린터
inland bill 국내어음
inland bill of exchange 내국환어음
Inland Revenue 영국국내세입청
innocent misrepresentation 선의의 부실표시
innocent purchaser 선의의 매주
innovation 혁신; 갱정
innovative competition 혁신적인 경쟁
innovative efficiency 혁신적인 효율
innovator group 이노베이터집단
input coefficient 투입계수
input variable 투입변수
input-output analysis 투입산출분석
input-output table 투입산출표
inquiry agency 신용조사기관
inquiry for the balances 잔고조회
inquisition 심문
inquisitor 검증관
inscribed bond 기명채권
inscribed stock certificate 기명주권
insecurity clause 저당약관
insert 끼워 넣다

insert editing 인서트 편집
inside build-up 책임준비금증가액
inside information 내부정보
inside the room 장내
insider 인사이더
insider trading 인사이더거래
insolvency 채무초과
insolvency of debtors
　　채무자의 반제(返濟) 불능
insolvent corporation 지불불능회사
insolvent debtor 파산자
inspection 검사
inspection certificate 검사증명서
inspection of corporate record
　　회사기록을 검사함
inspection of documents 문서열람
inspection of property 재산검사
inspection report 검사보고서
inspection status 검사상태
installation 설치
installation work 설치공사
installment 할부
installment basis 할부기준
installment credit 할부채권
installment method 할부기준
installment payment 분할지불
installment plan 할부판매법
installment purchase 할부구매
installment receivable 할부외상금
installment sale 월부판매
installment savings 정기예금
installment settlement 분할지불
installment time deposit 적립정기예금
installments receivable 할부미수입금
instance 신청
instanter 즉시에
Institute cargo clauses 협회화물약관
Institute clauses 협회약관
Institute of Chartered Financial Analyst
　　미국공인증권분석가협회
Institute of Internal Auditors

　　미국내부감사인협회
Institute of London Underwriters
　　런던보험업자협회
institutes 주석서
institution 기관; 제도
institution buying 법인매입
institution of law suits 소송
institutional advertisement 기업광고
institutional advertising 제도광고
institutional analysis 제도분석
institutional arbitration 기관중재
institutional buying 기관매입
institutional decentralization
　　유통기관을 분산화함
institutional delivery 대체결제
institutional investors 기관투자가
institutional investors' index option
　　기관투자가지수옵션
institutional school 제도학파
institutional selling 기관매출
institutional stock purchase 기관매입
institutional stockholder 법인주주
institutionalized saving 제도적인 저축
instore merchandising 인스토어머천다이징
instruction 지시
instruction to bidders 입찰자에 대한 지시서
instrument 상품
instrument trust 사후신탁
instruments for buying operation
　　매입대상채권
insubordination 반항
insufficient funds 잔고부족
insurable interest 피보험이익
insurable interest in property 물상피보험이
　　익
insurable risk 보험대상이 되는 리스크
insurable value 보험가액
insurance 보험
insurance accounting 보험회계
Insurance Accounting and Statistical
　　Association 보험회계통계협회

I
J

insurance activities 보험사업
insurance against death 사망보험
insurance amount 보험금액
Insurance Board 보험청
insurance broker 보험브로커
insurance broker's liability insurance
　보험브로커책임보험
Insurance Brokers Registration Council
　보험브로커등록평의회
insurance business 보험업
insurance carrier 보험업자
insurance cartel 보험카르텔
insurance claims 미수보험금
insurance claims unsettled 미결산보험금
insurance clause 보험약관
insurance collector 보험수금원
insurance companies blanket bond
　보험회사포괄보증증권
insurance company 보험회사
insurance contract law 보험계약법
insurance control 보험통제
Insurance Council 보험심의회
insurance expense 보험료
insurance expense exhibit 보험경비명세서
insurance group 보험그룹
insurance law 보험감독법
insurance management 보험관리
insurance market 보험시장
insurance of medical expenses 의료보험
insurance of substandard lives
　표준하체보험계약
insurance on mortgagee's interest 저당보험
insurance payable at death 사망보험
insurance policy 보험증권
insurance pool 보험풀
insurance premium 보험료
insurance premium deduction 보험료공제
insurance prepaid 전불보험료
insurance principle 보험원리
insurance product firm 보험상품취급업자
insurance proposal form 보험계약신청서

insurance scheme 보험형연금
insurance science 보험학
insurance syndicate 보험신디케이트
insurance tax 보험세
insurance to value 전부보험
insurance value 보험가액
insurance with bonus 특별배당금보험
insurance with settlement options
　선택권부 보험
insured 피보험자
insured amount 보험금액
insured event 보험사고
insured peril 피보험위험
insured plan 보험형연금
insurer 보험자
intaglio 요판, 오목판
intake of foreign capital 외자도입
intake value 구입가격
intangible assets 무형자산
intangible capital 무형자본
intangible depreciable assets
　무형감가상각자산
intangible depreciable property
　무형상각자산
intangible effects 무형효과
intangible fixed assets 무형고정자산
intangible property 무형재산
intangibles 무형고정자산
integer programming 정수계획법
integral part 중요한 부분
integrated circuit card IC 카드
integrated organization 종합조직
integrated production 일관생산
integrated services digital broadcasting
　종합디지털방송
integration 통산
integration of business 사업통합
intellectual property right 지적소유권
intelligent building 인텔리전트빌딩
intelligent encoding 지적부호화
intelligent manufacturing system IMS

intelligent network 인텔리전트네트워크
intemperance 몹시 취함
intendant 감독관
intendment of law 법의 진의
intensive distribution 개방적인 유통
intensive investment 집중투자
intention 의사
intention of concept 개념을 내포함
intention to purchase 구입의사
intentional 고의의
inter alia 그 중에서도
inter industry analysis 산업연관분석
inter-bank 은행 간의
inter-bank deposit 은행 간 예금
inter-bank exchange transaction 인터뱅크 환
    거래
inter-bank market 인터뱅크장
inter-bank rate 은행 간 상장
inter-enterprise credit 기업 간 신용
industry-relations table 산업연관표
inter-market spread 시장 간 스프레드
inter-market trading system
    시장 간 거래시스템
inter-office account 본지점 계정
inter-office exchange adjustment account
    환끝환산차금
inter-office rate 본지점 레이트
inter-period tax allocation 연도간 세 배분
interaction 쌍방향성
interaction approach 상호작용
interactive 쌍방향
interactive television 쌍방향텔레비전
interbank loan 인터뱅크론
interbank rate 인터뱅크 상장
interbranch account 지점상호계정
interbranch loss 지점 상호 간 손실
interbranch profit 지점 상호 간 이익
interchangeability 호환성
intercommon 상호입회하다
intercompany account 회사 간 계정
intercompany elimination 회사 간 제거

intercompany loss 회사 상호 간 손실
intercompany profit 회사 간 이익
intercompany transfer variance
    내부대체차액
interconnection 상호접속
interdepartment account 부문 간 계정
interdepartmental profit 내부대체이익
interdiction 금치산
interdisciplinary 학제
interest 지분; 이해관계; 이권
interest advance 선불이자
interest after the maturity 기한 후 이자
interest arbitrage 금리재정
interest arrears 지연이자
interest bearing 이자부
interest bearing issuance 유리발행
interest bill 이자부 어음
interest burden 이자부담
interest cap trading 금리캡거래
interest capitalization method
    원가(元加) 방식
interest claims 이자클레임
interest cost 이자비용
interest cover 이자비용
interest coverage ratio 금리부담율
interest differential 금리차
interest during construction 건설이자
interest earned 수취이자
interest equalization tax 금리평형세
interest for arrears 지연이자
interest for delay 연체이자
interest for delinquency 연체이자
interest futures 금리선물
interest in arrears 연체이자
interest included 원리합계
interest income 이자소득
interest incurred during construction
    건설이자
interest method 이자법
interest on bond 사채이자
interest on borrowed 차입금이자

I
J

interest on borrowed fund 부채이자
interest on call loans 콜론이자
interest on call money 콜머니이자
interest on deposit 예금금리
interest on external bond 외채이자
interest on foreign currency deposits
　외화예금이자
interest on government bond 공채이자
interest on government securities 국채이자
interest on guaranty cap 기금이자
interest on interest 이자에 대한 이자
interest on loans and discount 대출금이자
interest on loans on bills 어음대부이자
interest on loans rebated 대부금이자반려
interest on overdrafts for export bills
　환당좌대이자
interest on postal savings 우편예금이자
interest on public bond 공채이자
interest on refund 환부가산금
interest on savings deposit 저금금리
interest on securities 유가증권이자
interest option transaction 금리옵션거래
interest parity 금리평가
interest payable 미불이자
interest payment 이자지불
interest payment method 이자지불방법
interest payments on foreign debt
　대외채무이자지불
interest per annum 연리
interest prepaid 선불이자
interest rate 금리
interest rate abroad 해외금리
interest rate arbitrage 금리재정
interest rate arbitrage transaction
　금리재정거래
interest rate change 이자율변화
interest rate collar 금리칼라
interest rate control 금리조작
interest rate differential 금리차
interest rate floor 금리플로어
interest rate fluctuation 금리변동

interest rate futures 금리선물
interest rate futures contracts 금리선물계약
interest rate futures option trading
　금리선물옵션거래
interest rate minded 금리마인드
interest rate movement 금리동향
interest rate on borrowing 차입금리
interest rate on inter-bank deposit
　은행 간 예금금리
interest rate on loans 대출금리
interest rate on loans secured by time deposit
　정기예금담보대출금리
interest rate on the Eurocurreney market
　유로금리
interest rate on time deposit 정기예금금리
interest rate option 금리옵션
interest rate policy 금리정책
interest rate raise 이자인상
interest rate risk 금리리스크
interest rate sensitive items 금리감응 항목
interest sensitive products 금리감응형 상품
interest rate sensitive stock 금리민감주
interest rate sensitivity 금리감응도
interest rate spread 금리마진
interest rate swap 금리스와프
interest rate parity theory 이자평가이론
interest receivable 수취이자
interest receivable on bank deposits
　미수은행예금이자
interest received 수취이자
interest sensitivity of the pension surplus
　연금잉여의 금리감응도
interest skimming 인터레스트스키밍
interest spread 금리차
interest surplus 이차익
interest swap 금리스와프
interestrate parity theory 이자평가이론
interest swap bond 금리 스와프 채
interest tax 이자세
interest tax on delayed payment
　연납과 관련된 이자세

interest-bearing bank debenture 이자금융채
interest-bearing bond 이자부채
interest-bearing debt 이자부 부채
interest-bearing security 이자부 증권
interested party 이해관계자
interference with trade 영업방해
interfirm analysis 기업 간 분석
interim 임시의; 중간의
interim account 중간계정
interim audit 기중(期中) 감사
interim call 중간분담금입금청구
interim closing 중간결산
interim dividend 중간배당
interim financial statements 중간재무제표
interim interest payment 중간지불이자
interim loan 입금 예정의 공백을 메우기 위해
　서 받는 융자
interim measure 경과조치
interim meeting 중간회의
interim premium adjustment
　예납보험료 잠정조정
interim receipt 가영수서
interim report 중간보고
interim return form 중간신고서
interim sales 중간매상
interim statement 중간계산서
interim tax return 중간신고
interlace 서로 엇갈리게 짜다
interlineation 행간기입
interlocking 운동
interlocking directors 겸임중역
interlocking stockholding 주식비율
interlocutory 중간의
interlocutory judgment 중간판결
intermarket 시장 간
intermarket trading system 시장 간 거래
intermediary 중개자
intermediary bank 중개은행
intermediary trade 삼국 간 무역
intermediate accounting 중급회계학
intermediate lag 중간 래그

intermediate market 중간 시장
intermediate target 운영목표
intermediate tariff 중간세율
intermediate term market outlook 중기예상
intennediating financial institution
　금융중개기관
intern 억류하다
internal allocation 내부할당
internal analysis 내부분석
internal audit 내부감사
internal audit report 내부감사보고서
internal audit standard 내부감사기준
internal audit system 내부감사제도
internal auditing 내부감사
internal auditor 내부감사인
internal business analysis 내부경영분석
internal check 내부견제
internal check system 내부견제제도
internal consistency 내부정합성
internal control 내부통제
internal debt 내채
internal evidence 내부증거
internal exposure hazard 내부연소위험
internal factor 내부요인
internal financing 내부금융
internal information 내부정보; 내부자료
internal investment management 자가운용
internal labor market 내부노동시장
internal liability 내부부채
internal operation 내부운용
internal rate of return 내부수익률
internal reporting 내부보고
internal reporting system 내부보고제도
internal reserve 내부유보금
internal revenue bond 소득세지불보증증권
Internal Revenue Code 미국내국세입법
Internal Revenue Service 미국내국세입청
internal rule 사내규정
internal structure 내부구조
internal tax 내국세
internal transaction 내부거래

internal transfer profit 사내대체이익
internalized order 내부화주문
international accounting 국제기업회계
international accounting standards
  국제회계기준
International Accounting Standards
  Committee 국제회계기준위원회
international agency bond 국제기관채권
international agreed specialization 합의에 따
  른 국제분업
International Air Transport Association
  국제항공운송협회
international asset management
  국제자산운용
International Atomic Energy Agency
  국제원자력기관
international balance of payment 국제수지
international bank for economic cooperation
  국제경제협력은행
international bank for investment
  국제투자은행
international banking facility 국제은행업무
international banking operation
  국제은행업무
international broking 국제브로킹
international comparison 국제비교
international capital 국제자본
international capital market 국제자본이동
international capital movement
  국제자본이동
international cartel 국제카르텔
International Center for Settlement of
  Investment Disputes
  투자분쟁해결국제센터
International Chamber of Commerce
  국제상공회의소
International Chamber of Shipping
  국제해운회의소
International Civil Aviation Organization
  국제민간항공기관
international commodity agreement

  국제상품협정
International Confederation of Free Trade
  국제자유노동조합연합
International Congress of Actuaries
  국제액추어리협회
international consortium 국제인수단
International Court of Justice
  국제사법재판소
International Criminal Police Organization
  국제형사경찰기구
international currency 국제통화
international currency system 국제통화제도
international custom 국제관습법
International Depositary Receipts
  국제예탁증서
International Development Association
  국제개발협회
international distribution 국제유통
international diversified investment
  국제분산투자
international division of labor 국제분업
international double taxation 국제이중과세
international economics 국제경제학
International Energy Agency
  국제에너지기관
international exchange 국제환
International Federation of Stock Exchanges
  국제증권거래소연합
international finance 국제금융
International Finance Corporation
  국제금융공사
international financial institution
  국제금융기관
international financial market 국제금융시장
international financial system 국제금융제도
international fund 국제자금
International Fund for Agricultural
  Development 국제농업개발기금
international indebtedness 국제대차
international interest-spread 내외금리차
international investment 국제투자

international investment bank 국제투자은행
international investment trust 국제투자신탁
International Labor Organization
　국제노동기관
international law 국제법
International Law Association 국제법협회
international lease 국제리스
international liquidity 국제유동성
international long-termcapital movement
　국제장기자본이동
international managed currency system
　국제관리통화제도
International Marine Satellite
　Telecommunication Organization
　국제해사위성통신기구
International Maritime Organization
　국제해사기관
international market 국제시장
international market price 국제시장가격
international marketing 국제마케팅
international marketing research
　국제시장조사
international merchandise 국제상품
international monetary exchanges
　국제금융거래소
International Monetary Fund 국제통화기금
international monetary turmoil 국제통화불안
international money management
　국제적인 금융관리
international money market 국제금융시장
international movements of funds
　국제자금이동
international normals 국제노멀포트폴리오
International Olympic Committee
　국제올림픽위원회
International Organization of Consumer's
　Unions 국제소비자기구
International Organization of Employers
　국제경영자단체연맹
International Organization of Journalists
　국제저널리스트

International Organization of Securities
　Commissions 국제증권거래위원회기구
International Peace Bureau 국제평화국
international portfolio 인터내셔널포트폴리오
international portfolio diversification
　국제분산투자
international public law 국제공법
international recognized standard 국제기준
International Red Cross 국제적십자
international relations 국제관계
International Resources Bank 국제자원은행
international securities 국제증권
International Securities Clearing Corporation
　국제결제기관
international settlement 국제결제
international settlement currency
　국제결제통화
international short-term capital transaction
　국제단기자본거래
international short-term money market
　국제단기금융시장
International Social Security Association
　국제사회보장협회
international spread of risk
　국제적으로 위험을 분산시킴
International Standardization Organization
　국제표준화기구
international stock 국제주권
International Swap Dealers Association
　국제스왑딜러
international syndicate 국제신디케이트
international tax law 국제조세법
International Telecommunication Satellite
　Consortium 인텔샛; 국제상업통신위성기구
International Telecommunication Union
　국제전기통신연합
International Trade Commission
　국제무역위원회
international transaction currency
　국제거래통화
international underwriting group 국제인수단

I
J

International Union Aviation Insurers
국제항공보험연합
**International Union of Credit and Investment
Insurers** 국제수출신용보험기구
International Union of Marine Insurance
국제해상보험연합
international unit 국제단위
internationalization 국제화
Internet 인터넷
interorganizational system 조직간 시스템
interperiod income tax allocation
소득과세를 기간상호배분함
interpersonal perception 대인지각
interpleader 권리자확인
interpolation 보간법, 내삽법
interpretation clause 해석조항
interpretation of cash flows 캐시플로해석
interregional analysis 지역연관분석
interrogation 취조
interruption effect 방해효과
interruption of business 영업정지
interruption of prescription 시효중단
intersegment sales 사업구분간매상
interstate commerce 주제(州際)통상
Interstate Commerce Commission
주제(州際)통상위원회
intertype competition 이업종간경쟁
interunit pricing 부문간의 대체가격을 결정함
interunit transfer 부문간 대체
intervene 소송에 참가하다
intervening variable 중개변수
intervention 개입
intervention against market 역풍개입
intervention by selling dollars 달러매출개입
intervention currency 개입통화
intervention following market 순풍개입
intervention level 개입수준
intervention operation 개입조작
intervention point 개입점
intervention purchase 개입구입
intervention rate 개입금리

intra vires 권한 내에서
intra-contract spread 상품간 스프레드
intra-day high and low 하루중 고저치
intracompany transfer 내부대체
intracompany transfer price 내부대체가격
intrafirm analysis 기업내 분석
intramarginal intervention
허용변동폭 내 개입
intramarket 시장내
intraperiod income tax
기간 내의 소득과세배분
intraperiod tax allocation 기간 내의 세금배분
intrapreneuring 사내기업
intraventure 사내벤처
intrinsic deposit 본원예금
intrinsic value 본원적인 가치
introduced stock 공개주
introducing 중개
introducing firm 주문중개업자
introduction 소개
introductory period 도입기
intrusion 불법점유
invalid card 무효카드
invalid coupon 효력이 없는 쿠폰
invention 발명
inventories of merchandise and supplies
저장품
inventory 재고자산
inventory adjustment 재고조정
inventory assets 자고자산
inventory audit 재고정리자산감사
inventory capital 재고자산
inventory carrying cost 보관비
inventory certificate 재고증명서
inventory change 재고변동
inventory control 재고정리
inventory cycles 재고순환
inventory financing 재고금융
inventory investment 재고투자
inventory loss 재고손
inventory method 재고자산계산법

inventory model 재고모델
inventory of security 담보목록
inventory profit 재고자산이익
inventory recession 인벤토리리세션
inventory reserve 재고자산평가준비금
inventory sheet 재고표
inventory shipments ratio 재고율
inventory tag 재고표
inventory turnover 재고자산회전율
inventory unit 재고단위
inventory valuation 재고자산평가
inventory valuation adjustment 재고평가조정
inventory valuation method
    재고자산평가방법
inventory valuation reserves
    재고자산평가준비금
inventory value 재고평가액
inventory variation 재고자산증감
inventory-sales ratio 재고율
inventoryless system 무재고방식
inverse demand pattern 역수요패턴
inverse floater 역플로터채
inverse matrix 역행렬
inverse matrix table 역행렬표
inverse yield 역이익
inverted market 시중은행의 할인율상회시장
inverted scale 역전스케일
inverted yield curve 역이율
inverted yield curve phenomena 역이율 현상
invested assets 운용자산
invested capital 투하자본
investigation of cause 원인조사
investigator 국세사찰관
investing activities 투자활동
investing public 대중투자가
investment 출자
investment abroad 해외투자
investment account 투자계정부문
investment advisor 투자고문
investment advisory industry 투자고문업계
investment advisory law 투자고문법

investment analysis 투자분석
investment and loan 투자융자업계
investment bank 투자은행
Investment Banking Financing Company
    투자은행금융기관
investment boom 투자경기
investment buying 투자매
investment by foreign investors 외국인투자
investment climate 투자환경
investment club 투자클럽
investment committee 투자위원회
investment company 투자회사
investment counselor 투자카운셀러
investment credit 투자공제
investment criteria 투자척도
investment currency 투자통화
investment curve 투자곡선
investment decision 투자결정
investment demand 투자수요
investment dollar 투자달러
investment environment 투자환경
investment expenditure 투자지출
investment expense 투자경비
investment flexibility 투자유연성
investment function 투자함수
investment function of profit principle type
    이윤원리형 투자함수
investment fund 투자신탁
investment grade 투자적격
investment grade corporate 투자대상기업
investment horizon 소유기간
investment in affiliates 관계회사출자금
investment in capital 출자금
investment in kind 현물출자
investment in money 현금출자
investment in plant and machinery 설비투자
investment in securities 투자유가증권
investment in stocks 주식투자
investment income 투자소득
investment information sources 투자정보원
investment ledger 유가증권원장

J

investment letter 투자목적확인서
investment management company
　투자고문회사
investment manager 투자매니저
investment market 투자시장
investment multiplier 투자승수
investment objectives 투자목표
investment of life insurance fund
　생보자금투자
investment opportunities 투자기회
investment outlet 투자대상
investment overseas 해외투자
investment period 투자기간
investment philosophy 투자철학
investment policy 투자정책
investment profit 자기계정매매익
investment program 투자계획
investment propensity 투자성향
investment purchased register
　유가증권매입기입장
investment result 투자성과
investment return 이익
investment securities 투자유가증권
investment security 투자증권
investment selection summary 투자선택개괄
investment skeleton 기대에서 벗어난 증권
investment sold register 유가증권매각기입장
investment stock 투자주
investment strategy 투자전략
investment tax credit 투자세액공제
investment trust 투자신탁
investment trust management company
　투자신탁위탁회사
investment trust on securities 증권투자신탁
investment value 투자가치
investment year method 투자연도별 방식
investor 출자자
investors relations 인베스터즈릴레이션즈
invisible assets 무형자산
invisible hand 보이지 않는 손
invisible trade 무역외

invisible trade balance 무역외수지
invitation 유인
invitation telex 권유텔렉스
invoice 송장; 청구서
invoice book 청구서
invoice method 인보이스방식
invoice-book inward 상품구입장
invoice-book outward 상품발송장
involuntary 자발적이 아닌
involuntary bankruptcy 강제파산
involuntary conversion 강제교환
involuntary exchange 교환처분
involuntary insolvency 강제지불불능
involuntary transfer 강제양도
involuntary unemployment 비자발적인 실업
involvement 관여
inwards reinsurance 내부재보험
ipso facto 사실상
ipso jure 법률상
irrational tax 악세
irrecoverable cost 회수불능원가
irredeemable bond 불상환채
irregular installment payment 불균등지불
irregular practices 부정행위
irrelevant 관련성이 없는
irreparable injury 회복할 수 없는 침해
irretrievable deprivation 가망이 없는 상실
irrevocable 철회할 수 없는
irrevocable letter of credit 취소불능신용장
irrevocable license 취소할 수 없는 허가
irrigation right 수리권(水利權)
island reversal pattern 아일랜드리버설패턴
issuance of bond 채권발행
issue 쟁점; 발행
issue at face value 액면발행
issue at intermediate price 중간발행
issue at market price 시가발행
issue at par 퍼 발행
issue by tender 입찰발행
issue management 문제처리방법
issue market 발행시장

issue of bond 기채
issue of public bonds 공공채발행
issue of the wall between banking and
 security business 은행증권간의 담장논쟁
issue on a tap basis 탭채로 발행하다
issue on fact 사실문제에 대한 쟁점
issue price 매출가격
issue standards 적채기준
issue tax 발행세
issue terms 발행조건
issue used in the average 평균주가채용문제
issue value 발행가격
issued capital stock 발행필 주식자본금
issued shares 발행필 주식
issuer 발행회사
issuer's cost 발행자비용
issues paper 토의보고서

issues to shareholders 주주할당
issuing bank 발행은행
issuing corporation 발행회사
issuing house 발행상사
item 항목
item depreciation 개별상각
item in transit 미달항목
item of account 계정항목
item parameter 항목특성치
itemization 내역
itemized account 분개계정; 명세계정
itemized bill 내역계정서
itemized deduction 개별공제
items of business 영업종목
items of payment 지불항목
items of tax 세목**

I
J

J curve effect J 커브 효과
jacket 일반문서
jeopardy 위험
job 공사
job contents 직무내용
job cost 개별원가
job cost system 개별원가계산
job description 직책
job enlargement 직무확대
job enrichment 직무충실
job evaluation 직무평가
job lot 싸구려물건
job order 작업지도서
job order cost system 개별원가계산법
job order costing 개별원가계산
job rotation 직무순회
job slip 작업전표
job specification 직무명세
job ticket 작업표
jobber 중매인
jobber's turn 중매인의 가격차이
jobbing 중매행위
joinder 병합
joinder of cause of action 소송원인을 병합함
joinder of offenses 범죄를 병합함
joinder of parties 당사자병합
joinder of protests 병합심리
joint 공동의
joint account 공통계정
joint advertisement 공동광고
joint agreement 연합협약
joint and several 연대

joint and several bond 연대증서
joint and several guarantee 연대보증
joint and several liability 연대책임
joint and several obligation 연대채무
joint and several obligation of tax payment
　연대납부책임
joint audit 공동감사
joint beneficiary 공동수취인
joint bond 합동사채
joint cost 결합비용
joint currency float 공동변동상장
joint development 공동개발
joint enterprise cooperative 기업조합
joint financing 공동융자
joint float 공동플로트
joint floating exchange rate 공동변동상장
joint guarantee 공동보증
joint insureds 공동피보험자
joint investment 합병
joint labor management conference
　노사협의
joint liability 공동책임
joint life annuity 연생연금
joint life insurance 연생보험
joint marketing 공동판매
joint obligation 합유채권
joint ownership 공유
Joint Photographic Expert Group JPEG
　이미지 파일의 한 종류
joint probability 동시 확률
joint product 연산품
joint project 공동사업

joint return 공동신고

joint right 합유

joint sales 공동판

joint stock company 주식회사

joint surety 연대보증인

joint tenancy 합유부동산권

joint tenant 공동보유

joint trust 합동운용신탁

Joint venture 합변사업

joint-floating market system 공동변동상장

journal 분개장

journal entry 분개기입

journal ledger 대체원장

journal slip 대체전표

journal voucher 대체영수증

journalizing 분개

judge 판사

judge's chambers 판사실

judging 심사

judgment 판결

Judgment creditor 판결채권자

judgment debtor 판결채무자

judgment in rem 대물판결

judgment nil dicit 무소답으로 인한 결석판결

judgment nisi 가판결

judgment of definite liabilities 채권확정판결

judgment of exclusion on shareholders rights
  주권제권판결

judgment on merits 사실판결

judgment on the verdict 평결에 따른 판결

judgment record 판결기록

judgment set-off 판결채권이 상쇄됨

judicature acts 재판소법

judicial bond 법령보증

judicial confession 재판상의 자유

judicial convention 재판상의 협정

judicial costs 재판비용

judicial economy 소송경제

judicial judgment 사법심사

judicial legislation 재판에 따른 입법

judicial notice 법원의 당연한 확신

judicial power 사법권

judicial proceedings 사법절차

judicial sale 사법상의 매각

judicial valuation 법정평가

"Jumbo" clause 거액위험약관

jumbo risk 거대위험

jump process 점프과정

jumping juvenile 자동증액소아보험

junior accountant 회계사보

junior bond 후순위채권

junior creditor 후순위채권자

junior director 청년중역

junior execution 수반집행

junior issue 하위증권

junior mortgage 후순위저당

junior securities 열후증권

junior security 후순위담보

junior subordinated 하위열후

junk bond 정크본드

jurat 맺음말

Juridical person 법인

juridical person for public interest 공익법인

juridical person in a public law 특수법인

juridical personality 법인격

jurisdiction 관할

jurisdictional defect 관할차이

jurisprudence 법률학

juristic act 법률행위

juror 배심원

Jury 배심

jury box 배심원석

jury trial 배심원재판

jus in rem 대물권

Just after the opening 시작하자마자

just compensation 정당한 보상

just-in-time system 저스트인타임 방식

justice 판사

justifiable act 정당행위

justifiable reason to apply
  적용하는 정당한 이유

justification 정당화

juvenile comprehensive insurance
  어린이종합보험

I
J

keep the books 기장하다
keep-out price 저지가격
keep-well agreement 건전성 유지계약
Keogh Plan 자영업자 퇴직연금
key account 주요거래처
key currency 기축통화
key executive insurance 경영자보험
key factor 주요원인
key industry 기간산업
key reversal day 상장의 대전환일
key station 키국(局)
keymoney 권리금
Keynesian 케인스학파
Keynesian revolution 케인스혁명
keystone bond funds 키스톤채권
kick back 킥백
killing 큰 벌이

kilo bit 킬로비트
kilo byte 킬로바이트
kind of income 소득의 종류
Kingston Regime 킹스턴체제
kinked demand curve 굴절수요곡선
Kitchen cycles 단기파동, 키친사이클
kite 융통어음
knock out 담합경매
knock-down product 녹다운제품
knock-on effect 파급효과
knock-out option 정지조건부 옵션
knockdown price 최저가격
knowledge 인식
knowledge engineering 지식공학
knowledge intensive industry 지식집약산업
Kondratieff wave 콘드라티에프파(주기)

labeled price 매가
labor account 임금계정
labor agreement 노동협약
labor audit 노무감사
labor coefficient 노동계수
labor cost 노임
labor credit associations 노동금고
labor income 노동소득
labor laws 노동법
labor legislation 노동입법
labor management 노무관리
labor market 노동시장
labor & material payment bond
　　임금하청대금지불보증증권
labor productivity 노동생산성
labor rate standard 임률표준
labor rate variance 임률차이
labor regulations 노동법규
labor relative share 노동분배율
labor saving investment 노동력절약투자
labor share 노동분배율
labor time variance 작업시간차이
labor trouble 노동분쟁
labor turnover 노동자이동
labor union group insurance
　　노동조합단체보험
labor variance 노무비차이
laborage 공임
laboratory test 실험실조사
lacuna 공백
Latter curve 래터곡선

lag 뒤떨어지다
lag analysis 래그분석
lag effect 래그효과
lag indicator 지행지수
laggard 전반적인 경기회복수준보다 회복이 더
　　딘 경제분야
lagging series 지행계수
laid down cost 도착원가
laissez-faire 무간섭주의
lame duck 제명회원
land 토지
land and building 토지건물
land category 지목(地目)
land charges 토지부담
land cost 용지비
land development tax 택지개발세
land expropriation 토지수용
land expropriation right 토지수용권
land for residence 주택용 토지
land for sale in lots 분양권
land improvement 토지개량
land improvement enterprise 토지개량사업
land improvement expenses 토지개량비
land ledger 토지대장
land lot 토지
land lot without construction 갱지(更地)
land ownership 토지소유
land purchase for specified business
　　특정사업의 용지매수
land reform 토지개량
land registration 토지등기

land registry 토지등기소
land tax 지조(地租)
land tax register book 토지과세대장
land taxation 토지세제
land-tenant 토지보유자
land tenure 토지보유
land-value tax 토지가격세
landed estate 부동산; 토지
landed property 토지
landed proprietor 토지소유자
landing tax 입국세
landlord 지주
landlords' contingent liability policy 지주미
　　필배상책임보험
landlords' liability policy 지주배상보험
languish 활기를 잃다
lapping 결정적인 책임을 지지 않다
　　(외상 출금의)
laps 집행
lapse 보험계약에 실패함
lapse of the leasehold 차지권의 기간이 경과함
lapse ratio 실효권
lapsed days 경과일수
lapsed share 실효주
lapsed time 경과시간
lapsing schedule of fixed assets
　　고정자산증감명세표
large amount deposit interest 거액예금금리
large amount time deposit 거액정기
large amount transaction 거액거래
large credit 고액채권
large depreciable property 대규모상각자산
large institutional investors 큰 기관투자가
large investment bank 대투자은행
large order 거액주문
large risks 거대리스크
large scale retail store law
　　대점법(대규모 소매점포에 대한 법률)
large-capital stock 대형주
large-scale bond issue 채권을 대량발행함
large-scale retailer 대규모소매업자

laser printer 레이저프린터
Laspeyres formula 라스파이레스방식
last close 전일종가
last cost method 최종구입원가법
last heir 최종상속인
last price 종가
last purchase method 최종구입원가법
last quotation 막장
last resort 라스트리조트
last resort lender 최후의 대주(貸主)
last survivor annuity 최종생존자연금
last trading day 최종거래일
last-in first-out basis 후입선출기준
late payment charge 지연손해금
late presentation 제시지연
late shipment 선적지연
latent assets 비밀적립금
latent call option 잠재적인 콜옵션
latent demand 잠재수요
latent equity holdings 보유주포함
latent loss 비밀손실
latent return 비밀수익
latent unemployment 잠재실업
latent variable 잠재변수
latent warrant 잠재워런트
lateral diversification 수평형 다각화
lateral thinking 수평사고
latter half 하반기
latter half of the year 후기
lattice approach 격자법
launch date 발행개시일
launching 기채; 모집발표
laundered money 위장자금
law change 법률변경
law enforced territory 법시행지
law for foreign securities company
　　외국증권업법
law of a maximum interest rate 이자제한법
law of commerce 상법
law of diminishing return 수익체감의 법칙
law of exception 예외원칙

law of increasing public expenditures
경비팽창의 원칙
law of indifference
일물일가(一物一價)의 법칙
law of large numbers 대수의 법칙
law of nations 국제법
law of nature 자연법
law of obligations 채권법
law of ship's flag 기국법; 선적국법
law of subscription 출자법
law of substitution 대체법률
law of succession 상속법
law of the forum 법정지법
law office 법률사무소
law on bills 어음법
law reports 판례집
law with expiration date 시한입법
lawful 적법의
lawful age 성년
laws of realty 물권법
lawsuits 소송
lawyer 변호사
lawyer's fee 변호사료
lawyer's liability 변호사책임
lawyer's liability insurance
변호사배상책임보험
lay 풋내기의
lay off 레이오프
lay underwriter 레이언더라이터
lay-days 상륙기간
lay-up 간단한 거래
lay-up refund 휴항환불보험료
lead 이르게 하다; 이끌다
lead auditor 주임감사원
lead manager 주간사
leader merchandising 특매상품전략
leader of long side 구입장본인
leader of short side 매출장본인
leaders 주도주
leading case 지도적인 판례
leading counsel 주임변호인

leading index of business conditions
경기선행지수
leading indicator 경기선행지수
leading questions 유도심문
leading series 선행계열
leading share 선두주
leading underwriter 주도보험자
leads and lags 리즈앤드래그즈
leak of know-how 노하우누설
lean production method 린 생산방식
leap 대폭증가
learning curve 학습곡선
lease 임차권; 리스
lease bond 임대보증증권
lease contract bond 임대차계약보증증권
lease in perpetuity 영대차지권
lease of land 차지증
lease of premises 토지건물임차계약
lease of property 자산임대
lease period 리스기간
lease tenant right 차지권
lease-holder 차지인
leased land 임차지
leasehold 차지권을 부여하는 계약
leasehold estate 임차부동산
leasehold interest insurance 임차권보험
leaseholder 차지권자
leasing business 리스업무
leasing company 리스회사
leasing contract 리스계약
least less developed countries
후발발전도상국
least-squares method 최소제곱법
leave order 지정가격주문
ledger 원장
ledger account 원장계정
ledger assets 원장자산
ledger balance 원장잔고
ledger clerk 원장계
ledger folio 원장페이지수
ledger transfer 원장대체**

left-hand 자산담보의
legacy 유산
legacy duty 유산세
legal 적법의
legal ability person 능력자
legal adviser 법률고문
legal aid services 법률상담
legal benefit 법정급부
legal capacity 행위능력
legal capital 법정자본
legal channeling of liability
　　법률상의 책임집중제도
legal contract 적법계약
legal cost 소송비용
legal counsel 법률상담
legal department 법무부
legal document 법률서류
legal durable years 법정내용연수
legal duty 법률상의 의무
legal earned surplus reserve 법정이익준비금
legal entity 법적실체
legal evidence 법률상의 증거
legal exemption from income tax 기초공제
legal fee 변호사 보수
legal fiction 가정
legal guardian 법정후견인
legal heir 가독(家督)
legal interest 법정이자
legal investment 투자적격대상
legal jeopardy 법적위험
legal lending limit 법정대출한도화
legal liability 법정책임; 법적채무
legal liability insurance 법정책임보험
legal lien 선취특권
legal liquidation 법적정리
legal mortgage 보통법상의 모기지
legal notice 적법한 통지
legal opinion 변호사의 의견서
legal organ 정당한 권한이 있는 기관
legal person 법인
legal portion of legacy 법정상속분

legal possession 법률상의 점유
legal presumption 법률상의 추정
legal procedure 재판절차
legal process 합법적인 절차
legal rate 법정이율
legal rate of interest 법정금리
legal relations 법률관계
legal representative 법정대리인
legal reserve 법정준비금
legal reserve life insurance company
　　법정준비금적립생명보험회사
legal subrogation 법정대위
legal tax cut 감세
legal tender 법정통화
legal term 법정기한
legal title 보통법상의 소유권
legal valuation 법정평가
legal valuation method of inventory
　　법정재고평가법
legal welfare expense 법정복리비
legally secured portion of succession
　　유류분(遺留分)
legatee 유산수취인
leges non scriptae 불문법
leges scriptae 성문법
legislative act 입법기관제정법
legislative action 법적조치
leisure expenditures 여가지출
leisure industries 레저산업
lender bank 대출은행
lender's preference 대출자의 선호
lender's risk 대출자의 위험
lending 대부
lending a street name 명의대여
lending loss 대손금
lending operation 대출업무
lending policy 대출정책
lending rate 대출금리
lending securities 대증권
lending stock 대주
lending terms 대출조건

lending window 대부창구
length of service 재직기한
Leontief's paradox 레온체프의 역설
less than carload 소액취급
lessee 임차인
lesser evil 문제가 적은 제도
lessor 임대인
lessor owner 출자자
letter form 자체, 글꼴
letter of allotment 할당장
letter of attorney 위임장
letter of award 낙찰결정서
letter of confirmation of collateral
　담보차입증
letter of credit 신용장
letter of credit confirming bank
　신용장확인은행
letter of credit margin money
　신용장개설보증금
letter of guarantee 보증장
letter of indemnification 보상계약서
letter of indemnity 손해보전계약서
letter of intent 합의확인서
letter of license 지불기일연기서면
letter of subrogation 권리이전증
letter of undertaking 각서
letter securities 비등록사모채
letter stock 매각제한주식
lettered rule 문자규칙
letters patent 특허증
letting out 계약체결
level 수준
level net premium 평준순보험료
level of consumption 소비수준
level of employment 고용수준
level of income 소득수준
level of interest rate 금리수준
level of significance 유의수준
level of society 사회수준
level of transaction 거래수준
level pay floating rate note

　정액지불변동이부채
level payment 원리균등분할반제
level premium 평준보험료
level premium insurance 평준보험료식 보험
level premium normal cost on entry age
　가입연령식 평준표준보험료
leveling of income 이익평준화
leverage 자금효율
leverage effect 레버리지효과
leverage factor 레버리지지수
leverage factor ratio 레버리지비율
leverage ratio 레버리지비율
leveraged buyout 레버리지드바이아웃
leveraged holding 레버리지드홀딩
leveraged lease 레버리지드리스
leveraged option 레버리지드옵션
leveraged position 레버리지드포지션
leveraged recapitalization 레버리지드리캐피
　털리제이션
leveraged stock 레버리지드스톡
leviable property 집행재산
levy 과세
levy in kind 물납세
levy of attachment 재산차압
lex loci delictus 범죄지법
lex loci rei 소재지법
Lexis's principle 렉시스의 원칙
liabilities account 부채계정
liabilities and capital 부채 및 자본
liabilities exceeding assets 채무초과
liabilities for guarantee 보증채무
liabilities for guarantee against repairs
　수선보증예비금
liabilities off the book 장부외채무
liabilities on guaranties 보증채무
liability 채무; 책임
liability insurance 손해배상책임보험
liability management 부채관리
liability of estimated amount
　견적에 따른 채무
liability reserve 책임준비금

liability reserves 부채성 준비금
liability side 부채측
liability swap 채무스와프
liability with interest 유리자부채
liaison office 주재원사무소
libel (문서에 의한) 명예훼손
libel liability insurance
　명예훼손배상책임보험
libelant 원고
liberalization of capital transactions
　자본거래자유화
liberalization of exchange control 환자유화
liberalization of interest rate 금리자유화
liberalization of trade 무역자유화
liberate 보석자인도영장
liberty of contract 계약자유의 원칙
license 허가
license fees 면허료
license insurance 라이센스보험
license tax 면허세
licensed tax accountant 세리사
licensing system 면허제
lie in grant 증서이전이 되는
lien 선취특권; 리엔
lien of partners 조합원 선취득권
lien theory 선취특권이론
lienor 선취특권자
life annuity 종신연금
life annuity certain and continuous
　보증기간부 연금
life annuity due 시기지불연금
life annuity fund 생명연금적립금
life annuity insurance 종신연금보험
life annuity payable in arrears
　기말지불생명연금
life annuity with no refund 무상환종신연금
life insurance 생명보험
life insurance company 생명보험회사
life insurance company purchase 생보구입
life insurance credit 생명보험료공제
life insurance medicine 생명보험의학

life insurance policy 생명보험증권
life insurance premium 생명보험료
life insurance premiums deduction
　생명보험료공제
life insurance trust 생명보험신탁
life reinsurance 생명보험의 재보험
life table 생명표
life tenant 영대차지인
life time policy 종신보험증권
life-interest 평생 동안의 권리
life-long education 평생교육
life-to-call 기전상환까지의 거치기간
LIFO adaptation of retail method
　후견선출매가환원법
LIFO reserve 후입선출법준비금
lifting charges 취급수수료
lifting of gold embargo 금수출해금
light and fuel expenses 광열비
light mortality 저사망율
light oil delivery tax 경유거래세
light vehicle tax 경차세
lighting model 광원모델
like goods 동종상품
limit calculation 가격지정산정법
limit deviation 한계수치
limit high 스톱고(高)
limit low 스톱저(低)
limit of age 가입연령범위
limit of cession 출재한도액
limit of cover 인수한도액
limit of credit 신용한도
limit of indemnity 손해보전한도액
limit of liability 배상책임한도액
limit of overdrawn account 수표발행한도
limit of retention 보유한도액
limit on foreign investors' holdings of stocks
　외국인지주제한
limit order 지정가격주문
limit to credit reserve for bad debts
　대손준비금계정편입한도액
limitation of actions 출소기한

limitation on dividend 배당제한
limitation on interlocking 업무겸업제한
limitation on issue principle 쟁점주의
limitation on proprietary right of land 토지
limitational factor 제한요인
limitations of price theory 가격이론의 한계
limited annuity 유한연금
limited audit 한정감사
limited branching 특정지역지점설치
limited company 유한책임회사
limited convertibility 제한적인 교환성
limited damages 확정손해배상액
limited distribution 한정적인 판로
limited guarantee 제한적인 보증
limited income method 소득원천세
limited legal tender 제한법화
limited liability 유한책임
limited obligation bond 특정재원채
limited partnership 유한책임조합
limited payment life policy 단기불입생명보험
limited policies 제한적인 보험
limited premium payment 유한불입
limited private company 유한회사
limited tax liability 제한납세의무
limited tax rate 제한세율
limited-life assets 유한내용연수자산
limiting factor 한정요인
line card 계약자카드
line feed 라인피드
　(모니터의 커서를 한 줄 아래로 내림)
line guide 인수한도표
line of business 영업과목
line of credit 대출예약한도
line organization 라인조직
line production 직선생산
line space 행간
lineal warranty 승계담보
linear accelerator 선형가속도계수
linear combination 선형결합
linear discriminant analysis 선형판별분석
linear discriminant function 선형판별함수

linear programming 선형계획법
linear regression 선형회귀
linked bond 링크채
linked long term 가격변동과 연동된 생명보험
liquid assets 유동자산
liquid capita 유동자본
liquid crystal display 액정디스플레이
liquid deposit 유동성예금
liquid part 유동부분
liquid ratio 유동비율
liquid reserve 유동성준비금
liquid stock 유통문제
liquid yield option note 해약옵션채권
liquid-asset hypothesis 유동자산가설
liquidate 현금화하다
liquidated account 확정계정
liquidated company 청산회사
liquidated damages 손해배상금
liquidated debt 확정채무
liquidating dividend 청산배당
liquidating partner 청산인
liquidation 현금화; 청산
liquidation accounts 청산계정
liquidation affairs 청산사무
liquidation balance sheet 청산대차대조표
liquidation by compromise 해소하다
liquidation dividend 청산배당
liquidation final return 청산확정신고
liquidation income 청산소득
liquidation income from dissolution
　해산에 따른 청산소득
liquidation matter 청산사무
liquidation of claim 채권변제
liquidation of duties 관세사정
liquidation of special bad debts
　채권상각특별계정제거
liquidation of speculative accounts
　투기계정을 정리함
liquidation office 청산사무소
liquidation preference 청산우선권
liquidation price 청산치**

K
L

liquidation proceedings 청산수속
liquidation profit and loss 청산손익
liquidation tax 청산소득세
liquidation value 청산가치
liquidator 청산인
liquidity 유동성
liquidity creation 유동성창출
liquidity differential 유동성격차
liquidity dilemma 유동성딜레마
liquidity diversification 유동성분산
liquidity effect 유동성효과
liquidity in hand 소지한 유동성
liquidity index 유동지수
liquidity management 유동성관리
liquidity of the banking system 은행유동성
liquidity position 유동성포지션
liquidity preference theory 유동성선호이론
liquidity premium 유동성프리미엄
liquidity ratio 유동성비율
liquidity risk 유동성리스크
liquidity scarcity 유동성부족
liquidity trap 유동성의 함정(계략)
liquidity-driven issue 유동성상장주
liquidity-driven market 유동성지향상장
liquidity-motivated transactions 유동성동기
　로 인한 매매
liquor tax 주세
lis pendens 계속 중인 소송
list of members 회원명부
list of property 재산목록
list of shareholders 주주명부
list quotation 상장표
listed bond market 상장채권시장
listed company 상장회사
listed futures 상장선물
listed issue 상장문제
listed option 상장옵션
listed product 상장상품
listed securities 상장증권
listed stock 상장주
listing 상장

listing agent 상장대리인
listing requirements 상장심사기준
listing standard 상장기준
litigant 소송당사자
litigation 소송추행; 소송수행
litigation bond 소송보증증권
litigation expense insurance 소송비용보험
litigation officer 소송담당관
litigious right 계쟁권
little 소액투자가
living 생계
living cost 생계비
living trust 생전신탁
Lloyd's broker 로이드중개인
Lloyd's survey report 로이드검사인 보고서
Lloyd's surveyor 로이드검사인
Lloyd's underwriter 로이드보험자
load 판매수수료
load up 가득 채워 넣다
loading 부가보험료
loading charges 적재비용
loading for expense 경비부가보험료
loading profit 비용차익
loading surplus 부가익
loan 융자
loan account 대부계정
loan agreement 금전대차계약
loan application 융자신청
loan association 금융조합
loan business on real property 부동산대부업
loan capital 차입자본
loan claims 론채권
loan extension 차관공여
loan for carrying unsold inventory 체화융자
loan for consumption 소비론
loan for education 교육론
loan for exchange 교환대차
loan from banks 은행차입
loan insurance 대부금보험
loan interest rate 대출이율
loan ledger 대부원장

loan limit 융자한도
loan loss 대손금
loan of subscription payment funds
　불입융자대부
loan on bill 어음대부
loan on deeds 증서대부
loan on personal guarantee 보증대출
loan on real property 부동산대부
loan on security 담보대출
loan participation 대부지분참가
loan payable 차입금
loan rate 대출금리
loan receivable in securities 대부유가증권
loan received 차관수령
loan restrictions 융자규제
loan sales 론채권매매
loan secured by deposit 예금담보대부
loan secured by government bonds corporate
　debentures 공사채담보대부
loan secured by real estate 부동산저당대부금
loan secured by securities
　유가증권담보대부금
loan shark 고리대
loan society 금융조합
loan spread 론스프레드
loan stock 대금주
loan subparticipation 대출채권분매
loan to affiliated companies 계열융자
loan to financial institutions 금융기관대부금
loan to subsidiary 자회사대부금
loan transaction 대차거래
loan trust 대부신탁
loan value 대부한도
loan value method 대부가치법
loan with third party's guarantee 보증부 대부
loan without interest 무이자대부
loan-deposit ratio 예금대출율
loanable fund 대부자금
loanable funds theory 대출자금이론
loanable resources 대출자금
loanable value 담보

loans and bills discounted 대출금
loans and bills discounted accounts
　대출금계정
loans and discounts by industry
　업종별 대출통계
lobbying 원외운동
lobbying contract 원외계약
lobster trap 랍스터트랩
local 지방
local allocation tax 지방분여세
local area network 기업내 고속정보통신망
local authorities 지방자치체
local autonomy 지방자치
local bond 지방채
local competition 지역경쟁
local content 로컬컨텐트
local content ratio 현지조달율
local court 지방법원
local credit 로컬크레디트
local currency 현지통화
local custom 지방의 관습
local expenditure 지방비
local finance bureau 재무국
local government 지방자치체
local government bond 지방채
local grant tax 지방교부세
local law 지역법
local media 지방광고매체
local national 로컬내셔널
local production factory 현지생산공장
local public entity 지방자치체
local public finance 지방재정
local road tax 지방도로세
local stock exchange 지방증권거래소
local tax 지방세
local transfer tax 지방양여세
local transport expenses 교통비
locals 로컬즈
location 소재지
location clause 집적손해제한약관
location of industry 산업입지

K
L

location of loss or damage 손실발생지
location policy 입지정책
lock-in 확정
lock-up option 록업옵션
lock-up period 록업기간
locked market 동결시장
loco price 현장인도가격
locomotive theory 기관차 이론
locus sigilli 날인개소
logarithmic calculation 대수계산
logarithmic spiral 등각나선, 로그스파이럴
logistic function 로지스틱함수
lognormal distribution 대수정규분포
lollipop tactic 롤리폽 전술
Lombard Street 롬바르드가
London clearing banks
　런던어음교환소가맹은행
London Club 런던클럽
London Depositary Receipts 런던예탁증서
London Inter-bank Bid Rate
　런던은행 수취레이트
London Inter-Bank Offered Rate
　런던은행 수취금리
London refinance 런던리파이낸스
long 강세
long account 매매계약을 하였으나 아직 결제
　하지 않은 주식이나 상품
long and medium-term interest rate
　장중기금리
long butterfly spread transaction
　롱버터플라이스프레드거래
long calendar spread transaction
　롱캘린더스프레드거래
long call 롱콜
long condor 롱콘더
long coupon 롱쿠폰
long exchange 장기환
long hedge 매입헤지
long hedging 매입헤징
long position 매입보유
long position risk 매입보유리스크

long put 롱풋
long service allowance 근속수당
long-term postponement of credit
　채권을 뒤로 미룸
long treasury bond 미국재무부 장기채권
long waves 장기파동
long-dated bill 장기어음
long-dated forwards 장기선도거래
long-form report 장문식 보고서
long-run equilibrium 장기균형
long-term accounts payable in foreign
　currency 장기외화유통채무
long-term accounts receivable foreign
　currency 장기외화유통채권
long-term bill 장기어음
long-term bond 장기채
long-term borrowing 장기차입금
long-term business 장기사업
long-term buying 장기구입
long-term capital 장기자본
long-term capital balance 장기자본수지
long-term capital gains 장기양도소득
long-term capital transaction 장기자본거래
long-term comprehensive insurance
　장기종합보험
long-term contract 장기청부공사
long-term credit 장기신용
long-term debt 장기채무
long-term debt assumed 장기채무증가
long-term finance 장기금융
long-term forward exchange agreement
　장기환예약
long-term fund 장기자금
long-term government bond 장기국채
long-term interest rate 장기금리
long-term investment 장기투자
long-term loan payable 장기차입금
long-term loan receivable 장기대부금
long-term money market 장기금융시장
long-term national bond of England
　영국장기국채

long-term prime rate 장기프라임레이트
long-term solvency 장기지불능력
long-term suspended claims 장기연기채권
long-term wage agreement 장기임금협정
long term lease 장기임대차계약
long term yield 장기이율
look-back option 룩백옵션
loop 루프
loose leaf book 루즈리프식 장부
lord chief justice 수석판사
Lorenz curve 로렌츠곡선
losers game 패자의 게임
loss 손실
loss adjustment 손해사정
loss and gain 손익
loss and gain account 손익계정
loss and gain statement 손익계산서
loss carryback 이연손실
loss cut 손해를 피해 철수하다
loss due to spoiled work 손해비용
loss expense 손해조사비
loss experience 손해경험
loss factor 손해팩터
loss for the current term 당기손실금
loss frequency 손해발생률
loss from bad debts 대손손실
loss from capital reduction 감자차손
loss from putting on reserve for deferred
    income tax 압축준비금편입손
loss function 손실함수
loss leader 특가품(싸게 파는)
loss making operations 적자경영
loss of income benefit 소득상실급부
loss of productivity claims 생산성상실클레임
loss of profits insurance 이익보험
loss of work 작업손실
loss on assets 자산손실
loss on foreign exchange 외국환차손
loss on property abandoned 자산폐기손
loss on property destroyed 자산상실비
loss on property revaluation 자산평가손

loss on retirement of fixed assets 제거손실
loss on sale of fixed assets 고정자산매각손
loss on sale of real estate 부동산매각손
loss on securities 유가증권매각손
loss payable clause 제삼자지불약관
loss portfolio 로스포트폴리오
loss ratio 손해율
loss reserve 손실준비금
loss retention 보유손해액
loss statistics 손해통계
loss-making division 불채산부문
losses ejusdem generis
    동종위험으로 인한 손해
losses on insurance claims 보험금차손
lost card 분실카드
lost instrument bond 분실증권보증증권
lot 거래고
lot consolidation 단주정리
lot sampling 로트샘플링
lot-money 경매수수료
lottingout 분양
Louvre accord 루브르합의
low capital intensive industry
    자본집약성이 낮은 산업
low context 저맥락
low earth orbit 저고도궤도
low earth orbit communication 저궤도통신망
low grade stocks 저위주
low growth 저성장
low income countries 저소득국
low input sustainable 저투입지속형의
low interest loan 저금리론
low price 싼값
low risk stocks 안전성이 높은 주식
low-cost strategy 저비용전략
low-dividend stock 저배주
low-involvement purchases
    적게 관여하는 형태의 구매
low-par issue 저액면주식
lower closing quotation 저고정가격
lower end of the market 저가격시장

K
L

lower in quotation 저가격
lower limit rate 하한상장
lower price 하한상장
lower order goods 저가재
lower-of-cost-or-market method 저가법
lower-priced stock 저위주
lowering of interest rate 금리인하
lowest taxable limit 과세최저한
loyalty rebate 특약리베이트
lucrative capital 영리자본
luminance 휘도

luminance signal 휘도신호
lump-sum contract 정액청부계약
lump-sum freight 총괄운임
lump-sum payment 일괄지불
lump-sum payment of dividends at maturity
　수익만기지불
lump-sum pension 일시불연금
lump-sum purchase 일괄구입
lump-sum settlement 보험금일괄지불
luxury tax 사치세
lying down 계약이행거절

M2+CD Statistics M2+CD 통계
Maastricht Treaty 마스트리히트조약
machine bookkeeping 기계부기
machine plate 인쇄판
machine tool 기계공구
machine-hour rate 기계시간율
machine-hour rate method
　기계시간율 배부법
machinery 기계
machinery and equipment 기계장치
machinery and tool 기기
machinery insurance 기계보험
macroeconomic 거시경제적
macroeconomic factor 매크로경제요인
macroeconomic model 매크로경제모델
macrofunction 매크로기능
macrohedge 매크로헤지
macroview 대세관
magistrate 하급판사
magnet optical disk 광자기디스크
magnet store 핵점포
mail confirmation 메일컨퍼메이션
mail credit 메일크레디트
mail credit facility 메일크레디트퍼실리티
mail days 우편일수
mail exchange bill 문서환
mail transfer 보통발송송금; 우편환
mail transfer payable 송금환
mail-order 통신판매
mail-order loan 메일론
mailing cost 우송료

main account 주요계정
main books 주요장부
main budget 본예산
main customer 주요거래
main income earner 주소득자
main materials 주요원재료
main office 주사무소; 본사
maintainability 보전성
maintained markup 판매가와 원가의 차액
maintenance 유지
maintenance and repairs 수선비
maintenance bond 하자보수보증증권
maintenance call 추가증거금
maintenance clause 부양약관
maintenance cost 유지비
maintenance department 보수과
maintenance expense 유지비; 계약유지비
maintenance fee 관리비
maintenance funds 유지자금
maintenance lease 메인터넌스리스
maintenance margins 유지증거금
maintenance of books and records
　장부서류를 정리하고 보존함
maintenance of capital 자본유지
maintenance of competence 능력유지
maintenance of financial capital
　화폐자본유지
maintenance of membership 조합원자격유지
maintenance of physical capital
　실제자본유지
maintenance reserve 유지준비금

major 큰; 주요한
major bottom 기초; 토대
major casualties 주요사고
major cycles 주순환
major economic power 경제대국
major hospitalization insurance
　고액입원비보험
Major Import Agreement
　주요수입화물요율협정
major industry 주요산업
major market index 메이저마켓지수
major medical expense insurance
　고액의료비보험
major move 메이저무브
major multinational grain firms 곡물메이저
major order 대량수주
major peak 메이저피크
major product 주제품
major raw materials 주요한 원재료
major relationship bank 주력은행
major stockholders 주요주주
major trend 주요트렌드
majority 다수
majority control 과반수지배
majority-owned subsidiary
　과반수소유종속회사
make a downward revision 하향수정하다
make good 배상하다
make two-sided markets 양방향가격결정
make up 메이크업
make-ready time 준비시간
make-up 구성
maker 작성자
making up of a deficit 적자보전
mala fides 악의
malefactor 유죄가 확정된 자
malice 범죄의사
malicious 악의적인 행위
malicious arrest 부당체포
malicious damage clause
　악의적인 손해담보약관

malign neglect 해로운 태만
malpractice 의료과실; 부당행위
malpractice coverage 과실담보
malpractice insurance 전문직과실책임보험
malversation 배임; 유용
man-power development 능력개발
man-to-man system 대인비교법
managed crawling peg 크롤링페그를 관리함
managed currency 관리통화
managed currency system 관리통화제도
managed floating rate system 관리플로트
managed fund 합동운용펀드
managed liabilities 관리채무
managed price 관리가격
managed trade 관리무역
management 관리자
management accounting 관리회계
management agreement 경영위탁계약
management area 관리영역
management audit 경영감사
management business of investment trust
　투자신탁위탁업무
management buyout 매니지먼트바이아웃
management by objective 목표관리
management capacity 관리능력
management company 투자신탁위탁
management concept 경영이념
management consultant 경영컨설턴트
management consulting 기업진단
management contract 매니지먼트계약
management cycle 매너지먼트사이클
management effect 관리효과
management fee 간사수수료
management function 관리직능
management group 인수간사단
management hierarchy 관리계층
management information system
　경영정보시스템
management labor relations 노사관계
management of collateral 담보관리
management of indirect cost 간접부문합리화

management of juristic act 법무처리
management of property 재무처리
management of supply 공급관리
management participation 경영참가
management participation right 경영참가권
management philosophy 경영이념
management plan 경영계획
management principles 관리원칙
management resources 경영자원
management responsibility 경영자책임
management review 경영감사
management service for bill for collection
　수금어음관리서비스
management simulation
　매너지먼트 시뮬레이션
management strategy 경영전략
management supervisor 감독관
management through figures 계수관리
management tool 관리수단
management grid 관리자그리드
manager 간사
manager's contribution 매니저의 기여도
manager-client relations
　투자관리자와 고객의 관계
managerial resources 경영자원
managers 간사단
managing bank 간사은행
managing committee 경영위원회
managing underwriter 간사증권
mandate 명령
mandate on remission 환송명령
mandatory 위임통치국
mandatory clause 필수조건
mandatory control 법적규제
mandatory injunction 강제금지명령
mandatory redemption 강제상환
mandatory securities valuation reserve
　법정유가증권평가준비금
mandatory sinking fund requirement
　강제적인 감책기금조항
mandatory valuation reserve

　법정평가손적립금
manifest 적재목록
manifesto 선언
manipulation 조작
manipulation of stock price 주가조작
manipulation of the market 가격조작
manner of amortization 상각방법
manpower accounting 인적회계
manpower plan 인원계획
manual manipulator 매뉴얼매니퓰레이터
manufacture order 제조지도서
manufactured goods 제품
manufactured imports 제품수입
manufacturer's risks 제조자리스크
manufacturing accounting 공업회계
manufacturing bookkeeping 공업부기
manufacturing burden 제조간접비
manufacturing cost accounting 제조원가계산
manufacturing department 제조부문
manufacturing expenses 제조경비
manufacturing expenses budget
　제조간접비예산
manufacturing expenses ledger
　제조간접비원장
manufacturing license 제조허가
manufacturing process 제조공정
manufacturing statement 제조원가보고서
manufacturing taxation 제조과세
manufacturing-retailer alliance 제판동맹
margin 위탁증거금; 차금; 중간이윤
margin account 증거금계정; 신용거래구좌
margin buying 신용구입
margin call 추가증거금
margin collateral margin debt 증거금부채
margin deficiency 증거금부족
margin money 유지증거금
margin money system 증거금제도
margin of safety 안전여력
margin of solvency 지불여력
margin on commodity futures
　상품선물거래의 증거금

margin rate 증거금율
margin ratios 이익률
margin required method 필요증거금법
margin requirements 위탁보증금율
margin trading 신용거래
margin transaction 증거금거래
marginal analysis 한계분석
marginal balance 한계이익
marginal capital coefficient 한계자본계수
marginal capital expenditure 한계자본지출
marginal clauses 난외약관
marginal condition 한계조건
marginal cost 한계비용
marginal cost curve 한계비용곡선
marginal cost of production 한계생산비
marginal costing 한계원가계산
marginal credit 한계신용
marginal deduction system 한계공제제도
marginal effect 한계효과
marginal efficiency 한계효율
marginal factor 한계요소
marginal income statement 한계손익계산
marginal loan-deposit ratio 한계예대율
marginal net suitability 한계순적합도
marginal principle 한계원리
marginal production 한계생산
marginal productivity 한계생산성
marginal profit 한계이익
marginal profit ratio 한계이익률
marginal propensity to consume
   한계소비성향
marginal propensity to import 한계수입성향
marginal propensity to save 한계저축성향
marginal rate of return 한계수익률
marginal ratio 한계비율
marginal returns 한계수익
marginal revenue 한계수입
marginal rise 미미하게 늘어남
marginal seal 난외에 찍어두는 도장
marginal tax rate 한계세율
marginal theory 한계이론

marginal unit cost 한계단위원가
marginal utility 한계효용
marginal value 한계가치
marginal value curve 한계가치곡선
margins of solvency 지불여력
marine adventure 항해사업
marine and transport insurance
   해상 및 운송보험
marine cargo insurance 화물해상보험
marine cargo policy 화물해상보험증권
marine casualty 해난
marine clause 해상보험조항
marine hull insurance 선박해상보험
marine insurance 해상보험
marine insurance account 해상보험계정
marine insurance 해상보험증권
marine perils 해상위험
marine protest 해난보고서
marine surveyor 해사검사인
marine transportation 해운
mariner 선원
maritime 해사의
maritime association 해사협회
maritime belt 영해
maritime court 해사재판소
maritime hypothecation 해사저당
maritime law 해사법
maritime lien 해사선취특권
maritime perils 해상위험
maritime traffic 해운
mark bond 마크채
mark down 가격인하
mark to market 마크투마켓
mark to the market 시가평가
mark up 이익을 더하다, 가격을 인상하다
mark-on required 필요가산이익
marked cheques 기호수표
market 시장; 상장
market analysis 시장분석
market area 시장지역
market basket contract 마켓바스켓방식

market basket trading 바스켓거래
market beta 시장베타
market capitalization 시가총액
market claim 시장클레임
market conduct 시장행동
market control 시장지배
market crash 상장의 하락
market creating effect 시장창조효과
market cycle 시장의 주기
market demand 시장수요
market demand curve 시장수요곡선
market demand function 시장수요함수
market development 시장개발
market dynamics 시장역학
market economy 시장경제
market economy model 시장경제모델
market efficiency 시장의 효율성
market equilibrium 시장균형
market equilibrium curve 시장균형곡선
market expansion effect 시장확장효과
market expectation 시장예측
market extinction 시장삭감
market failure 시장의 실패
market hours 입회시간
market impact 시장에 대한 영향
market index 시장지수
market information center 시황정보센터
market interest rate 시중금리
market leaders 시장의 주도주
market maker 마켓메이커
market making condition 마켓메이킹 상황
market making function 마켓메이킹 기능
market manipulation 상장조종
market maturity 시장성숙
market mechanism 시장기구
market method 시가법
market milking 시장을 조종함
market momentum 시장의 힘
market multiple 시장배율
market niche strategy 마켓니치전략
market on close 종가지정주문

market opening 시장개방
market order without limit 성행주문
market out clause 마켓아웃조항
market overt 공개시장
market overview 시장개황
market penetration 시장침투
market portfolio 시장포트폴리오
market potential 시장잠재력
market prediction 시장예측
market price 시장가격
market price basis 시가주의
market price of risk 리스크의 시장가격
market price of stock 주가
market principle 시장원리
market psychology 시장심리
market quotation 시장분위기
market rate 시장상장; 실세레이트
market rate of interest 시장이자율
market recovery 시장회복
market report 시장보고
market research 시장조사
market rhythm 시장의 기조
market risk 가격리스크; 시장리스크
market sector 시장 섹터
market segment 시장구분
market segmentation 마켓세그멘테이션
market sensitivity 시장감응도
market sentiment 시장센티멘트
market share 시장점유율
market stabilization 시장안정조작
market standing 시장내의 지위
market structure 시장구조
market survey 시장조사
market timing 마켓타이밍
market timing assessment
　　시장타이밍을 평가함
market transaction 거래
market valuation 시장평가
market value 시장가격
market value basis 시가주의
market value clause 시장가액약관

market value method 시가법
market value of inventory 재고자산의 시가
market value weighted index
　시장가격가중평균지수
market yield 시장이율
market-if-touched order 마켓이프터치드오더
market-on-close order 마켓온클로즈오더
market-oriented 시장지향형
marketability 시장성
marketable debt securities
　시장성이 있는 채권
marketable securities 시장성증권
marketable title 매매에 적합한 권리
marketing 마케팅
marketing agreement 판매협정
marketing channel 판매경로
marketing channel selection 마케팅경로선정
marketing control 마케팅통제
marketing control system 마케팅통제시스템
marketing cost 판매비
marketing cost accounting 마케팅원가계산
marketing cost analysis 마케팅원가분석
marketing decision 마케팅결정
marketing decision support system
　마케팅의사결정지원시스템
marketing decision variable 마케팅결정변수
marketing environment 마케팅환경
marketing expense 마케팅비
marketing force 마케팅요인
marketing function 마케팅기능
marketing intermediary 마케팅중개업자
marketing monopoly 마케팅독점
marketing opportunity 마케팅기회
marketing organization 마케팅조직
marketing performance 마케팅성과
marketing phenomena 마케팅현상
marketing practices 마케팅관행
marketing relativism 마케팅상대주의
marketing research company 시장조사회사
marketing research control 시장조사계약
marketing risk 마케팅위험

marketing stimuli 마케팅자극
marketing structure 마케팅구조
marketing tactics 마케팅전술
marketing theory 마케팅이론
markup cancellation 가산이익정정
markup pricing 가산이익에 따른 가격결정
markup reduction planning 가격인하계획
marry 매리
marrying transaction of securities company
　증권매리
marshal 집행관
marshaling assets 재산의 우선순위를 결정함
marshaling securities
　담보권행사의 우선순위를 결정함
Marshall curve 마샬곡선
Marshallian demand curve 마샬수요곡선
masking 매스킹
mass consumption society 대중소비사회
mass culture 대중문화
mass distribution 대량유통
mass media 매스미디어
mass merchandiser 매스머천다이즈
mass merchandising strategy
　매스머천다이징 전략
mass production 대량생산
mass risks 대중리스크
mass sales 대량추천판매
mass society 대중사회
mass transportation 대량수송
master letter of credit 원신용장
master plan 기본계획
master policy 일괄증권
match 일치시키다
match making 균형
matched book 매매일치
matched maturities 기간일치
matched order 담합매매
matching 대응
matching costs and revenues
　비용과 수익의 대응
matching ratio 조회적합률

matching swap 대응스와프
matching transaction 매칭거래
mate's receipt 본선인수증
material 원료
material allegation 중요한 주장
material alternation 중요한 변수
material control 재료관리
material cost 재료비
material cost budget 재료예산
material damage 물적손해
material evidence 중요한 증거
material fact 중요사실
material for repair 수리용 재료
material in process 중도재료비
material misrepresentation 중대한 부실표현
material price variance 재료 가격 차이
material quantity variance 재료 수량 차이
material requirement program
    자재소요량계획
material variance 실질적인 차이
materiality 중요성
materiality principle 중요성 원칙
materials budget 재료예산
materials department 자재부
materials distribution sheet 재료분개장
materials for investigation 조사자료
materials in storage 저장원재료
materials inventory 재료재고
materials ledger 재료원장
materials on hand 소유자재
materials price standard 재료표준가격
materials purchased 재료구입고
materials purchased report 원재료구입보고서
materials received report 원재료인수보고서
materials requirements planning
    자재요구계획
materials returned report 원재료반환표
materials specification 재료사양서
materials usage curve 자재사용곡선
materials variance 재료비차액
maternity benefit 출산급부

maternity insurance 임신출산보험
mathematical economics 수리경제학
mathematical expectation
    산술적인 기대수치
mathematical model 수학모델
mathematical program 수리계획법
mathematical reserve 수리적인 책임준비금
mathematical statistics 수리통계
matrimonial domicile 혼인상의 주소
matrimony 혼인상태
matrix 매트릭스
matrix algebra 매트릭스대수
matrix multiplier 행렬승수
matrix organization 매트릭스조직
matter 기초사실
matter in deed 증서사항
matter in issue 쟁점사항
matter of record 기록사항
mature 기한이 오다
mature company 성숙기업
mature economy 성숙경제
mature phase 성숙단계
mature plans 성숙한 플랜
mature product strategy 성숙제품전략
matured bill 만기어음
matured bond 만기채권
matured liability 만기채무
maturing liability 만기가 된 채무
maturity 만기
maturity basis 만기일기준
maturity date 반제일
maturity distribution range 만기분포의 차이
maturity gap exposure
    운용과 조달 사이의 기간 차이
maturity list 만기일표
maturity repayment 만기반려금
maturity stripping 매츄리티스트리핑
maturity structure 만기일구성
maturity value 상환가액
maturity-designated time deposit
    기일지정정기예금

maultichannel access radio system MCA 무선
maverick risk 이단자리스크
maximal collateral 근저당
maximin criterion 최대최소척도
maximization 최대화
maxims 법률 격언
maximum and minimum tariff system
　최고최저세율제
maximum demand 최대수요
maximum effort plan 최대세력계획
maximum inventory 최대재고량
maximum limit for interest rate
　이자부 최고한도
maximum limit of fluctuation 스톱치
maximum limit of overdraft 대출초과한도액
maximum limit system 최고발행액제한제도
maximum loan value 대출한도액
maximum operating stock 최대운전재고량
maximum possible loss 발생가능최고손해액
maximum price change limit 가격변동폭제한
maximum probable loss 최고손해액
maximum retention 최고보유액
maximum special depreciation allowance
　특별상각한도액
maxmil rate 맥시밀레이트
mayhem 신체상해
mean absolute deviation 평균절대편차
mean absolute error 평균절대오차
mean curve 평균곡선
mean deviation 평균편차
mean difference 평균차
mean price 중간값
mean reversion 평균회귀
mean reverting 평균재귀
mean reverting process 평균회귀과정
mean squared error 평균제곱오차
mean sum insured 평균보험금액
mean test 수입조사
mean time between failures 평균고장간격
mean time to repair 평균수복시간
mean value 중간치

means for hedging 헤지수단
means of foreign payment 대외지불수단
measure for monetary ease 금융완화조치
measure of association 속성상관
measure of central tendency 대표치
measure of dispersion 분산도
measure of indemnity 손해보전한도
measure of investment 투자척도
measure of productivity 생산성측정
measure of return 수익률측정
measure of risk 리스크측정
measure of value 태도측정
measurement contract 측정계약
measurement control 측정관리
measurement of attitude 유효성
measurement of effectiveness 유효성 측정
measuring effectiveness 계측 유효성
measuring results 계측결과
mecena 메세나; 기업후원
mechanical efficiency 기계효율
mechanical recorder method
　기계장치기록방식
mechanical trading 기계화거래
mechanism 기구
mechanization method 기계화방식
mechanized accounting 기계화회계
mechatronics 메카트로닉스
media 매체; 미디어
media advertising 매체광고
media control 매체지배
media decision 매체의 결정
media effect 매체효과
media mix 매체믹스
media selection model 미디어선택모델
median 중앙치
mediate descent 간접상속
mediate powers 부수권한
Medicaid 영방의료부조제도
medical assistance 의료보조금
medical certificate 의사진단서
medical corporation 의료법인

medical credit 의료비공제

medical examination 진사(생명보험을 계약할 때 피보험인의 건강상태를 조사함)

medical expense insurance 의료비보험

medical expenses 의료비

medical expenses deduction 의료비공제

medical jurisprudence 법의학

medical malpractice 의료과실

medical payment coverage 의료비담보

medical payments insurance 의료비지불보험

medical professional liability
　의료손해배상책임

medical selection 의학적인 선택

medical treatment clause 의료신고약관

medical underwriting 의료사정

medicalinsurance 유진사(有診査)보험

medico-actuarial science 의료수리학

medium of capital transfer 자본이전수단

medium-term government bond fund
　중기국채펀드

medium-term bond 중기채

medium-term fixed rate government bond
　중기이자부국채

medium-term government bond fund
　중국펀드

medium-term loan 중기대부

medium-term note 미디엄텀노트

medium-term outlook 중기전망

meeting of bond-holders 사채권자집회

meeting of promoters 발기인회

meeting of representative holders
　사원총대회

meeting of shareholders 주주총회

mega byte 메가바이트

mega transport network
　메가트랜스포트네트워크

megamarketing 메가마케팅

megaselling 메가셀링

melon cutting 고액배당

member bank 가맹은행

member bank of the Second Association of

Regional Banks 제2 지방은행

member banks of the clearing house
　어음교환소가맹은행

member firm 회원회사

member organization 회원회사

member's fee 거래소회비

member's store 가맹점

member's voluntary winding-up
　주주에 의한 임의청산

membership 가맹권

membership business 회원비즈니스

membership fee 회비

membership group 소속단체

membership in the capacity of a corporation
　회사명의의 회원

memorandum
　협정서; (조합의)규약; 정관(회사의)

memorandum decision 메모랜덤디시전

memorandum for offering 모집요강

memorandum goods 시매품

memorandum of alteration
　특허에 대한 일부포기각서

memorandum of association 기본정관

memorandum of balance sheet audit
　대차대조표감사의 각서

memorandum of protest 거절증서

memorandum price 비방가액

memorandum value 비망가격

memorandum-check 제시하지 않는 특약수표

memorial dividend 기념배당

memory 기억

mens legislatoris 입법취지

menu approach 메뉴어프로치

mercantile agency 상사대리

mercantile block insurance
　판매업자일괄보험

mercantile credit 기업간신용

mercantile law 상업법

mercantile paper 상업어음

mercantile partnership 상업조합

mercantile risk 상품위험

M N

merchandise 상품
merchandise account 상품계정
merchandise assortment 상품구비
merchandise book 상품매매장
merchandise bookkeeping 상업부기
merchandise budget 상품예산
merchandise certificate account 상품권계정
merchandise control 상품관리
merchandise cost 상품원가
merchandise in transit 미달상품
merchandise inventory 상품재고; 재고상품
merchandise knowledge 상품지식
merchandise ledger 상품원장
merchandise loss 상품로스
merchandise management 상품관리
merchandise mart 머천다이즈마트
merchandise of approval floater
　　사용상품포괄보험
merchandise procurement cost 상품조달원가
merchandise resources 구입처
merchandise turnover ratio 상품회전율
merchandiser 머천다이저
merchandising 머천다이징
merchant bank 머천트뱅크
merchant banker 투자은행가
merchant fee 가맹점수수료
merchant guild 상인길드
merchant insurance 상인보험
merchant law 상업법
merchant protective bond 상인보호보증증권
merchantable 시장성이 있는
mere jus 점유를 수반하지 않는 권리
merely nominal persons 단순명의인
merger 합병; 혼동
merger and acquisition 합병; 매수
merger of guaranty
　　보증계약을 혼동하여 소멸함
merger terms 합병조건
merit goods 가치재(價値財)
merit increase 성공보수
merit rating 보장요율제

merits 실체
mesne 중간의
message area 단위통화구역
message channel 메시지경로
message effect 메시지효과
messenger floater 메시지포괄보험
meta-communication 메타커뮤니케이션
metamarketing 메타마케팅
meta-need 메타요구
metalized lithography 금속평판
metes and bounds 토지경계
method 수법
method of bonus allocation 계약자배당방식
method of comparative analysis 비교분석법
method of fixed percentage on cost 정율법
method of policy dividend allocation
　　계약자배당방식
method of price of last purchase
　　최종구입원가법
methodical approach 계통적인 어프로치
methodology 방법론
metromarket 수도권시장
metropolitan 수도의
metropolitan inhabitant tax 도민세
mezzanine bond 열후사채
mezzanine bracket 메자닌브라켓
mezzanine debt 메자닌채무
mezzanine finance 메자닌파이낸스
mezzanine money 전환사채
microanalysis 마이크로분석
microbehavioral sales model
　　마이크로행동적인 판매모델
microcomponent sales model
　　마이크로구성요소 판매모델
microhedge 마이크로헤지
mid-term cancellation 중도해약
middle class 중간층
middle rate 중간수치
middle-sized stock 중견주
middleman 중간업자
military government 군정

military jurisdiction courts 군사법원
milline rate 밀라인레이트
million instruction per second
  밉스; MIPS(컴퓨터의 연산속도)
Milne's table 밀룬의 생명표
mind share 마인드쉐어
mine 광산
mineral product tax 광산세
mineral properties mining right 광업권
mini. max. bond 미니맥스채
mini-refunding 미니리펀딩
minimil rate 미니밀레이트
minimum age requirement 최저수급연령
minimum capital system 최저자본금제도
minimum cost principle 최소비용원칙
minimum cost rule 원가비교법
minimum denomination on which interest is
  calculated 이자 단위
minimum exempt income 최저면세소득
minimum fluctuation unit 최소변동단위
minimum freight 최저운임
minimum funding standard 최저적립기준
minimum inventory 최저재고
minimum lease payment 최저리스지불액
minimum lending rate 최저대출비율
minimum liability 최소부채
minimum liquidity ratio 최저유동성비율
minimum margin 최저이폭
minimum margin requirement 최저증거금율
minimum marginal cost 최소한계비용
minimum payment 최저지불액
minimum premium 최저보험료
minimum profit 최소이윤
minimum quantity 최저주문량
minimum rate 최저요율
minimum rate of interest 최저이율
minimum sacrifice 최저의 희생
minimum service requirement 최저의무기간
minimum stock 최저재고
minimum surplus 자본의 최저한도
minimum tax 최저과세

minimum value 최소치
minimum wage 최저임금
minimum wage system 최저임금제도
mining accounting 광업회계
mining concession 채굴권
mining lease 광업임차권
mining license 광업권
mining location 광업권취득
mining partnership 광업조합
mining property 광업자산
mining rights 채굴권
mining royalty 광구사용료
mining tax 광업세
ministerial ordinance 부령(部令)
ministerial power 사무권한
minor 미성년자
minor account 미성년자의 거래계좌
minor cycle 소순환
minor loss 소손해
minor rally 본래 상태로 조금 되돌아감
minor service 이류서비스
minor tax credit 미성년자공제
minority control 소수지배
minority group 소수파집단
minority interest 소수주주지분
minority representation 소수대표법
minority shareholders 소수주주
minority shareholders' right 소수주주권
mint par of exchange 법정평가
mint price 주조가격
minus factor 마이너스요인
minus growth 마이너스성장
minus tick 마이너스틱
minus-ceiling 마이너스실링
minute book 소송기록서
minutes 의사록
misappropriation 착복
misappropriation of funds 부당지출
misappropriation of goods 물품횡령
misbranding 부당표시
miscalculation 계산착오**

M
N

miscellaneous accounts payable 여러 미불금
miscellaneous accounts 여러 미수금
miscellaneous assets 잡자산
miscellaneous bond 잡종보증증권
miscellaneous expenses 잡비
miscellaneous gains 잡익
miscellaneous income 잡소득
miscellaneous local taxes 잡종세
miscellaneous losses 잡손
miscellaneous movable articles floater
　　각종 동산포괄보험
miscellaneous receipts 잡수입
miscellaneous revenue 잡수익
misconduct 위반행위
misdemeanor 경죄
misery index 경제불쾌지수
misfeasance 불법행위
misfit return 부적합리터닝
misfit risk 부적합리스크
misfit-portfolio 부적합포트폴리오
mismatch between assets and liabilities
　　자산과 부채의 미스매치
mismatch risk 미스매치리스크
mismatching 미스매칭
misnomer 성명오기
mispricing 미스프라이싱
misprision 오기
misredemption 오상환
misrepresentation 부실표시
missing the market 시장상실
mission 사명
mistake 착오
mistake of fact 사실착오
mistake of law 법률착오
mitigation 경감
mitigation of damage 손해경감
mixed 혼성의; 엇갈린
mixed account 혼합계정
mixed action 혼합소송
mixed assets 혼합자산
mixed contract 혼합계약

mixed economy 혼합경제
mixed gift 혼합증여
mixed insurance 혼합보험
mixed inventory 혼합재고정리
mixed nuisance 혼합불법방해
mixed policy 혼합보험
mixed property 혼합재산
mixed question of law and fact
　　법률과 사실이 혼재된 문제
mixed quota-surplus reinsurance
　　비례·초과액혼합재보험
mixed reserve 혼합준비금
mixed surplus 혼합잉여금
mixed transaction 혼합거래
mixed trust 미스트러스트
mixed undertaking 공사(公私)혼합기업
mixed variance 혼합차이
mobile franchise 이동형 프랜차이즈
mobile shop 이동점포
mobility barrier 이동장벽
mobilization 동원
mock auction 경매
modal shift 모달시프트
mode 최빈치, 최빈값
mode of transportation 수송방법
model analysis 모델분석
model of consumer behavior
　　소비자행동 모델
model of diffusion process 보급과정모델
model of response to price 가격반응모델
model safety-responsibility bill
　　사고방지책임모범법안
model stock plan 모델스톡계획
modem 모뎀
modern portfolio theory
　　현대 포트폴리오 이론
modern utility theory 근대 효용이론
modernization of smaller enterprise
　　중소기업의 근대화
modestly-priced 적당한 가격의
modification 수정

modified accelerated cost recovery system
수정가속상각법
modified all-inclusive theory 수정포괄주의
modified capitalism 수정자본주의
modified cash refund annuity
수정현금반환부 연금
modified duration 모디파이드듀레이션
modified endowment 수정양로보험계약
modified file and use system
수정요율계출사용제도
modified net premium 수정순보험료
modified pass-through securities
모디파이드패스스루증권
modified preliminary term reserve
수정초연정기식 책임준비금
modified prior approval system
수정요율사전승인제도
Modigliani-Miller theory
모딜리아나-밀러의 명제
modular fixtures 모듈러비품
moiety 일부
moment 모멘트
momentum oscillator 모멘텀오실레이터
monetarism 통화주의
monetary aggregate 통화총량
monetary agreement 통화협정
monetary analysis 화폐분석
monetary and financial policy 통화금융정책
monetary approach 모네터리어프로치
monetary assets 금융자산
monetary authority 통화당국
monetary control 통화관리
monetary crisis 통화위험
monetary ease 금융완화
monetary expansion 금융확대
monetary financial assets 통화성 금융자산
monetary growth 금융확대
monetary growth model 화폐성장모델
monetary illusion 화폐환상
monetary instability 통화불안
monetary interest rate 화폐이자율

monetary items 금전항목
monetary liabilities 금전채무
monetary management 통화관리
monetary policy 금융정책
monetary policy for easing 금융완화정책
monetary reform 통화개혁
monetary reserve 통화준비
monetary restraint policy 금융긴축정책
monetary stability 통화안정
monetary standard 본위제도
monetary standard policy 본위정책
monetary stringency
돈의 융통이 막힘; 자금이 딸림
monetary survey 모니터리서베이
monetary system 화폐제도
monetary target 모니터리타겟
monetary tightening 금융긴축
monetary transfer 모니터리트랜스퍼
monetary union 통화동맹
monetary unit 통화단위
monetization of government bonds
국채의 화폐화
money and securities broad form
금전유가증권종합보험증권
money appropriated 충당금
money at call 단기융자
money bill 금전법안
money borrowed for short-term 단기차입금
money broker 금전업자
money center bank 대형전국은행
money changer 환전상
money claim 금전채권
money demand 금전청구
money deposited 예금
money earmarked 충당금
money flow 자금순환
money flow analysis 머니플로분석
money flow table 머니플로표
money game 머니게임
money illusion 화폐환각
money in bank 예금

M
N

money in trust 위탁금
money income 현금수입
money judgment 금전판결
money laundering 자금세정
money lender 금융업자
money lending business 금전대부업
money manager 자산운용자
money market 단기금융시장
money market account 단기금융계정
money market broker 단기업자
money market certificate
　시장금리연동형 정기예금
money market conditions index
　금융시장정세지표
money market data 금융시장데이터
money market dealer 단자회사
money market deposit account
　단기금융시장예금계정
money market fund 단기금융상품투자신탁
money market index 단기금융시장지수
money market instrument 단기금융상품
money market intervention
　금융시장에 대한 개입
money market management 금융조절
money market preferred stock
　머니마켓우선주
money market rate 시중금리
money market securities 금융시장증권
money market unit trust
　머니 마켓 유닛 트러스트
money multiplier 통화승수
money of adieu 계약금
money of the world 세계화폐
money order 송금환
money orders and counterfeit paper currency
　coverage 소액우편환 및 위조지폐손해담보
money paid-in part 내금
money paid temporarily 일시금
money position 머니포지션
money purchase plan 보험료기준연금제도
money rate 금리

money received 입금
money spread 머니스프레드
money stock 통화스톡
money supply 통화공급량
money supply control 머니서플라이관리
money trust 금전신탁
money-flow tables 자금순환표
money-lending business 금전대부업
money-making 영리
money-veil theory 화폐베일이론
monitoring 감시
monitoring of delivery 인도감시
mono line 모노라인
mono-purpose credit card 단일목적 카드
monochronic 모노크로닉
monography 계산도표
monopolistic competition 독점적인 경쟁
monopoly 점유권
monopoly assessment 전매과세
monopoly 독점자본
monopoly price 독점가격
monopoly pricing 독점가격설정
monopoly profit 전매이익
monopsony 수요독점
monopurpose credit card 단일목적 카드
monorate of exchange system 단일환시장제
Monroe Doctrine 먼로주의
montage 몽타쥬
month order 먼스오더
month-end 월말
month-end average method
　이월평균단가불출법
month-end delivery 월말인도
monthly accounting 월말결산
monthly allotment of depreciable period 감
　가상각의 월할계산
monthly average method 월차총평균법
monthly balance sheet 월차대차대조표
monthly chart 매달 차트
monthly debit industry
　데빗 시스템 월불 간이보험

monthly debit ordinary
　데빗 시스템 월불 보통보험
monthly diminishing clause 월차체감약관
monthly income statement 월차손익계산서
monthly installment 월부
monthly installment sales 월부판매
monthly investment plan 월부투자계획
monthly payment 매월지불
monthly prorata fraction system
　월차비례배분방식
monthly prorata return premium
　월부반환보험료
monthly report 월보
monthly reversal 먼스리리버설
monthly statement 월차계산서
monthly statement of account 월계표
monthly trial balance 월차시산표
mook 무크
moral consideration 도덕상의 약인
moral hazard 도덕적 해이
moral obligation 자연채무
moral obligation bond
　도의적인 지불보증채권
moral risks 모랄리스크
moral suasion 도의적인 설득
moral turpitude 부도덕행위
morale survey 도의조사
moratorium 지불정지; 모라토리엄
moratorium period 지불유예기간
moratory interest 손해배상이자
more margin 증거금
more or less terms 수량과부족용인조건
morning session 전장(前場)
morphing 모핑
mortality 폐기물
mortality curve 사망률커브
mortality loss 사차손
mortality profit 사차익
mortality table 생명표
mortgage 저당권; 모기지
mortgage backed bond 모기지담보채권

mortgage backed securities 모기지증권
mortgage bank 저당은행
mortgage bond 물상담보부사채
mortgage bond coupon 모기지사채금리
mortgage clause 저당권설정약관
mortgage collateral 모기지담보형태
mortgage company 저당금융회사
mortgage credit 주택저당세액공제
Mortgage Credit Association 저당신용조합
mortgage credit bond 저당신용채
mortgage creditor 모기지권자
mortgage debenture 저당신용채
mortgage debentures trust law
　담보부 사채신탁법
mortgage debtor 저당권설정자
mortgage documents 저당증서류
mortgage guarantee insurance 저당증권보험
mortgage insurance 저당보험
mortgage investment trust 담보부 투자신탁
mortgage loan 저당론
mortgage of goods 동산모기지
mortgage of ship 선박저당권
mortgage pass-through certificate
　부동산저당패스스루증권
mortgage payable 저당차입금
mortgage pool 모기지풀
mortgage securities 저당증권
mortgage service 모기지관리
mortgageable chattels 저당이 될 수 있는 동산
mortgagee 저당권자
mortgagees' interest 담보이익
mortgages receivable 담보부 대부금
mortgagor 저당권설정자
mortgagor's completion bond 저당권설정자
　완성보증증권
mortuary bonus 사망시 배당
most deliverable bond 인도최적채권
most favored nation clause 최혜국조항
most favored nation treatment 최혜국대우
most favored reinsurer clause
　최혜재보험자약관

MN

most recent purchase method 최종구입원가법
most seriously affected countries
　최대피영향국
mother fund 마더펀드
motion 신청; 동의
motion day 신청심리일
motion for directed verdict
　지시평결을 신청함
motion for judgment 판결신청
motion for new trial 재심리신청
motion model 운동모델
motion study 동작연구
motion to strike out 삭제신청
motivating factor 동기부여인자
motivation 동기부여
motivation level 동기부여수준
motivation research 동기조사
motive 동기
motor hull insurance 자동차차량보험
motor insurance 자동차보험
motor third party insurance
　자동차배상책임보험
motor vehicle passenger insurance
　자동차승객보험
mounting 설치
movable and immovable assets account
　동산부동산계정
movable band 무버블밴드
movable property in trust 동산신탁
movables 동산
movables comprehensive insurance
　동산종합보험
move 제안하다
movement of funds 자금이동
movement of price 가격변동
moving average 이동평균
moving average convergence divergence
　trading method
　이동평균수속분산 트레이딩법
moving average cost method 이동평균법
moving average deviations 이동평균치

moving average index 이동평균지수
moving average method 이동평균법
moving average model 이동평균모델
moving averages 이동평균
moving downward 하강
Moving Picture Expert Group
　엠페그; MPEG (동화상압축방식)
moving weighted average method
　이동가중평균
multiattribute model 다속성모델
multibank holding company
　복수은행지주회사
multibrand strategy 복수브랜드전략
multichannel society 고도선택사회
multicurrency clause 통화선택권
multicurrency intervention 복수통화개입
multicurrency loan 멀티커런시론
multidivisional company
　여러 사업부를 소유한 기업
multidomestic 멀티도메스틱
multifactor model 복수요인모델
multilateral agreement 다국간협정
multilateral clearing agreement
　다각적 청산협정
Multilateral Investment Guarantee Agency
　다수국간투자보증기관
multilateral trade negotiations
　다각적 무역교섭
multilevel marketing system 멀티상법
multimedia 멀티미디어
multimedia personal computer
　멀티미디어컴퓨터
multinational corporation 다국적기업
multinational marketing 다국적 마케팅
multinationalim 다국적주의
multiperiod model 다기간모델
multiple answer 복수회답
multiple banking system 복수은행제도
multiple brand entries 복수브랜드참가
multiple channel 복합경로
multiple choice 다항목선택법

multiple correlation 다중상관

multiple decremental table 다중탈퇴잔존표

multiple evidence 다원적인 증거

multiple indemnity policy ~배(培) 보장 생명보험

multiple line 멀티플라인

multiple line agent
생명손해보험동시판매외무원

multiple line policy 멀티플라인보험증권

multiple location risk insurance
다수소재지물건보험

multiple management 복합경영

multiple maturity deposit 복수만기예금

multiple option funding facilities
멀티플옵션펀딩퍼실리티

multiple payment credit card 할부카드

multiple perils insurance for cinemas
영화관종합보험

multiple protection policy
~배(培) 보장 생명보험

multiple purpose bank account 종합계좌

multiple regression analysis 다중회귀분석

multiple step 구분식

multiple sub-nyquist sampling encoding
뮤즈방식

multiple tariff system 복합세제

multiple tax rate 복수세율

multiple-step form 다단계식

multiple-step income statement
구분손익계산서

multiple-step statement 복수구분계산서

multiplication rule 승법규칙

multiplicity of action 소송중복

multiplied effect 파급효과

multiplier analysis 승수분석

multiplier effect 승법효과

multiplier theory 승수이론

multisectoral analysis 다부문분석

multisourcing 멀티소싱

multitask 멀티태스크

multivariate analysis 다변량분석

multiwill 다수자유언

multiwindow 멀티윈도

municipal accounting 관청부기

municipal bond fund 지방공공단체채권펀드

municipal bonds 지방채

municipal by-laws 조례

municipal corporation 지방공공단체

municipal courts 시재판소

municipal futures 지방채선물

municipal inhabitants tax 시읍면세

municipal law 조례

municipal ordinance 시조례

municipal property tax 고정자산세

municipal securities dealer 공공채딜러

municipal tobacco tax 시읍면담배세

muniments 권리증

mute 침묵

mutilated check 훼손수표

mutual account 상호계산

mutual adjustment 상호조정

mutual agreement procedure 상호협의

mutual aid 공제

mutual aid contract for retirement allowance
퇴직금공제계약

mutual aid money 공제금

mutual aid organization for specific retirement
allowance 특정퇴직금공제단체

mutual aid premiums 공제부금

mutual aid system 공제금제도

mutual association 상호보험조합

mutual benefit association 공제조합

mutual benefit society 상호조합

mutual company 상호회사

mutual condition 상호조건

mutual covenant 상호날인계약

mutual credits 상호대차

mutual debt 상대채무

mutual fund 뮤츄얼펀드

mutual fund redemption value insurance
투자신탁상환가격보증보험

mutual fund underwriters
뮤츄얼펀드인수업자

M
N

mutual installment 상호부금
mutual insurance 상호보험
mutual insurance company 상호생명보험회사
mutual insurance society 상호보험조합
mutual offset system 상호결제제도
mutual pension 공제연금
mutual promise 상호약속
mutual reinforcement 상호보강효과
mutual savings bank 상호저축은행
mutual 상호유언
mutual-type associations
　상호주의 성격의 보험단체

mutualism 상호주의
mutuality of insurance institution
　보험제도의 상호성
mutuality of obligation 채무의 상호성
mutuality of remedy 구제의 상호성
mutualization 상호화
mutually exclusive event 상호독립적인 사건
myopia 근시안적인 사고방식
Mysigma profitability graph
　미시그마의 수익 그래프
mysterious disappearance 분실

nail damage 네일대미지
nailed down 초저가격광고상품
naked call 네이키드콜
naked confession 불완전자유
naked contract 무상계약
naked option 네이키드옵션
naked position 네이키드포지션
naked warrant 네이키드워런트
name 이름
name list 인명부
name of the corporation 상호
name share 기명주
name transfer 명의서환
named bill 기명어음
named insured 기명피보험자
named nonowner policy 기명비소유자보험
named peril 특정위험
named peril insurance 열거위험담보보험
named schedule bond 기명식 보증증권
nano-second 나노초
narrative form 보고식
narrow 축소하다
narrow based stock index 업종별 주가지수
narrow market 한산시장
narrow market security 물량이 적은 주
narrow movement 소폭왕래
narrow range 소폭
narrow seas 해협
narrow spread
　　시세변동으로 매매차익금이 적어지다
narrowcasting 내로우캐스팅

narrowing of spread
　　시세변동으로 매매차익금이 적어지다
NASDAQ Composite Index 나스닥
nation 국가
national balance sheet 국민대차대조표
national bank 국민은행
national bond futures market 국채선물시장
national brand 전국브랜드
national capital 국민자본
national capital account 국민자본계정
national capital sheet 국민자본표
national certification 국가인정
national credit 국가신용
national debt 국가채무
national debt service expenditure 공채비
national economic accounting 국민경제재산
national finance 국가재정
national full line firm 종합증권회사
National Futures Association
　　전미(全美)선물협회
national government debts 정부채무
National Health Insurance Law
　　국민건강보험법
national health insurance tax 국민건강보험세
national income 국민소득
national income accounting 국민소득회계
national income accounts 국민소득계정
national income analysis 국민소득분석
national income distributed 분배국민소득
national income expended 지출국민소득
national income produced 생산국민소득

national income statistics 국민소득통계
national information structure
　전미(全美)정보기반
national pension 국민연금
national property 국유재산
national subsidy 국고보조금
national tariff 국정세율
national tax 국세
national tax procedure law 국세통칙법
national treasury 국고
national treatment 내국민대우
national wealth 국부(國富)
national wealth statistics 국부통계
nationalization 국유화
nationalized reinsurance 국영재보험
natural boundary 자연경계
natural business year 자연영업연도
natural capital 자연자본
natural classification 자연발생적 분류
natural disaster relief loans 천재자금
natural gas pipeline 천연가스파이프라인
natural heirs 혈연상속인
natural infancy 유년
natural language system 자연언어체계
natural law 자연법
natural liberty 자연적인 자유
natural person 자연인
natural premium 자연보험료
natural presumption 자연적인 추정
natural rate of interest 자연이자율
natural rate of unemployment 자연실업률
natural rights 자연권
natural support 자연적 지지
natural year 역년(曆年)
naturalization 귀화
nature and degree 성질과 정도
nature of business 사업종류
navigable 항행가능한
ne exeat 난국금지영장
ne varictur 동일성을 인정함
near future 머지않아

near maturity 만기에 가까운
near money 준통화
near the money 니어더머니
near time prospect 전망
near-panic market 공황상장
near-term bond 만기에 가까운 채무
nearest month 가장 가까운 달
necessaries 생활필수품
necessary evidence documents
　필요한 증거서류
necessary expense 필요경비
necessary household furniture 필수가구
necessary party 필요당사자
necessary tax procedure 필요한 세무수속
necessity 긴급피난
neck line 네크라인
need hierarchy 요구계층
need-satisfaction approach 요구충족 어프로치
needs 니즈
needs test 필요조사
needs theory 욕구이론
negative adaptation 음성순응
negative assets 소극자산
negative assurance 소극적인 보증
negative averments 소극적인 주장
negative capital 부채
negative carry 네거티브캐리
negative clause 담보보류조항
negative confirmation 소극적인 확인
negative covenant 경쟁제한특약
negative duration 부정적인 듀레이션
negative effect 부정적인 효과
negative evidence 소극적인 증거
negative factor 마이너스요인
negative film 네거필름
negative goodwill 소극적인 주
negative growth 마이너스성장
negative income tax 역소득세
negative interest 역금리
negative interest rate spread
　시중은행의 할인율 상회

negative leverage effect 부정적인 레버리지

negative list 신용불량자 리스트

negative monetary position 금전채무상태

negative option sales 네거티브옵션판매

negative plea 소극적인 항변

negative pledge clause 담보제한조항

negative pledge pari passu clause
　네거티브 플레지 패리 패스 조항

negative prescription 소멸시효

negative property 소극재산

negative reaction 거절반응

negative reserve 소극적인 적립금

negative statute 금지법

negative testimony 소극적인 증언

negative valuation accounts
　소극적인 평가계정

negative yield curve 부(負)의 이율곡선

negligence 과실

negligence clause 면책조항

negligence liability 과실책임

negligible in amount 무시할 수 있는 가격

negotiable 양도가능

negotiable certificate of deposit
　양도가능정기예금증서

negotiable instrument 유통증권

negotiable letter of credit 매입가능신용장

negotiable order of withdrawal account
　양도가능환불지도예금계정

negotiable securities 유가증권

negotiable time certificates of deposits
　양도가능정기예금증서

negotiated 상대

negotiated contracts 수의계약

negotiated market 상대매매시장

negotiated transaction 상대거래

negotiated underwriting 협의인수

negotiating bank 어음유통은행

negotiation 유통

negotiation charge 어음유통수수료

negotiation credit 외국환유통신용장

negotiation effect 교섭효과

negotiation for budget draft 부활절충

negotiation on terms and conditions
　조건교섭

neighborhood benefits 인지자의 수익

nemine contradicente 전원일치

neo-behaviorism 신행동주의

neo-functionalism 신기능주의

neo-quantity theory of money 신화폐수량설

nervous 신경질적인

nervous shock 정신적인 충격

net 그물

net amount after provision for loss
　대손준비금공제후의 금액

net amount principle 순액주의

net asset per share 일주당 순자산

net asset value 순자산가치

net asset value per unit 유닛당 순자산가치

net asset worth per share 일주당 순자산

net assets 순자산

net assets value 순자산가액

net avails 순수취액

net balance 넷밸런스

net base 순액(純額)베이스

net block flow 넷블록플로

net book value 순장부가액

net borrowed reserves 순차입준비

net budget 예산순계

net capital stock 스톡 조자본스톡

net carry-over cost 순이월비용

net cash 넷캐시

net cash flow 넷캐시플로

net cash inflows 순현금유입

net changes in each element 과목별 순변동액

net collectible amounts 순회수가능액

net commodity terms of trade
　순상품교역조건

net cost 순원가

net creditor country 넷채권국

net current assets 순유동자산

net cycle time 순운전시간

net damaged value 손해시가

net debt 순부채
net deposit 실세예금
net earned surplus forwarded
　이월이익잉여금
net earnings 순이익
net equity assets 순지분자산
net export 순금융수입
net external assets 대외순자산
net financial income 순금융수입
net free reserves 순자유준비
net income 순익
net income ratio 순이익률
net income to sales 매상순이익률
net interest 순이자
net interest cost 순이자비용
net interest income 순수취이자
net investment 순투자
net lease 넷리스
net level premium reserve
　평준순보험료식 책임준비금
net liabilities 순부채
net line 순소지금액
net liquidity balance 순유동성 수지
net loss 순손실
net loss carried forward 이월결손금
net mark-on 순가산이익액
net monetary items 순금전항목
net monetary position 순화폐포지션
net national product 국민순생산
net national welfare 국민복지지표
net of 제외하고
net of reserves 대손준비금공제후 수취채권
net open position 넷오픈포지션
net operating cycle 순영업순환일수
net operating earnings 경상순익액
net operating loss 순영업손실
net operating profit 순영업이익
net operation profit 업무순익
net outgo 순지출
net pay 급료
net position 넷포지션

net premium 순수입보험료
net premium payable 순지불보험료
net premiums written 순계상보험료
net present value 순현재가치
net price 순가격
net price index 넷프라이스인덱스
net price trading 넷프라이스트레이딩
net proceeds 순수취액
net production value 순생산고
net profit 순이익
net profit after depreciation 상각후 순이익
net profit before corporation tax
　법인세공제전 순이익
net profit before depreciation 상각전 순이익
net profit for the year 당기순이익
net profit margin 매상순이익률
net profit on sales 매상순익
net profit or loss 순손익
net profit or loss account 순손익계산
net profit or loss section 순손익구분
net profit ratio 순익률
net profit to net worth 자기자본이익률
net profit to sales 매상순이익률
net purchase 매입초과; 순구입고
net quick assets 순당좌자산
net realizable value 순실현가능가격
net receipt 순수취금
net return 순수익
net sales 순매상고
net saving 순저축
net settlement 차금결제
net short hedging 순매연결
net succession 순상속재산
net supply of industrial funds
　산업자금공급상황
net surplus 순잉여금
net tangible asset ratio to long-term debt
　장기부채순고정자산
net tangible assets 순고정자산
net taxable assets 순과세재산
net trading volume 넷거래고

net value 순가격
net working capital 순운전자본
net worth 순자산
net worth equity 순자산
net worth equity capital 자기자본
net worth method 자산부채증감법
net worth of collateral 담보여력
net worth tax 부유세
net worth to debts 자본부채비율
net worth to fixed capital 자본고정비율
net yield 세인이율
netdown 상쇄
netting 네팅
network architecture 네트워크아키텍처
network broadcast 네트워크분석
network control unit 순제어장치
network of credit 신용네트워크
neural computing 뉴럴컴퓨팅
neutrality 중립성
neutrality of taxation 조세의 중립성
never-out list 상비상품리스트
new 신규
new account 신규계정
new banking law 신은행법
new bond 신발채
new common carrier 뉴커먼캐리어
new design 신안
new face bond 신안채
new field 신규분야
new foreign exchange law 신외국환관리법
new high 신고치
new industrial revolution 신산업혁명
new issue 신규발행
new issue of stocks 신주발행
new listing 신규상장
new loan 신규대출
new low 신저치
new media community 뉴미디어커뮤니티
new monetary adjustment system 신금융조절
new mortgage 신규모기지
new order 신규수주

new premium 신규프리미엄
new print film 차세대사진필름
new product failures 신제품이 실패함
new product introduction 신제품소개
new product screening 신제품을 체분류함
new share 신주
new share issuing expense 신주발행비
new share off 신주하락
new social indicators 국민생활지표
new stock issuing expenses 신주발행비
new trial 재심
new type of gold standard 신형 금본위제
new welfare economics 신후생경제학
New York acceptance credit 뉴욕인수신용장
New York Stock Exchange 뉴욕증권거래소
newly industrialized countries 신공업국군
newly issued corporate bond 신규발행사채
next closing of account 차기결산
next day fund 익일자금화 자금
next friend 대리인; 후견인
next time 차기
next to kin 근친자
niche 니치
niche market 니치마켓
niche strategy 니치전략
Nielsen research 닐슨조사
nient comprise 해당사실없음
nient dedire 부인하지 않음
nient le fait 작성부인의 항변
nifty fifty 인기50문제
night deposit safe 야간금고
night duty allowance 숙직료
nil dicit 무답변
nine bond rule 나인본드룰
no action letter 노액션레터
no claim return 무사고반환
no consideration 무약인항변
no effect 무효
no fault automobile insurance
　노폴트 자동차보험
no franchise 면책보합부 적용약관

no limit order 성행주문
no load fund 노로드펀드
no protest 거절증서가 필요없음
no return rule 노리턴룰
no-down 노다운
no-par-value stock 무액면 주식
NOB spread NOB스프레드
Nobel Foundation 노벨재단
node 절점
node method 노드방식
noise 노이즈
noise gate 노이즈게이트
noise reduction 노이즈리덕션
nominal account 명목계정
nominal amount 액면가액
nominal assets 명목자산
nominal assured 명의상의 피보험자
nominal capital 명목자산
nominal coupon 표면이율
nominal damages 명목상의 손해배상액
nominal GNP 명목GNP
nominal gross deposit 표면예금
nominal income 명목수입
nominal interest rate 표면금리
nominal liabilities 명목부채
nominal partner 명목상의 파트너
nominal price quotation 호가
nominal profit 명목이익
nominal proxy 무권대리
nominal quotation 분위기, 흐름
nominal rate 표면금리
nominal rate of discount 명목할인율
nominal rate of interest 명목이율
nominal rate of protection 명목보호율
nominal rate of return 명목수익률
nominal scale 명의척도
nominal transaction 명목상거래
nominal value 액면가; 공칭가
nominal wage 명목임금
nominal wealth tax 명목상의 재산세
nominal yield 명목이율

nominalism 명목주의
nominate 지명하다
nominated subcontractor 지정하청업자
nominee 명의인
nonamortizable securities 일시불유가증권
nonassessable insurance 비부과식 보험
nonassessable policy 보험료추징불요증권
nonassumpsit 비인수답변
nonaverage insurance 실손전보계약
nonbank 논뱅크
nonbank financial institution 비은행금융기관
nonbasic shareholder of family corporation
　비동족주의
nonboard company 과율산정기관불참가회사
nonbordereau agreement 논보르드로 특약
nonborrowed reserve 여잉준비
nonborrowed reserves 비차입준비
nonbusiness activity 비사업활동
nonbusiness expenses 사업외경비
nonbusiness property 비영업용 자산
noncallable 이연하는, 연기하는
noncancellable 해약할 수 없는
noncancellable insurance
　해약할 수 없는 보험계약
noncash assets 비현금자산
noncash investing activities
　수지를 수반하지 않는 투자활동
nonclaim 청구불이행
noncommercial enterprise 비영리회사
noncommercial insurance 비영리보험
noncommercial trader 비상업 트레이더
noncompensatory model 비보정모델
noncompetitive tender 비경쟁입찰
nonconcealed assets 장부외자산
nonconcurrency 이위성(異位性)
nonconcurrent policies 이위계약
nonconforming product 부적합제품
nonconformity 부적합
noncontinuous policy 보험금액감소보험
noncontrollable cost 관리불능원가
noncost items 비원가항목

noncumulative dividend 비누적형 배당
noncumulative preferred stock
　비누적형 우선주식
noncurrent assets 비유동자산
noncurrent liabilities 장기채무
nondeclarant 미선언자
nondeductible franchise 무공제면책률
nondeductible taxes 손금불산입 조세과금
nondelivery 인도불이행
nondepreciable assets 비상각자산
nondetachable warrant 분리불능 워런트
nondiversified investment company
　비분산투자형 투자회사
nondividend 무배
nondraft export 외화를 주고받지 않는 수출
nondraft import 외화를 주고받지 않는 수입
nonduplication of benefits 이중급부배제
nondurables 비내구재
nonexclusive 비독점적
nonexpendable fund 사용불능자금
nonfamily corporation 비동족회사
nonfeasance 불이행
nonfinancial accounts 비금융계정
nonfinancial assets 비금융자산
nonfinancial market 비금융시장
nonfinancial transaction 비금융거래
nonfleet insured 논플리트계약자
nonforfeiture act 불몰수법
nonfulfillment 불이행
nonfulfillment of a contract 계약불이행
nonfund transactions
　수지를 수반하지 않는 거래
nongenuine agreement 이면계약
nongovernment bond 민간채
nonhomogeneity 비동질성
noninstallment 비할부
noninterest-bearing bond 비이자부채
noninterest-sensitive item 금리비감응항목
noninvestment cooperative association
　비출자조합
nonjoinder 불병합

nonjuridical organization
　법인격이 없는 단체
nonledger assets 미기장자산
nonlegal standards 법률이 아닌 기준
nonlicensed micropower broadcasting
　미약전파방송
nonlife insurance 손해보험
nonlife insurance agent 손해보험대리점
nonlife insurance company 손해보험회사
nonliquid assets 비유동성자산
nonmarine agency system 논마린 대리점제도
nonmarket economy 비시장경제
nonmarket risk 비시장성 리스크
nonmarket risk sources
　비시장성 리스크의 원천
nonmarketable securities 비시장성증권
nonmarking 가격표생략
nonmember firm 비회원증권회사
nonmonetary indirect security
　비화폐간접증권
nonmonetary items 비금전항목
nonmonetized economy 비화폐경제
nonmoney trust 금외신탁
nonnegotiable 유통성이 없는
nonnegotiable bill 이서금지어음
nonnegotiable endorsement 이서금지이서
nonnegotiable instrument 비유통증권
nonnegotiable safekeeping receipts
　양도불능보호예금
nonoperating 영업외의
nonoperating expenditure 영업외비용
nonoperating expenses 영업외경비
nonoperating gains and loss 영업외손익
nonoperating revenue 영업외수익
nonoperating section 영업외손익구분
nonopinion report 무한정감사보고서
nonorder bill 지도금지어음
nonpar stock 무액면주
nonpar-value stock 무액면주식
nonparametric test 논파라메트릭 검사
nonparticipating fund 무배당보험자산

nonparticipating preferred stock
비참가우선주식
nonparticipating premium 무배당보험료
nonpayment protest 부도통지
nonpayments 미납
nonperformance 불이행
nonpermanent resident 비영주자
nonpersonal family corporation
비동족의 동족회사
nonpersonnel expenses 물건비
nonpolicy writing agent 비발권대리점
nonprice competition 비가격경쟁
nonprobability sample 비확률표본
nonprofit corporation 비영리회사
nonprofit foundation 공익법인
nonprofit institution 비영리기관
nonprofit-making activity 공익사업
nonprofit-making business 비영리사업
nonprofit-making company 비영리회사
nonprofit-making organization 비영리조직
nonprogrammed decision
비정형적인 의사결정
nonproportional reinsurance
비례할당하지 않는 재보험
nonpurpose loan 비특정대부
nonrate earnings assets 비금리자산
nonrate-paying liability 비금리부채
nonrate-sensitive liability 금리비감응부채
nonreciprocal 비상호적
nonreciprocal reinsurance 일방적인 재보험
nonrecourse 논리코스
nonrecurrent item 임시손익항목
nonrecurring cost 경상외비용
nonrecurring profit 임시이익
nonrecurring profit and loss 경상외 손익
nonregistered 등기미제
nonresident foreign currency account
비거주자외화예금계정
nonresident won account
비거주자 원예금계정
nonresident won deposit 비거주자 원예금

nonrisk assets 비위험자산
nonrisk interest rate 비위험이자율
nonselling area 비매장면적
nonsettled 비계약자
nonsigner 비계약자
nonstochastic model 비확률모델
nonstrategic division 비전략부문
nonsuit 소송각하
nonsystematic risk 논시스티매틱리스크
nontax payment 세외부담
nontax receipts 세외수익
nontaxable corporation 비과세법인
nontaxable document 비과세문서
nontaxable exchanges of properties 수용환지
nontaxable goods 면세품
nontaxable income 비과세소득
nontaxable interest income 비과세이자소득
nontaxable property 비과세재산
nontaxable receiving 미납세인수
nontaxable savings 비과세저축
nontaxable securities 면세증권
nontaxable transaction 비과세거래
nontaxable-goods for special use
특수용도면세
nontie-up loan 비제휴론
nontraditional asset class
비전통적인 애셋클래스
nonuser 행사하지 않음
nonvoting stock 의결권이 없는 주
noon clause 정오조항
Nordic Council 북유럽협의회
Nordic Council of Ministers 북유럽각료회의
Norin Chukin Bank (일본의)농림중앙금고
norm 노르마
normal and average use hours 통상사용시간
normal asset mix 노멀애셋믹스
normal auditing procedures 정규감사절차
normal balances 정상잔고
normal burden rate 정상배부율
normal cost 정상원가
normal depreciation 정상상각

normal distribution 정규분포
normal market 노멀마켓
normal operating cycle 정상상업순환
normal probability curve 정규확립분포곡선
normal probability distribution 정규확률분포
normal procedure 정규절차
normal profit 정상이윤
normal rate of exchange 정상환상장
normal return 정상이익
normal standard cost 정상표준원가
normal stock 정상재고고
normal target allocation 노멀타겟앨로케이션
normal tax 보통세
normalization 규준화
normalized EPS 표준 EPS
normative change 표준적인 변화
normative influence 규범적인 영향
normative theory 규범론
norms in society 사회규범
norms of behavior 행동규범
North America Free Trade Agreement
　북미자유무역협정
North Atlantic Assembly 북대서양의회
North Atlantic Free Trade Area
　북대서양자유무역지역
North Atlantic Treaty Organization
　북대서양조약기구
North Brent 북해 브렌트
north-south problem 남북문제
north-south trade 남북무역
Northampton table 노샘프턴 생명표
nostro 자국
Nostro account 당방계정
not excessive 너무 과도해도 안되며
not inadequate 너무 부정당해도 안되며
not otherwise provided 별도의 규정이 없는 한
not possessed 점유하지 않은
not proven 증거불충분
not unfairly discriminatory
　차별해서는 안되며
not yet delivered 도착하지 않은

notarial charges 공증료
notarial deed 공정증서
notarial document 공정증서
notary 공증인
notary public liability policy
　공증인배상책임보험
note 노트
note at sight 일람불약속어음
note endorsed 이서양도어음
note for payment of tonnage dues
　톤세 납부서
note issuance facility 노트이슈언스퍼실리티;
　NIF
note of payment 지불통지서
note of protest 거절각서
note payable register 지불어음기입장
note purchase agreement 채무매입계약
note received discounted 할인어음
note register 어음기입장
notes and accounts payable 지불채무
notes and accounts receivable 수취채권
notes and bills discounted 할인어음
notes and bills endorsed 이서어음
notes and bills payable 지불어음
notes and bills receivable 수취어음
notes endorsed for payment 이서양도어음
notes payable to banks 은행차입금
notes receivable register 수취어음기입장
notes to financial statement 재무제표각주
noteworthy 주목할 만한
notice 통지
notice deposit 통지예금
notice of abandonment 위임통지
notice of demand to guarantor 납부최고서
notice of determination 결정통지서
notice of lien 선취특권통지
notice of loss and damage 사고통지
notice of redemption 상환통지
notice of seizure 차압통지서
notice to produce 문서제출요구서
notice to quit 해약예고

M
N

notification 최고서
notification in writing 문서를 통한 통지
notification of appropriation of refund
　환부금충당통지서
notification of audit 사전조사통지
notification of claim 구상통지
notification of depreciation method
　상각방법을 신고함
notification of incorporation 설립계
notification of opening of business
　개업계(開業屆)
notification of payment of refund
　환부금지불통지서
notification of tax agent 납세관리인을 신고함
notification of tax payment 납세고지서
notification of the taxable year
　사업연도를 신고함
notification of transfer of place of tax
　payment 납세지이동을 신고함
notification procedure 통고처분
notifying bank 통지은행
noting protest 거절각서를 작성함
notional amount 명목원본
notional certificate 의제증서
notional income 관념상의 소득
notorious possession 공공연한 점유
novelty 신안(新案)
nuclear accident 원자력 사고

nuclear damage 원자력손해
nuclear energy hazard 원자력위험
nuclear energy liability insurance
　원자력손해배상책임보험
nuclear energy property insurance
　원자력재산보험
nuclear installation 원자력시설
nudge 주의환기
nuisance 불법방해
null and void 무효의
null hypothesis 귀무가설, 영가설
nullity 무효
number of days' purchases in accounts
　payable 외상채권회전일수
number of days' sales in inventories
　재고정리자산회전일수
number of days' sales in receivables
　매상채권회전일수
number of machines installed 설치대수
number of scheduled payments 반제회수
number of stocks held 보유주식수
number of stocks issued 발행필 주식수
number of years elapsed 경과연수
numbered accounts 번호계좌
numeraire 평가기준
numerical integration 수치적분법
numerical rating method 점수사정법
numerical techniques 수치기법

oath 선서
object 물건
object cost 요소별 원가
object of taxation 과세물건
object oriented database
  오브젝트지향 데이터베이스
object space 오브젝트공간
object tax 목적세
objection 이의
objective 요소별의
objective evidence 객관적인 증거
objective function 목적함수
objective indicator 객관지표
objective probability 객관적인 확률
objective statement 요소별 계산서
objective value 객관적인 가치
obligation 채무
obligation fees 부담비
obligation of bookkeeping 기장업무
obligation of contract 계약상의 권리
obligation to disclose 고지의무
obligation to file return 신고의무
obligations incurred 발생채무부담
obligatory insurance 강제보험
obligatory reinsurance 의무재보험
oblige line 오블라이지라인
obligee 채권자
obligor 채무자
obliteration 말소
observation 관찰결과; 입회
observed depreciation 견적감가상각

observed life table 견적내용연수표
observed value 관찰치
obsolescent depreciable property
  진부화 상각자산
obsolete 쓸모없게 된, 진부한
obsolete assets 진부화 자산
obsolete property 진부화 자산
obstruction of justice 사법방해
obstruction of navigation 항행(航行)방해죄
obtain in advance 미리 얻다; 미리 차용하다
obtainer of employment income 급여소득자
occasional income 일시소득
occasional income deduction
  일시소득특별공제
occupancy 자주점유
occupancy terms 점유기간
occupant 점유자
occupation 영업
occupation tax 영업비
occupational accident 직업재해
occupational pension 기업연금
occupational tax 영업면허세
odd date 정형화이외거래기간
odd price 단수가격
odd-lot consolidation 단주정리
odd-lot dealer 단주업자
odd-lot shares 단주
odd-lot theory 단주이론
odd-lot transaction 단주거래
of like grade and quality 품질이 같은
off balance 오프밸런스

off limit 출입금지
off market swap 오프마켓스와프
off talk service 오프토크 통신서비스
off-balance sheet transaction
　오프밸런스시트거래
off-board market 장외시장
off-market 오프마켓
off-setting account 상쇄계정
offense 범죄
offensive strategy 공격적인 전략
offer 제출; 신청
offer by subscription 예약공모
offer curve 오퍼곡선
offer for sale 팔다
offer price 오퍼가격
offer side 오퍼사이드
offered rate 오퍼레이트
offering 모집
offering circular 모집안내서
offering for sale 매출
offering price 매출가격
office 사무소; 직무
office audit 책상조사
office copy 관제등본
office expense account 영업비계정
office expenses 사무비
office expenses book 영업내역장
office furniture 영업용집기
office grant 강제이행
office hours 영업시간
office landscape 오피스계획
office manual 사무규정
office or other fixed place of business
　사무소 또는 다른 일정한 사업소
office overhead 사무소제경비
office regulation 사내규정
officer de jure 법률상의 직원
officer's bonus 임원상여금
officer's compensation 임원보수
officer's salary 임원급료
officers retiring allowance 임원퇴직금

official assessment 부과과세제도
official check 은행수표
official deposit 공금예금
Official Development- Assistance
　정부개발원조
official discount rate 공정률
official exchange market 공정시장
official exchange rate 공정환상장
official foreign exchange reserves
　외화준비고
official information 공보
official inspection 임검
official intervention 공적개입
official invoice 공용 인보이스
official power 직권
official receiver 관선수익관리인
official reserve transactions balance
　공적결제수지
official retain 영치
official to receive national tax
　국세수납관리
offset 상쇄
offset account 상쇄계정
offset error 상쇄오진
offset item 상쇄항목
offset printing 오프셋인쇄
offshoot 자회사
offshore account 오프쇼어계정
offshore banking center 오프쇼어뱅킹센터
offshore banking facility 오프쇼어은행간시장
offshore banking unit 오프쇼어뱅킹유닛
offshore center 오프쇼어센터
offshore fund 오프쇼어펀드
offshore lease 오프쇼어리스
offshore market 오프쇼어시장
offshore production 오프쇼어해외시장
offshore trade 삼국간무역
oil concession 석유채굴권
oil money 오일머니
oil pollution liability insurance
　원유오염배상책임보험

oil refinery 석유정제업
old account 잔존계정
old age pension 노령연금
old bank act 구은행법
old bond 올드본드
old person allowance 노년자공제
old share 구주
old-age pension 노령연금
old-aged, survivor and disability insurance
　노령유족장애자연금
oligopolistic competition 과점경쟁
oligopolistic control 과점지배
oligopolistic economy 과점경제
oligopolistic interdependence
　과점적인 상호의존
oligopoly 과점
oligopoly industry 과점산업
oligopoly price 과점가격
ombudsman 옴브즈맨
omitted dividend 무배당
omnibus account 공동계정
omnibus building 잡거빌딩
omnibus clause 총괄조항
on a simple interest basis 단리(單利) 베이스
on account 외상판매
on air test 온에어테스트
on balance 온밸런스
on balance volume 온밸런스볼륨
on board notation 선적이서
on call 청구한 즉시
on cost 제조비
on demand 요구지불
on demand selling rate 도착지불판매상장
on hook dial 온후크다이얼
on or before 기일 또는 기일전에
on our risk 당방부담
on passage 운송중
on the books 외상장부에서
on the job accidents 업무상의 사고
on-balance-sheet transaction 온 밸런스 거래
on-line 온라인

on-shore 자국내
on-shore market 온쇼어마켓
oncost 제경비
one bank holding company 단일 은행 지주회사
one day contract 일일계약
one day skipped 영업일이 지나서
one hundred percent income statement
　백분율손익계산서
one name paper 단명어음
one pass scan 선순차방식
one share shareholder 일주주주
one shot customer 일회성 고객
one sided hedge 편도헤지
one way 편도
one year budget principle 예산단년도주의
one year rule 일년기준
one's own convenience 자기사정
one's own house system 지가제도(持家制度)
one-bank holding company
　단일은행지주회사
one-factor 단일요인
one-factor model 단일요인모델
one-man company 일인회사
one-time rate 단발요금
one-write policy 원라이트증권
onerous contract 유상계약
onerous gift 부담부증여
ongoing assessment 계속평가
onomastic 자필서명한
onus of proof 입증책임
open 미결산
open account 미결계정
open air market 야외시장
open and current account 상호계산계정
open bid 일반경쟁입찰
open board of broker 공개거래회관
open book 오픈북
open buying 신규구입
open check 보통수표
open contract 특약이 없는 계약
open corporation 공개회사

O
P

open court 공개법정
open cover 오픈커버; 포괄보험
open down 오픈다운
open economy 개방경제
open group 개방단체
open house 오픈하우스
open inflation 개방형 인플레이션
open insurance 포괄예정보험
open interest 미결제거래잔고
open interest on buyer's side
　매입 측의 거래잔고
open interest on seller's side
　매출 측의 거래잔고
open investment trust 오픈형 투자신탁
open ledger 미결제원장
open letter of credit 매입은행무지정신용장
open market 공개시장
open market operations 공개시장조작
open market quotation 시중상장
open market rate 시중금리
open market selling operation
　매출오퍼레이션
open media framework
　오픈미디어프레임워크
open money market 공개단기금융시장
open mortgage 해방담보
open mortgage clause 단순저당채권자불약관
open order 무조건주문
open outcry method 공개경쟁매매방식
open plan office 오픈플랜오피스
open policy 포괄보험증서
open question 미해결 문제
open rate method 오픈레이트방식
open repo 공개시장조작
open selling 신규매출
open tendering 일반경쟁입찰
open theft 현행절도죄
open-end 개방식의
open-end bond investment trust
　공사채투자신탁
open-end fund 오픈엔드형 펀드

open-end investment trust 오픈형 투자신탁
open-end lease 오픈엔드형 리스
open-end mortgage 개방식 담보
open-end mortgage bond 개방식 담보부사채
open-up of money market 금융시장개방
opener 신용장발행의뢰인
opening balance 기초잔고
opening balance account 개시잔고계정
opening bank 개설은행
opening charge 신용장발행수수료
opening commission 발행수수료
opening entry 이월기장
opening inventory 기초재고고
opening market 시장개방
opening of branch 지점개설
opening price 오프닝프라이스
opening price point 최저가격라인
opening quotation 기부단가
opening rate 시가
opening session 오프닝시즌
opening statement 모두진술
opening tone 오프닝톤
opening words 모두문서
operand 연산수
operated days 조업일수
operating 영업활동의
operating accounts 영업활동계정
operating activities 영업활동
operating assets 운용자산
operating budget 영업예산
operating business 영리회사
operating capital 운전자금
operating characteristics curve
　운전특성곡선
operating condition 영업상황
operating cost 운전비용
operating cycle 영업순환
operating cycle rule 영업순환기준
operating earning rate 경영자본이익률
operating efficiency 경영효율
operating expenses 영업경비

operating income 영업수익
operating income to sales 영업이익률
operating lease 오퍼레이팅리스
operating ledger 영업원장
operating leverage analysis
　오퍼레이팅레버리지 분석
operating leverage effect 영업면의 증익효과
operating loss 영업손실
operating margin 영업이익률
operating performance ratios 업적비율
operating profit 영업이익
operating profit and loss 영업손익
operating profit level 영업이익단계
operating profit margin 영업이익률
operating profit on sales 매상고영업이익률
operating profit or loss 영업손익
operating rate 조업도
operating ratio 가동률
operating receipt 영업수입
operating report 영업보고
operating reserve 영업준비금
operating results 영업성적
operating revenue 영업수익
operating section 영업손실구분
operating standing 영업상태
operating statement 영업활동계산서
operating surplus 영업잉여
operating system 오퍼레이팅시스템; OS
operating target 조작목표
operation 조업
operation capacity 조업도
operation efficiency 작업능률
operation expenses 작업비
operation in the secondary market
　유통시장조작
operation ratio 조업률
operation variance 조업도차이
operational decision 업무의사결정
operational efficiency 효율성
operational procedure 실시수순
operations audit 업무감사

operations for stabilizing the stock market
　price 주가안정조작
operations research 오퍼레이션리서치
operative clause 주문
operative words 효력발생문언
opinion 변호사의견서
opinion of auditors 감사의견서
opinion of independent certified public
　accountant 감사보고서
opinion survey 의견조사
opportunity analysis 기회분석
opportunity cost 기회비용
opportunity 기회이익
opportunity loss 기회손실
opposite accounts 반대계정
opposite party 상대방
oppression 직권남용죄
optical character recognition
　광학적인 문자인식
optical computing 광컴퓨팅
optical fiber cable 광케이블
optimal condition 최적조건
optimal growth model 최적성장모델
optimal information 최적정보
optimal operating ratio 최적조업도
optimal policy mix 최적폴리시믹스
optimal scale 최적규모
optimal strategy index 최적전략지수
optimal threshold return 적성상한계수익률
optimization 최적화
optimum advertisement cost 최적광고비
optimum allocation of resources
　최적자원배분
optimum currency 최적통화지역
optimum distribution 최적분배
optimum foreign exchange reserves
　적정외화준비고
optimum inventory 최적재고량
optimum network 최적네트워크
optimum output 최적생산량
optimum rate of growth 최적성장률

O
P

optimum rate of interest 최적이자율
optimum rate of operations 최적조업도
opting-out 옵팅아웃
option 옵션; 선택권
option bond 옵션부채
option buyer 옵션바이어
option clearing corporation 옵션청산회사
option combination 풋콜조합옵션
option delivery 풋콜인도
option expiration date 옵션만기일
option market 옵션시장
option money 특권료
option performance index 옵션퍼포먼스지수
option period 선택권행사가능기간
option pool 옵션풀
option position 옵션포지션
option premier 옵션프리미엄
option pricing model 옵션가격결정모델
option pricing theory 옵션가격결정이론
option seller 최적규모
option spreads 옵션스프레드
option to double 배액감채약관
option transaction 옵션거래
option warrants 주식매수권증서
option writer 옵션매도자
optional assessment 원천선택과세
optional calling plan 선택통화요금
optional cancellation 임의해약
optional cargo 양륙지선택화물
optional court bond 임의재판보증증권
optional perils 선택가능위험
optional redemption 임의상환
optional repayment provision 선택상환조항
options on stock index futures
　주가지수선물옵션
oral testimony 구두증언
orbital structure 활동범위구조
order and disposition 명의상의 소유
order backlog 수주잔
order bill of lading 지도인식 선하증권
order book official 오더북피셜

order book trading 주문부거래
order by telephone 전화주문
order for attachment of property 차압명령
order for collection 징수명령
order for relief 구제명령
order frequency 주문빈도
order increase 수주증가
order nisi 가명령
order of application 적용순서
order of credit 채권순위
order of filiation 인지명령
order of liquidity 유동성배열법
order of preference 선호순위
order paper 지시증권
order stock 현품주문
order to outside manufacturer 외주
order to pay 지불명령
order turnaround 주문회송
order volume 수주액
ordering cost 발주비
ordering point 발주점
orderly export marketing 질서있는 수출
orderly marketing agreement
　시장질서유지협정
orders in hand 수주잔고
ordinal scale 순서척도
ordinance 조례
ordinance by local government 조례
ordinary 경상
ordinary agent 생명보험외무원
ordinary and normal recurring operations
　통상운용
ordinary annual expenditure 경상세출
ordinary annual revenue 경상세입
ordinary bank 보통은행
ordinary bill 통상어음
ordinary care 통상주의
ordinary charges 통상비용
ordinary collection 보통징수
ordinary conveyance 통상양도증서
ordinary corporation 보통법인

ordinary corporation income 보통소득
ordinary deposit 일반예금
ordinary depreciation 보통상각
ordinary dividend 보통배당
ordinary expenditure 경상비용
ordinary foreign tax credit 통상외국세액공제
ordinary franchise 무공제면책보합
ordinary general meeting 통상총회
ordinary income 경상수입
ordinary income with recurrent nature
　경상소득
ordinary insurance 보통보험
ordinary interest rate 통상이자율
ordinary life insurance 보통생명보험
ordinary local grant tax 보통교부세
ordinary tosses 통상손해
ordinary partnership 보통조합
ordinary payment 통상결제
ordinary private company 일반적인 사회사
ordinary profit 경상이익
ordinary profit and loss 경상손익
ordinary remittance 보통송금
ordinary risks of employment
　사업상의 통상위험
ordinary share 보통주
ordinary tax 경상세
ordinary temperature 상온
ore-leave 채굴면허
organ 기관지
organic composition of capital
　유기적인 자본구성
organic growth 유기적 성장
organismic model 유기체모델
organization 창립
organization committee 창립위원
organization development 조직개발
organization expenses amortize 설립상각비
Organization for Asian Economic
　Cooperation 아시아경제협력기구
Organization for European Economic
　Cooperation 유럽경제협력기구

organization meeting 창립총회
Organization of Arab Petroleum Exporting
　Countries 아랍석유수출국기구
Organization of Pacific Economic
　Cooperation 태평양지역경제협력기구
organization office 창립사무소
organizational buyer 조직구매자
organizational change 조직변경
organizational goal 조직목표
organizational strategy 조직전략
organizational structure 조직구조
organizations of primary commodity
　producers 일차산품생산국기구
organizer 창립자
organizing 조직하다
original 원본
original capital 원시자본
original cost 취득원가
original cost method 취득원가법
original credit 원신용장
original document 원본
original entry 원시기입
original equipment manufacturing OEM
original goods 오리지널상품
original insurance 원보험
original issue discount 발행시할인
original jurisdiction 제1심 관할권
original money 본원화폐
original package 원포장
original policy 원보험증권
original purchaser 당초구입자
original rate 원보험요율
original register 원부
originator 발기인
orthogonal 직교, 직각
orthogonal factor 직교인자
oscillation theory 진동이론
oscillator 오실레이터
OTC company 장외등록기업
other account 타회사
other charges 영업외 비용

O
P

other income 잡수익
other insurance clause 타보험 조항
other reserve 별도적립금
other revenues 잡수익
our account 당방계정
our side 당방
out line 아웃라인
out of date 기한경과
out of term 폐정기; 법정을 닫는 시기
out of the money 아웃오브더머니
out town bill 타소불어음
out town check 타소불수표
out town delivery 타소인도
out-cycle work 기계휴지시작업
out-of-court settlement 시담해결
out-of-date check 실효수표
out-of-pocket cost 현금지불비용
out-of-pocket expense 현금지출비
out-of-work pay 실업수당
out-sourcing 아웃소싱
outbuilding 부속건물
outdoor advertising 옥외광고
outgo 지출
outlaw strike 불법쟁의
outlay 지출
outlay cost 지출원가
outlay expiration 지출소비
outlay for advertisement 광고비
outlay tax 간접세
outlet store 아웃렛스토어
outline font 아웃라인폰트
outlook for consumer spending 소비예상
output 생산고
output coefficient 산출계수
output cost 제조원가
output method 생산고비례법
output reduction 조업단축
output variable 아웃풋변수
outright base 무조건오퍼
outright forward delivery with option
　옵션부 순월인도

outright forward fixed date delivery
　순월확정일인도
outright forward rates fixed date
　순월확정일상장
outright purchase 매절
outright sales 품절
outright transaction 아웃라인거래
outside capital 타인자본
outside day 아웃사이드데이
outside dealing 장외거래
outside environment 외부환경
outside manufacturer 외주업자
outside money 외부화폐
outside premises coverage 구외담보
outside pressure 외압
outside product 외주제품
outside test 외부시험
outsider 장소에 어울리지 않는 사람
outsider director 사외중역
outstanding 미불의
outstanding account 미결제계정
outstanding amount 발행잔고
outstanding balance 융자잔고
outstanding balance of issue amount
　발행잔고
outstanding balances 잔존원본
outstanding bond 발행필 채권
outstanding capital 발행필 자본
outstanding capital stock 자본금현재고
outstanding contract amount 계약잔고
outstanding debt 한도를 넘은 차용
outstanding liabilities 미불부채
outstanding premiums 미수보험료
outstanding principal 잔존원본
outstanding shares 발행필 주식
outstanding title 제 3자의 권원
outward freight 왕로운임
outward investment 대외투자
over and short account 과부족계정
over drive processor 오버드라이브프로세서
over funding 오버펀딩

over par 오버퍼
over time 시간경과에 따른
over time price of bond
　시간경과에 따른 채권가격
over transfer 과잉진입
over-the-counter currency option
　장외통화옵션
over-the-counter market 장외시장
over-the-counter option 장외옵션
over-the-counter stock 장외주
over-the-counter transaction 장외거래
over-the-month delivery 익월인도
overabsorbed burden 간접비배부초과액
overabsorbed cost 배부초과원가
overabsorption 초과배부
overall balance 종합수지
overall balance of foreign exchange
　외환보유고
overall effective tax rate 종합효과세율
overall evaluation method 종합평가법
overall position 종합지고
overborrowing 차입초과
overbought market 과잉매입상장
overbought position 과잉매입포시션
overbuying 과잉매입
overcapacity 설비과잉
overcapitalization 과대자본
overcarrying cost 과잉소지비
overcompetition 과당경쟁
overdepreciation 상각초과; 초과상각
overdraft 당좌초과인출
overdraft economy 초과인출경제
overdraft facilities 당자대월약정
overdraft interest 초과발행이자
overdrafts for export bills 환당좌대출
overdrawing 초과대출
overdrawn 초과대부
overdrawn account 초과대출계정
overdressing 과도한 분식
overdue 연체의
overdue account 기한경과계정

overdue bill 기한경과어음
overdue check 기한경과수표
overdue interest 연체이자
overdue interest on loan on bills
　어음대부연체이자
overdue interest per diem 연체일변, 연체일보
overdue loan 기한경과대부
overdue payment 기일도래채권
overestimate 과대평가
overestimation of goods traded
　보상판매상품을 과대평가함
overestimation of inherited assets
　인계자산을 과대평가함
overestimation of investment in kind
　현물출자를 과대평가함
overexuberant economy 과열경제
overfunded 자금이 크게 팽창된
overhauling 수선
overhead 제경비
overhead allocation 제조간접비배부
overhead cost 간접비
overhead cost distribution 간접비배부
overhead distribution basis 간접비배부기준
overhead distribution sheet 부문비계산표
overhead expenses 경상비
overhead rate 간접비배부율
overhead variance 간접비차이
overheated economy 과열경제
overheating of business activity 경기과열
overhedge 과대헤지
overhung 달러과잉
overindebted person 다액채무자
overinsuance by double insurance 중복보험
overinsurance 초과보험
overinvestment 과잉투자
overissue 제한외발행주식
overland freight 육상운송비
overlapping account 중복계정
overlapping debt 중복채무
overlapping time 오버래핑타임
overloan 대출초과

overman 조정인
overmonth loan 익월물
overnight 익일반제
overnight delivery 익일인도
overnight money 익일불대부
overnight rate 오버나이트레이트
overnight repo 익일물레포
overnight transaction 오버나이트거래
overpaid 과불의
overpayment 과오납금; 과납
overprivilege 과잉특권
overproduction 생산과잉
overreaching clause 소유권유보조항
overriding commission 특별수수료
overrule 각하
overs and shorts 과부족
overseas affiliated firm 해외관계회사
overseas assets 해외자산
overseas business 해외사업
overseas interest rate 해외금리
overseas interests 대외이권
overseas investment 대외투자
overseas investment loss reserve
　해외투자손실준비금
overseas investment report 해외투자보고서
overseas legal reserves 해외법정준비금
overseas liabilities 해외부채
overseas major market 해외주요시장
overseas production capacity 해외생산능력
overseas production ratio 해외생산비율
overseas transaction 해외거래
overseas transactions for technique
　기술해외거래
overseas travel accident insurance
　해외여행상해보험
overseas travel sickness insurance
　해외여행질병보험
overseas traveling expense 해외여행비
overseas undertaking corporation
　해외사업법인

overselling 초과매출
overshoot 지나친 행위
overshoot method 오버슈트법
oversold 초과매출의
oversold position 매출이 매입보다 많은 상태
overspeculation 과당투기
overstatement 과대표시
overstatement of taxable income 과대신고
overstock 과잉재고
oversupply 공급과다
overt 명백한; 공공연한
overt act 명백한 행위
overtime allowance 잔업수당
overtime duties 잔업
overtime working 잔업
overtrading 초과매매
overtransfer 과잉불입
overused hours 초과사용시간
overvaluation 과대평가
overvalued 과대평가한 선물
overvalued futures 과대평가한 선물
owing 지불해야 할
owing to bank 은행차입
own account 자기계정
own bill 자행인수
own capital 자기자본
own usance 자행유전스
own-named cards 자사카드
owned capital 자기자본
owner 소유자
owner control 소유자지배
owner of record 명의상의 주주
owner trustee 오너트러스티
owner's capital 주주자본
owner's equity 소유주지분
owner's equity to total assets 자기자본비율
owner's risk 하주위험부담
ownership 소유권
ownership certificate 소유권증
ownership of expiration 만기표소유권

Paasche formula 파쉐계산식
Pac-man defense 팩맨디펜스
pacific blockade 평시봉쇄
package automobile policy 자동차종합보험
package deal 일괄거래
package lease 패키지리스
package policy 패키지폴리시
package-deal contract 패키지딜
packet communication 패킷통신
packet switching 패킷교환
packing 포장비
packing a jury 배심원선정을 속임
packing and wrapping expenses 포장비
packing charge 포장비
packing list 포장명세서
pact 협약
page description language 페이지설명언어
paid cash book 현금지불장
paid check 지불필 수표
paid-in capital 불입자본
paid-in capital in excess of par
    주식불입잉여금
paid-in capital increase 유상증자
paid-in surplus 불입잉여금
paid-up addition
    계약자배당에 따라 보험금액이 증가함
paid-up capital 불입자본
paid-up insurance 보험료 지불을 마친 보험
paid-up-policy value
    보험료 지불을 마친 보험의 금액
painting the tape 가격조작

pair cable 쌍케이블
paired comparison 한 쌍 비교법
pairing-off 상호포기협정
palletization 팔레트화
panel 배심원명부
panel decision 위원회결
panel doctor 보험의
panel patient 국민보험환자
panel research 패널조사
panic market 공황시장
panic sale 공황적인 매출
panicky selling 난매
paper audit 서면감사
paper company 페이퍼컴퍼니
paper crisis 종이홍수
paper currency 지폐
paper days 구두변론일
paper profit 가공이익
paper-book 소송기록서
paperless trading 페이퍼리스트레이딩
par 주식액면
par bond 액면매매사채
par forward 파포워드
par issue 액면발행
par price 액면가격
par value 액면가격
par yield 파일드
par-value capital stock 액면주식
par-value share 액면주식자본금
paradigm 규범; 패러다임
paradox of conceptualization 개념화의 역설

paragraph 항, 단락
paralanguage 준언어
parallel import 평행수입
parallel issue 평행기채
parallel loan 상호대출
parallel market 패럴렐마켓
parallel money market 평행시장
parallel rate shift 금리평행이동
parallel shift 평행이동
parallel transaction 평행거래
parameter 매개변수; 파라미터
parametric design 파라메트릭디자인
parametric test 파라메트릭테스트
paramount right 우월한 권리
parcel 토지 한 필
parent company 친회사
parent guaranteed 친회사보증부
parent store 본점
parenthetical notes 본체주기
pareto's constant 파레토 상수
pari passu 동순위로
pari-mutuel betting 경마식 도박
Paris Club 파리클럽
Paris Union 파리동맹
parity 평가
parity account 패리티계산
parity index 패리티지수
parity line 패리티직선
parity of official exchange rate 공정평가
parity quotation 평준상장
parity rate of exchange 액면평가
parity value 패리티가치
parity-grid 패리티그리드
parking 피난
parliament 국회
parol contract 구두계약
parol license 구두허가
part finished product 반제품
part performance 일부이행
part-owners 공유자
part-timer 파트타임으로 근무하는 사람

partial abandonment 일부위탁
partial acceptance 일부인수
partial assignment 일부양도
partial audit 부분감사
partial correlation 부분상관
partial costing 부분원가계산
partial delivery 일부인도
partial elasticity 편탄력성
partial legal tender 불완전법화
partial loss 분손
partial payment 일부지급
partial proprietor 부분소유자
partial reserve system 일부준비제도
partial shipment 분할선적
partial tax transfer to local government
　지방분여세
partially finished goods 반제품
partially finished goods ledger 반제품원장
participant 참가자
participating annuity 이익배당부연금
participating bond 이익참가사채
participating collision 연쇄충돌
participating preferred stock 참가우선주식
participating premium 이익배당부 연금
participating stock 이익배당주
participation 참가
participation bank 참가은행
participation certificate 참가증권
participation group 참가집단
participation in seizure 참가차압
participation loan 참가융자
participation method 참가방식
participation preferred stock 참가우선주
particular average 단독해손
particular average warranty 분손약관
particular charges 특별비용
particular loss 분손
particulars 내역
particulars of account 계정명세
parties to lawsuit 소송당사자
partition 공유물분할

partition of corporation 회사분할
partition of the estate 유산분할
partly paid bond 일부불입채권
partner 출자사원
partner shaft 파트너샤프트
partners 조합원
partnership 조합
partnership assets 조합재산
party 당사자
party insuring 보험계약자
pass book 원장
pass dividend 무배당으로 하다
pass on 전가하다
pass-along deal 가격인하거래
pass-through securities 패스스루증권
passage 통과
passage of title 소유권이전
passbook 통장
passbook savings account 통장저축예금계좌
passed dividend 무배당
passenger traffic receipts 여객수입
passengers liability insurance
　　승객배상책임보험
passengers tax 통행세
passing off 사칭통용
passing ratio 추이율
passive bond 무이자사채
passive debt 무이식채무
passive investment management
　　소극적인 투자관리
passive learning 소극적인 학습
passive management 소극적인 관리
passive strategy 안전형 운용
passive trust 소극신탁
passive waste 소극적인 훼손
password 패스워드
past due interest 연체이식
past performance 과거실적
past performance control 과거실적관리
past service benefit 과거근무급부
past service credits 과거근무가산

past service liability 과거근무채무
past service pension 과거근무연금
pasteurization 저온멸균
patent 특허권
patent ambiguity 의미가 명백하게 불명료함
patent applied for 특허출원중
patent attorney 특허변리사
patent fee 특허료
patent infringement 특허권침해
patent law 특허법
patent pending 특허출원중
patent period 특허유효기간
patent right 특허권
patentability 특허자격
patented article 특허품
patentee 특허권자
patentor 특허권수여자
path 경로
pattern of consumption 소비패턴
pattern of portfolio return
　　포트폴리오의 수익패턴
pattern variable 패턴변수
pauper 빈곤자
pause 조정
pawn 저당물
pawn-shop 전당포
pawnee 질권자
pawnor 담보잡히는 사람
Pax Americana 팍스아메리카나
pay after tax 세금공제급여
pay by card 카드결제
pay down 현금지불
pay on application 확인지불
pay pause 임금동결
pay per view 페이퍼뷰
pay roll audit 급료감사
pay television 페이텔레비전
pay-as-you-go-system 부과방식
pay-back period 회수기간
pay-freeze 임금동결
pay-off 일괄완제

pay-off diagram 페이오프다이어그램
pay-roll register 임금급료지불부
pay-through bond 페이스루채권
pay-up 추가지불
payable 지불기일이 도래한
payable at sight 일람불
payable on a fixed date 확정일불
payable on demand 요구불
payable register 지불전표기입장
payable to bearer 지참인불
payable to holder 소지인불식; 소지인출급식
payable to order 지도식 또는 소지인불식
payables 매입채무
payables to sales ratio 매상채무비율
payback analysis 자본회수분석
payback period 회수기간
payday 수도일
paydown 페이다운
payee 수취인
payer 지불인
paying agent 지불대리인
paying bank 지불은행
paying in slip 입금전표
paying tax 납부
paying & warrant agency agreement
　　지불워런트 대리인계약서
paymaster 회계주임, 경리담당자
payment 결제
payment account agreement
　　지불준비계정계약
payment against acceptance 인수불
payment against document 서류상환지급
payment at regular fixed times 정시불
payment at short date 단기불
payment bond 지불보증증권
payment book 지불기입장
payment by beneficiary 수익자부담금
payment by bill 어음지불
payment by cash 현금지불
payment by installment 분할지불
payment by rough estimate 개산지불

payment by the result 성과배분
payment for another 대납
payment handling bank 불입취급은행
payment in advance 선금으로
payment in full 전액불입
payment in installments 분할납부
payment in kind 물납
payment in lump sum 일시불입
payment in part 일부지급
payment in subrogation 대위납부
payment in substitution 대물변제
payment into court 공탁
payment of tax 세금납부
payment of tax in kind 현물납부
payment on account 일부지급
payment on delivery 선불
payment order 지불지도
payment periods 반제기간
payment record 지불조서
payment regarded as dividends 간접배당
payment slip 출금전표
payment statement 지불명세
payment stop 지불정지
payment supra 참가지불
payment system 결제수단
payment terms 지불조건
payment to nonresidents 비거주자의 급여소득
payment-in-kind preferred stock
　　페이먼트인카인드 우선주
payoff 페이오프
payoff matrix 이득행렬
payoff pattern 페이오프패턴
payola 비합법적인 보수
payout 배당지불
payout ratio 배당성향
payroll 급료; 임금지불장
payroll deduction 임금공제
payroll deduction type investment trust
　　급여공제형 투신
payroll savings life insurance
　　급료적립생명보험

payroll tax 임금세

peaceable possession 평온한 점유

peak 경기의 최고점

pearl harbor file 펄하버파일

peculiar benefits 특수수익

pecuniary considerations 금전적인 보수

pecuniary damage 금전적인 손해

pecuniary legacy 금전유증

pecuniary relation 금전상의 관계

pecuniary transaction 금전거래

pedigree 가계(家系)

peer 동료

pegged exchange 고정된 환상장

pegged exchange rate system
고정환상장제도

pegged market 고정상장

pegged stock 고정주

pegging 가격안정화

pen position 종합상태

penal 형사상의

penal action 형사소송

penal interest 위약이자

penal regulations 벌칙

penal servitude 징역

penal statute 형사법규

penal sum 위약금액

penalty 위약금

penalty against employer and employee
양벌규정, 쌍벌규정

penalty and fine 벌금

penalty on delayed delivery 연체보상금

penalty rate 벌칙금리

penalty tax 가산세

pendency 미정

pendente lite 소송계속중인

pending 미결의

penetration 삽입; 보급률

penetration chart 시장침투도

penetration price 침투가격

penetration price strategy 침투가격전략

pennant 페넌트

penny stock 저가주 【영】; 값싼 주식

pension 연금

pension and life insurance schemes
기업연금, 기업보험

pension assets 연금자산

pension expense 연금비용

pension financing method 재정방식

pension fund 연금기금

pension fund management 연금기금관리

pension fund spread 연금기금 스프레드

pension fund surplus 연금기금잉여

pension plan 연금계획

pension scheme 연금제도

pension trust 연금신탁

pensionable age 지급개시연령

pent road 막다른 길

people meter 피플미터

People's Finance Corporation 국민금융공고

People's Insurance Company of China
중국인민보험공사

peppercorn rent 명목상의 지대

per annum 일년당

per annum rate 연리

per capita 일인당

per capita gross national product
일인당 국민총생산

per capita levy 균등할세율

per capita rate 일인당 세율

per contra account 대조계정

per contra noted discounted account
할인보증계정

per contra-account 보증계정

per diem 일일당

per incuriam 부주의로 인해

per procuration 대리로

per quod 그것에 의해

per se 본질적으로

per se illegal 그 자체로 무효

per share data 일주당 수치

per share earning ratio 주가수익률

per-diem allowance 일일당

per-diem rate for call loan 콜이율
perceived risk 인지된 리스크
perceived value 인지된 가치
percent distribution 구성비
percent of capacity use 가동율
percentage 수수료
percentage analysis 구성비율
percentage balance sheet 백분율대차대조표
percentage depletion 비율법감모상각
percentage lease 퍼센티지리스
percentage method 백분율법
percentage of capital structure 자본구성비율
percentage of completion basis 공사진행기준
percentage of credit losses 대손율
percentage of debt collection 회수율
percentage of delinquency 연체율
percentage of each classification of assets to total assets 자산구성비율
percentage of profits available on net worth 자기자본이익률
percentage of working force 노동비율
percentage on diminishing value plan 정율상각법
percentage statements 백분율재무제표
percentage table 백분율표
percentage variation method 백분율변이법
percentage-of-completion method 공사진행기준
perception 점유하다
perceptual selectivity 지각선택성
perennial tax 영구세
perennial tenant right 영대(永代)소작권
perfect competition 완전경쟁
perfect obligation 완전채무
perfect title 완전권원
perfecting bail 보석완료
perfection standard cost 완전표준원가
perform well 호전개가 되다
performance 운용성적
performance analysis 성과분석
performance attribution 퍼포먼스특성

performance basis 업무수행기준
performance bond 이행보증증권
performance bond insurance 이행보증보험
performance characteristic 성능특성
performance evaluation 업적평가
performance fund 퍼포먼스펀드
performance guarantee 이행보증
performance guarantee deposit 이행증거금
performance margin 퍼포먼스증거금
performance measurement 퍼포먼스측정
performance of business 사업수행
performance of obligations of guarantee 보증채무이행
performance rating 인사고과
performance-based fee system 퍼포먼스비례보수체계
peril 위험
peril clause 위험약관
peril point 위험점
perils ejusdem generis 동종위험
perils excepted 면책위험
perils not covered 중성위험
perils of the sea 해상고유의 위험
period 기한
period analysis 기간분석
period call market 정기콜시장
period charge 기간비용
period cost 기간원가
period expense 기간비용
period for tax 납기
period of economic growth 경제성장기
period of economic stability 경제안정기
period of integration 통합기
period of request for reconsideration 심사청구기간
periodic actual inventory 정기실지재고
periodic audit 정기감사
periodic average method 총평균법
periodic balance sheet 기말대차대조표
periodic income 기간이익
periodic inventory 정기재고조사

periodic pension cost 연금의 기간원가
periodic trial balance 기말시산표
periodical accounting 기간계산
periodical deposits 정기적금
periodical return 정기수익
periodical transaction 정기거래
periodicals 정기간행물
perishable property 부패하기 쉬운 물건
perishable tool 소모공구
permanent account 영구계정
permanent address 본적
permanent assets 영구자산
permanent auditor 상임감사역
permanent change 항구적인 변경
permanent debt 영구공채
permanent difference 영구차이
permanent disability 영구고도장해
permanent employment system 종신고용제
permanent establishment 항구적인 시설
permanent exhibit 상설전시
permanent facility 항구적인 시설
permanent financing 영구대출
permanent health insurance 종신건강보험
permanent income 항상소득
permanent income hypothesis 상설소득가설
permanent injunction 영구금지명령
permanent liabilities 영구부채
permanent life insurance 종신보험
permanent tenant right 영대소작권
permanent trespass 계속적인 침해
permeation of tight money policy
　금융긴축이 침투함
permissible error 허용오차
permissible loss ratio 허용손해율
permutation 교환
pernor of profits 수익자
perpetual annuity 종신연금
perpetual bond 영구권
perpetual fire insurance policy
　영구화재보험증권
perpetual injunction 영구금지명령

perpetual inventory 계속재고
perpetual inventory method 계속기록법
perpetual lease 영대차지권
perpetual lessee 영대차지인
perpetual merchandise control
　계속적인 상품통제
perpetual warrant 영구워런트
perpetuating testimony 증언을 증거로 보전함
perpetuity 영구구속
perquisite 임시수입
persistency rate 계속률
person adjudged incompetent 금치산자
person receiving employment income
　급여소득자
personable 계약능력자
personal accident insurance 상해보험
personal accident mutual insurance
　상해상호보험
personal account 인명계정
personal action 인적소송
personal assets 동산
personal attribute 개인특성
personal average tax rate 평균개인세율
personal bankruptcy 개인파산
personal bias 개인적인 편향
personal bill 개인어음
personal checking account 개인당좌계정
personal communication network
　개인통신망
personal consumption expenditure 개인소비
personal contact 대인접촉
personal contract 동산계약
personal covenant 인적 약관
personal credit 개인신용
personal deposit 개인예금
personal disposable income 개인가처분소득
personal distress 동산차압
personal dividend income 개인배당소득
personal estate 동산
personal exclusion from taxation
　인적과세제외**

O
P

personal exemption 기초공제
personal expenditure 개인지출
personal expenses 인건비
personal family corporation
　동족주주의 동족회사
personal financing 개인금융
personal guarantee 개인보증
personal handyphone system 간이휴대전화
persona hereditament 인적상속재산
personal holding company 동족회사
personal identification number 비밀번호
personal immunity 개인의 비밀보유권
personal income 개인소득
personal income from property 개인재산소득
personal income tax 개인소득세
personal influence 개인적인 영향
personal insurance 개인보험
personal interest income 개인이자소득
personal judgment 인적판결
personal knowledge 직접인식
personal ledger 인명원장
personal liability 개인부채
personal liability insurance
　개인배상책임보험
personal liberty 인신의 자유
personal lines statistical plan
　가계보험통계플랜
personal loan 개인론
personal media 인적미디어
personal opinion 자기의견
personal pension 개인연금
personal pension scheme 개인연금제도
personal property 개인재산
personal property floater 가재포괄보험
personal rental income 개인임대료소득
personal saving 개인저축
personal sector 개인부문
personal security 인적담보
personal service 역무
personal tax 동산세
personal taxation 인적과세

personal valuation 개인적인 평가
personality inventory 인물평가법
personality system 퍼스널리티체계
personality trait 인격특성
personation 성명사칭
personification theory 의인화이론
personnel audit 인사감사
personnel division 인사부
personnel floater 개인소유물포괄보험
personnel inspector 국세청감찰관
personnel management 인사관리
personnel reshuffle 인사이동
personnel strategy 인사전략
persons in overseas service 국외근무자
persons in parental authority 친권자
persuasibility 피설득성
petit jury 소배심
petition 청원
petition in bankruptcy 파산신청
petition of right 권리청원
petitioner 신립인
petrobond 원유가격연동형 사채
petroleum act 석유업법
petroleum gas tax 석유가스세
petroleum tax 석유세
petty average 소규모 해손
petty cash 소액현금
petty cash book 소액현금출납장
petty cash payment 소액현금지불
petty cash system 소액현금제도
petty current deposit 소액현금예금
petty deposits 소액예금
petty expense analysis book 잡비내역장
petty expenses 잡비
petty imprest 소액전도금
petty loss and profit 잡손익
petty-sum depreciable property
　소액상각자산
petty-sum wasting property 소액감모자산
phantom market 영치시장
phantom shopper 가상매물객

phase change printer 용해형 프린터
phase shifter 페이즈시프터
phased construction 단계적인 건설
phases of economic cycle 경기순환국면
phatic communication 교감적인 언어사용
Philadelphia plan 필라델피아플랜
philanthropy 자선
Phillips curve 필립스곡선
photo diode 포토다이오드
photoconductor device 광전도체디바이스
photomechanical process 사진제판
phototype setting 사진식자
physical access member
  입회장에서 거래할 수 있는 회원
physical capital 실체자본
physical contingency 물리적인 예비비
physical delivery 현실인도
physical depreciation 물리적인 감가
physical destruction 실체적인 멸실
physical distribution 물류
physical distribution function 물류기능
physical distribution responsibility 물류책임
physical distribution strategy 물류전략
physical inventory 실지재고정리
physical life 물리적인 내용연수
physical safety 물적 안전성
physical variance 추량차이
physical wear and tear 물리적인 감모
physically handicapped person 신체장애자
physically handicapped person allowance
  장애자 공제
physician's expense insurance 치료비보험
physiological drive 생리적인 동인
physiological needs 생리적인 욕구
pica 파이카(활자 크기의 한 종류)
pick up 상승
pick-up of inflation rate 인플레율이 상승함
pick-up of yield 이익개선
picker 도둑; 소매치기
picketing 피케팅
pickup bond 피크업본드

pico second 피코초
pictogram 픽토그램; 그림도표
pie chart 분원도
pignorative contract 질권설정계약
pilot marketing 파일럿마케팅
pilot plant 파일럿플랜트
pilot unit 시작기
pilotage 수로안내료
pin number 비밀번호
pioneering stage 개척단계
pip 피프
pit 피트
pit reporter 피트리포터
pixel 화소
place for tax payment 납세지
place of adjustment 공동해손정산지
place of business 사업소
place of delivery 인도장소
place of fiduciary 수탁취급장소
place of issue 발행지
place of payment 지불지
place of tax payment 납세지
placement 배치; 고용
placement advertisement 인재모집광고
placer claim patent 채광권
placing memorandum 사모요령
plain deal 플레인딜
plain language 보통주
plain vanilla 플레인바닐라
plaint 소송신청서
plaintiff 원고
plaintiff legislation 원고보호입법
plaintiffs bond 원고보증
plan 설계도
plan assets 연금자산
plan beneficiaries 플랜가입자
plan documents 연금플랜규정서
plan termination insurance
  연금제도종료보험
planned economy 계획경제
planning delivery 계획배송

O
P

planning hierarchy 계획계층
planning unit 계획단위
plant 공장
plant account 공장설비계정
plant and equipment 공장설비
plant capacity 생산설비
plant fund 설비자금
plant investment 설비투자
plant ledger 고정자산원장
plantation 대농원
plasma display 플라즈마디스플레이
plastic money 플라스틱머니; 신용카드
plasticity of demand 수요의 유연성
plateauing 플라토성향
platform 플랫폼
playing cards tax 트럼프세
playright 흥행권
Plaza accord 플라자합의
plea bargaining 사법거래
plea in abatement 각하항변
plea in bar 방소항변
plea of guilty 유죄답변(절차)
plea side 민사부
plead 소답하다
pleading 소답
pledge 저당(담보)물
pledged assets 저당자산
pledged security 차입유가증권
pledgee 동산질권자
pledgeholder 질물수탁자
pledger 질권설정자
pledgery 보증
pledging 플레징
pledger 질권설정자
plenipotentiary 전권
plottage 토지평가
plowing-back 이익을 재투자함
plug 짧은 광고방송
plum 특별배당
plunger 뛰어드는 사람
pluralistic competition 다원적인 경쟁

plus-tick 플러스 틱
point and figure method 포인트앤드피규어법
point estimate 점추정
point of indifference 무차별점
point of purchase POP; 구매시점
point of sales 판매시점정보관리
point scoring 점수기록제
point system 점수법
points 주장의 요점
points reserved 보류논점
poison pills 포이즌필
police court 간이형사재판소
policies for promoting competition
　　경쟁촉진정책
policies for restricting competition
　　경쟁제한정책
policy 보험증권
policy asset allocation 폴리시어셋앨로케이션
policy asset mix 폴리시어셋믹스
policy assignment 정책수단을 할당함
policy coordination 정책협조
policy depreciation 정책인인 감가상각
policy dividend 계약자배당금
policy fee 증권발행수수료
policy formulation 방침책정
policy jacket 보험증권의 본문
policy loan 보험증권대부
policy mix 폴리시믹스
policy number 보험증권번호
policy objective 최종목표
policy of the law 공서양속
policy proof of interest 이익보험증권
policy reserve 책임준비금
policy state 정책포지션
policy summary 계약개요
policy territory 증권적용지역
policy valuation 협정보험가액
policy value 보험증권가액
policy writing agent 보험증권발행대리점
policy year basis 인수연도별 계산
policyholder 보험계약자

policyholder's dividend 보험계약자배당금
policyholder's reserve 계약자준비금
policyholder's surplus 계약자잉여금
political corporation 정치단체
political crime 정치범죄
political office 정치적인 관직
political rights 정치적인 권리
political risk 정치리스크
political system stability index 정치안정지수
political turmoil 정치적인 혼란
poll tax 인두세
pollution control facilities 공해예방시설
pollution control reserve 공해방지준비금
polycentrism 현지지향
polychronic 폴리크로닉
polynomial-trend 다항식 경향선
pool account 풀계산
pool of fund approach 자금풀법
pool operation 풀조작
pool reinsurance 풀재보험
pool treaty 풀특약
pooled buying 공동구입
pooled common stock account
　합동보통주계정
pooled first mortgage 공동제일저당권
pooled income fund 합동수익기금
pooled marketing 공동마케팅
pooled private placement bond account
　합동사모(私募)채계정
pooled publicly traded bond account
　합동공모채계정
pooled real property account
　합동부동산계정
pooling arrangement 재보험풀
pooling contracts 공동계산계약
pooling of interests 지분풀링
poor laws 구빈법
popular action 민중소송
popular stock 인기주
population composition 인구구성
population density 인구밀도

population mortality 국민사망표
port charges 항만료
port dues 입항세
port risks insurance 계선(係船)보험
port toll 양륙세
portable pension 이동계속연금
portage 운임
portfolio 운용자산
portfolio analysis 포트폴리오 분석
portfolio approach 포트폴리오 수법
portfolio balance approach
　포트폴리오 밸런스 어프로치
portfolio bond 소지채권
portfolio characteristic line
　포트폴리오의 특성선
portfolio engineers 포트폴리오 엔지니어
portfolio investment 자산운용투자
portfolio management 포트폴리오 관리
portfolio method 전자산합동방식
portfolio mix 포트폴리오 믹스
portfolio monitoring 포트폴리오 모니터링
portfolio of investment trust 투신상표
portfolio optimization 포트폴리오 최적화
portfolio premium 포트폴리오 보험료
portfolio pricing methodology
　포트폴리오 가격 결정법
portfolio reinsurance 포트폴리오 재보험
portfolio restructuring 포트폴리오 재편
portfolio revision 포트폴리오 수정
portfolio risk model 포트폴리오 리스크 모델
portfolio selection 자산선택
portfolio view 포트폴리오 뷰
position 환보유고
position blanket bond 직무별 포괄보증증권
position bookkeeping 평형부기
position delta 포지션델타
position floating policy 직무별 포괄신용보험
position gamma 포지션감마
position instruction 포지션지도
position media 위치매체
position sheet 운용장

O
P

position trader 포지션 트레이더
position trading 포지션 매매
positioning 위치결정
positioning analysis 포지셔닝 분석
positive 실정의
positive adjustment policies
　　적극적인 조정정책
positive carry 포지티브캐리어
positive condition 적극조건
positive confirmation 적극적인 확인
positive credit file 포지티브정보
positive figure 흑자
positive Film 포지필름
positive financial policy 적극재정, 팽창재정
positive law 실정법
positive leverage effect
　　긍정적인 레버리지 효과
positive marketing 실증적인 마케팅
positive marketing 금전채권의 초과상태
positive prescription 취득시효
positive property 적극재산
positive yield 순 이일드
positive yield curve 긍정적인 이율곡선
positivism 실증주의
possession 점유
possession in deed 현실점유
possession in law 법정점유
possession of land 토지점유
possession of property 자산소유
possession utility 소유효용
possessory action 점유소송
possessory interest 단순점유권
possibility 불확정권
post 전기하다
post-audit 사후감사
post-close account 마감후 계정
post-closing entry 마감후 기입
post-closing trial balance 이월계산표
post-decision dissonance
　　의사결정후의 불협조
post-due bill 기한경과어음

post-entry 추가기입
post-facto 사후의
post-industrial society 탈공업화 사회
post-production 생산후의
post-qualification 사후자격심사
post office annuity 우편연금
post office life insurance 간이생명보험
post to the ledger 원장에 옮겨 적다
postage 우송료
postage paid 우송료 지불필
postage to be paid on delivery 우송료선불
postal money order 우편환
postal savings deposit 우편저축예금
postal transfer account 대체계좌
postdate 사후일부
postdated check 사후일부 수표
posted price 공시가격
posterior analysis 사후분석
posterior probabilities 경험적인 확률
posting 옮겨 적기
postmortem dividend 사후배당
postponement 연기
postponement of investment 투자연기
postponement of payment 지불유예
postponement of tax collection 징수유예
postponement of tax payment 연납
postretirement benefit 퇴직후 급부
postscript graphic 포스트스크립트그래픽
postulate of accounting period
　　회계연도를 공준함
postulate of business entity
　　기업실체를 공준함
potential competition 잠재적인 경쟁
potential customer 잠재고객
potential demand 잠재수요
potential existence 잠재적인 존재
potential injury 잠재적인 가해
potential oversupply produced by new issues
　　증자압박
pound bloc 펀드블록
pound crisis 펀드위기

pound sterling commercial paper
영국펀드 CP

pound sterling currency futures
영국펀드 통화선물

pound sterling depositary interest futures
영국펀드 예금금리선물

pound sterling time deposit
영국펀드 정기예금

poundage 집행수수료

poverty line 빈곤선

power 권한

power appendant 부종적인 지명권

power curve 검출력곡선

power expense 전력비

power in gross 독립지명권

power of appointment 지명권

power of attorney 위임장

power of collection 징수권

power of sale 매각권

power structure 권력구조

practicable 실무적으로 가능한

practical economy 실천경제

practice 실행하다; 영위하다

practitioner 실무가

pragmatics 실천론

pragmatism 프래그머티즘

prayer 청구취지신청

preacquisition profit 취득일 이전의 유보이익

preamble 서문

preappointed evidences 법이 예정한 증거

preapproach 예비접근

preaudience 우선발언권

preaudit 사전감사

prebid agreement 프레비드계약

precarious right 불확실한 권리

precaution 경계; 예방책

precautionary motive 예비동기

precedence 우위

precedence rule on tax collection 징수순위

precedent 선례

preceding fiscal year 전년도

preceding 이전의

preceding taxable year 전사업연도

preceding year 전년

precept 명령

precision 정밀도

preclusive specification 배타적인 사양

precognition 증인예비심문

precontract 선계약

precontract assessment 계약전 평가

predate 전일부로 하다

predecessor company 피합병회사

predetermined burden rate 예정배부율

predetermined cost 예정원가

predetermined cost system 예정원가계산

predicted cost 예상원가

prediction error 예측오차

prediction of investment return
투자수익을 예측함

prediction validity 예측타당성

predictors of default 채무불이행 예측지표

preemption 우선매수권

preemption entry 선취권을 등록, 신청함

preemptive right 신주우선인수권

preemptory 전제적인

preemptory instruction 결정적 설시

preemptory nonsuit 결정적 각하

prefabrication 사전가공

prefectural bond 지방채

prefectural inhabitants tax 지방세

prefectural tax 도시세

preference 선호; 우선권

preference dividend 우선배당

preference for interest rate 금리선호

preference income 우선소득

preference of financial assets 금융자산선호

preference segmentation
선호에 따른 세분화

preference share 우선주

preferential 특혜적인

preferential creditor 우선채권자

preferential duty 특혜관세**

preferential payment in bankruptcy
파산우선지불
preferential reinsurance 우선재보험
preferential right 우선권
preferential tariff 특혜관세
preferred creditor 우선채권자
preferred dividend 우선배당
preferred dividend coverage ratio
우선배당부담배율
preferred liability 우선채무
preferred risk 우량물건
preferred stock 우선주
prejudice 권리훼손; 편견
preliminary advice 사전조언
preliminary audit 예비감사
preliminary balance sheet 예비대차대조표
preliminary bordereau 예정 보르드로
preliminary claim 예비클레임
preliminary disclosure of settlement of
  accounts 결산예비발표
preliminary examination 예비심문
preliminary information 예비정보
preliminary investigation 예비조사
preliminary prospectus 사업설명서
preliminary review 예비심사
premature death 조기사망
prematurity redemption 조기상환
premerger notification 사전신고제
premise of a going concern
  계속기업을 전제로
premises 전술한 사항
premises coverage 구내담보
premium 권리금; 보험료
premium adjustment clause 보험료조정조항
premium base 기준보험료
premium bill 보험료청구서
premium bordereau 보험료보르드로
premium condition 보험료프리미엄
premium deposit 특약재보험예금
premium discount 보험료현장반환
premium discount for good risks
  우량물건할인

premium due 지불기일이 온 보험료
premium in arrears 미수보험료
premium income 수입보험료
premium issue 프리미엄발행
premium loan 보험료대체대부
premium on bonds payable 사채할증발행차금
premium on capital stock 주식불입잉여금
premium over conversion value
  전환가격을 넘는 금액
premium payment of a retirement annuity
  퇴직연금부금
premium pricing strategy 특별가격전략
premium quotation system 프리미엄시가방식
premium sale 경품부 판매
premium statement 보험료정산서
premium tax 보험료세
premium trust fund 보험료신탁기금
premium written 계상보험료
prenegotiation 사전교섭
preopening expenses 창립준비비
preoperating cost and similar deferrals
  이연자산
prepaid 선불의
prepaid card 프레페이드카드
prepaid expense 선불비용
prepaid freight 선불운임
prepaid income 선불이익
prepaid income taxes 선불법인세
prepaid insurance 선불보험료
prepaid insurance premiums 미경과보험료
prepaid interest 선불이자
prepaid rents on buildings 선불가임
prepaid salaries and wages 선도임금
preparatory audit 사전조사
prepay 선불하다
prepayment 도중상환
prepayment of income tax 예정납세
prepayment of premiums 보험료일괄선불
prepayment of tax 조세예납
prepayment option 선불옵션

prepayment projection 조기상환예상
prepayment risk 조기상환리스크
preprint 초벌인쇄
preproduction cost 시작품원가
prequalification 사전자격심사
presale order 사전판매
prescript 법령
prescription 시효
prescription 취득시효
prescription extinctive 소멸시효
present data analysis 현상분석
present of money in token of sympathy 위문금
present price 현재가격
present value 현재가치
present value discounted at compound interest 복리현가
present value method 현가법
present value rate 현가율
present worth 현재가치
presentation 증여
presentation bill 일람불어음
presentation for acceptance 인수증여
presentation for payment 지불증여
presentation period for payment 지불증여기간
presenting bank 증여은행
presentment 제출; 신청
presentment of bill of exchange 환어음을 증여함
presents 본증서
preservation 보존
preservative attachment 채권보전
preservative security 보전담보
preservative seizure 보전차압
president 총재
press law 출판법
press release 신문발표
pressure group 압력단체
prestige price 명예가격
presumption 추정

presumption of a real obtainer of income 소득귀속을 추정함
presumption of fact 사실상의 추정
presumptive evidence 추정증거
presumptive heir 법정추정상속인
pretax accounting income 세금공제전 회계이익
pretax income 세금공제전 이익
pretax income to sales 매상세금공제전 이익률
prevailing price 일반가격
prevailing value 재조달가치
prevailing wage 일반임금
preventional cost 예방코스트
preventive action 예방처리
preventive justice 예방사법
preventive law 예방법학
preventive maintenance 예방보전
previous close 전일종치
previous illness 기왕증
previous indorsements guaranteed 선행이서의 진정성을 증명함
previous insurers 선순위보험자
previous term 전기
previous year 전년
price action 가격행동
price adjustment 가격조정
price agreed upon 협정가격
price agreement 가격협정
price analysis 가격분석
price auction 가격입찰
price bargaining 가격교섭
price before tax 세전가격
price book-value ratio 주가순자산배율
price boost 가격상승
price cartel 가격카르텔
price cashflow ratio 캐시플로
price competition 가격경쟁
price concession 가격양보
price contingency 인플레예비비
price contract 가격계약
price control 가격통제

price cutting 가격인하
price determination 가격결정
price discrimination 가격차별
price divergence 가격차이
price effect 가격효과
price elasticity 가격탄력성
price elasticity of demand 수요가격
price equalization 가격균등화
price factor 가격계수
price filter 프라이스필터
price fixing 가격결정
price flexibility 가격신축성
price fluctuation 가격변동
price fluctuation reserve 가격변동준비금
price freeze 가격동결
price guaranty 가격보증
price hike 가격인상
price image 가격이미지
price including tax 세입가격
price index 물가지수
price indication method 가격표시방법
price information 가격정보
price leader 프라이스리더
price level 물가수준
price limit 가격 폭 제한
price limit on commodity futures
　상품선물거래가격폭제한
price line 가격폭제한
price line of futures price 선물가격곡선
price maker 프라이스메이커
price margin 가격차익
price mechanism 가격 메커니즘
price mix 가격믹스
price movement limit 가격 폭 제한
price movement of stocks 주가동향
price of corporate bond 사채가격
price of introduced stock 공개가격
price pattern 가격패턴
price priority 가격우선
price protection 가격보호
price pyramid 가격피라미드

price quotation 시세; 시가; 가격표
price range 가격 폭
price revision 가격개정
price risk 가격리스크
price spread 가격차이
price stabilization 가격안정
price stabilization policy 물가안정정책
price strategy 가격전략
price structure 가격구조
price supporting 가격안정조작
price system 가격체계
price theory 가격이론
price variation 물가변동
price volatility 가격변동률
price war 가격전쟁
price weighted index 평균가격가중지수
price-support subsidy 가격차이보조금
price-trend on stocks 주가트렌드
price-yield curve 가격-이율곡선
prices less tax 세공제가격
pricing 금리결정; 가격결정
pricing calculation 가격계산
pricing decision 가격결정
pricing model 가격결정모델
pricing strategy 가격결정전략
pricing tool 가격결정툴
prima 얼핏 보기에는
primage 운임할증
primage duty 수입부가세
primaries 예산
primary account 일차계정
primary advance 일차적인 부동산이동행위
primary beneficiary 일순위 보험금수취인
primary capital 일차자본
primary data 일차데이터
primary dealer 프라이머리딜러
primary deposit 본원적인 예금
primary distributions 일차분매
primary election 예비선거
primary goods 일차산품
primary industry 일차산업

primary industry product export
　일차산품수출
primary liability 일차부채
primary market 기채시장
primary materials 원재료
primary mortgage market
　신규모기지발행시장
primary processed goods 주요가공품
primary regulation notice 기본통달
primary reserve assets 일차준비자산
primary securities 직접증권
primary securities market 증권발행시장
primary stimuli 일차자극
primary user 주요이용자
prime bankers acceptance 일류은행인수어음
prime bill 우량어음
prime contract 원계약
prime corporate bonds 일류사채
prime cost 구입원가
prime cost method 직접원가배부법
prime factor 주요인
prime interest rate 프라임레이트
prime name bank 초일류은행
prime paper 우량어음
prime product 주제품
prime rate 우선대출금리; 프라임레이트
principal 원본; 본인
principal amortization schedule
　원본상환방법
principal amount 원금
principal and interest 원리
principal books 주요장부
principal component analysis 주성분분석
principal guaranteed 원본보증
principal paying 주지불
principal paying agent 주지불대리인
principal payment 원본지불
principal place of business 영업상의 본거
principal production order 주요제조지도서
principal products 주제품
principal sum 기본보험금액

principal tax 본세
principle of ascertained claim 권리확정주의
principle of balanced budget 건전재정주의
principle of clarity 명료성의 원리
principle of comparative advantage
　비교우위의 원리
principle of conservatism 보수주의의 원칙
principle of consistency 계속성의 원칙
principle of cost allocation 비용배분의 원칙
principle of cross liabilities 교차책임주의
principle of disclosure 공개성의 원칙
principle of effective demand
　유효수요의 원리
principle of equilibrium 대차평균의 원리
principle of equivalence 수지상등의 원칙
principle of gross budget accounting
　총액예산주의
principle of increasing risk 위험체증의 원리
principle of least effort 최소세력의 원리
principle of matching 대응의 원칙
principle of materiality 중요성의 원칙
principle of need 필요성원칙
principle of orderly system of bookkeeping
　정규부기의 원칙
principle of perennial tax 영구세주의
principle of priority of national tax claim
　국세채권우선의 원칙
principle of priority to first seizure
　차압선착순주의
principle of realization 실현주의의 원칙
principle of single budget 예산단일주의
principle of single liability 단일책임주의
principle of surplus section
　잉여금구분의 원칙
principle of taxation 조세원칙
principle of taxation on actual beneficiary
　실질주의
principle of the freedom of contract
　계약자유의 원칙
principle of truth 진실성의 원칙
principle of unified accounting 회계단일원칙

O
P

principle of valuation 평가원칙
principles of consolidation 연결방침
print media 인쇄매체
printed matter 인쇄물
printing plate 쇄판
prior approval 사전인가제도
prior distribution 사전분포
prior lien 선취유치권
prior lien bond
　　선취특권채; 우선담보권부사채
prior period adjustment 전기손익수정
prior preferred stock 제일우선주
prior probability 사전확률
prior redemption 만기전 상환
prior service cost 과거근무비용
prior taxable year 전사업연도
prior use 우선사용
prior year adjustment items
　　전년도손익수정항목
priori probability 선험적인 확률
priority 우선성
priority creditor 우선채권자
priority of attachment 우선차압권
priority of mortgage 저당우선권
priority of taxes 조세우선권
priority order of application 충당순위
priority rate of duty 실행관세율
priority reinsurance 우선재보험
prisoner's dilemma 죄수의 딜레마
private account 개인명의계좌
private accountant 사적회계사
private automobile policy 자가용 자동차보험
private bill 개인어음
private bond 민간채
private branch exchange 구내교환기
private brand
　　자가브랜드; 프라이베이트브랜드
private capital 민간자본
private company 비공개기업
private consumption 민간소비
private contract 수의계약

private convertible note 사모(私募)전환사채
private corporation 민간회사
private delivery system 자사배송시스템
private enterprise 민영사업
private holding company 동족회사
private insurance 자가보험
private insurance company 민영보험회사
private international law 국제사법
private label card 제휴자사카드
private ledger 사용(私用)원장
private member 개인회원
private note 사모채
private nuisance 사적 불법방해
private offering 사모(私募)
private passthrough 프라이베이트패스스루
private pension 기업연금
private pension plan 기업연금제
private placement 사모(私募)발행
private placement bond 연고채
private placement local government bond
　　연고지방채
private placement securities 사모(私募)증권
private placement special bond 연고특별채
private placement straight bond
　　사모(私募)보통사채
private right 사권(私權)
private risk 프라이베이트리스크
private sale 폐쇄매각
private settlement 시담
private subscription 연고모집
private telecommunication network
　　사설통신회선
private tender 지명입찰
private trust 개인신탁
private undertaking 민간사업
private use 사적인 사용
privately placed bond 비공모채
privatization 민영화
privilege 특권면책
privilege of conversion 전환특전
privilege tax 영업세

privileged allocation of issuance to
  stockholders 주주우선배정
privileged debts 우선지불채무
privileges and immunities 특권 및 면제
privity of contract 계약관계
prize offered for advertisement of the
  business 사업광고를 위한 상품
pro hac vice 이 경우에 한하여
pro rata distribution clause
  보험금액할당조항
pro rata payment 비례지불
pro se 자기자신의
pro-trade biased growth 무역에 편향된 성장
proactive strategy 선행형 전략
probabilistic brand choice
  확률론적 브랜드 선택
probabilistic characteristic lines
  확률에 따른 특성선
probabilistic forecasting 확률적 예측
probabilistic model 확률론적 모델
probabilistic model of preference
  확률론적 선호모델
probability curve 확률곡선
probability distribution 확률분석
probability mass function 확률함수
probability of loss or damage 손해확률
probability sample 확률표본
probable 확률이 높은
probable cause 상당한 이유
probable dividend 예상배당
probable life 예상내용연수
probable maximum loss 예상최대손해액
probable yield 예상이익
probate 검증
probate bond 검인보증증권
probation 집행유예
problem detection study 문제발견법
problem identification 문제를 선별함
procedural audit 절차감사
procedure 소송절차
procedures of tax adjustments 세무조사절차

proceeding 소송절차
proceeds 수취고; 지불보험금
proceeds account agreement
  지불준비계정계약
proceeds from disposals 처분수입
proceeds from external bond issuance
  외채발행대금
proceeds from long-term debt
  장기차입에서의 자금증가
proceeds of life insurance 생명보험금
proceeds of sale 매상고
process 소송절차
process analysis 공정분석
process capacity 공정능력
process color 프로세스컬러
process control 공정관리; 프로세스관리
process cost accounting 공정별 원가계산
process cost system 종합원가계산
process costing 공정별 원가계산
process for the recovery of taxes in arrears
  세금체납처분
process innovation 프로세스이노베이션
process modification 프로세스변경
process of garnishment 채권절차
process of inspection 검사공정
process parameter 공정파라미터
process production 일관생산
process quality audit 공정품질관리
process specification 공정사양서
process study 공정분석
process variable 프로세스관리특성
process verbal 조서
processed material 프로세스제품
processing 가공
processing cost 가공비
processing deal trade 가공무역
processing expenses 가공비
processing tax 가공세
proctor 사무변호사
procuration 대리인을 세움
procurement 수당

procurement cost 조달비
producer market 생산자시장
producer price index 생산자물가지수
producer's cartel 생산국가르텔
producer's goods 생산재
producer's surplus 생산자잉여
producing departments cost 제조부문비
product 제품
product assortment 제품구비
product attribute 제품특성
product attribute curve 제품속성곡선
product category 제품카테고리
product classification 제품분류
product cost accounting 제품별 원가계산
product cycle theory 프로덕트사이클론
product deletion 제품삭제
product development 상품개발
product differentiation 제품차별화
product diversification 제품다양화
product family 제품군
product image 제품이미지
product improvement 제품개량
product innovation era 상품혁신의 시대
product liability 제조물책임
product liability insurance 제조물책임보험
product life cycle 제품라이프사이클
product maturity 제품성숙
product mix 제품믹스
product motive 제품동기
product planning 제품계획
product portfolio 제품 포트폴리오
product portfolio management
　　제품 포트폴리오 매니지먼트
product positioning 제품포지셔닝
product price 제품가격
product proliferation 제품증식효과
product quality 제품품질
product recall 제품회수
product research 제품조사
product satisfactions 제품만족
product space 제품공간

product warranties 제품보증
product-oriented 생산지향
production 생산고; 연출
production account 생산계정
production base 생산거점
production budget 제조예산
production capital 생산자본
production card 작업표
production control 생산관리
production control system 생산관리시스템
production cost 제조간접비
production department 제조부문
production efficiency variance
　　제조능률 차이
production equipment 제조설비
production expenses 제조경비
production facility 생산설비
production function 생산함수
production goods 생산재
production labor cost 생산노무비
production level 조업도
production loan 프로덕션론
production method 생산고비례법
production order 제조지도서
production order cost accounting
　　개별원가계산
production orientation 생산지향
production permit 생산허가
production process 생산공정
production release 생산개시
production report 생산고보고서
production sharing 생산분배
production statement 제조보고서
production statistics 제품통계
production upon order 주문생산
productive wages 직접임금
productivity 생산성
productivity inflation 생산성격차인플레
productivity measurement 생산성측정
productivity of capital 자본생산성
productivity of labor 노동생산성

productivity ratio 생산성지표
products 생산물
products and completed operation liability
    insurance 생산물배상책임보험
profession 직업
professional accountant 직업회계사
professional auditor 직업감사인
professional liability insurance 전문직업인배
    상책임보험
professional publication 전문지
professional's market 전문적인 상장
professionals 전문가
profit 이익
profit account 이익계정
profit accruing from insurance 보험차익
profit accruing from refund of bonds and
    debentures 공사채상환익
profit accured from valuation 평가익
profit after expenses 경비공제후 이익
profit after tax 세공제후 이익
profit and commissions form
    이익 및 수수료담보양식
profit and loss 손익
profit and loss account 손익계정
profit and loss break-even point 손익분기점
profit and loss carried forward 이월손익
profit and loss equation 손익계산서등식
profit and loss method 손익법
profit and loss report 손익보고
profit and loss statement 손익계산서
profit and loss transaction 손익거래
profit available for dividend 배당가능이익
profit before tax 세공제전 이익
profit center 프로핏센터
profit chart 이익도표
profit commission 이익반환
profit control 이익관리
profit control chart 이익도표
profit corporation 영리법인
profit curve 이익곡선
profit debenture 수익사채

profit equation 이익방정식
profit form amalgamation 합병차익
profit from capital reduction 감자차익
profit from consolidation 합병차익
profit from merger 합병차익
profit from private funds offered 사재제공익
profit from redemption 상환차익
profit from sales of stocks 주식매각익
profit from the difference between new and
    old official prices 가격차익금
profit from trust 신탁이익
profit from valuation of assets 자산평가익
profit function 이익함수
profit goal 목표이익
profit growth 이익신장
profit growth rate 이익성장률
profit impact 수익효과
profit increase 증익
profit inflation 이윤인플레이션
profit insurance 이익보험
profit making business 영리사업
profit management 이익관리
profit margin 이폭
profit maximization 이윤극대화
profit motive 이윤동기
profit on redemption of discount bond
    할인채상환익
profit on sale 매각익
profit on sale of real estate 부동산매각익
profit or loss on foreign exchange
    외환환산손익
profit per share 일주당 이익
profit planning 이익계획
profit potential 잠재이익
profit prior to consolidation 연결전 이익
profit prior to incorporation
    회사설립전 이익
profit profile 수익구조
profit quota 이익할당
profit rate of total liabilities and net worth
    총자본수익률

profit ratio 이익률
profit ratio of capital 자본이익률
profit responsibility 이익책임
profit slide 이익감소
profit taking 가격차이로 이익얻기
profit tax 수익세
profit transferred 대체이익
profit volume graph 한계이익도표
profit-driven market 업적상장
profit-making business 영리사업
profit-sharing 이익분배(제)
profit-sharing bond 이익분배사채
profit-sharing system 이익분배제도
profit-sharing securities 이윤증권
profit-sharing trust 이윤분배신탁
profit-volume ratio 매상고한계이익률
profitability 수익성
profitability and investment analysis ratio
  수익성 분석
profitable 수익률이 높은
profitable line of business 채산라인
profiteer 부당이득자
protits from immovables transactions
  부동산매매익
proforma 견적
proforma account sales 견적매상계정서
proforma amount 참고수치
proforma balance sheet 견적대차대조표
proforma bill/draft 견적한 어음
proforma estimated cost 견적
proforma statement 견적재무제표
program budgeting 프로그램예산
program evaluation and review technique
  PERT; 퍼트
program supplier 프로그램공급업자
program trading 프로그램매각
programed instruction 프로그램학습
programming method 프로그래밍방식
progress payment 생산고지불
progressive average inventory method
  총평균법

progressive cost 체증비
progressive income tax 누진소득세
progressive ledger 연속원장
progressive obsolescence 점진적인 진부화
progressive tax rate 누진세율
progressive taxation 누진과세
prohibited risks 인수금지물건
prohibition of deposit transfer 예금양도금지
prohibition of endorsement 이서금지
prohibitive tax 금지세
prohibitory injunction 금지명령
project finance 프로젝트파이낸스
project simulator 프로젝트시뮬레이터
projected balance sheet 견적대차대조표
projected benefit obligation 예측급부채무
projected demand 예측수요량
projected dividend 예상배당
projected financial statements 견적재무제표
projected holding period rate of return
  기대보유기간수익률
projected income statement 견적손익계산서
projective methods 투영법
proliferation 확산
prolixity 불요한 진술
promisee 수약자
promisor 약속자
promissory note 약속어음
promissory warranty 약속담보
promoter 발기인
promoter's share 발기인주
promoting mergers tax credit
  합병촉진세액공제
promotion expenses 창업비
promotion mix 프로모션믹스
promotional strategy 프로모션전략
promotools 프로모션용구
promulgation 반포, 공포, 선전
proof 증거
proof of loss 손해를 증명함
propaganda 선언
propensity to consume 소비성향

propensity to import 수입성향
propensity to investment 투자성향
propensity to savings 저축성향
proper card 자사카드
proper journal 보통분개장
proper law 준거법
proper value 고유치
property 재산
property 취득자산
property and equipment 고정자산
property and liability insurance 손해보험
property damage 재물손괴
property depreciation insurance 신가보험
property for advertisement 광고선전용 자산
property for exchange 교환용 자산
property for experimental and research
　　시험연구용 자산
property for residence 거주용 자산
property for substitution 대체자산
property for transfer 양도자산
property income 재산소득
property insurance 동산보험
property ledger 재산원장
property life insurance 재산생명보험
property replaced by purchase 매환자산
property reserved 준비필 재산
property right 재산권
property subject to seizure 차압대상재산
property tax 고정자산세
property tax cadaster 고정자산과세대장
property ward 재산구
proportional calculation 비례원가계산
proportional expenses 비례비
proportional method 일괄비례배분방식
proportional reinsurance 비례재보험
proportional reserve method 비례준비금
proportional reserve system 비례준비제도
proportional tax 비례세
proportional taxation 비례과세법
proportional equal terms 비례평등조건
proportionally variable cost

비례적인 가변비용
proposal letter 프로포절레터
proposal method 프로포절방식
propound 제안하다
proprietary account 자본주계정
proprietary company 사회사
proprietary insurance company
　　비상호조직보험회사
proprietary right 소유권
proprietary trading 자기계정매매
proprietor 소유자
proprietor deduction 사업주공제
proprietor of a business 사업주
proprietor punishment 업무주처벌제도
proprietors special expense reserve
　　사업주특별경비준비금
proprietorship 개입기업; 소유주지분
proprietorship account 소유주계정
proration 비례할당
prorogation 폐회
prose model 산문모델
prosecuting attorney 검찰관
prosecutors office 검찰청
prospective cash receipts 입금예측액
prospective dividend rate 예상배당율
prospective method 장래법
prospective profit 기대이익
prospective rating 경험요율법
prospective return 예상수익률
prospective usable 사용가능기간
prospective yield 예상이익
prospective yield average 예상평균이익
prospectus 설립취지서; 내용설명서
prospectus of promotion 회사설립취지서
prosperous days 호경기시대
protecting the currency 통화방위
protection 보호영장
protection of investor 투자자보호
protective duty 보호관세
protective order 보호명령
protective put trading 프로텍티브풋 거래

O
P

protective tariff 보호관세
protective trust 보호신탁
protectorate 보호령
protest 거절증서
protest charges 거절증서작성수수료
protestation 이의신청
protested check 부도수표
protester 비판적인 시청자
protestor 거절자
protocol 조약의정서; 프로토콜
provable debt 입증할 수 있는 채권
prove 증명하다
provident benefit 공제급부금
provision 조건; 준비금
provision account 준비금계정
provision for bad debts 대손준비손
provision for surplus 적립이월
provision for tax 납세준비금
provisional attachment 가차압
provisional budget 잠정예산
provisional disposition 가처분
provisional execution 가집행
provisional insurance 예정보험
provisional liquidator 잠정청산인
provisional order 가명령
provisional policy 예정보험
provisional rating 일시적인 가격설정
provisional registration 가등기
provisional residence 가주소
provisional return 예정신고
provisional risk book 예정보험인수부
provisional seizure 가차압
provisional settlement of account 가결산
provisional sum 프로비저널섬; PS단가
provisional tariff 잠정세율
proviso 조건; 단서
provisory clause 단서조항
provocation 도발
proxemics 근접학
proximate cause 주원인
proximate damage 직접손해

proximo 다음달의
proximo terms 익월일부조건
proxy 대리
proxy currency 대용통화
proxy fight 위임장쟁탈전
proxy solicitation 위임장근유
proxy statement 주주총회소집통지
proxy variable 대수변수
proxy vote 위임장투표
prudence 주의
prudent man rule 신중인원칙
prudent person rule 수탁자책임
psychic income 심리소득
psychological consumer behavior
    심리학적 소비자행동
psychological element 심리적인 요소
psychological laws 심리법칙
psychological line 사이콜로지컬라인
psychological theory of exchange 환심리설
psychometrics 계량심리학
public acceptance 퍼블릭억셉턴스
public accountant 공인회계사
public acknowledgment 인지
public address 장내방송장치
public and corporate bond 공사채
public and corporate bond investment trust
    공사채투자신탁
public assistance 생활보호
public auction 공매
public bidding 공개입찰
public body 공공단체
public bond dealing 공채매매
public bond investment trust 공사채투자신탁
public company 공개기업
public compensation bond 교부공채
public corporation 공사, 공단
public corporation bond 공사채
public debt securities 공공채
public disclosure 공시
public domain software
    퍼블릭 도메인 소프트웨어

public dues 공과
public economics 공공경제학
public enterprise 공적기업
public expenditure 공공지출
public facilities tax 공동시설세
public finance 국가재정
public finance corporation 공고
public finance law 재정법
public goods 공공재
public health service 공중보건기관
public hearing 공청회
public impost 공과
public information 공개정보
public institution 공개기관
public insurance 공영보험
public interest corporation 공익법인
public investment 공공투자
public issue 공모채
public law 공법
public liability coverage
　일반손해배상책임담보
public market 대중상장
public measurer 공인검량인
public monopoly 전매
public notary 공증인
public notification 공시최고
public notification of auction 공매광고
public notification of returns 신고서공시
public offering 공모
public offering business 공모업무
public order 공공질서
public pension 공적연금
public policy 공익
public relations 공중관계활동; PR
public responsibility 공공책임
public sale 공개매각
public service 공공사업
public spending 공공지출
public subscription 공모
public summons 공시최고
public telecommunication business
　공공통신사업
public trust 공익신탁
public utility 공공사업
public utility accounting 공익사업회계
public utility bond 공익사업채
public utility charges 공공요금
public welfare 공공복지
public work 공공사업
publicly held stock 공개주
publicly offered share 매출주
publicly subscribed share 공모주
publicly traded company 상장회사
publicly-held company 공개회사
publising advertising 출판물광고
publishing cost 출판비
publishing law 출판법
publishing right 출판권
puffer 경매인의 한통속
puffing 과장
pull strategy 풀전략
pulling-back 후퇴
pulse code modulation 펄스코드변조
pulse code modulation broadcasting
　PCM 방송
pump-priming effect 마중물효과; 실마리 효과
punishment on penalty tax 추징처분
punitive damages 징벌적인 손해배상
punitive tariff 제재관세
purchase 구매
purchase acquisition 흡수합병
purchase agent 매입대리인
purchase agreement 매수계약서
purchase allowance 구입가할인
purchase amount 구입고
purchase and assumption 예금승계방식
purchase and sale statement 매입계산서
purchase behavior 구매행동
purchase book 구입장
purchase commission 구입수수료
purchase commitments 구입약정
purchase contract 선물매수계약

O
P

purchase cost 구입원가
purchase discount 구입할인
purchase face amount 매수액면금액
purchase frequency 구매빈도
purchase fund 매입자금
purchase 매입그룹
purchase investigation 매수를 임의조사함
purchase ledger 구입처원장
purchase method 매수법
purchase money 구입대금
purchase on credit 외상구입
purchase payment fund 외상적립기금
purchase price 구입대금
purchase return 구입반품
purchase tax 구입세
purchase-money mortgage 토지대금양도저당
purchase-money obligation 매입대금채무
purchased parts 매입부품
purchaser 매주
purchases and sales 매매
purchases budget 구입예산
purchases rebate 구입환불
purchasing cost 구입원가
purchasing expenses 구입비용
purchasing manager 구매부장
purchasing power gain or loss
    구매력변동손익
purchasing power of money 화폐의 구매력
purchasing power parity theory
    구매력평가설
purchasing power risk 구매력리스크
purchasing price 구입단가
purchasing redemption 구입상환
purchasing units 구매단위

pure cap 퓨어캡
pure deferred life annuity
    순수거치종신연금
pure discount bond 순할인채
pure endowment 생존보험
pure endowment insurance 생존보험
pure oligopoly 순수과점
pure risk 순수위험
purpose loan pursue 사용목적특정대부
purview 본문
push money 보상금
push phone telephone line 푸쉬회선
push pull 푸쉬풀
put 풋
put bond 상환청구권부 채권
put diagram 풋다이어그램
put holder 풋보유자
put option 풋옵션
put ratio back spread trading
    풋레이쇼백스프레딩
put swaption 풋스왑션
put-call ratio 풋콜비율
put-value line 풋가격선
putative 추정의
puttable bond 푸터블채권
puttable swap 푸터블스와프
puttable swaption 푸터블스왑션
putting-out system 전대제도
pyramid management method
    관리방식 피라미드형 관리방식
pyramid marketing system 멀티상법
pyramiding 개서, 보험누적채무
pyramiding process 피라미딩 과정

quadratic cost function 이차비용함수
quadratic demand function 이차수요함수
quadratic loss function 이차손실함수
quadratic programing 이차계획서
qualification 한정사항; 적격성; 면책사항
qualification criteria 자격기준
qualification laws 자격법
qualification process 적격성확인프로세스
qualified 적격인
qualified acceptance 조건인수
qualified acceptance heritage 한정상속
qualified acceptance of bill 부단순인수
qualified acceptance of inheritance 한정상속
qualified audit certificate 한정감사보고서
qualified endorsement 한정이서
qualified inheritance 한정상속
qualified opinion 한정의견
qualified pension contract 적격퇴직연금계약
qualified pension funds 적격퇴직연금적립금
qualified pension plan 적격퇴직연금
qualified pension system 적격퇴직연금제도
qualified privilege 제한적인 면책특권
qualified property 제한적인 재산권
qualified report 한정보고서
qualified spouse for deduction
　　공제대상배우자
qualifying activity 유망결결정
qualifying dimensions 제특성
qualifying reserve 한정준비금
qualifying stock option 종업원자사주구입권
qualitative analysis 정성분석

qualitative credit control 질적인 금융통제
qualitative criteria 정성기준
qualitative economic policy 질적인 경제정책
qualitative substantiality test
　　질적실질성의 원칙
quality 격
quality awareness 품질의식
quality class 고품질클래스
quality control 품질관리
quality cost approach 품질코스트법
quality description 품질설명
quality effect 품질효과
quality improvement 품질개선
quality loop 품질루프
quality loss 품질로스
quality objective 품질목표
quality of earnings 이익의 질
quality paper 고급지
quality policy 품질방침
quality record 품질기록
quality related cost 품질관련코스트
quality surveillance 품질감시
quality system 품질시스템
quality variable 품질변수
quantification 수량화
quantitative analysis 정량분석
quantitative approach 정량적인 어프로치
quantitative asset allocation
　　정량적인 애셋앨로케이션
quantitative boom 수량경기
quantitative economic policy 양적인 경제정책

quantitative market analysis
　정량적인 시장분석
quantitative model 정량모델
quantitative monetary indicator
　양적인 금융지표
quantitative substantiality test
　수량실질성의 원칙
quantitative tool 수량화수단
quantity adjustment 수량조정
quantity discount 수량할인
quantity discount system 단계식 할인방법
quantity limit 수량제한
quantity of production 생산량
quantity sold 판매수량
quantity standard 수량표준
quantity theory of money 화폐개량설
quantity variance 추정량차이
quantize 양자화하다
quantum evaluation 금전적인 평가
quantum mechanics 양자역학
quarter 4반기
quarter-days 4계지불지급일
quarterly real growth rate
　4반기 베이스의 실질성장률
quarterly reports 4반기보고서
quash 각하하다
quasi-arbitrator 준중재인
quasi-chain 준체인
quasi-compulsory saving 준강제저축
quasi-contract 준계약
quasi-currency 준통화
quasi-delict 준불법행위
quasi-easement 준지역권
quasi-equity 준주식
quasi-estoppel 준금반언(準禁反言)

quasi-final return 준확정신고
quasi-incompetent person 준금치산자
quasi-insurance 준보험
quasi-integration 반통합
quasi-judicial power 준사법권력
quasi-loan for consumption 준소비대차
quasi-member 준회원
quasi money 준화폐
quasi-public corporation 제3섹터
queuing 대기행렬
queuing model 대기행렬모델
quick assets 당좌자산
quick assets ratio 당좌비율
quick assets to year's cash expenses
　연간지출당좌비율
quick liabilities 단기부채
quick ratio 당좌비율
quick ring 퀵링
quiet market 보합상장
quit 면책된
quitting of business 사업폐지
quorum 법정수
quota 출자할당액
quota sample 할당표준
quota sampling 할당추출법
quota share treaty reinsurance
　비례특약재보험
quotation 상장
quotation exchange center 시세정보교환센터
quotation of over-the-counter issue 장외시세
quotation on overseas markets 해외상장
quote (가격·시세를) 부르다; 어림치다
quote reporter 쿼트리포터
quoting high 시세를 높게 부르다

rack focus 랙포커스

racketeering 무리하게 억지로 청함

radian 라디안, 호도

radio communication 무선통신

raider 적대적인 매수를 고려하는 주식취득자

raiding the market 시장을 어지럽힘

rail transportation 철도수송

railroad bonds 철도채

raising of funds 자금조달

raising of interest rate 금리인상

rally 시세가 회복복되다

random access memory RAM

random effect model 변량효과모델

random fluctuation 불규칙변동

random numbers 난수

random price changes 불규칙한 가격변동

random sampling 무작위추출법

random variable 확률변동

random walk theory 랜덤워크이론

range 변동폭

range forward contract 레인지포워드거래

rank order 계급순위

ranking system 서열법

ransom insurance 납치보험

rapid expansion 급증

rare stock 희귀주

raster 래스터(텔레비전 브라운관의 형광면 위에 나타나는 주사선에 의한 가로줄무늬)

ratable distribution 비례배당

ratable value 과세견적가격

rate 요율; 세금

rate card 매체요율표; 과금표

rate covenant 금리조항

rate cut 요율인하

rate down 요율저하

rate in foreign currency 외화통화유통

rate in home currency 자국통화유통

rate in overseas market 해외상장

rate of change 변화율

rate of estimated expenses 개산경비율

rate of increase 상승률

rate of inflation 인플레율

rate of listed bond 공사채를 상장한 상장

rate of operating 가동률

rate of output 조업도

rate of premium 보험료율

rate of return 수익률

rate of stock-turn 상품회전율

rate of technical progress 기술진보율

rate of temporary duty 잠정세율

rate of turnover 회전율

rate of variable expenses 변동비율

rate of wage increase 임금상승률

rate papers 납세고지서

rate payment 지방세

rate scale 시청률측정기준

rate sensitive assets 금리감응자산

rate sensitive liability 금리감응부채

rated policy 고요율적용계약

rated value 정격치

ratepayer 조세부담자

ratification 비준

rating 등급을 정함; 시청률
rating agency 평가기관
rating of bond 채권의 등급을 매김
rating organization tariffs 산정회요율
rating system 등급제도
ratio 비; 비율
ratio analysis 비율분석
ratio call spread transaction
  레이쇼 콜 스프레드 거래
ratio method 비율분석법
ratio of direct and indirect taxes 직간접비율
ratio of earnings to dividends
  이익금 대 배당비율
ratio of Rxed liabilities to net worth
  고정부채비율
ratio of general expenses to current income
  일반경비율
ratio of gross profit to inventory investment
  교차비율
ratio of gross profit to net sales
  매상총이익률
ratio of net worth to total capital
  자기자본비율
ratio of operating profit to revenue
  영업이익률
ratio of personnel expenses 인건비율
ratio of profit to capital 자본이익률
ratio of profit to net sales 매상고이익률
ratio of receivable to inventories
  인수계정 대 재고자산비율
ratio of replacement 자산갱신률
ratio of shareholding 지주비율
ratio of special depreciation deduction
  특별상각률
rational motivation 합리적인 동기부여
rational valuation 합리적인 평가
rationalization 합리화
rationalization of production 생산합리화
rationing 배급제도
raw and processed materials 원재료
raw material 재료

raw material inventory 원재료재고
reach 도달범위; 누적도달률
reaching the top price 최고가격에 도달하다
reaction 반락
reaction curve 반응곡선
reactionary fall 반락
read only memory 롬(ROM)
readership survey 열람율조사
readjusting entry 재수정기입
readjustment of taxation system 세제정리
ready money 현금
ready reckoner 계산조견표
real account 실재계정
real action 대물소송
real assets 실물자산
real balance effect 실질화폐잔고효과
real capital 실물자본
real chattels 물적동산
real contract 대물계약
real cost 실질원가
real credit 대물신용
real deposits 실질예금
real disposable income 실질가처분소득
real distress 부동산차압
real earnings 실질소득
real economy 실체경제
real entity theory of corporation 법인실재설
real estate 부동산
real estate acquisition tax 부동산취득세
real estate broker 부동산브로커
real estate held for sale 판매용 토지
real estate in trust 부동산신탁
real estate income 부동산소득
real estate investment trust 부동산투자신탁
real estate loan receivable
  부동산저당장기대부금
real estate mortgage 부동산모기지
real estate security 부동산담보
real estate tax 고정자산세
real evidence 물적증거
real growth 실질성장

real growth rate 실질성장률
real guarantee 물상보증
real hereditament 물적상속재산
real income 실질소득
real income earner 실질소득자
real interest rate 실질금리
real investment 실물투자
real investment return 실질투자수익률
real obtainer of dividend income
　배당소득으로 귀속됨
real obtainer of interest income
　이자소득으로 귀속됨
real property 부동산
real property acquisition tax 부동산취득세
real rate 실질이율
real right 물권
real term 실질단위
real time 리얼타임
real time communication 순시통신
rate-real time processing 리얼타임처리
real unit labor cost 실질단위노동코스트
real wage 실질임금
real world computing 실세계컴퓨팅
real yield 실질이율
real-bills doctrine 상업어음주의
realignment 재조정
realignment negotiation 재조정교섭
realizable value 실현가능가액
realization 환가
realization basis 실현주의
realization of gains 수익실현
realization of tax liability 납세의무성립
realization principle 실현주의
realization sales 환금판매
realized appreciation 실현증가액
realized depreciation 실현감가상각
realized profit 실현이익
realized revenue 실현수익
realized volatility 실현가격변동률
realized yield 실효이율
really rightful person 진실로 정당한 권리자

realm of being 존재영역
realty business 부동산업
reappraisal 재평가; 재검토
reappraisement 재평가
rearrangement of budget item 예산항목이체
reason for dishonor 부도사유
reasonable 상당한
reasonable depreciation 상당한 상각
reasonable doubt 합리적인 의문
reassessment 재평가
reassessment of taxes 과세갱정결정
rebalance 재평가
rebalancing strategies 리밸런싱전략
rebate 리베이트; 환불
rebate of premium 보험료환불
rebate on business 구입반려
rebate on sales 매상반려
rebound 반등
rebut 반증을 들다
rebutting evidence sit 반증
recall 회수
recall method 회상법
recapitalization 자본형성; 자본수정
recaption 자력으로 되찾음
recapture 탈환, 회복
recapture clause 상환조항
receipt and payment bookkeeping 수지부기
receipt in full 전액영수서
receipt slip 입금전표
receipts and disbursements break-even point
　수지분기점
receipts and payments 수지지출
receivables 수취채권
receivable and payable contract
　채권채무계약
receivable from affiliate 관계회사외상금
receivables turnover 매상채권회전률
receive slip 입금전표
received margin 수입증거금
receiver 파산관재인
receiver in bankruptcy 파산관재인

Q
R

receivership 채권자구제수속
receiving 수납계정
receiving bank 피발송은행
receiving inspection 구입검사
receiving monitor 수입 감시
receiving order 재산관리명령
receiving quotation 수취계정기준상장
receiving report 수납보고서
reception stamp 수납인
recession 경기후퇴; 불황
recession cartel 불황카르텔
recession period 경기후퇴기
recipient 수취인
reciprocal 상호의, 호혜적인
reciprocal account 대응계정
reciprocal consignment 상호위탁판매
reciprocal contract 쌍무계약
reciprocal credit 상호신용장
reciprocal decision 상호결정
reciprocal demand 상호수요
reciprocal demand curve 상호수요곡선
reciprocal distribution method 상호배부법
reciprocal duties 호혜관세
reciprocal exchange 상호보험
reciprocal reinsurance 교환재보험
reciprocal transfer of property 상호자산교환
reciprocal treaty 교환재보험특약
reciprocity 교환재보험; 상호주의
recital clause 설명문언
recklessness 부주의
reclaimed land 매립지
reclaimed materials 재생원재료
reclamation 개발; 재생
reclassification 재분류
recognition of sales 매상고를 인식함
recognitive dissonance 인지불협화음
recognizance 서약
recognized private operating agency
　민간전기통신사업자
recommended standard
　RS232C(직렬 로트)

recommended stock 추천주
reconcilement 조합
reconciliation 조정
reconciliation item 조정항목
reconciliation of surplus 잉여금조정서
reconciliation statement for current account
　당좌조회표
reconciling type 잔고조정식
reconstruction expense 개축비
reconstruction works 개축공사
recontinuance 상속재산회복
reconversion 재전환
reconveyance 양도저당
record 등록
record a profit 이익을 계상하다
record date 기준일
record high 사상최고
record low 사상최저
record of conviction 유죄판결기록
record of payment 지불조서
record of seizure 차압조서
record on appeal 상소기록
record on removal 이송신청기록
record price 고치(高値)
record retention 기록유지
recorded cost 장부원가
reorder 기록관
recoup 손해를 회복하다
recoupment 공제권
recourse 구상권
recourse loan 리코스론
recourse right 파급권
recover high 고가로 회복
recoverable 회수가능한
recovery 회수; 회복
recovery cost 회수가능원가
recovery expenditure 회수가능지출
recovery of bad debt 대손금회수
recovery of credits 채권회수
recovery of legal status 복권
recovery of loss 결손회수

recovery value 회수가능가치
recreation plan 리크리에이션관리
recruiting expense 모집비
rectangular coordinates 직교좌표
recurring profit 경상이익
recurring profit and loss 경상손익
recusation 기피
recycle strategy 자원재이용전략
red B/L 적선하증권
red clause credit
　　레드클로즈 신용장; 전대신용장
red figure 적자
red green blue
　　RGB 적, 녹, 청(컬러화상의 3원색)
red herring 적자잔고
red tape 관료주의
red-balance 적자잔액
redeem 저당재산을 되찾다
redeem before maturity 앞당겨 상환하다
redeemable bond 상환채권
redeemable preferred stock 상환우선주식
redeemable stock 상환주식
redemption 상환
redemption at fixed date 정시상환
redemption at market value 시가상환
redemption at maturity 만기상환
redemption before maturity 중도환금
redemption by lottery 추첨상환
redemption by purchase 매입상각
redemption by yearly installment 연부상환
redemption date 상환기일
redemption from tax sale 공매에서 되찾음
redemption of bond 채권기일
redemption of external loan 외채상환
redemption of government securities
　　정부증권상환
redemption of pledge 저당을 되찾음
redemption premium 상환프리미엄
redemption profit 상환익
redemption value 상환가격
redevelopment 재개발

redirect examination 재직접심문
rediscount 재할인
rediscount policy 재할인정책
rediscount rate 재할인금리
redistributed cost 재배부원가
redistribution of income 소득재분배
redress 구제
reduce holding ratio 재구성비율을 인하하다
reduce to practice 실시화
reduced asset price 감자산가격
reduced instruction set computer RISC
reduced old-age benefit 감액노령연금급부
reduced paid-up insurance 감액완납보험
　　(이후의 보험료 지불을 중지하고 그 시점에
　　서의 해약금 바탕으로 일시불보험료를 산정
　　하여 새롭게 보험금액을 결정함)
reduced rate contribution clause
　　감소율분담조항
reduced tax rate 경감세율
reduced tax rate on dividendpaid 배당경과
reduced tax rate on specified medical
　　corporation 특정의료법인의 특별세율
reducing balance method 체감잔고법
reducing unemployment rate 실업률감소
reduction 공제; 감면
reduction and exemption of taxes 감면
reduction in price 가격인하
reduction of incidence 부담경감
reduction of operation 조업단축
reduction of stock 감자
reduction of taxes 감세
reduction or exemption of tax 조세감면
reduction surplus 감자잉여금
reductions in long-term debt 장기차입반제액
redundancy 과잉, 여분
reengineering 리엔지니어링
referable name 확인해야 할 곳
referee bond 조정인보증증권
referee in bankruptcy 파산심리인
referee ill case of need 예비지불인
reference 조합; 중재합의

Q
R

reference bank 조회처은행
reference behavior 준거행동
reference index 지표가 되는 지수
reference on consent 합의하여 사건을 위탁함
reference period 참고기간
reference range 참고상장권
reference rate 기준금리
reference zone 참고상장권
referral premium 소개사찰
refinance system 리파이낸스방식
refinancing 자금재조달
refinancing bond 차환채
refinancing issue 차환발행
refix date 갱신일
reflation 통화재팽창
reflation policy 경기부양책
reflection 반사광
reflow 환류
reform of the administrative structure
　행정개혁
reformation 정정
refresher 추가사례금
refund 환부금
refund annuity 상환식 연금
refund bond 전불금반환보증증권
refund by final return 확정신고에 따른 환금
refund deferred life annuity
　상환거치종신연금
refund of overpayment 과오납금환부
refund of principal 원본상환
refund of taxes 세금환부
refund tax 환부세
refunded corporation tax 환부법인세
refunding 자금재조달
refunding bond 상환보증증권
refunding securities 차환증권
refundment 반려금
refundment guarantee 전불금반환보증
refusal to deal 거래거부
regional analysis 지역분석
regional bank 지방은행

regional bank card 뱅크카드
regional brand 지역브랜드
regional differences 지역격차
regional economy 지역경제
regional exchange 지방거래소
regional issue 지방판
regional market 지방시장
regional office 지방사무소
regional plan 지역계획
regional portfolio 특정지역 포트폴리오
regional station 지방국
regional taxation bureau 국세청
regionalism 지역주의
regionals 지방업자
regioncentrism 지역지향
register 등기부
register of cancellation of attachment
　차압지소등기
register of government bonds 국채등록부
register of settlement of mortgage
　저당권설정등기
registered 등기필
registered bond 기명사채; 등록채
registered design 의장권
registered form 기명식
registered gilts 등록길트채
registered issues 등록명
registered number 등기번호
registered office 본사사무소
registered owner 등록명의인
registered public accountant 경리사
registered representative 증권외무원
registered securities 기명식 증권
registered share 등록주
registered society 등록조합
registered stock 기명주식
registered trade-mark 등록상표
registered trader 등록트레이더
registrar 등록기관
registrar of companies 회사등기소
registration 등기

registration agency 등록기관
registration and license tax 등록면허세
registration certificate 권리증
registration fee 등기료
registration formalities 등기수속
registration of alteration 변경등기
registration of copyright 판권등록
registration of design 의장등록
registration of establishment 설립등기
registration of incorporation 회사설립등기
registration of the right of pledge 질권등기
registration of transfer 이전등기
registration statement 유가증권계출서
registration tax 등록세
registry 등기부
regrating 독점
regression 회귀식
regression analysis 회귀분석
regression analysis method 회귀분석법
regression coefficient 회귀계수
regression correlation 회귀상관
regression equation 회귀방정식
regression model 회귀모델
regressive expectations 회귀기대
regressive taxation 역진과세
regular assortment 정번상품
regular audit 정시감사
regular delivery 통상인도
regular dividend 보통배당
regular fee 통상비용
regular member 정회원
regular panel 소집배심원명부
regular settlement 익영업일인도
regular transaction 보통거래
regular wage 기본급
regular wage standard 기준내임금
regular way 보통거래
regular way of delivery 통상인도
regulated interest rate 규제금리
regulated investment company 규제투자회사
regulation 규칙

regulation by government 정부규제
regulation of debt collection 회수규제
regulation of industrial structure 산업조정
regulation of lending 융자규제
regulation of retirement allowance
  퇴직급여규정
regulation of stock price 주가규제
regulations of financial statements
  재무제표규칙
regulations on foreign banks 외국은행규제
regulatory agencies 감독기관
regulatory measure 규제조치
rehabilitation 갱생
rehearing 재심리
rehypothecation 재담보설정
reimburse 상환하다
reimbursed expenses 입체경비
reimbursement 환불
reimbursement authorization 보상지불수권서
reimbursement benefit 보상급부
reimbursement method 생산고지불제
reimbursing bank 상환은행
reinforcement of response 반응강화
reinstatement clause 부활조항
reinsurance 재보험
reinsurance agreement 재보험계약
reinsurance bordereau 재보험보고서
reinsurance broker 재보험중매인
reinsurance by coinsurance method
  공동보험식 재보험
reinsurance by quota 할당재보험
reinsurance clause 재보험조항
reinsurance commission 재보험수수료
Reinsurance Exchange 렉스
reinsurance pool 재보험풀
reinsurance premium 재보험료
reinsurance premium rate 재보험요율
reinsurance recovery 재보험금
reinsurance return 재보험반려금
reinsurance treaty 재보험특약
reinvested earnings 이익잉여금

Q
R

reinvestigation organization 이의심리청
reinvestment 재투자
reinvestment rate 재투자이율
reinvestment risk 재투자리스크
rejected check 지불거절수표
rejection 기각
rejection certificate 거절증서
related businesses 관련사업
related cost 관련원가
related goods 관련재
related issue 관련상표
related-item sales 관련상품판매
relation 효과파급
relation income 상대소득
relationship management system
　거래처종합관리
relationship models 관련모델
relative 상대
relative costs 상대적인 코스트
relative deprivation 상대적인 박탈
relative error 상대오차
relative excepted risk 상대적인 면책위험
relative income 상대소득
relative income hypothesis 상대소득가설
relative market share 상대적인 마켓쉐어
relative measures 상대적인 측도
relative performance 상대적인 퍼포먼스
relative price 상대가격
relative quality 상대적인 품질
relative revenue 상대수익
relative revenue curve 상대적인 수익곡선
relative share 분배율
relative strength 상대적인 강약도
relative viewing distance 상대시거리
relator 고발인; 소추대행자
relax 늦추다; 완화하다
relaxation 완화
relaxation of tight money policy
　금융완화정책
release from debts 채무면제
release of libel bond 차압해제청구보증증권

release of lien 리엔방기
release of security 담보해제
release of seizure 차압해제
relegation 추방
relevancy 관련성
relevant information 적절정보
relevant range 적합범위
relevant risk 관련리스크
reliability engineering 신뢰성공학
relief merger 구제합병
relief method 제거법
religious corporation 종교법인
relinquishing of business 사업폐지
remain buoyant 지속적인 호조
remain in surplus 지속적인 흑자
remainder 잔고
remainder price 비망가격
remainder type 차액식
remaining period 잔존기간
remaining useful life 잔존내용연수
remand of further proceedings 반송
remargin 추가수익
remarkably low price 현저하게 낮은 가격
remeasurement 재측정
remedy 구제방법
remedy for violation of private right
　권리구제제도
reminder advertising 리마인더광고
remittance abroad 외국송금
remittance bill 송금환
remittance check 송금수표
remittee 수취인
remitter 권원회복
remitting bank 발송은행
remnant 잔존물
remodel 개조
remote area 벽지
remote cause 원인
remote sensing 원격탐사
removal 이전
removal expenses 제거비용

removal of seasonal effect
계절적인 영향을 제거함

remove 이전

removed assets 철거자산

remuneration 보수

render 언도하다

rendering of service 역무제공

rendition of judgment 판결언도

renewable term insurance 갱신조건부 정기보험

renewal 갱신

renewal after the maturity 기한후 자동지속

renewal charge 갱신료

renewal commission 갱신수수료

renewal expenses 대체비용

renewal fee 갱신료

renewal of bills and notes 어음갱신

renewal premium 계속보험료

renewal projects 리뉴얼프로젝트

renounce 거절하다

rent 지대(地代)

rent arrears 연체지대(地代)

rent charge 지대(地代)부담

rent income 임대료수입

rent on real estate 부동산임대료

rent payable 지불임대료

rent reasonably fixed 정당한 지대(地代)

rent roll 지대표(地代表)

rent-paying capacity 임차료지불능력

rental 임대료

rental agents' commissions 임차수수료

rental allowance 가임수당

rental expense 렌탈비용

rental income 가임(家賃)소득

rental income insurance 가임(家賃)보험

rental market value 가임(家賃)상장

rental of real property 부동산대부

rental revenue 리스료

rental service 임대업

rental value 임대가격

rentier class 불로소득자층

rents and royalties 임대료 및 사용료수입

rents of assize 정액지대

rents received 부동산수입

renumeration 보수

reopen 다시 열다

reorganization 재건

reorganization of corporation 회사갱생

reorganization proceedings 갱생수속

reorganization scheme 재건계획

repackage bond 리패키지채

repair 수선

repair equalization reserve 수선평균적립금

repair-shop 수선공장

repairing budget 수선비예산

repairing expenses 수선비

repairing risks insurance 선박수선보험

repairs and maintenance 수선유지비

reparation 손해배상액

repatriation 이익회수

repayment 반제

repayment money 환부금

repeal 취소

repeat purchase model 반복구매모델

repeated calculation 반복계산

repeating audit 반복감사

repercussion effect 파급효과

repetition research 반복조사

replaced property 대치자산

replacement 교체

replacement assets 교체자산

replacement by purchase 대치

replacement cost 교체원가

replacement cost accounting 교체원가회사

replacement cost coverage 재조달비용보험

replacement demand 대치수요

replacement expense 교체비용

replacement fertility 대치번식력

replacement in kind 현물보상

replacement investment 갱신투자

replacement method 50%상각법

replacement of business property
사업용 자산을 대치함

Q
R

replacement of collateral 대체담보
replacement of loan 차관반제
replacement of property 자산대치
replacement potential 대치잠재력
replacement price 교체가격
replacement property by purchase
  대체를 통한 자산교환
replacement rate 결손보충율
replacement reserve 설비갱신준비금
replacement risk 재취득리스크
replacement unit 교체단위
replacement value 교체가치
replacement value insurance 신가보험
replacing 교체
replenish 보충하다
replenishing cost 보충발주비
replenishment 보충
replenishment of stock 재고보충
replevin 동산점유회복소송
replicate 모조
report 보고서
report form 보고식
report form balance sheet 보고식 대차대조표
report of independent auditors 감사보고서
report on examination 검사보고서
report system 보고제도
reporting audit standards 감사보고기준
reporting currency 보고통화
reporting standards 감사보고기준
repossession 철수; 반환
representation 표명
representation work 표시작업
representative 대표자
representative democracy 대표민주제
representative director 대표이사
representative liquidator 대표청산인
representative money 대표화폐
representative of corporation 법인의 대표자
representative office 주재원사무소
representative sample 표준견본
representative suit 대표소송

representing issue 대표문제
repression 억압
reprieve 집행연기
reprimand 견책; 징계
reprisal 배상금
reproduction 재생산
reproduction cost 재생산원가
reproduction on a diminishing scale
  축소재생산
repudiation 거절; 방기
repugnancy 모순
repurchase 되사기
repurchase agreement 환매조건부 거래
repurchase obligation 환매의무
repurchase price 환매가; 재취득가격
repurchase 환매청구권
reputation 평가
reputed owner 명의상의 소유자
request 청구
request for correction 갱정청구
request for decision 품의
request for reconsideration 심사청구
request for reinvestigation 이의제기
request for share distribution 교부요구
request for wage increase 임상요구
request payment by securities 증권위탁납부
request repeat system 재송정정방식
requested return 의뢰반송
required accuracy 요구정도
required capital coefficient 필요자본계수
required quality 요구품질
required reserve 법정준비금
required reserve ratio 법정준비율
required reserves 소요준비
requirements 요건
requirements contract 납입계약
requirements of society 사회적인 요구사항
requisite 필요요건
requisition 요구
res adjudicata 기판력
resale 재판

resale price 재판가격
resale price maintenance 재판가격유지
resale price method 재판매가격기준법
rescheduling 리스케줄링
rescission 해약
rescue 불법탈환
research and development 연구개발
research and development expenditures
  연구개발비
research cost 연구비
research expenditure 조사비
research method 조사수법
research objectives 조사목적
research on prices 가격조사
research opportunity 조사기회
reseller 재판매업자
reservation 유보사항
reservation of ownership 소유권보류
reserve 적립금
reserve account 준비금계정
reserve adequacy 준비금의 타당성
reserve against decline in price
  가격변동준비금
reserve assets 준비자산
reserve bank 준비은행
reserve cash 현금준비
reserve currency 준비통화
reserve deposit requirement system
  준비예금제도
reserve for accidents 재해준비금
reserve for additions 증설적립금
reserve for amortization 상각준비금
reserve for bad loan 대도준비금
reserve for bonus payment 상여준비금
reserve for bonuses allotted
  보험계약이익배당준비금
reserve for compensation for completed
  works 완성공사보상준비금
reserve for compensation for default loss
  위약손실보상준비금
reserve for construction 신축적립금

reserve for contingency 우발손실준비금
reserve for corporation tax 법인세준비금
reserve for deferred income tax 압축준비금
reserve for depreciation 감가상각준비금
reserve for electronic computer programs
  프로그램보증준비금
reserve for foreign exchange fluctuation
  외국환변동준비금
reserve for guarantee far completed work
  제품보증준비금
reserve for intercompany profit 진체이익준
  비금
reserve for inventory fluctuation
  가격변동준비금
reserve for liability 부채준비금
reserve for loss on goods unsold
  반품조정준비금
reserve for losses 결손전보적립금
reserve for outstanding claims 지불준비금
reserve for overhead 간접비준비금
reserve for overseas investment loss
  해외투자손실준비금
reserve for pension fund 퇴직급여적립금
reserve for prevention of 공해방지준비금
reserve for price fluctuation 가격변동준비금
reserve for retirement of preferred stock
  우선주상환준비금
reserve for self-insurance 자가보험준비금
reserve for special depreciation
  특별상각준비금
reserve for specific purpose 목적적립금
reserve for tax payment 납세준비금
reserve fund 적립금
reserve investments 준비금투자
reserve on gross premium method
  영업보험료식 책임준비금
reserve on net premium method
  순보험료식 책임준비금
reserve position 준비포지션
reserve rate 지불준비율
reserve requirement operation 준비율조작

reserve requirement policy 지불준비율정책
reserve requirements system 지불준비제도
reserve system 준비제도
reserve tranche 리저브트랑슈
reserved common stock 유보주식
reserved surplus 준비잉여금
reset date 금리갱신일
reset frequency 갱신빈도
residence liability policy
　주택손해배상책임보험
resident 거주자
resident alien 거주외국인
resident auditor 주재감사인
resident foreign corporation 거주외국법인
residential investment 주택투자
residential property 거주용 재산
residents tax 주민세
residual 잔여, 재방송할증요금
residual claim 잔여청구권
residual cost 잔여원가
residual equity 잔여지분
residual net income 잔여순이익
residual profits 잔여이익
residual property 잔여재산
residual quantitative import restriction
　잔존수입제한
residual ratio 잔존율
residual return 잔차수익률
residual share 잔여배분
residual standard deviation 잔차표준편차
residual value 잔존가격
residuary estate 잔여재산
residuary outlay 잔여지출
residue 잔여부분
resiliency 신속한 조정
resistance level 관문
resistance line 저항선
resolution 해상도; 결의
resource allocation 자원배분
resources 자원
resources on business 경상자원

respite 변제를 연기함
respondent 피공소인
respondent superior 사용자책임
response elasticity 반응탄력성
response error 회답오차
response function 반응함수
response rate 회답률
responsibility accounting 책임회계
responsibility costing 책임원가계산
responsible and recognized dealer
　주요 딜러
rest 휴식하다; 잔여
restitution in integrum 원상회복
restitution of conjugal rights 동거명령
restoration 복원
restraining order 금지명령
restraint 제지; 억제
restraint measures 억제정책
restraint of trade 영업제한
restraint on alienation 양도금지
restraint on anticipation 미수이익 처분금지
restrict sales 한정매출
restricted account 제한부 계정
restricted distribution policy
　한정적인 판로정책
restricted letter of credit 매입은행지정신용장
restricted receipts 특정수입고
restricted share 제한주
restricted surplus 제한부 잉여금
restriction of price range 치폭제한
restriction of transfer 양도제한
restriction on the growth of bank loans
　대출증가액규칙
restriction on transfer of shares
　주식양도제한
restrictive covenant 한정조항; 부작위약관
restrictive financial covenant 재무제한조항
restrictive monetary policy 금융긴축정책
restructuring 재구축
restructuring related stock
　리스트럭처링 관련주

rests 결산기
resulting trust 추정신탁; 복귀신탁
results of business 영업실적
results of operations 영업성적
results of ordinary operations 경상손익
results of the tax examination 세무조사결과
resumption of dividend 복배, 부배
retail 소매
retail accounting 소매업회계
retail and consumer spending sector stock
　소비지출관련주
retail bank 소매은행
retail banking 리테일뱅킹
retail broker 소매브로커
retail cost 소매원가
retail credit 소매신용
retail excise 소매세
retail inventory method 재고조사법
retail investor 최종투자가
retail method 매가환원법
retail price inflation 소매물가인플레이션
retail prices structure 소매가격구조
retail sales 소매매상고
retail selling price 소매매가
retail stores location strategy
　소매점포입지전략
retailing competition 소매경쟁
retailing function 소매기능
retailing strategy 소매업전략
retained earnings 이익잉여금
retained line 보유액
retained premium 보유보험료
retained profit 내부유보
retained surplus 유보이익
retainer 변호사위임계약
retaining fee 변호사고문료
retaining lien 변호사리엔
retaliation 보복
retaliatory duties 보복관세
retention 보유
retention money 유보금

retention schedule 리텐션스케줄
retention time 보관기간
retentive advertising 유지광고
retire 기증상환하다; 퇴직하다
retired employee 퇴직한 종업원
retired equipment 폐잔설비
retirement 소각
retirement accounting 제거회계
retirement allowance 퇴직급여
retirement allowance in a lump sum
　퇴직금을 일괄지급함
retirement allowance regulations
　퇴직급여규정
retirement annuity 퇴직연금
retirement annuity business 퇴직연금업무
retirement annuity reserve 퇴직연금적립금
retirement by purchase 매입상각
retirement cost 제거비
retirement income 퇴직소득
retirement income deduction 퇴직소득공제
retirement income 퇴직소득부 보험
retirement lump sum grants 퇴직일시금
retirement method 폐기법
retirement of bonds 사채상환
retirement of shares 주식상각
retirement pay 퇴직금
retirement pension 퇴직연금
retirement plan 퇴직금제도
retirement price 제거가액
retirement unit 제거단위
retour sans protet 거절증서불요
retracement 되돌아감; 회고
retractable maturity 단기가능만가
retreat buying 반복구매
retroactive adjustments 소급수정
retroactive levy 소급징수
retroactive restatement 소급수정보고서
retrocession treaty 재재보험특약
retrogressive accounting 소구계산
retrospective law 소급법
retrospective policy 소급보험

Q
R

return 환원; 이익
return after due date 기한후 신고
return and payment 신고 및 납부
return blank 신고용지
return commission 환급수수료
return day 확정일
return form for retirement income
　퇴직소득신고서
return freight 반환운임
return inward 반품
return line 리턴라인
return maximizer 리턴극대자
return on assets 총자산수익률
return on equity capital 주주자본이익률
return on investment 투자수익
return on investment ratios 투자이익률
return on loll §.term liabilities plus equity
　capital 자익자본이익률
return on total assets 총자산이익률
return outward 반품
return premium for cancellation 해약반려금
return to equilibrium 평형으로 회귀함
return to nature 자연회귀
returned goods unsold 반품
returned materials report 원재료반환표
returned sales 반품
returned unsold goods reserve
　반품조달비금
returning of premium 프리미엄환원
returning officer 선거관리자
returns 보수
revaluation 절상; 재평가; 평가절상
revaluation excess 재평가차액
revaluation profit 재평가익
revaluation surplus 재평가잉여금
revaluation surplus reserve 재평가적립금
revealed preference 현시선호
revenue 매상(비제조업)
revenue account 수입계정
revenue agency 세입대리점
revenue and expenditure budget

　세입세출예산
revenue bond 특정재원채
revenue curve 수익곡선
revenue deficit 세입결함
revenue expenditure 수익지출
revenue from government enterprise
　관영수입
revenue from leases 리스수익
revenue from operations 영업수익
revenue from public bond 공채수입
revenue maximization hypothesis
　매상고최대화가설
revenue officer 수세관
revenue realization 수익실현
revenue recognizing standard 수익인식기준
revenue reserve amount 수익적립금액
revenue stamp 수입인지
revenue tax 소득세
reversal 상장의 반전
reversal cost method 역산법
reversal day 반전일
reversal of judgment 판결을 파기함
reversal of surplus 적립금반환
reversal of taxation 과세처분취소
reversal pattern 반전패턴
reverse direction 역방향
reverse distribution 역유통
reverse for extraordinary casualties
　이상위험준비금
reverse hedge 역헤지
reverse income tax 역소득세
reverse offset 역상태
reverse operation 역산
reverse remittance 역송금
reverse repo 리버스레포
reverse split 역분할
reverse split of stocks 주식병합
reverse telegraphic transfer 전신거래환
reverse zero coupon swap
　리버스제로쿠폰스왑
reverse-order perception 가격역전인지현상

reversed swap 역스와프
reversing entry 반대기입
reversing trade 반대매매
reversion 복귀권
reversionary annuity 생잔연금
reversionary bonus system
　　보험금증액배당방법
review 심사
review criteria 실적평가기준
revised average stock price 수정평균주가
revised budget 수정예산
revised statutes 수정법률
revision 정정
revision of office regulation 내규개정
revival 보험계약이 부활함
revival of judgment 판결부활
revived quotation 급등한 가격
revocable beneficiary 변경가능보험금수취인
revocable letter of credit 취소가능신용장
revocation 철회
revocation of probate 검인철회
revocation suit 취소소송
revoke 취소하다
revolving collateral 근담보
revolving credit 회전신용장; 리볼빙크레딧
revolving fund 회전자금
revolving guarantee 근보증
revolving letter of credit 회전신용장
revolving line of credit 한계대부선
revolving loan 리볼빙론
revolving trade 회전무역
revolving underwriting facility
　　리볼빙 언더라이팅 퍼실리티
reward 보수
rework 재생산; 재가공
rewriting 고쳐 쓴; 다시 쓴
ride down 떨어뜨리다
rider 부가조항
right and interest 이권
right in rem 물권
right of access 엑세스권

right of access to courts 재판청구권
right of auditing 감사권
right of avoidance 부인권
right of beneficiary 수익권
right of cancellation 해약권
right of claim 청구권
right of collective bargaining 단체교섭권
right of credit availability 크레딧이용권
right of demanding compensation 구상권
right of first refusal 최우선인수권
right of indemnity 구상권
right of inheritance 상속권
right of lease 임차권
right of nullification 기피권
right of petition 청원권
right of pledge 질권
right of priority 선취권
right of recourse 상환청구권
right of redemption 권리반환권
right of taxation 과세권
right of telephone 전화가입권
right of trademark 상표권
right of use 사용권
right of way 우선토지사용권
right person in a right position 적재적소
right to begin 개시권
right to counsel 변호사의 도움을 받을 권리
right to obtain foreign money 외화할당권
right to revoke fraudulent act
　　사해행위취소권
rights 권리
rights and liabilities of members 사원권
rights existing on real property
　　부동산상의 권리
rights for profit-sharing 공익권
rights of repurchase 환매권
rights off 권리하락
rights offering 주주할당
rights on 권리부
rigidity of price 가격경직성
ring 링

rise above 오르다; 치솟다
rise in price 가격상승
rise on stock price 주가상승
rise-and-fall market 왕래상장
rising of the court 폐정
rising quotation 상승상장
risk 보험사고
risk absolutely excluded 절대적인 면책위험
risk arbitrage 리스크를 수반한 재정거래
risk asset ratio 위험자산비율
risk assets 위험자산
risk aversion 위험회피
risk capital 위험자본리스크
risk characteristic 리스크특성
risk covered 피보험위험
risk disclosure statement 리스크개시서
risk exposure 위험노출
risk free 신용리스크가 없는
risk hedge 위험회피; 리스크헤지
risk lover 위험선호자
risk management 리스크매니지먼트
risk minimization 리스크를 최소화함
risk penalty 리스크페널티
risk preference 리스크선호도
risk premium 리스크프리미엄
risk premium insurance 위험보험료식 보험
risk reduction measure 리스크경감수단
risk reduction strategy 리스크경감전략
risk sector 리스크섹터
risk sensitive index 리스크감응도지표
risk structure 리스크구조
risk structure of discount rate
　　할인율의 리스크구조
risk taking 리스크부담
risk tolerance 리스크허용도
risk weight 리스크웨이트
risk-based capital 리스크기반자본금
risk-controlled 리스크제어
risk-free 무리스크의
risk-free assets 무리스크자산
risk-free interest rate 무리스크금리

risk-free securities 무리스크증권
risk-neutral valuation 무리스크뉴트럴
risk-return group 리스크수익그룹
risk-return relationship
　　리스크와 수익의 관계
risk-return trade-off
　　리스크와 수익의 트레이드 오프
risk-weighting 리스크웨이트
riskless arbitrage 무리스크재정
riskless assets 안전자산
riskless transaction 리스크가 없는 거래
risky 리스크가 큰
risky assets mix 위험자산 믹스
risky securities 리스크증권
risky shift phenomenon 위험전가현상
rival brands 경합브랜드
road blocking 로드블로킹
robot teller 로드텔러
rocket scientist 하이테크상품개발자
rogatory letters 촉탁서
role commitment 역할커미트먼트
role differentiation 역할요구
role involvement 역할관여
role playing 역할연기법
role theory 역할이론
roll 인명부
rollback 롤백
roller coaster swap 롤러코스터스와프
rolling readjustment 파동조정
rolling yield 롤링일드
rolling-forward procedure 선송법
rolling-over 구르다
rollover date 금리갱신일
rollover loan 롤오버론
Rome club 로마클럽
Roosa bond 로자본드
root cause 근본원인
root of title 권원의 기초
roster 인명부
rotated merchandise control
　　순번상품재고관리

rotation effect 로테이션효과
rotten boroughs 부패선거구
rough balance sheet 개산대차대조표
rough cost 개산원가
rough cost book 원가개산표
rough number 어림값
round lot 최저거래단위
round turn 반대매매
round-the-clock market 24시간거래시장
roundabout production 우회생산
roundabout trade 우회무역
rounding error 끝수처리오차
rounding off in calculation 끝수계산
rounding reversal pattern 라운딩리버설패턴
route sales 루트세일즈
router 루터
routing 절차
royalties received for use of patents
　특허권사용료
royalty 로얄티
royalty as to knowhow 노하우사용료
royalty interest 소유권이권
royalty of the copyright 저작권사용료
royalty on a book 인세
royalty to be paid every fixed time
　정시불사용료
rule 규칙
rule absolute 절대명령
rule against accumulations 영구적립금지규칙
rule day 명령일
rule 가명령
rule of ejusdem generis 동종원칙

rule of law 법의 지배
rule of reason 합리원칙
role of securities trading 매매방법
rule to show cause 이유개시명령
rules 동의제출기
rules for construction of policy
　보험증권해석규칙
rules for the preparation of financial
　statements 재무제표준칙
rules of court 재판소규칙
rules of thumb 경험적인 상식
ruling 결정
ruling coalition 여당연합
run 조업
run the book 장부관리
run upon a bank 단골은행
run-down 상장표요약
run-off 재보험특약기간 종료후의 잔존책임
runaway gap 런어웨이갭
running account 당좌계정
running cost 운전비
running inventory 상시재고
running inventory method 계속재고법
running of the market 시황상황
running policy 계속보험
running price 시가
running royalty 계속사용료
running stock 정상재고
rural-urban shift of population
　지방도시인구이동
rush order 주문이 쇄도함

sabotage 사보타주; 태업
sacrifice sale 투매; 헐값으로 팔기
saddle point 안상점
saddle stitching 철사로 박는 제본방식
safe custody 안전보호
safe deposit box insurance 대금고보험
safe harbor lease 세이프하버리스
safe keeping 보관
safe-pledge 보석보증인
safeguard provision 세이프가드조항
safekeeping deposit 보호예금
safety control 안전관리
safety envelop 세이프티엔벨롭
safety loading 안전할증
safety margin 안전계수
safety nets 예금자보호시스템
safety stock 안전재고
safety valve 안전밸브
sag 처짐, 늘어짐
salaries 급료
salaries and wages 임금
salary from secondary source
　　이차재원에서 급여를 지급함
salary plus commission 비율병용급여제
salary scale 급여지수
sale 판매
sale amount 매상고
sale and lease-back 세일앤드리스백
sale and purchase on credit 외상매매
sale and return 해제조건부 매매
sale bond 판매보증증권

sale by agent 대리판매
sale by brand 브랜드매매
sale by bulk 일괄매매
sale by description 표시를 통한 매매
sale by grade or type 규격매매
sale by specification 사양서매매
sale by subscription 예약판매
sale for cash 현금판매
sale in gross 일괄매출
sale on account 외상매출
sale on an underwriting basis 인수매출
sale on commission 위탁판매
sale on standard 표준품매매
sale or return 반환권부 매매
sale price 거래가격
sales 매상
sales account 매상계정
sales accounting 판매회계
sales activity index 판매활동지수
sales allowance 매출에누리
sales amount 판매금액
sales analysis 매상분석
sales and purchases on commission
　　수수료매매
sales basis 매상기준
sales book 매상장
sales commission 판매수수료
sales contract 매매계약
sales cost 매상원가
sales cost ratio 매상원가율
sales credit 외상거래채권

sales discount 판매할인
sales earnings 영업수입
sales finance 판매금융
sales finance company 판매금융회사
sales force 판매력
sales force management 판매원관리
sales force performance analysis
　판매원성과분석
sales forecasting 매상고예측
sales growth rate 매상성장률
sales invoice 매상송장
sales journal 매상분개장
sales ledger 매상원장
sales method 판매방법
sales mix 세일즈믹스
sales network 판로
sales of corporate bonds by purchasers
　사채소화상황
sales office 영업소
sales on approval 시용판매
sales on consignment 수탁판매
sales opportunity 판매기회
sales performance 판매성과
sales price 매출가격
sales proceeds 매상액
sales profit ratio 매상이익률
sales promotion 판매촉진
sales promotion expense 판매촉진비
sales quota 판매할당
sales rebate 매상환불
sales record 판매장부표
sales response function 매상고반응함수
sales returns 매상되돌림
sales revenues 매상수익
sales slip 매상전표
sales subsidiary 판매자회사
sales targets 판매목표액
sales tax 매상세
sales to accounts receivable 외상채권율
sales to cash 현예금회전율
sales to fixed assets 고정자산매상률

sales to inventories 재고정리자산매상률
sales to receivables 외상채권회전율
sales to total assets 총자산매상률
sales to working capital 운전자본매상률
sales under agreement to repurchase
　환매를 조건으로 매각함
sales volume 생산고
sales volume budget 매상고예산
sales worth ratio 외상채권회전율
sales-force recruitment 판매원모집
sales-type leases 판매리스
salesman 판매원
salesman training 세일즈맨교육
salient ratio 특수비율
Sallie Mae 미국장학자금금고; 샐리메이
salutary products 살루터리제품
salvage charges 구조비용
salvage value 처분가치
same day effective order 당일유효주문
same day settlement 동일결제
same day transaction 당일거래
sample 상품견본
sample error 표본설비
sample means 표본평균치
sample shipment 견본적송품
sample variance 표본분산
samples accuracy 표본정밀도
samples expense 견본비
samples floater 상품견본포괄보험
sampling 견본추출
sampling error 표본추출오차
sampling inspection 발취검사
sampling precision 표본추출정밀도
sampling sound module 샘플링음원
sampling survey 표본조사
samurai bond 사무라이채
sanction 제한조치
sandwich spread 샌드위치스프레드
sans recourse 상환청구에 응하지 않은
satellite cable network 새틀라이트케이블넷
satellite communication 위성통신

S
T

satellite market 위성시장
satellite news gathering
　새틀라이트뉴스개더링
satisfaction of mortgage 모기지개방증서
satisfactory 만족할 만한
saturation 채도
saturation campaign 집중캠페인
Saturday Night Special
　새터데이나이트스페셜
saucer 소스
saving account 저축계정
saving clause 유보사항
saving function 저축함수
savings and loan association 저축대부기관
savings at call 통지예금
savings bank 저축은행
savings bank life insurance
　저축은행생명보험
savings bond and debenture 저축채권
savings deducted at source 공제저금
savings deposit 저축예금
savings ratio 저축률
savings-for-tax association 납세저축조합
savings-type insurance 적립보험
scab 파업을 깨뜨리는 사람
scale merit 규모의 이익
scale method 척도법
scale of central and local public finance
　재정규모
scale order 등급주문
scale trading 평가하기 어려운 매매
scalper 당장의 이윤을 노려 사고파는 사람
scalping 스캘핑(당장의 이윤을 노려 사고팜)
scan 주사(走査)
scan panel 스캔패널
scan panel research 스캔패널 조사
scandalous matter 추문
scanner 스캐너
scanning line 주사선
scarce currency clause 희소통화조항
scarce resources 희소자원

scarce stock 적은 주
scarcity of stock 주부족
scenario analysis 시나리오분석
scenario writing 시나리오라이팅
schedule 각종명세
schedule form 보고식
schedule of bonds payable 사채명세표
schedule of capital 자본금명세표
schedule of concessions 관세양허표
schedule of depreciation 감가상각비명세표
schedule of securities 유가증권명세표
schedule of tangible fixed assets
　유형고정자산명세표
schedule of the marginal efficiency of capital
　자본한계효율표
schedule of transactions 거래명세
scheduled cost 표시원가
scheduled payment 약정반제
scheduled personal property floater 명세서부
　동산포괄보험
scheduled policy 담보조항선택방식증권
scheduled property floater
　명세서부 고가품포괄보험
scheduled repayment 정시상환
scheduler income taxation 분류소득세
schedules of financial statements
　재무제표부속명세표
scheme of arrangement 채무정리계획
scheme of operation 사업방법서
scheme of reproduction 재생산표식
school district 학교구
science park 사이언스파크
scienter 고의로
scientific management 과학적인 관리
scientific method 과학적인 방법
scintilla of evidence 미미한 입증
scissors-form difference in price
　가위형태의 가격차이
scope 감사범위
scope of assessment 과세범위
scope of audit 감사범위

scope of authority 권한범위
scope of business 사업범위
scope of exemption of property tax
　고정자산세비과세범위
scope of securities 유가증권의 범위
scorched earth defense 초토작전
score a deficit 구멍을 뚫다
scotchlite 스카치라이트
scrap 찌꺼기; 토막
scrap equipment 폐잔설비
scrap value 잔존가액
scrapped property 제거자산
scrapping 제거
scrapping of equipment tax credit
　특정설비폐기세액공제
screen angle 스크린각도
screen ruling 스크린선수
screen tone 스크린톤
screening 심사
screening of application for loan 대출심사
scrip certificate 가주권
scrip dividend 증서배당
script 원문서
scrutiny 심사
scuttling 고의적인 침몰
sea brief 중립선증명서
sea law 해사법규
sea peril 해상위험
sea-letter 중립국선증명서
seal 검인
seal impression 인감
sealed instrument 날인증서
seaman 선원
search 수색
search goods 정밀조사상품
season dating 계절일부
season sale 계절매출
seasonal adjustment 계절조정
seasonal average 계절평균
seasonal discount 계절할인
seasonal duties 계절관세

seasonal fluctuation adjustment
　계절변동조정
seasonal fund 계절자금
seasonal goods 계절상품
seasonal index 계절지수
seasonal merchandise 계절상품
seasonal model 계절변동형 모델
seasonal selling pressure 계절적인 매출압력
seasonal unemployment
　계절적인 요인으로 인한 실업
seasonal variation 계절변동
seasonally adjusted 계절변동조정제
seasoned bond 만기에 가까운 채권
seasoned issue 통상거래증권
seat 회원권
seaworthy 항해에 견디는
second deliverance 재인도
second generation on-line system 이차온라인
second half of the year 하반기
second mortgage 이차저당
second section 시장 제2부
second surplus treaty 이차초과액특약
second-distress 이차차압
secondary activities 부수업무
secondary beneficiary 이순위보험금수취인
secondary bond dealing
　유통시장에서의 채권딜링
secondary boycott 이차보이콧
secondary conveyance 이차부동산이전행위
secondary data 이차데이터
secondary distribution 이차분매
secondary drive 이차동인
secondary evidence 이차적인 증거
secondary financing 이차저당금융
secondary group 이차집단
secondary industry 이차산업
secondary liability 이차부채
secondary market 유통시장
secondary needs 이차적인요구
secondary offering 매출
secondary rally 이차부채

secondary stimulus 이차자극
secondary tax liability 이차납세의무
secondary trend 이차트렌드
secrecy agreement 수비의무계약
secret account 비밀계정
secret commission 비밀수수료
secret language 암호
secret liability 비밀부채
secret partnership 익명조합
secret reserve 비밀적립금
secret service expenses 기밀비
secret trust 비밀신탁
secretariat 총무처; 사무국
Secretary of State 국무장관
section 분할; 절개
section of revenue 수세과
sectional calculation 부문계산
sectional development 지구개발
sectional income statement 구분손익계산서
sectional journal 분할분개장
sectional ownership 구분소유권
sectional surface rights 구분지상권
sector 섹터
sector balance sheet 부문별 대차대조표
sectoral approach 섹터방식
secular 세속의
secular boom 영속적인 효과
secular economic growth 장기적인 경제성장
secured account 보증계정
secured advance 담보부 대부
secured bond 저당권부 사채
secured credit 담보 부대출
secured debenture 담보부 부채
secured debt 담보부 대출
secured liabilities 담보부 부채
secured loan 담보대출
secured loan on securities 증권담보론
secured party 담보권자
secured securities 담보부 증권
secured transactions 담보부 거래
securities 유가증권

securities account 유가증권계정
securities acquired by the specified
　investment in kind 특정현물출자증권
securities administration 증권행정
securities administration trust
　유가증권관리신탁
Securities and Exchange Commission
　미국증권거래위원회
securities and exchange law 증권거래법
securities borrowed 차입유가증권
securities business 증권업
securities business tax law 증권거래세법
securities capital 증권자본
securities company 증권회사
securities deposited as collateral
　담보차입유가증권
securities deposited from others
　보관유가증권
securities exchange 증권거래소
securities exchange commission
　증권거래심의회
securities finance company 증권금융회사
securities financing 증권금융
securities for fiduciary issue 보증준비
securities for sale 매각가능증권
securities futures 증권선물거래
securities holdings 보유증권
securities house dealer 증권회사딜러
securities in foreign currency 외화증권
securities in portfolio 소지증권
securities in trust 유가증권신탁
securities industry 증권업계
securities inventory
　증권회사가 판매를 위해 보유한 채권
securities investment 증권투자
securities investment advisory service
　증권투자상담
securities investment trust 증권투자신탁
securities investment trust sales company
　투자신탁판매회사
securities issue 증권발행

securities issued by government related agency 정부계 기관증권
securities ledger 유가증권원장
securities loan 증권금융
securities loaned 대부유가증권
securities market 증권시장
securities market line 증권시장선
securities of affiliated company 관계회사유가증권
securities on property 물적증권
securities purchase 유가증권매입
securities received as collaterals 보관유가증권
securities received for guarantee 세금유가증권
securities register 유가증권기입장
securities regulations 증권규칙
securities reserve 유가증권준비
securities transaction loss reserve 주식매각손실준비금
securities transaction tax law 유가증권거래세법
securities transfer tax 유가증권거래세
securities underwriting business law 유가증권인수업법
securities yield 증권이율
securitization 증권화
security 담보
security account 보증계정
security analyst 증권분석전문가
security credit 증권금융
security credit by banks 은행을 통한 증권금융
security deposits 담보예금
security for costs 소송비용담보
security for obligation 채권담보
security for tax payment 납세담보
security income and expense 유가증권손익
security interest 담보권
security loan 증권담보대부
security of tax payment 납세보증
security 담보권

security risk curve 증권리스크
security suretyship 보증인
security yield curve 증권이익곡선
security-specific risk 증권고유리스크
sedition 난동죄; 선동죄
seed money 초기투입자금
seeds 시즈
segment reporting 사업구분별 손익보고
segmental breakdown 부문별 내역
segmental information 세그먼트정보
segmental sales 부문별 매상
segmental sales breakdown 부문별 매상내역
segmentation 세분화; 세그멘테이션
segmentation theory 시장분단이론
segregation 격리
segue 세이그웨이
seisin 점유
seized 점유한
seized goods 차압물건
seizor 차압인
seizure 차압
seizure note 차압통지서
select table 선택표
selected issue 선정문제
selection 선정
selection of depreciation method 상각방법을 선정함
selection of risk 위험선택
selection of valuation method 평가방법을 선택함
selection process 선택과정
selective benefits 선택급부
selective bid 지명경쟁입찰
selective buying 물색매매
selective channel 선택적인 채널
selective competition 선택적인 경쟁
selective credit regulation 선택적인 신용규제
selective demand 선택적인 수요
selective exposure 선택적인 노출
selective financing 선별융자
selective function 선택적인 기능

S
T

selective perception 선택적인 지각
selective selling 특약판매
selective tendering 지명경쟁입찰
self-accounting system 독립회계제
self-actualization 자기실현
self-addressed check 자기앞수표
self-assessed income tax 신고소득세
self-assessment 자기시고
self-assessment of taxation 신고납세
self-assessment system 자기신고납부제도
self-balancing 독자평균
self-balancing type 증감대조식
self-concept 자기개념
self-consumption 자가소비
self-defense 정당방위
self-disserving evidence 자신에게 불리한 증거
self-employed 자영의
self-employment income 자가영업소득
self-enforcement 자력집행권
self-finance ratio 자기금융·비율
self-inspection 자주검사
self-insurance 자가보험
self-insurance fund 자가보험기금
self-insurance plan 자가보험제도
self-insurance reserve 자가보험준비금
self-liquidating 자기정산의
self-mailer 셀프메일러
self-maintaining growth 자립성장
self-management 자영
self-owned capital ratio 자기자본비율
self-produced fixed assets
  자기생산에 관련된 고정자산
self-produced inventories
  자기제조에 관련된 재고자산
self-regarding evidence 자신에 대한 증거
self-regulation 자주규제
self-regulatory organization 자주규제기관
self-restraint 자주규제
self-restraint agency 자주규제기관
self-restraint interest 자주규제금리
self-return 자기신고

self-return system 자기신고제
self-service retailing 셀프서비스식 소매업
self-serving declaration
  자기에게 이익이 되는 공술
self-support accounting 독립채산
self-support subsistence 독립생계
self-supporting accounting system
  독립채산제
self-sustained personal accident insurance
  자손사고보험
sell back 되팔다
sell low 싸게 팔다
sell off 떨이로 팔다
sell on credit 외상으로 팔다
sell on the spot 즉매하다
sell order 매주문
sell signal 매신호
sell-and-lease agreement 대차계약
seller 파는 쪽
seller structure 판매자구조
seller's monopoly 판매자독점
seller's option 매주(파는 자)선택
seller's option trading 셀러즈옵션거래
seller's price 부르는 값
sellers' market 파는 자의 시장
sellers over 전매장
selling 셀링업무
selling agreement 판매계약
selling charges 판매비용
selling climax 셀링클라이막스
selling commission 매상수수료
selling concept 판매콘셉트
selling concession 판매수수료
selling contract 매예약
selling cycle 판매순환
selling exchange 판매환
selling expense variance 판매비차이
selling expenses 판매비
selling group 판매단
selling group agreement 판매단계약서
selling off 투매

selling offer 판매오파
selling on a consignment basis 위탁판매
selling on a rising scale 매상
selling on balance 평균매출
selling on credit 외상매출
selling on rally 되팔기
selling on spurt 급등매출
selling operation under repurchase agreement 환매조건부 매출오퍼레이션
selling opportunity 매장
selling order 매주문
selling out 처분매출
selling overhead 판매간접비
selling pressure 매압력
selling price 파는 값
selling price clause 판매가액약관
selling price inventory 매가재고조사법
selling price per unit 일품당 매가
selling rate 매상장
selling right 파는 권리
selling sample 매출견본
selling short 공매
selling side 매출사이드
selling support 매출인기
sellout 매진
semantic differential 의미분별법
semantic differential method 일대비교법
semantic differential scale 의미분별법의 기준
semantics 의미론
semi-annual closing of accounts 중간결산
semi-annual compounding calculation 반년마다 하는 복리계산
semi-annual coupon 반년불쿠폰
semi-annual report 반기(半期)보고서
semi-endowment insurance 만기반액지불양로보험
semi-facultative reinsurance 임의출자재보험
semi-finished goods 반제품
semi-fixed cost 준고정비
semi-inflation 준인플레이션
semi-installment 반기지불

semi-Tontine dividend 준톤티식 배당
semi-variable charge 준변동비
semi-variable cost 준변동원가
semi-variable expenses 준변동비항목
senior 선순위의
senior accountant 상급회계사
senior bond 상위사채
senior citizen 연금생활자
senior co-manager 상급부간사
senior creditor 선순위채권자
senior debt 우선채무
senior issue 상위증권
senior mortgage 선순위양도저당
senior mortgage bond 선순위담보부사채
senior securities 우선증권
seniority order wage system 연공서열임금제도
seniority system 연공제
sensitive market 민감한 시장
sensitivity 감응성
sensitivity adjustment 감응도조정
sensitivity analysis 감응도분석
sensitivity coefficient 감응도계수
sensitivity training 감수성훈련
sensory characteristic 감응특성
sentiment 감정; 정서
sentiment index 센티멘트지표
separable cost 분리가능원가
separate account 별도계정
separate bill 별계정
separate financial statements 단독재무제표
separate investment account 분리계정
separate maintenance 별거수당
separate property 특유재산
separate return 개별신고서
separate trading of registered interest and principal of securities 스트립채
separate valuation 분리평가
separate withholding tax 분리과세
separate withholding taxation at source 원천분리과세

S
T

separated taxation on dividend income
배당분리과세
separation between capital and administration
자본경영분리
separation negative 분색 네거티브
sequence of deduction 공제순서
sequence of tax credits 세액공제순서
sequenced entry 단계적인 참가
sequenced strategy 단계적인 전략
sequencer 시퀀서
sequencing 순서배열
sequential cost system 공정별 종합원가계획
sequential sampling 연속표본추출법
serial advertisement 시리즈광고
serial bond 연속상환채권
serial correlation 계열상관
series bond 연속발행채권
service 노무
service area 서비스에어리어
service by public notification 공시송달
service contribution 역무출자
service cost 용역원가
service delivery 서비스제공
service department 보조부문
service departmental charge 보조부문비
service division 보조부문
service economy 서비스경제
service function 서비스함수
service life 내용연수
service mark 서비스마크
service office 영업소
service organization 서비스조직
service report 서비스보고서
service trade 서비스무역
service transaction 서비스거래
service unit 용역단위
serviceability 서비스성
services output method 용역생산고법
servitude 지역권; 노역
servitude for use of water 용수지역권
servitude holder 지역권자

servo mechanism 서보기구
session 회기
session period 입회시간
set aside 취소하다
set of accounts 회계장표
set of exchange 조수표
set off 상쇄
setback 하락
sets in use 스위치가 장착된 수신기의 비율
setting 설정
setting up overdraft 대월설정
settle 청산하다
settle accounts 결산하다
settled account 청산계정
settled additional tax due amount
갱정결정으로 확정한 추가세액
settlement 청산
settlement account 결제계정
settlement date 결제일
settlement day 인도일
settlement discount 결제할인
settlement method 결제방식
settlement of accounts 수지결산
settlement of balance 평균결제
settlement of claim 채권변제
settlement of debt 정산
settlement of easement 지역권설정
settlement of leasehold 차지권설정
settlement of mortgage 저당권설정
settlement of subsidy 보조금반제
settlement of superficies 지상권설정
settlement of tax amount 세액확정
settlement options 보험금지불수단을 선택함
settlement out of court 시담
settlement price 결산가격
settlement risk 인도리스크
settlement trade 거류지무역
settling 청산
settling term 결산기
settlor 신탁설정자
setup costs 조직편제비용

setup time 조직편제시간
sever 분리하다
several contract 분할계약
several covenant 가분조항
several fishery 단독어업권
several liability 개별책임
several ownership 분할소유권
severally 가분으로; 단독으로
severally but not jointly 비연대보증
severally liable 개별책임의
severance 분리
severance benefit 퇴직수당
severance of actions 소송을 분리함
shade 조정
shadow account 새도우어카운트
shadow price 잠재가격
shaking-out 투매
shape 형태
share 주식
share account 주식계정
share allotment certificate 주식할당증서
share allotment letter 주식할당통지
share broker 주식브로커
share capital 주식자본
share consolidation 주식합병
share draft account 주식어음계정
share holding ratio 주식보유율
share in expense of public service
　공공시설부담액
share index 주가지수
share of audience 시청자수 쉐어
share of the residual property 잔여재산여분
share oriented 쉐어지향
share price 주가
share price performance 주가동향
share split-down 주식합병
share split-up 주식분할
share-issuing expense 신주발행비
shared monopolies 공동독점
shareholder 주주
shareholder activism 주주행동주의

shareholder resolution 주주결의
shareholder's equity 주주자본
shareholder's interest 주주지분
shareholder's list 주주명부
shareholder's meeting 주주총회
shareholder's right 주주권
shareholders ledger 주주원장
shareholders of record 주주명부상의 주주
shareholdings 지분주
shares outstanding 발행필 주식
shark repellent 기업매수방지책
sharp advance market 급등상장
sharp decline 격감
sharp decline market 급락상장
sharp drop 폭락
sharp fall 급락
sharp increase 급등
sharp rally 반등
sharp rise 급등
sharp setback 급반락
sharp upward revision 대폭상향수정
shelf life 보관기한
shelf redemption 일괄상환
shelf registration 발행등록
shell branch 겉보기가격
shell corporation 페이퍼컴퍼니
shift system 교체근무제도
shiftability theory 전가성이론
shifting charge 하조비용, 옮겨쌓기 비용
shifting of business center 영업본거이동
shifting of tax burden 조세를 전가함
shinkin bank 신용금고
ship's bill 선장용 선하증권
ship's husband 선박관리인
ship's paper 선박비부서류
shipment 적송품
shipped quality terms 선적품질조건
shipper 적송인
shipper's usance 수출신용
shipping 해운
shipping articles 선원고용계약서

S
T

shipping charge 운송비
shipping commissioners 해사고용감독관
shipping document 선적서류
shipping expense 발송비
shipping market 해운시장
shipping marks 하인(荷印)
shipping receipts 해운수입
shipping tax 선박세
ships and vessels 선박
shogun bond 쇼군채
shop 공장
shop act 상점법
shop book rule 상품장부원칙
shop cost 공장원가
shop inspection 공장검사
shop talk language 암호
shopping around 쇼핑어라운드
shopping behavior 쇼핑행동
short 쇼트
short account 쇼트어카운트
short bond 단기채권
short book 쇼트북
short call 쇼트콜
short coupon 쇼트쿠폰
short covering 환매결제
short covering at a loss
　값을 어림짐작하여 매기다
short delivery 부족
short drawing 쇼트드로잉
short fall 단기투자이익
short form 간이형
short form audit report 단문식 감사보고서
short forward position 선물매출포지션
short hedge 매출헤지
short interest 차입주잔주, 차주잔고
short loan 단기대부
short market 단기상장
short paper 단기증권
short period 단기
short period insurance 단기보험계약
short position 쇼트포지션

short position risk 쇼트포지션리스크
short put 쇼트풋
short rate table 단기요율표
short sale against the box
　시세를 예상하여 매각함
short sale ratio 공매비율
short selling 공매
short squeeze 쇼트스퀴즈
short strangle 쇼트스트랜글
short strap 쇼트스트랩
short strip 쇼트스트립
short supply 공급부족
short swap 단기스와프
short swing 단기거래
short swing profits 단기매매익
short the swap 스와프를 단기로 하다
short title 약칭
short-covering 공매환매
short-form report 단문식 보고서
short-lined rally 일시적인 반등
short-period cost 단기비용
short-run equilibrium 단기균형
short-run optimizing principle
　단기최적화원리
short-run supply curve long-run supply curve
　단기공급곡선, 장기공급곡선
short-term 단기
short-term bond 단기채
short-term borrowing 단기차입
short-term capital 단기자본
short-term capital balance 단기자본수지
short-term capital 단기양도소득
short-term capital transaction 단기자본거래
short-term credit market 단기금융시장
short-term debt 단기차입금
short-term economic survey of all businesses
　전국기업단기경제관측
short-term economic survey of principal
　enterprises 주요기업단기경제관측
short-term facility rate 단기자금레이트
short-term finance 단기금융

short-term fund 단기자금

short-term government bond 단기국채

short-term government securities
　정부단기증권

short-term interest rate 단기금리

short-term investment 단기투자

short-term investment account 단기투자계정

short-term liabilities 단기부채

short-term liquidity factor 단기유동성요인

short-term loan 단기대부

short-term loan payable 단기차입금

short-term loan receivable 단기대부

short-term money house 단자업자

short-term money market 단기금융시장

short-term note 단기채권

short-term oriented 단기지향

short-term prime rate 프라임레이트

short-term returns 단기투자수익

short-term solvency 단기지불능력

short-term transaction 단기거래

short-term field 단기이율

short-time loan 단기대부

shortage 부족액

shortage economy 부족경제

shortage of funds 자금부족

shortage of special depreciation
　특별상각부족액

shortening 단축

shotgun approach 샷건어프로치

show scan system 쇼스캔시스템

showstopper 매수저지소송

shrinkage barrier 수축장벽

shrinkage of market 시장수축

shut for dividend 명의변경저지

shyster 사기꾼

sic 원문 그대로

sickness benefit 질병급부

side judge 배석판사

side liner 부업대리점

side stitching 인쇄물을 철사로 엮는 방법

sight 일람

sight bill 일람불환어음

sight credit 사이트크레디트

sight draft 일람불어음

sight letter of credit 일람불신용장

sight note 일람불약속어음

sight of a bill 어음사이트

sight rate 일람불환상장

sight selling rate 일람불상장

sight-seeing tax 관광세

sign manual 자서

sign of fragility 취약성

signal to noise ratio 신호잡음비

signature and seal 기명날인

signed and sealed 서명날인

signed check 기명식 수표

signed transfer 기명양도

significance level 유의수준

significant 중요한

significant amount 중요한 금액

significant difference 유의차

significant subsidiaries 중요한 자회사

silence 침묵

silent base 익명참가베이스

silent participation 익명참가

silent partner 익명참가자

silver exchange 은환

silver standard 은본위제

similar goods 유사품

similar investment media 유사한 투자매체

simple accounting 단식부기

simple 단순총화

simple arbitrage 단순재정

simple arithmetic average index
　단순산술평균지수

simple average 단순해손; 단순평균

simple average method 단순평균법

simple average stock price 단순평균주가

simple contract 약식계약

simple correlation coefficient 단순상관관계

simple cost accounting 단순종합원가계산

simple guarantor 단순보증인

S
T

simple hypothesis 단순가설
simple index 단순지수
simple interest 단리
simple journal 단순분개장
simple jump model 단순점프모델
simple moving average 단순이동평균
simple multiplier 단순승수
simple obligation 단순채무
simple random sample 단순확률표본
simple regression model 단순회귀모델
simple reproduction 단순재생산
simple reserve method 단순준비법
simple tariff system 단일세율제
simple trust 단순신탁
simplex method 심플렉스법
simplification 단순화
simplified bookkeeping system 간이부기
simplified employee pension
　간이종업원퇴직연금
simplified method of depreciation 간편상각
simplified tax system 간이과세제도
simulation 시뮬레이션
simulcast 동시방송
simultaneous distribution 동시분포
simultaneous tax audit 동시조사
simultaneous transmissive communication
　동보통신
sine qua non 필수조건
sine die 무기한으로
sine qua non 필수조건
single account system 단회계제도
single balance sheet 단일대차대조표
single banking license 단일은행면허
single bill 채무부담날인채무증서
single correlation coefficient 단일상관관계
single entry 단식기입
single entry bookkeeping 단식부기
Single European Act 단일유럽의정서
single exchange rate 단일환레이트
single expression 단식
single index method 단일지수법

single index model 단일지표모델
single interest policy 단일이익담보보험
single liability basis 단일책임주의
single life annuity 단일연금
single limit on insurer's liability
　단일전보한도액
single lump sum credit 일괄지불
single name 단명
single name paper 단명어음
single option 싱글옵션
single payment 일괄지불
single payment annuity 일시지불
single payment loan 일회불대부
single premium 일시불보험료
single premium annuity 보험료일시불연금
single premium deferred annuities
　일시불거치연금
single premium insurance 보험료일시불보험
single premium 일시불종신보험
single purpose 전용의
single rate 단일요율
single step 무구분식
single sum 일시금
single tariff 단일세율
single tax 단일세
single transaction 단일거래
single-customer separate account
　단일고객분리계정
single-employer defined benefit pension plan
　단일사업주형 급부건연금제도
single-maturity deposit 단일만기예금
single-order term 일정기한지불
single-step income statement
　단일구분손익계산서
single-step statement 단일구분계산서
singular concept 단순개념
singular proposition 단칭명제
sinking 침몰
sinking fund 감채기금
sinking fund date 감채기금상환일
sinking fund insurance 감채기금보험

sinking fund method 상각기금법
sinking fund requirements 감채기금적립순
sinking fund reserve 감채기금적립금
sister company 자매회사
sister publications 자매출판물
site 소재지
site audit 현장감사
site survey 실지조사
situation analysis 상황분석
situational variable 상황변수
sizzle 질감
skeleton form account T자형 계정
skewness 뒤틀림; 왜곡
skill inventory 스킬인벤토리
skill measurement 기능검정
skimming price 스킴가격
skimming price strategy 상징흡수가격전략
skip-day settlement 3일정산
skunk work 스컹크워크
skyrocketing 급상승
skyrocketing price 급상승가격
slack 완만한
slacken 느슨한, 줄인
slackness of money market 금융완만
slander of title 권리비방
slaughter sale 투매
sleeper effect 수면효과
sleeping account 휴면구좌
sleeping member 휴면회원
sliding cheap 슬라이딩침
sliding rate 슬라이드예금
sliding scale 슬라이드제
sliding tariff 슬라이드관세
slight negligence 경과실
slight tightening 가벼운 긴장
slight ups and downs 소부동
slightly firmer 작은 가게
slimmer profit margins 이익률저하
slip 무너지다
slip bookkeeping 전표식 부기
slip system 전표제도

slip system of accounting 전표식회계법
slope risk 경사리스크
slow 늦다
slowdown 둔화
sluggish 완만한
slumpflation 슬럼프플레이션
small 스몰(100만달러단위의 거래)
small-and medium enterprise modernization activities 중소기업근대화시책
small-and medium-sized enterprises 중소기업
Small Business Corporation 중소기업사업단
Small Business Finance Corporation 중소기업금융공고
small capital stock 소형주
small computer system interface 스카시; SCSI
small enterprise mutual aid plan 소규모기업공제
small group theory 소집단이론
small investor 소액투자가
small loan 소액금융
small loan company blanket bond 소액대부회사포괄보증증권
small lot order 소액주문
small margin 소폭
small revaluation 소폭절상
small sample 소표본
small savers certificate 소액예금증권
small sized business proprietor 소규모기업자
small spread 스몰스프레드
small sum and important property 소액중요자산
small sum deferred assets 소액거치자산
small sum properties 소액자산
small sums of deposits and savings 소액예저금
small sums of depreciable property 소액상각자산
small sums of dividend income 소액배당소득

S
T

small sums of pension paid to old-age
  persons 소액노령연금
small sums of savings 소액예금
small talk 잡담
small trend 소규모 트렌드
smallest space analysis 최소공간분석
smart money 현명한 투자가
Smithsonian system 스미소니언체제
smoothing constant smorgasbord plan
  평활정수
smoothing operation 안정화개입
smoothing out operation
  스무딩 아웃 오퍼레이션
smorgasbord plan 스모가스보드제
smuggling 밀수
snake in the tunnel 터널 속의 뱀
snapper 스내퍼
snipe 스나이프
snob effect 스놉효과
snowballing 눈사람현상
soar 급등
soaring market 고등시장
social accounting 사회회계
social and entertainment expenses provided
  in lump sum 적정교환비
social assumption 사회적인 가정
social audit 사회감사
social capital 사회자본
social climate 사회풍토
social club 사교클럽
social concerns 사회문제
social contract 사회계약
social cost 사회비용
social dependent consumer
  사회의존형 소비자
social ecology 사회생태학
social ethic 사회이론
social evolution 사회진화
social expenses 교제비
social insurance 사회보험
social insurance premiums 사회보험료

social insurance premiums deduction
  사회보험료공제
social insurance tax 사회보험세
social interaction 사회적인 상호행위
social judgment theory 사회판단이론
social mobility 사회이동
social movements 사회운동
social multiplier effect 사회승수효과
social overhead capital 사회자본
social psychology 사회심리학
social responsibility of enterprise
  기업의 사회적 책임
social security 사회보장
social security number 사회보장번호
social security system 사회보장제도
social stimuli 사회적인 자극
social system 사회체계
social unrest 사회불안
social value 사회적인 가츠
social wants 사회적인 욕구
social wealth 사회적인 부
social welfare function 사회적인 후생함수
socialization 사회화
socially integrated consumer
  사회융화형 소비자
societal environment 사회환경
society 조합
Society for Worldwide International
  Financial Telecommunications 스위프트
sociodemographic variable
  사회인구총계적인 변수
socioeconomic classification
  사회경제적인 분류
socioeconomic process 사회경제적인 과정
sociogram 소시오그램
sociologist 사회학자
sociometric technique 소시오메트릭기법
sociometry 소시오메트리
sociostasis 사회정체
soft currency 연화; 교환불능통화
soft currency country 연화국

soft dollar 소프트달러
soft landing 소프트랜딩
soft loan 소프트론
soft market 연조(軟調)시장
soil bank 지방증진금융
sola bill 솔라빌(1통만의 수출어음)
sold bill 할인어음
sold book 상품매상장
sold ledger 외상매출금원장
sold-out market 물량이 적은 상장
sole agent 독점권
sole proprietorship 개인기업
sole right 독점권
solicit 권유
solicitation 교사
soliciting 권유모집
solid model 솔리드모델
solidity ratio 고정비율
solution optical communication
　광솔린톤통신
solution provider 솔루션프로바이더
solvency 지불능력
solvency margin 솔벤시마진
solvent 지불능력이 있는
sound banking 건전한 은행업무
sound effects 효과음
sound logo 사운드로고
soundness 건전성
source and disposition statement
　원천 및 도중계산서
source effects 정보원효과
source of funds 자금원
source of income 소득원천
source of information 정보원
source of revenue 재원
source of taxation 세원
sources 원천
South Asian Association for Regional
　Cooperation 남아시아지역협력연합
South Commission 남위원회
South Pacific Commission 남태평양위원회

South Pacific Forum 남태평양포럼
sovereign 주권국
sovereign act 통치행위
sovereign immunity 외국주권면제
sovereign loan 소브린론
sovereign of taxation 과세주체
sovereign power 주권
sovereign rating 소브린비율
sovereign risk 주권리스크
sovereignty 주권
space actualization 시장잠재력실현
space arbitrage 스페이스재정
span of control 관리한계
spare plant capacity 유휴설비
speaker 의장
special 한정된
special account 특별회계
special account for inward portfolio
　investment 증권특별계정
special account of gains on insurance claim
　보험차익특별계정
special assessment 특별과징금
special audit 특별감사
special automobile policy
　자가용자동차종합보험
special bad debts reserve 채권상각특별계정
special bank account firm 특별은행계정업자
special benefit theory of taxation 특별편익설
special bills for installment sales credit 할부
　판매전용어음
special bond 특별채
special bracket group 스페셜브래킷그룹
special charges 특별비용
special clause 특별약관
special clearance 특별청산
special collecting agent 특별징수의무자
special collection 특별징수
special committee for public and corporate
　bond 공사채전문위원회
special conditions of the contract 특별조건서
special contingency reserve 우발손실준비금

S
T

special corporation 특수회사
special corporation surtax 법인특별세
special cost studies 특수원가조사
special credit 스페셜크레디트
special credit of corporation tax
　법인세액특별공제
special crossed check 특정횡선수표
special damage 실해(實害)
special damages 특별손해
special day delivery transaction
　특약일결제거래
special deduction 특별공제
special deduction for blue return
　청색신고특별공제
special deduction for occasional income
　일시소득특별공제
special deposit scheme 특별예금제도
special deposits 별단예금
special depreciation 특별상각
special depreciation method 특별한 상각방법
special depreciation reserve 특별상각준비금
special dividend 특별배당
Special Drawing Rights 특별인출권
special economic benefit 특별한 경제적 이익
special endorsement 기명식 이서
special event 특별보도방송
special examiner 특별국세조사관
special exchange 특별교환
special exemption for spouse 배우자특별공제
special expenses 특별비
special features 스페셜피처즈
special incentive measures 촉진세제
special income tax 특별소득세
special indorsement 기명식 이서
specal initial depreciation 특별상각
special interest group 특정이해집단
special interest publishing 특정관심층출판
special intermediary institution 특별매개기관
special item 특별항목
special journal 특수분개장
special landholding tax 특별토지보유세

special letter of credit 매입은행지정신용장
special loan account interest rate
　특별대부계정금리
special local consumption tax 특별지방소비세
special local grant tax 특별지방교부세
special loss 특손(特損)
special margin 특별증거금요건
special methods of computing depreciation
　특별한 감가상각방법
special non-taxable treatment on small
　government bond 특별공채이자과세제도
special outlay 별도지출
special participant 특별참가자
special payment 특별결제
special performance 특정이행
special policy 개별보험증권
special process 특수공정
special product firm 전문상품취급업자
special production order 특정제조지도서
special profit and loss 특별손익
special prosecutor 특별검찰관
special quotation 특별청산지수
special repair expenses 특별수선비
special reserve 특별적립금
special reserve fund 별도적립금
special resolution 특별결의
special revenue officer 특별국세징수관
special risks 특별위험
special status system 자격제도
special surplus fund 특별적립잉여금
special tax bond 특별목적세채권
special tax reduction bond 특별감세국채
special tax treatment 특례
special taxation measures 조세특별조치
special tonnage due 특별톤세
special treatment 특례
special valuation method 특별한 평가법
special ward 특별구
special ward inhabitants tax 특별구민세
special-purpose financial statement
　특정목적재무제표

specialist 스페셜리스트
specialist block purchases 특별대행구매
specialist book 스페셜리스트북
specialist insurer 개인보험자
specialist staff 전문스텝
speciality advertising 스페셜리티광고
specialization 전문화; 특화
specialized foreign exchange bank
　외국환전문은행
specialized fund 특정전문투자신탁
specialty store 전문점
specie money 정화(正貨)
specie points 금의 현송점
specie reserve 정화준비(正貨準備)
specific charge 특정담보
specific consumption tax 개별소비세
specific cost 개별원가
specific duty 종량세
specific foe 특정경쟁상대
specific insurance 물건특정보험
specific media 특수매체
specific performance 특정이행
specific policy 특정보험계약
specific productive factors 특수생산요소이론
specific property tax 개별재산세
specific reinsurance 개별재보험
specific risk 고유리스크
specific storage 종량보관료
specific tariff 종량세율
specific-order cost system 개별원가계산제도
specification 명세서; 시방서
specification cost 시방서원가
specified assets 특정자산
specified disease insurance 특정질병보장보험
specified donation 특정기부금
specified interest 특정이자
specified investment in kind 특정현물출자
specified medical corporation 특정의료법인
specified money in trust 특정금전신탁
specified portion 지정상속분
specified requirement 지정요건

specified stock 특정주
speculating for difference 차금거래
speculation 투기
speculation for difference
　가격차액으로 이익을 얻음
speculation for margin 차금거래
speculation in stocks 주식투기
speculation transaction 투기거래
speculative buyers 투기꾼
speculative buying 투기구매; 매점매석
speculative dealing 투기전
speculative demand 가수요
speculative enthusiasm 투기열
speculative gain 투기이윤
speculative import 가수입
speculative market 투기시장
speculative money 투기자금
speculative motive 투기동기
speculative risk 투기리스크
speculative stock 투기주(株)
speculative transaction 투기거래
speculator 투기꾼
speculator buying 투기구입
speed resistance line 스피드레지스턴스라인
speedy trial 신속한 재판
spending 지출
spending variance 예산차이
spendthrift trust 낭비자신탁
spike 감당할 수가 없는
spill over 스필오버
spin out 스핀아웃
spin-off 스핀오프
spinarama 스피나라마
spiral theory 스파이럴이론
split 스플릿
split ledger account 분할원장계정
split order 대량주문을 소량집행함
split rating 다른 비율
split run 분할테스트법
split sale 분할판매
split-dollar plan 보험료분담플랜

split-funding 분할각출
split-off 스플릿오프
split-ups of stocks 주식분할
splining a cause of action 청구원인분할
spoilage 손상(물)
spoilage expenses 손상품비
sponsor 스폰서
sponsor selectivity 스폰서의 선택력
sponsor tolerance to risk
　스폰서의 리스크 허용도
sponsor's role 스폰서의 역할
sponsored research 위탁연구
spontaneous combustion 자연발화
sports gambling 스포츠도박
spot 직물
spot delivery 현물인도
spot exchange 현물환
spot exchange rate 현물상장; 직물환상장
spot forward 스폿포워드
spot fund 스폿펀드
spot market 현물시장
spot next 스폿넥스트
spot operation 직물거래
spot period 스폿기간
spot position 직물위치
spot price 현물가격
spot quotation 현물상장
spot rate 현물상장
spot sale 즉매
spot share 현주
spot transaction 직물거래
spot value 현재가격
spotty 드문드문한
spread 가격차
spread 스프레드
spread banking 스프레드뱅킹
spread effect 파급효과
spread loan 스프레드론
spread loss cover 스프레드로스커버
spread toss reinsurance 초과손해재보험
spread sheet 스프레드시트

spread trading 스프레드트레이딩
spread transaction 스프레드거래
spreader 스프레더
spring offensive 춘투
spurious contagion 의사감염
spurious correlation 의사상관
spurt 급증
square 스퀘어
square an account 계정을 마감하다
square 스퀘어포지션
squeeze 스퀴즈
squeeze-out 스퀴즈아웃
stability 안정성
stability condition 안정조건
stability of the foreign exchange market
　환수급안정성
stabilization clause 안정조항
stabilization operation 안정조작
stabilization transaction 안정조작거래
stabilized accounting 안정가치회계
stabilizing 안정촉진적인
stabilizing transaction 안정조작
stable dividend 안정배당
stable dollar assumption 화폐가치일정공준
stable economic growth 안정경제성장
stable growth 안정성장
stable money principle 안정화폐론
stable stock 안정주
stable stockholder 안정주주
stable stockholder 주주안정공작
staff function 스탭직능
stag 스태그
stagflation 스태그플레이션
staggered schedule 스태거드스케줄
staggering maturity 만기분산
stagnant industry 정체산업
stagnant market 저속상장
stakeholder 이해관계자
stale bill of lading 시기경과선하증권
stale cheque 연체수표
stalemated industry 막다른 산업

stallage 매장설치권; 지대

stamp 인지

stamp duty 인지세

stamp duty law 수입인지세법

stamp revenue 인지수입

stamping bureau 요율감사부

stand alone investment 단순한 투자대상

stand in debt 채무가 있는

standard 기준; 표준물

standard burden rate 표준배부율

standard coin 본위화폐

standard cost 표준원가

standard cost accounting 표준원가계산

standard cross default provision
표준크로스디폴트조항

standard currency basket system 표준 바스킷

standard date 표준일

standard deduction 개산공제

standard depletion expenses 표준손료

standard deviation of volatility
변동율표준오차

standard documentation 표준서식

standard error 표준오차

standard error of beta 베터표준오차

standard error of estimate 추정치표준오차

standard industrial classification
표준산업분류

standard interest rate 표준금리

standard labor cost 표준노무비

standard lives 표준체

standard machine time 표준기계시간

standard manufacturing expense
표준제조간접비

standard material cost 표준재료비

standard metropolitan statistical areas
통계표준도시시권

standard money 본위화폐

standard of price 도량표준

standard part 표준부품

standard policy conditions 표준보험약관

Standard & Poor's Stock Price Index

스탠더드 앤드 푸어 주가지수

standard population 표준인구

standard profit 표준이익

standard quantity of materials consumed
재료표준소비량

standard rate 기준요금

standard score 표준득점

standard silver dollar 표준 은 달러

standard stocks 표준주

standard system 본위제도

standard tax rate 표준세율

standard values 표준치

standard wage 기준임금

standard-normal distribution 표준정규분포

standard-run quantity 표준생산량

standardization 표준화

standardized financial statements
표준재무제표

standardized slip 통일전표

standardized volatility 표준화 볼라틸리티

standby agreement
잔액인수; 스탠드바이인수

standby arrangement 차입예약

standby credit 스탠드바이·크레디트;
스탠드바이 신용장

standby facilities 스탠드바이퍼실리티

standby underwriting
청부모집; 잔액인수발행

standing agent 전환부대리인

standing auditor 상임감사역

standing charge 항상비용

standing cost 항상단가

standing expenses 고정비

standing order 계속주문

standing production order 계속제도명령서

standing proxy 상임대리인

standstill 스탠드스틸

standstill agreement 변제유예

standstill provision 스탠드스틸조항

staple items 항상상품

star system 스타시스템

S
T

stare decisis 선열구속력의 원칙
starting-load cost 당초부담원가
state bank 주법은행
state bankruptcy 국가파산
state branching 주내지점설치
state capital 국가자본
state capitalism 국가자본주의
state enterprises 국영사업
state franchise tax 주법인세
state government bond and debenture
　주정부채권
state government securities 주정부증권
state income tax 주소득세
state indemnification 국가보상
state insurance 국영보험
state insurance department 주보험국
state monopoly payment 전매납부금
state of the art 최신의
state of the union message 일반교서
state-chartered association 주면허조직
stated capital 확정자본금
stated liabilities 표시부채
stated value 장부기재가격
stated value no-par stock 기재식 무액면주식
statement 계산서
statement analysis 재무제표분석
statement classified by account title
　계정과목내역명세서
statement of account 결산보고
statement of cash flow 자금수지표
statement of cash receipts and disbursement
　자금조표
statement of changes in financial position
　재정상태변동표
statement of facts 합의사실기재서
statement of income and retained earnings
　잉여금결합계산서
statement of intent 고지서
statement of items 내역서
statement of liquidations 청산서
statement of operation earnings

　경상이익계산서
statement of principles 기본방침
statement of production cost 제조원가보고서
statement of realization and liquidation
　처분청산계산서
statement of retained earnings
　이익여잉금계산서
statement of source and application of funds
　자금운용표
statement of stockholders' equity
　주주지분계산서
statement of surplus 잉여금계산서
statement on auditing procedures 감사수속서
static analysis 정태분석
static market 정태시장
static model 정학모델
static multiplier 정학승수
static ratio 정태비율
static risk 정태리스크
static statistics 정태통계
staling part 주요부분
stationary state 정상상태
statistical analysis 통계분석
statistical assumption 통계가정
statistical decision theory 통계가정이론
statistical laws 통계법칙
statistical procedure 통계처리
statistical sampling 통계샘플링
statistical technique 통계방법
statistical terminology 통계용어
statistics 통계학
statistics of foreign currency reserves
　외화준비통계
statistics on international balance of payment
　국제수지통계
statistics on money supply analysis
　머니서플라이분석통계
statistics on national income 국민소득통계
status quo 현상
status system 지위체계
statute 제정법

statute book 법령전서
statute of limitation 시효
statute of limitations on collection
　징수권소멸시효
statute of limitations on refund claim
　환부청구권시효
statutes at large 법령집
statutory 법령에 의한
statutory accounting principle 법정회계원칙
statutory audit 법정감사
statutory bond 법정보증증권
statutory company 사법률에 의한 회사
statutory debt limit 법정발행한도액
statutory depletion method 법정상각법
statutory deposit 법정공탁금
statutory depreciation method 법정상각방법
statutory due date of tax payment
　법정납기한
statutory merger 강제합병
statutory notice 법정통지서
statutory rate of interest 법정이율
statutory reserve 법정준비금
statutory tariff 법정세율
statutory useful life 법정내용연수
statutory valuation method 법정평가방법
statutory valuation method of securities
　유가증권을 법정평가하는 방법
stay of execution 형집행정지
stay of proceedings 소송중지
steady 견고
steady market 견고한 시황
steady rise 착실한 신장
steady sales 순조로운 매상
steady state 항상상태
step function 단계함수
step-ladder payment method 스텝상환
step-up bonus 생존급부금
step-up coupon 스텝업쿠폰
step-up swap 스텝업스와프
stepped cost 단계원가
stepped coupon bond 단계이부채

stereogram 실체화, 입체화
sterling balance 본드잔고
sterling exchange standard 본드환본위제
stet processus 소송종결기재
steward 토지관리인
stiffen 경화시키다; 완고하게 하다
stimulated demand 자극된 수유
stimulatory marketing 자극판매
stipulated damage 약정손해배상액
stipulated price 협정가격
stipulated security 약정담보권
stipulation 조항
stochastic calculus 확률해석
stochastic method 확률방법
stochastic model 확률모델
stochastic process 확률프로세스
stochastics 추측통계학
stock 주식; 재고
stock abbreviation 주식약어
stock account 자본계정
stock acquired by the investment in kind
　현물출자취득주
stock acquisition 주식매수;
　주식구입에 의한 매수; 주식취득
stock adjustment 스톡조정
stock allotted to third persons 제삼자할당주
stock arbitrage 주식제정거래
stock at par 액면주
stock authorized 수권자본
stock bonus plan 스톡보너스플랜
stock book 재고품대장; 주식대장
stock broker 주식중매인
stock buyback 주식환매
stock capitalization 자본금
stock certificate 주권
stock certificate to bearer 무기명주권
stock clearing corporation 대체결제회사
stock collateral loan 주식담보금융
stock compensation plan 주식보상제도
stock controlling other business
　기업지배주식

S
T

stock cum rights 증자권리부 주식
stock dealing 주식거래
stock dealing on credit 주식신용거래
stock dividend 주식배당
stock equity 주주지분
stock equity value 주식지분가치
stock exchange 주식거래소
Stock Exchange Automated Quotation
　런던증권거래소시황정보시스템
stock exchange clearing house
　주식청산소
stock exchange daily official list
　주식거래소공보
stock exchange holiday 주식거래소휴일
stock exchange loan 주식거래소대부
stock exchange panic 주식공황
stock exchange seat 주식거래소회원권
stock exchange share 당소주(當所株)
stock exchange transaction 거래소거래
stock for guarantee 보증주
stock for inflation hedging 인플레헤지주
stock for margin trading 신용거래주
stock futures transaction 주식선물거래
stock holding ratio of foreigners
　외국인지주비율
stock in hand 현재품
stock in process 제작중인 물건
stock ill the inventory 재고품
stock index 주가지수
stock index futures 주가지수선물
stock inflation 스톡인플레이션
stock investment 주식투자
stock investment trust 주식투자신탁
stock issue at market price 시가발행주식
stock issue expenses 신주발행비
stock ledger 주식대장
stock level 소지재고수준
stock loan 주권대부
stock loan market 대주시장
stock manipulation 주가조작
stock market 주식시장

stock market fluctuation 주식시장의 변동
stock mind 스톡마인드
stock name 주식명
stock of affiliated company 관계회사주식
stock on hand 소지주
stock option 주식매입선택권; 스톡옵션
stock option plan 주식구입선택권
stock power 주권양도위임장
stock price 주가
stock price analysis 주가분석
stock price average 평균주가
stock price index 주가지수
stock price index arbitrage transaction
　주가지수재정거래
stock price index futures trading
　주가지수선물거래
stock price index option transaction
　주가지수옵션거래
stock price manipulation 주가조작
stock purchase option 주식매입옵션
stock purchase plan 주식구입계획
stock purchase warrant 신주인수권
stock quotations 주가정보
stock rating 주식비율
stock receipt 주권양도증
stock recommended for purchase
　권장주, 추천주
stock register 주식원장
stock repurchase plan 주식환매계획
stock right 증자신주매수권
stock risk estimation 주식리스크추정
stock speculation 주식투기
stock split-up 주식분해
stock subscription 주식응모
stock swap 주식스와프
stock symbol 주식심볼
stock taking 실제재고
stock transfer 명의변경
stock turnover 재고회전율
stock used in the average 평균주가채용주
stock valuation 주식평가

stock valuation based on dividend
배당환원주식평가

stock valuation summary 주식평가개요

stock warrants 스톡워런트

stock with par value 액면주식

stock without par value 무액면주식

stock yield 주식이율

stock-book 상품소유

stock-flow 스톡플로우

stock-market crash 주식공황

stock-to-sales ratio 재고율

stockdraw 비축철거

stockholder 주주

stockholder's 자본주계정

stockholder's right 주주권

stockholding limit for foreign investors
외국인지주제한

stockpile financing 체화금융

stockpower 위임장

stocks 저장품

stocks in hand 소유주

stolen check 도난수표

stop loss cover 초과손해율보험

stop loss order 손절주문

stop loss reinsurance 초과손해재보험

stop order 공탁금지불금지명령; 지정가격주문

stop-and-go policy 스톱앤드고정책

stop-limit order 역지정가격주문

stop-loss order 손실한정주문

stop-payment order 지불정지통지

stoppage of business 영업정지

storage 보관료

storage accounts receivable 미수보관료

storage charges 보관비

storage costs 저장경비

storage management 저장품관리

storage of inventories 재고자산보관

store arrangement 점포배열

store audit 점포감사

store business interruption insurance
점포휴업보험

store modernization 점포근대화

store preference 점포선고

store saturation 점포포화상태

store traffic 장내교통

storecasting 장내방송

stored and forward switching 축적교환

stored goods 저장품

storekeepers' comprehensive insurance
점포종합보험

stores ledger 원재료원장

stores purchase book 재료구입장

storyboard 영화의 주요 장면을 간단히 그린 일
련의 그림을 붙인 패널

stowage 하적료

straddle 스트래들

straddle position transaction
스트래들포지션거래

straight average cost method 단순평균법

straight bankruptcy 단순파산

straight bill of lading 기명식 선하증권

straight bond 보통사채

straight climb 수직상승

straight commission 수수료제도

straight corporate bond 보통사채

straight credit 매입불능신용장

straight currency swap
스트레이트커런시스와프

straight fall 시세가 폭락함

straight government bond 보통국채

straight life annuity 종신연금

straight life insurance 보통종신보험

straight-line depreciation 정액감가상각법

strait-line method 직선법

stranding 좌초

stranger 제삼자

strangle 스트랭글

strangle position transaction
스트랭글포지션거래

strap 스트랩

strategic advantage 전략우위제

strategic advertisement 전략광고

strategic alliance 전략적인 제휴; 전략동맹
strategic beachhead 전략적 교두보
strategic business unit 전략사업단위
strategic competition 전략적인 경쟁
strategic decision 전략적인 의사결정
strategic field 전략분야
strategic group 전략적인 집단
strategic information system 전략정보시스템
strategic management 전략경영
strategic performance 전략성과
strategy 전략
strategy analysis 전략분석
strategy development 전략개발
strategy formulation 전략형성
stratification 계층화
stratified sampling 계층화추출
stratum 계층
straw bail 공보증인
straw man 위증자
street 금융가
street broker 장외중매인
street name 명의
street price 인수후 상장
strengthen 해결하다
strengthening 정리; 해결
strengthening of managerial function
　관리기능강화
strict construction 엄격해석
strict foreclosure 대물변제담보물을 취득함
strict liability 엄격책임
strike a balance 대차를 공제하다
strike price 권리행사가격
stringent policy a lifts 강경정책
strip player 스트립플레이어
strip yield 스트립일드
stripped cap 스트립캡
stripped interest rate cap 스트립금리캡
stripped zero-coupon 스트립제로쿠폰
strips 스트립채
strong and weak 강약
strong feeling 강한 느낌

strong form 스트롱폼
strong growth 강한 성장
strong incentive 호재료
strong market 강세시황
strong sentiment 강한 느낌
strong tone 시세가 오를 듯한 기세
strong won 원고
structural 구조적인
structural adjustment facility 구조조정융자
structural analysis 구조분석
structural change 구조변화
structural determinant 구조요인
structural equation 구조방정식
structural factor 구조인자
structural flexibility 구조상의 탄력성
structural impediments initiative talks
　구조협의
structural inflation 구조적인 인플레이션
structural outline 구도
structural unemployment 구조적인 실업
structural-functional analysis 구조기능분석
structure 구축물
structure of industry 산업구조
structure of interest rates 금리구조
structure of price 가격구조
structured transaction 구조거래
struggle for existence 생존경쟁
stuck 스택상태의
student comprehensive insurance
　학생종합보험
student's distribution 스튜던트분포
studio standard 스튜디오규격
stuffer 첨부광고
style sheet 스타일시트
sub-contrary 작은 반대명제
subcenter 부도심(副都心)
subcontract 하청
subcontract factory 하청공장
subcontractor 하청업자
subculture 하위문화
subduct 제거하다

subheading 부표제
subject 과목
subject market 서브젝트마켓
subject-matter 계쟁물(係爭物)
subject-matter of insurance 보험의 목적
subjective perception 주관적인 지각
subjective probability 주관적인 확률
sublease 부동산전대차
sublet 전대하다
subliminal 서브리미널
subliminal advertisement 서브리미널광고
subliminal advertising 잠재의식광고
subloan 서브론
submission 중재부탁합의
subobjective 하위목적
suboptimization 부분최적화
subordinate debenture 예속조항부 사채
subordinate ledger 보조원장
subordinated 예속의
subordinated bond 하위사채
subordinated clause 예속조항
subordinated creditor 하위채권자
subordinated debenture 하위사채
subordinated debt 하위채권
subordinated payment-in-kind bond
　하위페이먼트인카인드채
subordinated stock 하위주
subordinated unsecured debenture
　하위성 무담보사채
subordination 종속; 하위
subparticipation 대리참가
subrogated performance 대위변제
subrogated right 대위채무
subrogation 대위
subrogation arising out of salvage
　잔존물대위
subrogation payment 대위납부
subrogation receipt 대위영수서
subrogation right of obligee 채권자대위권
subscribe 서명하다
subscribed capital stock 미불입자본

subscriber's yield 응모자이율
subscription 출자
subscription agreement 모집계약
subscription blank 주식신청서
subscription book closed 주식모집마감
subscription book open 주식모집개시
subscription certificate 출자증권
subscription for shares 주식응모
subscription money 신청금
subscription period 판매기간
subscription price 응모가격
subscription right 신주인수권
subscription television 유료방송
subscription warrant 신주인수권증서
subscription's receivable account
　주식인수계정
subscriptions 불입을 끝내지 않은 자본금
subsequent events 후발사상
subsequent measurements 사후측정
subsequent taxable year 다음 사업연도
subsidiary 자회사
subsidiary accounts 보조원장계정
subsidiary book 보조장부
subsidiary coin 보조화폐
subsidiary company 자회사
subsidiary corporation 관계회사
subsidiary department 보조부문
subsidiary journal 보조기입장
subsidiary ledger 보조원장
subsidiary material cost 보조재료비
subsidiary money 보조화폐
subsistence money 생계비
substance 본질
substance over form 실질우선
substandard 표준하체
substandard loan 회수에 문제가 있는 대부
substantial damages 실질손해배상금
substantial evidence 실질적인 증거
substantial performance 실질이행
substantive 주요
substantive evidence 실질증거

S
T

substantive law 실체법
substitute assets 대체자산
substitute certificate for government bond
　국채대용증서
substitute fixed assets 대체고정자산
substitute property 대체자산
substitute securities 대용유가증권
substituted expenses 대체비용
substitution 대체
substitution curve 대체곡선
substitution effect 대체효과
substitution of land lot 환지처분
substrategy 하위전략
subsystem 서브시스템
subtitle 견출
subtraction 공제
subunderwriting 대리인수
suburban paper 교외지
suburban population 교외인구
suburban store 교외점포
subvention 보조
subzero growth 마이너스성장
succession 승계
succession of endorsement 이서연속
succession of liabilities 채무인계
succession of national tax liability
　국세채무승계
succession of property 유산상속
succession of right of taxation 과세권승계
succession of tax liability 납세의무계승
successive inheritance 상차상속
successor 후계자
suck 핥다; 빨아먹다
suction to cash 현금에 부착함
sue and labor charges 손해방지비용
sue and labor clause 손해방지조항
sue out 신청하여 취득하다
suffer 허용하다
suffrage 투표행위
suggested resale price 권장재판매가격
suggestion scheme 제안제도

sui generis 자기고유의
suit 소송
suitor 소송인
Sullivan Principle 설리반의 원칙
sum 총액
sum insured 보험금액
sum insured left 잔존보험금액
sum insured method 보험금액비례주의
sum payable at death 사망보험금
sum total 합계
sum up 계상하다
sum-of-the-years-digits method 산술급수법
summary 종합계정; 요약
summary account 집계계정
summary journal 종합분개장
summary judgment 즉결판결
summary measure 집약척도
summary of earnings 영업성적
summary procedure 감독절차
summary proceeding 약식소송절차
summary reports 개략보고
summary sheet 집계표
summary statement of business
　사업개황설명서
summated rating 평정가산법
summer time 서머타임
summing-up 증거요약
summons 호출장
sundry account 잡계정
sundry expenses 제잡비
sundry goods 잡화
sundry income 잡수입
sundry supplies 소모품
sunk cost 회수불능원가
super 301 Article 슈퍼 301조
super floater swap 플로터스와프
super gold tranche 슈퍼골드트랜시에
super impose 슈퍼임포즈
super majority provision 슈퍼메이저터리조항
super NOW account 슈퍼나우계정
super prime rate 슈퍼프라임레이트

superannuation 노령퇴직자연금
superannuation payment 퇴직금적립금
supercargo 화물관리인
superficiary 지상권자
superficium 지상물
superior character 상급문자
superior courts 상급법원
superior obligation 재단채권
superior risks 우수물건
supernational bond 국제기관사채
supersede 대체하다
supertax 부가세
supervisor 슈퍼바이저
supplemental 보충의
supplemental contract 부수계약
supplementary budget 보정예산
supplementary call 보충분담금
supplementary cost 간접원가; 보충비용
supplementary financial measure 보충융자
supplementary income statement information
　손익계산서의 보충자료
supplementary insurance 보조보험
supplementary payment 보조급료
supplementary proceedings 보충절차
supplementary regulations 부칙
supplementary special deposits scheme
　추가특별예금제도
supplementary statement 부속명세서
supplier's credit 연불신용
supplies 부장품
supplies expenses 소모품비
supply 지급
supply and demand 수급
supply bond 공급보증증권
supply function 공급함수
supply of investible funds 자금공급
supply-side economics 서플라이사이드경제학
support 지탱
support buying 급격한 시세변동을 막음
support line 하치지시선
support operation 급격한 시세변동을 막음

support price 유지가격
support trust 부조신탁
supporter 부양자
supporting documents 부속서류
supporting order 매매유지주문
suppression of deposition
　공술녹취서를 금지함
suprafinn 슈프라펌
Supreme Court 최고법원
supreme law of the land 국가의 최고법규
surcharge 가중세; 과징금
surety 보증인
Surety Association of America
　미국보증보험협회
surety bond 보증증권
surety company 보증회사
surety money 보증채무
surety obligation 구상권
suretyship 보증
surface communication
　표면적인 커뮤니케이션
surface model 표면모델
surface right 지상권
surgical expense insurance 수술비 보험
surplus 잉여금
surplus account 잉여금계정
surplus adjustment 잉여금수정
surplus analysis 잉여금분석
surplus appropriated for redemption fund
　채무상환적립금
surplus appropriation statement
　잉여금처분계산서
surplus at liquidation 청산잉여금
surplus available for dividend 배당가능이익
surplus charge 잉여금부과
surplus equipment 유휴설비
surplus finance 흑자재정
surplus from capital reduction 감자잉여금
surplus from consolidation 연결잉여금
surplus from merged company 합병차익
surplus from revaluation 재평가잉여금

surplus funds 잉여금
surplus insurance 잉여인슈런스
surplus line 주내보험자의 소화가 안되는 보험
surplus profit 잉여익금
surplus reserves 잉여적립금
surplus reserves transferred to income
　적립금 반려
surplus section 잉여금구분
surplus statement 잉여금계산서
surplus transaction 잉여금거래
surplus treaty reinsurance 초과액특약재보험
surplus value 잉여가치
surplusage 과잉
surprises in earnings 예상외의 이익변동
surrender 권리방기
surrender charge 해약공제
surrender profit 해약익
surrender provisions 해약조항
surrender ratio 해약률
surrender value 해약반려금
surtax 과징금
surtax on land tax 지조부가세
surtax on national tax 국세부가세
surveillance 감시
survey bias 조사선입견
survey fee 감정료
survey repot 감정보고서
surveying 측량
surveying fee 감정료
surveyor 사정인
survival bond 서바이벌본드
survival of the fittest 적자생존
surviving company 존속회사
surviving entity 존속실체
survivor annuity 유족연금
survivor benefit 유족급부금
survivorship 생존자에 대한 권리의 귀속
survivorship annuity 생잔연금
sushi bond 스시본드
suspended trading 매매정지
suspense account 미결계정

suspense payment account 가불금계정
suspense payments 가불금
suspense receipts 가수금
suspense receipts account 가수금계정
suspension 정지
suspension of banking transaction
　은행거래정지처분
suspension of business 사업중지
suspension of convertibility 교환성정지
suspension of execution 집행정지
suspension of payment 지불정지
suspension of prescription 정지시효
suspension of right 권리정지
suspension of seizure 차압유예
suspension of statute of limitations 시효정지
suspension of transactions 입회정지
suspension of work claims 중단클레임
suspicion 혐의
sustain 유지하다
sustainable equilibrium exchange rate
　유지가능한 균형상장
sustainable growth 지속성장
sustainable growth rate 지속성장률
sustaining program 스폰서가 없는 프로그램
sustenance 생계
swap 스와프
swap agreement 스와프협정
swap broker 스와프브로커
swap cost 스와프코스트
swap coupon 스와프쿠폰
swap fund 스와프채
swap loan 스와프론
swap of bond 채권스와프
swap portfolio 스와프채포트폴리오
swap rate 스와프채레이트
swap strike 스와프채스트라이크
swap trading 스와프채거래
swap-in-arrears 에어리어스와프
swaption 스왑션
sweat 땀에 젖음
sweep 시청률조사

sweep account 스윕어카운트
sweetener 조미료
swing 스윙
swing line 신용공여화
switch 환승
switch finance 스위치금융
switch from won to dollars 원달러시프트
switch pitch 스위치피치
switch reversal 역입체
switch trade 스위치무역
switching cost 구입선변경코스트
syllabus 판결적요
symbiosis 공생
symbol system of accounts 계정기호법
symbolic communication 심볼릭커뮤니케이션
symbolic delivery 상징적인 인도
symbolic logics 기호논리학
symbolic model 기호모델
symbolic simulation 심볼릭시뮬레이션
symmetrical distribution 대칭분포
symmetrical triangle pattern 대칭트라이앵글
symptomatic behavior 징후형 행동
synchromarketing 동조형 마케팅
synchronize 동기(同期)로 하다
synchronizer 싱크로나이저
synchronousity broadcasting 동기방송
syndic 파산관재인
syndicate 인수단
syndicate of banks 은행단
syndicate survey 신디케이트조사
syndicate underwriting 신디케이트인수
syndicated loan 신디케이트론
syndicated term loan 중장기협조융자
syndication 신디케이트단
synergy 상승
synergy effect 상승효과

synopsis sheet 개요시트
synthesis tax rate 종합세율
synthetic assets 합성자산
synthetic bond 신세틱채권
synthetic cash arbitrage transaction
　합성현물재정거래
synthetic cash instrument 신세틱캐시
synthetic instrument 복합상품
synthetic long 신세틱론
synthetic position 합성포지션
synthetic propositions 종합명제
synthetic put 신세틱풋
synthetic rubber 합성고무
synthetic short 신세틱쇼트
synthetic useful life 종합내용연수
system approach 시스템어프로치
system audit 시스템
system engineering 시스템공학
system issue 시스템문제
system of accounts 회계조직
system of blue return 청색신고제도
system of fixed rate of exchange 고정상장제
system of interest rates 이자율체계
System of National Account 신국민경제체계
system of note issue 발권제도
system of taxation 조세체계
system operation 시스템조작
system repos 시스템 레포
system risk 시스템리스크
systematic analysis 조직적인 분석
systematic calculation 계통적인 계산
systematic risk 시스티매틱리스크
systematic sampling 계통표본
systemic 계통적인
systems competition 시스템 간 경쟁

S
T

T form account T자형 계정
table 계산표
table of present value 현가표
table of price factors 환산계수테이블
table of random numbers 난수표
tabloid size 타블로이드판
tabular cash book 다행식 현금출납장
tabular ledger 표식원장
tabular standard 계산본위
tabulating machine 회계기
tabulation 제표
tachistoscope 순간노출기
tacit 묵시의
tacit collusion 암묵의 공모
tacking 후순위저당우선
tact system 택트시스템
tactical asset allocation 전술적인 자산배분
tactical planning 전술계획
tail hedge 테일헤지
tailgating 상승
tailing 테일링
tailor made 특주의
take a capital stake in 자본출자하다
take-home pay 세금공제급여
take-off strategy 초기단계전략
take-ones 테이크원즈
take-or-pay contract
　　산출물인수 혹은 지불계약
takeout 차액수입
takeout loan 테이크아웃론
takeover 매입

takeover bid 주식공개매입
taking a bath 투기전에서 손해를 봄
taking a flier 투기함
takings 매상
talk down 구두개입(하락)
talk up 구두개입(상승)
tally 조합
tally audit 검수감사
tally man 검수인
tangible assets 유형자산
tangible depreciable property 유형상각자산
tangible fixed assets 유형고정자산
tangible loss 유형손실
tangible property 유형고정자산
tangible value 유형자산가치
tap 탭발행
tap bills 탭빌
tap issue 탭발행
tap stock 탭채
tapping of resources 자원개발
target assets value 대상자산가액
target company 대상회사
target cost 목표원가
target group 표적집단
target income 목표이익
target issue 타겟발행
target payout ratio 목표배당성향
target portfolio 목표포트폴리오
target price 목표가격
target profit 목표이익
target range 목표변동폭

target securities 대상상품
target stock 대상주식
target yield 목표이율
target zone 타겟존; 목표상장권
tariff 관세
tariff autonomy 관세자주권
tariff barrier 관세장벽
tariff by agreement 협정요율
tariff commission 세율위원회
tariff escalation 경사관세
tariff harmonization 관세조화화
tariff in jeopardy 긴급관세
tariff negotiations 관세교섭
tariff premium 영업보관료
tariff quota 관세할당
tariff quota system 관세할당제도
tariff rate 관세율
tariff war 관세전략
taritfication 관세화
tarnished halo 역헤일로효과
task 사업
task environment 태스크환경
task method 태스크방법
tax 조세
tax accountant examination 세리사시험
tax accountant fee 세리사보수
tax accounting 세무회계
tax adjustments 세무조사
tax administration system 세무행정조직
tax advisor 세무고문
tax agency 세무대리
tax agent 납세관리인
tax amount 과세액
tax amount settled 조정세액
tax and public dues 공조공과
tax and stamp revenues 조세 및 인지수입
tax anticipation bill 조세준비증권
tax arbitrage 세금재정
tax assessment 조세사정
tax audit 세무감사
tax authorities 세무당국

tax avoidance 조세회피
tax base 과세기준
tax basis 과세표준
tax bearer 담세자
tax bearing capacity 담세력
tax benefit 조세특전
tax bond 세수채
tax bracket 세율등급
tax burden 조세부담
tax burden rate 세부담율
tax burden ratio 조세부담율
tax claims 조세채권
tax clause 세금조항
tax collection 징세
tax collection by stamp 증지징수
tax collection system 징세기구
tax collector 수세관
tax computation basis 세액계산기준
tax consultation 세무상담
tax convention 조세조약
tax court 세무법원
tax credit 세액공제
tax credit for dividend 배당공제
tax credit for minor 미성년자공제
tax criminal 조세범
tax cut by law 감세
tax cutback 택스컷백
tax deductible items 과세공제비목
tax deductions 세공제
tax deed 공매증서
tax delinquency 체납
tax dispute 세무쟁소
tax documents 세무서류
tax due 납세액
tax effect 세효과
tax effect accounting 세효과회계
tax evasion 탈세
tax examination 세무조사
tax exempt 비과세
tax exempt bond 면세채
tax exemption 면세

tax exemption for agricultural income
농업소득면세

tax exemption for dependents 부양공제

tax exemption for specific use 특정용도면제

tax exemption limit 면세점

tax for default 가산세

tax for transfer of securities 유가증권이전세

tax forms 납세신고용지

tax free 비과세

tax free article 비과세품

tax free corporation 비과세법인

tax free purchase 비가세구입

tax haven 택스헤븐; 세금피난처

tax in arrears 연체세

tax in jeopardy 긴급과세

tax in kind 물납세

tax incentive 세리상의 우대조치

tax incidence 조세귀착

tax increase 증세

tax items 세목(稅目)

tax jurisprudence 세법학

tax law 세법

tax lease 택스리스

tax liability 납세의무

tax lien 조세선취특권

tax loss carry-forward 결손금이월

tax loss carryback 결손금 되풀이

tax manager 납세관리인

tax obligation 납세의무

tax office 세무서

tax on admission 입장세

tax on bank note system 태환권발행세

tax on capital 캐피탈게인과세

tax on construction 건축세

tax on deposit 예금이자세

tax on dividend 이익배당세

tax on excess issue 제한외발행세

tax on goods and possessions 물세

tax on property 자산세

tax on redemption profit 상환차익과세

tax on the write-up 자산재평가세

tax on undistributed profits
유보소득에 대한 세

tax on unutilized land 미이용지세

tax oriented transaction 절세거래

tax papers 납세고지서

tax paradise 택스파라다이스; 조세피난처

tax payable 미불세금

tax payable account 미불세금계정

tax payer's suit 납세자소송

tax payment 납세

tax payment by securities 증권납부

tax payment by self-assessment 신고납세

tax payment by stamp 인지납부

tax payment by transfer account 대체납세

tax payment in kind 현물납부

tax payment in money 금전상납

tax payment place 납세지

tax payment slip 납부서

tax policy 조세정책

tax practitioner 세리사

tax procedures 세무상의 수속

tax proxy 세무대리

tax rate 세율

tax rate applied to upper part of income
상적세율(上積稅率)

tax rate higher than standard 초과세율

tax rate of gift tax 증여세율

tax rebate 환불세

tax reduction 감세

tax reform 세제개혁

tax refunded 환급된 조세

tax regulations 세법

tax relief 조세부담경감

tax relief bonds 감세채권

tax requisition 과세요건

tax reserve 세금준비금

tax resort 택스리조트; 세금휴양소

tax return form 납세신고서

tax revenue 세수

tax roll 과세대장

tax rule 세법규

tax sale 환가처분
tax saving 절세
tax saving association 납세저축조합
tax seal 세인
tax selling 세금을 위한 매각
tax shelter 세금회피수단
tax sparing credit 간주외국세액공제
tax state 조세국가
tax structure 조세구조
tax suit 세무소송
tax surcharge 부가세
tax swap 택스스와프
tax system 세제
tax system council 세제조사회
tax table 세액표
tax take 세금으로 빼앗기는 금액
tax threshold 과세최저한
tax treaty 조세조약
tax tribunal examiner 국세심사관
tax unpaid 납세미제
tax value 과세가격
tax-free small-sum public bond investment system 소액공채별 비과세제도
tax-free small-sum savings system 소액저축비과세제도
tax-gathering season 세수기
taxable 과세할 수 있는
taxable amount 과세가격
taxable capacity 세부담능력
taxable depreciation 유세상각
taxable document 과세문서
taxable estate 과세유산
taxable goods 과세품
taxable income 과세소득
taxable item 과세대상
taxable minimum of property tax 고정자산세면세점
taxable period 과세기간
taxable property 과세재산
taxable purchases 과세구입
taxable sales 과세매상

taxable undistributed profits 과세대상유보금액
taxable unit 과세단위
taxable value 과세가격
taxable year 사업연도
taxable year of merger 합병사업연도
taxanticipation note 세수보증어음
taxanticipation warrant 세수보증워런트
taxation 과세
taxation allowance for life insurance premium 생명보험료공제
taxation allowance for nonlife insurance premium 손해보험료공제
taxation at the source 원천과세
taxation at time of receipt from bonded area 인수과세
taxation by applying upper bracket 상적과세
taxation by estimate 추계과세
taxation division 수세과
taxation of income basis 소득할과세
taxation on a per capita basis 균등할과세
taxation on aggregate income 종합과세
taxation on capital 캐피탈게인과세
taxation on corporation tax basis 법인세할과세
taxation on enterprise 기업과세
taxation on government monopoly 전매과세
taxation on retirement annuity 퇴직연금과세
taxation on shipment 이출과세
taxation on small business 소기업과세
taxation rate 세율
taxation system 세제
taxation upon the general-public 대중과세
taxation upon total income 종합과세
taxbenefit rule 세효과 규칙
taxcollector 세무관
taxdodging 탈세
taxes 공과
taxes and rates 국세 및 지방세
taxes assessed by taxpayers 신고세
taxes collected 세금예금

S
T

taxes receivable 미수세
taxexempt organization 비과세기관
taxflation 택스플레이션
taxfree income 면세소득
taxfree investment 면세투자
taxfree reserve 비과세준비금
taxpayer 납세자
taxpayer filing a blue return 청색신고자
taxpayer identification number system
　납세자번호제도
taxpayer with limited tax liability
　제한납세의무자
taxpayer's association 납세조합
taxpayer's option 납세자의 선택
taxpayer's suit 납세자소송
teaser advertising 티저광고
technical analysis 기술적인 분석
technical assistance 기술지원
technical change 사선으로 교차된 줄무늬
technical cooperation 기술제휴
technical forecast 기술적인 예측
technical graph 기술분석용 그래프
technical index 기술지표
technical indicator 기술분석지표
technical innovation 기술혁신
technical position 시장내부요인
technical progress 기술진보
technical quality 기술의 질
technical rally 기술적인 반등
technical reaction 기술적인 반응
technical rebound 자율반등
technical specification 기술시방서
technical theory 기술이론
technical trading 테크니컬트레이딩
technocrat 기술관료
technological changes 기술진보
technological forecasting 기술예측
technological gap 기술격차
technology assessment 테크놀로지어세스먼트
technology transfer 기술이전
technology transfer agreement 기술이전계약

telecine translation 텔레시네변환
telecommunication business 전기통신사업
telecomputing 텔레컴퓨팅
telegraphic transfer 전신환
telegraphic transfer buying rate 전신매상장
telegraphic transfer payable 송금환
telegraphic transfer receivable 수금환
telegraphic transfer selling rate 전신매상장
telematique 텔레마티크
telephone market 텔레폰마켓
telephone rates 전화요금
telephone subscription right 전화가입권
teleport 텔레포트
teletext 문자다중방송
television conference 텔레비전회의
television system 텔레비전방식
teller 현금출납계
temporal law 시간법칙
temporal method 속성법
temporary 잠정적
temporary account 임시계정
temporary advance 일시입체
temporary annuity 정기생명연금
temporary bond 템퍼러리본드
temporary boom 일시적인 호황
temporary borrowing 일시차입금
temporary income 임시소득
temporary injunction 임시금지명령
temporary investment 일시투자
temporary layoff 일시이직
temporary leave from work 일시귀휴
temporary loan 일시대부금
temporary loan before bond flotation
　기채연결융자
temporary loan on property
　일시적인 자산대부
Temporary Money Rates Adjustment Law
　임시금리조정법
temporary payment 가불금
temporary rally 일시적인 반등
temporary receipts 가수금

temporary receipts account 가수금계정
temporary repairs 가수선
temporary residence 거소
temporary seal 가봉
temporary tariff rate 잠정세율
temporary tax accountan 임시세리사
temporary use 일시사용
10-K report 10-K레포트
10-Q report 10-Q 사반기보고서
tenancy 부동산권
tenancy in common 전구성원이 공유함
tenant 차지인
tenant right 차지권; 대차권
tender 입찰인수; 견적사양서
tender bill 텐더빌
tender clause 입찰약관
tender offer 주식공개매부
tender panel 텐더패널
tender security 입찰증권
tenement 보유재산
tenor 상환기한
tension 긴장
tentative agreement 잠정합의
tentative balance sheet 가대차대조표
tentative budget 잠정예산
tentative validity 공정력
tenure of office 재직기한
term 기간; 조건
term annuity 정기연금
term bonds 단일만기채
term deposits 정기예금
term fed 텀페드
term federal fund 텀페더럴펀드
term financing 중장기파이낸스
term financing rate 기간차입금리
term for evaluation 평가시기
term insurance 정기보험
term loan 텀론
term of execution 집행기간
term of insurance 보험기간
term of office 재직기한

term of payment 지불기한
term of validity 유효기한
term policy 정기생명보험계약
term risk 기간리스크
term sheet 조건개요서
term structure 기간구조
term-end 기말
term-end account 기말계정
term-end settlement of accounts 기말결산
terminal dividend 소멸배당
terminal funding 연금원가적립방식
terminal funding method 연금현물충족방식
terminal pay allowance 퇴직수당
terminal reserve 연말책임준비금
termination 기간만료
termination claim 만기청구액
termination dividend 계약종료배당
terms and conditions 조건
terms of delivery 인도조건
terms of trade 교역조건
terrier 토지대장
territorial multiplier 지구배율
territorial right 지구특약권
territorial waters 영해
tertiary beneficiary 삼순위보험금수취인
tertiary industry 삼차산업
test data 시험데이터
test marketing 시험판매
test of hypothesis 가설검정
testament 유언
testify 증언하다
testimonial advertising 추천광고
testimony 증언
testing 시험
testing audit 시험조사
testing expenses 시작비
testing hypothesis 검정가설
text editor program 텍스트편집프로그램
their account 선방계정
theoretical 이론적
theoretical economics 이론경제학

S
T

theoretical future price 이론선물가격
theoretical hypothesis 이론적인 가설
theoretical price 이론가격
theoretical rate of exchange 이론적인 환상장
theoretical support 이론적인 지시
theoretical value 이론가치
theories of insurance 보험학설
theory of achievement motivation
　달성동기부 이론
theory of action 행위이론
theory of approximation 근사치이론
theory of asset valuation 자산평가론
theory of comparative cost 비교생산비설
theory of consumption 소비이론
theory of games 게임이론
theory of indemnity 손해보상이론
theory of international indebtedness
　국제대차설
theory of liabilities taxation
　조세채무관계설
theory of multiplier 승수이론
theory of optimum tariff 최적관세이론
theory of portfolio selection 자산선택이론
theory of rate-making 보험요율결정이론
theory of role enactment 역할실현이론
theory of tax accounting 세무회계론
theory of ultimate cause 최후조건설
therblig 서블리그
thesaurus 지식의 보고(백과사전 등)
thin 한산
thin capitalization 과소자본
thin industry 취약산업
thin margin 소규모차액이익금
thing in action 무체동산
things real 부동산
think tank 두뇌집단
third country bill 삼국어음
third generation 삼차
third generation on-line system
　3차 온라인시스템
third market 장외거래시장

third party 제삼자
third party claimant bond
　제삼자이의신청소송보증증권
third party legal liability insurance
　제삼자법적배상책임보험
third party liability cover
　제삼자배상특약보험
third party liability insurance
　제삼자배상책임보험
third party sales credit 할부구입알선
third sect 제3구역
third world countries 제3세계 각국
threat 협박
3D scanner 입체스캐너
three digit PER 세자리수 주가수익률
three line converting method 삼선전환법
three-fourths loss clause 4분의3 보전약관
three-month moving average 3개월이동평균
threshold 한계
threshold of divergence 괴리한도
through bill of lading 통과선하증권
through transportation 일관수송
through-put contract 스루풋조항
throughout accounting 일관회계
throughout the target issues 대상문제전체의
throw-back rule 스로우 백 원칙
throwaway product 일회용 제품
thumbnail 엄지손톱, 간결한
tick 틱
tick-test rule 틱테스트룰
ticker 주식상장표시판
ticket 전표
ticket of leave 가석방허가증
ticket sale finance 티켓판매금융
tie-in 포합의
tie-in sale 포합판매
tie-up loan 제휴론
tied loan 조건부 융자
tied-agent 전속중개자
tier 계층
tight 단단히

tight budget 긴축재정
tight fiscal policy 재정긴축정책
tight money policy 금융긴축정책
tightened inspection 엄격한 검사
tightening 협박, 긴축
tighter monetary policy 긴축정책
tightness of money 자금이 딸림
till-forbid 틸포비드
timber delivery tax 목재거래세
timber income 산림소득
time bargains 정기거래
time bias 타임바이어스
time bill 기한부 어음
time card 타임카드
time cost 시간원가
time decay 타임디케이
time deposit 정기예금
time deposit account 정기예금계정
time deposit certificate 정기예금증서
time division multiple access 시분할다원접속
time draft 일람후 정기불환어음
time expired 기한무효
time filter 타임필터
time for tax payment 납기한
time horizon 거래기간
time limit 기한
time limitation 기간제한
time limited 기일
time loan 정기대부
time of adoption 채용시간
time of presentation 제시기간
time of receipts 수입시기
time of recognizing gain 수익계상시기
time of recognizing loss 손실계상시기
time perception 시간인식
time policy 기간보험
time preference 시간선호
time priority 시간우선의 원칙
time rate system 시간임금제
time sales 할부판매
time series analysis 시계열분석

time series behavior of earnings
　이익의 시계열변동
time series data 시계 열 데이터
time span 타임스팬
time spread 시간스프레드
time study 시간연구
time to expiration 잔여기간
time to maturity 잔존기간
time transaction 정기거래
time value 시간가치
time value of option 옵션의 시간가치
time variance 시간차이
time-series analysis 시계열분석
time-series behavior 시계열변동
time-weighted return 시간가중수익률
timely disclosure 때맞춤 정보개시
times per year 연간회전횟수
times-interest earned 이자부담배율
times-interest earned ratio 이자부담배율
timing differences 기간차이
timing option 타이밍옵션
tip 정보누설
title deeds 권원
title insurance 부동산권이서
title insurance company 권원보험; 소유권보증
title of account 소유권보험회사
title paramount 계정과목
tobacco consumption tax 담배소비세
token order 명목발주
tokkin 토킨펀드
tolerance 허용차; 공차
tolerance limit 허용한도
toll 통행료
toll charges 통행세
toll gate 도로요금소
toll traverse 사유지통행료
tomorrow-next 익일차입, 삼일후 반제
tone 시황
tonnage due 톤세
Tontine dividend 톤틴배당
tool 수법

S
T

tool for analysis 분석도구
top 상위
top bidder 최고가입찰자
top management 수뇌부
top straddle 톱스트래들
top vertical combination 톱버티컬컴비네이션
top-down forecasting 톱다운
top-down technique 톱다운기법
top-reversal 톱리버설데이
topless 주가가 천정부지로 치솟음
topography 지형
topology 위상
topping out 토핑아웃
tort 불법행위
total 합계
total amount of insurance in force 보유계약
total asset turnover ratio 총자산회전율
total assets 총자산
total audience 총시청자
total buying contract 총매입계약
total capital 자본금합계
total capital profit ratio 총자본수익률
total capitalization 총장기자금
total correlation 전상관
total cost 전부원가
total cost curve 총비용곡선
total cost of transaction 거래총비용
total costing 전부원가계산
total deposit 총예금
total earnings 총수익
total liabilities and net worth 총자본
total loss 전손
total loss only 전손만의 담보
total market delta 총시장델타치
total market value 총시장가액
total maximum liability 책임한도액
total money supply 총통화공급고
total net income 총소득금액
total net worth 자기자본합계
total payment of installments 할부가격
total rate of return 총수익률

total receipts 총수입
total receivables 미수수취계정합계
total reserve system 전액정화준비제도
total reserves 총준비
total return 종합이율
total sales 총매상고
total selling contract 총매출계약
total stocks issued 총발행제주식수
total sum 총계
total taxable income 과세총소득금액
total turnover 총생산고
touching the bottom 최저시세로 떨어짐
tourist income 관광수입
tourist tax 여행자세
tout 과잉추천
towage 예선료
town 마을
town planning scheme 도시계획
traceability 트레이서빌리티
traceable cost 추적가능원가
traceable theory 귀속이론
tracking 트래킹
tracking error 연동오차
trade 영업
trade acceptance 수출인수어음
trade acceptances payable 인수어음
trade account 영업계정
trade account payable 외상매입금
trade account receivable 외상매출금
trade advertising 유통광고
trade against the trend
　　인기가 높을 때 팔고 낮을 때 삼
trade assets 영업자산
trade associations 증권거래업자협회
trade balance 무역수지
trade by agreement 협정무역
trade channel 거래경로
trade claim 무역클레임
trade contractor 직별업자
trade control 무역통제
trade creation effect 무역창출효과

trade credit 무역금융
trade creditor 구입처
trade date 약정일
trade debtor 외상판매처
trade deficit 무역적자
trade description 상품설명
trade discount 업자할인
trade expansion 통상확대법
trade expenses 영업비
trade figure 무역수지실적
trade friction 무역마찰
trade imbalance 무역불균형
trade liability 영업채무
trade logic 트레이드로직
trade mark 상표
trade matrix analysis 무역연관분석
trade name 상호
Trade Negotiations Committee
  무역교섭위원회
trade on commission 위탁무역
trade on one's own account 스스로 붙임
trade payables 지불채무
trade receivable 매상채권
trade rights 영업권
trade secrets 기업비밀
trade sharing 적취비율
trade show 견본시
trade statistics 무역통계
trade surplus amount 무역수지흑자폭
trade tax 영업세
trade terms 정형무역조건
trade ticket 트레이드티켓
trade union 노동조합
trade-in 신품을 고가로 인수함
trade-in articles 고가로 인수한 신품
trade-mark infringement 상표권침해
trade-mark registration law 상표등록법
trade-off 트레이드오프
trade-related investment measures
  무역관련투자조치
traded securities 유통증권

trader 트레이더
trading 거래
trading account 매매계정
trading area 상세권
trading conditions 거래조건
trading day 거래일
trading down 박리다매
trading firm finance 상사금융
trading floor 거래소
trading halts 거래정지
trading know-how 거래노하우
trading limit 가격폭제한
trading market 유통시장
trading on equity 자기자본대용
trading on the over-the-counter market
  장외거래
trading partner 무역상대국
trading pool 트레이딩풀
trading post 거래포스트
trading profit 증권매매익
trading profit and loss account
  매매손익계정
trading range 거래범위
trading securities 트레이딩목적유가증권
trading stamp 트레이딩스탬프
trading system 거래시스템
trading tax 거래세
trading unit 거래단위
trading volume 생산고
trading-up 고리소회전
traditional channel 전통적인 경로
traditional market 전통시장
traffic personal accident insurance
  교통사고상해보험
trailing PER 실적기준 PER
training expenses 훈련비
training program 훈련계획
training within industry 감독자훈련
traitor 신뢰를 배신한 자
tramper 부정기선
tranche 분할발행

tranche issue 트란시방식
transaction 거래
transaction account 결제계정
transaction approach
　개별거래마다 리스크를 평가함
transaction characteristics 거래특성
transaction cost 거래코스트
transaction fee 거래수수료
transaction in assets 자산거래
transaction motive 거래동기
transaction of near delivery 기근물거래
transaction on a dealer basis 자기매매
transaction on exchange 거래소거래
transaction shift 거래소시프트
transaction tax 거래세
transaction with delayed settlement 착지거래
transactional efficiency 거래효율
transactions tax 거래세
transcript 등본
transfer 양도
transfer account 한계정
transfer agent 명의변경대리인
transfer at low price 저액양도
transfer books closed 주권명의변경정지
transfer books open 주권명의변경정지해제
transfer contract 양도계약
transfer depot 이송데포
transfer effect 이전효과
transfer entry 환기입
transfer expenditure 이전경비
transfer expenses 양도비용
transfer fee 양도수수료
transfer income 이전소득
transfer ledger 환원장
transfer machine 트랜스퍼머신
transfer mechanism 트랜스퍼메카니즘
transfer number 환번호
transfer of a share-certificate 주권명의변경
transfer of assets 자산양도
transfer of business 영업양도
transfer of current account 당좌계정부체

transfer of endorsed note 이서양도
transfer of fixed assets given in pledge
　담보부 고정자산양도
transfer of fund 자금이동
transfer of land tax 지대위양
transfer of name 명의변경
transfer of operations 영업양도
transfer of property 자산양도
transfer of real property 부동산양도
transfer of rights 이권양도
transfer of securities 유가증권양도
transfer of seized goods 차압물인도
transfer of transferable credit 신용장양도
transfer payment 이전지출
transfer price 양도가격
transfer pricing 이전가격조작
transfer pricing taxation 이전가격세제
transfer problem 트랜스퍼문제
transfer profit 환이익
transfer risk 환위험
transfer savings account 환저금계좌
transfer slip 환전표
transfer tax 양도세
transfer transactions 환거래
transferable account 환가능계정
transferable credit 양도가능신용장
transferable loan 양도가능대출
transferable loan facility 양도가능대부
transferable RUF 양도가능러프
transferee 양수인
transferee corporation 합병법인
transferor 양도인
transferor corporation 피합병회사
transferred debt 이관채권
transfers between geographic areas
　지역간 대체
transformation of tax transit 세금소전
transgression 침해
transient rate 단발요금
transit account 미달계정
transit advertising 교통광고

transit clause 운송약관

transit insurance 운송보험

transit trade 통과무역

transition 경과조치

transition matrix 천이확률행렬

transition model 추이모델

transition period 과도기

transition probability 추이확률

transitional benefit 과도적인 급부

transitional measure 경과조치

transitory 일시적인

transitory income 변동소득

translation adjustments 환환산조정

translation method at historical rates
취득시 환산표

translation of foreign currency statements
외화표시부분을 환산함

transmission mechanism 파급경로

transmitting bank 단골은행

transnational corporation 초국적기업

transponder 중계증폭기

transport 수송

transport insurance 운송보험

transportation 운송

transportation business 운송업

transportation charges 운송료

transportation claim 운송클레임

transportation company 운송업자

transportation cost 수송비

transportation equipment 운송설비

transportation in bond 보세운송

transportation insurance 운송보험

transportation model 수송모델

transposition 배치전환

transshipment 짐을 옮겨실음

transvection 트랜스벡션

travel advances 전불여비

travel tax 통행세

traveling audit 순회감사

traveling benefits 여비수당

traveling expenses 여비교통비

traveling expenses for business 출장여비

traveling salesman 순회판매인

traveling tax 통행세

traveller's letter of credit 여행신용장

traverse 부인하다

treason 반역죄

treasurer 재무부장

treasury 출납소

treasury auction 국채입찰

Treasury Bill 재무부증권; 재무부단기증권

Treasury Bill issued
재무부증권발행 재무부발행증권

Treasury Bond 재무부장기증권

Treasury Bonds Investment Series
재무부투자채권

Treasury Certificate of Indebtedness
재무부채무증서

Treasury Euro-dollar spread TED 스프레드

treasury fund remittance 국고금송금

treasury investment and loan 재정투융자

Treasury Note 재무부중기증권

Treasury Savings Notes 재무부중기저축채권

treasury securities market 재무부증권시장

treasury stock 자기주

treasury surplus 국고여유금

treasury tax and loan account 조세공채계정

treasury yield 재무부증권이율

treating 교섭하다

treaty 조약

treaty reinsurance 특약재보험

treaty shopping 트리티쇼핑

treaty wording 재보험특약서

treble indemnity 세배보상

treble tariff 삼중관세율

tree structure 트리구조

trend 추세

trend analysis 추세분석

trend channel 트렌드채널

trend follower 트렌드플라워

trend line 트렌드라인

trend model 경향형 모델

trend of earnings 수익경향
trend pattern 경향선
trend series 경향지수
trend towards luxury spending
　고급품소비지향
trespass 침해소송
trespass for mesne profits
　중간이득반환청구소송
trespasser 침해자
trial 시산
trial at bar 공판
trial balance of balances 잔고시산표
trial balance of totals 합계시산표
trial balance of totals and balances
　합계잔고시산표
trial balance sheet 시산표
trial consignments 위탁품
trial employment period 시용기간
trial manufacture 시작
trial product 시작품
trial running expenses 시운전비
trial running of manufacturing equipment
　생산설비를 시운전함
triangle 트라이앵글
triangle reversal patterns
　트라이앵글리버설패턴
triangular trade 삼각무역
tribunal 심판기관
trickle down 통화침투설의
trigger price 트리거가격
trilemma 삼도논법
trimming 트리밍
tripartite agreement 삼국간 협정
triple bottom 삼중바닥
triple crossover method 트리플크로스오버법
triple merit 삼중익
triple settlement 4일후 인도
triple top 트리플톱
trouble shooter 트러블슈터
trough 경기의 저점
trover 동산침해소송

truck system 현물급여
true and fair 진실하며 공정함
true group insurance 정규단체보험
true installment premium 정규분할불보험료
true panel 순수패널
true reserve 진정준비금
trust 신탁
trust account 신탁계정
trust accounting 신탁업회계
trust accounts of all banks 전국은행시탁계정
trust agreement 신탁계약
trust assets 신탁재산
trust bank 신탁은행
trust by act of law 법정신탁
trust company 신탁회사
trust company administered pension plan
　신탁은행이용형 기업연금
trust contract 신탁약관
trust deed 신탁증서
trust deposit 신탁예금
trust estate 신탁재산
trust fee 신탁보수
trust for value 유상신탁
trust fund 신탁기금
trust fund bureau 자금운용부
trust fund plan 신탁형연금
trust indenture 신탁증서
trust joint 합동
trust money 위탁금
trust property 신탁재산
trust receipt 수입담보화물보관증
trust under agreement 계약신탁
trust-fund plan 신탁식연금제도
trustee 수탁자
trustee company 수탁회사
trustee for bond issuance 사채발행수탁자
trustee group insurance 수탁자단체보험
trustee in bankruptcy 파산관재인
trusteed plan pension 신탁형 연금
trusteed surplus 신탁잉여금
trustor 신탁설정자

truth in lending 진성대부법
tungsten light 텅스텐라이트
turn around 반전
turn to red figures 적자전락
turn-key contract 턴키계약
turndown 갑자기 떨어지다(무역, 소비가)
turning point 전환점
turnover 생산고
turnover increase rate 매상증가율
turnover of capital 자본회전율
turnover of commodity 상품회전수
turnover of funds 자금회전율
turnover of payables 매입채무회전율
turnover of receivables 인수계정회전율
turnover of total capital 총자본회전율
turnover of total operating assets
    경영자본회전율
turnover period 회전기간
turnover rate 회전율
turnover rate of capital 자본회전율
turnover ratio 회전율
turnover ratio of capital 자본회전율
turnover ratio of total liabilities
    타인자본회전율
turnover ratios 회전율

turnover tax 거래고세
turnovers of net worth 자기자본회전율
twig 소규모지점
twin deficits 쌍둥이적자
twin-card 트윈카드
twisting
    (왜곡된 권유로 인한) 부당생명보험계약
two factor contribution plan
    두 가지 요소로 인한 이원별 배당
two tier market 이중구조시장
two way account 상호계정
two way price 쌍방시세
two-item form 이항목방식
two-level inventory control system
    2단계 재고컨트롤시스템
two-tailed test 양측검정
two-tier offer 이단계오퍼
two-way layout 이원배치
two-way market 투웨이마켓
tying arrangement 구속부 협정
type 활자
type face 서체
type of holding 보유형태
typology 유형론

U.S. dollar short-term interest futures
달러단기금리선물
U.S. Japan financial talks 일미금융협의
U.S. Japan framework talks 일미포괄협의
U.S. savings bond 미국저축채
U.S. term 미국방식
ugly foreigner approach
어글리포리너어프로치
ulterior motive 은닉동기
ultimate consumer 최종소비자
ultimate fact 주요사실
ultimate objectives 최종목적
ultimate table 종국사망표
ultra definition television 초고화질텔레비전
ultra high frequency UHF
ultra long-term national bond 초장기국채
ultra vires activities 월권행위
umbrella cover 포괄보험계약
umbrella liability policy
기업포괄배상책임보험; 포괄책임보험
umpire 심판인
una voce 전원일치로
unabsorbed burden 가접비배부부족액
unadmitted asset 비공인자산
unallocated benefit 포괄급부
unallocated claim expense 이차사정비
unallocated funding instrument
비할당적립방식
unamortized 미상각
unamortized bond discount 미상각사채할인
unamortized cost 미상각원가

unamortized debt discount and expenses
사채발행차금
unamortized discount on debenture accounts
채권이연계정
unamortized interest during construction
미상각건설이자
unamortized premium on bonds
사채발행차익
unanimous 전원일치
unappropriated deficit 미처리결손금
unappropriated earned surplus
미처분이익잉여금
unappropriated earned surplus for current
term 당기미처분이익잉여금
unappropriated income 미처분이익
unappropriated retained earnings
미처분잉여금
unappropriated surplus 미처분이익잉여금
unassigned surplus 미분배잉여적립금
unaudited 비감사
unauthorized card 무권카드
unauthorized member 무효회원
unauthorized use 부정사용
unavoidable accident 불가피한 사고
unavoidable circumstances 부득이한 사정
unavoidable cost 회피불가능원가
unavoidable dangers 불가피한 위험
unbalanced 미결산의
unbalanced account 미결산계정
unbalanced book 미결산장부
unbalanced budget 적자예산

unbalanced open 미결산

uncertain
시세가 불투명하여 매매가 활발하지 못한

uncertain factor 불투명요인

uncertainty 불투명

unchange 수준유지

unchanged to slightly higher 강세수준유지

unchanged to slightly lower 약세수준유지

unclaimed 소유자불명의

unclaimed dividends 미청구배당금

unclaimed wages 미불임금

unclassified expenses 잡비

unclear energy insurance 원자력보험

unclear energy liability insurance
원자력손해배상책임보험

uncollected balance 미수금

uncollected commission 미수수수료

uncollected funds 미수자금

uncollected income 미수수익

uncollected interest 미수이자

uncollected premium 미수보험료

uncollected rent 미수지대

uncollected revenue 미수수익

uncollectible accounts 대손계정

uncollectible loan 언콜렉터블론

uncompleted works 미완성공사

unconditional 무조건의

unconditional contract 단순계약

unconditional debt 무조건채무

unconditional drawing right 무조건인출권

unconditional estimate 무조건추정

unconditional liquidity 무조건유동성

unconditional operation 무조건오퍼레이션

unconditional reserve 별도적립금

unconfirmed credit 불확인신용장

unconsolidated subsidiaries 비연결자회사

unconstitutional 위헌의

uncontrollable expenses 관리불능비

uncorrelated return 무상관수익률

uncovenanted benefit 무계약급부

uncovered interest arbitrage
언커버드금리제정

uncovered option 언커버드옵션

uncovered position 언커버드포지션

uncrossed check 보통수표

undated bill 무일부어음

undepreciated balance 미상각잔고

undepreciated wasting property
미상각감모자산

under absorbed 배부부족

under development 개발중

under hedge 과소헤지

under insurance 일부보험

under liquidity 과소유동성

under par 액면할

under protest 지불거절

under repair 수선중

under reserve 유보조건

under separate cover 별봉(別封)으로

underage cost 품절코스트

undercapitalization 과소자본

underdepreciation 과소상각

underemployment 과소고용

underemployment equilibrium 과소고용균형

underemployment multiplier
불완전고용승수

underestimation 과소평가

underground economy 지하경제

underground money 지하자금

underhedging 과소헤지

underinsurance 일부보험

underinvestment 과소투자

underlease 경비차이

underlining security 현물증권

underlying 원자산의

underlying assets 원자산

underlying index 대상지표

underlying premium 기준보험료

underlying retention 보유손해액

underlying securities 원증권; 대상증권

underlying stock 대상주식

underlying swap 대상스와프

underpayment 과소납부
undertaker 사업자
undertaking 약속
undertaking of corporate bonds 사채응모
undertenant 전차인
undertone 전반적인 시황
undervaluation 과소평가
undervalued 값이 쌈
underwrite 인수하다
underwriter 인수업자
underwriting 인수업무
underwriting account balance
　영업계정수지잔고
underwriting agreement 인수계약서
underwriting business 인수업무
underwriting by the Bank of Korea
　한은(韓銀) 인수
underwriting commission 인수수수료
underwriting company 인수회사
underwriting contract 증권인수업자수수료
underwriting firm 인수회사
underwriting group 인수단
underwriting of government securities
　국채인수
underwriting of new issue securities
　신증권인수
underwriting spread 발행비용
undischargeable claim 파면책채권
undisclosed reserve 비밀적립금
undisposed 미처분
undisposed deficit 미처분결손
undistributed profits 유보금액
undivided 미처분
undivided bequest 미분할유산
undivided interest 불가분권
undivided profits 미처분이익
undue influence 부당위압
unduplicated audience
　중복되지 않은 시청자수
unearned 미수
unearned discount 미경과할인료

unearned income 불로소득
unearned interest 미경과이자
unearned premium 미경과보험료
unearned premium reserve
　미경과보험료준비금
unearned revenue 전수익금
unemployment benefit 실업급부
unemployment insurance 실업보험
unemployment rate 실업율
unequal probability 불균등확률
unexpected property loss 임시자산손실
unexpired 미경과
unexpired cost 미소비원가
unexpired expenses 미경과비용
unexpired insurance premium 미경과보험료
unexpired interest 미경과이자
unfair advantage 부정이익
unfair call 부당이행청구
unfair competition 부정경쟁
unfair dismissal 부당해고
unfair labor practice 부당노동행위
unfair trade 부당영업행위
unfavorable balance 지불초과
unfavorable factor 악재료
unfavorable leverage effect
　부정적인 증익효과
unfilled orders 현품주문
unfixed interest bearing 불확정이자부
unforeseen event 예견되지 않은 사고
unfunded debt 단기채무
unified brand 통일상표
uniform 일률적
uniform accounting regulations
　통일경리기준
uniform accounting system 통일회계제도
Uniform Commercial Code 통일상사법전
uniform cost accounting 통일원가계산
uniform cost accounting system
　통일원가계산제도
unilateral 국내법상
unilateral contract 편무계약

unilateral record 일방적인 기록
unilateral transaction 일방적인 거래
unimodal 단봉형의
unincorporated company 법인격이 없는 회사
unincorporated joint venture
　비회사형 합변사업
uninscribed stock 무기명주식
uninsured peril 비담보위험
union 조합
union label 조합증표
union mortgage clause
　표준저당권자 지불약관
union shop 유니온숍
unique chattel 대체할 수 없는 물건
unique factor 고유인자
unissued capital stock 미발행자본
unissued certificate 예비주권
unissued stock 미발행주식
unit 단위
unit banking 단일은행제도
unit banking system 단일은행제도
unit benefit plan 연금액기준방식
unit cost 단위원가
unit depreciation 개별상각
unit investment trust company 투자회사
unit linked life insurance 유닛링크보험
unit load 유닛로드
unit merchandise planning 단품상품계획
unit method 개별감가상각법
unit of account 계산단위
unit of account bond 유닛오프어카운트채
unit of production method 생산고비례법
unit of taxation 과세단위
unit of trading 매매단위
unit price 단가
unit pricing 단가적산법
unit sales 매상수령
unit type investment trust 단위형 투신
unit-price contract 단가계약
unitary taxation 합산과세
United Nations Capital Development Fund

　국제연합자본개발기금
United Nations Conference on Trade and
　Development 국제연합무역개발회의
United Nations Economic Development
　Administration 국제연합경제개발국
United States trustee 연방관재관
unity of seisin 점유통합
unity of title 권원합동
universal agent 총대리인
universal banking 유니버설뱅킹
universal legacy 포괄유증
universal life policy 유니버설생명보험
universal notation 국제공통기호
unjust disbursement 부당지출
unjust enrichment 부당이득
unjustified 부당한
unknown clause 부지약관
unlawful 불법인
unlawful act 불법행위
unlawful assembly 불법집회
unlawful detainer 불법유치
unlawful entry 불법점유
unlawfulness 불법
unless otherwise specified 다른 결정이 없는 한
unlimited legal tender 무제한법화
unlimited liability 무한책임
unlimited liability company 무한책임회사
unlimited partnership 합명회사
unliquidated claim 불확정채권
unliquidated damages 불확정손해배상액
unlisted assets 부외자산
unlisted company 비상장회사
unlisted liability 부외채무
unlisted loan 부외차금
unlisted securities 장외증권
unlisted stock 비상장주
unloading 물건이나 주식을 팔아서 큰 이득을
　보고 물러남
unmatched book 언매치드북
unofficial capita night 비공식자본이 유출됨
unpaid 미불

U
V

unpaid capital 미불입자본
unpaid claims 미불보험금
unpaid dividend 미불배당금
unpaid donation 미불기부금
unpaid draft 부도어음
unpaid returns 미불반려금
unpaid tax 미불세금
unproductive capital 미가동자본
unprofitable company 실적이 좋지 않은 회사
unqualified financial statements
　미감사재무제표
unqualified opinion 무한정의견
unrealizable assets 환가불능자산
unrealized gross profit on installment sales
　할부매상미실현익
unrealized income 미실현이익
unrealized revenue 미실현수익
unreasonable taxation 부당과세
unreasonably 현저하게
unrecovered cost 미회수원가
unregistered 미등기
unregistered stock 무등록주
unrelated business income 비관련사업이익
unsalable stock 매잔재고
unsealed deposit 개봉예금
unseasoned security 발행직후의 증권
unseaworthy 내항력이 없는
unsecured 무담보의
unsecured account 무담보계정
unsecured bond 무담보사채
unsecured credit 무담보신용
unsecured creditor 일반채권자
unsecured liability 무담보부채
unsecured loan 무담보융자
unsecured trading 무담보거래
unsettled 미결제의
unsettled account 미결제계정
unsold 팔다남은
unsual casualty reserve 이상위험준비금
unsubordinated 비열후
unsystematic risk 비(非)시스티매틱리스크

untied loan 언타이드론
untrue 사실에 반한
unused buildings 유휴건물
unused land 유휴토지
unused land tax 미이용지세
unusual gains or losses 임시손익
unusual item 이상항목
unusual loss 이상손실
unusual profit or loss item 이상손익항목
unusual risks reserve 이상위험준비금
unvalued policy 미평가보험
unwind a trade 거래관계를 청산하다
unwritten law 비제정법
up and put option 업앤드풋옵션
up front 일괄전불
up gap 업갭
up load 업로드
up-down ratio 등락레이쇼
up-front payment 계약일시금
up-front premium 선불프리미엄
up-pressure 상승력
up-tick 상향
update 갱신하다
upkeep 유지비
ups and downs 성쇠
upset price 최저경매가격
upstairs market 계상시장
upswing 상승
upswing on business results 실적상승
uptrend 업트렌드
upturn 호전
upward pressure 상승압력
upward revision 상향수정
upwards 기조를 올림
urban fringe 도시주변지대
urban remodeling enterprise 도시개량사업
urbanization 도시화
Uruguay Round 우루과이라운드
usable years 사용기간
usage 관습
usage rate 사용요금

usance 유전스
usance bill 기한부 환어음
usance bill rate 기한부 어음상장
usance buying rate 기한부 어음매상장
usance granted by foreign banks
　외국은행유전스
usance letter of credit 기한부 신용장
usance rate 유전스레이트
use and file 사용후 계출제
use and occupancy insurance 사업중단보험
use of funds 자금사용
use value 사용가치
used hours 사용시간
used property 중고자산
useful life 내용연수
useful life table 내용연수표
user 소비자
user cost 사용자원가
user instruction 취급설명서
user-active 유저액티브
usual covenants 통상약관

usufruct 사용수익권
usurer 고리채
usury 법정이율초과이자
usury law 이자제한법
utilities bond 전력채
utilities stock 전력가스주
utility 공익기업; 유용성
utility consumption 유틸리티소비
utility curve 효용곡선
utility function 효용함수
utility maximization 효용최대화
utility model 실용신안
utility model patent 실용신안권
utility service 용역제공
utility theory 효용이론
utility value 사용가치
utilization variance 조업도차이
utilized cost 이용원가
utmost good faith 최대선의
utter 행사하다; 발행하다

vacant land tax 공간지세
vacant lot 공지
vacation 비워 줌, 내줌
vacation pay 휴가수당
vacation with pay 유급휴가
vacuum packing 진공포장
valid 유효한
validate 정당하다고 인정하다
validation 타당성확인
validation test 타당성시험
validity 정당성
valuable consideration 유가약인(有價約因)
valuation 평가액
valuation account 평가계정
valuation actuary 보험계리인
valuation at cost 원가법
valuation at selling price 시가법
valuation basis 평가기준
valuation by multiplier 배율평가
valuation by road rating
　　노선가방식에 따른 평가
valuation characteristics 평가특성
valuation clause 보험평가액조항
valuation form 적하가격신고서
valuation item 평가과목
valuation loss 평가손
valuation modeling 평가모델
valuation of assets 자산평가
valuation of bond 공사채평가
valuation of call option 콜옵션평가
valuation principle 평가원칙

valuation profit 평가익
valuation reserve 평가성준비금
valuation standards 평가기준
value 가액
value added 부가가치
value added advantage 부가가치우위
value added chain 부가가치연쇄
value added network 부가가치통신망
value added tax 부가가치세
value analysis 가치분석
value approach 밸류어프로치
value 평가하다
value chain 가치연쇄
value date 기산일(起算日)
value declared 신고가격
value diagram 밸류다이어그램
value engineering 가치공학
value exchange system 가치교환시스템
value in use 사용가치
value investor 가치 목적의 투자가
value judgment 가치판단
value line average 밸류라인평균
value line composite index 밸류라인 종합지수
value line index 밸류라인인덱스
value line option 밸류라인옵션
value line ranking 밸류라인랭킹
value next month 익월인도
value of assessment 과세가격
value received 대가수령
value today 당일인도
value tomorrow 익일인도

value variance 가액차이

vampire video 뱀파이어비디오

variability 불안정성

variable 변수

variable annuity 변액연금

variable budget 변동예산

variable capital 가변자본

variable cash reserve requirements
　가변적인 현금준비제도

variable charge 변동비

variable constant 가변상수

variable cost and expenses 변동비

variable cost ratio 변동원가율

variable costing 변동소득계산

variable expenses 변동비

variable insurance 변액보험

variable interest rate 변동이율

variable investment tax 가변투자세

variable life insurance 변액생명보험

variable overhead 변동관리비

variable premium 변동보험료

variable profit 변동이익

variable rate mortgage loan
　변동금리형 부동산론

variable universal life insurance
　변액유니버설보험

variable zone 변동가격권

variance 차이

variance account 원가차액계정

variance analysis 분산분석

variance of cost 원가차액

variance of the estimate 평가차액

variation from budget 예산차이

variation margin 변동증거금

various kinds of income 각종소득

various kinds of tax benefits 세법상의 특전

varying annuity 예정변액연금

vector 벡터

vehicle selection 매체선택

velocity 속도

velocity of circulation 유통속도

vendee 구입자

vendor 판매자

vendor analysis 구입처분석

venture 사업

venture business 벤처비즈니스

venture capital 벤처캐피탈

venue 행위지

verbal 구두의

verdict 평결

verification 검증

verification by telephone 전화확인

verification of a seal impression 인감조회

versus ～와 대비하여

vertical analysis 수직분석

vertical angle of view 수직화각(垂直畵角)

vertical blank interval 수직귀선 소거기간

vertical channel system 수직경로시스템

vertical integration 수직형 통합

vertical marketing system
　수직인인 마케팅시스템

vertical merger 수직합병

vertical publication 전문업계지

vertical specialization 수직적인 국제분업

vertical spread 버티컬스프레드

vertical spread transaction
　버티컬스프레드거래

vertical territorial customer restrictions
　수직적인 고객제한

vertical trade horizontal trade
　수직무역, 수평무역

very high frequency VHF

vessel 선박

vessel unknown
　적재한 선박의 이름을 알지 못함

vest 권리를 주다

vested benefit 기득이익

vested benefit obligation 확정급부채무

vested in interest 발생확정시키다

vested in possession 현재 소유한

vested interest 확정권리

vested interests 기득권

vested remainder 확정잔여권
vesting 수급권부여
vesting deed 계승재산부여증서
vesture 토지점유
veto 거부
viable 성장할 수 있는
vicarious liability 사용자책임
vice chairman 부의장
vice president 부총재
vice-consul 부영사
vicinity of the upper limit 천정권
vicious member merchant 악질가맹점
video dial tone service 비디오다이얼서비스
video display terminal 비디오단말
video editing 비디오편집
video on demand 비디오온디맨드
video random access memory V-RAM
video system control architecture
　비디오컨트롤아키텍처
video tape recorder VTR
video tex 비디오텍스
video transmission service 영상전송서비스
view 검증
view of lowering interest rate
　금리가 낮으리라 예상함
viewfinder adopter 시야조절
viewing distance 시거리
viewing model 시야모델
viewing transformation 시야변환
vintage 평균자본연령
violation 권리침해
violation of a contract 계약위반
violence 불법행위
violent fluctuation (시세의) 난조
virtual interface environment workstation
　가상환경 워크스테이션
virtual private network 가상전용선
virtual reality 가상현실
virtually unchanged 큰 변화가 없는
virus 바이러스
vis major 불가항력

visible supply 유형공급
visual curve-fitting method 작도법
vital statistics 인구동태통계
voice 발언
voice mail 보이스메일
voice over 보이스오버
voice recognition 음성인식
voice recognition & response system
　음성응답시스템
void 무효의
void agreement 무효합의
void contract 무효계약
void transaction 효력이 없는 법률행위
voidable 무효로 하다
void dire 예비심분
volatile market 변동시장
volatility 변동율
volatility value 볼라틸리티
volume 조업도; 생산고
volume accumulation 누적생산고
volume accumulator
　볼륨어큐뮬레이터 (누적지표의 한 종류)
volume cost 양산원가
volume discount 수량할인
volume efficiency 양산효과
volume indicator 조업도지수
volume of business 거래고
volume of inventories 재고량
volume of issuance 발행규모
volume of over-the-counter transaction
　장외매매고
volume of sales 매상고
volume of trading 매매고
volume ratio 볼륨레이쇼
volume variance 조업도차이
voluntary 임의의; 약인없이
voluntary accumulation plan
　임의형 계속투자플랜
voluntary additions 임의편입액
voluntary adjustment 자기부인
voluntary association 자발적인 조직

U
V

voluntary audit 임의감사
voluntary bankruptcy 자기파산
voluntary chain 볼런터리체인; 임의연쇄점
voluntary conveyance 무상양도
voluntary depreciation 임의상각
voluntary depreciation method 임의상각법
voluntary dissolution 임의해산
voluntary export restraint 수출자주규제
voluntary insurance 임의보험
voluntary liquidation 임의정리
voluntary partnership 임의조합
voluntary place of tax payment 임의납세지
voluntary reserve 임의준비금
voluntary restraint program 자주규제계획
voluntary restriction of export 수출자주규제
voluntary saving 자발적인 저축
voluntary settlement 무상승계적인 부동산처분
voluntary tax payment 자주납부

voluntary unemployment 자발적인 실업
voluntary waste 적극적 훼손
voluntary winding 임의해산
volunteer 무상취득자
Vostro account 상대편계정
voting 투표
voting company 결의권회사
voting right 의결권
voting stock 의결권주식
voting trust 의결권신탁
voting trust certificate 의결권신탁증서
vouch 증명하다
voucher 전표
voucher for disbursement 불출증표
voucher payable register 지불전표기입장
voucher system 지출전표제도
vouching 전표대조
voyage policy 항해보험

wage according to job evaluation 직능급
wage assignment 급료공제
wage ceiling 상한임금설정
wage contract 임금협정
wage cut 임금컷
wage disparity 임금격차
wage earner 임금생활자
wage freeze 임금동결
wage in kind 현물급여
wage income 임금소득
wage increase 임금인상
wage level 임금수준
wage negotiation 노사교섭
wage rate 임율
wage stabilization system 안정임금제
wage structure 임금체계
wage unit 임금단위
wage variance 임금차이
wage-bracket table 간이세류표
wage-hike drive 임금투쟁
wage-price control 임금물가통제
wage-price guideline 임금물가 가이드라인
wage-push inflation 임금인플레이션
wages attached to a post 직무급
wages ledger 임금원장
wages on job evaluation 직능급
wages payable 미불임금
wait and see 시황관망
wait for reaction 반응을 기다림
waiting for further development
　　전개를 기다림
waiting period 대기기간
waiver 권리방기
waiver clause 권리방기조항
waiver of obligation 채무면제
waiver of premium 보험료불입면제
walk-out
　　물건을 사지 않고 값만 묻고 다니는 고객
wall flower 인기가 떨어진 물건
Wall Street 월가
Walrasian auctioneer 왈라스경매인
want of procesution 소송을 추행하지 않음
wanton negligence 무관심과실
wantonness 무시
war clause 전쟁약관
war perils 전쟁위험
warehouse charges 차고료
warehouse expenses 보관료
warehouse fee 창고료
warehouse financing 창고금융
warehouse receipt 예금증권
warehouse rent 보관료
warehousing 입고
warrant 위임장; 워런트
warrant agent 워런트대리인
warrant agreement 워런트계약서
warrant bond 워런트채
warrant in bankruptcy 파산자 재산차압명령
warrant of attachment 차압명장
warrant of attorney 위임장

warrant parity 워런트패러티
warranted rate of growth 적정성장률
warranty 보증
warranty of legality 적법성담보
wash order 와시오더
wash sale 가장매매
waste 폐기물
waste circulation 웨이스트서큐레이션
wasting assets 감모자산
watch list 요주의명부
water concession 수리권
water expense 수도료
water right 수리권
water-bailiff 수로주변감시관
water-utilization tax 수리지익세
watered assets 수증자산
watered capital 의제자본; 수할자본
watered stock 수증주식
wave editing soft 음원편집소프트
wave function 파동함수
wave posting 웨이브포스팅
Wave Theory 웨이브이론
waveform 파형
way 통행권
ways and means 재원
weak form 위크폼
weak stockholders 부동주주
weak tone 약한 시세
weaken 약해지다
weaker economy 경기후퇴기
weaker U.S. dollar 달러약세
weakness 연조(軟調)
wealth tax 부유세
wear and tear 손모
weather insurance 날씨보험
wedge 웨지
wedge formation 웨지포메이션
Wednesday-factor 수요일요인
week order 위크오더
weekend effect 주말효과
weekly accounting 주차결산

weekly chart 매주의 차트
weekly payment 일주간지불
weekly reversal 위클리리저벌
weight of evidence 증거의 무게
weighted 가중
weighted arithmetic average 가중산술평균
weighted average 가중평균
weighted average cost method
    가중평균원가법
weighted average method 가중평균법
weighted average number of common share
    outstanding 가중평균보통주수
weighted average of market capitalization
    시가총액가중평균치
weighted basis trade 가중평균베이스무역
weighted index 가중지수
weighted mean 가중평균
weighted mean method 가중평균법
weighted stock price average 가중평균주가
weighting 편입률
welfare economics 후생경제학
welfare expense 복리후생비
welfare facilities 복리후생시설
welfare pension 후생연금
welfare pension insurance 후생연금보험
welfare program 복리후생
Western European Union 서유럽연합
Western Hemisphere Free Trade Area
    미주자유무역권
wharfage 부두세
wheel of retailing 소매회전
when-issued basis 발행일기준
when-issued transaction 발행일거래
while clause 위험부담정지약관
whisky tax 위스키세
white knight 백마 탄 왕자; 매수위기의 기업을
    구하기 위해 개입하는 제3의 기업
white list 우량자 리스트
white paper on economic cooperation
    경제협력백서
white return 백색신고

W
X

whole issued stock 총발행필주식수
whole life annuity 종신연금보험
whole life insurance 종신보험
wholesale 도매량
wholesale accounting 도매회계
wholesale bank 홀세일뱅크
wholesale business 도매업
wholesale dealer 도매상
wholesale establishment 도매사업
wholesale group insurance 단체급계약
wholesale price 도매가격
wholesale price index 도매물가지수
wholesale trade 도매업
wholesaler 도매업자
wholly owned subsidiary 완전소유자회사
wide area distribution center 광역물류센터
wide fluctuation of market 난조시장
widening gap 확대되는 격차
wider band 변동폭이 있는 고정제
wider margin 확대상장변동
widow 미망인
widow deduction 미망인공제
widow-and-orphan stock 안정배당주
width of assortment 상품구비폭
width of currency movements 환변동폭
wild card option 와일드카드옵션
willful 고의의
willful false 고의적인 허위
willful misconduct 고의적인 불법행위
willful negligence 고의적인 과실
willingness to pay 반제의지
wind storm and flood insurance 풍수해보험
windfall loss 예상 밖의 손출
windfall loss or gain 우발적인 손익
windfall profit 뜻밖의, 행운의
winding up 해산
winding-up by the court 강제청산
winding-up of pending affairs 잔무정리
winding-up order 청산명령
window 창구
window dressing 분식(粉飾)

window dressing deposit 분식예금
window dressing financial statement
　분식재무제표
window dressing settlement 분식결산
window guidance 창구지도
wire houses 개인고객을 상대하는 증권회사
wire transfer 전신송금
with a proviso 조건부
with average 분손담보
with discount 액면이하
with holding tax 원천소득세
with premium 액면이상
with recourse credit
　상환의무를 면제하지 않는 신용장
with warrants 권리부
withdrawal of portfolio
　포트폴리오의 미경과부분을 일괄인양함
withdrawal plan 인출플랜
withdrawals 철수
withholding 공제
withholding agent 원천징수의무자
withholding and payment 원천징수와 납부
withholding at source 원천징수
withholding exemption certificate
　원천징수표
withholding income tax 원천징수소득세
withholding of customs appraisement
　관세평가금지
withholding system 원천징수제도
withholding tax on income 원천소득세
withholding tax option 원천선택
withholding tax system 원천징수제도
within-group stratification 집단내 계층분화
without compensation 무보수
without credit at sight buying rate
　신용장 없는 일람불어음매입상장
without prejudice 권리를 손상치 않고
without prejudice to preliminary
　기득권을 범하지 않고
without recourse 상환의무를 지지 않는
without recourse credit 상환의무면제신용장

without reserve 가격무제한

witness 증거

witnessing part 증서본문

word of mouth 입으로 전해지는 소문

words of limitation 내용표시문언

work 작업

work in process ledger 제작 중인 물건의 원장

work instruction 작업지시서

work order 제조지도서

work rules 취업규제

work sheet 정산표

work study 작업연구

workable competition 유효경쟁

workaholism 일중독

worker's property accumulation savings
재형저축

workers' accident comprehensive insurance
노동재해종합보험

workers union 종업원조합

working account 활계정

working assets 운용자산

working balance 운용잔고

working budget 실행예산

working capital 운전자금

working capital analysis 운전자본분석

working capital control 운전자금관리

working capital position 운전자본상태

working capital ratio 유동비율

working condition 작업조건

working cost 영업비

working days 작업일수

working document 작업문서

working fund 운전자금

working hour curtailment 작업시간단축

working hours 작업시간

working hypothesis 작업가설

working interest 임차권이권

working inventory 운전재고자산

working place 사업장

**working rules of audit procedures in
reporting** 감사보고준칙

working student 근로학생

working student allowance 근로학생공제

working trial balance sheet 시산표

working year 영업연도

working-capital ratio 운전자본비율

working-hours method 운전시간법

workmanship 만들어낸 솜씨

workmen's compensation acts
노동자재해보상법

workmen's compensation insurance
노동자재해보상보험

workmen's compensation law 노동자배상법

worksheet method 정산표방식

workshop 작업장

World Bank 세계은행

world company 세계기업

world crisis 세계공황

world enterprise 세계기업

world index 월드인덱스

World Intellectual Property Organization
세계지적소유권기관

world market portfolio 포트폴리오

world market price 국제시장가격

world marketing 세계마케팅

World Trade Organization 세계무역기구

World Wide Fund for Nature
세계자연보호기금

worth and fixed assets ratio
자본고정자산비율

worth debts ratio 자본부채비율

wreck 난파

writ of entry 부동산점유회복소송

write-down 잘라버림

write-off 상각

write-up 평가증가

writer 매출자

writing 주식신용거래나 상품선물거래에서 성
립된 판매주문

written agreement 서면계약

written application 서면신청

written assignment 양도증서**

W
X

written contract 서면계약
written decision 재결서
written examination 필기시험
written inquiry 서면문의
written premium 계상보험료

written-down value 평가감후 가격
wrong 위법행위
wrong doing 부정행위
wrongful dismissal 부당해고

Yankee bond 양키본드
Yankee bond market 미국달러채시장
yard transportation 공장내 운송비
year 연도
year end stock 기말재고
year in brief 당년도의 개황
year's opening session 대발회
year-end 년말
year-end dividend 기말배당
year-end market 연말상장
year-end settlement 연말조정
year-to-year changes 경년변동율
year-to-year percentage change
    전년대비변화율
yearly earnings 연간총익
yearly installment 연부(年賦)
yearly taxation 연세주의(年稅主義)
yeas and nays 찬반투표
yield 생산고; 이율
yield auction 이율입찰
yield based on weighted average
    가중평균이익
yield book 이익표
yield by simple interest 단리이익
yield curve 일드커브

yield curve risk 이율곡선리스크
yield curve swap 일드커브스와프
yield differential 이익격차
yield factor 이익요인
yield for average life 평균잔존연한이익
yield for holding period 소유기간이익
yield improvement switch 이익개선스위치
yield on already issued bond 기발채이익
yield on bond 채권이익
yield on investment 운용이익
yield on public and corporate bond
    공사채응모자이익
yield rate 이율비
yield spread 이익격차
yield standard 이익수준
yield structure 이익구조
yield to call 임의상환이익
yield to maturity 만기이익
yield to subscriber 응모자이익
yield-to-call 조상상환이익
yield-to-put 매입청구이익
yo-yo stock 요요주식
yours 유어즈(팔았을 때)
youth orientation 젊은 층 지향

zapping 급속채널이동
zero cost option 제로코스트옵션
zero defects 무결함운동
zero-beta portfolio 제로베타포트폴리오
zero-cost collar 제로코스트칼라
zero-cost option trading 제로코스트옵션거래

zero-coupon bond 제로쿠폰채
zero-coupon curve 제로쿠폰커브
zero-order model 제로발주모델
zero-plus tick 제로펄스틱
zero-sum game 제로섬게임
Zillmerized reserve 질멜식 책임준비금

ㄱ

가가칩 giga chip
가감법 add-back method
가격개정 price revision; price determination; price fixing; pricing decision
가격결정모델 pricing model
가격결정전략 pricing strategy
가격결정툴 pricing tool
가격경쟁 price competition
가격경직성 rigidity of price
가격계산 pricing calculation
가격계수 price factor
가격계약 price contract
가격교섭 price bargaining
가격구조 price structure; structure of price
가격균등화 price equalization
가격대비성능비 cost performance
가격동결 price freeze
가격리스크 price risk
가격리스크; 시장리스크 market risk
가격메카니즘 price mechanism
가격무제한 without reserve
가격믹스 price mix
가격반응모델 model of response to price
가격변동 movement of price; price fluctuation
가격변동과 연동된 생명보험 linked long term
가격변동률 price volatility
가격변동수정 adjustment for price fluctuations
가격변동준비금 price fluctuation reserve; reserve against decline in price; reserve for inventory fluctuation; reserve for price fluctuation
가격변동폭제한 maximum price change limit
가격보증 price guaranty
가격보호 price protection
가격분석 price analysis
가격상승 price boost; rise in price
가격수준변동회계 accounting for price-level change
가격신축성 price flexibility
가격안정 price stabilization
가격안정조작 price supporting
가격안정화 pegging
가격양보 price concession
가격역전인지현상 reverse-order perception
가격우선 price priority
가격이론 price theory
가격이론의 한계 limitations of price theory
가격이미지 price image
가격-이율곡선 price-yield curve
가격인상 price hike
가격인하 mark down; price cutting; reduction in price
가격인하거래 pass-along deal
가격인하계획 markup reduction planning
가격인하불안 downsizing
가격인하여지 downside risk
가격입찰 price auction
가격전략 price strategy

가격전쟁 price war
가격정보 price information
가격조사 research on prices
가격조작 manipulation of the market; painting the tape
가격조정 price adjustment
가격지정산정법 limit calculation
가격차 spread
가격차별 price discrimination
가격차액으로 이익을 얻음 speculation for difference
가격차이 price divergence; price spread
가격차이로 이익얻기 profit taking
가격차이보조금 price-support subsidy
가격차익 price margin
가격차익금 profit from the difference between new and old official prices
가격체계 price system
가격카르텔 price cartel
가격탄력성 elasticity of price; price elasticity
가격통제 price control
가격패턴 price pattern
가격폭 price range
가격폭제한 price limit; price line; price movement limit; trading limit
가격표생략 nonmarking
가격표시방법 price indication method
가격피라미드 price pyramid
가격하락 falling in price
가격하향경직성 downward rigidity of price
가격행동 price action
가격협정 price agreement
가격효과 price effect
가결산 provisional settlement of account
가결산일 assumed settling day
가계 household
가계(家系) pedigree
가계보험통계플랜 personal lines statistical plan
가계부 family bookkeeping; household sector
가계비 household expenses; housekeeping expenses
가계소비지출 household consumption expenditure
가계조사(家計調査) family income and expenditure survey
가공 fictitious; processing
가공매상전표 fictitious sales slip
가공명의예금 fictitious name deposit
가공무역 processing deal trade
가공비 conversion cost; cost of processing; processing cost; processing expenses
가공세 processing tax
가공이익 fictitious profit; paper profit
가구집기 furniture and fixture
가능성 조항 availability clause
가대차대조표 tentative balance sheet
가독(家督) legal heir
가동률 operating ratio; rate of operating; percent of capacity use
가동시간 hours worked
가동이익 income earned
가득 채워넣다 load up
가득(稼得)기준 earned income
가등기 provisional registration
가령 ~라 해도 arguendo
가망이 없는 상실 irretrievable deprivation
가맹권 membership
가맹은행 member bank
가맹점 affiliated store; member's store
가맹점수수료 merchant fee
가맹중간업자 affiliated middleman
가명령 order nisi; provisional order; rule
가법감산 additive substruction
가벼운 긴장 slight tightening
가변금리 floating rate of interest
가변보험 convertible
가변상수 variable constant
가변자본 variable capital
가변적인 현금준비제도 variable cash reserve requirements
가변정기보험 convertible term insurance

가변투자세 variable investment tax
가봉 temporary seal
가분계약 divisible contract
가분으로; 단독으로 severally
가분조항 several covenant
가분채권 divisible claim
가분채무 divisible obligation
가불 borrowing in advance
가불금 suspense payments; temporary payment
가불금계정 suspense payment account
가사관련비 expenses incurred for maintaining household
가산세 additional tax; penalty tax; tax for default
가산이익에 따른 가격결정 markup pricing
가산이익정정 markup cancellation
가상매물객 phantom shopper
가상전용선 virtual private network
가상현실 virtual reality
가상환경 워크스테이션 virtual interface environment workstation
가석방허가증 ticket of leave
가설검정 test of hypothesis
가속도계수 acceleration coefficient
가속도원리 acceleration principle
가속법 accelerated method
가수금 suspense receipts; temporary receipts
가수금계정 suspense receipts account; temporary receipts account
가수선 temporary repairs
가수선비 cost of temporary repair
가수요 anticipatory demand; fictitious demand; imaginary demand; speculative demand
가수입 speculative import
가스세 gas tax
가스수도세 gas and water expenses
가액 value
가액차이 value variance
가열하는; 가열 heating

가영수서 interim receipt
가위형태의 가격차이 scissors-form difference in price
가이드라인 guideline
가임(家賃)보험 rental income insurance
가임(家賃)상장 rental market value
가임(家賃)소득 rental income
가임수당 rental allowance
가입연령 age at entry
가입연령방식 entry age cost method
가입연령범위 limit of age
가입연령식 평준표준보험료 level premium normal cost on entry age
가장 가까운 달 nearest month
가장 유망한 상품 creaming merchandise
가장매매 chumming; wash sale
가장행위 disguised act
가재도구 furniture and household goods; household goods
가재포괄보험 personal property floater
가전(家電) consumer electronics
가접비배부부족액 unabsorbed burden
가정 assumptions; legal fiction
가정의료비보험 family medical expense policy
가정이익 but-for income
가족고용공제 deduction for family employees
가족보험 family insurance
가족상해보험 family persona accident policy
가족수당 dependent allowance; family allowance
가족특성 family characteristics
가주권 scrip certificate
가주소 commorancy; provisional residence
가중 weighted
가중사유 aggravation
가중산술평균 weighted arithmetic average
가중세; 과징금 surcharge
가중지수 weighted index
가중평균 weighted average; weighted mean
가중평균법 weighted average method;

weighted mean method
가중평균베이스무역 weighted basis trade
가중평균보통주수 weighted average number of common share outstanding
가중평균원가법 weighted average cost method
가중평균이익 yield based on weighted average
가중평균주가 weighted stock price average
가증서, 보험인수증 cover note
가집행 provisional execution
가차압 ancillary attachment; provisional attachment; provisional seizure
가처분 provisional disposition
가처분소득 disposable income
가처분이익 available profit; disposable profit
가치 목적의 투자가 value investor
가치공학 value engineering
가치교환시스템 value exchange system
가치를 높이다 enhance
가치분석 value analysis
가치연쇄 value chain
가치재(價値財) merit goods
가치판단 value judgment
가트; 관세와 무역에 관한 일반협정 General Agreement on Tariffs and Trade
가판결 judgment nisi
가평균 guessed mean
각국통화단위 denominated in each currency
각서 binder; letter of undertaking
각종동산포괄보험 miscellaneous movable articles floater
각종명세 schedule
각종소득 classified income; various kinds of income
각주 foot note
각하(却下) overrule; dismissal; dismissal without prejudice
각하하다 ignore; quash
각하항변 plea in abatement
간단한 거래 lay-up

간사 manager
간사단 managers
간사수수료 management fee
간사은행 managing bank
간사증권 managing underwriter
간이과세제도 simplified tax system
간이보험 industrial insurance
간이부기 simplified bookkeeping system
간이생명보험 home service life insurance; industrial life insurance; post office life insurance
간이생명표 abridged life table
간이세류표 wage-bracket table
간이수속 informal proceeding
간이종업원퇴직연금 simplified employee pension
간이형 short form
간이형사재판소 police court
간이휴대전화 personal handyphone system
간접금융 indirect financing
간접노무비 indirect labor cost
간접매매 indirect sales
간접무역 indirect trade
간접발행 indirect issue
간접배당 payment regarded as dividends
간접법 indirect method
간접보증 indirect guarantee
간접부문합리화 management of indirect cost
간접부수비용 indirect incidental expenses
간접부채 indirect liability
간접비 business commencement expenses; indirect expenses; overhead cost
간접비(원재료와 노무비 이외) burden on cost
간접비배부 overhead cost distribution
간접비배부기준 overhead distribution basis
간접비배부율 distribution rate of overhead cost; overhead rate
간접비배부초과액 overabsorbed burden
간접비분배 distribution of overhead cost
간접비준비금 reserve for overhead

간접비차이 overhead variance
간접비할부율 application rate of overhead cost
간접상각 indirect method of depreciation
간접상속 mediate descent
간접생산 indirect production
간접세 indirect tax; outlay tax
간접세협력단체 cooperative association on indirect taxes
간접손해 consequential damage
간접송달 constructive service
간접수요; 파생수요 derived demand
간접예금 indirect deposit
간접외국세액공제 indirect foreign tax credit
간접원가; 보충비용 supplementary cost
간접원인 causa remota
간접이익 indirect yield
간접임금 indirect wage
간접재료비 indirect material cost
간접재정 indirect exchange arbitrage
간접증거 indirect evidence
간접증권 indirect securities
간접투자 indirect investment
간접표시 indirect presentation
간주교부금 deemed bounty
간주기부금 deemed donations
간주배당 consent dividend; constructive dividends; deemed dividend
간주사업연도 deemed accounting period
간주상속재산 deemed inherited property
간주심사청구 deemed request for reconsideration
간주양도 deemed transfer
간주외국세액공제 tax sparing credit
간주인가규정 deemer clause
간판만 걸어둔 가게 brass-plate office
간편상각 simplified method of depreciation
간행허가 imprimatur
갈고리모양의 hooked
갈고리손 hook damage
감가상각 depreciation

감가상각가능한 depreciable
감가상각기금 depreciation fund
감가상각기초액 depreciation base
감가상각누계액 cumulative amount of depreciation
감가상각누적액 accumulated depreciation
감가상각단위 depreciation unit
감가상각발생액 accrued depreciation
감가상각법 depreciation method
감가상각부담 depreciation burden
감가상각비 depreciation expense
감가상각비누계 aggregate of depreciation deduction
감가상각비명세표 schedule of depreciation
감가상각수당금 depreciation allowance
감가상각연수 depreciation period
감가상각예비금 allowance for depreciation
감가상각율 depreciation rate
감가상각의 월할계산 monthly allotment of depreciable period
감가상각자산 depreciable assets
감가상각자산취득가액 acquisition cost of depreciable assets
감가상각준비금 depreciation reserve; reserve for depreciation
감가상각준비금비율 depreciation reserve ratio
감가상각타당성 depreciation adequacy
감가상각특례 exception to depreciation deduction
감가상각필 fully depreciated
감가상각회계 depreciation accounting
감가상각후 가액 depreciated value
감가상각후 원가 depreciated cost
감가상각후 원시원가 depreciated original cost
감가수당금 depletion allowance
감가율에 따른 상각 depreciation by depreciation rate
감가정율법 fixed percentage method
감당할 수가 없는 spike
감독관 intendant; management supervisor

감독기관 regulatory agencies
감독자 foreman
감독자훈련 training within industry
감독절차 summary procedure
감리위원회 board of supervisors
감마보정 gamma correction
감마익스포저 gamma exposure
감면 reduction and exemption of taxes
감면세액공제 deduction for tax reduction
감모가능한 depletable
감모상각 depletion
감모상각비 cost depletion
감모상각원가법 cost method of depletion
감모자산 depletion assets; wasting assets
감배 dividend cut; dividend decrease age
감사 audit
감사결정 audit adjustment
감사결정에 따른 보험계약 audit policy
감사결제보험료차액 audit premium
감사계획 audit program
감사권 right of auditing
감사기관 auditing organization
감사기준 auditing standards; general audit standards
감사목적 audit objective
감사범위 extent of audit; scope; scope of audit
감사법인 audit corporation
감사보고기준 reporting audit standards; reporting standards
감사보고서 accountant report; audit report; opinion of independent certified public accountant; report of independent auditors
감사보고준칙 working rules of audit procedures in reporting
감사보수 audit fee
감사빈도 audit frequency
감사상각원가 depreciable cost
감사수속서 statement on auditing procedures
감사실시기준 field-work audit standards
감사역 auditor; comptroller

감사연도 audit year
감사원의 독립성 independence of auditor
감사원의 일관성 consistency of auditor
감사의견 audit opinion
감사의견서 opinion of auditors
감사의견서; 각서(비공식)감사의견서; 각서 comfort letter
감사인의 의견 auditor's opinion
감사절차 audit procedure
감사절차위원회 committee on auditing procedure
감사증명 audit certificate; certification of audit
감사필 연차재무보고서 annual audited financial statement
감사필 재무제표 certificated financial statement
감성 affectivity
감세 legal tax cut; reduction of taxes; tax cut by law; tax reduction
감세국채 government bond for tax
감세채권 tax relief bonds
감소율 attrition rate
감소율분담조항 reduced rate contribution clause
감속경향 decelerating trend
감수 decreased receipts
감수성훈련 sensitivity training
감시 monitoring; surveillance
감액 abatement
감액노령연금급부 reduced old-age benefit
감액완납보험(이후의 보험료 지불을 중지하고 그 시점에서의 해약금 바탕으로 일시불보험료를 산정하여 새롭게 보험금액을 결정함) reduced paid-up insurance
감응도계수 sensitivity coefficient
감응도분석 sensitivity analysis
감응도조정 sensitivity adjustment
감응성 sensitivity
감응특성 sensory characteristic
감자 capital decrease; capital reduction;

decrease of capital; reduction of stock

감자산가격 reduced asset price

감자잉여금 reduction surplus; surplus from capital reduction

감자차손 loss from capital reduction

감자차익 gains from stock retirement; profit from capital reduction

감자회사 company with reduced capital

감정 appraisal

감정; 정서 sentiment

감정료 survey fee; surveying fee

감정보고서 survey repot

감정서 appraisal report

감정인; 평가인 assessor

감정적인 동기 affectional drives

감채기금 sinking fund

감채기금보험 sinking fund insurance

감채기금상환일 sinking fund date

감채기금적립금 sinking fund reserve

감채기금적립순 sinking fund requirements

감추다 harbor

감춘 이익을 처분함 hidden profit distributions

갑자기 떨어지다(무역, 소비가) turndown

갑작스럽게 떼어놓음 avulsion

값싼 증권 cabinet security

값을 깎아 내려가는 경매 Dutch auction

값을 끌어올림 bidding up

값을 어림짐작하여 매기다 short covering at a loss

값이 쌈 undervalued

값이 오른 이익 capital appreciation

강경정책 stringent policy a lifts

강등 demotion

강보합 firmer; gaining

강세 bullish tone; long

강세근성 bull clique

강세매입 bull buying

강세수준유지 unchanged to slightly higher

강세스프레드거래 bull spread transaction

강세시장 bull market

강세시황 strong market

강약 strong and weak

강약지수 bull and bear index

강요 extortion

강제감사 compulsory audit

강제경매 compulsory sale by auction; forced auction

강제교환 involuntary conversion

강제금지명령 mandatory injunction

강제력 coercive power

강제매각 forced sale

강제배상보험 compulsory liability insurance

강제보험 compulsory insurance; obligatory insurance

강제사임 enforced vacation

강제상해보험 compulsory accident insurance

강제상환 mandatory redemption

강제소송참가 cross claim

강제양도 involuntary transfer

강제이전 forced transfer

강제이행 office grant

강제잉여금 compulsory surplus

강제재판보증증권 compulsory bond

강제저축 forced saving

강제적 compulsory

강제적인 감책기금조항 mandatory sinking fund requirement

강제적인 자산양도 compulsory or involuntary transfer of property

강제전환 forced conversion

강제조사 criminal investigation

강제지불불능 involuntary insolvency

강제집행 compulsory execution; forcible execution

강제채무증서 bill obligatory

강제처분 forcible disposition

강제처분가치 forced-sale value

강제청산 compulsory winding-up; forced liquidation; winding-up by the court

강제파산 involuntary bankruptcy

강제하다 enforce

강제합병 statutory merger
강제해약 compulsory cancellation
강제화의 compulsory composition
강제환가 compulsory conversion into money
강하게 부인하다 forswear
강한 느낌 strong feeling; strong sentiment
강한 성장 strong growth
강한 재료 bullish factor
강한 저항선 bullish resistance line
강한 지지선 bullish support line
강한 채널 bullish channel
강행가능 enforceable
강행규정 forcible provisions
개구; 인접지 frontage
개념을 내포함 intention of concept
개념틀짜기 conceptual framework
개념형성 concept formation; formation of
    concept
개념화의 역설 paradox of conceptualization
개략보고 summary reports
개량 iniproveiiient
개량비 improvement expense
개량지수익 approvement
개량특허 improvement patent
개발; 재생 reclamation
개발격차 development gap
개발부담금 charge for development
개발비 cost for development; development
    cost; development expenses
개발수입 develop and import scheme
개발업자 developer
개발자금 development fund
개발중 under development
개방경제 open economy
개방단체 open group
개방식 담보 open-end mortgage
개방식 담보부사채 open-end mortgage bond
개방식의 open-end
개방적인 유통 intensive distribution
개방하다 affranchise
개방형 인플레이션 open inflation

개별감가상각법 unit method
개별거래마다 리스크를 평가함 transaction
    approach
개별계약단체보험 franchise group insurance
개별공제 itemized deduction
개별과세 individual taxation
개별기업 individual firm
개별기업고유의 company-specific
개별내용연수 individual useful life
개별매매방식 individual dealing system
개별법 identified cost method
개별보증증권 individual bond
개별보험 individual insurance
개별보험연금계획 individual policy pension
    trust
개별보험증권 special policy
개별상각 individual depreciation; item
    depreciation; unit depreciation
개별생산 individual production
개별소비세 specific consumption tax
개별신고서 separate return
개별신원보증증권 individual Fidelity bond
개별원가 job cost; specific cost
개별원가계산 job cost system; job order
    costing; production order cost accounting
개별원가계산법 job order cost system
개별원가계산제도 specific-order cost system
개별재보험 specific reinsurance
개별재산세 specific property tax
개별중재 ad hoc arbitration
개별책임 several liability
개별책임의 severally liable
개봉예금 unsealed deposit
개산가격 approximate price; approximate
    value
개산경비공제 deduction of estimated expenses
개산경비율 rate of estimated expenses
개산공제 standard deduction
개산대차대조표 rough balance sheet
개산요구 estimate of budget requests
개산원가 approximate cost; estimated cost;

rough cost

개산지불 payment by rough estimate

개서, 보험누적채무 pyramiding

개선 amelioration; betterment

개설은행 opening bank

개시 disclosure; discovery

개시권 right to begin

개시원칙 disclosure philosophy

개시잔고계정 opening balance account

개업계(開業屆) notification of opening of business

개업비 expenses incurred for opening of business; initial cost of business

개요시트 synopsis sheet

개인가처분소득 disposable personal income; personal disposable income

개인건강보험 individual health insurance

개인고객을 상대하는 증권회사 wire houses

개인공제 individual exclusion

개인금융 personal financing

개인기업 sole proprietorship

개인당좌계정 personal checking account

개인론 personal loan

개인명의계좌 private account

개인배당소득 personal dividend income

개인배상책임보험 personal liability insurance

개인변액연금 individual variable annuity

개인보증 personal guarantee

개인보험 personal insurance

개인보험업자 individual underwriter

개인보험자 specialist insurer

개인부문 personal sector

개인부채 personal liability

개인소득 personal income

개인소득세 individual income tax; personal income tax

개인소비 personal consumption expenditure

개인소유물포괄보험 personnel floater

개인신용 personal credit

개인신용정보 consumer's credit

개인신탁 private trust

개인어음 personal bill; private bill

개인연금 individual annuity; personal pension

개인연금제도 personal pension scheme

개인예금 personal deposit

개인의 비밀보유권 personal immunity

개인이자소득 personal interest income

개인임대료소득 personal rental income

개인재산 personal property

개인재산소득 personal income from property

개인저축 personal saving

개인적인 영향 personal influence

개인적인 편향 personal bias

개인적인 평가 personal valuation

개인주민세 individual inhabitant tax

개인주주 individual stockholder

개인지출 personal expenditure

개인통신망 personal communication network

개인퇴직계정 individual retirement account

개인특성 personal attribute

개인파산 personal bankruptcy

개인회원 private member

개입 intervention

개입구입 intervention purchase

개입금리 intervention rate

개입기업; 소유주지분 proprietorship

개입수준 intervention level

개입점 intervention point

개입조작 intervention operation

개입통화 intervention currency

개장비(改裝費) betterment expense

개정중 in session

개조 remodel

개척단계 pioneering stage

개축공사 reconstruction works

개축비 reconstruction expense

객관적인 가치 objective value

객관적인 증거 objective evidence

객관적인 확률 objective probability

객관지표 objective indicator

갠트차트 Gantt chart

갭법 gap management technology

갭분석 gap analysis
갱생 rehabilitation
갱생수속 reorganization proceedings
갱생회사 corporation in need of reorganization
갱신 renewal
갱신료 renewal charge; renewal fee
갱신빈도 reset frequency
갱신수수료 renewal commission
갱신일 refix date
갱신조건부 정기보험 renewable term insurance
갱신차금 difference by renewal
갱신투자 replacement investment
갱신하다 update
갱정 등의 효력 effect of correction
갱정; 조정 correction
갱정결정으로 확정한 추가세액 settled additional tax due amount
갱정이나 결정을 담당하는 관청 authority of correction or determination
갱정청구 claim for correction; request for correction
갱지(更地) land lot without construction
거대리스크 large risks
거대위험 jumbo risk
거래 market transaction; trading; transaction
거래가격 sale price
거래거부 refusal to deal
거래경로 trade channel
거래고 dealings; lot; volume of business
거래고세 turnover tax
거래관계를 청산하다 close one's position; unwind a trade
거래관계를 해소하다 closed out method
거래기간 time horizon
거래노하우 trading know-how
거래단위 trading unit
거래동기 transaction motive
거래명세 schedule of transactions
거래범위 trading range
거래세 trading tax; transaction tax; transactions tax

거래소 trading floor
거래소 유러피언옵션거래소 European Options Exchange
거래소, 경마장에서 부당이익을 얻는 사람 bucketeer
거래소거래 exchange transactions; stock exchange transaction; transaction on exchange
거래소거래세 bourse tax
거래소매입 exchange acquisition
거래소법 exchange law
거래소별세 exchange tax
거래소분배 exchange distribution
거래소세 bourse transaction tax
거래소시장 exchange market
거래소시프트 transaction shift
거래소중매인 commission broker
거래소회비 member's fee
거래소회원 exchange member
거래수수료 transaction fee
거래수준 level of transaction
거래시스템 trading system
거래약정서 customer's agreement and consent
거래일 trading day
거래일계표 blotting book
거래정지 trading halts
거래정지처분 disposition by suspension of business
거래조건 business terms; trading conditions
거래처 clients; customers
거래처계정 customer's account
거래처선불금 advance to vendor
거래처종합관리 relationship management system
거래총비용 total cost of transaction
거래코스트 transaction cost
거래특성 transaction characteristics
거래포스트 trading post
거래효율 transactional efficiency
거류지무역 settlement trade
거리개념 distance concept

거미집순환 cobweb cycle

거부 veto

거소 temporary residence

거시경제적 macroeconomic

거액거래 large amount transaction

거액예금금리 large amount deposit interest

거액위험약관 "Jumbo" clause

거액정기 large amount time deposit

거액주문 large order

거절; 방기 repudiation

거절각서 note of protest

거절각서를 작성함 noting protest

거절반응 negative reaction

거절자 protestor

거절증서 memorandum of protest; protest; rejection certificate

거절증서가 필요없음 no protest

거절증서불요 retour sans protet

거절증서작성수수료 protest charges

거절하다 renounce

거주외국법인 resident foreign corporation

거주외국인 resident alien

거주용 자산 property for residence

거주용 재산 residential property

거주자 resident

거주자유러엔채 Euroyen bond for resident

거출금; 분담금 contribution

거출식 질병보험 contributory sickness fund

거출잉여금 contributed surplus

거출자금 contributed stock

거출제도 contribution plan

거출제연금 contributory annuity

거치; 미수 deferred

거치기간 grace period

거치저금 deferred savings

거치종신연금 deferred life annuity

건강보험 health insurance

건강보험료 health insurance premium

건강진단 health examination

건물 및 대부금포괄보증증권 building and loan blanket bond

건물감가상각 depreciation of building

건물세 house duty

건물용 부지 building lot

건물전대인 house farmer

건물파괴약관 fall of building clause

건설가계정 construction in process account

건설공사 construction work

건설공사보험 contractors' all risks insurance

건설공사수입 construction work revenue

건설공사전도금 advance on construction

건설국채 construction bond; government bond for the purpose of public works

건설비계정 construction account

건설이자 interest during construction; interest incurred during construction

건설조성금 construction subsidy; government subsidy for capital expenditure

건설중인 건물 building under construction

건설지출 construction expenditure

건설청부업자 기계기구포괄보험 contractors' equipment floater

건설청부업자 미필배상책임보험 contractors' contingent liability insurance

건설청부업자 책임보험 contractors' liability insurance

건설클레임 construction claim

건전성 soundness

건전성 유지계약 keep-well agreement

건전재정주의 principle of balanced budget

건전한 은행업무 sound banking

건조중량 dry weight

건축가배상책임보험 architect's liability policy

건축계정 building account

건축기준법 Construction Standard Law

건축대부조합 building and loan association

건축대차권 building lease

건축비 building expenses; construction cost

건축세 building tax; tax on construction

건축조합 building societies

검사 inspection

검사공정 process of inspection

검사보고서 inspection report; report on examination
검사상태 inspection status
검사위원회 committee of inspection
검사증명서 inspection certificate
검색항변권 defense right of attachment
검수감사 tally audit
검수인 tally man
검인 seal
검인보증증권 probate bond
검인재판소 court of probate
검인철회 revocation of probate
검정가설 testing hypothesis
검증 probate; verification; view
검증관 inquisitor
검찰관 prosecuting attorney
검찰청 prosecutors office
검출력곡선 power curve
것 시장상실 missing the market
겉보기가격 shell branch
게·플랜 game plan
게시판체계 bulletin board system
게임이론 theory of games
겐사키시장 Gensaki
계산조견표 calculator
격 quality
격감 sharp decline
격리 segregation
격자법 lattice approach
격차균등화 equalizing divergences
격탁매매 group auction
견고 steady
견고한 시황 steady market
견본비 samples expense
견본시 trade show
견본적송품 sample shipment
견본추출 sampling
견적 estimation; proforma; proforma estimated cost
견적감가상각 observed depreciation
견적공사원가 estimated cost of construction work
견적금액변경 changes in estimates
견적내용연수 estimated useful life; expected life
견적내용연수표 observed life table
견적대차대조표 budgeted balance sheet; estimated balance sheet; proforma balance sheet; projected balance sheet
견적매상계정서 proforma account sales
견적비용 estimated expenses
견적세액 estimated tax
견적손익계산서 estimated profit and loss statement; projected income statement
견적에 따른 채무 liability of estimated amount
견적원가계산 estimated cost accounting
견적원가계산제도 estimated cost accounting system
견적원가제도 estimating-cost system
견적이익 estimated profit
견적재무제표 proforma statement; projected financial statements
견적채무 estimated liabilities
견적하다 assess
견적한 어음 proforma bill/draft
견조(堅調); 사업법인 firm
견책; 징계 reprimand
견출 subtitle
결과책임 absolute liability
결론 conclusion
결론을 내는 법 conclusion drawing
결론의 근거 basis for conclusions
결사의 자유 freedom of association
결산 closing account
결산가격 settlement price
결산기 rests; settling term
결산보고 statement of account
결산분개 closing entries
결산수속 account closing procedure
결산예비발표 preliminary disclosure of settlement of accounts
결산일 account day; closing date

결산정리 closing adjustment
결산조정 adjustment in settling accounts
결산하다 settle accounts
결손 deficiency
결손계정 deficiency account
결손금 되풀이 tax loss carryback
결손금계산서 deficit statement
결손금계정 deficit account
결손금이월 carryover of deficit; tax loss carry-forward
결손금처리계산서 deficit disposition statement; deficit reconciliation statement
결손금환급 carryback of deficit
결손보충율 replacement rate
결손전보적립금 reserve for losses
결손회수 recovery of loss
결의권회사 voting company
결정 decision; ruling
결정계수 coefficient of determination
결정기술 decision technology
결정변수 decision variable
결정의 유효성 decision effectiveness
결정적 각하 preemptory nonsuit
결정적 설시 preemptory instruction
결정적인 책임을 지지 않다(외상 출금의) lapping
결정적인 추정 conclusive presumption
결정적인 확신 abiding conviction
결정통지서 notice of determination
결정표 casting vote
결정함수 determination coefficient
결제 closing-out; payment
결제계정 settlement account; transaction account
결제방식 settlement method
결제성 예금 checkable deposit
결제수단 payment system
결제수지 balance of clearing
결제시 clearing time
결제일 delivery date; settlement date
결제할인 settlement discount

결함품; 하자품 defective goods; defective work
결합대차대조표 combined balance sheet
결합비용 joint cost
결합상각법 combined depreciation
결합손익계산서 combined profit and loss statement
결합재무제표 combined financial statement
겸임중역 interlocking directors
경감 extenuation; mitigation
경감세율 reduced tax rate
경감하는 infirmative
경계 bounds; fear
경계; 예방책 precaution
경계선 boundary
경계자세 cautious stance
경계전략 boundary strategy
경계체 borderline risk
경계표현 boundary representation
경과계정 deferred and accrued accounts
경과보험료 earned premium
경과시간 lapsed time
경과실 slight negligence
경과연수 elapsed years; number of years elapsed
경과이자 accrued interest
경과일수 lapsed days
경과재보험료 earned reinsurance premium
경과조치 interim measure; transition; transitional measure
경기 business climate; business conditions
경기과열 overheating of business activity
경기동향조사 business survey
경기동향지표 diffusion index
경기변동 economic fluctuation
경기부양책 reflation policy
경기선행지수 leading index of business conditions; leading indicator
경기순환 business cycle; economic cycle
경기순환국면 phases of economic cycle
경기순환주 business cyclical stock

ㄱ

경기순환형 기업 business cyclical company
경기예측 business forecast
경기의 저점 trough
경기의 최고점 peak
경기자극책 business stimulating measure
경기조정 business adjustment
경기증대 boost
경기지수 business barometer
경기지표 business indicator
경기회복 economic recovery
경기후퇴 economic recession; economic slump
경기후퇴; 불황 recession
경기후퇴기 recession period; weaker economy
경년변동율 year-to-year changes
경력개발프로그램 career development program
경력정체 career plateau
경로 path
경로개발 channel development
경로비용분석 channel cost analysis
경로시스템 channel system
경로의존형 파생상품 history-dependent derivative
경로통제 channel control
경로환경 channel environment
경로효율 channel efficiency
경리과 accounting department
경리사 registered public accountant
경리의 하이라이트 financial highlights
경마식 도박 pari-mutuel betting
경매 auction sale; mock auction
경매수수료 lot-money
경매시장 auction market
경매인 auctioneer
경매인의 한통속 puffer
경매조건 conditions of sale
경비개선비용 cost improvement cost
경비공제후 이익 profit after expenses
경비내역장 expense analysis book

경비보상금 compensation for expense and loss
경비부가보험료 loading for expense
경비삭감 curtailment of expenditure
경비예산 estimated appropriation; expenses budget
경비원장 expense ledger
경비절감 financial retrenchment
경비차액 factory expenses variance
경비차이 underlease
경비팽창의 원칙 law of increasing public expenditures
경비할당 expenses quota
경사관세 tariff escalation
경사도가 심한 이율곡선 elbow
경사리스크 slope risk
경상 ordinary
경상(經常); 당좌의 current
경상거래 current transaction
경상계정수지 balance of current account
경상계획 business plan
경상관리자연금 Executive pension
경상달러 current dollar
경상분석 business analysis
경상비 overhead expenses
경상비용 current expenses; ordinary expenditure
경상세 ordinary tax
경상세입 ordinary annual revenue
경상세출 ordinary annual expenditure
경상소득 ordinary income with recurrent nature
경상손익 ordinary profit and loss; recurring profit and loss; results of ordinary operations
경상수입 ordinary income
경상수지 current account balance; current balance
경상수지계정 balance on current account
경상수지흑자 favorable balance on current account

경상순익액 net operating earnings
경상예산 current budget
경상외비용 nonrecurring cost
경상외손익 nonrecurring profit and loss
경상이익 ordinary profit; recurring profit
경상이익계산서 statement of operation
    earnings
경상이전 current transfer
경상자원 resources on business
경상자지향 businessman's orientation
경상지불 current payment
경상지출 current expenditure
경상통계 business statistics
경상판단의 원칙 business judgment principle
경영감사 management audit; management
    review
경영계획 management plan
경영분석 analysis of the affairs of a business
경영위원회 managing committee
경영위탁계약 management agreement
경영위험 business risk
경영이념 management concept; management
    philosophy
경영자보험 key executive insurance
경영자본이익률 operating earning rate
경영자본회전율 turnover of total operating
    assets
경영자원 management resources; managerial
    resources
경영자책임 management responsibility
경영자판단 executive judgment
경영전략 management strategy
경영정보시스템 management information
    system
경영지배권 controlling interest
경영참가 management participation
경영참가권 management participation right
경영컨설턴트 management consultant
경영하다 carry on
경영효율 operating efficiency
경유거래세 light oil delivery tax

경쟁가격 competitive price
경쟁관할권 concurrent jurisdiction
경쟁광고 competitive advertising
경쟁매장 auction
경쟁압력 competitive pressure
경쟁입찰 bid by advertising; competitive
    tender
경쟁자분석 competitor analysis
경쟁적인 평가절하 competitive depreciation
경쟁전략 competition strategy
경쟁제품 emulative product
경쟁제한정책 policies for restricting
    competition
경쟁제한특약 negative covenant
경쟁촉진정책 policies for promoting
    competition
경쟁판매 competitive sale
경쟁품취급금지계약 exclusive dealing
경제개발검토위원회 Economic and
    Development Review Committee
경제개혁 economic reform
경제계 economic circles
경제계획 economic plan
경제공황 economic crisis
경제구조조정 economic structural adjustment
경제권 economic bloc
경제기능 economic function
경제기초조건 중시파 fundamentalist
경제기초조건; 펀드멘털즈 fundamentals
경제대국 economic big power; major
    economic power
경제동맹 economic union
경제리스크 economic risk
경제마찰 economic friction
경제모델 economic model
경제백서 economic white paper
경제봉쇄 economic blockade
경제불쾌지수 misery index
경제산업자문위원회 Business and Industry
    Advisory Committee
경제상호작용 economic interaction

경제상황 economic conditions
경제생활 economic life
경제성 공학 economic engineering
경제성장 economic growth
경제성장기 period of economic growth
경제성장률 economic growth rate
경제성장모델 economic growth model
경제성장정책 economic growth policy
경제센터 economic center
경제순환 circular flow of economic system
경제심의회 Economic Deliberation Council
경제안전보장 economic security
경제안정기 period of economic stability
경제연보 annual economic review
경제예측 economic forecast; economic
  outlook; economic prediction
경제우선 economic priority
경제원가 economic cost
경제원조 economic aid
경제윤리 economic ethics
경제의 귀결 economic consequence
경제의 연속성 economic continuity
경제의 흐름 economic tide
경제인 economic man
경제재(經濟財) economic goods
경제적 모방단계 economic emulation stage
경제적 수요곡선 empirical demand curve
경제적 이익 economic earnings
경제적 이익의 베타수치 economic earnings
  beta
경제적인 낭비 economic waste
경제적인 성숙 economic maturity
경제적인 진부화 economic obsolescence
경제적인 책임이 집중됨 economic
  channeling of liability
경제적인 편익 economic benefits
경제전망 economic prospect
경제전쟁 economic war
경제정보 business information
경제정보서비스 business information service
경제정책 economic policy

경제제재 economic sanction
경제조직 economic organization
경제주체 economic unit
경제지수 economic index
경제지표 economic barometer; economic
  figure; economic indicator
경제지표효과 economic number effect
경제진보 economic progress
경제질병 economic malaise
경제질서 economic order
경제집중 economic channeling
경제철학 economic philosophy
경제체제 economic regime; economic system
경제통계 economic statistics
경제통합 economic integration
경제표 economic table
경제품질 economic quality
경제학과 economic science
경제해석 economic interpretation
경제협력 economic assistance; economic
  cooperation
경제협력백서 white paper on economic
  cooperation
경제활동 economic activity
경제활동자극책 economic activity stimulating
  measure
경제활력 economic viability
경제효용 economic utility
경죄 misdemeanor
경차세 light vehicle tax
경품부 대매출 gift enterprise
경품부 판매 premium sale
경합과실 concurrent negligence; culpa
  concurrens
경합브랜드 rival brands
경합타사정보 competitive intelligence
경합패턴 competitive pattern
경합하다 compete; consolidate
경향선 trend pattern
경향지수 index-number trend series; trend
  series

경향형 모델 trend model

경험곡선 experience curve

경험분류요율표 experience grading and rating schedule

경험요율 experience rating

경험요율법 prospective rating

경험적 어프로치 empirical approach

경험인인 상식 rules of thumb

경험적인 확률 posterior probabilities

경험표 experience table

경험효과 experience effects

경화시키다; 완고하게 하다 stiffen

계급순위 rank order

계량경제모델 econometric model

계량모델예측 forecast by the econometric model

계량분석 econometric analysis

계량심리학 psychometrics

계산가격 computed price

계산기수 commutation function

계산기초 basis of calculation

계산다툼 footing

계산단위 unit of account

계산도표 monography

계산본위 tabular standard

계산서 statement

계산서; 고객 account

계산서류 financial documents

계산소송 action for accounting

계산절차 computation procedure

계산조견표 ready reckoner

계산차이 errors in calculation

계산착오 miscalculation

계산표 table

계산하다 calculate

계상보험료 accrued premium; premium written; written premium

계상시장 upstairs market

계상이익 declared profit

계상하다 appropriate; sum up

계선(係船)보험 port risks insurance

계속개시 continuous disclosure

계속기간 duration

계속기록법 perpetual inventory method

계속기업을 전제로 premise of a going concern

계속률 persistency rate

계속보험 running policy

계속보험료 renewal premium

계속사업부문이익 earnings from continuing operations

계속사용료 running royalty

계속성의 원칙 principle of consistency

계속시장; 연속거래 continuous market

계속재고 perpetual inventory

계속재고법 running inventory method

계속적인 상품통제 perpetual merchandise control

계속적인 신용공여 evergreen credit

계속적인 침해 permanent trespass

계속제도명령서 standing production order

계속주문 standing order

계속중인 소송 lis pendens

계속평가 ongoing assessment

계수 coefficient

계수관리 management through figures

계승재산부여증서 vesting deed

계약 contract

계약; 약정 agreement

계약각서 articles of agreement

계약개요 policy summary

계약곡선 contract curve

계약관계 privity of contract

계약구조 contract salvage

계약구조료 contract salvage charges

계약규모 contract size

계약금 contract money; money of adieu

계약기간 contract term

계약내용수정 amendment to a contract

계약내용을 실행함; 인출 closing

계약내용확인 contract review

계약능력 capacity to contract

계약능력자 personable

계약당사자 contracting party
계약률 contract ratio
계약모집대리점 acquisition agent
계약모집비 acquisition cost
계약모집수수료 acquisition commission
계약배상책임보험 contractual liability policy
계약보전 administration of insurance contract
계약보증 contract bond
계약불이행 nonfulfillment of a contract
계약비용 bargaining cost
계약사양서 contract specification
계약상의 ex contractu
계약상의 권리 obligation of contract
계약상의 권리침해 impairment of contract
계약서 contractual documents; indenture
계약선수금 advance received on contract
계약성립 done
계약수수료 contract charge
계약시장 contract market
계약신탁 trust under agreement
계약운임제 contract rate system
계약위반 breach of contract; violation of a
  contract
계약을 해약함 cancellation of contract
계약의 목적을 달성하지 못함 frustration
계약이전재보험 assumption reinsurance
계약이행 fulfillment of a contract
계약이행거절 lying down
계약인수능력; 행위능력 capacity
계약일보 daily bordereau
계약일시금 up-front payment
계약자배당 dividend to policyholders
계약자배당금 policy dividend
계약자배당방식 method of bonus allocation;
  method of policy dividend allocation
계약자배당에 따라 보험금액이 증가함
  paid-up addition
계약자유의 원칙 liberty of contract; principle
  of the freedom of contract
계약자잉여금 policyholder's surplus
계약자준비금 policyholder's reserve

계약자카드 line card
계약잔고 contract balance; outstanding
  contract amount
계약전 평가 precontract assessment
계약전도금 advance made on contract;
  contract deposit paid; contract deposit
  received
계약조건 contract terms
계약종료배당 termination dividend
계약증거금 earnest money
계약채무; 계약의무 commitment
계약책임 contractual liability
계약체결 conclusion of a contract; letting out
계약체결후 감사 audit after the contract
계약초과금액 excess receipt over contract
  price
계약포지션 contract position
계약해당일 anniversary date
계약해제 annulment of a contract
계약해제약관 cancellation clause
계약해제효과 effect of rescission
계약형 contract type
계약형 계속투자플랜 contract type
  accumulative investment plan
계약형 수직적 마케팅 contractual vertical
  marketing
계약형 투자신탁 contract type investment
  trust
계열금융기관 affiliated financial institute
계열상관 serial correlation
계열위험 allied line risks
계열위험담보계약 allied line cover
계열융자 loan to affiliated companies
계열화 affiliation
계쟁권 litigious right
계쟁물(係爭物) subject-matter
계절관세 seasonal duties
계절매출 season sale
계절변동 seasonal variation
계절변동조정 seasonal fluctuation adjustment
계절변동조정제 seasonally adjusted

계절변동조정필 adjusted to seasonal variations

계절변동형 모델 seasonal model

계절상품 seasonal goods; seasonal merchandise

계절일부 season dating

계절자금 seasonal fund

계절적인 매출압력 seasonal selling pressure

계절적인 영향을 제거함 removal of seasonal effect

계절적인 요인으로 인한 실업 seasonal unemployment

계절조정 seasonal adjustment

계절지수 seasonal index

계절평균 seasonal average

계절할인 seasonal discount

계정; 계좌 counting

계정과목 account headings; account title; title paramount

계정과목내역명세서 statement classified by account title

계정과목번호 account number

계정과목번호표시법 account number plan

계정과목분류표 classification of item of accounts

계정과목일람표 account chart; classification of account

계정과목표 card of accounts; chart of accounts

계정구 check-out counter

계정기호법 symbol system of accounts

계정대조표 account reconcilement

계정명세 particulars of account

계정분석 account analysis

계정서 account statement

계정시스템 account system

계정식 account form; balanced form

계정식 손익계산서 account form income statement; account form profit and loss statement

계정을 마감하다 square an account

계정항목 item of account

계좌대체 account transfer

계좌자동대체 automatic fund transfer

계출후 사용제 file and use

계측결과 measuring results

계측유효성 measuring effectiveness

계층 stratum; tier

계층이론 hierarchical theory

계층화 stratification

계층화추출 stratified sampling

계통적인 systemic

계통적인 계산 systematic calculation

계통적인 어프로치 methodical approach

계통표본 systematic sampling

계획경제 planned economy

계획계층 planning hierarchy

계획단위 planning unit

계획배송 planning delivery

고가 high; high price; higher in quotation; higher quotation

고가격시장전략 above the market strategy

고가로 인수한 신품 trade-in articles

고가로 회복 recover high

고가상품 big ticket merchandise

고가주 high-priced stock

고객 한 쌍 dyad customer

고객계정을 보유한 브로커 carrying broker

고객관계 customer relations

고객단가 customer transaction

고객단말 consumer premises equipment

고객동원력 customers mobilizing power

고객만족도 customer's satisfaction

고객믹스 customer mix

고객보고 customer repos

고객상실률 decay rate

고객시장 customer market

고객원장 account receivable ledger

고객을 엄선함 customer preference

고객을 합리화함 customer rationalization

고객이월효과 customer holdover effect

고객전수금 advance by customers

고객조사 customer research

고객주문 customer's order
고객지향 customer oriented
고객효과 clientele effect
고금리 high interest rate
고금리시대 era of high interest rate
고금리정책 dear money policy; high interest rate policy
고급지 quality paper
고급품소비지향 trend towards luxury spending
고대수로 ancient watercourse
고도가공품 advanced processed
고도로 긍정적인 상관관계 high degree of positive correlation
고도선택사회 multichannel society
고도장애 disability
고도장애급부 disability benefits
고도장애급부보험 disability benefits insurance
고도장애연금 disability annuity
고도정보통신시스템 information network system
고도화텔레비전 advanced television
고등시장 soaring market
고리대 feneration; loan shark
고리부 사채 high-interest-bearing debenture
고리소회전 trading-up
고리채 usurer
고맥락 high context
고문서 ancient writing
고밀도 high density
고발 accusation
고발인; 소추대행자 relator
고보합 holding high
고수준 healthy trend
고수준의 경기 high level of business activity
고스트 ghosting
고액납세자 high income brackets; high taxpayers
고액배당 melon cutting
고액신탁증권 high income trust security
고액의료비보험 major medical expense insurance
고액입원비보험 major hospitalization insurance
고액채권 large credit
고요율적용계약 rated policy
고용 employment
고용기회균등 equal employment opportunities
고용수준 level of employment
고용승수 employment multiplier
고용시장 employment market
고용자퇴직급여금 employees' retirement allowance
고용절차 employment producers
고용조정 employment adjustment
고용지수 employment index
고유리스크 specific risk
고유위험 inherent hazard
고유인자 unique factor
고유치 proper value
고유하자 inherent defect
고율적용제도 higher interest rates application system
고의로 scienter
고의의 intentional; willful
고의적인 과실 willful negligence
고의적인 불법행위 willful misconduct
고의적인 침몰 scuttling
고의적인 허위 willful false
고이율채 high yield bond
고장모드 failure mode
고장어음 foul bill
고장영향완화 benign failure
고장트리해석 fault tree analysis
고저법 high-low method
고전파경제학 classical school of economics
고정 fixing
고정(苦情); 고소 complaint
고정가격 fixed price
고정금리 fixed rate
고정금리기준모기지 graduated payment

mortgage

고정금리부채 fixed-rate liability

고정금리자산 fixed-rate assets

고정금리증권 fixed income security

고정금리지불인 fixed-rate payer

고정급 fixed salary; fixed wages

고정단위형 투자신탁 fixed unit trust

고정달러증권 fixed dollar security

고정대부금 fixed loan

고정된 환상장 pegged exchange

고정부채 fixed liabilities

고정부채비율 ratio of Rxed liabilities to net worth

고정비 constant cost; constant expenses; fixed costs and expenses; fixed expenses; fixed overhead; standing expenses

고정비용부담배율 fixed-charge coverage ratio

고정비율 fixed asset to net worth ratio; fixed ratio; solidity ratio

고정비율법 constant percentage method

고정비율성장모델 constant-growth rate model

고정비율성장평가모델 constant-growth rate valuation model

고정상장 pegged market

고정상장제 system of fixed rate of exchange

고정성 배열 fixed-first type

고정성 배열법 capital arrangement; fixed arrangement

고정세율 fixed general tariff

고정수입 fixed income

고정수치를 각 항목에 분배해서 선호도를 나타냄 constant sum scale

고정유동비율제도 fixed liquidity reserve requirements

고정이율증권 fixed return securities

고정자본 fixed capital

고정자본투자 fixed capital investment; fixed investment

고정자산 fixed assets; property and equipment

고정자산과세대장 property tax cadaster

고정자산납세기한 due date of property tax

payment

고정자산대장 fixed asset ledger

고정자산매각손 loss on sale of fixed assets

고정자산매각익 gains from sale of fixed assets

고정자산매상률 sales to fixed assets

고정자산명세표 fixed-asset schedule

고정자산비율 fixed asset ratio

고정자산세 fixed asset tax; municipal property tax; property tax; real estate tax

고정자산세면세점 taxable minimum of property tax

고정자산세비과세범위 scope of exemption of property tax

고정자산원장 plant ledger

고정자산자기자본율 equity capital ratio to fixed assets

고정자산증감명세표 lapsing schedule of fixed assets

고정자산처분 disposal of fixed assets

고정자산평가익 gains from revaluation off fixed assets

고정자산회전율 fixed asset turnover ratio

고정주 pegged stock

고정차입금 fixed debt

고정채시장; 채권시장 fixed income market

고정평가제 fixed parity system

고정환상장제도 pegged exchange rate system

고정환율 fixed exchange rate

고정환율제도 fixed exchange rate system

고지서 statement of intent

고지의무 duty of disclosure; obligation to disclose

고지의무위반 concealment

고지효과 announcement effect

고차재(高次財) higher order goods

고참변호사 ancients

고쳐 쓴; 다시 쓴 rewriting

고충처리기관 grievance machinery

고충처리위원회 grievance committee

고치(高値) record price

고품질클래스 quality class
고화질텔레비전; **HDTV** high definition
　television
곡물메이저 major multinational grain firms
곡물시장 grain market
곡손 bending
골드러시 gold rush
골드센터 gold center
골드트란시 gold tranche
골든크로스 golden cross
골든패러슈트 golden parachute
골든핸드커프스 golden hand cuffs
골칫거리; 곤란한 것(사람) annoyance
골퍼보험 golfers' insurance
공간지세 vacant land tax
공개가격 price of introduced stock
공개거래회관 open board of broker
공개경쟁매매방식 open outcry method
공개기관 public institution
공개기업 public company
공개단기금융시장 open money market
공개매각 public sale
공개법정 open court
공개성의 원칙 principle of disclosure
공개시장 market overt; open market
공개시장조작 open market operations; open
　repo
공개입찰 public bidding
공개정보 public information
공개주 introduced stock; publicly held stock
공개초안 exposure draft
공개회사 open corporation; publicly-held
　company
공격적인 전략 offensive strategy
공격적인 증권 aggressive securities
공격적인 투자 aggressive investment
공고 ban; government financial corporation;
　public finance corporation
공공경제학 public economics
공공단체 public body
공공복지 public welfare

공공사업 public service; public utility; public
　work
공공사업비 expenditure for public works
공공시설건설부담액 allotted amount in
　constructing public facility
공공시설부담액 share in expense of public
　service
공공연한 점유 notorious possession
공공요금 public utility charges
공공재 public goods
공공지출 public expenditure; public spending
공공질서 public order
공공채 public debt securities
공공채딜러 municipal securities dealer
공공채발행 issue of public bonds
공공책임 public responsibility
공공통신사업 public telecommunication
　business
공공투자 public investment
공과 duties; public dues; public impost; taxes
공권을 박탈하다 disfranchise
공금예금 official deposit
공급과다 oversupply
공급관리 management of supply
공급보증증권 supply bond
공급부족 short supply
공급탄성치 elasticity of supply
공급함수 supply function
공기연장 extension of time for completion
공동감사 joint audit
공동개발 joint development
공동계산계약 pooling contracts
공동계정 common account; omnibus account
공동광고 joint advertisement
공동구입 group buying; pooled buying
공동독점 shared monopolies
공동마케팅 pooled marketing
공동모의 conspiracy
공동발행인 co-maker
공동법정상속인 co-heir
공동변동상장 joint currency float; joint

floating exchange rate; joint-floating market system

공동보유 joint tenant

공동보증 joint guarantee

공동보증인 cosurety

공동보험 coinsurance

공동보험수취계정 coinsurance account receivable

공동보험식 재보험 reinsurance by coinsurance method

공동보험인수비율 coinsurance share

공동보험인수한도 coinsurance limit

공동보험자 coinsurer

공동보험지불계정 coinsurance account payable

공동사업 joint project

공동수취인 joint beneficiary

공동시설세 public facilities tax

공동시장 common market

공동신고 joint return

공동융자 co-finance; joint financing

공동으로 in concert

공동의 joint

공동인수 club deal

공동작업 common employment

공동장부 counterrolls

공동제일저당권 pooled first mortgage

공동주간사 co-lead-manager

공동채권매입기구 Cooperative Credit Purchase Corporation

공동책임 joint liability

공동체 community

공동판 joint sales

공동판매 combination sale; cooperative marketing; joint marketing

공동플로트 joint float

공동피보험자 joint insureds

공동해손 general average

공동해손맹약서 average bond; general average bond

공동해손부담가액 contributory value

공동해손분담액 general average contribution

공동해손비용 general average expenditure

공동해손이 아닌 해손 average unless general

공동해손정산고 general average balance

공동해손정산지 place of adjustment

공동해손희생손해 general average sacrifice

공동행위 concerted activity

공매 public auction; selling short; short selling

공매광고 public notification of auction

공매보증금 deposit for public auction

공매비율 short sale ratio

공매에서 되찾음 redemption from tax sale

공매증서 tax deed

공매처분 disposition by public sale

공매환매 short-covering

공모 confederacy; public offering; public subscription

공모; 통모(通謀) collusion

공모업무 public offering business

공모입찰 bidding for public offering

공모주 publicly subscribed share

공모채 public issue

공모한 부동산회복소송 common recovery

공무원 civil servant; civil service

공무집행방해죄 crime of interference with execution of official duty

공문서 archives

공민 citizen

공민권 civil rights

공백 lacuna

공백기간 "black out" period

공법 public law

공보 official information

공보증인 straw bail

공분산 covariance

공분산분석 covariance analysis

공사 job

공사(公私)혼합기업 mixed undertaking

공사, 공단 public corporation

공사공단채 authority bond

공사관리 care of works
공사미수금 construction work account receivable
공사부담금 contribution in aid of construction
공사비 cost of construction
공사수입 construction revenue
공사완성기준 completion basis
공사전도금 deposits paid on construction work
공사진행기준 percentage of completion basis; percentage-of-completion method
공사채 government bonds and corporate debentures; public and corporate bond; public corporation bond
공사채담보금융 bond collateral loans
공사채담보대부 loan secured by government bonds corporate debentures
공사채를 상장한 상장 rate of listed bond
공사채상환익 profit accruing from refund of bonds and debentures
공사채응모자이익 yield on public and corporate bond
공사채전문위원회 special committee for public and corporate bond
공사채투자신탁 bond investment trust; open-end bond investment trust; public and corporate bond investment trust; public bond investment trust
공사채평가 valuation of bond
공사청부인 contractor
공사청부인 보험증권 contractors' insurance policy
공생 symbiosis
공서양속 policy of the law
공소 appeal
공소재판소 court of appeal
공수 air transportation
공수로 highway
공술녹취서를 금지함 suppression of deposition
공술하다 depose
공시 announcement; public disclosure

공시가격 posted price
공시기능 disclosing function
공시송달 service by public notification
공시자본 declared capital
공시제도 disclosure system
공시최고 public notification; public summons
공식 formula
공식연금 formal plan annuity
공업국 industrialized countries
공업단지 industrial estate
공업디자인 industrial design
공업부기 factory bookkeeping; industrial bookkeeping; manufacturing bookkeeping
공업생산 industrial production
공업소유권 industrial proprietorship; industrial right
공업재단 industrial foundation
공업주 industrial stock
공업회계 industrial accounting; manufacturing accounting
공영보험 public insurance
공용 인보이스 official invoice
공용수용하다 condemn
공용징수 appropriation; expropriation
공유 co-ownership; joint ownership
공유물분할 partition
공유자 part-owners
공유자산 common property
공익 public policy
공익권 rights for profit-sharing
공익기업; 유용성 utility
공익법인 corporation in public interest; corporation of public utility; juridical person for public interest; nonprofit foundation; public interest corporation
공익사업 nonprofit-making activity
공익사업채 public utility bond
공익사업회계 public utility accounting
공익사업회사예금 deposits with public utility corporations
공익신탁 charitable trust; public trust

공인검량인 public measurer
공인딜러; 지정판매점 authorized dealer
공인의 chartered
공인재산재해보험사 chartered property casualty underwriter
공인증권분석전문가 chartered financial analyst
공인회계사 certified public accountant; chartered public accountant; public accountant
공인회계사법 certified public accountant Law
공임 laborage
공장 factory; plant; shop
공장간접비 factory burden
공장검사 shop inspection
공장계정 factory account
공장내 운송비 yard transportation
공장물건 factory risk; industrial risk
공장비품 factory furnitures and fixtures
공장설비 plant and equipment
공장설비계정 plant account
공장용 소모품 factory supplies
공장용 집기 factory furniture
공장원가 factory cost; ground price; shop cost
공장원가계정 factory ledger account
공장원장 factory ledger
공장유치 attraction of factory
공장인도 ex works
공장재단 industrial factory foundation
공장주상호보험 factory mutual insurance
공장회계 factory accounting
공적개입 official intervention
공적결제수지 official reserve transactions balance
공적기업 public enterprise
공적불법방해 common nuisance
공적연금 public pension
공적연금공제 deduction for public pension
공정가격 fair price
공정가치 fair value
공정거래국 fair trade bureau

공정거래위원회 Fair Trade Commission
공정과 형평 fair and equitable
공정관리; 프로세스관리 process control
공정내 관리 in-process inspection
공정능력 process capacity
공정데이터 calibration data
공정력 tentative validity
공정률 official discount rate
공정별 원가계산 process cost accounting; process costing
공정별 종합원가계산 conversion cost system; departmental process cost system
공정별 종합원가계획 sequential cost system
공정분석 process analysis; process study
공정사양서 process specification
공정상품 equity products
공정시장 official exchange market
공정시장가격; 시가 fair market value
공정원칙 fairness doctrine
공정율할인율조작 discount rate policy
공정증서 notarial deed; notarial document
공정파라미터 process parameter
공정평가 parity of official exchange rate
공정품질관리 process quality audit
공정한 경쟁 equal footing
공정한 이익 equity margin
공정할인율인하 discount rate cut
공정환상장 official exchange rate
공제 check-off; deduction; mutual aid; subtraction; withholding
공제; 감면 reduction
공제권 recoupment
공제금 mutual aid money
공제금제도 mutual aid system
공제급부금 provident benefit
공제단체 benefit association
공제대상배우자 qualified spouse for deduction
공제면책금액 deductible
공제면책보합 deductible franchise; excess franchise
공제면책조건부 담보방식 deductible

coverage
공제보험 fraternal insurance
공제부금 mutual aid premiums
공제순서 sequence of deduction
공제액 amount deducted
공제연금 mutual pension
공제저금 deposit through deduction from monthly pay; savings deducted at source
공제조합 aid societies; benefit society; fraternal benefit society; mutual benefit association
공제조항 deductible clause
공제해야 하는 채무 deductible liabilities
공제후의 상황 after-session undertone
공조공과 tax and public dues
공중관계활동; PR public relations
공중보건기관 public health service
공증료 notarial charges
공증인 notary; public notary
공증인배상책임보험 notary public liability policy
공지 vacant lot
공지조항 clear space clause; distance clause
공집합 empty set
공채 government debt
공채관리정책 debt management policy
공채매매 public bond dealing
공채발행 flotation of government bond
공채비 expenditure for public bond; national debt service expenditure
공채수입 revenue from public bond
공채이자 interest on government bond; interest on public bond
공채정리 consolidation of public loans
공청회 public hearing
공칭자본금 capital stock registered
공탁 payment into court
공탁금지불금지명령; 지정가격주문 stop order
공탁물 deposited article
공탁법 deposit law

공탁소 deposit office
공탁자 depositor
공통계정 joint account
공통기금 common fund
공통기반 common background
공통기사; 틀에 박힌 문구 boilerplate
공통담보 common collateral
공통선신호방식 common signaling channel
공통요인리스크 common factor risk
공통원가 common cost
공판 trial at bar
공평성 fairness
공평하게 fairy and impartially
공평한 과세 impartial taxation
공평한 납세 equalization of tax payment
공평한 징수 equalization of tax collection
공하(空荷)운임 dead freight
공항관리자 배상책임보험 airport owner's or operator's liability insurance
공해(公海) high seas
공해방지준비금 pollution control reserve; reserve for prevention of
공해예방시설 pollution control facilities
공헌이익 contribution margin; contributory margin
공헌이익식 contribution margin form
공황 crisis
공황상장 near-panic market
공황시장 panic market
공황적인 매출 panic sale
과거근로채무의 상각액 amortization of prior service cost
과거근무가산 past service credits
과거근무급부 past service benefit
과거근무비용 prior service cost
과거근무연금 past service pension
과거근무채무 past service liability
과거실적 past performance
과거실적관리 past performance control
과거의 수요 backward needs
과거의 수치폭 historical trading range

과거의 실적 historical earnings

과당경쟁 excessive competition; overcompetition

과당투기 overspeculation

과대신고 exaggerated final return; overstatement of taxable income

과대자본 overcapitalization

과대평가 overestimate; overvaluation

과대평가한 선물 overvalued; overvalued futures

과대표시 overstatement

과대헤지 overhedge

과도기 transition period

과도적인 급부 transitional benefit

과도한 매매권유 churning

과도한 분식 overdressing

과목 subject

과목별 순변동액 net changes in each element

과반수소유종속회사 majority-owned subsidiary

과반수지배 majority control

과부족 excess and deficiency; overs and shorts

과부족계정 over and short account

과불의 overpaid

과세 imposition; levy; taxation

과세가격 dutiable value; tax value; taxable amount; taxable value; value of assessment

과세갱정결정 reassessment of taxes

과세견적가격 ratable value

과세공제비목 tax deductible items

과세구입 taxable purchases

과세권 right of taxation

과세권승계 succession of right of taxation

과세금 assessed tax

과세기간 taxable period

과세기준 tax base

과세단위 taxable unit; unit of taxation

과세대상 taxable item

과세대상유보금액 taxable undistributed profits

과세대장 tax roll

과세매상 taxable sales

과세문서 taxable document

과세물건 object of taxation

과세범위 scope of assessment

과세소득 assessable income; taxable income

과세액 tax amount

과세연기 deferment of taxation

과세요건 tax requisition

과세원부 assessment roll

과세유산 taxable estate

과세재산 taxable property

과세주체 sovereign of taxation

과세처분취소 reversal of taxation

과세총소득금액 total taxable income

과세최저한 lowest taxable limit; tax threshold

과세평가심사위원회 Board of Review

과세표준 base of taxation; tax basis

과세품 article subject to taxation; taxable goods

과세할 수 있는 taxable

과소고용 underemployment

과소고용균형 underemployment equilibrium

과소납부 underpayment

과소상각 underdepreciation

과소신고가산금 additional charge for deficient return

과소신고가산세 additional tax for deficient returns

과소유동성 under liquidity

과소자본 inadequate capital; thin capitalization; undercapitalization

과소투자 underinvestment

과소평가 underestimation; undervaluation

과소헤지 under hedge; underhedging

과실 culpa; fault; gross error; negligence

과실담보 malpractice coverage

과실상쇄 compensation culpae

과실을 범하다 culpable

과실책임 negligence liability

과열경제 overexuberant economy; overheated

economy
과열장세 feverish market
과오납금; 과납 overpayment
과오납금환부 refund of overpayment
과율산정기관불참가회사 nonboard company
과잉 surplusage
과잉, 여분 redundancy
과잉거래 excessive trading
과잉구매고 amount overbought
과잉달러 dollar overhung
과잉매입 overbuying
과잉매입상장 overbought market
과잉매입포시션 overbought position
과잉매출고 amount oversold
과잉불입 overtransfer
과잉설비; 과잉능력 excess capacity
과잉소비 excessive consumption
과잉소지비 overcarrying cost
과잉유동성 excess liquidity; excessive liquidity
과잉융자 excessive lending
과잉재고 overstock
과잉저축 excessive savings
과잉주 excessive stocks
과잉진입 over transfer
과잉추천 tout
과잉투자 overinvestment
과잉특권 overprivilege
과장 puffing
과장광고 brag and boast commercial;
    exaggerated advertisement
과점 oligopoly
과점가격 oligopoly price
과점경쟁 oligopolistic competition
과점경제 oligopolistic economy
과점산업 oligopoly industry
과점적인 상호의존 oligopolistic
    interdependence
과점지배 oligopolistic control
과제폐지 avoidance of sections
과징금 surtax
과학적인 관리 scientific management

과학적인 방법 scientific method
관계자 affiliate
관계회사 affiliated company; concerns
    interested; subsidiary corporation
관계회사사채 bond of affiliated company
관계회사외상금 receivable from affiliate
관계회사외상매출금 account receivable due
    from affiliated company
관계회사유가증권 securities of affiliated
    company
관계회사주식 stock of affiliated company
관계회사채권 indebtedness of affiliates
관계회사출자금 contributions to affiliated
    company; investment in affiliates
관광세 sight-seeing tax
관광수입 tourist income
관념상의 소득 notional income
관련리스크 relevant risk
관련모델 relationship models
관련사업 related businesses
관련산업 correlative industry
관련상표 related issue
관련상품판매 related-item sales
관련성 relevancy
관련성이 없는 irrelevant
관련원가 related cost
관련재 related goods
관료주의 red tape
관리가격 administered price; managed price
관리가격인플레이션 administered-price
    inflation
관리가능원가 controllable expenses
관리감사 administrative audit
관리계층 management hierarchy
관리기구 control mechanism
관리기능강화 strengthening of managerial
    function
관리능력 management capacity
관리무역 managed trade
관리방식 피라미드형 관리방식 pyramid
    management method

관리불능비 uncontrollable expenses
관리불능원가 noncontrollable cost
관리비 maintenance fee
관리상의 불확실성 administrative uncertainty
관리수단 management tool
관리영역 management area
관리요소 element of control
관리원칙 management principles
관리자 management
관리자그리드 management grid
관리적합 administrative fit
관리절차 control procedure
관리직능 management function
관리채무 managed liabilities
관리책임; 재물관리 care and custody
관리통화 controlled currency; managed currency
관리통화제도 managed currency system
관리플로트 managed floating rate system
관리한계 control limit; span of control
관리회계 administrative accounting; management accounting
관리효과 management effect
관문 resistance level
관보 gazette
관선수익관리인 official receiver
관세 customs duty tariff; tariff
관세가 사중손실됨 dead weight loss of customs duty
관세교섭 tariff negotiations
관세동맹 customs union
관세면제품 article on the free list
관세사정 liquidation of duties
관세서 cocket
관세양허표 schedule of concessions
관세율 tariff rate
관세율표 customs tariff table
관세자주권 customs autonomy; tariff autonomy
관세장벽 tariff barrier
관세전략 tariff war
관세조화화 tariff harmonization

관세평가금지 withholding of customs appraisement
관세할당 tariff quota
관세할당제도 tariff quota system
관세화 taritfication
관세환부제도 customs duty refund system
관세환불 drawback
관습 consuetude; usage
관습가설 habit persistence hypothesis
관습법 common law; custom
관습법신탁 common-law trust
관습법주식회사 common-law corporation
관습상의 보유 customary tenure
관습상의 보유권 customary tenure estates
관여 involvement
관영수입 revenue from government enterprise
관용 covenance
관이벤트 crown event
관재인 administrator
관제등본 office copy
관찰결과; 입회 observation
관찰치 observed value
관청부기 government bookkeeping; municipal accounting
관청회계 government accounting
관할 jurisdiction
관할구 districts
관할세무서 competent taxation office
관할이전 change of venue
관할차이 jurisdictional defect
관행 customary practice; habit
광고 advertisement
광고결정 advertising decision
광고규제 advertising regulation
광고기술 advertising technology
광고기회 advertising opportunity
광고기획자 account executive
광고노출 advertisement exposure
광고대리점 advertisement agency
광고대리점망 advertising network; agency network

광고매체 advertisement media; advertising media

광고메시지 advertising message

광고목표 advertising objectives

광고비 advertising expenses; outlay for advertisement

광고비비율 advertising sales ratio

광고비판 advertising criticism

광고사회 advertising society

광고선전비 advertising and general publicity expenses

광고선전용 자산 property for advertisement

광고세 advertisement tax

광고소구 advertising appeals

광고소스 advertisement source

광고심리학 advertising psychology

광고예산 advertising appropriation

광고예산편성 advertising budgeting

광고원고 advertising copy

광고의 환상 advertising fantasy

광고전략 advertising strategy

광고전략가 account planner

광고조사 advertising research

광고주제 advertisement theme; advertising theme

광고지원금 advertising allowance

광고집단 advertising group

광고쪽지 flyer

광고쪽지; 등귀 flier

광고차별화 advertising differentiation

광고캠페인 advertising campaign

광고탄력성 elasticity of advertising

광고평가 advertising evaluation

광고표시가격 advertised price

광고활동을 통합함 advertisement mix

광고회사의 총매상 gross billing

광고효과 advertising effect

광고효과테스트 advertising testing

광공업생산지수 industrial production index

광구사용료 mining royalty

광범위한 시장지표 broad market index

광산 mine

광산세 mineral product tax

광솔린톤통신 solution optical communication

광업권 mineral properties mining right; mining license

광업권취득 mining location

광업세 mining tax

광업임차권 mining lease

광업자산 mining property

광업조합 mining partnership

광업회계 mining accounting

광역물류센터 wide area distribution center

광열비 fuel and light prices; light and fuel expenses

광원모델 lighting model

광자기디스크 magnet optical disk

광전도체디바이스 photoconductor device

광컴퓨팅 optical computing

광케이블 optical fiber cable

광학적인 문자인식 optical character recognition

괴리 divergence

괴리지표 divergence indicator

괴리한도 divergence threshold; threshold of divergence

교감적인 언어사용 phatic communication

교란적인 자본이동 disequilibrating capital flows

교묘하게 회피함 end run

교부공채 government compensation bond; public compensation bond

교부국채 delivery bond; delivery of government bond

교부금 bounty

교부요구 request for share distribution

교사 solicitation

교섭력 bargaining power

교섭하다 treating

교섭효과 negotiation effect

교양비 expenses for education and culture

교역조건 terms of trade

교외인구 suburban population
교외점포 suburban store
교외지 suburban paper
교육론 loan for education
교육비 education expense
교육수준 educational level
교정쇄 galley proof
교제비 entertainment and social expenses; social expenses
교제비공제 deduction of entertainment expenses
교차비율 ratio of gross profit to inventory investment
교차신청 cross offer
교차책임주의 cross liabilities basis; principle of cross liabilities
교차탄력성 cross elasticity
교차통화금리스와프 cross-currency interest rate swap
교체 alternation; replacement; replacing
교체가격 replacement price
교체가치 replacement value
교체근무제도 shift system
교체단위 replacement unit
교체비용 replacement expense
교체원가 replacement cost
교체원가회사 replacement cost accounting
교체자산 replacement assets
교통광고 transit advertising
교통비 local transport expenses
교통사고상해보험 traffic personal accident insurance
교환 access; permutation
교환가능통화 hard currency
교환공문 exchange of notes
교환대차 loan for exchange
교환방정식 equation of exchange
교환비율 convertible ratio
교환성정지 suspension of convertibility
교환용 자산 property for exchange
교환잔고표 clearing-house balance

교환재보험 reciprocal reinsurance
교환재보험; 상호주의 reciprocity
교환재보험특약 reciprocal treaty
교환차금 difference from exchange of property
교환차익 gains from exchange of properties
교환처분 involuntary exchange
교환효율 exchange efficiency
구관세 antique customa
구관습세 antique customs
구금 imprisonment
구내교환기 private branch exchange
구내담보 premises coverage
구도 structural outline
구두개입(상승) talk up
구두개입(하락) talk down
구두계약 parol contract
구두변론일 paper days
구두의 verbal
구두증언 oral testimony
구두허가 parol license
구르다 rolling-over
구매 purchase
구매단위 purchasing units
구매대전도금 advance for purchase
구매력 buying power
구매력리스크 purchasing power risk
구매력변동손익 purchasing power gain or loss
구매력지수 buying power index
구매력침식 erosion in purchasing power
구매력평가설 purchasing power parity theory
구매부장 purchasing manager
구매빈도 purchase frequency
구매습관 buying habit
구매신청 buying offer
구매심리학 buying psychology
구매오퍼레이션 buying operation
구매자 bargainee
구매자세분화 buyer segmentation

구매자차관 buyer's guide
구매자행동 buyer behavior
구매장 buying opportunity
구매정보 buying information
구매행동 purchase behavior
구멍을 뚫다 score a deficit
구법률 antiqua statuta
구분소유권 sectional ownership
구분손익계산서 multiple-step income
  statement; sectional income statement
구분식 multiple step
구분식 시산표 classified trial balance
구분지상권 sectional surface rights
구빈법 poor laws
구상 claim for compensation
구상권 guarantor's right of indemnity;
  recourse; right of demanding compensation;
  right of indemnity; surety obligation
구상기간 claim period
구상무역 compensating trade or transactions;
  compensation trade
구상액 amount of claim
구상은행 claiming bank
구상통지 notification of claim
구성 make-up
구성관리 configuration management
구성부분 building block
구성비 component ratio; percent distribution
구성비율 component percentages; distribution
  ratio; percentage analysis
구성비율분석 component analysis
구속력이 있는 binding
구속부 협정 tying arrangement
구속잔고 compensating balance
구속조항 binding clause
구심적인 시장 centripetal market
구역외의 extramural
구외담보 outside premises coverage
구은행법 old bank act
구입가격 buying price; cost price; intake
  value

구입가할인 purchase allowance
구입검사 receiving inspection
구입고 purchase amount
구입과정 buying process
구입기간 buying period
구입기준 buying criteria
구입능력 buying ability
구입단가 purchasing price
구입대금 purchase money; purchase price
구입대리점 buying agent
구입반려 rebate on business
구입반품 purchase return
구입비용 purchasing expenses
구입상환 purchasing redemption
구입선변경코스트 switching cost
구입선불대금 advance on account of sellers
구입세 purchase tax
구입수수료 purchase commission
구입실패 buying error
구입약정 purchase commitments
구입에너지 buying energy
구입예산 purchases budget
구입운임 freight inward; freight-in
구입원가 buying cost; cost of goods
  purchased; first cost; prime cost; purchase
  cost; purchasing cost
구입의사 intention to purchase
구입자 vendee
구입장 purchase book
구입장본인 leader of long side
구입전불대금 deposits paid to trade creditors
구입절차 buying procedure
구입조건 buying terms
구입주문 buying order
구입지원 buying support
구입처 merchandise resources; trade creditor
구입처분석 vendor analysis
구입처원장 creditors ledger; purchase ledger
구입총액 gross purchase
구입측 buying side
구입캘린더 buying calendar

구입할인 purchase discount
구입환불 purchases rebate
구제 redress
구제명령 order for relief
구제방법 remedy
구제의 상호성 mutuality of remedy
구제조치 bailout
구제합병 relief merger
구제합병방식 assisted acquisition
구조거래 structured transaction
구조기능분석 structural-functional analysis
구조방정식 structural equation
구조변화 structural change
구조분석 structural analysis
구조비용 salvage charges
구조상의 탄력성 structural flexibility
구조요인 structural determinant
구조인자 structural factor
구조적인 structural
구조적인 실업 structural unemployment
구조적인 인플레이션 structural inflation
구조조정융자 structural adjustment facility
구조협의 structural impediments initiative talks
구주 old share
구축물 structure
국(局) bureau
국가 nation
국가보상 state indemnification
국가신용 national credit
국가신용도 country risk
국가예산누적적자 cumulative fiscal deficit
국가의 최고법규 supreme law of the land
국가의 행위 act of state
국가인정 national certification
국가자본 state capital
국가자본주의 state capitalism
국가재정 national finance; public finance
국가채무 national debt
국가파산 state bankruptcy
국경세 frontier tax

국경세조정 border tax adjustment
국경없는 경제 borderless economy
국경인도 delivered at frontier
국경인도가격 delivered at frontier price
국고 fisc; national treasury
국고 대 민간수지 government fund transactions with the public
국고금송금 treasury fund remittance
국고보조금 national subsidy
국고수지 government fund transactions
국고여유금 treasury surplus
국고재무대리인 fiscal agent for treasury fund
국내국채 government bonds in domestic currency
국내균형 domestic equilibrium
국내기관투자가 domestic institutional investor
국내론방식 domestic loan system
국내법상 unilateral
국내사업 domestic operations
국내생산 home production
국내어음 inland bill
국내원천 domestic source
국내원천소득 domestic source income; income accrued from domestic sources
국내위성통신 domestic satellite communication
국내지출 domestic expenditure
국내지향 ethnocentrism
국내총생산 gross domestic product
국내총자본형성 gross domestic capital formation
국내투자 domestic investment
국무장관 Secretary of State
국민건강보험법 National Health Insurance Law
국민건강보험세 national health insurance tax
국민경제재산 national economic accounting
국민금융공고 People's Finance Corporation
국민대차대조표 national balance sheet
국민보험환자 panel patient
국민복지지표 net national welfare

국민사망표 population mortality
국민생활지표 new social indicators
국민소득 national income
국민소득계정 national income accounts
국민소득분석 national income analysis
국민소득순환 circulation of national income
국민소득통계 national income statistics; statistics on national income
국민소득회계 national income accounting
국민순생산 net national product
국민연금 national pension
국민은행 national bank
국민자본 national capital
국민자본계정 national capital account
국민자본표 national capital sheet
국민총생산 gross national product
국민총자산 gross national wealth
국민총지출 gross national expenditure
국별한도 country limit
국부(國富) national wealth
국부통계 national wealth statistics
국산품 domestic goods
국선변호인 assigned counsel
국세 national tax
국세 및 지방세 taxes and rates
국세부가세 surtax on national tax
국세사찰관 investigator
국세수납관리 official to receive national tax
국세심사관 tax tribunal examiner
국세심판관 appeals
국세조사관 examiner
국세채권우선의 원칙 principle of priority of national tax claim
국세채무승계 succession of national tax liability
국세청 regional taxation bureau
국세청감찰관 personnel inspector
국세통칙법 national tax procedure law
국세환부가산액 additional amount to a refund of national tax
국영보험 state insurance

국영사업 state enterprises
국영재보험 nationalized reinsurance
국외근무자 persons in overseas service
국유재산 national property
국유화 nationalization
국적부여 denization
국정세율 national tariff
국제개발부흥은행협정 Agreement of the International Bank for Reconstruction and Development
국제개발협회 International Development Association
국제거래통화 international transaction currency
국제결제 international settlement
국제결제기관 International Securities Clearing Corporation
국제결제은행 Bank for International Settlements
국제결제통화 international settlement currency
국제경영자단체연맹 International Organization of Employers
국제경쟁 foreign competition
국제경제학 international economics
국제경제협력은행 international bank for economic cooperation
국제경제협력회의 Conference on International Economic Cooperation
국제공법 international public law
국제공통기호 universal notation
국제관계 international relations
국제관리통화제도 international managed currency system
국제관습법 international custom
국제금융 international finance
국제금융거래소 international monetary exchanges
국제금융공사 International Finance Corporation
국제금융기관 international financial

institution

국제금융시장 international financial market; international money market

국제금융제도 international financial system

국제기관사채 supranational bond

국제기관채권 bond of international agency; international agency bond

국제기업회계 international accounting

국제기준 international recognized standard

국제노동기관 International Labor Organization

국제노멀포트폴리오 international normals

국제농업개발기금 International Fund for Agricultural Development

국제단기금융시장 international short-term money market

국제단기부동자금; 핫머니 hot money

국제단기자본거래 international short-term capital transaction

국제단위 international unit

국제대차 balance of international indebtedness; international indebtedness

국제대차설 theory of international indebtedness

국제리스 international lease

국제마케팅 international marketing

국제무역위원회 International Trade Commission

국제민간항공기관 International Civil Aviation Organization

국제민간항공조약 Convention on International Civil Aviation

국제법 international law; law of nations

국제법협회 International Law Association

국제복합운송조약 Convention on International Combined Transport

국제분산투자 international diversified investment; international portfolio diversification

국제분업 international division of labor

국제브로킹 international broking

국제비교 international comparison

국제사면위원회 Amnesty International

국제사법 private international law

국제사법재판소 International Court of Justice

국제사회보장협회 International Social Security Association

국제상공회의소 International Chamber of Commerce

국제상품 international merchandise

국제상품협정 international commodity agreement

국제소비자기구 International Organization of Consumer's Unions

국제수지 balance of international payments; international balance of payment

국제수지조정과정 adjustment process of balance of payments

국제수지탄력성 elasticity of the balance of payments

국제수지통계 balance of payments statistics; statistics on international balance of payment

국제수지흑자 favorable balance of payments

국제수출신용보험기구 International Union of Credit and Investment Insurers

국제스왑딜러협회 International Swap Dealers Association

국제시장 international market

국제시장가격 international market price; world market price

국제시장조사 international marketing research

국제신디케이트 international syndicate

국제액추어리협회 International Congress of Actuaries

국제에너지기관 International Energy Agency

국제연합경제개발국 United Nations Economic Development Administration

국제연합경제사회이사회 Economic and Social Council of the United Nations

국제연합무역개발회의 United Nations Conference on Trade and Development

국제연합아프리카경제위원회 Economic Commission for Africa

국제연합자본개발기금 United Nations Capital Development Fund

국제예탁증서 International Depositary Receipts

국제올림픽위원회 International Olympic Committee

국제원자력기관 International Atomic Energy Agency

국제유동성 international liquidity

국제유통 international distribution

국제은행업무 international banking facility; international banking operation

국제이중과세 international double taxation

국제인수단 international consortium; international underwriting group

국제자금 international fund

국제자금이동 international movements of funds

국제자본 international capital

국제자본이동 international capital market; international capital movement

국제자산운용 international asset management

국제자원은행 International Resources Bank

국제자유노동조합연합 International Confederation of Free Trade

국제장기자본이동 international long-termcapital movement

국제저널리스트 International Organization of Journalists

국제적십자 International Red Cross

국제적으로 위험을 분산시킴 international spread of risk

국제적인 금융관리 international money management

국제전기통신연합 International Telecommunication Union

국제조세법 international tax law

국제주권 international stock

국제증권 international securities

국제증권거래소연합 International Federation of Stock Exchanges

국제증권거래위원회기구 International Organization of Securities Commissions

국제카르텔 international cartel

국제통화 international currency

국제통화기금 International Monetary Fund

국제통화기금협정 Agreement of the International Monetary Fund

국제통화불안 international monetary turmoil

국제통화제도 international currency system

국제투자 international investment

국제투자신탁 international investment trust

국제투자은행 international bank for investment; international investment bank

국제평화국 International Peace Bureau

국제표준화기구 International Standardization Organization

국제항공보험연합 International Union Aviation Insurers

국제항공운송협회 International Air Transport Association

국제해사기관 International Maritime Organization

국제해사위성통신기구 International Marine Satellite Telecommunication Organization

국제해상보험연합 International Union of Marine Insurance

국제해운회의소 International Chamber of Shipping

국제형사경찰기구 International Criminal Police Organization

국제화 internationalization; international exchange

국제환경 foreign environment

국제회계기준 international accounting standards

국제회계기준위원회 International Accounting Standards Committee

국채 government bond

국채대용증서 substitute certificate for

government bond
국채대체결제제도 government bond book-entry system
국채등록부 register of government bonds
국채모집인수단컨소시엄 consortium
국채선물시장 national bond futures market
국채의 화폐화 monetization of government bonds
국채이자 interest on government securities
국채인수 underwriting of government securities
국채입찰 treasury auction
국회 parliament
국회제정법 act of parliament
군사법원 military jurisdiction courts
군정 military government
군중; 대중; 동아리 crowd
굳히다; 경화하다 harden
굴신(屈伸)제한제도 elastic limit system
굴절수요곡선 kinked demand curve
권고요율 advisory rates
권력구조 power structure
권리 rights
권리구제제도 remedy for violation of private right
권리금 foregift; keymoney
권리금; 보험료 premium
권리담보자 common vouchee
권리담보조항 covenant of seisin
권리락; 신주락으로(의) ex-new
권리를 박탈하다 forejudge
권리를 부여하다 entitle
권리를 손상치 않고 without prejudice
권리를 주다 vest
권리반환권 right of redemption
권리방기 abandonment of right; surrender; waiver
권리방기조항 waiver clause
권리부 rights on; with warrants
권리비방 slander of title
권리상실소장 bill for foreclosure

권리서 abstract of title
권리서기탁 deposit of title-deeds
권리수록 acquisition of right
권리이전증 letter of subrogation
권리자확인 interpleader
권리장전 bill of rights
권리정지 suspension of right
권리증 muniments; registration certificate
권리증권 document of title
권리증서 deed of title
권리청원 petition of right
권리침해 infringement; violation
권리하락 rights off
권리행사 exercise
권리행사가 인정된 거래량 exercise limit
권리행사가격 strike price
권리확보 entitlement
권리확정주의 principle of ascertained claim
권리훼손; 편견 prejudice
권면; 디노미네이션 denomination
권원 title deeds
권원(權原)구입 buying title
권원담보문서 dedi et concessi
권원보험; 소유권보증 title insurance company
권원의 기초 root of title
권원합동 unity of title
권원회복 remitter
권유 solicit
권유모집 soliciting
권유장을 내어 판매함 follow-up selling
권유텔렉스 invitation telex
권장재판매가격 suggested resale price
권장주, 추천주 stock recommended for purchase
권한 authority; power
권한내에서 intra vires
권한담보조항 covenant for title
권한범위 ambit; scope of authority
권한부여 delegation
권한수용설 acceptance theory

권한위임 delegation of authority
권한을 수여하다 authorize
권한이 없는 de son tort
권한이 없는 임원집행자 executor be son tort
권한이 있는 당국 competent authority
귀납적인 통계 inductive statistics
귀납적인 통계모델 inductive statistical model
귀무가설, 영가설 null hypothesis
귀속가격 imputed price
귀속가치 imputed value
귀속소득 imputed income
귀속시키는 impute
귀속원가; 부가원가 imputed cost
귀속이론 traceable theory
귀속이자 imputed interest
귀속주의 attributable income principle
귀책과실 imputed negligence
귀화 naturalization
규격매매 sale by grade or type
규격외허가 deviation permit
규모의 경제성 economies of scale
규모의 불경제성 diseconomies of scale
규모의 이익 scale merit
규범; 패러다임 paradigm
규범론 normative theory
규범사례 base case
규범적인 영향 normative influence
규제금리 regulated interest rate
규제완화 deregulation
규제조치 regulatory measure
규제투자회사 regulated investment company
규준화 normalization
규칙 regulation; rule
균등가중평균 equal-weighted average
균등평준연차배당 equivalent level annual
　　dividend
균등할과세 taxation on a per capita basis
균등할세율 per capita levy
균분 equally divided
균일가격설정 group marketing
균일가격점 five-and-dime store

균일수수료 flat commission
균일요율; 균일레이트 flat rate
균일의; 배당락의 flat
균일이자배당 flat yield
균일환예약 flat exchange contract
균형 match making
균형가격 equilibrium price
균형경제학 equilibrium economies
균형성장 balanced growth
균형세력 balanced power
균형예산 balanced budget
균형예산정리 balanced budget theorem
균형이자율 equilibrium rate of interest
균형재고 balanced stock
균형재정 balanced finance
균형환상장 equilibrium rate of exchange
그 자체 in return; in se
그 자체로 무효 per se illegal
그 중에서도 inter alia
그 지방에 대한 재투자 community
　　reinvestment
그 집의 상인인; 호주상속 family estate
그것에 의해 per quod
그라비아인쇄 gravure printing
그래픽액셀러레이터 graphic accelerator
그래픽을 통한 사용자 중심의 인터페이스
　　graphical user interface GUI
그랜트엘리먼트 grant element
그레샴의 법칙 Gresham's law
그레이터풀이론 greater fool theory
그로스거래고 gross trading volume
그로스레이팅포인트; **GRP** gross rating point
그로스업방식 gross up method
그로스펀드포지션 gross fund position
그룹과세 consolidated tax return system
그룹웨어 groupware
그리드 grid
그린마케팅 green marketing
그린메일 green mail
그린슈조항 green shoe clause
그린카드제도 green card system

그린필드 green field
그물 net
근거있는 조항 grounding clause
근담보 revolving collateral
근대효용이론 modern utility theory
근로소득공제 earned income allowance
근로소득세 earned income tax
근로학생 working student
근로학생공제 allowance for working student;
  deduction for working student; exemption
  for working student; working student
  allowance
근린궁지화 정책 beggar-my-neighbor policy
근보증 revolving guarantee
근본원인 root cause
근사치이론 theory of approximation
근속수당 long service allowance
근시안적인 사고방식 myopia
근인주의 cause proximate
근저당 fixed collateral; flexible mortgage;
  maximal collateral
근저당권 fixed mortgage
근접의 adjoining
근접학 proxemics
근친자 next to kin
글로벌노트퍼실리티 global note facilities
글로벌마케팅 global marketing
글로벌무기명예탁증서 global bearer
  certificate
글로벌본드 global bond
글로벌체스 global chess
글로벌트레이딩 global trading
글로벌포트폴리오 global portfolio
금구입와런트 gold purchase warrant
금기준치결정 gold fixing
금리 interest rate; money rate
금리가 낮으리라 예상함 view of lowering
  interest rate
금리감응도 interest rate sensitivity
금리감응부채 rate sensitive liability
금리감응자산 rate sensitive assets

금리감응항목 interest rate sensitive items
금리감응형 상품 interest sensitive products
금리갱신일 reset date; rollover date
금리결정; 가격결정 pricing
금리구조 structure of interest rates
금리동향 interest rate movement
금리리스크 interest rate risk
금리마인드 interest rate minded
금리마진 interest rate spread
금리민감주 interest rate sensitive stock
금리변동 interest rate fluctuation
금리부담율 interest coverage ratio
금리비감응부채 nonrate-sensitive liability
금리비감응항목 noninterest-sensitive item
금리선도거래 forward rate agreement
금리선물 interest futures; interest rate futures
금리선물계약 interest rate futures contracts
금리선물옵션거래 interest rate futures option
  trading
금리선호 preference for interest rate
금리세금공제전 이익 earnings before interest
  and taxes
금리수준 level of interest rate
금리스와프 interest rate swap; interest swap
금리스와프채 interest swap bond
금리옵션 interest rate option
금리옵션거래 interest option transaction
금리인상 raising of interest rate
금리인하 lowering of interest rate
금리자유화 liberalization of interest rate
금리재정 interest arbitrage; interest rate
  arbitrage
금리재정거래 interest rate arbitrage
  transaction
금리정책 interest rate policy
금리조작 interest rate control
금리조항 rate covenant
금리차 interest differential; interest rate
  differential; interest spread
금리칼라 interest rate collar
금리캡거래 interest cap trading

금리평가 interest parity
금리평행이동 parallel rate shift
금리평형세 interest equalization tax
금리플로어 interest rate floor
금리하락 falling interest rate
금반언(禁反言) estoppel
금보유고 gold holdings
금본위제 gold standard
금본위제도붕괴 fall of gold standard
금불태화정책 gold sterilization policy
금선물계약 gold bullion futures contract
금선물옵션 gold futures option
금속평판 metalized lithography
금수출해금 lifting of gold embargo
금액가중수익율 dollar-weighted return
금약관 gold clause
금언 gnome
금외신탁 nonmoney trust
금융 finance
금융가 street
금융거래 financial transaction
금융계정 balance of monetary movements; cash account; financial accounts
금융공황 financial crisis; financial panic
금융규제 bear-squeeze; financial regulation
금융기관 banking facilities; financial institution
금융기관대부금 loan to financial institutions
금융기관예금 deposit at financial institutions
금융기관의 알선 good offices of banking facilities
금융긴박 financial strain and stress
금융긴축 credit squeeze; monetary tightening
금융긴축이 침투함 permeation of tight money policy
금융긴축정책 monetary restraint policy; restrictive monetary policy; tight money policy
금융난 financial difficulty
금융리스 financial lease
금융면의 결단 financial decision

금융모델 financial model
금융보증보험회사 Financial Guaranty Insurance Company
금융부담 financing burden
금융부채 financial liability
금융붕괴 financial collapse
금융비용 finance charge; financial charges; financial expenses; financing charge
금융상의 역선택 adverse financial selection
금융상품 financial instrument; financial product
금융서비스 financial facilities; financial service
금융선도계약 financial forward contract
금융선물 financial futures
금융선물거래 financial futures transaction
금융선물계약 financial futures contract
금융선물상품 financial futures instrument
금융선물시장 financial futures market
금융선물옵션 financial futures option
금융수단 financing vehicle
금융수익 financial profit
금융시장 financial market
금융시장개방 open-up of money market
금융시장데이터 money market data
금융시장분석 financial market analysis
금융시장에 대한 개입 money market intervention
금융시장정세지표 money market conditions index
금융시장증권 money market securities
금융어음 finance paper; financing bill
금융업 financial operations
금융업자 money lender
금융연구소 financial research center
금융옵션 financial option contract
금융옵션시장 financial option market
금융완만 slackness of money market
금융완화 monetary ease
금융완화정책 monetary policy for easing; relaxation of tight money policy

금융완화조치 measure for monetary ease
금융원조 financial aid
금융자본 finance capital; financial capital
금융자본시장자유화 deregulation of financial and capital market
금융자산 financial assets; monetary assets
금융자산부채잔고표 financial assets and liabilities account
금융자산선호 preference of financial assets
금융자유화 financial liberalization
금융자유화정책 financial liberalization policy
금융자회사 captive finance company
금융정책 financial policy; monetary policy
금융정책에 변경이 없는 상태 even keel
금융제도 financial system
금융조절 money market management
금융조합 loan association; loan society
금융주 financial sector stocks
금융중개기관 financial intermediaries or brokers; intennediating financial institution
금융중심지 financial center
금융채 bank debenture
금융채권 financial claim
금융채무 financial obligation
금융크로스 crossing for the purpose of financing
금융통계 financial statistics
금융항목 financial item
금융혁명 financial revolution; financial innovation
금융협정 financial agreement
금융확대 monetary expansion; monetary growth
금융환경 financial environment
금융활동 financial activities
금융회사 finance company; financing corporation
금은복본위제도 gold and silver bimetallism
금의 현송점 specie points
금전거래 pecuniary transaction
금전대부업 money lending business; money-lending business
금전대차계약 loan agreement
금전법안 money bill
금전상납 tax payment in money
금전상의 관계 pecuniary relation
금전상의 손실 financial damages
금전신탁 money trust
금전신탁이익 income from trust deposits
금전업자 money broker
금전유가증권종합보험증권 money and securities broad form
금전유증 pecuniary legacy
금전의 인환권 exchange check for money
금전적인 보수 pecuniary considerations
금전적인 손해 pecuniary damage
금전적인 평가 quantum evaluation
금전채권 money claim
금전채권의 초과상태 positive marketing
금전채무 monetary liabilities
금전채무상태 negative monetary position
금전채무인증서 due bill
금전청구 money demand
금전판결 money judgment
금전항목 monetary items
금지금본위제 gold bullion standard
금지명령 prohibitory injunction; restraining order
금지법 negative statute
금지세 prohibitive tax
금채권 gold bond
금치산(禁治産) interdiction; incompetency
금치산자 person adjudged incompetent
금태환 conversion to gold
금평가 gold parity
금폐화(金廢貨) demonetization of gold
금풀 gold pool
금현송점(金現送點) gold points
금화본위제 gold coin standard
금환본위제 gold exchange standard
금환준비 gold exchange reserve
급격한 시세변동을 막음 support buying;

support operation

급등 high rise; sharp increase; sharp rise; soar

급등매출 selling on spurt

급등상장 sharp advance market

급등한 가격 revived quotation

급락 sharp fall

급락상장 sharp decline market

급료 net pay; salaries

급료; 임금지불장 payroll

급료감사 pay roll audit

급료공제 wage assignment

급료선불 advance of salary

급료적립생명보험 payroll savings life insurance

급반락 sharp setback

급별생산물생산 class-product production

급부 benefit

급상승 skyrocketing

급상승가격 skyrocketing price

급상승상장 buoyant market

급속채널이동 zapping

급송료 dispatch money

급여공제형 투신 payroll deduction type investment trust

급여기준 basis on the amount of salary

급여소득 employment income

급여소득공제 deduction for employment income; employment income deduction; employment income exemption

급여소득자 employment income earner; obtainer of employment income; person receiving employment income

급여지수 salary scale

급증 considerable rise; rapid expansion; spurt

급파하다; 급파 dispatch

긍정적인 affirmative

긍정적인 레버리지효과 positive leverage effect

긍정적인 약인 affirmative covenants

긍정적인 이율곡선 positive yield curve

긍정적인 증익효과 favorable leverage effect

긍정표시 affirmative charge

기가바이트 giga byte

기각 rejection

기간; 조건 term

기간계산 periodical accounting

기간구조 term structure

기간내의 세금배분 intraperiod tax allocation

기간내의 소득과세배분 intraperiod income tax

기간리스크 term risk

기간만료 effluxion of time; termination

기간보험 time policy

기간분석 period analysis

기간비용 period charge; period expense

기간산업 key industry

기간세 fundamental tax

기간원가 period cost

기간이 정해지지 않은 고용계약 employment

기간이익 periodic income

기간일치 matched maturities

기간제한 time limitation

기간지표 current coupon

기간차이 timing differences

기간차입금리 term financing rate

기간효과 extension effect

기계 machinery

기계공구 machine tool

기계보험 machinery insurance

기계부기 machine bookkeeping

기계시간율 machine-hour rate

기계시간율배부법 machine-hour rate method

기계운전시작업 in-cycle work

기계장치 machinery and equipment

기계장치기록방식 mechanical recorder method

기계화거래 mechanical trading

기계화방식 mechanization method

기계화회계 mechanized accounting

기계효율 mechanical efficiency

기계휴지시작업 out-cycle work

기관; 제도 institution

기관구매 equity purchases by institutions

기관구입 buying by institutional investors

기관매입 institutional buying; institutional stock purchase

기관매출 institutional selling

기관중재 institutional arbitration

기관지 organ

기관차 이론 locomotive theory

기관투자가 institutional investors

기관투자가간 시장 fourth market

기관투자가지수옵션 institutional investors' index option

기구 mechanism

기국법; 선적국법 law of ship's flag

기근물거래 transaction of near delivery

기금 endowments

기금; 자금; 펀드 fund

기금이자 interest on guaranty cap

기기 apparatus; machinery and tool

기념배당 commemorative dividend; memorial dividend

기능 function

기능검정 skill measurement

기능별 계산서 functional statement

기능별 조직 functional organization

기능별 회계 functional accounting

기능분석 functional analysis

기능적산법 functional pricing

기능적인 감가 functional depreciation

기능적인 어프로치 functional approach

기능적인 전문화 functional specialization

기능적인 효과 functional effect

기능통화법 functional currency method

기대가설 expectation hypothesis

기대갭 expectation gap

기대만기이율 expected yield-to-maturity

기대만족 expected satisfaction

기대보유기간수익률 expected holding-period rate of return; projected holding period rate of return

기대불일치효과 disconfirmation of expectations

기대상속인 expectant heir

기대수요 expected demand

기대수익 expected earnings

기대에서 벗어난 증권 investment skeleton

기대이론 expectancy theory; expectation theory

기대이윤 expected profit

기대이익 prospective profit

기대이익성장률 expected earnings growth rate

기대총수익률 expected total rate of return

기대치 expected value

기대치이론 expected value theory

기대탄력성 elasticity of expectations

기득권 acquired right; vested interests

기득권을 범하지 않고 without prejudice to preliminary

기득권조항 grandfather provision

기득이익 vested benefit

기록 anagraph

기록결손주장 alleging diminution

기록관 recorder

기록미제출 failing of record

기록사항 matter of record

기록유지 record retention

기말 term-end

기말감사 completed audit; final audit

기말결산 term-end settlement of accounts

기말계정 term-end account

기말대차대조표 periodic balance sheet

기말배당 year-end dividend

기말시산표 periodic trial balance

기말잔고 closing balance; ending balance

기말잔고; 최종잔고 final balance

기말재고 year end stock; closing inventories

기말정리 adjustment at term-end

기말지불생명연금 life annuity payable in arrears

기명날인 signature and seal

기명비소유자보험 named nonowner policy

기명사채; 등록채 registered bond

기명식 registered form
기명식 보증증권 named schedule bond
기명식 선하증권 straight bill of lading
기명식 수표 signed check
기명식 이서 special endorsement; special indorsement
기명식 증권 registered securities
기명양도 signed transfer
기명어음 named bill
기명주 name share
기명주권 inscribed stock certificate
기명주식 registered stock
기명채권 inscribed bond
기명피보험자 named insured
기밀비 secret service expenses
기밀성 confidentiality
기발채이익 yield on already issued bond
기본계획 master plan
기본권리 fundamental rights
기본규제 fundamental rules
기본급 base pay; basic salary; regular wage
기본기간 basic period
기본단위 elementary unit
기본방침 statement of principles
기본보험금액 principal sum
기본서비스 basic service
기본요건구성 basic assortment
기본정관 charter; memorandum of association
기본증거금 initial margin
기본통달 primary regulation notice
기부금 손금산입한도액 deduction limit applicable to donation
기부금공제 contribution deduction; deduction for contributions; deduction for donation
기부금의 손금산입한도액 deductible amount for donation
기부단가 opening quotation

기산일(起算日) initial date in reckoning; value date
기소 indictment

기소결정기관 accusatory body
기소부분 accusatory part
기소서류 accusatory instrument
기소자 accuser
기소할 수 있는 과실 actionable negligence
기술격차 technological gap
기술관료 technocrat
기술데이터 descriptive data
기술분석용 그래프 technical graph
기술분석지표 technical indicator
기술시방서 technical specification
기술예측 technological forecasting
기술의 질 technical quality
기술이론 technical theory
기술이전 technology transfer
기술이전계약 technology transfer agreement
기술적인 반등 technical rally
기술적인 반응 technical reaction
기술적인 분석 technical analysis
기술적인 예측 technical forecast
기술제휴 technical cooperation
기술지원 technical assistance
기술지표 technical index
기술진보 technical progress; technological changes
기술진보율 rate of technical progress
기술해외거래 overseas transactions for technique
기술혁신 technical innovation
기시불연금 annuity certain due
기어링비율 gearing ratio
기어링효과 gearing effect
기어전동장치; 기어링 gearing
기억 memory
기업 business concern
기업가정신 entrepreneurship
기업가지향 entrepreneurial orientation
기업간 신용 credit among corporations
기업간분석 interfirm analysis
기업간신용 inter-enterprise credit; mercantile credit

기업거래 business transaction
기업결합 business combinations
기업결합회계 accounting for business combinations
기업경영 corporate management
기업경제 enterprise economy
기업과세 taxation on enterprise
기업광고 institutional advertisement
기업구조 business structure
기업금융 business finance; corporate banking; corporation finance
기업내 고속정보통신망 local area network
기업내 교육 in-house training
기업내 분석 intrafirm analysis
기업농업 agribusiness
기업담보권 enterprise mortgage
기업도메인 corporate domain
기업매수방지책 shark repellent
기업매수자 corporate raider
기업문화 corporate culture
기업부문 corporation sector
기업비밀 trade secrets
기업사취 corporate ripoff
기업성장 business growth
기업소비자 business consumer
기업시민성 corporate citizenship
기업실체를 공준함 postulate of business entity
기업안정 corporate settlement
기업연금 business annuity; corporate pension; industrial pension; occupational pension; private pension
기업연금, 기업보험 pension and life insurance schemes
기업연금제 private pension plan
기업연합 corporate alliance
기업원가 enterprise cost
기업유치지역 area of welcome enterprise
기업의 구매활동 business buying
기업의 비공개화 going private
기업의 사명 corporate mission
기업의 사회적 책임 social responsibility of enterprise

기업의 신규합병 consolidation of corporations
기업이미지 corporate image
기업이미지통합전략 corporate identity
기업이익조정 adjustment of business income
기업재고 business inventory
기업재무담당자 corporate treasurer
기업전략 corporate strategy
기업전체의 리스크를 평가함 enterprise approach
기업조합 joint enterprise cooperative
기업지배주식 stock controlling other business
기업진단 management consulting
기업집단재무제표 group financial statement
기업집중 concentration of enterprise
기업책임 business responsibility
기업태도 business attitude
기업투자 business investment
기업포괄배상책임보험; 포괄책임보험 umbrella liability policy
기업프로필 corporate profile
기업형 corporation type
기업형 투자신탁 corporation type investment trust
기업형태 forms of enterprise
기업홍보 corporate communication
기업활력 corporate vitality
기업회계 business accounting; corporate accounting; enterprise accounting
기업회계심의회 Business Accounting Deliberation Council; Financial Accounting Deliberation Council
기업회계원칙 accounting principles for business enterprise; business accounting principle; corporate accounting principles; financial accounting standards for business enterprise
기여분 contributory shares of estate
기여침해 contributory infringement
기왕증 previous illness

기왕증, 병력 anamnesis
기일 appointed day; date; time limited
기일 또는 기일전에 on or before
기일도래원본 credit past due date
기일도래채권 overdue payment
기일지정정기예금 maturity-designated time deposit
기입 entry
기입하다 enter
기장기 book-keeping machine
기장업무 obligation of bookkeeping
기장장소 booking center
기장하다 keep the books
기재식 무액면주식 stated value no-par stock
기재하다 enter in an account-book
기전상환까지의 거치기간 life-to-call
기점가격제 basing-point pricing
기조를 올림 upwards
기존자산 existing assets
기존채무 another debt; existing debt
기존특혜 existing preferential duties
기준; 표준물 standard
기준가격 base price
기준계열 base series
기준금리 reference rate
기준기간 base period
기준내임금 regular wage standard
기준레이트 base rate
기준보험료 base premium; premium base; underlying premium
기준상장; 기본요율 basic rate
기준설정권 criteria rights
기준연도 base year; basic taxable year
기준요금 standard rate
기준일 date of record; record date
기준임금 standard wage
기준재고법 base-stock method
기준통화 base currency
기준표준원가 base standard cost
기준할인레이트 basic discount rate
기중(期中)감사 interim audit

기중상환하다; 퇴직하다 retire
기증자 donator
기채 bond flotation; flotation of loan; issue of bond
기채; 모집발표 launching
기채시장 bond flotation market; primary market
기채연결융자 temporary loan before bond flotation
기채조정 coordination of bond issues
기초(期初) initial; beginning of period
기초; 토대 major bottom
기초공제 basic allowance; basic deduction; basic exemption; legal exemption from income tax; personal exemption
기초금융상품어프로치 fundamental financial approach
기초를 둔; 근거있는 grounded
기초불균형 fundamental disequilibrium
기초비용견적 base cost estimate
기초사실 matter
기초수익 base earnings
기초수지 basic balance
기초연구 fundamental scientific research
기초율 experience assumptions
기초자본 initial capital
기초잔고 beginning balance; initial balance; opening balance
기초재고고 opening inventory
기초재고자산 beginning inventories; initial inventories
기초정리 fundamental theorem
기초제작중인 물건 initial goods in process
기초제작품계정 initial work in process account
기초퇴직연금기금 basic retirement funds
기축통화 key currency
기탁회사 deposit company
기판력 res adjudicata
기프트광고 gift advertisement
기피 challenge; recusation

기피권 right of nullification
기하평균 geometric average
기한 end of the year; period; time limit
기한경과 out of date
기한경과계정 overdue account
기한경과대부 overdue loan
기한경과수표 overdue check
기한경과어음 overdue bill; post-due bill
기한만료 expiry
기한무효 time expired
기한부 신용장 usance letter of credit
기한부 어음 time bill
기한부 어음매상장 usance buying rate
기한부 어음상장 usance bill rate
기한부 어음을 매입함 credit buying
기한부 환어음 usance bill
기한이 끝난 카드 expired card
기한이 오다 become due; mature
기한이익상실 acceleration
기한이익의 상실사유 event of default
기한전 defcased
기한전 지불할인 anticipation discount
기한전 처분 anticipation
기한전 행사 early exercise
기한전의 계약위반 anticipatory breach of
    contract
기한후 신고 return after due date
기한후 이자 interest after the maturity
기한후 자동지속 renewal after the maturity
기호논리학 symbolic logics
기호모델 symbolic model

기호수표 marked cheques
기회분석 opportunity analysis
기회비용 opportunity cost
기회손실 opportunity loss
기회이익 opportunity
긴급경보방송 emergency warning system
긴급과세 tax in jeopardy
긴급관세 emergency; emergency duty; tariff
    in jeopardy
긴급구입 dawn raid
긴급상각 emergency amortization
긴급융자 emergency loan
긴급입법 emergency legislation
긴급추적 hot pursuit
긴급피난 necessity
긴장 tension
긴축예산 austere budget
긴축재정 austere fiscal policy; tight budget;
    tighter monetary policy
길모퉁이땅 corner lot
길트에지채 gilt-edged bond
길트에지채; 금연증권 gilt-edged securities
깁슨의 역설 Gibson paradox
깃발 flag
꼭 필요한 만큼만 구입함 hand-to-mouth
    buying
끝수계산 rounding off in calculation
끝수처리오차 rounding error
끼워 넣다 insert
끼워 넣어진 imbedded

ㄴ

나노초 nano-second
나스닥 NASDAQ Composite Index
나인본드룰 nine bond rule
낙담 disappointing
낙성계약 consensual contract; contract entered into by mutual consensus
낙찰결정서 letter of award
낚시보험 anglers' insurance
난국금지영장 ne exeat
난동죄; 선동죄 sedition
난매 panicky selling
난수 random numbers
난수표 table of random numbers
난외약관 marginal clauses
난외에 찍어두는 도장 marginal seal
난조(시세의)난조 violent fluctuation
난조시장 wide fluctuation of market
난파 wreck
날씨보험 weather insurance
날인; 브랜드설정 branding
날인개소 locus sigilli
날인의 인장조회 collation of seals
날인증서 charta; deed; sealed instrument
날인증서계약위반 breach of covenant
남북무역 north-south trade
남북문제 north-south problem
남아시아지역협력연합 South Asian Association for Regional Cooperation
남용 abuse
남위원회 South Commission
남태평양위원회 South Pacific Commission

남태평양포럼 South Pacific Forum
납기 period for tax
납기연장 extension of due date
납기한 due date for tax payment; time for tax payment
납부 paying tax
납부독촉 demand for tax payment
납부서 tax payment slip
납부위탁 consignment of tax payment
납부최고서 notice of demand to guarantor
납세 tax payment
납세고지서 notification of tax payment; rate papers; tax papers
납세관리인 administrator of tax payment; tax agent; tax manager
납세관리인을 신고함 notification of tax agent
납세기일 day for paying taxes
납세담보 security for tax payment
납세미제 tax unpaid
납세보증 security of tax payment
납세부담 burden of paying tax
납세신고서 tax return form
납세신고용지 tax forms
납세액 tax due
납세예비금 accrued taxes on income
납세위탁 consignment ledger; consignment of tax liability
납세의무 tax liability; tax obligation
납세의무가 있는 법인 corporation liable to taxation
납세의무계승 succession of tax liability

납세의무성립 realization of tax liability
납세의무자분류 classification of a taxpayer
납세의무확정 establishment of tax liability
납세자 taxpayer
납세자번호제도 taxpayer identification number system
납세자소송 tax payer's suit; taxpayer's suit
납세자의 선택 taxpayer's option
납세저축조합 savings-for-tax association; tax saving association
납세제 duty-paid
납세조합 taxpayer's association
납세준비금 provision for tax; reserve for tax payment
납세준비예금 deposit for tax
납세증명서 certificate of tax payment
납세지 place for tax payment; place of tax payment; tax payment place
납세지변경 change of the place of tax payment
납세지이동을 신고함 notification of transfer of place of tax payment
납세지지정 designation of place for tax payment
납세필 증서 certificate of compliance
납입계약 requirements contract
납치방지 black check
납치보험 ransom insurance
낭비자신탁 spendthrift trust
낭비함 frivolity
낳다 bear
내구소비재 consumers' durables; durable consumer goods
내국민대우 national treatment
내국법인 domestic corporation
내국세 internal tax
내국환어음 inland bill of exchange
내규개정 revision of office regulation
내금 money paid-in part
내로우캐스팅 narrowcasting
내부감사 internal audit; internal auditing
내부감사기준 internal audit standard

내부감사보고서 internal audit report
내부감사인 internal auditor
내부감사제도 internal audit system
내부거래 internal transaction
내부견제 internal check
내부견제제도 internal check system
내부경영분석 internal business analysis
내부구조 internal structure
내부금융 internal financing
내부노동시장 internal labor market
내부대체 intracompany transfer
내부대체가격 intracompany transfer price
내부대체이익 interdepartmental profit
내부대체차액 intercompany transfer variance
내부보고 internal reporting
내부보고제도 internal reporting system
내부보고회계 accounting for internal reporting
내부부채 internal liability
내부분석 internal analysis
내부상호보조 cross subsidization
내부수익률 internal rate of return
내부연소위험 internal exposure hazard
내부요인 internal factor
내부운용 internal operation
내부유보 retained profit
내부유보금 internal reserve
내부재보험 inwards reinsurance
내부정보 inside information
내부정보; 내부자료 internal information
내부정합성 internal consistency
내부증거 internal evidence
내부통제 internal control
내부할당 internal allocation
내부화주문 internalized order
내생변수 endogenous variable
내생변화 endogenous change
내수 domestic demand
내수관련주 domestic demand related stock
내수산업 domestic demand oriented industry
내수진흥 domestic demand stimulation

내수확대 domestic demand expansion; increasing domestic demand

내역 break-down; itemization; particulars

내역계정서 itemized bill

내역서 detailed statement; statement of items

내외금리차 international interest-spread

내용연수 durable years; service life; useful life

내용연수계산 computation of useful years

내용연수표 useful life table

내용증명우편 content-certified mail

내용표시문언 words of limitation

내입금 initial down payment; initial installment; initial payment

내재변동성 implied volatility

내재적인 콜가격 implicit call price

내지근무 home service

내채 internal debt

내포금리 implicit interest

내항력이 없는 unseaworthy

내항화물해상보험 coastwise cargo insurance

냉각기간 cooling time

냉각시키기 위한 cooling-off

냉각효과 chilling effect

너무 과도해도 안되며 not excessive

너무 부정당해도 안되며 not inadequate

넓이 breadth

네거티브옵션판매 negative option sales

네거티브캐리 negative carry

네거티브플레지패리패스조항 negative pledge pari passu clause

네거필름 negative film

네이키드옵션 naked option

네이키드워런트 naked warrant

네이키드콜 naked call

네이키드포지션 naked position

네일대미지 nail damage

네크라인 neck line

네트워크분석 network broadcast

네트워크아키텍처 network architecture

네팅 netting

넷거래고 net trading volume

넷리스 net lease

넷밸런스 net balance

넷블록플로 net block flow

넷오픈포지션 net open position

넷채권국 net creditor country

넷캐시 net cash

넷캐시플로 net cash flow

넷포지션 net position

넷프라이스인덱스 net price index

넷프라이스트레이딩 net price trading

년말 year-end

노년자공제 old person allowance

노다운 no-down

노다지; 대성공 bonanza

노동계수 labor coefficient

노동금고 labor credit associations

노동력절약투자 labor saving investment

노동법 industrial law; labor laws

노동법규 labor regulations

노동분배율 labor relative share; labor share

노동분쟁 labor trouble

노동비율 percentage of working force

노동생산성 labor productivity; productivity of labor

노동소득 labor income

노동시장 labor market

노동입법 labor legislation

노동자나 소매상의 저축, 융자를 담당하는 금융기관 industrial bank

노동자배상법 workmen's compensation law

노동자이동 labor turnover

노동자재해보상법 workmen's compensation acts

노동자재해보상보험 workmen's compensation insurance

노동재해종합보험 workers' accident comprehensive insurance

노동쟁의 industrial dispute

노동조합 trade union

노동조합단체보험 labor union group insurance

노동협약 bargaining agreement; collective
agreement; labor agreement

노드방식 node method

노령연금 old age pension; old-age pension

노령유족장애자연금 old-aged, survivor and
disability insurance

노령자 aged person

노령자공제 allowance for old person;
deduction for old-age person; exemption for
aged person

노령퇴직자연금 superannuation

노로드펀드 no load fund

노르마 norm

노리턴룰 no return rule

노멀마켓 normal market

노멀애셋믹스 normal asset mix

노멀타겟앨로케이션 normal target allocation

노무 service

노무감사 labor audit

노무관리 labor management

노무비차이 labor variance

노벨재단 Nobel Foundation

노사관계 management labor relations

노사교섭 wage negotiation

노사협의 joint labor management conference

노샘프턴 생명표 Northampton table

노선가방식에 따른 평가 valuation by road
rating

노액션레터 no action letter

노이즈 noise

노이즈게이트 noise gate

노이즈리덕션 noise reduction

노인공양친족 aged dependent

노임 labor cost

노출강도 depth of exposure

노출빈도 exposure frequency

노트 note

노트이슈언스퍼실리티; NIF note issuance
facility

노폴트 자동차보험 no fault automobile
insurance

노하우누설 leak of know-how

노하우사용료 royalty as to knowhow

노화; 숙성 aging

녹다운제품 knock-down product

녹이다; 해산하다 dissolve

녹화 electronic video recording

논리코스 nonrecourse

논마린 대리점제도 nonmarine agency system

논뱅크 nonbank

논보르드로 특약 nonbordereau agreement

논시스티매틱리스크 nonsystematic risk

논쟁기간 contestable period

논파라메트릭 검사 nonparametric test

논플리트계약자 nonfleet insured

농기구포괄보험 agricultural machinery and
equipment floater

농림어업금융기관 financial institution for
agriculture forestry and fisheries

농림중앙금고(일본의)농림중앙금고 Norin
Chukin Bank

농산물시장 agricultural goods markets

농업금융 agricultural credit

농업기계보험 agricultural machinery insurance

농업보험 agricultural insurance

농업부기 agricultural bookkeeping

농업생산법인 agricultural production
corporation

농업선취특권 agricultural lien

농업소득 agricultural income

농업소득면세 tax exemption for agricultural
income

농업은행 agricultural bank

농업조정법 agricultural adjustment act

농업조합 agricultural society

농업회계 farm accounting

농장이 딸린 농가 homestead

높은 공산 high possibility

높은 사망률 high mortality

뇌물; 증회 bribery

뇌물수수, 부패 corruption

누가법 cumulative method

누적 accumulation
누적경험 cumulative experience
누적과세 cumulative taxation
누적급부채무 accumulated benefit obligation
누적배당 accumulated dividend; cumulative dividend
누적배당우선주식 accumulated preferred stock
누적배당형 주식 accumulative stock
누적변동성 historical volatility
누적생산고 volume accumulation
누적세 cascade tax
누적액 accumulated amount
누적우선주 cumulative preferred stock
누적위험 accumulative risk
누적유증 cumulative legacy
누적이율 historical yield
누적이익 accumulated income
누적적 누적적인 accumulative
누적적자 cumulative deficit
누적제한 cumulative limitation
누적지수 cumulative index
누적채무 debt accumulation
누적책임 cumulative liability
누적투자 accumulated investment
누적투자기간 accumulative investment period
누적투자유니트 accumulative investment unit
누적투자플랜 accumulative investment plan
누적투표 cumulative voting
누적판결 accumulative judgment
누적한도액기준 cumulative limit
누적형 거래고세 cascade-type turnover tax
누적흑자 cumulative surplus
누진과세 graduated taxation; progressive

taxation
누진세 graduated tax
누진세율 progressive tax rate
누진소득세 progressive income tax
눈금; 교정 calibration
눈사람현상 snowballing
뉴럴컴퓨팅 neural computing
뉴미디어커뮤니티 new media community
뉴욕연방준비은행 Federal Reserve Bank of New York
뉴욕인수신용장 New York acceptance credit
뉴욕증권거래소 Big Board; New York Stock Exchange
뉴커먼캐리어 new common carrier
느슨한, 줄인 slacken
능동적인 판단 conative judgment
능력 ability
능력개발 man-power development
능력유지 maintenance of competence
능력이 있는 당사자 competent parties
능력이 있음 competency
능력자 legal ability person
능률감사 efficiency audit
능률관리 efficiency management
능률급 incentive wage system
능률차이 efficiency variance
늦다 slow
늦추다; 완화하다 relax
니어더머니 near the money
니즈 needs
니치 niche
니치마켓 niche market
니치전략 niche strategy
닐슨조사 Nielsen research

ㄷ

다각경영 diversified management
다각적 무역교섭 multilateral trade negotiations
다각적 청산협정 multilateral clearing agreement
다각화기업 diversified company
다각화의 경제성 economies of scope
다각화전략 diversification strategy
다국간협정 multilateral agreement
다국적 마케팅 multinational marketing
다국적기업 multinational corporation
다국적주의 multinationalim
다기간모델 multiperiod model
다단계식 multiple-step form
다른 결정이 없는 한 unless otherwise specified
다른 계좌 different account
다른 비율 split rating
다목적대무재표 all-purpose financial statement
다변량분석 multivariate analysis
다부문분석 multisectoral analysis
다소 높은 유도 aggressively held up
다속성모델 multiattribute model
다수 majority
다수국간투자보증기관 Multilateral Investment Guarantee Agency
다수난전(亂戰)업계 fragmented industry
다수소재지물건보험 multiple location risk insurance
다수자유언 multiwill
다시 열다 reopen
다액채무자 overindebted person

다우식 상품지수 Dow-Jones Commodity Index
다우이론 Dow Theory
다우평균 Dow Jones Average
다운로드 download
다운앤드아웃옵션; 하향실격옵션 down-and-out option
다원적인 경쟁 pluralistic competition
다원적인 증거 multiple evidence
다음 사업연도 subsequent taxable year
다음달의 proximo
다이나믹데이터교환 dynamic data exchange
다이나믹영역 dynamic range
다이나믹전략 dynamic strategies
다이나믹프로그램 dynamic programming
다이나믹헤지 dynamic hedge scheme
다이렉트어음 direct paper
다이묘 본드 daimyo bond
다이버시티안테나 diversity antenna
다이아몬드반도체 diamond semiconductor
다이아몬드포메이션 diamond formation
다이얼회선 dial telephone line
다중상관 multiple correlation
다중채무 card-holic
다중탈퇴잔존표 multiple decremental table
다중회귀분석 multiple regression analysis
다지라인 Dodge Line
다항목선택법 multiple choice
다항식 경향선 polynomial-trend
다행식 시산서 artificial statement

다행식 현금출납장 tabular cash book
단가 unit price
단가계약 unit-price contract
단가적산법 unit pricing
단계식 할인방법 quantity discount system
단계원가 stepped cost
단계이부채 stepped coupon bond
단계적인 건설 phased construction
단계적인 경비 graded expense
단계적인 변화 gradation
단계적인 전략 sequenced strategy
단계적인 참가 sequenced entry
단계적인 평가변동방식 crawling peg system
단계함수 step function
단골은행 run upon a bank; transmitting bank
단기 short period; short-term
단기가능만가 retractable maturity
단기거래 short swing; short-term transaction
단기공급곡선, 장기공급곡선 short-run supply
  curve long-run supply curve
단기국채 short-term government bond
단기균형 short-run equilibrium
단기금리 short-term interest rate
단기금융 short-term finance
단기금융계정 money market account
단기금융상품 money market instrument
단기금융상품투자신탁 money market fund
단기금융시장 money market; short-term
  credit market; short-term money market
단기금융시장예금계정 money market deposit
  account
단기금융시장지수 money market index
단기대부 short loan; short-term loan;
  short-term loan receivable; short-time loan
단기로 매매하는 in-and-out trading
단기매매익 short swing profits
단기보험계약 short period insurance
단기부채 quick liabilities; short-term
  liabilities
단기불 payment at short date
단기불입생명보험 limited payment life policy

단기비용 short-period cost
단기상장 short market
단기스와프 short swap
단기양도소득 short-term capital
단기업자 money market broker
단기요율표 short rate table
단기유동성요인 short-term liquidity factor
단기융자 money at call
단기이율 short-term field
단기자금 short-term fund
단기자금레이트 short-term facility rate
단기자금조달비용 cost of short-term funds
단기자본 short-term capital
단기자본거래 short-term capital transaction
단기자본수지 short-term capital balance
단기증권 short paper
단기지불능력 short-term solvency
단기지향 short-term oriented
단기차입 borrowing short; short-term
  borrowing
단기차입금 bank loans; money borrowed for
  short-term; short-term debt; short-term loan
  payable
단기채 short-term bond
단기채권 short bond; short-term note
단기채무 unfunded debt
단기최적화원리 short-run optimizing principle
단기투자 current investment; short-term
  investment
단기투자가 day-to-day trader
단기투자계정 short-term investment account
단기투자수익 short-tenn returns; short fall
단기파동, 키친사이클 Kitchen cycles
단단히 tight
단독보유 entire tenancy
단독어업권 several fishery
단독재무제표 separate financial statements
단독해손 particular average
단독해손부담보; 분손부담보 free from
  particular average
단리 simple interest

단리(單利)베이스 on a simple interest basis
단리이익 yield by simple interest
단명 single name
단명어음 one name paper; single name paper
단문식 감사보고서 short form audit report
단문식 보고서 short-form report
단발요금 one-time rate; transient rate
단봉형의 unimodal
단서조항 provisory clause
단손부동산권으로 in fee
단수 fractional figure
단수가격 odd price
단수이자 fractional interest
단순가설 simple hypothesis
단순개념 singular concept
단순계약 unconditional contract
단순명의인 merely nominal persons
단순보증인 simple guarantor
단순부동산권 fee simple
단순분개장 simple journal
단순산술평균지수 simple arithmetic average index
단순상관관계 simple correlation coefficient
단순승수 simple multiplier
단순신탁 simple trust
단순이동평균 simple moving average
단순재생산 simple reproduction
단순재정 simple arbitrage
단순저당채권자불약관 open mortgage clause
단순점유권 possessory interest
단순점프모델 simple jump model
단순종합원가계산 simple cost accounting
단순준비법 simple reserve method
단순지수 simple index
단순채무 simple obligation
단순총화 simple
단순파산 straight bankruptcy
단순평균법 simple average method; straight average cost method
단순평균여명 curtate expectation of life
단순평균이율 arithmetic dividend yield

average
단순평균주가 arithmetic stock price average; simple average stock price
단순한 투자대상 stand alone investment
단순해손; 단순평균 simple average
단순화 simplification
단순확률표본 simple random sample
단순회귀모델 simple regression model
단식 single expression
단식기입 single entry
단식부기 bookkeeping by single entry; simple accounting; single entry bookkeeping
단위 unit
단위원가 unit cost
단위주 even lot
단위통화구역 message area
단위행렬 identity matrix
단위형 채권투자신탁 bond unit trust
단위형 투신 unit type investment trust
단일거래 single transaction
단일고객분리계정 individual separate account; single-customer separate account
단일구분계산서 single-step statement
단일구분손익계산서 single-step income statement
단일대차대조표 single balance sheet
단일만기예금 single-maturity deposit
단일만기채 term bonds
단일목적 카드 mono-purpose credit card; monopurpose credit card
단일사업주형 급부건연금제도 single-employer defined benefit pension plan
단일상관관계 single correlation coefficient
단일세 single tax
단일세율 single tariff
단일세율제 simple tariff system
단일연금 single life annuity
단일요율 single rate
단일요인 one-factor
단일요인모델 one-factor model

단일유럽의정서 Single European Act
단일은행면허 single banking license
단일은행제도 unit banking; unit banking
system
단일은행지주회사 one bank holding
company; one-bank holding company
단일이익담보보험 single interest policy
단일전보한도액 single limit on insurer's
liability
단일지수법 single index method
단일지표모델 single index model
단일책임주의 principle of single liability;
single liability basis
단일환레이트 single exchange rate
단일환시장제 monorate of exchange system
단자시장 call loan market; single liability
basis
단자업자 call loan broker; short-term money
house
단자회사 call loan dealer; money market
dealer
단주 odd-lot shares
단주거래 odd-lot transaction
단주업자 odd-lot dealer
단주이론 odd-lot theory
단주정리 lot consolidation; odd-lot
consolidation
단주주문 fractional order
단지보험 apartment dwellers' comprehensive
insurance
단체거치연금계약 group deferred annuity
contract
단체건강보험 group health insurance
단체교섭 collective bargaining
단체교섭권 right of collective bargaining
단체급계약 wholesale group insurance
단체기명식 보험 collective name schedule
policy
단체마크 collective mark
단체모기지보상생명보험 group mortgage
insurance

단체변액연금 group variable annuity
단체보유액 group retention
단체보험 collective insurance; group
insurance
단체상해보험 collective accident insurance;
collective personal accident insurance;
group accident insurance
단체생명보험 group life insurance
단체신용보험 group credit insurance
단체신용생명보험 creditor group insurance;
group credit life insurance
단체양로보험 group endowment insurance
단체연금 group annuity; group pension
단체연금보험 group annuity insurance
단체연금보험계약 group annuity insurance
contract
단체예탁관리계약 group deposit
administration contract
단체의료비보험 group medical expense
insurance
단체장기보험계약 group permanent
insurance contract
단체정기보험 group term insurance
단체종신보험 group permanent insurance
단체행동 association behavior
단체협약 collective bargaining agreement
단축 shortening
단칭명제 singular proposition
단품상품계획 unit merchandise planning
단회계제도 single account system
달러가중수익률 dollar-weighted rate of return
달러계정 dollar account
달러계좌개설서류 documents for opening a
U.S. dollar account
달러고기조 firm tone of the U.S. dollar
달러과잉 overhung
달러기준 denominated in U.S. dollar
달러기준전환사채 dollar convertible bond
달러기준채무 debt in U.S. dollar
달러단기금리선물 U.S. dollar short-term
interest futures

달러로 신주를 일부 유지함 free riding
달러매출개입 intervention by selling dollars
달러방위 defense of the dollar; dollar support
달러블록 dollar bloc
달러선호 dollar preference
달러시프트 dollar shift
달러약세 weaker U.S. dollar
달러위기 dollar crisis
달러콜옵션 dollar call option
달러평가 dollar parity
달러평균법 dollar average method
달러풋옵션 dollar put option
달러화약세 forward discount of U.S. dollar
달성동기 achieving need
달성동기부 이론 theory of achievement motivation
달성수준 achievement level
담; 울타리 enclosure
담배소비세 tobacco consumption tax
담보 collateral; gage; loanable value; security
담보 부대출 secured credit
담보가치 collateral value
담보관리 management of collateral
담보권 security; security interest
담보권자 secured party
담보권행사 exercise of security right
담보권행사의 우선순위를 결정함 marshaling securities
담보대부 collateral loan
담보대출 loan on security; secured loan
담보를 통한 은행차입 bank loans secured by mortgage
담보목록 inventory of security
담보물건의 가격보다 낮게 평가할 때의 비율 assessment rate of collateral
담보범위 coverage
담보보류조항 negative clause
담보부 거래 secured transactions
담보부 고정자산양도 transfer of fixed assets given in pledge
담보부 대부 secured advance

담보부 대부금 mortgages receivable
담보부 대출 secured debt
담보부 부채 secured debenture; secured liabilities
담보부 사채신탁법 mortgage debentures trust law
담보부 수입 collateral import
담보부 신탁채권 collateral trust bond
담보부 약속어음 collateral note
담보부 예금 collateral deposit
담보부 인수 acceptance on security
담보부 증권 secured securities
담보부 투자신탁 mortgage investment trust
담보설정 affection
담보여력 net worth of collateral
담보예금 security deposits
담보위반 breach of warranty
담보이익 mortgagees' interest
담보자산 hypothecated assets
담보잡히는 사람 pawnor
담보제한조항 negative pledge clause
담보조항선택방식증권 scheduled policy
담보차입동의서 hypothecation agreement
담보차입유가증권 securities deposited as collateral
담보차입자산 assets subject to lien
담보차입증 letter of confirmation of collateral
담보해제 release of security
담세력 tax bearing capacity
담세자 tax bearer
담수에 젖음 fresh water damage
담합경매 knock out
담합매매 matched order
당국 authorities
당기 current period; current taxable year; current year
당기결산 current term settlement
당기만기부분 current maturity
당기미처분이익잉여금 unappropriated earned surplus for current term
당기세액 current taxes

당기손실금 deficit for the current term; loss for the current term

당기순손실 current term net loss

당기순손익 current term net profit or loss

당기순이익 current term net profit; net profit for the year

당기순익 current term net income

당기업적주의 current operating performance basis; current operating performance theory

당기업적주의에 따른 손익계산서 current operating performance income statement

당기이익 bottom line; current income

당기지출원가 current-outlay cost

당년도의 개황 year in brief

당면의 유동성 immediate liquidity

당방 our side

당방계정 Nostro account; our account

당방부담 on our risk

당사자 party

당사자과실책임제도 adversary system

당사자병합 joinder of parties

당사자석 floor of the court

당소주(當所株) stock exchange share

당월에 한해 유효한 주문 good this month order

당일거래 same day transaction

당일결제거래 cash transactions

당일만 유효한 주문 day order

당일상환대출 day loan

당일유효주문 same day effective order

당일인도 value today

당자대월약정 overdraft facilities

당장의 이윤을 노려 사고파는 사람 scalper

당좌계정 account current; book account; checking account; current account; running account

당좌계정부체 transfer of current account

당좌대부 demand loan; cash credit

당좌비율 acid ratio; quick assets ratio; quick ratio

당좌수급자격 current insured status

당좌수표 current account cheek

당좌예금 cash at bank; checking deposits; current deposit; deposits in current account

당좌이월약정서 agreement for overdraft

당좌자금 current fund

당좌자산 quick assets

당좌조회표 reconciliation statement for current account

당좌초과인출 overdraft

당초구입자 original purchaser

당초부담원가 starting-load cost

대가 counter value

대가; 약인 consideration

대가수령 value received

대각스프레드 diagonal spread

대고객환상장 exchange quotation

대공황 great depression

대규모상각자산 large depreciable property

대규모소매업자 large-scale retailer

대금고보험 safe deposit box insurance

대금교환인도 cash on delivery

대금미불상품포괄보험 conditional sales floater

대금을 치를 생각 없이 물품을 대량으로 구매하여 사취함 confidence game

대금주 loan stock

대기기간 waiting period

대기오염지구 area polluted with soot and smoke

대기행렬 queuing

대기행렬모델 queuing model

대납 payment for another

대내간접투자 indirect inward investment; direct inward investment

대농원 plantation

대도준비금 reserve for bad loan

대등합병 amalgamation on an equal basis

대량가격매김 bulk marking

대량거래 block transaction

대량광고할인 bulk discount

대량구입 bulk purchase

대량매매거래 block sales
대량생산 mass production
대량수송 mass transportation
대량수주 major order
대량유통 mass distribution
대량주문을 소량집행함 split order
대량추천판매 mass sales
대륙식 원장마감수속 continental form of
　closing the ledger
대리 deputy; proxy
대리교환 clearing for nonmember
대리대부 agency loan
대리로 per procuration
대리수수료 agent commission
대리인 agent
대리인; 후견인 next friend
대리인부기 agency bookkeeping
대리인수 subunderwriting
대리인을 세움 procuration
대리인자금 afiency fund
대리점 agency; commercial agent
대리점경비 agency cost
대리점계약 agency contract
대리점계약자 agency agreement
대리점계정 agency accounts; agent account
대리점대여 agency account receivable
대리점대출 current credit accounts with
　agencies
대리점수수료 agency commission; agency fee
대리점원장 agency ledger
대리점제도 agency system
대리점활동 agency activity
대리참가 subparticipation
대리판매 sale by agent
대물계약 real contract
대물권 jus in rem
대물담보 impersonal security
대물배상보험 automobile property damage
　liability insurance
대물변제 accord and satisfaction; payment in
　substitution

대물변제담보물을 취득함 strict foreclosure
대물소송 action in rem; real action
대물신용 real credit
대물적 in rem
대물판결 judgment in rem
대발회 year's opening session
대배심 grand jury
대법정 court in bank
대변공제; 채권; 신용 credit
대변잔고 credit balance
대변전표 credit note
대부 lending
대부가치법 loan value method
대부계정 advance account; loan account
대부금 advance
대부금보험 loan insurance
대부금액 amount advanced
대부금이자반려 interest on loans rebated
대부금회수 collection of loans
대부미수이자 accrued interest on loan
대부신탁 loan trust
대부신탁예상배당률 expected return ratio of
　loan trust
대부예약 forward commitment
대부원장 loan ledger
대부유가증권 loan receivable in securities;
　securities loaned
대부자금 loanable fund
대부지분참가 loan participation
대부창구 lending window
대부한도 loan value
대상(大商) dramatic surge
대상; 큰장사 broad market
대상문제전체의 throughout the target issues
대상상품 target securities
대상스와프 underlying swap
대상자산가액 target assets value
대상주식 target stock; underlying stock
대상지표 underlying index
대상회사 target company
대세관 macroview

대손 bad loan; credit losses
대손계정 bad account; uncollectible accounts
대손금 bad debt loss; dead loan; desperate debt; lending loss; loan loss
대손금상각 charge-off
대손금회수 recovery of bad debt
대손상각 bad debt written-off
대손손실 loss from bad debts
대손예비금 allowance for bad debt; allowance for uncollectable accounts
대손율 percentage of credit losses
대손준비금 allowance for bad loan; allowance for doubtful accounts; bad debt provision; bad debt reserve
대손준비금계정편입한도액 limit to credit reserve for bad debts
대손준비금공제후 수취채권 net of reserves
대손준비금공제후의 금액 net amount after provision for loss
대손준비손 provision for bad debts
대수계산 logarithmic calculation
대수변수 proxy variable
대수의 법칙 law of large numbers
대수정규분포 lognormal distribution
대신 in lieu
대심(對審) confrontation
대심수속 adversary proceeding
대역압축 bandwidth compression
대외공통관세 common external tariff
대외균형 external equilibrium
대외순자산 net external assets
대외이권 overseas interests
대외지불수단 foreign means of payment; means of foreign payment
대외지불을 위한 환 exchange for means of foreign payment
대외채무의 주식화 debt-equity swap
대외채무이자지불 interest payments on foreign debt
대외투자 outward investment; overseas investment

대용유가증권 substitute securities
대용증권 collateral security
대용증권담보율 collateral value of substitute security
대용통화 proxy currency
대용할 수 있는 fungible
대월설정 setting up overdraft
대위 subrogation
대위구상권행사폐지 exclusion of subrogation
대위납부 payment in subrogation; subrogation payment
대위변제 subrogated performance
대위영수서 subrogation receipt
대위채무 subrogated right
대위통지서 advice of subrogation
대응 matching
대응계정 reciprocal account
대응구매 counter purchase
대응스와프 matching swap
대응의 원칙 principle of matching
대응조정 correlative adjustment
대인배상보험 automobile bodily injury liability insurance
대인비교법 man-to-man system
대인소송 action in personam
대인접촉 personal contact
대인지각 interpersonal perception
대인지역권 easement in gross
대점법(대규모 소매점포에 대한 법률) large scale retail store law
대조 collation
대조계정 contra account; per contra account
대조한 등본 examined copy
대주 lending stock
대주시장 stock loan market
대주주 big shareholder
대중과세 taxation upon the general-public
대중리스크 mass risks
대중문화 mass culture
대중사회 mass society
대중상장 public market

대중소비사회 mass consumption society
대중투자가 investing public
대증권 lending securities
대차거래 debt-credit transaction; loan transaction
대차계약 sell-and-lease agreement
대차계정 debtor and creditor accounts
대차대조표 balance sheet; financial position statement
대차대조표감사의 각서 memorandum of balance sheet audit
대차대조표분석 balance sheet analysis
대차대조표일후의 발생사항 event subsequent to balance sheet date; happening subsequent to balance sheet date
대차란 debtor side
대차를 공제하다 strike a balance
대차은행 debtor bank
대차평균의 원리 principle of equilibrium
대책 countermeasure; substitution
대체가격변동 alternative price change
대체가능성 fungibility; fungible goods
대체가능증권 fungible securities
대체결제 institutional delivery
대체결제회사 stock clearing corporation
대체계좌 postal transfer account
대체고정자산 substitute fixed assets
대체곡선 substitution curve
대체구입처 alternative sources
대체기입 cross entry
대체납세 tax payment by transfer account
대체담보 replacement of collateral
대체를 통한 자산교환 replacement property by purchase
대체믹스 alternative mixes
대체법률 law of substitution
대체비용 alternative costs; renewal expenses; substituted expenses
대체안 alternative plan; alternatives
대체영수증 journal voucher
대체원장 journal ledger

대체의료서비스공급시스템 alternative health care delivery system
대체이익 profit transferred
대체자산 property for substitution; substitute assets; substitute property
대체전표 cross slip; journal slip
대체제품 alternate product
대체탄력성 elasticity of substitution
대체하다 supersede
대체할 수 없는 물건 unique chattel
대체회계원칙 alternative accounting principles
대체효과 substitution effect
대출계정 creditor account
대출금 loans and bills discounted
대출금계정 loans and bills discounted accounts
대출금리 interest rate on loans; lending rate; loan rate
대출금이자 interest on loans and discount
대출란 creditor side
대출리스크 debt exposure
대출메모 credit memorandum
대출심사 examination of loan application; screening of application for loan
대출액 amount financed
대출약정평균금리 average contracted rates on loans and discounts
대출업무 lending operation
대출예약한도 line of credit
대출은행 creditor bank; lender bank
대출이율 loan interest rate
대출자금 loanable resources
대출자금이론 loanable funds theory
대출자의 선호 lender's preference
대출자의 우선권분석 analysis of lender's preference
대출자의 위험 lender's risk
대출정책 lending policy
대출조건 lending terms
대출조건명시 disclosure of terms and conditions of loans
대출준비금 borrowed reserves

대출증가액규칙 restriction on the growth of bank loans
대출채권 finance receivable
대출채권분매 loan subparticipation
대출초과 overloan
대출초과한도액 maximum limit of overdraft
대출한도액 maximum loan value
대출한도액 적용제도 credit ceiling application system
대출한도액; 신용한도 credit line
대치 replacement by purchase
대치번식력 replacement fertility
대치수요 replacement demand
대치자산 replaced property
대치잠재력 replacement potential
대칭변수 antithetic variable
대칭분포 symmetrical distribution
대칭트라이앵글 symmetrical triangle pattern
대투자은행 large investment bank
대폭 반등 big jump
대폭발 Big Bang
대폭상향수정 sharp upward revision
대폭의 할인 대폭할인 deep discount
대폭증가 leap
대표문제 representing issue
대표민주제 representative democracy
대표소송 representative suit
대표이사 representative director
대표자 representative
대표청산인 representative liquidator
대표치 measure of central tendency
대표화폐 representative money
대필; 대서 allograph
대학총장 chancellor of a university
대항 emulation
대항력 countervailing power
대행은행 agent bank
대행카드 credit cards issued by the agent
대형전국은행 money center bank
대형주 large-capital stock
더미회사 dummy company

더블업 double-up
더블크로스오버 double crossover
더빈-왓슨비 Durbin-Watson ratio
더빙 dubbing
더티플로트; 관리변동환율제도 dirty float
덤벨포트폴리오 dumbbell portfolio
덤핑 dumping
덤핑상품 distress merchandise
데드크로스 dead cross
데몬스트레이션효과 demonstration effect
데빗시스템 debit system
데빗시스템월불간이보험 monthly debit industry
데빗시스템월불보통보험 monthly debit ordinary
데스크톱뮤직 desk top music
데스크톱비디오 desk top video
데스크톱퍼블리싱 desk top publishing
데이터가공업무 data processing business
데이터검색 data retrieval
데이터방송 data broadcasting
데이터정리 data reduction
데이터통신; 데이터전송 data transmission
데트워런트채 bond with debt warrant; debt warrant
데트크로스 debt cross
데포이론 depot theory
덱홀더 deckholder
델타 delta
델타뉴트럴헤지 delta neutral hedge
델타수치 delta value
델타헤지 delta hedge
델피과정 Delphi process
델피법 Delphi method
도난보험 burglary insurance
도난수표 stolen check
도달범위; 누적도달률 reach
도덕상의 약인 moral consideration
도덕적 해이 moral hazard
도둑; 소매치기 picker
도떼기(고물, 벼룩)시장 flea market

도량표준 standard of price
도로요금소 toll gate
도매가격 wholesale price
도매량 wholesale
도매물가지수 wholesale price index
도매사업 wholesale establishment
도매상 wholesale dealer
도매상 리엔 factor's lien
도매업 wholesale business; wholesale trade
도매업자 wholesaler
도매회계 wholesale accounting
도미노효과 domino effect
도민세 metropolitan inhabitant tax
도발 provocation
도수곡선 frequency curve
도수분포 frequency distribution
도시개량사업 urban remodeling enterprise
도시계획 town planning scheme
도시계획세 city planning tax
도시세 prefectural tax
도시은행 city bank
도시주변지대 urban fringe
도시화 urbanization
도움 aid and comfort
도의적인 설득 moral suasion
도의적인 지불보증채권 moral obligation bond
도의조사 morale survey
도입기 introductory period
도입예금 deposit to be relet to a third party
도주범 fugitive from justice
도중상환 prepayment
도착원가 laid down cost
도착지불판매상장 on demand selling rate
도착하지 않은 not yet delivered
도착후 일람불어음 arrival draft
도청 eavesdropping
도함수 derived function
독립계약 independent audit
독립기관 independent agency
독립기업간가격 arm's length price
독립기업원칙 arm's length principle

독립변수 independent variable
독립생계 self-support subsistence
독립세 independent tax
독립점포 free-standing store
독립중개자 independent contractor
독립지명권 power in gross
독립채산 self-support accounting
독립채산제 business accountability; self-supporting accounting system
독립책임액비례주의 independent intermediary
독립투자 autonomous investment
독립판매조직 independent liability method; independent marketing organization
독립회계사 independent accountant
독립회계제 self-accounting system
독일무기명증서 German Bearer Certificate
독자평균 self-balancing
독점 regrating
독점가격 monopoly price
독점가격설정 monopoly pricing
독점권 exclusive privilege/right; sole agent; sole right
독점금지법 anti-monopoly law; anti-trust acts
독점대리점 exclusive agent
독점도 degree of monopoly
독점자본 monopoly
독점적인 경쟁 monopolistic competition
독점판매권 exclusive distributorship
독점판매대리점 exclusive selling agency
독촉료 charge for call
독촉장 collection letter
돈의 융통이 막힘; 자금이 딸림 monetary stringency
돌연한 방문판매 cold canvassing
동거명령 restitution of conjugal rights
동결계정 frozen account
동결시장 locked market
동결자산 frozen assets
동기 causa inducement; motive
동기(同期)로 하다 synchronize
동기방송 synchronousity broadcasting

동기부여 motivation
동기부여수준 motivation level
동기부여인자 motivating factor
동기분류 classification of motives
동기조사 motivation research
동남아시아국가연합 Association of
　South-East Asian Nations
동료 peer
동류증권그룹 homogeneous security group
동맹 alliance
동맹회사 allied company
동물보험 animal insurance
동보통신 simultaneous transmissive
　communication
동산 chattel; movables; personal assets;
　personal estate
동산계약 personal contract
동산대부 chattel loan
동산모기지 mortgage of goods
동산반환청구소송 detinue
동산보험 property insurance
동산부동산계정 movable and immovable
　assets account
동산세 personal tax
동산신탁 movable property in trust
동산신탁증서 equipment trust certificate
동산유증 bequest
동산의 불법수법 de bonis asportatis
동산인도청구소송 action of detinue
동산저당 chattel mortgage
동산점유회복소송 replevin
동산종합보험 movables comprehensive
　insurance
동산질권자 pledgee
동산차압 personal distress
동산침해소송 trover
동산회복소송 claim and delivery
동세대분석 cohort analysis
동순위로 pari passu
동순위선취특권 concurrent liens
동시거래정지 circuit breaker

동시방송 simulcast
동시분포 simultaneous distribution
동시이행약속 concurrent promises
동시적립방식 contemporaneous reserve
　accounting
동시조사 simultaneous tax audit
동시조사테스트 concurrent test
동시확률 joint probability
동심원적인 다각화 concentric diversification
동아시아경제협의체 East Asia Economic
　Caucus
동아프리카공동체 East African Community
동업조합 craft; guild
동원 mobilization
동위계약 concurrent policies
동위보험 concurrent insurance
동의 accord; consent
동의시킨; 일치하는; 조화된 accordant
동의제출기 rules
동의판결 consent judgment
동의하지 않음 disagreement
동일개설신용장 back to back credit
동일결제 same day settlement
동일사고사망자 commorientes
동일성 identity
동일성을 인정함 ne varictur
동일한 성장률 flat growth
동작연구 motion study
동조형 마케팅 synchromarketing
동족관계회사 affiliated family corporations
동족조합 family partnership
동족주주의 동족회사 personal family
　corporation
동족회사 closed corporation; family
　corporation; personal holding company;
　private holding company
동종상품 like goods
동종원칙 rule of ejusdem generis
동종위험 perils ejusdem generis
동종위험으로 인한 손해 losses ejusdem
　generis

동종의 in kind
동종제한의 원칙 "ejusdem generis" doctrine
동질성 homogeneity
동질시장 homogeneous market
동질적인 경쟁 homogeneous competition
동축케이블 coaxial cable
동태모델 dynamic model
동태분석 dynamic analysis
동태적 마케팅 dynamic marketing
동태적인 위험 dynamic risk
동학(動學)승수 dynamic multiplier
동학적인 산업연관분석 dynamic input-output
    analysis
동화이론 assimilation theory
되돌림재보험 declared back reinsurance
되돌아감; 회고 retracement
되사기 repurchase
되사다 buy back; buy-back
되팔기 selling on rally; sell back
두 가지 요소로 인한 이원별 배당 two factor
    contribution plan
두 회사의 독점 duopoly
두뇌집단 think tank
두자리수성장기조 double-digit recurring
    profit growth
둔조(鈍調)시장 heavy market
둔화 deceleration; slowdown
뒤떨어지다 lag
뒤틀림; 왜곡 skewness
듀레이션가중이익 duration-weighted yield
듀레이션매칭 duration-matching
듀레이션법 duration method
듀얼전환사채 dual convertible bonds
듀얼클로즈드엔드형 펀드 dual closed-end
    fund
듀얼펀드 dual fund
드래곤곡선 dragon curve
드러난 본문 bare body
드롭록채 drop-lock bond
드문드문한 spotty
등가 equivalence

등가계수 equivalent coefficient
등가관계 equivalence relationship
등가교환 equivalent exchangee; exchange of
    equivalents
등각나선, 로그스파이럴 logarithmic spiral
등간격추출법 equal interval sampling method
등귀 appreciation
등금액 포트폴리오 equal weighted portfolio
등급 degree; grade
등급거래 grading transaction
등급기능 grading function
등급별 수수료 graded commission
등급별 원가계산 group cost system
등급을 정함; 시청률 rating
등급제도 rating system
등급주문 scale order
등기 enrollment; entry under homestead laws;
    registration
등기료 registration fee
등기미제 nonregistered
등기번호 registered number
등기변경예고 caution
등기부 register; registry
등기수속 registration formalities
등기필 registered
등락레이쇼 up-down ratio
등락선 advance-decline line
등록 record
등록기관 registrar; registration agency
등록길트채 registered gilts
등록면제거래소 exempt stock exchange
등록면허세 registration and license tax
등록명 registered issues
등록명의인 registered owner
등록상표 registered trade-mark
등록세 registration tax
등록을 앞당김 acceleration of registration
등록정부증권 book-entry securities
등록조합 registered society
등록주 registered share
등록트레이더 registered trader

등본 duplicate tenor; transcript

디노미네이션관련주 denomination related stocks

디램; **DRAM** dynamic random access memory

디맨드풀인플레; 초과수요인플레 demand pull inflation

디버깅 debugging

디스인플레이션 disinflation

디스커버리베이시스 discovery basis

디스커버리본드 discovery bond

디스플레이광고 display advertising

디시전룸; 특별회의실 decision room

디오라마 diorama

디지탈영상효과 digital picture effect

디지털비디오인터랙티브 digital video interactive

디지털시그널프로세서 digital signal processor

디지털오디오워크스테이션 digital audio workstation

디지털콤팩트카세트 digital compact cassette

디지털피킹 digital picking

디퍼드스와프 deferred swap

디포지터리코러스폰던트; 예치환거래은행 depository correspondent

디폴트 default

디프디스카운트채 deep discount bond

디프라이미딩과정 depyramidding

디프록주의 deep rock doctrine

디프비드 deep bid

디프인더머니 deep in the money

디플레갭 deflationary gap

디플레기간 deflationary period

디플레기대 deflation expectation

디플레압력 deflationary pressure

디플레이션 deflation

디플레이션갭 deflation gap

디플레이터; 가격수정인자 deflator

디플레정책 deflation policy

디플레효과 deflationary effect

딕컬러 DIC color

딜러 dealer

딜러금융 dealer financing

딜러론 dealer loan

딜러수료 dealer's fee

딜러시장 dealer market

딜러어음 dealer paper

딜러옵션 dealer's option

딜러포지션 dealer's position

딜링거래시스템 computer assisted execution system

딜링리스크 dealing risk

따르다; ~을 지키다 abide by

땀에 젖음 sweat

때맞춤 정보개시 timely disclosure

(…의) 때문에 ad opus

떨어뜨리다 ride down

떨이로 팔다 sell off

뛰어드는 사람 plunger

뜻밖의, 행운의 windfall profit

뜻에 반하여 against the will

ㄹ

라디안, 호도 radian
라스트리조트 last resort
라스파이레스방식 Laspeyres formula
라운딩리버설패턴 rounding reversal pattern
라이센스보험 license insurance
라인조직 line organization
라인피드(모니터의 커서를 한 줄 아래로 내림) line feed
랍스터트랩 lobster trap
래그분석 lag analysis
래그효과 lag effect
래스터(텔레비전 브라운관의 형광면 위에 나타나는 주사선에 의한 가로줄무늬) raster
래터곡선 Latter curve
랙포커스 rack focus
랜덤워크이론 random walk theory
RAM random access memory
런던리파이낸스 London refinance
런던보험업자협회 Institute of London Underwriters
런던어음교환소가맹은행 London clearing banks
런던예탁증서 London Depositary Receipts
런던은행 수취금리 London Inter-Bank Offered Rate
런던은행 수취레이트 London Inter-bank Bid Rate
런던증권거래소시황정보시스템 Stock Exchange Automated Quotation
런던클럽 London Club

런어웨이갭 runaway gap
레드클로즈신용장; 전대신용장 red clause credit
레버리지드리스 leveraged lease
레버리지드리캐피털리제이션 leveraged recapitalization
레버리지드바이아웃 leveraged buyout
레버리지드스톡 leveraged stock
레버리지드옵션 leveraged option
레버리지드포지션 leveraged position
레버리지드홀딩 leveraged holding
레버리지비율 leverage factor ratio; leverage ratio
레버리지지수 leverage factor
레버리지효과 leverage effect
레온체프의 역설 Leontief's paradox
레이쇼콜스프레드거래 ratio call spread transaction
레이언더라이터 lay underwriter
레이오프 lay off
레이저프린터 laser printer
레인지포워드거래 range forward contract
레저산업 leisure industries
렉스 Reinsurance Exchange
렉시스의 원칙 Lexis's principle
렌탈비용 rental expense
로드블로킹 road blocking
로드텔러 robot teller
로렌츠곡선 Lorenz curve
로마클럽 Rome club

로스포트폴리오 loss portfolio
로얄티 royalty
로이드검사인 Lloyd's surveyor
로이드검사인 보고서 Lloyd's survey report
로이드보험자 Lloyd's underwriter
로이드중개인 Lloyd's broker
로이즈위원회 Committee of Lloy's
로이즈조합 Corporation of Lloyd's
로자본드 Roosa bond
로지스틱함수 logistic function
로컬내셔널 local national
로컬즈 locals
로컬컨텐트 local content
로컬크레디트 local credit
로테이션효과 rotation effect
로트샘플링 lot sampling
록업기간 lock-up period
록업옵션 lock-up option
론갱신 balance renewal
론스프레드 loan spread
론채권 loan claims
론채권매매 loan sales
롤러코스터스와프 roller coaster swap
롤리폽 전술 lollipop tactic
롤링일드 rolling yield
롤백 rollback
롤오버론 rollover loan
롬바르드가 Lombard Street
ROM read only memory
롱버터플라이스프레드거래 long butterfly
  spread transaction
롱캘린더스프레드거래 long calendar spread
  transaction
롱콘더 long condor
롱콜 long call
롱쿠폰 long coupon
롱풋 long put
루브르합의 Louvre accord
루즈리프식 장부 loose leaf book
루터 router
루트개발 development of route

루트분석 analysis of routes
루트세일즈 route sales
루프 loop
룩백옵션 look-back option
리뉴얼프로젝트 renewal projects
리마인더광고 reminder advertising
리밸런싱전략 rebalancing strategies
리버스레포 reverse repo
리버스제로쿠폰스왑 reverse zero coupon
  swap
리베이트; 환불 rebate
리베이트금지법 anti-rebate law
리볼빙론 revolving loan
리볼빙언더라이팅퍼실리티 revolving
  underwriting facility
리스계약 leasing contract
리스기간 lease period
리스료 rental revenue
리스수익 revenue from leases
리스업무 leasing business
리스케줄링 rescheduling
리스크가 없는 거래 riskless transaction
리스크가 큰 risky
리스크감응도지표 risk sensitive index
리스크개시서 risk disclosure statement
리스크경감수단 risk reduction measure
리스크경감전략 risk reduction strategy
리스크구조 risk structure
리스크기반자본금 risk-based capital
리스크를 수반한 재정거래 risk arbitrage
리스크를 최소화함 risk minimization
리스크매니지먼트 risk management
리스크부담 exposure to risk; risk taking
리스크분산 diversification of risks
리스크선호도 risk preference
리스크섹터 risk sector
리스크수익그룹 risk-return group
리스크와 수익의 관계 risk-return relationship
리스크와 수익의 트레이드 오프 risk-return
  trade-off
리스크웨이트 risk weight; risk-weighting

리스크의 시장가격 market price of risk
리스크제어 risk-controlled
리스크증권 risky securities
리스크측정 measure of risk
리스크특성 risk characteristic
리스크페널티 risk penalty
리스크프리미엄 risk premium
리스크허용도 risk tolerance
리스트럭처링 관련주 restructuring related stock
리스회계 accounting for leases
리스회사 leasing company
리얼타임 real time
리얼타임처리 rate-real time processing
리엔방기 release of lien

리엔지니어링 reengineering
리저브트랑슈 reserve tranche
리즈앤드래그즈 leads and lags
리코스론 recourse loan
리크리에이션관리 recreation plan
리턴극대자 return maximizer
리턴라인 return line
리테일뱅킹 retail banking
리텐션스케줄 retention schedule
리파이낸스방식 refinance system
리패키지채 repackage bond
린 생산방식 lean production method
링 ring
링크채 linked bond

마감세일 closing sale
마감시산표 closing trial balance
마감일 cutoff date
마감장의 고가 higher quotation at the close
마감필 계정 closed account
마감후 계정 post-close account
마감후 기입 post-closing entry
마구 팔기 bear the market
마더펀드 mother fund
마땅히 허용해야 하는 admissible
마샬곡선 Marshall curve
마샬수요곡선 Marshallian demand curve
마스트리히트조약 Maastricht Treaty
마을 town
마음을 사로잡는 engrossing
마이너스성장 minus growth; negative growth; subzero growth
마이너스실링 minus-ceiling
마이너스요인 adverse element; minus factor; negative factor
마이너스틱 minus tick
마이크로구성요소 판매모델 microcomponent sales model
마이크로분석 microanalysis
마이크로행동적인 판매모델 microbehavioral sales model
마이크로헤지 microhedge
마인드쉐어 mind share
마주침 come to terms
마중물효과; 실마리효과 pump-priming effect

마찰; 마찰손 chafing
마찰로 인한 실업 frictional unemployment
마케팅 marketing
마케팅결정 marketing decision
마케팅결정변수 marketing decision variable
마케팅경로선정 marketing channel selection
마케팅관행 marketing practices
마케팅구조 marketing structure
마케팅기능 functions of marketing; marketing function
마케팅기회 marketing opportunity
마케팅독점 marketing monopoly
마케팅비 marketing expense
마케팅상대주의 marketing relativism
마케팅성과 marketing performance
마케팅요인 marketing force
마케팅원가계산 marketing cost accounting
마케팅원가분석 marketing cost analysis
마케팅위험 marketing risk
마케팅의사결정지원시스템 marketing decision support system
마케팅이론 marketing theory
마케팅자극 marketing stimuli
마케팅전술 marketing tactics
마케팅조직 marketing organization
마케팅중개업자 marketing intermediary
마케팅통제 marketing control
마케팅통제시스템 marketing control system
마케팅현상 marketing phenomena
마케팅환경 marketing environment
마켓니치전략 market niche strategy

마켓메이커 market maker
마켓메이킹기능 market making function
마켓메이킹상황 market making condition
마켓바스켓방식 market basket contract
마켓세그멘테이션 market segmentation
마켓아웃조항 market out clause
마켓액세스 access to market
마켓온클로즈오더 market-on-close order
마켓이프터치드오더 market-if-touched order
마켓타이밍 market timing
마크채 mark bond
마크투마켓 mark to market
막 훔쳐낸 hot
막다른 길 pent road
막다른 산업 stalemated industry
막대그래프 bar chart
막장 last quotation
만기 Final maturity; maturity
만기가 된 채무 maturing liability
만기계산 entire day
만기반려금 maturity repayment
만기반액지불양로보험 semi-endowment
　　insurance
만기배액지불양로보험 double endowment
　　insurance
만기분산 staggering maturity
만기분포의 차이 maturity distribution range
만기상환 redemption at maturity
만기시 연령 age at expiry
만기어음 matured bill
만기에 가까운 near maturity
만기에 가까운 채권 seasoned bond
만기에 가까운 채무 near-term bond
만기이익 yield to maturity
만기일 due date; exercise date; expiration date
만기일괄상환 bullet maturity
만기일괄상환채 bullet bond
만기일구성 maturity structure
만기일기준 maturity basis
만기일표 maturity list
만기전 상환 prior redemption

만기전 인수 anticipated acceptance
만기전이서 before due endorsement
만기지불고 amount due
만기채권 matured bond
만기채무 matured liability
만기청구액 termination claim
만기통지 expiration notice
만기파일 expiration file
만기표소유권 ownership of expiration
만기후 이서 after maturity endorsement
만능의 all-purpose
만들어낸 솜씨 workmanship
만료 expiration
만리장성; 큰 방해물 Chinese wall
만성적 chronic
만성적인 디플레이션 chronic deflation
만성적인 인플레 deep-rooted inflation
만성적인 인플레이션 chronic inflation
만성적인 태업 chronic absenteeism
만족할 만한 satisfactory
말소 obliteration
말소회사 defunct company
망판(網版) half tone
매가 labeled price
매가재고조사법 selling price inventory
매가환원법 retail method
매각가능증권 securities for sale
매각권 power of sale
매각시반제 due on sale
매각원가 cost of products sold
매각익 profit on sale
매각제한주식 letter stock
매개변수; 파라미터 parameter
매너지먼트사이클 management cycle
매너지먼트시뮬레이션 management
　　simulation
매뉴얼매니퓰레이터 manual manipulator
매니저의 기여도 manager's contribution
매니지먼트계약 management contract
매니지먼트바이아웃 management buyout
매달 차트 monthly chart

매력주 glamor stock

매리 marry

매립지 reclaimed land

매매 bargain; buying and selling; purchases and sales

매매계약 sales contract

매매계약상의 양도 assignment of sales contract

매매계약선수금 advanced collection on sale contracts

매매계약을 하였으나 아직 결제하지 않은 주식이나 상품 long account

매매계정 trading account

매매고 volume of trading

매매기록 act of sale

매매단위 unit of trading

매매방법 role of securities trading

매매보고서 bought and sold note

매매손익계정 trading profit and loss account

매매수요 floating supply

매매에 적합한 권리 marketable title

매매유지주문 supporting order

매매일임계정 discretionary account

매매일임계정거래 discretionary account transaction

매매일치 matched book

매매정지 suspended trading

매매차익금 down spread

매매치폭 bid ask spread

매매폭 bit-ask spread

매매확인서 contract slip

매물 for sale

매부(買付)여행 buying trip

매부위탁서 주문서; 매입위탁서 indent

매부위탁입체금 advance on indent

매상 sales; selling on a rising scale; takings

매상(비제조업) revenue

매상계산기준 basis for recording sales

매상계산서 account of sales; account sales

매상계정 sales account

매상고 proceeds of sale; sale amount; volume of sales

매상고를 인식함 recognition of sales

매상고반응함수 sales response function

매상고영업이익률 operating profit on sales

매상고예산 sales volume budget

매상고예측 sales forcasting

매상고이익률 ratio of profit to net sales

매상고최대화가설 revenue maximization hypothesis

매상고한계이익률 profit-volume ratio

매상기준 sales basis

매상되돌림 sales returns

매상반려 rebate on sales

매상분개장 sales journal

매상분석 sales analysis

매상성장률 sales growth rate

매상세 sales tax

매상세금공제전 이익률 pretax income to sales

매상송장 sales invoice

매상수령 unit sales

매상수수료 selling commission

매상수익 sales revenues

매상순이익률 net income to sales; net profit margin; net profit to sales

매상순익 net profit on sales

매상액 sales proceeds

매상원가 cost of goods sold; sales cost

매상원가율 sales cost ratio

매상원장 sales ledger

매상이익률 sales profit ratio

매상장 sales book; selling rate

매상전표 sales slip

매상증가 gains of sales; increase of sales

매상증가율 turnover increase rate

매상채권 trade receivable

매상채권회수기간 average collection period

매상채권회전률 receivables turnover

매상채권회전일수 number of days' sales in receivables

매상채무비율 payables to sales ratio

매상총손실 gross loss on sales

매상총이익 gross margin; gross profit on sales

매상총이익률 ratio of gross profit to net sales

매상총익률 gross-profit ratio

매상환불 sales rebate

매수 buying over

매수계약서 purchase agreement

매수기회 aquisition opportunity

매수를 임의조사함 purchase investigation

매수법 purchase method

매수부담 buyer's risk

매수시장 buyer's market

매수액면금액 purchase face amount

매수여잉 buyer's surplus

매수율 bid rate

매수저지소송 showstopper

매수하다 buy out

매스머천다이즈 mass merchandiser

매스머천다이징 전략 mass merchandising strategy

매스미디어 mass media

매스킹 masking

매신호 buy signal; sell signal

매압력 selling pressure

매예약 selling contract

매월지불 monthly payment

매입 takeover

매입; 처분매입 buying

매입가능신용장 negotiable letter of credit

매입계산서 purchase and sale statement

매입그룹 purchase

매입대금채무 purchase-money obligation

매입대리인 purchase agent

매입대상채권 instruments for buying operation

매입보유 long position

매입보유리스크 long position risk

매입부품 purchased parts

매입불능신용장 straight credit

매입상각 redemption by purchase; retirement by purchase

매입선택권부 물품사용계약 hire purchase agreement

매입수수료 buying commission; commission for purchase

매입어음할인료 discounts on bills bought

매입외국환 foreign exchange bills bought

매입은행무지정신용장 general letter of credit; open letter of credit

매입은행지정신용장 restricted letter of credit; special letter of credit

매입을 미루다 hold off buying

매입을 촉진하여 급격한 시세 변동을 막다 holding the market

매입인수 bought deal; firm commitment underwriting

매입자금 funds for purchase; purchase fund

매입채무 payables

매입채무회전율 turnover of payables

매입청구이익 yield-to-put

매입초과; 순구입고 net purchase

매입측의 거래잔고 open interest on buyer's side

매입헤지 long hedge

매입헤징 long hedging

매잔재고 unsalable stock

매장 chance to sell; selling opportunity

매장설치권; 지대 stallage

매절 outright purchase

매점 buying up; cornering; hoarding

매주 emptor; purchaser

매주(買主)의 위험부담 caveat emptor; caveat venditor

매주(파는 자)선택 seller's option

매주문 sell order; selling order

매주의 차트 weekly chart

매주지불보증대리인 del credere agent

매진 sellout

매체; 미디어 media

매체광고 media advertising

매체믹스 media mix

매체분류 classification of media
매체선택 vehicle selection
매체요율표; 과금표 rate card
매체의 결정 media decision
매체지배 media control
매체효과 media effect
매초상수 field
매출 offering for sale; secondary offering
매출가격 issue price; offering price; sales price
매출견본 selling sample
매출사이드 selling side
매출어음 bill drawn for sale
매출에누리 sales allowance
매출오퍼레이션 open market selling operation
매출이 매입보다 많은 상태 oversold position
매출인기 selling support
매출자 writer
매출장본인 leader of short side
매출재보험 ceded reinsurance
매출주 publicly offered share
매출측의 거래잔고 open interest on seller's side
매출헤지 short hedge
매츄리티스트리핑 maturity stripping
매칭거래 matching transaction
매크로경제모델 macroeconomic model
매크로경제요인 macroeconomic factor
매크로기능 macrofunction
매크로헤지 macrohedge
매트릭스 matrix
매트릭스대수 matrix algebra
매트릭스조직 matrix organization
매판 comprador
매호치 asked rate
매환 exchange bought; exchange sold
매환자산 property replaced by purchase
맥시밀레이트 maxmil rate
맺음말 jurat
머니게임 money game

머니마켓우선주 money market preferred stock
머니마켓유닛트러스트 money market unit trust
머니서플라이관리 money supply control
머니서플라이분석통계 statistics on money supply analysis
머니스프레드 money spread
머니포지션 money position
머니플로분석 money flow analysis
머니플로표 money flow table
머지 않아 near future
머천다이저 merchandiser
머천다이즈마트 merchandise mart
머천다이징 merchandising
머천트뱅크 merchant bank
먼로주의 Monroe Doctrine
먼스리리버설 monthly reversal
먼스오더 month order
멀티도메스틱 multidomestic
멀티미디어 multimedia
멀티미디어컴퓨터 multimedia personal computer
멀티상법 multilevel marketing system; pyramid marketing system
멀티소싱 multisourcing
멀티윈도 multiwindow
멀티커런시론 multicurrency loan
멀티태스크 multitask
멀티풀라인 multiple line
멀티풀라인보험증권 multiple line policy
멀티풀옵션펀딩퍼실리티 multiple option funding facilities
메가마케팅 megamarketing
메가바이트 mega byte
메가셀링 megaselling
메가트랜스포트네트워크 mega transport network
메뉴어프로치 menu approach
메모랜덤디시전 memorandum decision
메세나; 기업후원 mecena
메시지경로 message channel

메시지포괄보험 messenger floater
메시지효과 effect of message; message effect
메이저마켓지수 major market index
메이저무브 major move
메이저피크 major peak
메이크업 make up
메인터넌스리스 maintenance lease
메일론 mail-order loan
메일컨퍼메이션 mail confirmation
메일크레디트 mail credit
메일크레디트퍼실리티 mail credit facility
메자닌브라켓 mezzanine bracket
메자닌채무 mezzanine debt
메자닌파이낸스 mezzanine finance
메카트로닉스 mechatronics
메타마케팅 metamarketing
메타요구 meta-need
메타커뮤니케이션 meta-communication
면세 duty exemption; exemption from taxation; tax exemption
면세소득 taxfree income
면세수입품 duty free imports
면세의 duty free; exempt from taxation
면세점 exemption point; tax exemption limit
면세증권 nontaxable securities
면세채 tax exempt bond
면세투자 taxfree investment
면세특권 extraterritoriality on tax laws
면세품 free article; free goods; nontaxable goods
면소를 언도하다 aquit
면역화 immunization
면제 immunity; imputation
면제사회사(私會社) exempt private company
면제증권 exempt securities
면책 exoneration; indemnity
면책되는 excusable
면책된 quit
면책문서 disclaimer
면책법 act of indemnity
면책보합부 적용약관 no franchise

면책선서 cornpurgation
면책약관 exceptions clause; exemption agreement
면책위험 excepted perils; excluded perils; perils excepted
면책율조항 franchise clause
면책조항 escape clause; exception clause; exculpatory clause; exemption clause; hedge clause; negligence clause
면책조항삭제 deletion of exclusion
면책주의 doctrine of immunity
면책특약 hold harmless agreement
면허료 fees and permits; license fees
면허보험자 authorized insurer
면허세 license tax; licensing system
명령 mandate; precept
명령계통 chain of command
명령불복종 contumacy
명령일 rule day
명령적인 법률 affirmative statute
명령하다 enjoin
명료성의 원리 principle of clarity
명목계정 nominal account
명목발주 token order
명목보호율 nominal rate of protection
명목부채 nominal liabilities
명목상거래 nominal transaction
명목상의 손해배상액 nominal damages
명목상의 재산세 nominal wealth tax
명목상의 지대 peppercorn rent
명목상의 파트너 nominal partner
명목수익률 nominal rate of return
명목수입 nominal income
명목원본 notional amount
명목이율 nominal rate of interest; nominal yield
명목이익 nominal profit
명목임금 nominal wage
명목자산 nominal assets; nominal capital
명목주의 nominalism
명목할인율 nominal rate of discount

ㅁ
ㅂ

명목 **GNP** nominal GNP
명백성 certainty
명백한 위험 apparent danger
명백한 행위 overt act
명백한; 공공연한 overt
명백한; 외견의 apparent
명세서; 시방서 specification
명세서부 고가품포괄보험 scheduled property floater
명세서부 동산포괄보험 scheduled personal property floater
명시계약 express contract
명시담보 express warranty
명시된 express
명시신탁 express trust
명시적 비용 explicit cost
명시조건 condition express; express condition
명시지역권 apparent easement
명시하지 않은 비용 implicit cost
명예가격 prestige price
명예계약 honorable agreement
명예박탈 infamy
명예보험증권 honor policy
명예훼손 defamation
명예훼손(문서에 의한) 명예훼손 libel
명예훼손배상책임보험 libel liability insurance
명예훼손이 될 만한 표시 actionable words
명의 artificer; street name
명의대여 lending a street name
명의변경 stock transfer; transfer of name
명의변경대리인 transfer agent
명의변경저지 shut for dividend
명의상의 소유 order and disposition
명의상의 소유자 reputed owner
명의상의 주주 owner of record
명의상의 피보험자 nominal assured
명의서환 name transfer
명의인 nominee
명의주 dummy stock
명의주배당 dividend on dummy stock

명의척도 nominal scale
모기지개방증서 satisfaction of mortgage
모기지관리 mortgage service
모기지권자 mortgage creditor
모기지담보채권 mortgage backed bond
모기지담보형태 mortgage collateral
모기지사채금리 mortgage bond coupon
모기지증권 mortgage backed securities
모기지풀 mortgage pool
모네터리어프로치 monetary approach
모노라인 mono line
모노크로닉 monochronic
모니터리서베이 monetary survey
모니터리타겟 monetary target
모니터리트랜스퍼 monetary transfer
모달시프트 modal shift
모델분석 model analysis
모델스톡계획 model stock plan
모뎀 modem
모두문서 opening words
모두진술 opening statement
모듈러비품 modular fixtures
모든 소비자 all buyers
모든 종류를 포함하는; 일괄의 across the board
모디파이드듀레이션 modified duration
모디파이드패스스루증권 modified pass-through securities
모딜리아니-밀러의 명제 Modigliani-Miller theory
모랄리스크 moral risks
모멘텀오실레이터 momentum oscillator
모멘트 moment
모순 repugnancy
모욕 contempt
모자형 투자신탁 family fund
모조 replicate
모집 offering
모집계약 subscription agreement
모집비 recruiting expense
모집안내서 offering circular

모집요강 memorandum for offering
모핑 morphing
모험 adventure
모험대차증권 bottomry bond
모호; 불명료함 ambiguity
목재거래세 timber delivery tax
목적세 earmarked tax; object tax
목적적립금 appropriation surplus; reserve for specific purpose
목적적합성 fitness for purpose
목적함수 objective function
목전 in the near term
목표가격 target price
목표갈등 goal conflict
목표관리 management by objective
목표배당성향 target payout ratio
목표변동폭 target range
목표변수 goal variable
목표원가 target cost
목표이율 target yield
목표이익 desired profit; profit goal; target income; target profit
목표일치 goal congruence
목표포트폴리오 target portfolio
몰수 confiscation; forfeiture
몰수된 impound
몹시 차가와지다 at low ebb
몹시 취함 intemperance
몽타쥬 montage
무가치증권 belly up
무간섭주의 laissez-faire
무결함운동 zero defects
무계약급부 uncovenanted benefit
무공제담보방식 first-dollar coverage
무공제면책률 nondeductible franchise
무공제면책보합 ordinary franchise
무관계한 impertinent
무관심과실 wanton negligence
무구분식 single step
무권대리 nominal proxy
무권카드 unauthorized card

무기명식 bearer form
무기명예탁증권 Bearer Depositary Receipts
무기명주권 stock certificate to bearer
무기명주식 bearer share; uninscribed stock
무기명채권 bearer bond
무기한보증 continuing guaranty
무기한으로 sine die
무기한차압 distress
무너지다 slip
무담보거래 unsecured trading
무담보계정 unsecured account
무담보부채 unsecured liability
무담보사채 unsecured bond
무담보신용 unsecured credit
무담보신용장 clean credit; documentary clean credit
무담보융자 unsecured loan
무담보의 unsecured
무답변 nil dicit
무등록주 unregistered stock
무력(無力)소송 faint action
무료배달우편 frank
무료신문 free paper
무리스크금리 risk-free interest rate
무리스크뉴트럴 risk-neutral valuation
무리스크의 risk-free
무리스크자산 risk-free assets
무리스크재정 riskless arbitrage
무리스크증권 risk-free securities
무리하게 억지로 청함 racketeering
무배 nondividend
무배당 omitted dividend; passed dividend
무배당보험료 nonparticipating premium
무배당보험자산 nonparticipating fund
무배당으로 하다 pass dividend
무버블밴드 movable band
무보수 without compensation
무부담 freedom from incumbrance
무사고반환 no claim return
무상계약 gratuitous contract; naked contract
무상관수익률 uncorrelated return

무상기탁 gratuitous bailment
무상승계인 부동산처분 voluntary settlement
무상양도 voluntary conveyance
무상취득자 volunteer
무상환사채 debenture stock
무상환종신연금 life annuity with no refund
무생물 bona vacantia
무선통신 radio communication
무세 free of taxation
무세품표 free list
무소답으로 인한 결석판결 judgment nil dicit
무시 wantonness
무시할 수 있는 가격 negligible in amount
무신고가산세 additional tax due to failure to file a return
무액면주 nonpar stock
무액면주식 nonpar-value stock; no-par-value stock; stock without par value
무약인항변 no consideration
무역관련투자조치 trade-related investment measures
무역교섭위원회 Trade Negotiations Committee
무역금융 foreign trade finance; trade credit
무역마찰 trade friction
무역불균형 trade imbalance
무역산업부 Department of Trade and Industry
무역상대국 trading partner
무역수지 balance of trade; trade balance
무역수지실적 trade figure
무역수지흑자 favorable balance of trade
무역수지흑자폭 trade surplus amount
무역에 편향된 성장 pro-trade biased growth
무역연관분석 trade matrix analysis
무역외 invisible trade
무역외수지 balance on invisible trade; invisible trade balance
무역자유화 liberalization of trade
무역장벽 barrier trade
무역적자 trade deficit

무역정책 foreign trade policy
무역지수 index of trade
무역창출효과 trade creation effect
무역클레임 trade claim
무역통계 foreign trade statistics; trade statistics; trade control
무이식채무 passive debt
무이자대부 loan without interest
무이자사채 passive bond
무일부어음 undated bill
무작위추출법 random sampling
무재고방식 inventoryless system
무제한법화 unlimited legal tender
무조건오퍼 outright base
무조건오퍼레이션 unconditional operation
무조건유동성 unconditional liquidity
무조건의 unconditional
무조건의; 절대로 absolute
무조건인도 absolute delivery
무조건인출권 unconditional drawing right
무조건주문 open order
무조건채무 unconditional debt
무조건추정 unconditional estimate
무조건판매 absolute sales
무진단증액특약 guaranteed insurability rider
무차별곡선 indifference curve
무차별점 point of indifference
무체동산 chose in action; thing in action
무체재산 incorporeal property
무크 mook
무한정감사보고서 nonopinion report
무한정의견 unqualified opinion
무한책임 unlimited liability
무한책임사원 general partner
무한책임파트너십 general partnership
무한책임회사 unlimited liability company
무해한 오진 harmless error
무형감가상각자산 intangible depreciable assets
무형고정자산 intangible fixed assets;

intangibles
무형상각자산 intangible depreciable property
무형자본 immaterial; intangible capital
무형자산 intangible assets; invisible assets
무형자산감가상각 amortization of intangibles
무형재산 immaterial property; intangible
  property
무형효과 intangible effects
무효 no effect; nullity
무효계약 void contract
무효라 할 수 없는 indefeasible
무효로 하다 voidable
무효로 할 수 있는 defeasible
무효의 null and void; void
무효카드 invalid card
무효판결 decree of nullity
무효합의 void agreement
무효화 annulment
무효회원 unauthorized member
무휴동산 incorporeal chattel
묵시담보 implied warranty
묵시신탁 implied trust
묵시의 tacit
묵시적인 약속 implied undertaking
묵시조건 condition implied; implied condition
묵시허용 implied license
묵인 acquiescence; connivance
묶음처리(자료) batch processing
문서관리 document control
문서를 통한 통지 notification in writing
문서열람 inspection of documents
문서위조 forgery
문서의 본문 body of an instrument
문서제출요구서 notice to produce
문서화 documentation
문서환 mail exchange bill
문자규칙 lettered rule
문자다중방송 teletext
문제가 적은 제도 lesser evil
문제를 선별함 problem identification
문제발견법 problem detection study

문제처리방법 issue management
문제해석 analysis of problem
문화경향 cultural influence
문화변용 cultural change
문화시너지 cultural synergy
문화융합 cultural assimilation
문화인류학법학 anthropological
  jurisprudence
문화적응 acculturation
문화적인 가치관 cultural values
물가 commodity price
물가변동 price variation
물가수준 price level
물가안정정책 price stabilization policy
물가지수 price index
물건 object
물건비 nonpersonnel expenses
물건을 사지 않고 값만 묻고 다니는 고객
  walk-out
물건을 사지 않고 눈요기하는 사람
  china eggs
물건이나 주식을 팔아서 큰 이득을 보고 물
  러남 unloading
물건특정보험 specific insurance
물권 real right; right in rem
물권법 laws of realty
물납 payment in kind
물납세 levy in kind; tax in kind
물량이 적은 상장 sold-out market
물량이 적은 주 narrow market security
물류 physical distribution
물류기능 physical distribution function
물류생산성 distribution productivity
물류전략 physical distribution strategy
물류책임 physical distribution responsibility
물리적인 감가 physical depreciation
물리적인 감모 physical wear and tear
물리적인 내용연수 physical life
물리적인 예비비 physical contingency
물물교환 barter
물산(物産) chose

물상담보부사채 mortgage bond
물상보증 real guarantee
물상피보험이익 insurable interest in property
물색매매 selective buying
물세 impersonal tax; tax on goods and possessions
물적 안전성 physical safety
물적공제 impersonal deduction
물적과세제외 impersonal exclusion from taxation
물적담보 collateral on property
물적동산 real chattels
물적분손절대부담보 free of damage absolutely
물적상속재산 real hereditament
물적손해 material damage
물적증거 real evidence
물적증권 securities on property
물품납부 delivery of articles
물품세 commodity excise; commodity tax; excise duty
물품세법 commodity tax law
물품을 통한 증여 gift in kind
물품화폐 commodity money
물품횡령 misappropriation of goods
뮤즈방식 multiple sub-nyquist sampling encoding
뮤츄얼펀드 mutual fund
뮤츄얼펀드인수업자 mutual fund underwriters
미가동자본 unproductive capital
미감사재무제표 unqualified financial statements
미결계정 open account; suspense account
미결산 open; unbalanced open
미결산계정 unbalanced account
미결산보험금 insurance claims unsettled
미결산의 unbalanced
미결산장부 unbalanced book
미결의 pending
미결제거래잔고 open interest
미결제계정 outstanding account; unsettled account

미결제수표 float
미결제원장 open ledger
미결제의 unsettled
미경과 unexpired
미경과광고료 advertising unexpired; prepaid insurance premiums; unearned premium; unexpired insurance premium
미경과보험료준비금 unearned premium reserve
미경과비용 expenses paid-in advance; unexpired expenses
미경과이자 unearned interest; unexpired interest
미경과할인료 unearned discount
미국경영자협회 American Management Association
미국공인증권분석가협회 Institute of Chartered Financial Analyst
미국공인회계사협회 American Institute of Certified Public Accountants
미국국무부 Department of State
미국규격협회 American National Standards Institute
미국내국세입법 Internal Revenue Code
미국내국세입청 Internal Revenue Service
미국내부감사인협회 Institute of Internal Auditors
미국노동총동맹 American Federation of Labor
미국달러채시장 Yankee bond market
미국대학교직원퇴직변액연금기금 College Retirement Equities Fund
미국방식 U.S. term
미국법률협회 American Law Institute
미국법조기금 American Bar Endowment
미국법조협회 American Bar Association
미국보증보험협회 Surety Association of America
미국보험교수연맹 Anicrican Association of University Teachers of Insurance

미국보험학회 American Risk and Insurance
Association

미국사법협회 American Judicature Socidty

미국사회사업가협회 American Association
of Social Workers

미국상무부 Department of Commerce

미국상품선물거래위원회 Commodity Futures
Trading Commission

미국상호보험회사협회 American Mutual
Insurance Alliance

미국생명보험협회 American Council of Life
Insurance; American Life Insurance
Association

미국액추어리협회 American Academy of
Actuaries

미국액추얼협회 Actuarial Society of America

미국연금가입자사망표 American Annuitants
Mortality Table

미국예탁증권 American Depositary Receipts

미국의료사회사업자협회 American
Association of Medical Social Workers

미국장학자금금고; 샐리메이 Sallie Mae

미국재무부 장기채권 long treasury bond

미국저축채 U.S. savings bond

미국정부주택저당 GNMA debenture

미국중재협회 American Arbitration
Association

미국증권거래소 American Stock Exchange

미국증권거래위원회 Securities and Exchange
Commission

미국지적소유권법협회 American Intellectual
Property Law Association

미국해상보험업자협회 American Institute of
Marine Underwriters

미국협회화물약관 American Institute Cargo
Clauses

미국형 American type

미국형 옵션 American option

미국회계사협회 American Institute of
Accountants

미국회계학회 American Accounting

Association

미국횡단의; 전미의 coast-to-coast

미기입장부 blank book

미기장자산 nonledger assets

미끼광고 bait advertising; bait ad; bait pricing

미납 nonpayments

미납세인수 nontaxable receiving

미니리펀딩 mini-refunding

미니맥스채 mini. max. bond

미니밀레이트 minimil rate

미달계정 account in transit; transit account

미달러지폐 green buck

미달상품 merchandise in transit

미달항목 item in transit

미달현금 cash in transit

미등기 unregistered

미디어선택모델 media selection model

미디엄텀노트 medium-term note

미래원가 future cost

미리 얻다; 미리 차용하다 obtain in advance

미망인 widow

미망인공제 allowance for widow; deduction
for widow; widow deduction

미미하게 늘어남 marginal rise

미미한 입증 scintilla of evidence

미발행자본 unissued capital stock

미발행주식 unissued stock

미분배잉여적립금 unassigned surplus

미분할유산 undivided bequest

미분할유산에 대한 상속세 inheritance tax on
undivided bequest

미불 unpaid

미불공임 accrued wages

미불금 accrued liabilities; amount in arrears;
debt service

미불급여 accrued payroll; employee
compensation

미불기부금 accrued donation; unpaid
donation

미불반려금 unpaid returns

미불배당금 dividend payable; unpaid

dividend
미불배당액 accrued dividend
미불법인세 income taxes payable
미불보험금 unpaid claims
미불부채 outstanding liabilities
미불비용 accrued charge; accrued expenses
　payable
미불세금 tax payable; unpaid tax
미불세금계정 tax payable account
미불수수료 accrued commission; commission
　payable
미불수입세 accrued income taxes
미불의 outstanding
미불이자 interest payable
미불임금 unclaimed wages; wages payable
미불입액 capital stock unpaid
미불입자본 subscribed capital stock; unpaid
　capital
미상각 unamortized
미상각감모자산 undepreciated wasting
　property
미상각건설이자 unamortized interest during
　construction
미상각사채할인 unamortized bond discount
미상각원가 unamortized cost
미상각잔고 amortized balance; undepreciated
　balance
미상환채권 bond outstanding
미선언자 nondeclarant
미성년자 infant; minor
미성년자공제 minor tax credit; tax credit for
　minor
미성년자의 거래계좌 minor account
미소비원가 unexpired cost
미수 unearned
미수금 accounts due; uncollected balance
미수급료 accrued salaries
미수배당 dividend receivable
미수보관료 storage accounts receivable
미수보증금 claim for guarantee
미수보험금 insurance claims

미수보험료 deferred premium; due and
　deferred premiums; outstanding premiums;
　premium in arrears; uncollected premium
미수세 taxes receivable
미수수수료 commission receivable;
　uncollected commission
미수수익 uncollected income; uncollected
　revenue
미수수취계정합계 total receivables
미수은행예금이자 interest receivable on bank
　deposits
미수이익 accrued income; accrued revenue
미수이익 처분금지 restraint on anticipation
미수이자 uncollected interest
미수임차금 accrued rent
미수자금 uncollected funds
미수지계정 accruals
미수지대 uncollected rent
미스매치리스크 mismatch risk
미스매칭 mismatching
미스트러스트 mixed trust
미스프라이싱 mispricing
미시그마의 수익그래프 Mysigma
　profitability graph
미실현수익 unrealized revenue; unrealized
　income
미약전파방송 nonlicensed micropower
　broadcasting
미완료거래 incomplete transaction
미완성공사 uncompleted works
미이용지세 tax on unutilized land; unused
　land tax
미정 pendency
미주자유무역권 Western Hemisphere Free
　Trade Area
미착품 goods in transit; goods to arrive
미처리결손금 unappropriated deficit
미처분 undisposed; undivided
미처분결손 undisposed deficit
미처분이익 unappropriated income;
　undivided profits

미처분이익잉여금 unappropriated earned surplus; unappropriated surplus

미처분잉여금 unappropriated retained earnings

미청구배당금 unclaimed dividends

미평가보험 unvalued policy

미필배상책임보험 contingent liability policy

미필수입세 duty contingency

미필영업중단보험 contingent business interruption insurance

미필운송임 freight contingency

미해결 문제 open question

미확정계약 executory contract

미활동계정 inactive account

미회수원가 unrecovered cost

민간사업 civilian enterprise; private undertaking

민간소비 private consumption

민간자본 private capital

민간전기통신사업자 recognized private operating agency

민간채 nongovernment bond; private bond

민간회사 private corporation

민감한 시장 sensitive market

민법 civil code; civil law

민사부 plea side

민사소송 civil action; common-law action

민사소송법전 code of civil procedure

민사의 civil

민사제일심재판소 court of nisi prius

민수 civilian demand

민영보험회사 private insurance company

민영사업 private enterprise

민영화 privatization

민중소송 popular action

밀라인레이트 milline rate

밀룬의 생명표 Milne's table

밀수 smuggling

밉스; **MIPS**(컴퓨터의 연산속도) million instruction per second

밑진 손해 benting

ㅁ
ㅂ

ㅂ

바닥 bottom
바닥값 bottom price
바닥시세 floor price
바닥짐(배의) ballast
바람직한 자금의 흐름을 산출하다
　generate favorable cash flows
바람직한 현금의 흐름 favorable cash flows
바베지의 생명표 Babbage's Table
바스켓 basket
바스켓거래 market basket trading
바스켓방식 basket system
바이너리파일 binary file
바이러스 virus
바이어즈크레디트 buyer's credit
바이오리듬 biorhythm
바이오컴퓨터 bio computer
바이트 byte
바젤협정 Basel Agreement
박리다매 trading down
박스젠킨스모형 box-Jenkins
박탈 amotion
박탈하다 disbar
반기(半期)보고서 semi-annual report
반기지불 semi-installment
반년마다 하는 복리계산 semi-annual
　compounding calculation
반년마다(의) half-yearly
반년불쿠폰 semi-annual coupon
반대계정 opposite accounts
반대기입 reversing entry

반대매매 closing transaction; reversing trade;
　round turn
반대상소 cross-appeal
반대선서진술서 counter-affidavit
반대소송 cross action
반대심문 cross examination;
　cross-examination
반대오퍼 counteroffer
반대의견 contrary opinion; dissenting opinion
반대증서 counter deed; counterdeed
반대청구 cross-demand
반대하다 dissent
반대항(답)변 counter-plea
반등 rebound; sharp rally
반락(反落) reaction; reactionary fall; ease
반려금 refundment
반복감사 repeating audit
반복계산 repeated calculation
반복구매 retreat buying
반복구매모델 repeat purchase model
반복범죄 cumulative of offenses
반복조사 repetition research
반사광 reflection
반소(反訴) counterclaim; demand in
　reconvention
반송 remand of further proceedings
반순환적 counter cyclical
반순환적인 contra-cyclical
반순환정책 counter cyclical policy
반실증주의 anti-positivism

반역죄 treason
반응강화 reinforcement of response
반응곡선 reaction curve
반응을 기다림 wait for reaction
반응탄력성 response elasticity
반응함수 response function
반입비 carrying-in expenses
반입인도 franco
반전 turn around
반전일 reversal day
반전패턴 reversal pattern
반제 repayment
반제기간 payment periods
반제의지 willingness to pay
반제일 maturity date
반제품 half-finished goods; part finished
    product; partially finished goods;
    semi-finished goods
반제품원장 partially finished goods ledger
반제회수 number of scheduled payments
반증 rebutting evidence sit
반증을 들다 rebut
반통합 quasi-integration
반포, 공포, 선전 promulgation
반품 goods returned to vendor; return inward;
    return outward; returned goods unsold;
    returned sales
반품조달준비금 returned unsold goods
    reserve
반품조정준비금 reserve for loss on goods
    unsold
반항 insubordination
반향원리 echo principle
반향효과 echo effect
반환권부 매매 sale or return
반환운임 return freight
발견기간 discovery period
발견위험의 원칙 doctrine of discovered peril
발권은행 bank of issue
발권제도 system of note issue
발기인 incorporator; originator; promoter

발기인주 promoter's share
발기인회 meeting of promoters
발매연기 adjourned sale
발명 invention
발생 accrual
발생가능최고손해액 maximum possible loss
발생주의 accrual basis; accrued basis; actual
    basis
발생주의회계 accrual accounting
발생채무부담 obligations incurred
발생확정시키다 vested in interest
발송비 delivery expenses; shipping expense
발송송금환 bill sent
발송운임 freight and cartage outward
발송은행 remitting bank
발송지 destination
발송지지입인도(관세입) delivered duty paid
발송지지입인도(관세제외) delivered duty
    unpaid
발언 voice
발주비 ordering cost
발주자면책조항 disclaimer clause
발주점 ordering point
발췌계산서 abstract of account
발취검사 sampling inspection
발표 deliverance
발행가격 issue value
발행개시일 launch date
발행고 amount issued
발행권 drawing right
발행규모 volume of issuance
발행등록 shelf registration
발행부수; 유통 circulation
발행비용 underwriting spread
발행상사 issuing house
발행세 issue tax
발행수수료 opening commission
발행시장 issue market
발행시할인 original issue discount
발행어음 drawn bill
발행예정채권 bond in a pipeline

발행은행 drawing bank; issuing bank
발행인 drawer
발행일거래 when-issued transaction
발행일기준 when-issued basis
발행자비용 issuer's cost
발행잔고 outstanding amount; outstanding balance of issue amount
발행전 유통시장 gray market
발행조건 conditions of issuance; issue terms
발행지 place of issue
발행직후의 증권 unseasoned security
발행필 자본 outstanding capital
발행필 자본금 capital stock issued
발행필 주식 issued shares; outstanding shares; shares outstanding
발행필 주식수 number of stocks issued
발행필 주식자본금 issued capital stock
발행필 주식총수 all issued stocks; capital stock
발행필 채권 bond issued; outstanding bond
발행회사 issuer; issuing corporation
발회 first session of the month
발효일 effective date
방계상속인 heir collateral
방계쟁점 collateral issue
방계혈족 collateral consanguinity
방관자 bystander
방기 desertion
방문판매 door-to-door sales
방문판매업자 call-sales merchant
방법론 methodology
방소항변 demurrer; plea in bar
방송광고 broadcast advertising; broadcast commercials
방송매체 broadcast media
방송업자 broadcaster
방송위성 broadcasting satellite
방위매입 defensive purchase
방위주 defensive stock
방위증권 defensive securities
방위채 defense bond

방위투자 defensive investment
방재 accident prevention
방출; 면책 discharge
방침책정 policy formulation
방해클레임 disruption claims
방해효과 interruption effect
방향성 directional movement
방향성지수 directional index
방화벽 fire wall
방화어음 bill in domestic currency
배(培)보장생명보험~배(培)보장생명보험 multiple indemnity policy; multiple protection policy
배가 뒤집힌; 전복된 capsized
배경사항 background information
배급제도 rationing
배달증명우편 delivery-certified mail
배당 dividend; dividend distribution
배당가능이익 profit available for dividend; surplus available for dividend
배당가능잉여금 divisible surplus
배당결정 determination of dividend
배당경과 reduced tax rate on dividendpaid
배당계정 dividend account
배당공제 credit for dividend; deduction for dividends; dividend credit; dividend exclusion; tax credit for dividend
배당금지불 delivery of dividends
배당능력 ability to pay dividend
배당락 dividend off; ex-dividend
배당락일 ex-dividend date
배당부 cum dividend; dividend on
배당분리과세 separated taxation on dividend income
배당사채 income bond
배당성향 dividend payout ratio; payout ratio
배당소득 dividend income
배당소득으로 귀속됨 real obtainer of dividend income
배당손금법 dividend-paid deduction method
배당예탁 accumulated dividend deposit

배당우선주식 dividend preferred stock

배당원천선택과세 alternative withholding tax on dividends

배당율 dividend rate

배당이익 dividend yield

배당이익이 없는데도 배당함 bogus dividend

배당재투자계획 dividend reinvestment plan

배당제한 limitation on dividend

배당주 dividend stock

배당준비적립금 dividend reserve

배당지불 dividend payment; payout

배당평균적립금 dividend equalization reserve

배당평균준비금 dividend equalization fund; equalizing dividends

배당플로 dividend flow

배당할인율 dividend discount rate

배당환원가액 capitalized value of stock

배당환원모델 dividend discount model

배당환원방식 dividend discount method

배당환원주식평가 stock valuation based on dividend

배리어프리 barrier free

배부계정 absorption account

배부부족 under absorbed

배부세 apportioned tax; distribution tax

배부절차 alloction procedure

배부초과원가 overabsorbed cost

배부필 제조간접비 absorbed burden

배분 admeasurement

배분기능 allocating function

배분기준 allocation on bases

배분지관리인 allotment warden

배분판결 decree of distribution

배상금 claims; indemnities; reprisal

배상금중복회수의 원칙 collateral source rule

배상책임집중 channeling of liability

배상책임한도액 limit of liability

배상청구를 인정받지 못하는 손해 damnum sine injuria

배상하다 make good

배석판사 side judge

배수사업지구 drainage district

배신 abuse of confidence

배심 Jury

배심선정관 elisors

배심심문저지신청 arrest of inquest

배심원 juror

배심원명부 panel

배심원석 jury box

배심원선정을 속임 packing a jury

배심원재판 jury trial

배심원호출 calling the jury

배액감채약관 option to double

배액정율법 double declining balance method

배우자공제 allowance for spouse; deduction for spouse; exemption for spouse

배우자특별공제 special exemption for spouse

배율평가 valuation by multiplier

배임; 유용 malversation

배제가능리스크 avoidable risk

배치; 고용 placement

배치거래시스템 batch trading system

배치전환 transposition

배타적인 사양 preclusive specification

백마 탄 왕자; 매수위기의 기업을 구하기 위해 개입하는 제 3의 기업 white knight

백분율대차대조표 common-size balance sheet; percentage balance sheet

백분율법 percentage method

백분율변이법 percentage variation method

백분율손익계산서 one hundred percent income statement

백분율재무제표 common-size financial statements; percentage statements

백분율표 percentage table

1/100퍼센트 basis point

백색신고 white return

백업라인 backup line

백업퍼실리티 back-up facility

백엔드라이트 back-end rights

백오피스; 배후부문; 비영업부문 back office

백지대 alba firma

백지식 이서 endorsement in blank
백지양도 assignment in blank
백지위임 carte blanche
백지이서 blank; blank endorsement
백지인수 blank acceptance
백지주식 blank stock
백투백론 back-to-back loan
백화점매상고 department store sales
백화점포괄보험 department store floater
밴드앤드크롤 band and crawl
밴드왜건효과 band wagon effect
밴콜 ban call
밸런스펀드 balanced fund
밸런스펀드포트폴리오 balanced fund portfolio
밸런스형 매니저 balanced manager
밸류다이어그램 value diagram
밸류라인 종합지수 value line composite index
밸류라인랭킹 value line ranking
밸류라인옵션 value line option
밸류라인인덱스 value line index
밸류라인평균 value line average
밸류어프로치 value approach
뱀파이어비디오 vampire video
뱅크라인 bank line
뱅크와이어 bankwire
뱅크카드 regional bank card
버스 bus
버즈세션; 버즈학습 buzz session
버터플라이스프레드거래 butterfly spread trading
버텀업어프로치 bottom-up approach
버텀업형 bottom-up process
버텀업형 예측 bottom-up forecasting
버티컬스프레드 vertical spread
버티컬스프레드거래 vertical spread transaction
버팅 butting
번호계좌 numbered accounts
벌금 amercement; fine; penalty and fine
벌금면제 abishering

벌칙 penal regulations
벌칙금리 penalty rate
범용카드 all purpose card
범유럽디지털전화방식 groupe speciale mobile
범죄 offense
범죄력 criminal record
범죄를 병합함 joinder of offenses
범죄보증증권 crime bond
범죄보험 crime insurance
범죄복합 duplicity
범죄의사 malice
범죄지법 lex loci delictus
범행을 방조하다 aid and abet
법 artificial
법규재량 controlled discretion
법령 prescript
법령보증 judicial bond
법령에 의한 statutory
법령전서 statute book
법령집 statutes at large
법률격언 maxims
법률고문 counselor; legal adviser
법률과 사실이 혼재된 문제 mixed question of law and fact
법률관계 legal relations
법률변경 law change
법률사무소 law office
법률상 de jure; ipso jure
법률상담 legal aid services; legal counsel
법률상담료 fee for legal advice
법률상의 사망 civil death
법률상의 의무 legal duty
법률상의 의제 fiction
법률상의 점유 legal possession
법률상의 증거 legal evidence
법률상의 직원 officer de jure
법률상의 책임집중제도 legal channeling of liability
법률상의 추정 legal presumption
법률서류 legal document
법률에 저촉됨 conflict of laws

법률에서 요구하는 형식 form required by law
법률위반 breach of law
법률위임 authorization by law
법률의 선언적인 부분 declaratory part of law
법률이 아닌 기준 nonlegal standards
법률적인 추정 artificial presumptions
법률착오 mistake of law
법률학 jurisprudence
법률행위 juristic act
법무관 Advocate General
법무부 legal department
법무장관 Attorney General
법무처리 management of juristic act
법시행지 law enforced territory
법외이익 exorbitant profit
법원 court; forum
법원소기관 court clerk
법원의 당연한 확신 judicial notice
법의 지배 rule of law
법의 진의 intendment of law
법의 평등한 보호 equal protection of the laws
법의 행위 act of law
법의학 forensic medicine; medical jurisprudence
법이 예정한 증거 preappointed evidences
법인 artificial person; corporation; Juridical person; legal person
법인격 juridical personality
법인격이 없는 단체 nonjuridical organization
법인격이 없는 회사 unincorporated company
법인고객 corporate customer
법인권 corporate right
법인단체 corporate body
법인매입 institution buying
법인보증인 corporate suretyship
법인사업세 enterprise tax on corporation
법인설립 establishment of corporation; incorporation
법인세 corporate tax
법인세공제 corporation tax credit; credit against corporation tax

법인세공제전 순이익 net profit before corporation tax
법인세액손금불산입 exclusion from expenses of corporation tax
법인세액특별공제 special credit of corporation tax
법인세준비금 reserve for corporation tax
법인세할과세 taxation on corporation tax basis
법인세할주민세 corporation levy
법인소득 corporate income
법인소득세비용 corporate income taxes expenses
법인소득세율 corporate income tax rate
법인신탁 corporate trust
법인실재설 real entity theory of corporation
법인예금 corporate deposit
법인의 대표자 representative of corporation
법인의제설 fictional theory of corporation
법인이득세 corporation profit tax
법인이론 entity theory
법인이익금 gross income of corporation
법인인감 corporate seal
법인저축 corporate savings
법인주주 corporate shareholder; institutional stockholder
법인카드 corporate card; corporation card
법인특별세 special corporation surtax
법인해산 dissolution of corporation
법적규제 mandatory control
법적실체 legal entity
법적위험 legal jeopardy
법적절차를 밟지 않고 in pais
법적정리 legal liquidation
법적조치 legislative action
법전 code
법정감사 statutory audit
법정공탁금 statutory deposit
법정금리 legal rate of interest
법정급부 legal benefit
법정기한 legal term
법정납기한 statutory due date of tax payment

법정내용연수 legal durable years; statutory useful life

법정대리인 legal representative

법정대위 legal subrogation

법정대출한도화 legal lending limit

법정발행한도액 statutory debt limit

법정변호사평의회 Council of the Bar

법정보증증권 statutory bond

법정복리비 legal welfare expense

법정상각방법 statutory depreciation method

법정상각법 statutory depletion method

법정상속동산 heir-looms

법정상속분 legal portion of legacy

법정상속인 heir apparent

법정상속하다 inherit

법정서체 court-hand

법정세율 statutory tariff

법정수 quorum

법정신탁 constructive trust; trust by act of law

법정에 출두하다 appear

법정유가증권평가준비금 mandatory securities valuation reserve

법정이율 legal rate; statutory rate of interest

법정이율초과이자 usury

법정이익준비금 legal earned surplus reserve

법정이자 legal interest

법정자본 legal capital

법정재고평가법 legal valuation method of inventory

법정점유 possession in law

법정조언자 amicus curiae

법정준비금 legal reserve; required reserve; statutory reserve

법정준비금적립생명보험회사 legal reserve life insurance company

법정준비율 required reserve ratio

법정지법 law of the forum

법정책임; 법적채무 legal liability

법정책임보험 legal liability insurance

법정책임액 초과배상책임보험 excess legal liability policy

법정추정상속인 apparent heir; presumptive heir

법정통지서 statutory notice

법정통화 legal tender

법정평가 judicial valuation; legal valuation; mint par of exchange

법정평가방법 statutory valuation method

법정평가손적립금 mandatory valuation reserve

법정회계원칙 statutory accounting principle

법정횡령 constructive conversion

법정후견인 legal guardian

법조협회 bar association

베어본드 bear bond

베어스프레드거래 bear spread trading

베어인덱스채 bear index bond

베어콜스프레드 bear call spread

베어허그(강한 포옹) bear hug

베이비펀드 baby fund

베이스머니 base money

베이시스 basis

베이시스갭 basis gap

베이시스거래 basis trading

베이시스리스크 basis risk

베이시스스와프 basis swap

베타 beta

베타계수 beta coefficient

베타수치 beta value

베타수치에 기반을 둔 정보원 information sources on beta value

베터표준오차 standard error of beta

벡터 vector

벤처비즈니스 venture business

벤처캐피탈 venture capital

벤치마크포트폴리오 benchmark portfolio

벨로우더마켓 below the market

벨형 곡선 bell-shaped curve

벽지 remote area

변경가능보험금수취인 revocable beneficiary

변경공사 change in work

변경등기 registration of alteration
변경불능보험금수취인 absolute beneficiary
변경비망록 alteration bordereau
변경클레임 change claims
변경할 수 있는 ambulatory
변동가격권 variable zone
변동계수 coefficient of variation
변동관리비 variable overhead
변동금리 floating rate
변동금리 CD floating rate certificate of deposit
변동금리대출 floating rate lending
변동금리모기지 adjustable rate mortgage
변동금리지불인 floating rate payer
변동금리지표 floating rate index
변동금리형 부동산론 variable rate mortgage loan
변동보험료 variable premium
변동비 variable charge; variable cost and expenses; variable expenses
변동비율 rate of variable expenses
변동상장 floating system
변동상한금리부 계정 floating interest rate account with ceiling
변동소득 fluctuating income; transitory income
변동소득 및 임시소득 fluctuating and extraordinary income
변동소득계산 variable costing
변동시장 volatile market
변동예산 variable budget
변동원가율 variable cost ratio
변동율 volatility
변동율표준오차 standard deviation of volatility
변동이율 adjustable rate; floating interest rate; variable interest rate
변동이율우선주 adjustable rate preferred stock
변동이익 variable profit
변동이자부 모기지 floating rate mortgage

변동이자부 채권 floating rate bond; floating rate note
변동조항 fluctuation clause
변동증거금 variation margin
변동폭 range
변동폭이 있는 고정제 wider band
변동폭제한 fluctuation limit
변동하다 fluctuate
변동환율 floating exchange rate
변동환율제 floating exchange rate system
변량효과모델 random effect model
변론 argument
변론기일 consilium
변명; 면책사유 excuse
변상 indemnification
변수 variable
변액보험 equities insurance; variable insurance
변액생명보험 variable life insurance
변액연금 variable annuity
변액유니버설보험 flexible-premium variable life insurance; variable universal life insurance
변제기일을 앞당기는 약관 acceleration clause
변제를 연기함 respite
변제유예 standstill agreement
변조 alteration
변조카드 forged cards
변존임차권 concurrent lease
변칙; 편차 anomaly
변호사 attorney; attorney at law; lawyer
변호사; 옹호자 advocate
변호사고문료 retaining fee
변호사도덕 etiquette of the profession
변호사료 lawyer's fee
변호사리엔 retaining lien
변호사배상책임보험 lawyer's liability insurance
변호사보수 legal fee
변호사위임계약 retainer
변호사의 도움을 받을 권리 right to counsel

ㅁㅂ

변호사의 의견서 legal opinion; opinion
변호사의뢰권 access to counsel
변호사자격박탈이유 grounds for disbarment
변호사책임 lawyer's liability
변화무쌍함 confounded variable
변화율 rate of change
변환계수 conversion factor
별거수당 separate maintenance
별계정 separate bill
별단예금 special deposits
별도계정 separate account
별도계정지불 extra
별도물건 general reserve
별도의 규정이 없는 한 not otherwise
  provided
별도적립금 general risk; other reserve;
  special reserve fund; unconditional reserve
별도지출 special outlay
별로 마음이 내키지 않음 dull
별명 alias
별봉(別封)으로 under separate cover
병위채 exchange bill payable
병존원인 concurrent cause
병합 annexation; joinder
병합심리 joinder of protests
보간법, 내삽법 interpolation
보강증거 corroborating evidence
보강하다 corroborate
보고서 account record; bulletin report; report;
보고식 narrative form; report form; schedule
  form
보고식 대차대조표 report form balance sheet
보고제도 report system
보고통화 reporting currency
보관 custody; safe keeping
보관계정 custodial account
보관기간 retention time
보관기한 shelf life
보관료 charges for custody; custody fee;
  storage; warehouse expenses; warehouse
  rent

보관비 inventory carrying cost; storage
  charges
보관유가증권 securities deposited from
  others; securities received as collaterals
보관은행 custodian bank
보관품 article in custody
보급 diffusion
보급과정 diffusion process
보급과정모델 model of diffusion process
보급률 diffusion rate
보급모델 diffusion model
보드거래 board trading
보류논점 points reserved
보복 retaliation
보복관세 retaliatory duties
보상계약서 letter of indemnification
보상금 indemnity allowance; push money
보상급부 reimbursement benefit
보상액; 보험금 claim paid or payable
보상액누증약관 accumulation clause
보상예금 compensatory deposit
보상융자 compensatory financing facility
보상의 약속을 하다 indemnify
보상재보험 indemnity reinsurance
보상제도 compensation system
보상지불수권서 reimbursement authorization
보상판매상품을 과대평가함 overestimation
  of goods traded
보색 complementary color
보석계약서 bail-piece
보석금 bail
보석금상실 forfeiture of bail
보석보증 bailbond
보석보증인 safe-pledge
보석보증증권 bail bond
보석완료 perfecting bail
보석자인도영장 liberate
보석허가명령 admission
보세운송 transportation in bond
보세지역 bonded area
보세항고내 화물 bonded goods

보수 compensation; fee; remuneration;
 renumeration; returns; reward
보수과 maintenance department
보수방식 compensation plan
보수성 conservatism
보수주의의 원칙 principle of conservatism
보수주의회계 concept of conservatism
보수한계량 critical mass of reward
보완수요 complementary demand
보완재 complementary goods
보완펀드 completeness fund
보유 retention
보유계약 total amount of insurance in force
보유기간상대가치 holding period
 value-relative
보유기간수익률 holding period return
보유보험료 retained premium
보유손익 holding gain or loss
보유손해액 loss retention; underlying
 retention
보유액 retained line
보유재산 tenement
보유주식수 number of stocks held
보유주포함 latent equity holdings
보유증권 securities holdings
보유채권 bond held
보유품 goods carried over
보유하다 hold
보유한도액 limit of retention
보유형태 type of holding
보이스메일 voice mail
보이스오버 voice over
보이지 않는 손 invisible hand
보장요율제 merit rating
보전담보 preservative security
보전성 maintainability
보전차압 preservative seizure
보전처분 injunction
보정모델 compensatory model
보정여잉 compensatory surplus
보정예산 additional budget; supplementary

 budget
보정예산정책 compensatory budget policy
보정재정정책 compensatory fiscal policy
보정항목 compensatory item
보정효과 compensatory effect
보조 help; subvention
보조공채 aid bond
보조금교부 delivery of subsidies
보조금반제 settlement of subsidy
보조금반환면제 exemption from return of
 subsidy
보조급료 supplementary payment
보조기능 facilitating functions
보조기입장 subsidiary journal
보조보험 supplementary insurance
보조부 auxiliary book
보조부 융자 buy-down loan
보조부문 service department; service
 division; subsidiary department
보조부문비 service departmental charge
보조원장 auxiliary ledger; subordinate ledger;
 subsidiary ledger
보조원장계정 subsidiary accounts
보조의 ancillary
보조의; 부(副)의 auxiliary
보조장부 auxiliary journal; subsidiary book
보조재료비 subsidiary material cost
보조제품 ancillary product
보조화폐 subsidiary coin; subsidiary money
보존 preservation
보증 guarantee; pledgery; suretyship;
 warranty
보증거치연금 guaranteed deferred annuity
보증계약 guaranty
보증계약을 혼동하여 소멸함 merger of
 guaranty
보증계정 per contra-account; secured
 account; security account
보증금 caution money; deposit received;
 guarantee deposits; guarantee money;
 guaranty money

보증기간 duration of guaranty
보증기간부 연금 life annuity certain and continuous
보증대출 loan on personal guarantee
보증론 guarantee loan
보증료 guarantee charge
보증발행 fiduciary issue
보증보험 guarantee insurance
보증보험신탁 guaranteed insurance trust
보증부 대부 loan with third party's guarantee
보증부 위임 commission del credere
보증부투자계약 guaranteed income contract
보증사채 assumed bond; guaranteed bond
보증스프레드 guaranteed spread
보증우선주 controlled preferred stock
보증운임 guaranteed freight
보증위탁계약 indemnity agreement
보증은행 guarantor bank
보증인 guarantor; security suretyship; surety
보증자본 guarantee capital
보증장 letter of guarantee
보증주 guaranteed stock; stock for guarantee
보증준비 securities for fiduciary issue
보증즉시연금 guaranteed immediate annuity
보증증권 guaranteed securities; surety bond
보증증권의 부본 duplicate policy
보증증권주식 bond form
보증차입유가증권 deposits of securities on contracts
보증채무 liabilities for guarantee; liabilities on guaranties; surety money
보증채무담보 customers' liabilities on guaranties
보증채무의 cautionary
보증채무이행 performance of obligations of guarantee
보증투자계약 guaranteed investment contract
보증회사 surety company
보충 replenishment
보충발주 Fill-ins
보충발주비 replenishing cost

보충분담금 supplementary call
보충융자 supplementary financial measure
보충의 supplemental
보충절차 supplementary proceedings
보충하다 replenish
보통거래 regular transaction; regular way
보통계약약관 general condition of contract
보통교부세 ordinary local grant tax
보통국채 straight government bond
보통금지명령 common injunction
보통발송송금; 우편환 mail transfer
보통배당 common dividend; ordinary dividend; regular dividend
보통법상의 모기지 legal mortgage
보통법상의 소유권 legal title
보통법인 ordinary corporation
보통보험 ordinary insurance
보통보험약관 general insurance clause
보통분개장 general journal; proper journal
보통사채 straight bond; straight corporate bond
보통상각 ordinary depreciation
보통생명보험 ordinary life insurance
보통세 general tax; normal tax
보통소득 ordinary corporation income
보통송금 ordinary remittance
보통수표 open check; uncrossed check
보통은행 ordinary bank
보통조합 ordinary partnership
보통종신보험 straight life insurance
보통주 ordinary share; plain language
보통주배당금 dividend on common stock
보통주식 common stock
보통주식일주당 순이익 earnings per share of common stock
보통주의 장부가격 common stock book value
보통징수 ordinary collection
보합상장 quiet market
보험 assurance; insurance
보험가액 insurable value; insurance value
보험가액할당 apportionment valuation

보험가액할당가능부분 apportionable part
보험감독법 insurance law
보험경비명세서 insurance expense exhibit
보험계리인 chief actuary; valuation actuary
보험계리인; 액추어리 actuary
보험계약법 insurance contract law
보험계약신청서 insurance proposal form
보험계약에 실패함 lapse
보험계약이 부활함 revival
보험계약이익배당준비금 reserve for bonuses allotted
보험계약자 party insuring; policyholder
보험계약자배당금 policyholder's dividend
보험관리 insurance management
보험그룹 insurance group
보험그룹의 보유액 fleet retention
보험금공제 deduction for insurance proceeds
보험금액 amount covered; amount insured; insurance amount; insured amount; sum insured
보험금액감소보험 noncontinuous policy
보험금액비례주의 sum insured method
보험금액자동복원조항 automatic reinstatement clause
보험금액증가 dividend addition
보험금액할당조항 pro rata distribution clause
보험금을 두배로 지불함 double indemnity
보험금일괄지불 lump-sum settlement
보험금증액배당방법 reversionary bonus system
보험금지불 claim settlement
보험금지불수단을 선택함 settlement options
보험금지불수수료 claim settling fee
보험금지불자금 claim settlement fund
보험금차손 losses on insurance claims
보험금청구서 debit note for premium
보험금청구자 claim note; claimant
보험금해외지불약관 claim payable abroad clause
보험기간 duration of insurance; term of insurance

보험기간조항 duration of risk clause
보험담당자 group representative
보험대상이 되는 리스크 insurable risk
보험료 insurance expense; insurance premium
보험료 지불을 마친 보험 paid-up insurance
보험료 지불을 마친 보험의 금액 paid-up-policy value
보험료공제 insurance premium deduction
보험료기준연금제도 money purchase plan
보험료대체대부 premium loan
보험료보르드로 premium bordereau
보험료분담제 contribution system; contributory plan
보험료분담플랜 split-dollar plan
보험료불입면제 waiver of premium
보험료세 premium tax
보험료신탁기금 premium trust fund
보험료율 rate of premium
보험료일괄선불 prepayment of premiums
보험료일시불보험 single premium insurance
보험료일시불연금 single premium annuity
보험료자동대체대부 automatic premium loan
보험료정산서 premium statement
보험료조정정산 annual premium adjustment
보험료조정조항 premium adjustment clause
보험료지불면제 exemption from payment of premium; free of premium
보험료지불정지 cessation of payment of premium
보험료집금 collection of premiums
보험료청구서 premium bill
보험료추징불요증권 nonassessable policy
보험료프리미엄 premium condition
보험료현장반환 premium discount
보험료환불 deferred rebate; rebate of premium
보험모집활동 agency work
보험법 general insurance law
보험브로커 insurance broker
보험브로커등록평의회 Insurance Brokers Registration Council

보험브로커책임보험 insurance broker's liability insurance

보험사고 event insured against; insured event; risk

보험사업 insurance activities

보험상품취급업자 insurance product firm

보험세 insurance tax

보험수금원 insurance collector

보험수리건전성 actuarial soundness

보험수리상의 기대치 actuarial expectation

보험시장 insurance market

보험신디케이트 insurance syndicate

보험심의회 Insurance Council

보험약관 insurance clause

보험업 insurance business

보험업자 insurance carrier

보험요율결정이론 theory of rate-making

보험요율계출제 File and use system

보험원리 insurance principle

보험을 통한 담보 cover

보험의 panel doctor

보험의 목적 subject-matter of insurance

보험의 종류 class of insurance

보험이익향수(享受)약관 benefit of insurance clause

보험인수증 acknowledgement of declaration; certificate of insurance

보험자 assecurator; insurer

보험재무분석가협회 Association of Insurance and Financial Analysts

보험제도의 상호성 mutuality of insurance institution

보험종류변경청구권 conversion privilege

보험증권 insurance policy; policy

보험증권가액 policy value

보험증권대부 policy loan

보험증권발행대리점 policy writing agent

보험증권번호 policy number

보험증권의 본문 policy jacket

보험증권해석규칙 rules for construction of policy

보험차익 gains on insurance claim; profit accruing from insurance

보험차익특별계정 special account of gains on insurance claim

보험청 Insurance Board

보험카르텔 insurance cartel

보험통제 insurance control

보험판매원 business canvasser; canvasser

보험평가액 agreed value

보험평가액조항 valuation clause

보험풀 insurance pool

보험학 insurance science

보험학설 theories of insurance

보험형연금 insurance scheme; insured plan

보험회계 insurance accounting

보험회계통계협회 Insurance Accounting and Statistical Association

보험회사 insurance company

보험회사포괄보증증권 insurance companies blanket bond

보호관세 protective duty; protective tariff

보호령 protectorate

보호명령 protective order

보호신탁 protective trust

보호영장 protection

보호예금 safekeeping deposit

복관세 dual tariff

복권 recovery of legal status

복귀권 reversion

복리 compound interest

복리방식 compound interest method

복리시설부담액 contribution to welfare facilities

복리연율 compound annual rate

복리이율 compound interest yield

복리할인 compound discount

복리현가 present value discounted at compound interest

복리후생 welfare program

복리후생비 welfare expense

복리후생시설 welfare facilities

복명(複名)어음 double name paper

복배, 부배 resumption of dividend

복본위제 bimetallism

복수구분계산서 multiple-step statement

복수기업이 주식을 소유함 cross-holding

복수만기예금 multiple maturity deposit

복수보험자 composite insurer

복수브랜드전략 multibrand strategy

복수브랜드참가 multiple brand entries

복수세율 multiple tax rate

복수영장 concurrent writs

복수요인모델 multifactor model

복수은행제도 multiple banking system

복수은행지주회사 multibank holding company

복수통화개입 multicurrency intervention

복수회답 multiple answer

복식기장법 bookkeeping by double entry

복식부기 double accounting; double-entry bookkeeping

복원 restoration

복잡한 구조작업 complex salvage operation

복제펀드 clone fund

복합거래 compound transaction

복합경로 multiple channel

복합경영 multiple management

복합기입 compound entry

복합머천다이징 dual merchandising

복합보험증권 combined policy

복합상품 synthetic instrument

복합세제 multiple tariff system

복합수송 complex transportation

복합운송서류 combined transport documents

복합증권 hybrid securities

본결산 full year business result

본국송환 extradition

본드잔고 sterling balance

본드증서의 증인 attestation witness

본드트레이더 bond trader

본드환본위제 sterling exchange standard

본래 상태로 조금 되돌아감 minor rally

본래의 가격을 밑돌다가 매각된 증권 bargain counter

본문 body copy; purview

본부집중구입 central buying

본사계정 head office account

본사사무소 registered office

본선(本船)지입인도 delivered ex ship

본선인도 free on board

본선인수증 mate's receipt

본세 principal tax

본소(本訴) formal lawsuits

본예산 main budget

본원예금 intrinsic deposit

본원적인 가치 intrinsic value

본원적인 예금 primary deposit

본원화폐 original money

본위정책 monetary standard policy

본위제도 monetary standard; standard system

본위화폐 standard coin; standard money

본적 permanent address

본점 head office; parent store

본증서 presents

본지점계정 inter-office account

본지점레이트 inter-office rate

본질 substance

본질적으로 per se

본체주기 parenthetical notes

본클레임 final claim

볼라틸리티 volatility value

볼런터리체인; 임의연쇄점 voluntary chain

볼록한 모양 convexity

볼륨레이쇼 volume ratio

볼륨어큐뮬레이터(누적지표의 한 종류) volume accumulator

봉쇄 blockade

봉쇄경제 closed economy

부(副)의 duplicate

부(負)의 이율곡선 negative yield curve

부가 addition

부가가치 added value; value added

부가가치세 value added tax

부가가치연쇄 value added chain
부가가치우위 value added advantage
부가가치통신망 value added network
부가계정 adjunct account
부가급부 additional benefit; fringe benefits
부가보험료 loading
부가서비스 accessorial service
부가세 supertax; tax surcharge
부가수정 adjustment of the carrying amount
부가위험 extraneous risk
부가익 loading surplus
부가조항 rider
부간사 co-manager
부과결정 assessment and decision
부과과세제도 official assessment
부과기일 base date for assessment
부과방식 current disbursement approach
부과방식 pay-as-you-go-system
부과식 보험 assessment insurance;
　assessment plan
부과식 상호보험조합 assessment mutual
　association
부과식 적립제 assessment system
　accumulation
부과실책임주의 doctrine of liability without
　fault
부과액 amount imposed
부과징수 assessment and collection
부기 bookkeeping
부기계 book keeper
부단순인수 qualified acceptance of bill
부담 burden
부담경감 reduction of incidence
부담금 burden charge
부담부증여 onerous gift
부담비 obligation fees
부담이익배율 earnings coverage ratios
부당계약 catching bargain
부당과세 unreasonable taxation
부당노동행위 unfair labor practice
부당생명보험계약(왜곡된 권유로 인한) 부당

생명보험계약 twisting
부당영업행위 unfair trade
부당위압 undue influence
부당이득 excessive profit; unjust enrichment
부당이득자 profiteer
부당이행청구 unfair call
부당지출 misappropriation of funds; unjust
　disbursement
부당체포 malicious arrest
부당평결 false verdict
부당표시 misbranding
부당한 unjustified
부당해고 unfair dismissal; wrongful dismissal
부대비용 charge extra; extra charges;
　incidental expenses;
부대세 additions to tax
부대소송 incidental appeal; incidental suit
부대약속 collateral promise
부대조건 collateral condition; condition
　collateral; incidental condition
부대증서 collateral bond
부도가 나다 go to protest
부도덕행위 moral turpitude
부도반각 bounce
부도사유 reason for dishonor
부도수표 dishonored check; protested check
부도심(副都心) subcenter
부도어음 dishonored bill; unpaid draft
부도통지 nonpayment protest
부동비 idle cost
부동산 fixed property; immovable property;
　real estate; real property; things real
부동산; 토지 landed estate
부동산계약 estate contract
부동산계정 immovables account
부동산공동보유 cotenancy
부동산권 tenancy
부동산권만료 determination
부동산권이서 title insurance
부동산담보 real estate security
부동산대부 loan on real property; rental of

real property
부동산대부업 business of renting property;
loan business on real property
부동산등기부등본 certified copy of real
estate register
부동산매각손 loss on sale of real estate
부동산매각익 profit on sale of real estate
부동산매매익 protits from immovables
transactions
부동산모기지 real estate mortgage
부동산복귀 escheat
부동산브로커 real estate broker
부동산상속순위법칙 canons of descent
부동산상의 권리 rights existing on real
property
부동산소득 real estate income
부동산수입 income from real estate; rents
received
부동산신탁 real estate in trust
부동산양도 transfer of real property
부동산양도취급인 conveyancer
부동산업 realty business
부동산업자 estate agent
부동산의 점유를 뺏다 disseise
부동산임대료 rent on real estate
부동산저당대부금 loan secured by real estate
부동산저당장기대부금 real estate loan
receivable
부동산저당패스스루증권 mortgage
pass-through certificate
부동산전대차 sublease
부동산점유침해 clausum fregit
부동산점유회복소송 writ of entry
부동산차압 real distress
부동산취득세 real estate acquisition tax; real
property acquisition tax
부동산투자신탁 real estate investment trust
부동산회복소송 ejectment
부동주주 weak stockholders
부두사용료 dockage
부두세 wharfage

부두지입인도 delivered ex quay
부득이한 사정 unavoidable circumstances
부령(部令) ministerial ordinance
부르는 값 seller's price
(가격·시세를) 부르다; 어림치다 quote
부메랑효과 boomerang effect
부문간 대체 interunit transfer
부문간계정 interdepartment account
부문간의 대체가격을 결정함 interunit
pricing
부문간접비 departmental overhead
부문간접비차이 department variance on
overhead
부문개별비 direct department cost
부문경영진 divisional management
부문계산 sectional calculation
부문구조 divisional structure
부문매상 divisional sales
부문별 내역 segmental breakdown
부문별 대차대조표 sector balance sheet
부문별 매상 segmental sales
부문별 매상내역 divisional sales breakdown;
segmental sales breakdown
부문별 손익 divisional breakdown
부문별 원가계산 cost accounting by
department; departmental cost accounting
부문별 원가계산 departmental costing
부문별 이익 departmental profit
부문부담비 departmental burden
부문비 departmental charge; departmental
expenses
부문비계산표 overhead distribution sheet
부문비예산 departmental expenses budget
부문원가 departmental cost
부분감사 partial audit
부분상관 partial correlation
부분소유자 partial proprietor
부분수익증권 certificate of beneficial interest
부분원가계산 partial costing
부분최적화 suboptimization
부산물 accessory product

부상사망보상금 compensation for injuries and deaths
부서 countersign
부속건물 accessory building; outbuilding
부속명세서 supplementary statement
부속서류 annex; annexed letter; supporting documents
부속설비 annexed structure
부속용도 accessory use
부속지역권 easement appurtenant
부속품 accessories; fittings
부수가스(천연가스의) associated gas
부수계약 accessory contract; supplemental contract
부수권한 mediate powers
부수소송 ancillary bill or suit
부수업무 secondary activities
부수적인 incidental
부수적인 금반언 collateral estoppel
부수적인 수입 incidental gains
부수채무 accessory obligation
부스 booth
부실표시 misrepresentation
부양가족 dependent; dependent family member
부양공제 allowance for dependent; deduction for dependents; exemption for dependents; tax exemption for dependents
부양약관 maintenance clause
부양의무 duty of support
부양자 supporter
부업대리점 side liner
부영사 vice-consul
부외자산 unlisted assets
부외차금 unlisted loan
부외채무 unlisted liability
부유세 net worth tax; wealth tax
부의장 vice chairman
부인 denial
부인권 right of avoidance
부인하다 traverse

부인하지 않음 nient dedire
부장품 supplies
부재 absence
부재소유권 absentee ownership
부재수요 absence of demand
부적법한 bad
부적합 nonconformity
부적합리스크 misfit risk
부적합리터닝 misfit return
부적합제품 nonconforming product
부적합포트폴리오 misfit-portfolio
부정경쟁 unfair competition
부정기선 tramper
부정기화물 중개업자 chartering broker
부정사용 unauthorized use
부정수단 fraud
부정수표 defective check
부정신고 false declaration
부정연금 contingent annuity
부정이득 fraudulent gains
부정이익 unfair advantage
부정적인 듀레이션 negative duration
부정적인 레버리지 negative leverage effect
부정적인 의견 adverse opinion
부정적인 증익효과 unfavorable leverage effect
부정적인 효과 negative effect
부정카드 fraudulent cards
부정행위 fraudulent act; irregular practices; wrong doing
부조기금 employees' relief fund
부조료 및 별거수당 alimony und separate maintenance payment
부조료과세 benefit taxation
부조신탁 support trust
부족 short delivery
부족경제 shortage economy
부족액 balance due; shortage
부족액보증 deficiency guarantee
부종적인 지명권 power appendant
부주의 recklessness

부주의로 인해 per incuriam
부지약관 unknown clause
부차적인 결과 by-product
부채 negative capital
부채 및 자본 liabilities and capital
부채계정 liabilities account
부채관리 liability management
부채기간 debt maturity
부채비율 creditor's equity to total assets; debt ratio
부채상각준비금 amortization fund
부채성 준비금 liability reserves
부채이자 interest on borrowed fund
부채이자공제 deduction of interest on borrowed fund
부채자본비율 debt-equity ratio
부채준비금 reserve for liability
부채측 liability side
부총재 deputy governor; vice president
부칙 supplementary regulations
부트스트랩매수 bootstrap acquisition
부패선거구 rotten boroughs
부패하기 쉬운 물건 perishable property
부표제 subheading
부호분할다원접속 code division multiple access
부활절충 negotiation for budget draft
부활조항 reinstatement clause
북대서양의회 North Atlantic Assembly
북대서양자유무역지역 North Atlantic Free Trade Area
북대서양조약기구 North Atlantic Treaty Organization
북미자유무역협정 North America Free Trade Agreement
북유럽각료회의 Nordic Council of Ministers
북유럽협의회 Nordic Council
북해 브렌트 North Brent
분개 journalizing
분개계정; 명세계정 itemized account
분개기입 covering entry; journal entry

분개장 journal
분권관리 decentralized management
분류 assorting
분류된 주식 classified stock
분류법 grade description system
분류소득세 classified income tax; scheduler income taxation
분리 severance
분리가능워런트 detachable warrant
분리가능원가 separable cost
분리계정 separate investment account
분리과세 separate withholding tax
분리불능 워런트 nondetachable warrant
분리저가법 cost or market whichever is lower basis
분리평가 separate valuation
분리하다 sever
분배 distribution
분배국민소득 national income distributed
분배율 relative share
분별연수 age of discretion
분산경로 decentralized channel
분산구매 decentralized buying
분산도 measure of dispersion
분산분석 variance analysis
분산주식투자포트폴리오 diversified portfolio on stock investment
분산책임 decentralized responsibility
분산투자 diversified investment
분산투자의 유효성 effectiveness of diversified investment
분산하다 diversify
분산형 마케팅 divergent marketing
분산형 보통주펀드 diversified type common stock fund
분산형 투자회사 diversified type investment company
분산형 포트폴리오 diversified type portfolio
분산화 diversification
분색 네거티브 separation negative
분석 analysis

분석가 analyst
분석데이터 analytical data
분석도구 tool for analysis
분석모델 analytical model
분석법학 analytical jurisprudence
분석수단 analytical tools
분석적 예측 analytical forecast
분석증명서 certificate of analysis
분손 partial loss; particular loss
분손계산 average loss settlement
분손담보 with average
분손손해 average claim
분손약관 average warranty; particular average warranty
분식(粉飾) window dressing
분식결산 window dressing settlement
분식예금 window dressing deposit
분식제무제표 window dressing financial statement
분신이론 alter ego doctrine
분실 mysterious disappearance
분실증권보증증권 lost instrument bond
분실카드 lost card
분양 lottingout
분양권 land for sale in lots
분양지 building lots for sale
분원도 pie chart
분위기 ambience
분위기, 흐름 nominal quotation
분쟁 dispute
분할 apportion
분할(계약의) apportionment
분할; 절개 section
분할각출 split-funding
분할계약 several contract
분할계좌 divided account
분할기준 basis to prorate local tax
분할납부 payment in installments
분할반제형 대부 amortization loan
분할발행 tranche
분할분개장 sectional journal

분할불 easy payment
분할불구입 hire purchase
분할상속제 division of succession
분할선적 partial shipment
분할소유권 several ownership
분할원장계정 split ledger account
분할인수 eastern account
분할지불 installment payment; installment settlement; payment by installment
분할테스트법 split run
분할판매 split sale
분할하다 allot
불가분권 undivided interest
불가분채권 indivisible credit
불가피한 사고 inevitable accident; unavoidable accident
불가피한 위험 unavoidable dangers
불가항력 act of God; force majeure; vis major
불가효력조항 force majeure clause
불경기 depression of business
불규칙변동 random fluctuation
불규칙한 가격변동 random price changes
불균등지불 irregular installment payment
불균등확률 unequal probability
불균형 disequilibrium; disparity; imbalance
불균형성장 disequilibrium growth
불납부가산세 additional tax on nonpayment
불능한 계약 impossible contract
불독본드; 외국기업이 런던시장에서 발행하는 파운드표시 채권 bulldog bond
불량대출 doubtful loan
불량물건 bad risk
불량물건할당계획 assigned risk plans
불량재고 dead stock
불량채권 bad debt; doubtful account
불량채권율 bad debt ratio
불량회원 bad member
불로소득 unearned income
불로소득자층 rentier class
불릿스와프 bullet swap
불명예로운 형벌 infamous punishment

불몰수법 nonforfeiture act
불문법 leges non scriptae
불법 illegality; unlawfulness
불법감금 false imprisonment
불법방해 nuisance
불법보수청구죄 exaction
불법유치 unlawful detainer
불법으로 손에 넣다 grab
불법의 illegal
불법인 unlawful
불법쟁의 outlaw strike
불법적인 권리확장 encroachment
불법점유 dispossession; intrusion; unlawful entry
불법점유자 deforceor
불법집회 unlawful assembly
불법침입 forcible entry
불법탈환 rescue
불법행위 delict; misfeasance; tort; unlawful act; violence
불베어채 bull bear bond
불변리스크 constant risk tolerance
불변자본 constant capital
불병합 nonjoinder
불복당사자 aggrieved party
불복신청 administrative protest
불복심사 administrative review
불상환채 irredeemable bond
불성실손해 dishonesty loss
불성실한 답변 frivolous answer
불안전의무 imperfect obligation
불안정성 variability
불안정한 erratic
불안정한 동요 erratic fluctuation
불완전경쟁 imperfect competition
불완전경쟁시장 imperfect competition market
불완전고용승수 underemployment multiplier
불완전법화 partial legal tender
불완전신탁 imperfect trust
불완전인도 bad delivery
불완전자유 naked confession

불완전한 defective
불완전확률변수 defective random variables
불요한 진술 prolixity
불이행 failure; nonfeasance; nonfulfillment; nonperformance
불이행자 defaulter
불이행포지션 fail position
불입부 cum call
불입융자대부 loan of subscription payment funds
불입을 끝내지 않은 자본금 subscriptions
불입일 due date of payment
불입잉여금 paid-in surplus
불입자본 capital paid-up; paid-in capital; paid-up capital
불입지정 designation for transfer
불입취급은행 payment handling bank
불채산부문 loss-making division
불출증표 voucher for disbursement
불투명 uncertainty
불투명요인 uncertain factor
불합리 absurdity
불확실한 권리 precarious right
불확인신용장 unconfirmed credit
불확정권 possibility
불확정손해배상액 unliquidated damages
불확정운송임 contingency freight
불확정이자 contingent interest
불확정이자부 unfixed interest bearing
불확정재산권 contingent estate
불확정채권 unliquidated claim
불환은행권 inconvertible bank note
불환지폐 inconvertible paper money
불황 depression
불황카르텔 recession cartel
붕괴 breakdown
붕락 crash
붙잡힌 청중 captive audience
브라운상품 brown goods
브랜드경쟁 battle of the brands
브랜드광고 brand advertising

브랜드라벨 brand label
브랜드로열티 brand loyalty
브랜드매매 sale by brand
브랜드변경 brand switch
브랜드비교 brand comparison
브랜드상품 brand-named item
브랜드상품화계획 brand merchandising
브랜드수용 brand acceptance
브랜드에퀴티 brand equity
브랜드이름짓기 brand naming
브랜드이미지 brand image
브랜드이행 brand switching
브랜드인식 brand recognition
브랜드인지 brand awareness
브랜드확장전략 brand-extension strategy
브레이크스루; 돌파구 breakthrough
브레턴우즈협정 Bretton Woods
브로커시장 brokered market
브로커업무 broker's business; brokerage
브로커즈론 broker's loan
브로커포괄보증증권 brokers blanket bond
브리지론; 연결융자 bridge loan
브리지환 bridging exchange
V-RAM video random access memory
VHF very high frequency
VTR video tape recorder
블라인드테스트(피시험자가 내용 모르고 실
  시하는 화학검사) blind test
블랙나이트 black knight
블랙리스트 blacklist
블랙먼데이 Black Monday
블랙박스 black box
블랙박스옥션 black box au box auction
블랙숄즈모형(옵션이론의 한 가지)
  Black-Scholes model
블록거래 block trading
블록경제 bloc economy
블록카피; 제판에 적합하게 정서한 원고
  block copy
블록포지셔너 block positioner
블록플로 block flow

블루칼라 blue-collar
비(非)시스티매틱리스크 unsystematic risk
비; 비율 ratio
비가격경쟁 nonprice competition
비가세구입 tax free purchase
비감사 unaudited
비거주자 원예금 nonresident won deposit
비거주자 원예금계정 nonresident won
  account
비거주자외화예금계정 nonresident foreign
  currency account
비거주자의 급여소득 payment to
  nonresidents
비거주제에 대한 감면 concessions for
  nonresident
비경쟁입찰 noncompetitive tender
비계약자 nonsettled; nonsigner
비공개기업 private company
비공개회사 closely-held company
비공모채 privately placed bond
비공식부문 informal sector
비공식연금 informal plan annuity
비공식자본이 유출됨 unofficial capita night
비공식조직 informal organization
비공식집단 informal group
비공인자산 assets not admitted; unadmitted
  asset
비과세 exclusion from taxation; exemption;
  tax exempt; tax free
비과세거래 nontaxable transaction
비과세기관 taxexempt organization
비과세문서 nontaxable document
비과세법인 corporation free from taxation;
  exempt corporation; nontaxable
  corporation; tax free corporation
비과세소득 exempt income; nontaxable
  income
비과세양도소득 capital gain free of taxation
비과세이자소득 nontaxable interest income
비과세재산 exempt property; nontaxable
  property

비과세저축 nontaxable savings
비과세준비금 taxfree reserve
비과세증여 exempt gift
비과세품 tax free article
비관련사업이익 unrelated business income
비교가능성 comparability
비교계산서 comparative statement
비교광고 comparative advertising
비교대차대조표 comparative balance sheet
비교마케팅 comparative marketing
비교문화 cross culture
비교분석 comparative analysis
비교분석법 method of comparative analysis
비교생산비설 theory of comparative cost
비교손익계산서 comparative income
  statement; comparative profit and loss
  statement
비교수지계산서 comparative statement of
  cash flows
비교우위 comparative advantage
비교우위의 원리 principle of comparative
  advantage
비교우위이론 comparative advantage theory
비교원가 comparative cost
비교원가조사 comparative cost studies
비교작용 comparative influence
비교재무제표 comparative financial statement
비교통계학 comparative statistics
비교표 comparison table
비금리부채 nonrate-paying liability
비금리자산 nonrate earnings assets
비금융거래 nonfinancial transaction
비금융계정 nonfinancial accounts
비금융시장 nonfinancial market
비금융자산 nonfinancial assets
비금융적 거래수지 balance on nonmonetary
  transactions
비금전항목 nonmonetary items
비내구재 nondurables
비누적형 배당 noncumulative dividend
비누적형 우선주식 noncumulative preferred
  stock
비담보위험 uninsured peril
비대칭바스켓방식 adjustable basket technique
비독점적 nonexclusive
비동맹국회의; 중립국회의 Conference of
  Non-Aligned Nations
비동족의 동족회사 nonpersonal family
  corporation
비동족주의 nonbasic shareholder of family
  corporation
비동족회사 nonfamily corporation
비동질성 nonhomogeneity
비등록사모채 letter securities
비디오다이얼서비스 video dial tone service
비디오단말 video display terminal
비디오온디맨드 video on demand
비디오컨트롤아키텍처 video system control
  architecture
비디오텍스 video tex
비디오편집 video editing
비례·초과액혼합재보험 mixed
  quota-surplus reinsurance
비례과세법 proportional taxation
비례배당 ratable distribution
비례보상계약 average policy
비례보상조항 average condition; averaging
  clause
비례비 proportional expenses
비례세 proportional tax
비례원가계산 proportional calculation
비례재보험 proportional reinsurance
비례적인 가변비용 proportionally variable
  cost
비례준비금 proportional reserve method
비례준비제도 proportional reserve system
비례증보 average
비례증보조항 condition of average
비례지불 pro rata payment
비례특약재보험 quota share treaty
  reinsurance
비례평등조건 proportional equal terms

비례할당 proration
비례할당하지 않는 재보험 nonproportional
　reinsurance
비망가격 memorandum value; remainder
　price
비매장면적 nonselling area
비목 expense item
비밀계정 secret account
비밀번호 personal identification number; pin
　number
비밀부채 secret liability
비밀손실 latent loss
비밀수수료 secret commission
비밀수익 latent return
비밀신탁 secret trust
비밀유지계약 confidentiality agreement
비밀유지의무 confidentiality of information
비밀적립금 latent assets; secret reserve;
　undisclosed reserve
비밀적립자산주 hidden assets stock
비밀절도 clandestine theft
비발권대리점 nonpolicy writing agent
비방가액 memorandum price
비보정모델 noncompensatory model
비부과식 보험 nonassessable insurance
비분산투자형 투자회사 nondiversified
　investment company
비사업활동 nonbusiness activity
비상각자산 nondepreciable assets
비상업 트레이더 noncommercial trader
비상장주 unlisted stock
비상장회사 unlisted company
비상해손(海損) extraordinary average
비상호적 nonreciprocal
비상호조직보험회사 proprietary insurance
　company
비선형 추세선 curving trend line
비시장경제 nonmarket economy
비시장성 리스크 nonmarket risk
비시장성 리스크의 원천 nonmarket risk
　sources

비시장성증권 nonmarketable securities
비실명예금 deposit in a fictitious name
비싸게 사다 buy high
비싼 값으로 구입 buying at top price
BA레이트 BA rate
비연결자회사 unconsolidated subsidiaries
비연대보증 severally but not jointly
비열후 unsubordinated
비영리기관 nonprofit institution
비영리보험 noncommercial insurance
비영리사업 nonprofit-making business
비영리조직 nonprofit-making organization
비영리회사 noncommercial enterprise;
　nonprofit corporation; nonprofit-making
　company
비영업용 상각자산 depreciable property for
　nonbusiness
비영업용 자산 nonbusiness property
비영주자 nonpermanent resident
비용 expenses
비용·조업도·이익분석 cost-volume-profit
　analysis
비용·편익분석 cost-benefit analysis
비용과 수익의 대응 matching costs and
　revenues
비용대비효과분석 cost effectiveness analysis
비용동향 cost behavior
비용배부 expense distribution
비용배분의 원칙 principle of cost allocation
비용보증계약 guaranteed cost contract
비용분류 cost classification
비용사정증 allocatur
비용수익대응의 원칙 cost matching income
　principle
비용차익 loading profit
비용함수 cost function
비용효율이 좋은 cost effective
비워 줌, 내줌 vacation
비원가항목 noncost items
비위험이자율 nonrisk interest rate
비위험자산 nonrisk assets

비유동성자산 nonliquid assets
비유동자산 noncurrent assets
비유동적 illiquid
비유통증권 nonnegotiable instrument
비율법감모상각 percentage depletion
비율병용급여제 salary plus commission
비율분석 ratio analysis
비율분석법 ratio method
비은행금융기관 nonbank financial institution
비이자부채 noninterest-bearing bond
비인기채권 inactive bond
비인수답변 nonassumpsit
비자발적인 실업 involuntary unemployment
비적격채 ineligible bill
비전략부문 nonstrategic division
비전통적인 애셋클래스 nontraditional asset class
비정형적인 의사결정 nonprogrammed decision
비제정법 unwritten law
비제휴론 nontie-up loan
비준 ratification
비중개 disintermediation
비즈니스게임 business game
비즈니스라운드테이블(미국내 대기업협의체) business round table
비즈니스오토메이션 business automation
비차입준비 nonborrowed reserves

비참가우선주식 nonparticipating preferred stock
비채무자예금 deposit of nondebtor
비축철거 stockdraw
비출자조합 noninvestment cooperative association
비특정대부 nonpurpose loan
비판기능 critical function
비판적인 시청자 protester
비품 fixtures; furnishings
비할당적립방식 unallocated funding instrument
비할부 noninstallment
비합법적인 보수 payola
비현금자산 noncash assets
비화폐간접증권 nonmonetary indirect security
비화폐경제 nonmonetized economy
비확률모델 nonstochastic model
비확률표본 nonprobability sample
비회사형 합변사업 unincorporated joint venture
비회원증권회사 nonmember firm
빈가족; 빈집 empty nest
빈곤선 poverty line
빈곤자 pauper
빌트인플렉서빌리티 built-in flexibility
빌패스 bill pass
빛 주위의 밝기 ambient light

ㅁ
ㅂ

ㅅ

사각 angle of view; dead corner
사건목록 cause list
사건부 cause-books
4계지불지급일 quarter-days
사고 accident
사고 1건당 보상한도액 combined single limit
사고방지책임모범법안
    model safety-responsibility bill
사고사급부금 accidental death benefit
사고통지 notice of loss and damage
사교클럽 social club
사권(私權) private right
사권박탈 attainder
사기 actionable fraud; cheat
사기꾼 shyster
사기양도 fraudulent conveyance; fraudulent
    transfer
사기죄 false pretense
사기채권자 fraudulent creditor
사기파산 fraudulent bankruptcy
사기표시 fraudulent misrepresentation
사내규정 internal rule; office regulation
사내기업 intrapreneuring
사내대체이익 internal transfer profit
사내벤처 intraventure
사내보 house organ
사는 쪽 bull; buyer
사단법인 aggregate corporation; corporate
    juridical person
사람의 감독하에 있는 alieni juris

사례금 honorarium
사례연구법 case method
사망기록 bill of mortality
사망률 death rate
사망률커브 mortality curve
사망보험 insurance against death;
    insurance payable at death
사망보험금 sum payable at death
사망시배당 mortuary bonus
사면위원회 board of pardons
사면하다 assoile
사명 mission
사모(私募) private offering
사모(私募)발행 private placement
사모(私募)보통사채 private placement
    straight bond
사모(私募)전환사채 private convertible note
사모(私募)증권 private placement securities
사모요령 placing memorandum
사모채 private note
사무간사회사 book runner
사무관리 administration
사무권한 ministerial power
사무규정 office manual
사무라이채 samurai bond
사무변호사 proctor
사무비 office expenses
사무소 또는 다른 일정한 사업소 office or
    other fixed place of business
사무소; 직무 office

사무소제경비 office overhead
4반기 베이스의 실질성장률
   quarterly real growth rate
4반기 quarter
4반기보고서 quarterly reports
사법거래 plea bargaining
사법권 judicial power
사법률에 의한 회사 statutory company
사법방해 obstruction of justice
사법상의 매각 judicial sale
사법심사 judicial judgment
사법적인 판단을 내리다 adjudge
사법절차 judicial proceedings
사법처분과 관계없는 매각 foreclosure under
   power of sale
사보타주; 태업 sabotage
4분의 3 보전약관 three-fourths loss clause
사상(事象) events
사상최고 record high
사상최저 record low
사선으로 교차된 줄무늬 technical change
사설통신회선 private telecommunication
   network
사실(私室) chambers
사실기재서 case stated
사실문제에 대한 쟁점 issue on fact
사실상 de facto; ipso facto
사실상 교환가능한 통화 currency convertible
   in fact
사실상의 추정 presumption of fact
사실에 반한 untrue
사실인정 finding of fact
사실조사 fact finding
사실착오 mistake of fact
사실판결 judgment on merits
사실확인 affirmation of fact
사양서매매 sale by specification
사양적합성 fitness for use
사업 business; enterprise; industry; task;
   venture
사업개황설명서 summary statement of

business
사업계속보험
   business continuation insurance
사업광고를 위한 상품 prize offered for
   advertisement of the business
사업구분간매상 intersegment sales
사업구분별 손익보고 segment reporting
사업금융 business loan; corporate finance
사업금융회사 business finance company
사업단위 business unit
사업대부 industrial loan
사업방법서 scheme of operation
사업방해 business interception
사업범위 scope of business
사업법 business law
사업법인 industrial corporation
사업보험 business insurance
사업부문제도 division system
사업부문제회사 divisionalized company
사업상의 통상위험 ordinary risks of
   employment
사업생명보험 business life insurance
사업설명서 preliminary prospectus
사업세 business tax; enterprise tax
사업소 business establishment; business
   place; place of business
사업소; 설정 establishment
사업소득 business income
사업소득계산 computation of business income
사업소비(事業所費) establishment expenses
사업소세 business office tax
사업수행 performance of business
사업신탁 business trust
사업아이디어를 발견하는 사람 business
   finder
사업에서 생기는 소득 income derived from
   business
사업연도 accounting period; business year;
   taxable year
사업연도개시일 beginning day of the taxable
   year

사업연도를 신고함 notification of the taxable year

사업연도변경 change of taxable year

사업연도지정 designation of accounting period

사업외경비 nonbusiness expenses

사업용 자산을 대치함 replacement of business property

사업자 undertaker

사업자금 business fund

사업장 working place

사업전환 change of business

사업종류 nature of business

사업주 business proprietor; proprietor of a business

사업주공제 proprietor deduction

사업주특별경비준비금 proprietors special expense reserve

사업중단보험 consequential loss insurance; use and occupancy insurance

사업중지 suspension of business

사업채 industrial bond; industrial debenture

사업통합 integration of business

사업폐쇄 closing business

사업폐지 quitting of business; relinquishing of business

사업협동조합 cooperative business association

사업확장 business expansion

사업환경리스크지수 business environment risk index

사업활동 active conduct of business

사업회사 business corporation

사외발행보통주식 common stock outstanding

사외이용자 external user

사외중역 outsider director

사용(私用)원장 private ledger

사용가능기간 estimated usable period; prospective usable

사용가능자금 good money

사용가치 use value; utility value; value in use

사용권 right of use

사용기간 usable years

사용목적특정대부 purpose loan pursue

사용불능자금 nonexpendable fund

사용수익권 usufruct

사용시간 used hours

사용시간비례법 hours-of-service method

사용요금 usage rate

사용용도불명금 expenditure unaccounted for

사용자 employer

사용자배상책임보험 employer's liability insurance

사용자원가 user cost

사용자책임 respondent superior; vicarious liability

사용후 계출제 use and file

사운드로고 sound logo

사원권 rights and liabilities of members

사원예금 employee deposits

사원총대회 general meeting of substitutional members

사원총대회 meeting of representative holders

사유지 allodium

사유지통행료 toll traverse

사이버네틱스 cybernetics

사이언스파크 science park

사이콜로지컬라인 psychological line

사이트크레디트 sight credit

사인(死因)증여 donation due to death

사인증여 gift causa mortis

4일후 인도 triple settlement

사재제공익 profit from private funds offered

사적 불법방해 private nuisance

사적인 사용 private use

사적회계사 private accountant

사전가격확인제도 advance pricing agreement

사전가공 prefabrication

사전감사 preaudit

사전계약자배당 advance dividend

사전교섭 prenegotiation

사전분석 ex-ante analysis

사전분포 prior distribution

사전상환 advanced redemption
사전신고제 premerger notification
사전인가제도 prior approval
사전자격심사 prequalification
사전적립방식 advance funding method
사전조달 advance refunding
사전조사 preparatory audit
사전조사통지 notification of audit
사전조언 preliminary advice
사전징수 advance collection
사전차압 advance seizure
사전청구 advance demand
사전판매 presale order
사전확률 prior probability
사정가액 assessed value
사정기관 assessing organ
사정소득액 assessed income
사정액 assessed amount
사정인 surveyor
사죄 apology
사죄광고 corrective advertising
사진식자 phototype setting
사진제판 photomechanical process
사차손 mortality loss
사차익 mortality profit
사찰제도 criminal investigation system
사채 bonds and mortgage; corporate bond;
 corporate debenture; corporate securities;
 corporation bond
사채가격 price of corporate bond
사채권 bond certificate; debenture bond
사채권신탁 debenture trust
사채권양도 debenture assignment
사채권자 bond holder
사채권자집회 meeting of bond-holders
사채명세표 schedule of bonds payable
사채미발행고 bond unissued
사채발행비 debenture-issuing expenses
사채발행비용 bond issue costs
사채발행수탁자 trustee for bond issuance
사채발행차금 debt discount and expenses;

discount on bond premium; unamortized
 debt discount and expenses
사채발행차금상각 amortization of bond
 premium
사채발행차익 unamortized premium on bonds
사채배당 bond dividend
사채상환 debenture redemption; retirement of
 bonds
사채상환차금 gains on bond retirement
사채소화상황 sales of corporate bonds by
 purchasers
사채원부 bond register
사채응모 undertaking of corporate bonds
사채이자 bond interest; debenture interest;
 interest on bond
사채이자지불자금 cash deposited for bond
 interest
사채최고발행한도 bond authorized
사채취득 acquisition of debenture
사채평가 bond valuation
사채할인발행차금 discounts on bonds payable
사채할증발행차금 premium on bonds payable
사채환산이율 corporate equivalent yield
사치세 luxury tax
사칭통용 passing off
사해행위취소권 right to revoke fraudulent act
사행계약 aleatory contract
사회감사 social audit
사회경제적인 과정 socioeconomic process
사회경제적인 분류 socioeconomic
 classification
사회계약 social contract
사회규범 norms in society
사회문제 social concerns
사회보장 social security
사회보장번호 social security number
사회보장제도 social security system
사회보험 social insurance
사회보험료 social insurance premiums
사회보험료공제 deduction for social
 insurance premiums; social insurance

premiums deduction
사회보험세 social insurance tax
사회불안 social unrest
사회비용 social cost
사회사 proprietary company
사회생태학 social ecology
사회수준 level of society
사회승수효과 social multiplier effect
사회심리학 social psychology
사회운동 social movements
사회융화형 소비자 socially integrated consumer
사회의존형 소비자 social dependent consumer
사회이동 social mobility
사회이론 social ethic
사회인구총계적인 변수 sociodemographic variable
사회자본 social capital; social overhead capital
사회적인 가정 social assumption
사회적인 가츠 social value
사회적인 부 social wealth
사회적인 상호행위 social interaction
사회적인 요구사항 requirements of society
사회적인 욕구 social wants
사회적인 자극 social stimuli
사회적인 후생함수 social welfare function
사회정체 sociostasis
사회진화 social evolution
사회체계 social system
사회판단이론 social judgment theory
사회풍토 social climate
사회학자 sociologist
사회화 socialization
사회환경 societal environment
사회회계 social accounting
사후(事後)의 ex post facto
사후감사 post-audit
사후광고 follow-up advertisement
사후배당 postmortem dividend
사후분석 ex-post analysis; posterior analysis

사후수치 ex-post alpha value
사후신탁 instrument trust
사후의 post-facto
사후일부 postdate
사후일부 수표 postdated check
사후자격심사 post-qualification
사후저축 ex-post saving
사후취득재산 after-acquired property
사후취득조항 after-acquired clause
사후측정 subsequent measurements
사후투자 ex-post investment
사후특성선 ex-post characteristic line
사후평가 ex-post assessment
삭제 erasure
삭제신청 motion to strike out
산림소득 forestry income; timber income
산림소득특별공제 forestry income deduction
산문모델 prose model
산성시험비율 acid test ratio
산술급수법 sum-of-the-years-digits method
산술적인 기대수치 mathematical expectation
산술평균 arithmetic average
산업공동화 deindustrialization
산업광고 industrial advertisement
산업구조 industrial composition; industrial structure; structure of industry
산업구조고도화 growth of industrial structure
산업구조정책 industrial structure policy
산업별 국민순생산 industrial origin of net national product
산업보호 industry protection
산업분류 industrial classification
산업사고준비금 industrial-accident reserve
산업스파이 industrial espionage
산업연관분석 inter industry analysis
산업연관표 industry-relations table
산업의 베타수치 industry beta value
산업입지 location of industry
산업자금 industrial fund
산업자금공급상황 net supply of industrial funds

산업자본 industrial cap
산업재유통 industrial distribution
산업정보 industry information
산업정책 industrial policy
산업조정 regulation of industrial structure
산업조직 industrial organization
산업집중 industry concentration
산업출판물 industrial publication
산업합리화 industrial rationalization
산업협력방식 industrial cooperation method
산업효과 industry effect
산정 calculation; computation
산정가격 appraised price
산정기간 computation period
산정회요율 bureau rates; rating organization
  tariffs
산출계수 output coefficient
산출물인수 혹은 지불계약 take-or-pay
  contract
산출세액 calculated tax amount
산학협동 cooperation between industry and
  academic organizations
살루터리제품 salutary products
삼각무역 triangular trade
3개월이동평균 three-month moving average
삼국간 협정 tripartite agreement
삼국간무역 intermediary trade; offshore trade
삼국어음 third country bill
삼도논법 trilemma
삼림개척 assart
삼림화재보험 forest fire insurance
삼선전환법 three line converting method
삼순위보험금수취인 tertiary beneficiary
3일정산 skip-day settlement
3입체스캐너 3D scanner
삼중관세율 treble tariff
삼중바닥 triple bottom
삼중익 triple merit
삼차 third generation
삼차산업 tertiary industry
삼차온라인시스템 third generation on-line

system
삽입; 보급률 penetration
상각 depreciation and amortization; write-off
상각가능한도액 Final depreciable limit
상각계정 depreciation account
상각기금법 sinking fund method
상각방법 manner of amortization
상각방법변경 change of depreciation method
상각방법을 선정함 selection of depreciation
  method
상각방법을 신고함 notification of
  depreciation method
상각범위 allowed depreciation
상각비배부 appointment of depreciation
상각비용 amortization cost
상각원가 amortized cost
상각자산 depreciable property; depreciation
  assets
상각전 순이익 net profit before depreciation
상각전의 이연자산 deferred charge before
  amortization
상각준비금 reserve for amortization
상각초과; 초과상각 overdepreciation
상각필 대손금을 회수함 collection of bad
  debts
상각하다 amortize
상각한도액 allowable limit for depreciation
  amount; allowed amortizable limit;
  depreciable limit
상각후 순이익 net profit after depreciation
상각후 원가 depleted cost
상공권 air right
상공업금융회사 commerce and industry
  finance company
상공회의소 Association Cambiste
  Internationale; board of trade; chamber of
  commerce
상관계수 coefficient of correlation;
  correlation coefficient
상관관계 correlation
상관도 correlation diagram

상관분석 correlation analysis
상관습법 customs of merchant
상관표 correlation table
상관행렬 correlation matrix
상급문자 superior character
상급법원 superior courts
상급부간사 senior co-manager
상급회계사 senior accountant
상급회계학 advanced accounting
상기(商機) business opportunity
상납금 aid
상당한 adequate; reasonable
상당한 상각 reasonable depreciation
상당한 이유 probable cause
상대 contra; negotiated; relative
상대가격 relative price
상대거래 negotiated transaction
상대계좌 corresponding account
상대기입 contra entry
상대매매시장 negotiated market
상대방 counterpart; opposite party
상대방당사자 adversary party
상대선택기능 receiving monitor
상대소득 relation income; relative income
상대소득가설 relative income hypothesis
상대수익 relative revenue
상대시거리 relative viewing distance
상대예금 corresponding deposit
상대오차 relative error
상대이익 adverse interest
상대적인 강약도 relative strength
상대적인 마켓쉐어 relative market share
상대적인 면책위험 relative excepted risk
상대적인 박탈 relative deprivation
상대적인 수익곡선 relative revenue curve
상대적인 측도 relative measures
상대적인 코스트 relative costs
상대적인 퍼포먼스 relative performance
상대적인 품질 relative quality
상대채무 cross debt; mutual debt
상대편계정 Vostro account

상륙기간 lay-days
상무회 council of managing directors
상법 commercial code; commercial law; law of commerce
상부조항 grandfather clause
상비상품리스트 never-out list
상사금융 trading firm finance
상사대리 mercantile agency
상사중재 commercial arbitration
상설소득가설 permanent income hypothesis
상설전시 permanent exhibit
상세권 trading area
상소관할 appellate jurisdiction
상소기록 record on appeal
상소법원 appellate court; court above
상소사실기재서 case on appeal
상소인 appellant
상속 inheritance
상속권 right of inheritance
상속법 law of succession
상속부동산 heritage
상속부동산점유회복소송 assize of mort d'ancestor
상속세 death duty; estate duty; inheritance tax
상속세공제 gift tax credit
상속세물납 inheritance tax paid in kind
상속인 heir; inheritor
상속재산 inherited property
상속재산공유 coparcenary
상속재산회복 recontinuance
상쇄 netdown; offset; set off
상쇄계정 offset account; off-setting account
상쇄관세 countervailing duty
상쇄오진 offset error
상쇄오차 compensating error
상쇄이자 compensating interest
상쇄항목 offset item
상수브로커 contra broker
상습관 business practice; custom of merchant
상승 ascending; pick up; synergy; tailgating; upswing

상승각 climbing angle
상승경향에 있는 in uptrend
상승력 climbing power; up-pressure
상승률 rate of increase
상승상장 rising quotation
상승압력 upward pressure
상승커브 ascending curve
상승폭 gains
상승효과 synergy effect
상시유효 always open basis
상시재고 running inventory
상업개발채권 industrial development bond
상업과실 carrier's risk
상업금융 commercial finance
상업대출 commercial loan
상업등기 commercial registration
상업등기부등본 certified copy of commercial registration
상업법 mercantile law; merchant law
상업보증 commercial guarantee
상업부기 commercial bookkeeping; merchandise bookkeeping
상업송장 commercial invoice
상업신용 commercial credit
상업신용보험 commercial credit insurance
상업신용장 commercial letter of credit
상업어음 commercial bill; commercial paper; mercantile paper
상업어음주의 real-bills doctrine
상업용 모기지 commercial mortgage
상업용 자동차보험 commercial automobile policy
상업용위조보험 commercial forgery policy
상업은행가 commercial banker
상업재판소 commercial court
상업조합 mercantile partnership
상업통계 census of commerce; commercial statistics
상업트레이더 commercial trader
상업포괄신원보증증권 commercial blanket primary bond

상업할인 commercial discount
상업회계 commercial accounting
상여 employee bonus
상여수당금 accrued bonuses
상여전 소득 income before employee bonus
상여준비금 bonus payment reserve; reserve for bonus payment
상온 ordinary temperature
상위 top
상위사채 senior bond
상위증권 senior issue
상인길드 merchant guild
상인보험 merchant insurance
상인보호보증증권 merchant protective bond
상임감사역 permanent auditor; standing auditor
상임대리인 standing proxy
상장 listing; quotation
상장관 forecast for market tendency
상장기준 initial listing requirement; listing standard
상장대리인 listing agent
상장문제 listed issue
상장상품 listed product
상장선물 listed futures
상장신청서 application ion for listing; application to list
상장심사기준 listing requirements
상장옵션 exchange traded option; listed option
상장의 대전환일 key reversal day
상장의 반전 reversal
상장의 움직임 action
상장의 하락 market crash
상장조종 market manipulation
상장주 listed stock
상장증권 listed securities
상장채권시장 listed bond market
상장폐지 delisting
상장표 list quotation
상장표요약 run-down

상장회사 listed company; publicly traded company

상적과세 taxation by applying upper bracket

상적세율(上積稅率) tax rate applied to upper part of income

상점법 shop act

상징적인 인도 symbolic delivery

상징흡수가격전략 skimming price strategy

상차상속 successive inheritance

상표 trade mark

상표간 격차 difference among issues

상표관리 brand management

상표권 right of trademark

상표권침해 infringement of trade-mark; trade-mark infringement

상표등록법 trade-mark registration law

상표선호 brand preference

상표전략 brand strategy

상표정책 brand policy

상품 commodity; instrument; merchandise

상품 또는 제품 goods and products

상품간 스프레드 intra-contract spread

상품개발 product development

상품거래 commodity transaction

상품거래계좌 commodity account

상품거래고문 commodity trading adviser

상품거래법 commodity exchange act

상품거래소 commodity exchange

상품거래책임준비금 commodity exchange responsibility reserve; commodity transaction responsibility reserve

상품거래할인 back-haul allowance

상품견본 sample

상품견본포괄보험 samples floater

상품계정 goods account; merchandise account

상품고객계약 commodity customers agreement

상품관리 merchandise control; merchandise management

상품구비 merchandise assortment

상품구비폭 breadth of assortment; width of assortment

상품구색구조 assortment structure

상품구색폭 assortment breadth

상품구색효용 assortment utility

상품구성 assortment

상품구입장 invoice-book inward

상품권계정 gift tickets account; merchandise certificate account

상품담보 collateral commodity

상품담보채권 commodity backed bond

상품로스 merchandise loss

상품매매장 merchandise book

상품매상장 sold book

상품발송장 invoice-book outward

상품분류 classification of goods

상품선물 commodity futures

상품선물거래가격 commodity futures price

상품선물거래가격폭제한 price limit on commodity futures

상품선물거래의 증거금 margin on commodity futures

상품선물거래청산소 clearinghouse for commodity futures

상품선물거래헤징 hedging on commodity futures

상품선물어드바이저 commodity futures trading adviser

상품선물지수 commodity futures index

상품설명 trade description

상품소유 stock-book

상품수요 commodity demand

상품시장 commodity market

상품연구 commodity approach

상품예산 merchandise budget

상품예산편성 dollar merchandise budgeting

상품옵션 commodity option

상품운임 commodity rate

상품원가 merchandise cost

상품원장 merchandise ledger

상품위험 mercantile risk

상품장부원칙 shop book rule

상품재고; 재고상품 merchandise inventory
상품조달원가 merchandise procurement cost
상품지식 merchandise knowledge
상품통계 commodity statistics
상품투자신탁 commodities investment trust
상품특성론 characteristic of goods theory
상품풀운영자 commodity pool operator
상품허위표시 false trade description
상품혁신의 시대 product innovation era
상품회전수 turnover of commodity
상품회전율 merchandise turnover ratio; rate of stock-turn
상한 ceding
상한금리 cap interest rate
상한임금설정 wage ceiling
상해건강보험 accident and health insurance
상해보상보험 accident and indemnity insurance
상해보험 accident insurance; personal accident insurance
상해상호보험 personal accident mutual insurance
상해질병보험 accident and sickness insurance
상행위 commercial transaction
상향 up-tick
상향수정 upward revision
상허보증증권 appeal bond
상호 business name; corporate name; name of the corporation; trade name
상호결정 reciprocal decision
상호결제제도 mutual offset system
상호계산 mutual account
상호계산계정 open and current account
상호계정 two way account
상호날인계약 mutual covenant
상호대차 mutual credits
상호대출 parallel loan
상호독립적인 사건 mutually exclusive event
상호무역협정 bilateral trade agreement
상호배부법 reciprocal distribution method
상호보강효과 mutual reinforcement

상호보험 mutual insurance; reciprocal exchange
상호보험조합 mutual association; mutual insurance society
상호부금 mutual installment
상호부조단체 beneficial association
상호부조조합 benevolent association
상호상관 cross correlation
상호생명보험회사 mutual insurance company
상호수요 reciprocal demand
상호수요곡선 reciprocal demand curve
상호신용장 reciprocal credit
상호약속 mutual promise
상호위탁판매 reciprocal consignment
상호유언 mutual
상호의, 호혜적인 reciprocal
상호입회하다 intercommon
상호자산교환 reciprocal transfer of property
상호작용 interaction approach
상호저축은행 mutual savings bank
상호접속 interconnection
상호조건 mutual condition
상호조정 mutual adjustment
상호조합 mutual benefit society
상호주의 mutualism
상호주의 성격의 보험단체 mutual-type associations
상호참조표 cross reference list
상호포기협정 pairing-off
상호협의 mutual agreement procedure
상호화 mutualization
상호회사 mutual company
상환 redemption
상환가격 call price; redemption value
상환가능주식 callable preferred stock
상환가액 maturity value
상환거치종신연금 refund deferred life annuity
상환기간까지 보유함 held to maturity
상환기일 redemption date
상환기한 tenor
상환면제 discharge of repayment; forgiveness

of repayment

상환보증증권 refunding bond

상환식 연금 annuity refund; refund annuity

상환연장 extension of the maturity

상환우선주식 redeemable preferred stock

상환은행 reimbursing bank

상환의무를 면제하지 않는 신용장 with recourse credit

상환의무를 지지 않는 without recourse

상환의무면제신용장 without recourse credit

상환익 redemption profit

상환조항 recapture clause

상환주식 callable shares; redeemable stock

상환준비예금 compulsory deposit as a condition for loans

상환차익 profit from redemption

상환차익과세 tax on redemption profit

상환채권 redeemable bond

상환청구 claim for reimbursement; claim of recourse

상환청구권 claim of redemption; right of recourse

상환청구권부 채권 put bond

상환청구에 응하지 않은 sans recourse

상환통지 notice of redemption

상환프리미엄 redemption premium

상환하다 reimburse

상황변수 situational variable

상황분석 situation analysis

상황적합이론 contingency theory

새도우어카운트 shadow account

새로이; 다시 de novo

새터데이나이트스페셜 Saturday Night Special

새틀라이트뉴스개더링 satellite news gathering

새틀라이트케이블넷 satellite cable network

색교정 color proof

색분해 color separation

색상명명법 color naming system

색상선별거울 dichroic mirror

색온도 color temperature

색차신호 chrominance signal

색참조표 color lookup table

색채조절 color dynamics

샌드위치스프레드 sandwich spread

샘플링음원 sampling sound module

생계 living; sustenance

생계비 living cost; subsistence money

생계잔고 balance in hand

생계현금 cash on hand

생계현금보유고 cash in hand

생리적인 동인 physiological drive

생리적인 욕구 physiological needs

생명보험 life insurance

생명보험금 proceeds of life insurance

생명보험료 life insurance premium

생명보험료공제 deduction for life insurance premiums; life insurance credit; life insurance premiums deduction; taxation allowance for life insurance premium

생명보험신탁 life insurance trust

생명보험외무원 ordinary agent

생명보험의 재보험 life reinsurance

생명보험의학 life insurance medicine

생명보험증권 life insurance policy

생명보험회사 life insurance company

생명손해보험동시판매외무원 multiple line agent

생명연금적립금 life annuity fund

생명표 life table; mortality table

생보구입 life insurance company purchase

생보자금투자 investment of life insurance fund

생보FP financial planner

생산개시 production release

생산거점 production base

생산계정 production account

생산고 crop; output; sales volume; trading volume; turnover

생산고; 연출 production

생산고; 이율 yield

생산고보고서 production report

생산고비례법 output method; production method; unit of production method

생산고원가 cost of work performed

생산고지불 progress payment

생산고지불제 reimbursement method

생산공정 production process

생산공학 industrial engineering

생산과잉 overproduction

생산관리 production control

생산관리시스템 production control system

생산국민소득 national income produced

생산국카르텔 producer's cartel

생산노무비 production labor cost

생산량 quantity of production

생산물 products

생산물배상책임보험 products and completed operation liability insurance

생산분배 production sharing

생산설비 plant capacity; production facility

생산설비를 시운전함 trial running of manufacturing equipment

생산성 productivity

생산성격차인플레 productivity inflation

생산성상실클레임 loss of productivity claims

생산성지수 index of productivity

생산성지표 productivity ratio

생산성측정 measure of productivity; productivity measurement

생산실적 actual production

생산요소 factors of production

생산자물가지수 producer price index

생산자본 production capital

생산자시장 producer market

생산자잉여 producer's surplus

생산자출하지수 indexes of producers' shipments

생산재 producer's goods; production goods

생산전량구입 bulk buying

생산지수 index number of production

생산지향 production orientation; product-oriented

생산함수 production function

생산합리화 rationalization of production

생산허가 production permit

생산후의 post-production

생성함수 generating function

생손보상호보험 all lines insurance

생잔연금 reversionary annuity; survivorship annuity

생전신탁 living trust

생전증여 gift during life

생존경쟁 struggle for existence

생존급부금 step-up bonus

생존보험 pure endowment; pure endowment insurance

생존자에 대한 권리의 귀속 survivorship

생태계 eco-system

생태적인 요인 ecological factor

생태학 ecology

생활보호 public assistance

생활비지수 cost of living index; cost-of-living index

생활필수품 necessaries

샷건어프로치 shotgun approach

서로 다투는 contentious

서로 엇갈리게 짜다 interlace

서류 document

서류상환지급 payment against document

서머타임 summer time

서면감사 paper audit

서면계약 written agreement; written contract

서면문의 written inquiry

서면신청 written application

서명날인 signed and sealed

서명하다 affix; subscribe

서문 preamble

서바이벌본드 survival bond

서보기구 servo mechanism

서브론 subloan

서브리미널 subliminal

서브리미널광고 subliminal advertisement

서브시스템 subsystem
서브젝트마켓 subject market
서블리그 therblig
서비스거래 service transaction
서비스경제 service economy
서비스마크 service mark
서비스무역 service trade
서비스보고서 service report
서비스성 serviceability
서비스에어리어 service area
서비스제공 service delivery
서비스조직 service organization
서비스함수 service function
서서히 절하 gradual devaluation
서약 adjuration; recognizance
서열 bracket
서열법 ranking system
서유럽연합 Western European Union
서체 type face
서커스스와프 circus swap
서킷교환 circuitswitching
서플라이사이드경제학 supply-side economics
석유가스세 petroleum gas tax
석유세 petroleum tax
석유업법 petroleum act
석유정제업 oil refinery
석유채굴권 oil concession
선가(船價)상각 depreciation of ship costs
선거관리자 returning officer
선거권자 constituent
선계약 precontract
선구주 forerunner stock
선권원(先權原) elder title
선금 advance payment
선금으로 payment in advance
선납보험료 advance premium
선도 forward delivery
선도가격 forward price
선도거래 forward agreement; forward transaction
선도결제 forward settlement

선도계약 forward contract
선도금리 forward rate
선도예금 forward deposit
선도임금 prepaid salaries and wages
선도환 forward exchange
선도환거래 forward exchange transaction
선두주 leading share
선량약인 good consideration
선례 precedent
선례가 없는 소송사건 case of first impression
선매 advance sale
선물(先物) futures
선물가격 futures price
선물가격곡선 price line of futures price
선물거래 futures trading
선물계약 futures contract
선물디스카운트 forward discount
선물딜러 futures dealer
선물레이트 futures rate
선물마진 forward margin; futures margin
선물매수계약 purchase contract
선물매출포지션 short forward position
선물상장 futures quotation
선물상품 futures product
선물시장 forward market; futures market
선물옵션 futures option
선물옵션시장 futures option market
선물중개업자 futures commission merchant
선물환거래 forward operation
선물환매매 forward bargain
선물환상장 forward exchange rate; forward quotation
선물환스프레드 forward rate spread
선물환예약 exchange forward contract; forward exchange contract
선물환포지션 forward position
선물환프리미엄 forward premium
선박 age of vessel; ships and vessels; vessel
선박건조보험 builders' risks insurance
선박관리인 ship's husband
선박보험 hull insurance

선박비부서류 ship's paper
선박세 shipping tax
선박수선보험 repairing risks insurance
선박양도증서 grand bill of sale
선박저당권 mortgage of ship
선박증명서 certificate of registry
선박해상보험 marine hull insurance
선방계정 their account
선별융자 selective financing
선불 payment on delivery
선불가임 prepaid rents on buildings
선불금반환보증증권 advance payment bond
선불급여 advance salary
선불로 cash before delivery; cash in advance
선불법인세 prepaid income taxes
선불보험료 prepaid insurance
선불비용 prepaid expense
선불옵션 prepayment option
선불운임 advance freight; prepaid freight
선불의 prepaid
선불이익 prepaid income
선불이자 interest advance; interest prepaid;
  prepaid interest
선불프리미엄 up-front premium
선불하다 prepay
선비(船費)보험 disbursements insurance
선서 oath
선서공술서 affidavit
선서공술자 deponent
선서관리관 commissioners for oaths
선-선레이트 forward-forward rate
선송법 rolling-forward procedure
선수금 advance received
선수수익 advance received profit
선순위담보부사채 senior mortgage bond
선순위보험자 previous insurers
선순위양도저당 senior mortgage
선순위의 senior
선순위채권자 senior creditor
선순차방식 one pass scan
선스타트스와프 forward swap

선언 manifesto; propaganda
선언규정 declaratory stipulation
선언적인 법률 declaratory statute
선언적인 판결 declaratory judgment
선열구속력의 원칙 stare decisis
선원 mariner; seaman
선원고용계약서 shipping articles
선원급료수취지도서 allotment note
선의계약 bona fide contracts
선의계약설 contract uberrimae fldei theory
선의소지자 bona fide holder
선의의 매주 innocent purchaser
선의의 부실표시 innocent misrepresentation
선의의 소지인 holder in good faith
선의의 제삼자 holder in due course
선의채권자 bona fide creditor
선의취득자 bona fide purchaser
선일부의 dating forward
선입선출법 first-in first-out method
선장용 선하증권 ship's bill
선저침수 bilged
선적서류 shipping document
선적이서 on board notation
선적지불 cash on shipment
선적지연 late shipment
선적통과 advice of shipment
선적품질조건 shipped quality terms
선적항 home port
선정 selection
선정문제 selected issue
선진국 advanced countries
선진국상장 중앙은행총재회의 Conference of
  Ministers and Governors
선진국수뇌회의 Economic Summit
선취권 right of priority
선취권을 등록, 신청함 preemption entry
선취유치권 prior lien
선취특권 legal lien
선취특권; 리엔 lien
선취특권이론 lien theory
선취특권자 lienor

선취특권채; 우선담보권부사채 prior lien bond
선취특권통지 notice of lien
선측(船側) 인도 선측인도 free alongside ship
선택가능위험 optional perils
선택계약 alternative contract
선택과정 selection process
선택권부 보험 insurance with settlement options
선택권부 환예약 exchange contract with option
선택권행사가능기간 option period
선택급부 selective benefits
선택상환조항 optional repayment provision
선택세 alternative duties
선택적인 경쟁 selective competition
선택적인 구제 alternative remedy
선택적인 기능 selective function
선택적인 노출 selective exposure
선택적인 수요 selective demand
선택적인 신용규제 selective credit regulation
선택적인 지각 selective perception
선택적인 채널 selective channel
선택주문 alternative order
선택채무 alternative obligation
선택통화요금 optional calling plan
선택표 select table
선택형 가격결정 alternative pricing
선하증권 bill of lading
선행 good behavior
선행계열 leading series
선행이서의 진정성을 증명함 previous indorsements guaranteed
선행형 전략 proactive strategy
선험적인 확률 priori probability
선형가속도계수 linear accelerator
선형결합 linear combination
선형계획법 linear programming
선형판별분석 linear discriminant analysis
선형판별함수 linear discriminant function
선형회귀 linear regression

선호; 우선권 preference
선호순위 order of preference
선호에 따른 세분화 preference segmentation
설계검증 design verification
설계관리 design control
설계도 plan
설계변경 design change
설계심사 design review
설계인정 design qualification
설리반의 원칙 Sullivan Principle
설립계 notification of incorporation
설립등기 registration of establishment
설립법 act of incorporation
설립상각비 organization expenses amortize
설립절차 formalities of incorporation
설립취지서; 내용설명서 prospectus
설명 clarification
설명기능 descriptive function
설명문언 recital clause
설명변수 explanatory variable
설명부 재무제표 descriptive financial statement
설명에 기반을 둔 승낙 informed consent
설명을 위한 통계 descriptive statistics
설명표시 descriptive labeling sea
설비 appliance; conveniences; equipment; facilities
설비가동률 capital utilization; capacity utilization rate
설비갱신준비금 replacement reserve
설비과잉 overcapacity
설비관리 equipment control
설비신규구입액 additions to plant and equipment
설비신탁 equipment trust
설비자금 equipment fund; plant fund
설비투자 capital investment; investment in plant and machinery; plant investment
설비투자 캐시플로비율 cash flow ratio to capital expenditures
설비투자계획 capital budgeting

설비투자의욕 capital investment intention
설정 setting
설치 installation; mounting
설치공사 erection work; installation work
설치대수 number of machines installed
성공보수 contingent fee; incentive fee; merit increase
성과배분 payment by the result
성과분석 performance analysis
성년 full age; lawful age
성년자 adult
성능특성 performance characteristic
성명사기 false personation
성명사칭 personation
성명오기 misnomer
성문법 leges scriptae
성분표시 ingredient labeling
성쇠 ups and downs
성숙경제 mature economy
성숙기업 mature company
성숙단계 mature phase
성숙제품전략 mature product strategy
성숙한 플랜 mature plans
성실 bona fides; good faith
성실히 in good faith
성장 순환성장 cyclical growth
성장률 growth rate
성장률변화 change in growth rate
성장벡터매트릭스 growth vector matrix
성장성 growth potential
성장전략 growth strategy
성장주 growth stock
성장통화 appropriate cash supply for economic growth; growing currency
성장할 수 있는 viable
성질과 정도 nature and degree
성질이 상실됨 alteration of species
성행관리 drifting management
성행주문 market order without limit; no limit order
세계공황 world crisis

세계기업 global corporation; world company; world enterprise
세계마케팅 world marketing
세계무역기구 World Trade Organization
세계은행 World Bank
세계자연보호기금 World Wide Fund for Nature
세계적인 시장 global market
세계지적소유권기관 World Intellectual Property Organization
세계지향 geocentrism
세계화 globalization
세계화폐 money of the world
세공제 tax deductions
세공제가격 prices less tax
세공제전 이익 profit before tax
세공제후 이익 profit after tax
세관 custom-house; customs house
세관수수료 custom free
세그먼트정보 segmental information
세금공제급여 pay after tax; take-home pay
세금공제전 이익 earnings before tax; income before income taxes; pretax income
세금공제전 회계이익 pretax accounting income
세금공제후 after tax
세금공제후 이익 after-tax income; after-tax yield
세금공제후 이익률 after tax profit rate
세금납부 payment of tax
세금배분회계 accounting for tax allocation; accounting for income tax allocation
세금분류 classification of tax
세금소전 transformation of tax transit
세금예금 taxes collected
세금유가증권 securities received for guarantee
세금으로 빼앗기는 금액 tax take
세금을 위한 매각 tax selling
세금이 붙는 물품 dutiable goods
세금재정 tax arbitrage
세금조항 tax clause

세금준비금 tax reserve
세금체납처분 process for the recovery of
　　taxes in arrears
세금포함 before tax
세금환부 refund of taxes
세금환원 amortization of taxes
세금회피수단 tax shelter
세대과세 household taxation
세델 cedel
세리사 licensed tax accountant; tax
　　practitioner
세리사보수 tax accountant fee
세리사시험 tax accountant examination
세리상의 우대조치 tax incentive
세목(稅目) items of tax; tax items
세목계정식 detailed account form
세무감사 tax audit
세무고문 tax advisor
세무관 taxcollector
세무당국 tax authorities
세무대리 tax agency; tax proxy
세무법원 tax court
세무사 certified tax accountant
세무사법 certified tax accountant law
세무사회 certified tax accountant association
세무상담 tax consultation
세무상의 수속 tax procedures
세무상의 특례 exceptional tax treatment
세무서 tax office
세무서류 tax documents
세무서장 chief of the taxation office
세무소송 tax suit
세무자문위원회 advisory tax board
세무쟁소 tax dispute
세무조사 audit and criminal investigation; tax
　　adjustments; tax examination
세무조사결과 results of the tax examination
세무조사절차 procedures of tax adjustments
세무조정 adjustment for taxable income
세무행정조직 tax administration system
세무회계 tax accounting

세무회계론 theory of tax accounting
세배보상 treble indemnity
세법 tax law; tax regulations
세법규 tax rule
세법상의 특전 various kinds of tax benefits
세법을 무시함 disregard of tax rule
세법학 tax jurisprudence
세부담능력 taxable capacity
세부담율 tax burden rate
세부담의 평준화 equalization of tax burden
세분화 breaking bulk; fragmentation
세분화; 세그멘테이션 segmentation
세분화하여 매입하다 buy on scale
세속의 secular
세수 tax revenue
세수기 tax-gathering season
세수보증어음 taxanticipation note
세수보증워런트 taxanticipation warrant
세수채 tax bond
세액계산 computation of tax amount
세액계산기준 tax computation basis
세액계산기준변경 cnange of tax computation
　　basis
세액공제 credit against tax; tax credit
세액공제순서 sequence of tax credits
세액사정액 assessment
세액직접공제 direct tax credit
세액표 tax table
세액확정 settlement of tax amount
세외부담 nontax payment
세외수익 nontax receipts
세원 source of taxation
세율 tax rate; taxation rate
세율등급 tax bracket
세율위원회 tariff commission
세이그웨이 segue
세이프가드조항 safeguard provision
세이프티엔벨롭 safety envelop
세이프하버리스 safe harbor lease
세인 tax seal
세인이율 net yield

세일앤드리스백 sale and lease-back
세일즈맨교육 salesman training
세일즈믹스 sales mix
세입 annual revenue
세입가격 price including tax
세입결함 revenue deficit
세입대리점 revenue agency
세입세출예산 revenue and expenditure budget
세자리수 주가수익률 three digit PER
세전가격 price before tax
세제 tax system; taxation system
세제개혁 tax reform
세제정리 readjustment of taxation system
세제조사회 tax system council
세출 annual expenditure
세포함 including tax
세환급증명서 customs debenture
세효과 tax effect
세효과규칙 taxbenefit rule
세효과회계 accounting for income taxes; tax effect accounting
섹터 sector
섹터방식 sectoral approach
센트럴레이트 central rate
센티멘트지표 sentiment index
셀러즈옵션거래 seller's option trading
셀룰러방식 cellular communication system
셀룰러어프로치 cellular approach
셀링업무 selling
셀링클라이막스 selling climax
셀프메일러 self-mailer
셀프서비스식 소매업 self-service retailing
소각 retirement
소개 introduction
소개사찰 referral premium
소구계산 retrogressive accounting
소구력 appeal power
소규모 트렌드 small trend
소규모 해손 petty average
소규모기업공제 small enterprise mutual aid plan

소규모기업공제 외상금공제 deduction for small enterprise mutual aid premiums
소규모기업자 small sized business proprietor
소규모지점 twig
소규모차액이익금 thin margin
소극신탁 passive trust
소극자산 negative assets
소극재산 negative property
소극적인 관리 passive management
소극적인 보증 negative assurance
소극적인 적립금 negative reserve
소극적인 주 negative goodwill
소극적인 주장 negative averments
소극적인 증거 negative evidence
소극적인 증언 negative testimony
소극적인 투자관리 passive investment management
소극적인 평가계정 negative valuation accounts
소극적인 학습 passive learning
소극적인 항변 negative plea
소극적인 확인 negative confirmation
소극적인 훼손 passive waste
소급법 retrospective law
소급보험 retrospective policy
소급수정 retroactive adjustments
소급수정보고서 retroactive restatement
소급징수 retroactive levy
소기업과세 taxation on small business
소답 pleading
소답하다 plead
소득감응계수 coefficient of income sensitivity
소득공제 deductions from income; exemption and deduction from income
소득과세를 기간상호배분함 interperiod income tax allocation
소득과세배분 income tax allocations
소득교역조건 income terms of trade
소득귀속을 추정함 presumption of a real obtainer of income

소득금액합산 aggregation of income amount
소득보상보험 disability insurance; income indemnity insurance
소득분포 income distribution
소득상실급부 loss of income benefit
소득세 income tax; revenue tax
소득세감액 decrease of income tax
소득세공제 income tax credit
소득세과세 imposition of income tax
소득세기본통달 fundamental directives of income tax
소득세법 income tax law
소득세속산표 income tax rapid calculation table
소득세신고 income tax return
소득세신고서 income tax return form
소득세액공제 credit for income tax
소득세연납 deferred payment of income tax
소득세율 income tax rate
소득세지불보증증권 internal revenue bond
소득소비곡선 income-consumption curve
소득수준 level of income
소득신고 declaration of income; income return
소득신고용지 income return blank
소득액을 신고하다 file income tax return
소득예금 income deposit
소득원천 source of income
소득원천세 limited income method
소득의 종류 kind of income
소득인플레이션 income inflation
소득재분배 redistribution of income
소득재분배효과 income redistribution effect
소득접근법 income approach
소득정책 income policy
소득창출효과 income-generating effect
소득층 income bracket
소득탄력성 income elasticity
소득평준화 income leveling off
소득할과세 taxation of income basis
소득효과 income effect

소매 retail
소매가격구조 retail prices structure
소매경쟁 retailing competition
소매기능 retailing function
소매매가 retail selling price
소매매상고 retail sales
소매물가인플레이션 retail price inflation
소매물가지수 index of retail price
소매브로커 retail broker
소매세 retail excise
소매신용 retail credit
소매업자 보증증권 dealer's bond
소매업전략 retailing strategy
소매업회계 retail accounting
소매원가 retail cost
소매은행 retail bank
소매점포입지전략 retail stores location strategy
소매회전 wheel of retailing
소멸 extinction
소멸배당 terminal dividend
소멸시킬 수 있는 피보험이익 defeasible interest
소멸시효 extinctive prescription; negative prescription; prescription extinctive
소멸원가 expired cost
소멸조건부 소유권 defeasible fee
소모 exhaustion
소모공구 perishable tool
소모품 consumables; sundry supplies
소모품비 supplies expenses
소문증거 hearsay evidence
소배심 petit jury
소부동 slight ups and downs
소브린론 sovereign loan
소브린비율 sovereign rating
소비가치 consumption values
소비동향 consumption trend
소비래그 consumption lag
소비론 loan for consumption
소비생활협동조합 consumer's cooperative

society

소비성향 propensity to consume

소비세 consumption tax

소비세신고 consumption entry

소비수요 consumption demand

소비수준 level of consumption

소비승수 consumption multiplier

소비양여세 consumption transfer tax

소비예상 outlook for consumer spending

소비이론 theory of consumption

소비자 user

소비자개척 consumer exploitation

소비자관련주 consumer sector stock

소비자광고 consumer advertisement

소비자교육 consumer education

소비자금융 consumer loan

소비자금융규제법 consumer credit control law

소비자금융생명보험 consumer credit life insurance

소비자금융의 금리 consumer credit rate

소비자금융회사 consumer credit company; consumer finance company

소비자단체 consumer's union

소비자단체생명보험 consumers group insurance

소비자리스 consumer leasing

소비자물가지수 consumer price index

소비자사고변수 consumer thought variable

소비자선택 consumer choice

소비자신용 consumer credit

소비자운동 consumer movement

소비자주의 consumerism

소비자지각 consumer perception

소비자지출 consumer expenditure; consumer spending

소비자테스트 consumer testing

소비자행동 consumer's behavior; consumer behavior

소비자행동모델 model of consumer behavior

소비자행동분석 consumer behavior analysis

소비지출관련주 retail and consumer spending sector stock

소비패턴 pattern of consumption

소비할당 consumption quota

소비함수 consumption function

소속단체 membership group

소손해 minor loss

소손해를 사정, 지불할 권한 draft authority

소손해면책 excess

소손해면책율 franchise

소송 bar; institution of law suits; lawsuits; suit

소송각하 nonsuit

소송경제 judicial economy

소송계속의 항변 autre action pendant

소송계속중인 pendente lite

소송교사 barratry

소송기록서 minute book; paper-book

소송담당관 litigation officer

소송당사자 litigant; parties to lawsuit

소송방기 abandonment of action; form of action

소송법 code of legal procedure

소송보증증권 litigation bond

소송비용 legal cost

소송비용담보 security for costs

소송비용보증증권 costs bond

소송비용보험 litigation expense insurance

소송비용상호보험 defense association

소송속행 further maintenance of the action

소송신청서 plaint

소송에 참가하다 intervene

소송원인 cause of action; ground of action

소송원인을 병합함 joinder of cause of action

소송원인이 발생함 accrual of cause of action

소송원조 champerty

소송을 분리함 severance of actions

소송을 위한 ad litem

소송을 추행하지 않음 want of procesution

소송이 각하될 만한 assessor cadere

소송인 suitor

소송절차 procedure; proceeding; process

소송절차비용 cost for judicial proceedings
소송종결기재 stet processus
소송종료판결 cassetur breve
소송중복 multiplicity of action
소송중지 stay of proceedings
소송추행; 소송수행 litigation
소수대표법 minority representation
소수주주 minority shareholders
소수주주권 minority shareholders' right
소수주주지분 minority interest
소수지배 minority control
소수파집단 minority group
소순환 minor cycle
소스 saucer
소시오그램 sociogram
소시오메트리 sociometry
소시오메트릭기법 sociometric technique
소액감모자산 petty-sum wasting property
소액거치자산 small sum deferred assets
소액공채별 비과세제도 tax-free small-sum
　public bond investment system
소액금융 small loan
소액노령연금 small sums of pension paid to
　old-age persons
소액대부회사포괄보증증권 small loan
　company blanket bond
소액배당소득 small sums of dividend income
소액상각자산 petty-sum depreciable
　property; small sums of depreciable
　property
소액예금 petty deposits; small sums of
　savings
소액예금증권 small savers certificate
소액예저금 small sums of deposits and
　savings
소액우편환 및 위조지폐손해담보 money
　orders and counterfeit paper currency
　coverage
소액자산 small sum properties
소액저축 등 이용자카드 green card
소액저축비과세제도 tax-free small-sum
　savings system
소액전도금 petty imprest
소액전불준비금 imprest cash fund
소액주문 small lot order
소액중요자산 small sum and important
　property
소액채권 baby bond
소액채권재판소 court of request
소액취급 less than carload
소액투자가 little; small investor
소액현금 petty cash
소액현금예금 petty current deposit
소액현금제도 petty cash system
소액현금지불 petty cash payment
소액현금출납장 petty cash book
소요준비 required reserves
소유권 ownership; proprietary right
소유권보류 reservation of ownership
소유권보험회사 title of account
소유권유보조항 overreaching clause
소유권이권 royalty interest
소유권이전 passage of title
소유권증 ownership certificate
소유권침해 infringement of ownership
소유기간 investment horizon
소유기간이율 horizon return
소유기간이익 yield for holding period
소유자 owner; proprietor
소유자불명의 unclaimed
소유자재 materials on hand
소유자지배 owner control
소유재고품 goods on hands
소유제품 finished goods on hand
소유주 stocks in hand
소유주계정 proprietorship account
소유주식 equity securities
소유주지분 owner's equity
소유효용 possession utility
소장 bill of complain
소재지 location; site
소재지법 lex loci rei

소지인 holder
소지인불식; 소지인출급식 payable to holder
소지재고수준 stock level
소지주 stock on hand
소지증권 securities in portfolio
소지채권 portfolio bond
소지한 유동성 liquidity in hand
소집단이론 small group theory
소집배심원명부 regular panel
소추하다 implead
소폭 narrow range; small margin
소폭상승 edge up
소폭왕래 narrow movement
소폭절상 small revaluation
소폭하락 edge down
소표본 small sample
소프트달러 soft dollar
소프트랜딩 soft landing
소프트론 soft loan
소형주 small capital stock
소화하다; 요약하다; 침지하다 digest
소환 annire; citation
소환절차 attachment of privilege
속도 velocity
속성 attribute
속성법 temporal method
속성상관 measure of association
속성열거법 attribute listing
속행 further directions
손금 charge against revenues; deductible
    expenses
손금불산입 exclusion from expenses
손금불산입 조세과금 nondeductible taxes
손금불산입교제비 entertainment expenses
    not qualifying for deduction
손금산입 inclusion in expenses
손금산입상여 bonus payment entered into
    expenses
손금산입외국세 foreign tax deductible as
    expenses
손금산입할 수 있는 준비금 deductible reserve

손모 wear and tear
손모료 dilapidations
손상(물) spoilage
손상가액 damaged value
손상성 damageability
손상품비 spoilage expenses
손실 loss
손실계상시기 time of recognizing loss
손실발생지 location of loss or damage
손실보상증서 back bond
손실신고서 final return in the case of loss
손실을 메꾸다 cover the loss
손실이월 carryover of loss
손실제외 exclusion of loss
손실준비금 loss reserve
손실한정주문 stop-loss order
손실함수 loss function
손실환급 carryback of loss
손익 income and expenses; income summary;
    loss and gain; profit and loss
손익거래 profit and loss transaction
손익계산서 earning statement; income
    statement; loss and gain statement; profit
    and loss statement
손익계산서감사 income statement audit
손익계산서계정 income statement account
손익계산서등식 profit and loss equation
손익계산서비율 income statement ratio
손익계산서어프로치 income statement
    approach
손익계산서원칙 income statement principles
손익계산서의 보충자료 supplementary
    income statement information
손익계정 general profit and loss account;
    income account; loss and gain account;
    profit and loss account
손익법 profit and loss method
손익보고 profit and loss report
손익분기도표 break-even chart
손익분기분석 break-even analysis
손익분기점 break-even point; profit and loss

break-even point

손익분기환상장 exchange rate at break-even point

손익통산 aggregation of profit and loss

손절주문 stop loss order

손해 damage

손해검사인 bureau adjuster

손해결제분석 claim settlement analysis

손해경감 mitigation of damage

손해경험 loss experience

손해담보계약 guaranty insurance

손해를 각오하고 처분하다 dump

손해를 증명함 proof of loss

손해를 피해 철수하다 loss cut

손해를 회복하다 recoup

손해발생률 loss frequency

손해발생확률 claim probability

손해방지비용 sue and labor charges

손해방지의무 duty to sue and labor

손해방지조항 sue and labor clause

손해배상 compensation for damage

손해배상금 liquidated damages

손해배상액 damages; reparation

손해배상이자 moratory interest

손해배상자력증명서 certificate of financial security

손해배상책임보험 liability insurance

손해배상청구 claim for damage

손해배상청구문서 ad damnurn

손해배상청구소송 action for damages

손해보상이론 theory of indemnity

손해보전계약서 letter of indemnity

손해보전한도 measure of indemnity

손해보전한도액 limit of indemnity

손해보험 damage insurance; nonlife insurance; property and liability insurance

손해보험공제 deduction for damage insurance; fire and other casualty insurance premiums deduction

손해보험대리점 nonlife insurance agent

손해보험료공제 taxation allowance for nonlife

insurance premium

손해보험회사 nonlife insurance company

손해분담 apportionment of loss

손해비용 loss due to spoiled work

손해빈도분석 claim frequency analysis

손해사정 adjustment; loss adjustment

손해사정국 adjustment bureau

손해사정비 adjustment costs

손해사정비용 claim expenses

손해사정인 adjuster

손해시가 net damaged value

손해율 claim ratio; loss ratio

손해전종목보험 general insurance

손해정산 claim adjustment

손해조사비 loss expense

손해통계 loss statistics

손해통지조항 claim notice clause

손해팩터 loss factor

손해확률 probability of loss or damage

솔라빌(1통만의 수출어음) sola bill

솔루션프로바이더 solution provider

솔리드모델 solid model

솔벤시마진 solvency margin

송금수표 remittance check

송금환 mail transfer payable; money order; remittance bill; telegraphic transfer payable

송달부 chitbook

송장; 청구서 invoice

쇄판 printing plate

쇠퇴산업 declining industry

쇼군채 shogun bond

쇼스캔시스템 show scan system

쇼트 short

쇼트드로잉 short drawing

쇼트북 short book

쇼트스퀴즈 short squeeze

쇼트스트랜글 short strangle

쇼트스트랩 short strap

쇼트스트립 short strip

쇼트어카운트 short account

쇼트콜 short call

쇼트쿠폰 short coupon
쇼트포지션 short position
쇼트포지션리스크 short position risk
쇼트풋 short put
쇼핑어라운드 shopping around
쇼핑행동 shopping behavior
수검성변동 convergent fluctuation
수검형 마켓팅 convergent marketing
수권법 enabling statute
수권자본 authorized capital; stock authorized
수권주식 authorized shares
수금불능예상액 estimated uncollectable
    amount
수금수수료 charge for collection
수금어음관리서비스 management service for
    bill for collection
수금채무 debt for collection
수금환 exchange for collection; telegraphic
    transfer receivable
수금환; 역환 bill receivable
수급 demand and supply; supply and demand
수급권부여 vesting
수급밸런스 demand-and-supply balance
수급조정 adjustment of supply to demand
수납계정 receiving
수납기관 agency to receive tax
수납보고서 receiving report
수납인 reception stamp
수뇌부 top management
수당 procurement
수도권시장 metromarket
수도료 water expense
수도연기금; 연전 backwardation
수도의 metropolitan
수도일 payday
수동적인 수탁자 bare trustee
수락 assent
수량경기 quantitative boom
수량과부족용인조건 more or less terms
수량실질성의 원칙 quantitative substantiality
    test

수량제한 quantity limit
수량조정 quantity adjustment
수량표 bill of quantities
수량표준 quantity standard
수량할인 quantity discount; volume discount
수량화 quantification
수량화수단 quantitative tool
수렴하다 converge
수령증 accountable receipt
수로안내료 pilotage
수로주변감시관 water-bailiff
수리경제학 mathematical economics
수리계획법 mathematical program
수리권(水利權) water concession; water right;
    irrigation right
수리보험료 actuarial contribution
수리손익 actuarial gains or losses
수리용 재료 material for repair
수리적인 책임준비금 mathematical reserve
수리지익세 water-utilization tax
수리통계 mathematical statistics
수면동기 dormant motive
수면효과 sleeper effect
수반집행 junior execution
수법 approach; method; tool
수비의무계약 secrecy agreement
수색 search
수석판사 chief justice; lord chief justice
수선 overhauling; repair
수선공장 repair-shop
수선보증예비금 liabilities for guarantee
    against repairs
수선비 cost of repairs; maintenance and
    repairs; repairing expenses
수선비예산 repairing budget
수선수당금 allowlince for repairs
수선유지비 repairs and maintenance
수선중 under repair
수선평균적립금 repair equalization reserve
수세과 section of revenue; taxation division;
    revenue officer; tax collector

수송 transport
수송모델 transportation model
수송방법 mode of transportation
수송비 transportation cost
수수료 charge; concession; percentage
수수료 각자지불 each way
수수료계정 commission account
수수료매매 commission sale; sales and
  purchases on commission
수수료사업 fee business
수수료수입 commission income
수수료원칙 fee basis
수수료제도 straight commission
수수료할인업자 discounters
수술비보험 surgical expense insurance
수신업무 deposit taking business
수신인 addressee
수신자요금부담통화; 프리다이얼 free dial
수약자 promisee
수요; 독촉 demand
수요가격 price elasticity of demand
수요곡선 demand curve
수요기 demand season
수요독점 monopsony
수요변화 demand changes
수요부족 demand deficiency
수요분석 demand analysis
수요예측 demand forecast
수요의 유연성 plasticity of demand
수요일요인 Wednesday-factor
수요자극 demand stimulation
수요중심점 center of demand
수요지수 demand index
수요창조 demand creation
수요탄력성 demand elasticity
수요탄성치 elasticity of demand
수요함수 demand function
수용과정 acceptance process
수용에 의한 보상금 compensation for
  expropriation
수용환지 nontaxable exchanges of properties

수월함 easier
수유자(受遺者) devisee
수의계약 negotiated contracts; private
  contract
수익 avails; earnings; fruit; gain
수익경향 trend of earnings
수익계상시기 time of recognizing gain
수익곡선 revenue curve
수익구조 profit profile
수익권 beneficial interest; beneficiary right;
  right of beneficiary
수익기업 beneficiary company
수익력 earning power
수익률 earning rate; rate of return
수익률교차 differential of return
수익률의 상관관계 correlation of return
수익률이 높은 profitable
수익률측정 measure of return
수익만기지불 lump-sum payment of
  dividends at maturity
수익면에서 in terms of revenue
수익모델 earnings model
수익보상금 compensation for revenue
수익사채 profit debenture
수익성 profitability
수익성 분석 profitability and investment
  analysis ratio
수익성장률 earnings growth rate
수익세 earning tax; profit tax
수익실현 realization of gains; revenue
  realization
수익안정성 earnings stability
수익예상 earnings forecast
수익예측컨센서스 consensus on earnings
  estimate
수익유보율 earnings retention rate
수익을 원본에 편입하는 형태의 투자신탁
  accumulation trust
수익인식기준 revenue recognizing standard
수익자 pernor of profits
수익자부담금 payment by beneficiary

수익자산 earning assets

수익적립금액 revenue reserve amount

수익증가 augmentation of earnings; earnings growth

수익증권 beneficiary certificate; beneficiary securities

수익지출 revenue expenditure

수익체감의 법칙 law of diminishing return

수익효과 profit impact

수입결제어음제도 import settlement bill system

수입계정 revenue account

수입과징금 import surcharge

수입규제 import restriction

수입금액 amount received

수입금융 import finance

수입금지품 contraband; contraband of import

수입담보화물보관증 trust receipt

수입대체 import substitute

수입무역관리 import control

수입물가지수 import price index

수입보험료 premium income

수입부가세 primage duty

수입분개장 cash-receipts journal

수입성향 propensity to import

수입세 import duty; import tax; impost

수입세표 import duties tariff

수입승인증 import license

수입시기 time of receipts

수입신고 declaration of import

수입어음 import bill

수입어음결제상장 acceptance rate

수입유전스 import usance

수입의존도 degree of dependence upon imports

수입인지 revenue stamp

수입인지세법 stamp duty law

수입인플레 imported inflation; inflation led by import

수입자금대부제도 import financing system

수입조사 mean test

수입증가 augmentation; increase of revenue

수입증거금 received margin

수입촉진지역 foreign access zone

수입할당 import quota

수입함수 import function

수입허가 import permit

수입현금 cash received

수정 amendment; modification

수정가속상각법 modified accelerated cost recovery system

수정기입 adjusting entry

수정기초액 adjusted basis

수정된 확률 corrected probability

수정법률 revised statutes

수정베타수치 adjusted beta value

수정분개 adjusting journal entry

수정사항결정 determining the necessary adjustments

수정순보험료 modified net premium

수정신고 amended return

수정양로보험계약 modified endowment

수정예산 amended budget; revised budget

수정요율계출사용제도 modified file and use system

수정요율사전승인제도 modified prior approval system

수정자본주의 modified capitalism

수정초연정기식 책임준비금 modified preliminary term reserve

수정총소득 adjusted gross income

수정취득원가 adjusted historical cost

수정평균주가 revised average stock price

수정포괄주의 modified all-inclusive theory

수정하다 amend

수정현금반환부 연금 modified cash refund annuity

수정회귀분석 adjusted regression analysis

수정후 순이익 adjusted net profit

수주액 order volume

수주잔 order backlog

수주잔고 orders in hand

수주증가 order increase
수준 level
수준유지 unchange
수중에 있는 채권 bond in portfolio
수증자 donee
수증자산 watered assets
수증주식 watered stock
수지결산 settlement of accounts
수지계정 balance of accounts
수지를 수반하지 않는 거래 nonfund transactions
수지를 수반하지 않는 투자활동 noncash investing activities
수지방정식 income and expenditure liquidation
수지부기 receipt and payment bookkeeping
수지분기점 cash break-even point; receipts and disbursements break-even point
수지분석 cash flow analysis
수지상등의 원칙 principle of equivalence
수지예측 cash forecasts
수지지출 receipts and payments
수직경로시스템 vertical channel system
수직귀선 소거기간 vertical blank interval
수직무역, 수평무역 vertical trade horizontal trade
수직분석 vertical analysis
수직상승 straight climb
수직적인 고객제한 vertical territorial customer restrictions
수직적인 국제분업 vertical specialization
수직적인 마케팅시스템 vertical marketing system
수직컴비네이션 bottom vertical combination
수직합병 vertical merger
수직형 통합 vertical integration
수직화각(垂直畵角) vertical angle of view
수집물포괄보험 collection floater
수축장벽 shrinkage barrier
수출관리규정 compliance program
수출금융 export financing

수출금지 embargo
수출금지품 contraband of export
수출드라이브 export drive
수출면세 export exemption
수출물가지수 export price index
수출변동보상융자제도 Cooperative Financing Facility
수출보험 export insurance
수출부조 disappointing export
수출세 export duties; export tax
수출승인증 export license
수출신고 export declaration
수출신용 export credit; shipper's usance
수출신용보험 export credit insurance
수출어음 bill of exchange; export bill
수출업자신용 export supplier credit
수출의 수익성 export profitability
수출의존도 degree of dependence upon exports; export dependence
수출인수어음 trade acceptance
수출입물가지수 export and import price index
수출입은행 export-import bank
수출자주규제 voluntary export restraint; voluntary restriction of export
수출장려금 export bounty
수출전대계정 export advanced account
수출전대금융 export advance loan
수출전도금 export advance
수출채권매입 export factoring
수출함수 export function
수취가임(受取家賃) house rent received
수취계정; 외상매출금; 미수금계정 account receivable
수취계정기준상장 receiving quotation
수취고; 지불보험금 proceeds
수취금 amount receivable
수취배당금 dividend earned; dividend received
수취배당금익금불산입 dividend excluded from income
수취수수료 commission earned

수취어음 notes and bills receivable

수취어음기입장 notes receivable register

수취이자 interest earned; interest receivable; interest received

수취인 payee; recipient; remittee

수취채권 notes and accounts receivable; receivables

수취할인료 discount earned

수치기법 numerical techniques

수치적분법 numerical integration

수탁 bailment

수탁매부전도금 advance received on indents

수탁자 assignee; bailee; bailor; consignee; fiduciary; trustee

수탁자고객포괄보험 bailees' customers floater

수탁자단체보험 trustee group insurance

수탁자배상책임보험 bailees' liability policy

수탁자보증증권 fiduciary bond

수탁자약관 bailee clause

수탁자책임 fiduciary responsibility; prudent person rule

수탁취급장소 place of fiduciary

수탁판매 sales on consignment

수탁판매입체금 advance on consignment-in

수탁품 goods on consignment-in

수탁회사 trustee company

수평구입 horizontal buy

수평무역 horizontal trade

수평분단 horizontal split

수평분석 horizontal analysis

수평분업 horizontal specialization

수평사고 lateral thinking

수평스프레드 horizontal spread

수평시장 horizontal market

수평적 horizontal

수평적인 감사 horizontal audit

수평적인 경쟁 horizontal competition

수평적인 국제분업 horizontal international specialization

수평적인 매입 horizontal acquisition

수평적인 협력 horizontal concurrence

수평합병 horizontal merger

수평형 다각화 lateral diversification

수평형 통합 horizontal integration

수평화각 horizontal angle of view

수표기입장 check register

수표발행지 check drawer

수표발행한도 limit of overdrawn account

수표법 check act

수표장 check book

수표장원부 checkbook stub

수표제도 checking system

수표지불인 check drawee

수표지정인 check holder

수학모델 mathematical model

수확기준 crop basis

수확물보험 crop insurance

수확전략 harvesting strategy

숙직료 night duty allowance

순 이일드 positive yield

순가격 net price; net value

순가산이익액 net mark-on

순간노출기 tachistoscope

순계상보험료 net premiums written

순고정자산 net tangible assets

순과세재산 net taxable assets

순교역조건지수 index of net terms of trade

순금융수입 net export; net financial income

순금전항목 net monetary items

순당좌자산 net quick assets

순매상고 net sales

순매상고총계 aggregate net sales

순매연결 net short hedging

순번상품재고관리 rotated merchandise control

순보험료식 책임준비금 reserve on net premium method

순부채 net debt; net liabilities

순분검정소 assay office

순상속재산 net succession

순상품교역조건 net commodity terms of

trade
순생산고 net production value
순서배열 sequencing
순서척도 ordinal scale
순소지금액 net line
순손실 net loss
순손실환급 carryback of net loss
순손익 net profit or loss
순손익계산 net profit or loss account
순손익구분 net profit or loss section
순수거치종신연금 pure deferred life annuity
순수과점 pure oligopoly
순수위험 pure risk
순수익 net return
순수입보험료 net premium
순수자가연금 company-administered annuity
순수채권 ex-warrant bond
순수취금 net receipt
순수취액 net avails; net proceeds
순수취이자 net interest income
순수패널 true panel
순시통신 real time communication
순실현가능가격 net realizable value
순액(純額)베이스 net base
순액주의 net amount principle
순영업손실 net operating loss
순영업순환일수 net operating cycle
순영업이익 net operating profit
순운전시간 net cycle time
순운전자본 net working capital
순원가 net cost
순월확정일상장 outright forward rates fixed date
순월확정일인도 outright forward fixed date delivery
순유동성 수지 net liquidity balance
순유동자산 net current assets
순이월비용 net carry-over cost
순이익 net earnings; net profit
순이익률 net income ratio
순이익에 대한 지분 equity in earnings

순이자 net interest
순이자비용 net interest cost
순익 absolute profit; net income
순익률 net profit ratio
순익처분 disposition of net income
순일수 clear days
순잉여금 net surplus
순자산 net assets; net worth; net worth equity
순자산가액 net assets value
순자산가치 net asset value
순자산인수액 acceptance price of net assets
순자유준비 net free reserves
순장부가액 net book value
순저축 net saving
순제어장치 network control unit
순조 favorable
순조로운 매상 steady sales
순조로운 매상신장 healthy revenue growth
순조로운 회복 brisk recovery
순지분자산 net equity assets
순지불보험료 net premium payable
순지출 net outgo
순차우선주취인 alternate preference beneficiaries
순차입준비 net borrowed reserves
순투자 net investment
순풍개입 intervention following market
순할인채 pure discount bond
순현금유입 net cash inflows
순현재가치 net present value
순화폐포지션 net monetary position
순환변동 cyclical fluctuation
순환불황 cyclical depression
순환주 cyclical stock
순회감사 traveling audit
순회수가능액 net collectible amounts
순회재판소 circuit court
순회판매인 traveling salesman
숫자상으로 in number
쉐어지향 share oriented
슈퍼 301조 super 301 Article

슈퍼골드트랜시에 super gold tranche
슈퍼나우계정 super NOW account
슈퍼메이저터리조항 super majority provision
슈퍼바이저 supervisor
슈퍼임포즈 super impose
슈퍼프라임레이트 super prime rate
슈프라펌 suprafinn
스나이프 snipe
스내퍼 snapper
스놉효과 snob effect
스로우백원칙 throw-back rule
스루풋조항 through-put contract
스모가스보드제 smorgasbord plan
스몰(100만달러단위의 거래) small
스몰스프레드 small spread
스무딩아웃오퍼레이션 smoothing out operation
스미소니언체제 Smithsonian system
스스로 in person
스스로 붙임 trade on one's own account
스시본드 sushi bond
스와프 swap
스와프론 swap loan
스와프를 단기로 하다 short the swap
스와프브로커 swap broker
스와프채 swap fund
스와프채거래 swap trading
스와프채레이트 swap rate
스와프채스트라이크 swap strike
스와프채포트폴리오 swap portfolio
스와프코스트 swap cost
스와프쿠폰 swap coupon
스와프협정 swap agreement
스왑션 swaption
스위치가 장착된 수신기의 비율 sets in use
스위치금융 switch finance
스위치무역 switch trade
스위치피치 switch pitch
스위프트 Society for Worldwide International Financial Telecommunications
스윕어카운트 sweep account

스윙 swing
스카시; **SCSI** small computer system interface
스카치라이트 scotchlite
스캐너 scanner
스캔패널 scan panel
스캔패널 조사 scan panel research
스캘핑(당장의 이윤을 노려 사고팜) scalping
스컹크워크 skunk work
스퀘어 square
스퀘어포지션 square
스퀴즈 squeeze
스퀴즈아웃 squeeze-out
스크린각도 screen angle
스크린선수 screen ruling
스크린톤 screen tone
스킬인벤토리 skill inventory
스킴가격 skimming price
스타시스템 star system
스타일시트 style sheet
스태거드스케줄 staggered schedule
스태그 stag
스태그플레이션 stagflation
스택상태의 stuck
스탠더드앤드푸어 주가지수 Standard & Poor's Stock Price Index
스탠드바이 · 크레디트; 스탠드바이신용장 standby credit
스탠드바이퍼실리티 standby facilities
스탠드스틸 standstill
스탠드스틸조항 standstill provision
스탭직능 staff function
스텝상환 step-ladder payment method
스텝업스와프 step-up swap
스텝업쿠폰 step-up coupon
스톡 조자본스톡 net capital stock
스톡마인드 stock mind
스톡보너스플랜 stock bonus plan
스톡워런트 stock warrants
스톡인플레이션 stock inflation
스톡조정 stock adjustment

ㅅ
ㅇ

스톡플로우 stock-flow
스톱고(高) limit high
스톱앤드고정책 stop-and-go policy
스톱저(低) limit low
스톱치 maximum limit of fluctuation
스튜던트분포 student's distribution
스튜디오규격 studio standard
스트래들 straddle
스트래들포지션거래 straddle position transaction
스트랩 strap
스트랭글 strangle
스트랭글포지션거래 strangle position transaction
스트레이트커런시스와프 straight currency swap
스트롱폼 strong form
스트립금리캡 stripped interest rate cap
스트립일드 strip yield
스트립제로쿠폰 stripped zero-coupon
스트립채 separate trading of registered interest and principal of securities; strips
스트립캡 stripped cap
스트립플레이어 strip player
스파이럴이론 spiral theory
스페셜리스트 specialist
스페셜리스트북 specialist book
스페셜리티광고 speciality advertising
스페셜브래킷그룹 special bracket group
스페셜크레디트 special credit
스페셜피처즈 special features
스페이스재정 space arbitrage
스포츠도박 sports gambling
스폰서 sponsor
스폰서가 없는 프로그램 sustaining program
스폰서의 리스크허용도 sponsor tolerance to risk
스폰서의 선택력 sponsor selectivity
스폰서의 역할 sponsor's role
스폿기간 spot period
스폿넥스트 spot next

스폿펀드 spot fund
스폿포워드 spot forward
스플릿 split
스프레더 spreader
스프레드 spread
스프레드거래 spread transaction
스프레드로스커버 spread loss cover
스프레드론 spread loan
스프레드뱅킹 spread banking
스프레드시트 spread sheet
스프레드트레이딩 spread trading
스플릿오프 split-off
스피나라마 spinarama
스피드레지스턴스라인 speed resistance line
스핀아웃 spin out
스핀오프 spin-off
스필오버 spill over
슬라이드관세 sliding tariff
슬라이드예금 sliding rate
슬라이드제 sliding scale
슬라이딩칩 sliding cheap
슬럼프플레이션 slumpflation
승객배상책임보험 passengers liability insurance
승계 succession
승계담보 lineal warranty
승계유산관리 de bonis non
승락; 인수 acceptance
승법규칙 multiplication rule
승법효과 multiplier effect
승수분석 multiplier analysis
승수이론 multiplier theory; theory of multiplier
승인 acknowledgment; approval; authorization; cognizance
승인되지 않은 자산 inadmitted assets
승인번호 authorization number
승인신청 application for approval
승인임원 approved person
시가 current price; opening rate; running price
시가개산액 approximate market price

시가발행 issue at market price
시가발행주식 stock issue at market price
시가발행증자 capital increase by new shares
　　at market price
시가방식 current cost method
시가법 market method; market value method;
　　valuation at selling price
시가상승 appreciated market price
시가상환 redemption at market value
시가전환 conversion at market price
시가주의 market price basis; market value
　　basis
시가주의 명목가치회계 current cost/nominal
　　dollar accounting
시가주의 안정가치회계 current cost/constant
　　dollar accounting
시가주의회계 fair value accounting
시가총액 aggregate market value;
　　capitalization of market price; market
　　capitalization
시가총액 가중인덱스 capitalization weighted
　　indices
시가총액가중평균치 weighted average of
　　market capitalization
시가평가 mark to the market
시가회계 current value accounting
시간가중수익률 time-weighted return
시간가치 time value
시간가치감가 depreciation of time value
시간경과에 따른 over time
시간경과에 따른 채권가격 over time price of
　　bond
시간법칙 temporal law
시간선호 time preference
시간스프레드 time spread
시간연구 time study
시간우선의 원칙 time priority
시간원가 time cost
시간인식 time perception
시간임금제 time rate system
시간차이 time variance

시거리 viewing distance
시계열데이터 time series data
시계열변동 time-series behavior
시계열분석 time series analysis; time-series
　　analysis
시기경과선하증권 stale bill of lading
시기지불연금 life annuity due
시나리오라이팅 scenario writing
시나리오분석 scenario analysis
시내경쟁사업자 competitive access provider
시담 private settlement; settlement out of
　　court
시담해결 out-of-court settlement
CD-ROM compact disk read only memory
CD시장 market CD
시료로 인한 공도 highway by prescription
시리즈광고 serial advertisement
시매품 memorandum goods
시뮬레이션 simulation
시민채권 citizen bond
시방서원가 specification cost
시분할다원접속 time division multiple access
시산 trial
시산표 trial balance sheet; working trial
　　balance sheet
시세; 시가; 가격표 price quotation
시세가 낮을 때 물러남 closing lower
시세가 내리는 상태 downward movement
시세가 내릴 것을 예상하고 증권을 매각함
　　going short
시세가 내릴 때 매입하다 buy on reaction
시세가 높을 때 물러남 closing high
시세가 떨어지다 ease off
시세가 불투명하여 매매가 활발하지 못한
　　uncertain
시세가 오를 것을 예상하고 증권을 매입함
　　going long
시세가 오를듯한 기세 strong tone; firmer
　　tone
시세가 조금씩 오르는 경향 creep back
　　upwards

ㅅ
ㅇ

시세가 폭락함 straight fall
시세가 회보복되다 rally
시세를 높게 부르다 quoting high
시세를 예상하여 매각함 short sale against the box
시세변동으로 매매차익금이 적어지다 narrow spread; narrowing of spread
시세수치 indicative price
시세수치; 표시 indication
시세에 파동을 일으키다 bull the market
시세정보교환센터 quotation exchange center
시세하락을 예상하고 매각함 hedge selling
시송품 goods on approval
시스크; 중앙처리장치의 한 종류 complex instruction set computer
시스템 system audit
시스템간 경쟁 systems competition
시스템공학 system engineering
시스템레포 system repos
시스템리스크 system risk
시스템문제 system issue
시스템어프로치 system approach
시스템으로 입회장에 액세스할 수 있는 회원 electric access member
시스템조작 system operation
시스티매틱리스크 systematic risk
시야모델 viewing model
시야변환 viewing transformation
시야조절 viewfinder adopter
시용기간 trial employment period
시용상품포괄보험 merchandise of approval floater
시용판매 approval sales; sales on approval
시용판매미수금 account due from sales on approval
시운전 commissioning; field test
시운전비 trial running expenses
시읍면담배세 municipal tobacco tax
시읍면세 municipal inhabitants tax
시인 affirmance
시작 trial manufacture

시작기 pilot unit
시작비 experimental manufacturing cost; testing expenses
시작품 trial product
시작품원가 preproduction cost
시작하자마자 Just after the opening
시장 제 2부 second section
시장; 상장 market
시장가격 market price; market value
시장가격가중평균지수 market value weighted index
시장가액약관 market value clause
시장가치가중 capitalization weighted
시장간 intermarket
시장간 거래시스템 inter-market trading system
시장간 스프레드 inter-market spread
시장간거래 intermarket trading system
시장감응도 market sensitivity
시장개발 market development
시장개방 market opening; opening market
시장개황 market overview
시장경제 market economy
시장경제모델 market economy model
시장구분 market segment
시장구조 market structure
시장균형 market equilibrium
시장균형곡선 market equilibrium curve
시장금리연동형 정기예금 money market certificate
시장기구 market mechanism
시장기구를 평가함 evaluation of market mechanism
시장내 intramarket
시장내부요인 technical position
시장내의 지위 market standing
시장동향 at the market
시장동향을 좌우하다 influence the market trend
시장방해 forestalling the market
시장배율 market multiple

시장베타 market beta
시장보고 market report
시장분단이론 segmentation theory
시장분석 market analysis
시장분위기 market quotation
시장분할 division of markets
시장삭감 market extinction
시장상장; 실세레이트 market rate
시장성 marketability
시장성숙 market maturity
시장성이 있는 merchantable
시장성이 있는 채권 marketable debt securities
시장성증권 marketable securities
시장섹터 market sector
시장센티멘트 market sentiment
시장수요 market demand
시장수요곡선 market demand curve
시장수요함수 market demand function
시장수축 shrinkage of market
시장심리 market psychology
시장안정조작 market stabilization
시장에 대한 영향 market impact
시장역학 market dynamics
시장연동형 우대금리 floating prime rate
시장예측 market expectation; market prediction
시장원리 market principle
시장을 어지럽히다 bear raiding
시장을 어지럽힘 raiding the market
시장을 조종함 market milking
시장의 기조 market rhythm
시장의 대부분을 점유하다 dominate the market
시장의 실패 market failure
시장의 주기 market cycle
시장의 주도주 market leaders
시장의 효율성 market efficiency
시장의 힘 market momentum
시장이율 market yield
시장이자율 market rate of interest

시장잠재능력별 할당 allocation by market potential
시장잠재력 market potential
시장잠재력실현 space actualization
시장적응제품 adaptive product
시장점유율 market share
시장조사 market research; market survey
시장조사계약 marketing research control
시장조사회사 marketing research company
시장지배 market control
시장지수 market index
시장지역 market area
시장지향형 market-oriented
시장질서유지협정 orderly marketing agreement
시장창조효과 market creating effect
시장침투 market penetration
시장침투도 penetration chart
시장클레임 market claim
시장타이밍을 평가함 market timing assessment
시장타이밍평가 assessment of market timing
시장평가 market valuation
시장포트폴리오 market portfolio
시장행동 market conduct
시장확장효과 market expansion effect
시장회복 market recovery
시재판소 borough courts; municipal courts
시정처치 corrective action
시조례 municipal ordinance
시중금리 market interest rate; money market rate; open market rate
시중대출 commercial bank credit
시중상장 open market quotation
시중은행; 상업은행 commercial bank
시중은행의 할인율상회 back spread; negative interest rate spread
시중은행의 할인율상회시장 inverted market
시즈 seeds
시청각교육 audio-visual education
시청각기기 audio-visual display

시청률조사 sweep
시청률측정기준 rate scale
시청자 천 명당 광고비 cost per thousand
시청자분석 audience analysis
시청자수 쉐어 share of audience
시카고상공회의소 Chicago Mercantile Exchange
시카고상품거래소 Chicago Board of Trade
시카고옵션거래소 Chicago Board Options Exchange
시퀜서 sequencer
시티; 도시 City
시한입법 law with expiration date
시행 enforcement
시행규칙 enforcement regulations
시행령 enforcement order
시행법 enforcement law
시행세칙 detailed enforcement regulations
시행일 date of enforcement
시험 testing
시험데이터 test data
시험연구비 experimental and research expense
시험연구비세액공제 experimental and research expense tax credit
시험연구용 자산 property for experimental and research
시험조사 testing audit
시험판매 test marketing
시황 tone
시황; 표견 color
시황관망 wait and see
시황상황 running of the market
시황정보센터 market information center
시효 prescription; statute of limitation
시효정지 suspension of statute of limitations
시효중단 interruption of prescription
식량증권 food bill
식별 identification
식별테스트 discrimination test
신가(新價)보험 depreciation insurance;

property depreciation insurance; replacement value insurance
신경질적인 nervous
신고 filing return
신고 및 납부 return and payment
신고; 배당발표 declaration
신고가격 value declared
신고기한 due date of filing return; due date of the tax return
신고납세 self-assessment of taxation; tax payment by self-assessment
신고납세액 income tax self-assessed
신고마감일 deadline for filing
신고서공시 public notification of returns
신고세 taxes assessed by taxpayers
신고소득세 assessment of income tax; self-assessed income tax
신고없이 creeping
신고용지 declaration form; return blank
신고의무 obligation to file return
신고조정 adjustment in filing a Final tax return
신고치 all-time high; new high
신공업국군 newly industrialized countries
신국민경제체계 System of National Account
신규 new
신규계정 new account
신규고객을 확보하기 위한 경품 account opener
신규구입 open buying
신규대출 new loan
신규매출 open selling
신규모기지 new mortgage
신규모기지발행시장 primary mortgage market
신규발행 new issue
신규발행사채 newly issued corporate bond
신규발행후 시장 after market
신규분야 new field
신규상장 new listing
신규수주 new order
신규주식공모 initial public offering

신규참가업자 entrant
신규프리미엄 new premium
신금융조절 new monetary adjustment system
신기능주의 neo-functionalism
신기원을 열다 blazing a trail
신디케이트단 syndication
신디케이트론 syndicated loan
신디케이트인수 syndicate underwriting
신디케이트조사 syndicate survey
신뢰계수 confidence coefficient
신뢰관계 confidential relation; fiduciary relation
신뢰구간신뢰계 confidence interval confidence coefficient
신뢰도 degree of confidence
신뢰를 배신한 자 traitor
신뢰성공학 reliability engineering
신뢰수치 confidence value
신뢰위반 breach of confidence
신립인 petitioner
신문발표 press release
신발채 new bond
신분증명서 identification card
신산업혁명 new industrial revolution
신상품 마케팅모델 adaptive planning and control sequence
신상품설명회 dog and pony show
신설합병 consolidation
신세틱론 synthetic long
신세틱쇼트 synthetic short
신세틱채권 synthetic bond
신세틱캐시 synthetic cash instrument
신세틱풋 synthetic put
신속하게 forthwith
신속한 재판 speedy trial
신속한 조정 resiliency
신시장개척 expansion of a new market
신안(新案) new design; novelty
신안채 new face bond
신외국환관리법 new foreign exchange law
신용 및 보증보험 credit and suretyship

insurance
신용감시시스템 credit watch system
신용거래 margin trading
신용거래대출 customer's loan
신용거래융자잔고 adjusted debit balance
신용거래주 stock for margin trading
신용격차 credit spread
신용경제 credit economy
신용공여 credit accommodation; granting credit
신용공여화 swing line
신용공황 credit crisis
신용구입 margin buying
신용구조 credit structure
신용금고 shinkin bank
신용기회균등 equal credit opportunity
신용네트워크 network of credit
신용대출 credit loan
신용도 credibility; credit quality
신용등급부여 credit rating
신용력 credit capability; credit worthiness
신용력이 있는 creditworthy
신용리스크가 없는 risk free
신용보증 credit guarantee
신용보증협회 credit guarantee corporation
신용보험 credit insurance; fidelity insurance
신용분석 analysis of credit
신용불량자 리스트 negative list
신용비율 credit ratio
신용상태 credit standing; credit standing condition
신용생명보험 credit life insurance
신용수령자 accreditee
신용어음 credit bill
신용완화 credit ease
신용외상거래처 credit customer
신용위험 commercial risk
신용장 circular note; letter of credit
신용장 없는 어음매입률 buying rate without credit
신용장개설보증금 letter of credit margin

money

신용장개설자 accrediting party

신용장발행수수료 opening charge

신용장발행의뢰인 accountee; accredited party; opener

신용장보증부 할인어음 documented discount note

신용장부 일람불어음매입률 at sight buying rate with credit

신용장양도 transfer of transferable credit

신용장없는 일람불어음매입상장 without credit at sight buying rate

신용장확인수수료 confirming charge

신용장확인은행 letter of credit confirming bank

신용정보 credit records

신용정책 credit policy

신용제도 credit system

신용제한 credit crunch; credit rationing

신용조건 credit terms

신용조사 credit investigation

신용조사기관 inquiry agency

신용조합 cooperative bank; credit association; credit union

신용조합단말 credit authorization terminal

신용조합환 credit union exchange

신용조회 credit inquiry; credit reference

신용증거금 credit margin

신용증서수표 due bill check

신용창조 credit creation

신용카드 credit card

신용카드업무 credit card business

신용카드회사 credit card company

신용판매계정 credit sales accounts

신용하지 않다 discredit

신용한도 credit ceiling; credit limit; limit of credit

신용한도제도 credit line system

신용화 demand line

신용화폐 credit money

신용환산계수 credit conversion factor

신원신용보험 fidelity guarantee insurance

신은행법 new banking law

신의신용채무 full-faith-and-credit debt

신임 confidence

신임장부호 accredit

신자원개발 exploitation of new resources

신저치 new low

신제품소개 new product introduction

신제품을 체분류함 new product screening

신제품이 실패함 new product failures

신종보험; 손해보증보험 casualty and surety insurance

신주 new share

신주 1주당 불입가액 amount paid per new stock paid per new stock

신주발행 capitalization issue; new issue of stocks

신주발행비 new share issuing expense; new stock issuing expenses; share-issuing expense; stock issue expenses

신주부 cum new

신주분배, 할당 ex-allotment

신주우선인수권 preemptive right

신주인수권 common stock preemptive right; stock purchase warrant; subscription right

신주인수권부 cum right

신주인수권부 사채 bond with subscription warrant

신주인수권증서 subscription warrant

신주하락 new share off

신중인원칙 prudent man rule

신증권인수 underwriting of new issue securities

신청 clamor; instance

신청; 동의 motion

신청금 application money; subscription money

신청심리일 motion day

신청인 applicant

신청증거금 advance on subscription

신청하여 취득하다 sue out

신체상해 bodily injury; mayhem
신체장애자 physically handicapped person
신축세율 flexible tariff
신축적립금 reserve for construction
신탁 trust
신탁계약 fiduciary contract; trust agreement
신탁계정 trust account
신탁권한 fiduciary power
신탁기금 trust fund
신탁보수 trust fee
신탁설정자 settlor; trustor
신탁수익자 cestui que trust
신탁수익자; 보험금수취인 beneficiary
신탁식연금제도 trust-fund plan
신탁약관 trust contract
신탁업회계 trust accounting
신탁예금 deposit in trust; trust deposit
신탁은행 trust bank
신탁은행이용형 기업연금 trust company administered pension plan
신탁의무 fiduciary duty
신탁이익 profit from trust
신탁잉여금 trusteed surplus
신탁재산 fiduciary estate; trust assets; trust estate; trust property
신탁증서 deed of trust; trust deed; trust indenture
신탁형 연금 trusteed plan pension; trust fund plan
신탁회계 fiduciary accounting
신탁회사 trust company
신품을 고가로 인수함 trade-in
신행동주의 neo-behaviorism
신형 금본위제 new type of gold standard
신호잡음비 signal to noise ratio
신화폐수량설 neo-quantity theory of money
신후생경제학 new welfare economics
신흥경제지역 emerging market
신흥도시 boom town
실가 actual value
실가법 actual value method

실가자산 actual assets
실권약관 forfeiture clause
실권주 forfeited share
실링방식 ceiling system
실무가 practitioner
실무수습생 articled clerk
실무적으로 가능한 practicable
실물자본 real capital
실물자산 real assets
실물투자 real investment
실비 actual expenses
실비정산계약 cost-plus contract
실세계컴퓨팅 real world computing
실세레이트 effective rate
실세예금 deposit minus checks and bills on hand
실세예금 deposit on a net basis; net deposit
실손전보 first-loss insurance
실손전보계약 nonaverage insurance
실수(實需)기준 earned basis
실수요 consumer demand
실수원칙 actual demand rule
실시권 enforcement right
실시수순 operational procedure
실시화 reduce to practice
실업급부 unemployment benefit
실업률감소 reducing unemployment rate
실업보험 unemployment insurance
실업보험지출 expenditure on unemployment benefit
실업수당 out-of-work pay
실업율 unemployment rate
실용신안 industrial new design; utility model
실용신안권 utility model patent
실재계정 real account
실적기준 PER trailing PER
실적상승 upswing on business results
실적을 예상한 하향수정 downward revision on business results
실적이 좋지 않은 회사 unprofitable company
실적평가기준 review criteria

실정법 positive law
실정의 positive
실제가격 actual price
실제가격변동율 effective volatility
실제거래행위 actual trading behavior
실제구입가액 actual purchase price
실제내용연수 actual life; actual useful life
실제배부율 actual burden rate
실제보다 전날일자로 하다 back dating
실제사망수 actual deaths
실제손해 actual loss
실제시장이율폭 current market yield spread
실제양도가액 actual transfer price
실제원가 actual cost
실제원가계산 actual costing
실제원가계산제도 actual cost accounting system
실제자본유지 maintenance of physical capital
실제재고 stock taking
실제제품 actual product
실제주의회계 actual basis accounting
실제채굴량 actual quantity of mining
실제취득원가주의 actual acquisition cost basis
실증 demonstration
실증분석 empirical analysis
실증연구 empirical study
실증적인 마케팅 positive marketing
실증주의 positivism
실지감사 field audit
실지재고 actual inventory
실지재고정리 physical inventory
실지조사 site survey
실질가처분소득 real disposable income
실질구매소득 effective buying income
실질금리 real interest rate
실질단위 real term
실질단위노동코스트 real unit labor cost
실질베이스로 in real terms
실질성장 real growth
실질성장률 real growth rate
실질소득 real earnings; real income

실질소득자 real income earner
실질소유자 beneficial owner
실질손해배상금 substantial damages
실질연리 actual annual percentage rate
실질예금 real deposits
실질우선 substance over form
실질원가 real cost
실질이율 real rate; real yield
실질이행 substantial performance
실질임금 real wage
실질적인 증거 substantial evidence
실질적인 차이 material variance
실질주의 principle of taxation on actual beneficiary
실질증거 substantive evidence
실질투자수익률 real investment return
실질화폐잔고효과 real balance effect
실천경제 practical economy
실천론 pragmatics
실체 entity; merits
실체경제 real economy
실체법 substantive law
실체자본 physical capital
실체적인 멸실 physical destruction
실체화, 입체화 stereogram
실체회계 entity accounting
실해(實害) special damage
실행관세율 priority rate of duty
실행기관 execution organ
실행예산 working budget
실행하다; 영위하다 practice
실험실조사 laboratory test
실험효과 experimental effect
실현가격변동률 realized volatility
실현가능가액 realizable value
실현감가상각 realized depreciation
실현수익 realized revenue
실현이익 realized profit
실현주의 realization basis; realization principle
실현주의의 원칙 principle of realization

실현증가액 realized appreciation
실효가격 effective price
실효권 lapse ratio
실효금리 effective interest rate
실효명령 actual instruction
실효보호율 effective rate of protection
실효세공제후 after effective tax
실효세율 effective tariff
실효수표 out-of-date check
실효약관 derogatory-clause
실효어드레스 effective address
실효이율 effective yield; realized yield
실효주 lapsed share
실효환상장 effective exchange rate
심도면접 depth interview
심리법칙 psychological laws
심리소득 psychic income
심리속행 further consideration
심리예정표 docket
심리적인 요소 psychological element
심리학적 소비자행동 psychological consumer behavior
심문 inquisition
심볼릭 시뮬레이션 symbolic simulation
심볼릭 커뮤니케이션 symbolic communication
심사 examination; judging; review; screening; scrutiny
심사재결 examination and decision
심사청구 claim for examination; request for reconsideration
심사청구기간 period of request for reconsideration

심층천연가스 deep earth natural
심판기관 tribunal
심판인 umpire
심플렉스법 simplex method
10-K 레포트 10-K report
10-Q 사반기 보고서 10-Q report
싱가폴예탁증서 Depository Receipts of Singapore
싱글옵션 single option
싱크로나이저 synchronizer
싸게 매입한 주를 시세가 올랐을 때 매각함 getting ashore
싸게 사다 buy on close
싸게 팔다 sell low
싸구려물건 job lot
싸구려상품 borax goods
CRT 투사 디스플레이 CRT projection display
싼 값 low price
쌍둥이적자 twin deficits
쌍무계약 bilateral contract; reciprocal contract
쌍무무역 bilateral trade
쌍방독점 bilateral monopoly
쌍방시세 two way price
쌍방향 interactive
쌍방향 커뮤니케이션 dyadic communication
쌍방향성 interaction
쌍방향시장 either way market
쌍방향텔레비전 interactive television
쌍케이블 pair cable
쓸모없게 된, 진부한 obsolete

ㅇ

아날로그를 디지털로 변환함 analog to digital conversion
아날로그방식 analog method
아랍마그레브연합 Arab Maghreb Union
아랍석유수출국기구 Organization of Arab Petroleum Exporting Countries
아랍연맹 Arab League
아메리카증권거래소 Amex Commodity Echange
아메리카증권거래소 주가지수 AMEX Index
아메리카트러스트 Americus Trust
아스키; 미국정보교환표준코드 American Standards Code for Information Interchange
아스피린이론 aspirin theory
아시아개발기금 Asian Development Fund
아시아개발은행 Asian Development Bank
아시아결제동맹 Asian Clearing Union
아시아경제협력기구 Organization for Asian Economic Cooperation
아시아극동경제위원회 Economic Commission for Asia and the Far East
아시아달러시장 Asian-dollar market
아시아달러채 Asian dollar bond
아시아보험감독관협회 Asian Insurance Commissioners Association
아시아아프리카공동시장 Afro-Asian Common Market
아시아재보험 Asian Reinsurance Pool
아시아준비은행 Asian Reserve Bank
아시아지불동맹 Asian Payment Union
아시아태평양경제사회위원회 Economic and Social Commission for Asia and the Pacific
아시아태평양경제협력회의 Asia Pacific Economic Cooperation
아시아통화단위 Asian Currency Unit; Asian Monetary Unit
아웃라인 out line
아웃라인거래 outright transaction
아웃라인폰트 outline font
아웃렛스토어 outlet store
아웃사이드데이 outside day
아웃소싱 out-sourcing
아웃오브더머니 out of the money
아웃풋변수 output variable
아이디코드 ID code
IC카드 integrated circuit card
IS곡선 · LM곡선 I-S curve · L-M curve
IMS intelligent manufacturing system
IMF차관 IMF loan
IMF평가 IMF par value
아이카메라 eye camera
아이캐처 eye catcher
아이콘 icon
아일랜드리버설패턴 island reversal pattern
아트디렉터 art director
아프리카개발은행 African Development Bank
악성인플레이션 galloping inflation
악세 irrational tax
악세수준유지 unchanged to slightly lower
악영향 adverse effects
악용 evil practice

악의 bad faith; mala fides

악의의 제삼자 holder in bad faith

악의적인 손해담보약관 malicious damage clause

악의적인 행위 malicious

악재료 bad news; unfavorable factor

악질가맹점 vicious member merchant

악화 deterioration

악화; 하강 downturn

안내광고 classified advertising

안데스공동시장 Andean Common Market

안상점 saddle point

안전계수 safety margin

안전관리 safety control

안전밸브 safety valve

안전보증신청 article of the peace

안전보호 safe custody

안전성이 높은 주식 low risk stocks

안전여력 margin of safety

안전자산 riskless assets

안전재고 safety stock

안전할증 contingency loading; safety loading

안전형 운용 passive strategy

안정가치 constant dollars

안정가치로 수정한 순이익 constant dollar net income

안정가치로 수정한 재무제표 common dollar statements

안정가치이익 constant-dollar profit

안정가치회계 constant-dollar accounting; stabilized accounting

안정경제성장 stable economic growth

안정구매력 constant purchasing power

안정구매력회계 constant power purchasing accounting

안정배당 consecutive dividend; stable dividend

안정배당주 widow-and-orphan stock

안정성 stability

안정성장 stable growth

안정임금제 wage stabilization system

안정조건 stability condition; stabilization operation; stabilizing transaction

안정조작거래 stabilization transaction

안정조항 stabilization clause

안정주 stable stock

안정주주 stable stockholder

안정촉진적인 stabilizing

안정화개입 smoothing operation

안정화폐론 stable money principle

안테나숍 antenna shop

안티덤핑코드 anti-dumping code

알러지전문의 allergist

알선인 arranger

RISC reduced instruction set computer

RS232C(직렬로트) recommended standard

알지 못함 ignorance

RGB 적, 녹, 청(컬러화상의 3원색) red green blue

알파벳펀드 alphabet fund

알파수치 alpha value

암딜링 black market dealing

암묵의 공모 tacit collusion

암묵적인 implied

암묵적인 니드 implied need

암묵적인 디플레이터 implicit deflator

암보험 cancer insurance

암시장 black market

암호 secret language; shop talk language

암호화하다 encode

압력단체 pressure group

압축기록 advanced depreciation

압축손 advanced depreciation deduction

압축준비금 reserve for deferred income tax

압축준비금편입손 loss from putting on reserve for deferred income tax

압축한도액 advanced depreciation limit

앞당겨 상환하다 redeem before maturity

앞서감; 프런트러닝 front running

애드버타이징스페셜티 advertising specialty

애드보커시광고; 자기를 옹호하는 광고 advocacy advertisement

애드온금리 add-on rate
애드온방식 add-on system
애로인플레이션 bottle-neck inflation
애버리지타입 선물환예약 averaged type forward contract
애버리징 averaging
애퍼처그릴 aperture grille
애퍼처그릴피치 aperture grille pitch
애프터로스 after loss
애프터리코딩 after recording
액면 face
액면가; 공칭가 nominal value
액면가격 par price; par value
액면가액 face value; nominal amount
액면금액 face amount
액면대로 at par
액면매매사채 par bond
액면발행 issue at face value; par issue
액면변경 change in par value
액면이 하락 arup below par
액면이상 with premium
액면이하 with discount
액면이하; 평가이하 below par
액면전환 conversion at par
액면전환사채 debenture convertible at par
액면주 stock at par
액면주식 par-value capital stock; stock with par value
액면주식자본금 par-value share
액면증서회사 face amount certificate company
액면초과금 capital in excess of par value
액면통액 aggregate face amount
액면평가 parity rate of exchange
액면할 under par
액세스차지 access charge
액세스카드 access card
액세스포인트 access point
액션프로그램 action program
액정디스플레이 liquid crystal display
액추얼관계 actuarial relationship

액추얼수학 actuarial mathematics
액추얼포지션 actual position
액티브리스크 active risk
액티브리스크 회피도 active risk aversion
액티브리턴 active return
액티브방식 active method
액티브포트폴리오 active portfolio
앳리스크 at risk
앳마켓 at-market
야간교환 exchange at night
야간금고 night deposit safe
야외시장 open air market
약세시세 bearish tone
약세시장 bearish market
약세의 감정(정서) bearish sentiment
약세의; 내림시세의 bearish
약세저항선 bearish resistance line
약세지지선 bearish support line
약세콘솔리데이션패턴 bearish consolidation patterns
약속 undertaking
약속담보 promissory warranty
약속어음 promissory note
약속자 promisor
약식계약 simple contract
약식기소장 criminal information
약식소송절차 summary proceeding
약식조사 informal investigation
약어 abbreviation
약인멸실 failure of consideration
약인조항 consideration clause
약정; 채무 engagement
약정가격 contracted price
약정금리 agreed interest rate; contracted interest rate
약정담보권 stipulated security
약정만기이익 agreed yield to maturity
약정반제 scheduled payment
약정반제부 스와프 amortizing swap
약정손해배상액 stipulated damage
약정수수료 commitment fee

약정이율 contracted rate

약정일 trade date

약정통지 contract notice

약칭 short title

약한 시세 weak tone

약한 채널 bearish channel

약해지다 weaken

양도 assignment; transfer

양도 및 이전 assignment and transfer

양도가격 transfer price

양도가능 negotiable

양도가능대부 transferable loan facility

양도가능대출 transferable loan

양도가능러프 transferable RUF

양도가능신용장 transferable credit

양도가능정기예금증서 certificate of deposit; negotiable certificate of deposit; negotiable time certificates of deposits

양도가능환불지도예금계정 negotiable order of withdrawal account

양도계약 transfer contract

양도금지 restraint on alienation

양도담보증서 bill of sale

양도무효조항 alienation clause

양도불능보호예금 nonnegotiable safekeeping receipts

양도비용 expenses incurred for the transfer; transfer expenses

양도세 transfer tax

양도수수료 assignment fee; transfer fee

양도이서 endorsement to transfer

양도인 alienator; transferor

양도자 assignor

양도자산 property for transfer

양도자산취득비용 cost of transferred properties

양도저당 reconveyance

양도저당이 병합됨 consolidation of mortgages

양도제한 restriction of transfer

양도조건 assignment clause

양도증서 common assurance; deed of conveyance; written assignment

양도채권 assigned accounts

양도하다 assign

양도할 수 없는 권리 inalienable rights

양동적인 가격설정 diversionary pricing

양로보험 endowment insurance

양륙세 port toll

양륙지변경경로 diversion charge

양륙지선택화물 optional cargo

양립성 compatibility

양방향가격결정 make two-sided markets

양벌규정, 쌍벌규정 penalty against employer and employee

양산원가 volume cost

양산효과 volume efficiency

양수인 alienee; assigns; transferee

양여자 grantor

양육비 expenses of bringing up children

양을 가늠하여 값을 부름 cuff quote

양자결정 adoption order

양자역학 quantum mechanics

양자화하다 quantize

양적인 경제정책 quantitative economic policy

양적인 금융지표 quantitative monetary indicator

양측검정 two-tailed test

양키본드 Yankee bond

양허계약 concession contract

어글리포리너어프로치 ugly foreigner approach

어긋난 정보 discrepant information

어레즈주가모델 Ahlers model

어리어스와프 arrears swap

어린이종합보험 juvenile comprehensive insurance

어림값 rough number

어베이러빌러티리스크 availability risk

어센딩 톱스 ascending tops

어셈블 편집 assemble editing

어셋베이스스와프 asset base swap
어셋스와프거래 asset swap transaction
어셋어프로치 asset approach
어셋클래스타겟 asset class target
어셋패스스루증권 asset-pass-through certificate
어업권 fishing right
어용조합 company union
어음갱신 renewal of bills and notes
어음계정 bill-book
어음교환 bill clearing; clearance
어음교환결산표 clearinghouse proof
어음교환결제 bank clearing
어음교환계정 clearing account
어음교환고 amount of clearing
어음교환소 clearing house; clearinghouse
어음교환소가맹은행 clearing bank; member banks of the clearing house
어음교환제도 clearing system
어음교환차액 clearing balance
어음기입장 note register
어음대부 advance on a promissory note; loan on bill
어음대부담보 collateral on loans on bills
어음대부연체이자 overdue interest on loan on bills
어음대부이자 interest on loans on bills
어음만기 due date of bills
어음매매레이트 bill buying and selling rate
어음매입수권서 authority to purchase
어음매입제도 bill buying system
어음발행 drawing of bill
어음발행인 drawer of bill
어음법 law on bills
어음브로커 bill broker
어음사이트 sight of a bill
어음소지자 bill bearer
어음수금기입 entering short
어음수금수수료 charge for collection of bill
어음수신인 drawee
어음유통수수료 negotiation charge

어음유통은행 negotiating bank
어음인수상사 accepting house
어음인수은행 accepting bank
어음지불 payment by bill
어음지불장소 domicile
어음취급업자 cambist
어음할인 discount on bill; discounting of a bill
어음할인료 discount on note
어음할인율 effective rate of discount
어음할인중개인 discount broker
어지러운 상황(商況) boom and bust
어카운트레포트서비스 account report service
어큐뮬레이션 방식 누적시스템 accumulation system
어패럴산업 apparel industry
어포인트상법 appointment sales
어프리시에이션스와프 appreciation swap
어필변환 affine transformation
억류하다 intern
억세스권 right of access
억압 repression
억제정책 restraint measures
억제조치 control measure
억측 guessing
언도하다 render
언론의 자유 freedom of speech
언매치드북 unmatched book
언커버드금리제정 uncovered interest arbitrage
언커버드옵션 uncovered option
언커버드포지션 uncovered position
언콜렉터블론 uncollectible loan
언타이드론 untied loan
얼핏 보기에는 prima
엄격책임 strict liability
엄격한 검사 tightened inspection
엄격해석 strict construction
엄숙한 선언 asseveration
엄지손톱, 간결한 thumbnail
업갭 up gap

업계 business circle; industry segments
업계기준 industry standard
업계단체 industry association
업계스페셜리스트 industry specialist
업계평균 industry average
업로드 up load
업무 affairs
업무감사 business audit; business operations audit; operations audit
업무겸업제한 limitation on interlocking
업무분석 activity analysis
업무상의 사고 on the job accidents
업무수행기준 performance basis
업무순익 net operation profit
업무의사결정 operational decision
업무주처벌제도 proprietor punishment
업앤드풋옵션 up and put option
업자간 상장 dealers' market; dealing market
업자에 의한 투기상장 broker's market
업자할인 trade discount
업적 achievement; earnings performance
업적부진의 ailing
업적비율 operating performance ratios
업적상장 profit-driven market
업적평가 performance evaluation
업적평가제도 appraisal system
업종 category of business
업종별 대출통계 loans and discounts by industry
업종별 주가지수 narrow based stock index
업종별 편입률 industry weighting ratio
업트렌드 uptrend
에너지리스크 energy risk
에너지주 energy sector stock
에누리 fictitious price
에듀테인먼트; 교육적이고 흥미있는 프로그램 edutainment
에스컬레이터조항 escalator clause
에스케이프시퀀스 escape sequence
에스크로계약 escrow agreement
에스크로계정 escrow account

에스크로보관증서예탁 escrow receipt depository
에스크로신용장 escrow credit
에스크로신탁계약 escrow and trust agreement
에어리어스와프 swap-in-arrears
ABC재고관리 ABC inventory management
에이전시마켓 agency market
에이전시이론 agency theory
에쿼티재판소 court of equity
FRB전문가 Fed watcher
에프엠 frequency modulation
에프엠음원 frequency modulation oscillator
엑조틱본드 exotic bond
엑조틱파생상품 exotic derivatives
NOB스프레드 NOB spread
엔트로피 entropy
엘고노믹스; 인간공학 ergonomics
엘리사법 Employee Retirement Income Security Act
엘리어트파동이론 Elliot Wave Theory
엘리트카드 elite card
MCA무선 maultichannel access radio system
MOF예탁금 deposit by the Ministry of Finance
M2+CD통계 M2+CD Statistics
엠페그; MPEG(동화상압축방식) Moving Picture Expert Group
여가지출 leisure expenditures
여객수입 passenger traffic receipts
여당연합 ruling coalition
여러 미불금 miscellaneous accounts payable
여러 미수금 miscellaneous accounts
여러 사업부를 소유한 기업 multidivisional company
여분공사클레임 extra work claims
여비교통비 traveling expenses
여비수당 traveling benefits
여신계약 credit agreement
여신공여량 credit availability
여신관리 credit control; credit exposure

management

여신리스크 credit risk

여신분석 credit analysis

여신업무 credit business

여유있는 성장 affordable growth

여유자금 excess cash

여영마진계정 excess margin account

여잉수익수취권 earn-out right

여잉이익을 분배하다 earn out

여잉준비 nonborrowed reserve

여잉현금 idle cash

여진 aftershock

여행령 cabinet order

여행신용장 traveller's letter of credit

여행자세 tourist tax

역광 backlighting

역금리 negative interest

역기능 dysfunction

역년(曆年) calendar year; natural year

역담보 counter-security

역무 personal service

역무계약 contract for service

역무제공 rendering of service

역무출자 service contribution

역발상에 능한 주식투자가 contrarian

역방향 reverse direction

역보증 counter guarantee

역분할 reverse split

역산 reverse operation

역산법 reversal cost method

역상태 reverse offset

역선택 adverse selection; antiselection

역소득세 negative income tax; reverse income tax

역송금 reverse remittance

역수요패턴 inverse demand pattern

역스와프 reversed swap

역월(1년의 12분의 1) calendar month

역월(曆月)인도 calender month delivery

역월(曆月)인도율 calender month delivery rates with option

역월도제 delivery system by calendar month

역월제(曆月制) 선물율 calender month delivery rate

역유통 reverse distribution

역이율 inverted yield curve

역이율현상 inverted yield curve phenomena

역이익 inverse yield

역일(자정에서 자정까지의 24시간) calendar day

역입체 switch reversal

역전된 시장 crossed market

역전스케일 inverted scale

역주기광고 countercyclical advertising

역지정가격주문 stop-limit order

역진과세 regressive taxation

역특혜 converse preference

역풍개입 intervention against market

역플로터채 inverse floater

역할관여 role involvement

역할실현이론 theory of role enactment

역할연기법 role playing

역할요구 role differentiation

역할이론 role theory

역할커미트먼트 role commitment

역행렬 inverse matrix

역행렬표 inverse matrix table

역헤일로효과 tarnished halo

역헤지 reverse hedge

역효과 disutility

역흡수합병 downstairs merger

연 1회후불 annual payment

연간소득 annual earnings

연간수입 annual income

연간이익처분액 annual profit disposition amount

연간정액지불법 equal-annual-payment method

연간지출당좌비율 quick assets to year's cash expenses

연간총익 yearly earnings

연간할부 annual installment

연간할부방식 annual payment budget facilities

연간회전횟수 times per year

연결계정 consolidated account

연결대차대조표 consolidated balance sheet

연결된 선의 consolidated goodwill

연결매상 consolidated sales

연결방침 consolidation policy; principles of consolidation

연결손익계산서 consolidated profit and loss statement

연결손익계산표 consolidated income statement

연결순손실 consolidated net loss

연결운전자금 consolidated working capital

연결원장 consolidation ledger

연결의 consolidated

연결이익 consolidated income

연결잉여금 consolidated surplus; surplus from consolidation

연결재무제표 consolidated financial statements

연결재무통계 consolidated financial statistics

연결전 이익 profit prior to consolidation

연결집단 consolidation group

연결초과액 consolidation excess

연계구입 buying hedge

연계원인 combination of causes

연고모집 private subscription

연고지방채 private placement local government bond

연고채 private placement bond

연고특별채 private placement special bond

연공서열임금제도 seniority order wage system

연공제 seniority system

연구개발 research and development

연구개발비 research and development expenditures

연구보조금 fellowship grant

연구비 research cost

연금 pension

연금계획 pension plan

연금구입요율 annuity purchase rates

연금급부액산정방식 benefit formula

연금기금 pension fund

연금기금 스프레드 pension fund spread

연금기금관리 pension fund management

연금기금의 역할 fund's mission

연금기금잉여 pension fund surplus

연금기금적립계약 funding instrument

연금기금적립기관 funding agency

연금보험 annuity insurance

연금부 보험 income endowment

연금비용 pension expense

연금생활자 senior citizen

연금수리비용계산방식 actuarial cost method

연금수취인 annuitant

연금신탁 pension trust

연금액기준방식 unit benefit plan

연금원가적립방식 terminal funding

연금유닛 annuity unit

연금의 기간원가 periodic pension cost

연금의 대가 annuity consideration

연금이회법 actuarial method

연금잉여의 금리감응도 interest sensitivity of the pension surplus

연금자산 pension assets; plan assets

연금자산실제운용수익 actual return on plan assets

연금제도 pension scheme

연금제도종료보험 plan termination insurance

연금플랜규정서 plan documents

연금현물충족방식 terminal funding method

연금회계 accounting for pension plan

연기 adjournment; postponement

연기, 거치 deferment

연기어음 extended bill

연기임차권 attendant term

연기하는 dilatory

연납 authorized deferred payment; deferment of payment; delayed payment;

postponement of tax payment

연납과 관련된 이자세 interest tax on delayed payment

연납세 deferred tax

연대 joint and several

연대납부책임 joint and several obligation of tax payment

연대보증 joint and several guarantee

연대보증인 joint surety

연대증서 joint and several bond

연대채무 joint and several obligation

연대책임 joint and several liability

연도 year

연도간 세배분 inter-period tax allocation

연도감사 annual audit

연도마감 annual closing

연동오차 tracking error

연령분포 age distribution

연령의 후퇴조정 age setback

연령제한 age limit

연료계정 fuel account

연료비 fuel expenses

연리 interest per annum; per annum rate

연말 end of the fiscal year

연말상장 year-end market

연말조정 year-end settlement

연말책임준비금 terminal reserve

연방공개시장위원회 Federal Open Market Commission

연방관재관 United States trustee

연방금융기관 federal credit agency

연방분권제도 federal decentralization

연방소득세 federal income tax

연방예금보험공사 Federal Deposit Insurance Corporation

연방자금금리 federal fund rate

연방자금시장 federal fund market

연방자문위원회 Federal Advisory Committee

연방저당금고 Federal National Mortgage Association

연방주택금융저당금고 Federal Home Loan Mortgage Corporation

연방주택대부은행 Federal Home Loan Bank

연방주택대부은행이사회 Federal Home Loan Bank Board

연방주택대부은행제도 Federal Home Loan Bank System

연방준비은행 Federal Reserve Bank

연방준비제도이사회 Board of Governors of the Federal Reserve System; Federal Reserve Board

연방준비지구 Federal Reserve District

연방중개신용은행 Federal Intermediate Credit Bank

연방토지은행 Federal Land Bank

연방통신위원회 Federal Communication Commission

연방파산법 Federal Bankruptcy Act

연복리수익율 compound annual return

연부(年賦) yearly installment

연부상환 redemption by yearly installment

연불기준 deferred payment basis

연불신용 supplier's credit

연불조건부 판매 deferred payment conditional sales; deferred payment sales

연불쿠폰 annual coupon

연산수 operand

연산품 joint product

연상테스트 association test

연생보험 joint life insurance

연생연금 joint life annuity

연서(連署) countersignature

연세주의(年稅主義) yearly taxation

연소위험 exposure hazard

연속매매 continuous trading

연속발췌 continuous sampling

연속발행채권 series bond

연속배당 continuous dividend

연속변수 continuous variable

연속복리 continuous compound interest rate

연속복리계산 continuous compounding calculation

연속사반기 consecutive quarters
연속상환채권 serial bond
연속생명연금 continuous annuity
연속생산 batch production; continuous manufacturing
연속시간 continuous time
연속원장 progressive ledger
연속표본추출법 sequential sampling
연속확률분포 continuous probability distribution
연속회기 continuous session
연쇄충돌 participating collision
연수익률 annual rate of returns
연역법 deductive method
연율의 퍼센테이지 annual percentage rate
연이율 annual interest rate
연장가능만기 extendible maturity
연장가능형 스와프 extensible swap
연장담보약관 extended cover clause
연장보험 extended insurance
연장정기보험 extended term insurance
연장클레임 extension of time claims
연조(軟調) heavy; weakness
연조(軟調)시장 soft market
연차결산 annual accounting
연차보고서 annual report
연차재무제표 annual financial statements
연차총회 annual meeting
연체가산금 additional arrearage charge
연체금 arrearage; back money
연체금거치쿠폰 arrears coupon
연체배당금 dividend in arrears
연체보상금 penalty on delayed delivery
연체보험료 aged account
연체세 deferred income taxes; delinquency tax; tax in arrears
연체세면제 discharge of delinquent tax
연체수표 stale cheque
연체율 percentage of delinquency
연체의 overdue
연체이식 past due interest

연체이자 daily interest for arrearage; default interest; deferred interest; delayed interest; interest for delay; interest for delinquency; interest in arrears; overdue interest
연체일변, 연체일보 overdue interest per diem
연체일수 days in arrears
연체지대(地代) rent arrears
연합개조(箇条) articles of union
연합규약 article of confederation; articles of confederation
연합시키다 associate
연합협약 joint agreement
연화; 교환불능통화 soft currency
연화국 soft currency country
연환산 annual basis
연회비 annual club due; annual dues
연회원 annual member
열거위험담보보험 named peril insurance
열거하다 enumerate
열람율조사 readership survey
열병합발전 cogeneration
열화자산 deteriorated assets
열후사채 mezzanine bond
열후증권 junior securities
염가구입권 bargain purchase option
염가예상 anticipation of falling market
영구계정 permanent account
영구고도장해 permanent disability
영구공채 permanent debt
영구구속 perpetuity
영구권 perpetual bond
영구금지명령 permanent injunction; perpetual injunction
영구대출 permanent financing
영구부채 permanent liabilities
영구세 perennial tax
영구세주의 principle of perennial tax
영구워런트 perpetual warrant
영구자산 permanent assets
영구적립금지규칙 rule against accumulations
영구차이 permanent difference

영구화재보험증권 perpetual fire insurance policy
영국국내세입청 Inland Revenue
영국무역진흥회 British Export Trade Research Organization
영국보험협회 British Insurance Association
영국식 경매 English auction
영국식 대차대조표 English form of balance sheet
영국은행협회 British Banker's Association
영국장기국채 long-term national bond of England
영국재무부증권 exchequer bills
영국증권거래소 British Stock Exchange
영국펀드 예금금리선물 pound sterling depositary interest futures
영국펀드 정기예금 pound sterling time deposit
영국펀드 통화선물 pound sterling currency futures
영국펀드CP pound sterling commercial paper
영년사용으로 인한 공도 highway by user
영대(永代)소작권 perennial tenant right
영대소작권 permanent tenant right
영대차지권 lease in perpetuity; perpetual lease
영대차지인 life tenant; perpetual lessee
영리 money-making
영리법인 corporation for profit; profit corporation
영리보험 commercial insurance
영리사업 commercial business; commercial enterprise; profit making business; profit-making business
영리자본 lucrative capital
영리회사 commercial company; operating business
영방의료부조제도 Medicaid
영사 consul
영사송장 consular invoice
영사재판소 consular courts

영상전송서비스 video transmission service
영속적인 효과 secular boom
영업 occupation; trade
영업경비 operating expenses
영업계정 trade account
영업계정수지잔고 underwriting account balance
영업과목 business line; description of business; line of business
영업권 goodwill; trade rights
영업권상각 amortization of goodwill
영업권소유자 concessionaire
영업권양도 assignment of business
영업내역장 office expenses book
영업면의 증익효과 operating leverage effect
영업면의 증익효과도 degree of operating leverage
영업면허세 occupational tax
영업방해 interference with trade
영업보고 business report; operating report
영업보고서 account of business
영업보관료 tariff premium
영업보험료식 책임준비금 reserve on gross premium method
영업본거이동 shifting of business center
영업비 business expenses; commercial expenses; occupation tax; trade expenses; working cost
영업비계정 office expense account
영업상의 본거 principal place of business
영업상태 operating standing
영업상황 operating condition
영업성적 business results; operating results; results of operations; summary of earnings
영업세 privilege tax; trade tax
영업소 sales office; service office
영업손실 operating loss
영업손실구분 operating section
영업손익 operating profit and loss; operating profit or loss
영업수익 operating income; operating

revenue; revenue from operations

영업수익세 business profit tax

영업수입 funds from operations; operating receipt; sales earnings

영업순환 operating cycle

영업순환기준 operating cycle rule

영업시간 business hours; office hours

영업실적 results of business

영업양도 transfer of business; transfer of operations

영업연도 working year

영업예산 operating budget

영업외경비 nonoperating expenses

영업외비용 nonoperating expenditure; other charges

영업외손익 nonoperating gains and loss

영업외손익구분 nonoperating section

영업외수익 nonoperating revenue

영업외의 nonoperating

영업용집기 office furniture

영업원장 operating ledger

영업이익 business profit; operating profit

영업이익단계 operating profit level

영업이익률 operating income to sales; operating margin; operating profit margin; ratio of operating profit to revenue

영업일 business day

영업일도 double settlement

영업일이 지나서 one day skipped

영업잉여 operating surplus

영업자산 trade assets

영업정지 interruption of business; stoppage of business

영업정책상 무리하게 맺은 계약 accommodation line

영업제한 restraint of trade

영업종목 items of business

영업준비금 operating reserve

영업중단보험 business interruption insurance

영업채무 trade liability

영업책임보험 business liability insurance

영업행위 doing business

영업활동 operating activities

영업활동계산서 operating statement

영업활동계정 operating accounts

영업활동의 operating

영업회의 business meeting

영주의사 animus manendi

영치 official retain

영치시장 phantom market

영토외관할권 foreign jurisdiction

영해 maritime belt; territorial waters

영향을 주다 affect

영화관종합보험 multiple perils insurance for cinemas

영화의 주요 장면을 간단히 그린 일련의 그림을 붙인 패널 storyboard

예견되지 않은 사고 unforeseen event

예금 deposit with other bank; money deposited; money in bank

예금감소 depreciation of deposit by inflation

예금금리 deposit interest rate; interest on deposit

예금기입장 deposit diary

예금담보대부 loan secured by deposit

예금대부 deposit loan

예금대체방식 deposit transfer

예금대출율 loan-deposit ratio

예금보증금 customers' deposits

예금보험제도 deposit insurance system

예금수부금 earnest money received

예금수입금융기관 depository institution

예금쉐어 deposit share

예금승계방식 purchase and assumption

예금양도금지 prohibition of deposit transfer

예금원장 deposit ledger

예금율 deposit-to-loan ratio

예금이율 deposit rate

예금이자세 tax on deposit

예금자보호 depositor protection

예금자보호시스템 safety nets

예금자위조보증증권 depositor's forgery bond

예금전표 deposit slip
예금정산불방식 deposit payoff
예금증권 warehouse receipt
예금증서 deposit certificate
예금지불준비율 cash reserve ratio
예금창구 deposit window
예금통화 deposit money; deposit of public money
예금현금 cash in banks and hand
예납보험료 잠정조정 interim premium adjustment
예대율 bank loan-deposit ratio
예방법학 preventive law
예방보전 preventive maintenance
예방사법 preventive justice
예방처리 preventive action
예방코스트 preventional cost
예비감사 preliminary audit
예비대차대조표 preliminary balance sheet
예비동기 precautionary motive
예비상품 back-up merchandise
예비선거 primary election
예비심문 preliminary examination
예비심분 void dire
예비심사 preliminary review
예비재고 back-up inventory
예비접근 preapproach
예비정보 preliminary information
예비조사 preliminary investigation
예비주권 unissued certificate
예비지불인 besoin; referee ill case of need
예비클레임 preliminary claim
예산 budget; primaries
예산계정 budgetary account
예산단년도주의 one year budget principle
예산단일주의 principle of single budget
예산배부와 집행 allocation and execution of budget
예산배분 budget allotment
예산순계 net budget
예산원가 budgeted cost

예산원칙 budget principle
예산위원회 Budget Committee
예산제도 budget system
예산차이 budget variance; spending variance; variation from budget
예산차이분석 analysis of budget variance
예산초과 cost overrun
예산총칙 general provisions of budget
예산통제 budgetary control
예산편성 budgetary process
예산항목이체 rearrangement of budget item
예상 expectation
예상 밖의 손출 windfall loss
예상내용연수 probable life
예상매상고 estimate of sales; forecast of sales
예상배당 probable dividend; projected dividend
예상배당율 prospective dividend rate
예상변동률 expected volatility
예상보유기간수익률 estimated holding period return
예상수익 anticipated profit
예상수익률 prospective return
예상외의 이익변동 surprises in earnings
예상원가 anticipated cost; predicted cost
예상이익 probable yield; prospective yield
예상최대손해액 probable maximum loss
예상평균이익 prospective yield average
예상함수 expectation function
예선료 towage
예속의 subordinated
예속조항 subordinated clause
예속조항부 사채 subordinate debenture
예약공모 offer by subscription
예약판매 sale by subscription
예외세율 exceptional rates of tax
예외없이 모두 all and singular
예외운임 exception rate
예외원칙 law of exception
예외의 원칙 exception principle
예저금 deposit and saving; deposits and

savings

예정, 예산 따위를 앞당겨 씀 front loaded

예정납세 estimated tax prepayment; prepayment of income tax

예정납세액독촉 claim of prepayment of income tax

예정납세액체납처분 disposition of failure to pay income tax in advance

예정납세제도 income tax prepayment system

예정배부율 predetermined burden rate

예정변액연금 varying annuity

예정보르드로 preliminary bordereau

예정보험 provisional insurance; provisional policy

예정보험인수부 provisional risk book

예정사망률 expected mortality rate

예정수입 expected income

예정신고 provisional return

예정원가 predetermined cost

예정원가계산 predetermined cost system

예정이율 assumed rate of interest

예측급부채무 projected benefit obligation

예측모델 expectancy-value model; forecasting model

예측수요량 projected demand

예측오차 error of prediction; prediction error

예측타당성 prediction validity

예탁계정 deposit account

예탁관리 deposit administration

예탁관리기금 deposit administration fund

예탁금 deposit; deposited money

예탁보증금 deposits on contract; deposits received for guarantees

예탁보험료 deposit premium

예탁우선주 depository preferred stock

예탁유가증권 deposited securities

예탁은행 depositary bank

예탁인 depositary

예탁자산 depositary assets

예탁주식 depositary shares

예탁증서 depositary receipts

오기 clerical mistake; misprision

오기하다 enter wrongly

오너트러스티 owner trustee

오더북피셜 order book official

오락 entertainment

오락설비 amusement

오류표시 false demonstration

오르다; 치솟다 rise above

오리지널상품 original goods

오바나이트거래 overnight transaction

오바나이트레이트 overnight rate

오버드라이브프로세서 over drive processor

오버래핑타임 overlapping time

오버슈트법 overshoot method

오버퍼 over par

오버펀딩 over funding

오브젝트공간 object space

오브젝트지향 데이터베이스 object oriented database

오블라이지라인 oblige line

오상환 misredemption

오스트레일리아국채 Australian National Bond

오실레이터 oscillator

50% 상각법 replacement method

오염손해 contamination damages

오염주식 dirty shares

OEM original equipment manufacturing

오일머니 oil money

오전장의 최초 가격으로 매입하다 buy on opening

오진을 정정함 correction of errors

오차탈루 errors or omissions

오차탈루제외 errors and omissions excepted

오퍼가격 offer price

오퍼곡선 offer curve

오퍼레이션리서치 operations research

오퍼레이트 offered rate

오퍼레이팅레버리지 분석 operating leverage analysis

오퍼레이팅리스 operating lease

오퍼레이팅시스템; **OS** operating system
오퍼사이드 offer side
오프닝시즌 opening session
오프닝톤 opening tone
오프닝프라이스 opening price
오프마켓 off-market
오프마켓스와프 off market swap
오프밸런스 off balance
오프밸런스시트거래 off-balance sheet
　　transaction
오프셋인쇄 offset printing
오프쇼어계정 offshore account
오프쇼어리스 offshore lease
오프쇼어뱅킹센터 offshore banking center
오프쇼어뱅킹유닛 offshore banking unit
오프쇼어센터 offshore center
오프쇼어시장 offshore market
오프쇼어은행간시장 offshore banking facility
오프쇼어펀드 offshore fund
오프쇼어해외시장 offshore production
오프토크 통신서비스 off talk service
오픈다운 open down
오픈레이트방식 open rate method
오픈미디어프레임워크 open media
　　framework
오픈북 open book
오픈엔드형 리스 open-end lease
오픈엔드형 펀드 open-end fund
오픈커버; 포괄보험 open cover
오픈플랜오피스 open plan office
오픈하우스 open house
오픈형 투자신탁 open investment trust;
　　open-end investment trust
오피스계획 office landscape
옥션시스템 auction system
옥외광고 outdoor advertising
온라인 on-line
온밸런스 on balance
온밸런스거래 on-balance-sheet transaction
온밸런스볼륨 on balance volume
온쇼어마켓 on-shore market

온에어테스트 on air test
온후크다이얼 on hook dial
올드본드 old bond
올리스크담보 all risks coverage
올리스크담보보험 all risks insurance
올리스크담보약관 all risks clause
옮겨적기 posting
옴브즈맨 ombudsman
옵션 더블옵션 double option
옵션; 선택권 option
옵션가격결정모델 option pricing model
옵션가격결정이론 option pricing theory
옵션거래 option transaction
옵션계약의 이서 endorsement for option
　　contract
옵션만기일 option expiration date
옵션매도자 option writer
옵션바이어 option buyer
옵션부 순월인도 outright forward delivery
　　with option
옵션부 전환사채 convertible bonds with
　　option
옵션부채 option bond
옵션스프레드 option spreads
옵션시장 option market
옵션의 시간가치 time value of option
옵션인도 delivery with option
옵션청산회사 option clearing corporation
옵션퍼포먼스지수 option performance index
옵션포지션 option position
옵션풀 option pool
옵션프리미엄 option premier
옵션헤징 hedging on option
옵팅아웃 opting-out
~와 대비하여 versus
와시오더 wash order
와일드카드옵션 wild card option
완공보너스 completion bonus
완만한 slack; sluggish
완만한 약세인(물가) easy
완매; 흡수합병 absorption

완매채권 absorbed bond

완성공사고 construction of completion

완성공사보상준비금 reserve for compensation for completed works

완성기준 completed contract method

완성매매계약 executed contract of sale

완성보증 completion guarantee

완성작업위험 completed operations hazard

완성품 finished goods; finished products

완성품검사 finished product verification

완전감사 complete audit

완전개시 full disclosure

완전경쟁 complete competition; perfect competition

완전고용 full employment

완전고용정책 full employment policy

완전권원 perfect title

완전법정통화 full legal tender

완전변제 direct payment

완전생명표 complete life table

완전서비스형 중간업자 full service middlemen

완전소유자회사 wholly owned subsidiary

완전수급자격 fully insured status

완전연금 complete annuity; full pension

완전원고 finished artwork

완전이용산출량 full capacity output

완전적합전략 completely adaptive strategy

완전즉시상환식 연금 full cash refund annuity

완전증명 full proof

완전채무 perfect obligation

완전특화 complete specialization

완전표준원가 perfection standard cost

완전합의조항 entire agreement clause

완전화폐 full-bodied money

완전히 in extenso

완충재고 buffer stock

완충재고융자 buffer stock financing facility

완화 easing; relaxation

왈라스경매인 Walrasian auctioneer

왕래상장 rise-and-fall market

왕로운임 outward freight

외견상의 변경 colorable alteration

외교관과세특권 fiscal privileges of diplomat

외국거래 foreign transactions

외국기업 foreign corporation company

외국대리점계정 foreign agents accounts

외국무역승수 foreign trade multiplier

외국무역통계 export and import statistics

외국법인 alien corporation; foreign corporation; foreign juridical person

외국법인세 foreign corporation tax

외국법인세액공제 foreign corporation tax credit

외국보험자 foreign insurer

외국보험회사 alien insurer

외국비상장주 foreign stocks unlisted

외국세액 foreign tax

외국세액공제 credit for foreign taxes; foreign tax credit

외국세액공제방식 foreign tax credit method

외국세액공제제도 foreign tax credit system

외국세액공제한도액 creditable amount of foreign taxes

외국세액면제방식 foreign tax exemption method

외국세액손금산입 deduction for foreign taxes

외국세액을 이월공제함 carryover of foreign tax credit

외국세액직접공제 direct foreign tax credit

외국소득면제방식 exemption method

외국소득세 foreign income tax

외국송금 remittance abroad

외국신용보험협회 Foreign Credit Insurance Association

외국어음 foreign bill

외국원천소득 income accrued from foreign sources

외국은행규제 regulations on foreign banks

외국은행유전스 usance granted by foreign banks

외국의 판결 foreign judgment

외국의; 예외적의 foreign

외국인 alien

외국인구매 foreign buying

외국인납세자 alien taxpayer

외국인재산 alien property

외국인지주비율 foreign stock holding ratio; stock holding ratio of foreigners

외국인지주제한 limit on foreign investors' holdings of stocks; stockholding limit for foreign investors

외국인투자 foreigner's investment; investment by foreign investors

외국인투자가 foreign investors

외국자회사 foreign subsidiary corporation

외국정산약관 foreign adjustment clause

외국주권면제 sovereign immunity

외국증권업법 law for foreign securities company

외국증권회사 foreign securities company

외국지점발송계정 foreign branch-our account

외국지점예금 due from foreign banks

외국지점피발송계정 foreign branch-their account

외국채권 foreign bond

외국타점예금 due to foreign banks

외국통화선물 foreign currency futures

외국통화선물계약 foreign currency futures contracts

외국환 foreign exchange

외국환계정 foreign exchange accounts

외국환공인은행 authorized foreign exchange bank

외국환관리 foreign exchange control

외국환금융기관 financial institution for foreign exchange

외국환변동준비금 reserve for foreign exchange fluctuation

외국환브로커 foreign exchange broker

외국환선물 foreign exchange futures

외국환시장 foreign exchange market

외국환시장개입 foreign exchange market intervention

외국환시장조작 foreign exchange market operation

외국환어음 foreign bill of exchange; foreign exchange bill

외국환예약 foreign exchange contract

외국환운영자금 fund for operation of foreign exchange

외국환유통신용장 negotiation credit

외국환율 foreign exchange rate

외국환은행 foreign exchange bank

외국환의 링크 exchange link

외국환자금증권 foreign exchange fund bill

외국환전문은행 specialized foreign exchange bank

외국환조작 foreign exchange operation

외국환차손 loss on foreign exchange

외국환차손익 foreign exchange gains and losses

외국환취급지점 branch handling foreign exchange business

외국환투기 foreign exchange speculation

외국환포지션 foreign exchange position

외국환포지션표 foreign exchange position sheet

외국환환산율 foreign exchange conversion rate

외국환환산표 foreign exchange conversion table

외무부 agency department

외무원개발시대 agent development era

외무직원 field underwriter

외부감사 external audit

외부감사인 external auditor

외부거래 external transaction

외부경제 external economy

외부금융 external financing

외부부채 external liabilities

외부성 externality

외부시험 outside test

외부실패 external failure

외부위험 external hazard
외부의 무형손실 external intangible loss
외부자원 external resources
외부적인 제약 external restraint
외부정보 external information
외부정합성 external consistency
외부증거 extraneous evidence; extrinsic evidence
외부품질감사 external quality audit
외부품질보증 external quality assurance
외부화폐 outside money
외부환경 outside environment
외삽법 extrapolation
외상거래 credit sales
외상거래가격 credit price
외상거래계정 credit account
외상거래채권 sales credit
외상계정 account of credit sales
외상구입 buying on credit; credit purchase; purchase on credit
외상매매 sale and purchase on credit
외상매입금 trade account payable
외상매출 sale on account; selling on credit
외상매출금 book credit; trade account receivable
외상매출금계정 charge account
외상매출금원장 customers' ledger; sold ledger
외상매출금회수 bill collection; collection of bill
외상보험 account receivable insurance
외상으로 판 상품 goods sold on credit
외상으로 팔다 sell on credit
외상장부에서 on the books
외상적립기금 purchase payment fund
외상채권매입업무; 팩터링 factoring
외상채권율 sales to accounts receivable
외상채권채무자 account debtor
외상채권회전율 sales to receivables; sales worth ratio
외상채권회전일수 number of days' purchases

in accounts payable
외상채무 account payable
외상판매 on account
외상판매처 trade debtor
외생변수 exogenous variables
외생변화 exogenous change
외생수요 exogenous demand
외선전화집중접수부 automatic call distributor
외압 external forces; outside pressure
외연적인 의미 denotative meanings
외자 foreign capital
외자계 소비자금융 foreign capital consumer finance company
외자계기업 foreign affiliate
외자도입 intake of foreign capital
외자법 Foreign Investment Law
외자비율소멸정책 fade-out policy
외자수입 foreign capital intake; importation of foreign capital
외자유입 inflow of foreign capital; influx of foreign capital
외자흡수 foreign capital inducement
외적인 증거 external evidence
외주 order to outside manufacturer
외주가공비 expense arising from outside manufacture
외주업자 outside manufacturer
외주제품 outside product
외채 external bond; external loan; foreign debt; foreign loan
외채모집 flotation of external loan
외채발행대금 proceeds from external bond issuance
외채상환 redemption of external loan
외채이자 interest on external bond
외화 foreign currency
외화거래 foreign currency transactions
외화계정 foreign currency account
외화국채 government bond in foreign currency
외화기준 denominated in foreign currency
외화기준계정항목을 환산함 conversion of

items in foreign currencies
외화기준상장 exchange rate in foreign currency
외화기준증권 foreign currency series securities
외화기준채권 claim in foreign currency; foreign currency-denominated bond
외화기준채무 debt in foreign currency
외화를 주고받지 않는 수입 nondraft import
외화를 주고받지 않는 수출 nondraft export
외화보유고 foreign currency holdings
외화어음 bill foreign currency; foreign money bill
외화예금 foreign currency deposit
외화예금계정 foreign currency deposit account
외화예금이자 interest on foreign currency deposits
외화예산 foreign exchange budget
외화예탁 foreign currency deposit with exchange bank
외화유입 foreign currency inflow
외화준비 external reserves; foreign currency reserves; foreign reserves
외화준비고 foreign exchange reserves; official foreign exchange reserves; sold and foreign exchange reserves
외화준비통계 statistics of foreign currency reserves
외화증권 foreign currency securities; securities in foreign currency
외화집중제도 foreign exchange centralization system
외화징수외국환 foreign currency bill receivable
외화채 foreign currency bond
외화통화유통 rate in foreign currency
외화표시부분을 환산함 translation of foreign currency statements
외화표시재무제표 foreign currency statements

외화할당권 right to obtain foreign money
외화할당제 foreign exchange allocation system
외화환산조정액 currency translation adjustments
외환법 foreign exchange law
외환보유고 overall balance of foreign exchange
외환환산손익 profit or loss on foreign exchange
요건 requirements
요구 requisition
요구계층 need hierarchy
요구불 payable on demand
요구불계정 demand account
요구불어음 demand note
요구불채무 demand debt
요구수준 aspiration level
요구정도 required accuracy
요구지불 on demand
요구충족 어프로치 need-satisfaction approach
요구품질 required quality
요금 dues
요물(要物)계약 contract in kind
요소별 계산서 objective statement
요소별 원가 object cost
요소별 원가계산 elementary cost accounting
요소별의 objective
요소비교법 factor comparison system
요소수익률 factor return
요약계정식 condensed account form
요약대차대조표 condensed balance sheet
요약보고식 condensed report form
요약손익계산서 condensed income statement
요역지(要役地) dominant estate
요요주식 yo-yo stock
요율; 세금 rate
요율감사부 stamping bureau
요율단계를 변경함 bracket creep
요율산정기관불참가회사 deviating company
요율산정가맹회사 bureau company

요율신청 bureau filing
요율인하 rate cut
요율자문기관 advisory organization
요율저하 rate down
요인분석 attribution analysis
요주의명부 watch list
요판, 오목판 intaglio
욕구이론 needs theory
용선계약; 용선료 charterage
용선계약 charterparty
용수 diversion of water
용수권 aquatic rights
용수지역권 servitude for use of water
용역단위 service unit
용역생산고법 services output method
용역원가 service cost
용역제공 utility service
용지비 land cost
용해형 프린터 phase change printer
우대조치기간 free-ride period
우량물건 good risk; preferred risk
우량물건할인 premium discount for good risks
우량어음 prime bill; prime paper
우량인 in good standing
우량자리스트 white list
우량주 blue chips
우루과이라운드 Uruguay Round
우발거래 contingent transaction
우발경비 accidental cost
우발비용 contingent charge
우발사상 contingency
우발손실 casual loss; contingent loss
우발손실준비금 reserve for contingency;
    special contingency reserve
우발이익 casual profit; contingent profit
우발자금 contingent fund
우발자산 contingent assets
우발적인 손익 windfall loss or gain
우발적인 위험 contingency risk
우발적인 좌초 accidental grounding
우발채무 contingent liabilities

우발채무적립금 contingent reserve
우선권 preferential right
우선대출금리; 프라임레이트 prime rate
우선매수권 preemption
우선발언권 preaudience
우선배당 preference dividend; preferred
    dividend
우선배당부담배율 preferred dividend
    coverage ratio
우선사용 prior use
우선성 priority
우선소득 preference income
우선재보험 preferential reinsurance; priority
    reinsurance
우선주 preference share; preferred stock
우선주배당금 dividend on preferred stock;
    dividend option
우선주상환준비금 reserve for retirement of
    preferred stock
우선주자본금 capital stock preferred
우선증권 senior securities
우선지불채무 privileged debts
우선차압권 priority of attachment
우선채권자 preferential creditor; preferred
    creditor; priority creditor
우선채무 preferred liability; senior debt
우선토지사용권 right of way
우송료 mailing cost; postage
우송료선불 postage to be paid on delivery
우송료지불필 postage paid
우수물건 superior risks
우애조합 friendly society
우연성 fortuity
우연손실보험 contingency insurance
우연한 사고 fortuitous event
우연한 재해 casus fortuitus
우월한 권리 paramount right
우위 precedence
우위적인 전략 dominated strategy
우편연금 post office annuity
우편예금이자 interest on postal savings

우편일수 mail days
우편저축예금 postal savings deposit
우편환 postal money order
우호적인 소송 amicable action
우회무역 roundabout trade
우회생산 roundabout production
운동 interlocking
운동모델 motion model
운동하여 in line with
운반비 haulage
운송 transportation
운송료 forwarding charges; transportation charges
운송료할증 additional charges
운송보험 transit insurance; transport insurance; transportation insurance
운송비 carriage; carrying cost; shipping charge
운송비·보험료포함 carriage and insurance paid to
운송비포함 carriage paid to
운송설비 transportation equipment
운송약관 transit clause
운송업 transportation business
운송업자 transportation company
운송업자책임보험 common carriers liability insurance
운송인인도 free carrier
운송인책임보험 carriers liability insurance
운송중 on passage
운송취급인 forwarding merchant
운송클레임 transportation claim
운영목표 intermediate target
운용과 조달 사이의 기간차이 maturity gap exposure
운용부분 cash value
운용설명서 evergreen prospectus
운용성적 performance
운용이익 yield on investment
운용자산 assets producing interest; employed assets; invested assets; operating assets; portfolio; working assets
운용자산액비례보수방식 compensation plans based on assets
운용잔고 working balance
운용장 position sheet
운임 cartage; fare; portage
운임·보험료포함 cost insurance and freight
운임보험 freight insurance
운임수입 freight receipts
운임유전스 freight usance
운임자금 circulating fund
운임전불 freight prepaid
운임포함 cost and freight
운임할인제 fidelity rebate system
운임할증 primage
운임환불제 deferred rebate system
운임후불 freight to collect
운전비 running cost
운전비용 operating cost
운전시간법 working-hours method
운전자금 operating capital; working capital; working fund
운전자금관리 working capital control
운전자금을 적용함 application of working capital
운전자배상책임보험 driver's liability policy
운전자본감소 deductions from working capital
운전자본구성 composition of working capital
운전자본매상률 sales to working capital
운전자본분석 working capital analysis
운전자본비율 working-capital ratio
운전자본상태 working capital position
운전재고 cycle stock
운전재고자산 working inventory
운전특성곡선 operating characteristics curve
워런트계약서 warrant agreement
워런트대리인 warrant agent
워런트채 bond with warrant; warrant bond
워런트패러티 warrant parity
원가 cost; initial cost
원가·보험료·운임포함 가격 CIF price

원가 및 비용 cost and expenses
원가(元加)방식 interest capitalization method
원가(이윤)가산방식 cost plus
원가가치 cost value
원가개산표 rough cost book
원가계산 cost accounting; costing
원가계산기간 cost accounting period; costing period
원가계산기준 cost accounting standards
원가계산단위 costing unit
원가계산서 cost card; cost statement
원가계산제도 cost accounting system
원가계산표 cost sheet
원가계정 cost account
원가고 high cost
원가관리 cost control
원가구성요소 components of cost
원가기준 cost standard
원가기준법 cost plus method
원가단위 cost unit
원가로 at cost
원가배당 allocation of cost
원가배부 circulation of cost
원가배분 cost distribution
원가법 cost method; valuation at cost
원가보고서 cost report
원가분석 cost analysis
원가비교법 minimum cost rule
원가삭감 cost savings
원가산정 cost finding
원가시스템 cost system
원가요소 cost element; element of cost
원가원장 cost ledger
원가율 cost rate
원가의식 cost consciousness
원가이하로 below cost
원가이하주의 cost-or-less principle
원가이하판매 below-cost sale
원가저감계획 cost-reduction programs
원가주의 cost basis; cost principle
원가주의회계 concept of historical cost

원가차액 cost variance; variance of cost
원가차액계정 variance account
원가차액조정 adjustment of cost variance; apportionment of cost variance; disposition of cost variance
원가차이분석 analysis of cost variances
원가회수 cost recovery
원가흡수 cost absorption
원격교육 distance learning
원격탐사 remote sensing
원계약 prime contract
원고 complainant; demandant; exchange rate in favor of won; libelant; plaintiff; strong won
원고 디플레 deflation caused by won appreciation
원고보증 plaintiffs bond
원고보호입법 plaintiff legislation
원고차익 exchange gain from the won appreciation
원고청구승낙서 cognovit note
원고호출 calling the plaintiff
원금 principal amount
원금상각보험사업 capital redemption business
원금증가형 스와프 accreting swap
원기준 denominated in won
원기준수출 export in terms of won
원달러시프트 switch from won to dollars
원라이트증권 one-write policy
원료 material
원료가격변동 fluctuations in prices of raw materials
원료구입대전도금 advance made for purchase of material
원료소비량 feed consumption
원리 principal and interest
원리균등반제 equal monthly payments with interest
원리균등분할반제 level payment
원리균등불방식 equal payment method

원리균등불채 annuity bond
원리균등상환방식 annuity repayment method
원리지불 debt servicing
원리합계 interest included
원망 열망 aspiration
원문 그대로 sic
원문서 script
원법원 court below
원보험 original insurance
원보험요율 original rate
원보험증권 original policy
원본 corpus; original; original document
원본; 본인 principal
원본균등불방식 equal installment repayment method
원본금리를 완전분리함 complete stripping between interest and principal
원본보증 principal guaranteed
원본상환 refund of principal
원본상환방법 principal amortization schedule
원본소유자이동 changes of owners of the principal
원본지불 principal payment
원부 original register
원산지손해 country damage
원산지증명 certificate of origin
원상회복 restitution in integrum
원수(元受)보험 direct insurance
원수(元受)보험료 direct premium; direct writing premium
원수(元受)보험료세 direct premium tax
원수(元受)회사 direct insurer
원시기입 original entry
원시기입부 book of original entry
원시자본 original capital
원신용장 master letter of credit; original credit
원심적인 시장 centrifugal market
원외계약 lobbying contract
원외운동 lobbying
원유가격연동형 사채 petrobond

원유선물옵션 crude oil futures
원유오염배상책임보험 oil pollution liability insurance
원인 cause; remote cause
원인제거 elimination of cause
원인조사 investigation of cause
원인채권 causal credit
원자력발전공사상각준비금 atomic power plant construction reserve
원자력보험 unclear energy insurance
원자력사고 nuclear accident
원자력손해 nuclear damage
원자력손해배상책임보험 nuclear energy liability insurance; unclear energy liability insurance
원자력시설 nuclear installation
원자력위험 nuclear energy hazard
원자력재산보험 nuclear energy property insurance
원자산 actuals; underlying assets
원자산의 underlying
원장 ledger; pass book
원장계 ledger clerk
원장계정 ledger account
원장대체 ledger transfer
원장마감 closing the ledger
원장에 옮겨적다 post to the ledger
원장의 각계정을 마감 closing all accounts in the ledger
원장자산 ledger assets
원장잔고 balance on ledger; ledger balance
원장체결 closing of the ledger
원장페이지수 ledger folio
원재료 primary materials; raw and processed materials
원재료구입보고서 materials purchased report
원재료를 보내다 feed
원재료반환표 materials returned report; returned materials report
원재료원장 stores ledger
원재료인수보고서 materials received report

원재료재고 raw material inventory

원저인플레 inflation caused by won depreciation

원적국주의; 본점감독주의 home country control

원조 assistance

원조금 aids

원조청원 aid prayer

원증권; 대상증권 underlying securities

원천 sources

원천 및 도중계산서 source and disposition statement

원천공제소득세 income tax withheld at source

원천과세 taxation at the source

원천분리과세 separate withholding taxation at source

원천선택 withholding tax option

원천선택과세 optional assessment

원천소득세 with holding tax; withholding tax on income

원천징수 amount withhold; withholding at source

원천징수소득세 withholding income tax

원천징수와 납부 withholding and payment

원천징수의무자 withholding agent

원천징수제도 withholding system; withholding tax system

원천징수표 withholding exemption certificate

원칙적인 납세지 general place of tax payment

원포장 original package

월가 Wall Street

월계표 monthly statement of account

월권행위 ultra vires activities

월드인덱스 world index

월말 end of the month; month-end

월말결산 monthly accounting

월말인도 month-end delivery

월보 monthly report

월부 monthly installment

월부반환보험료 monthly prorata return premium

월부투자계획 monthly investment plan

월부판매 installment sale; monthly installment sales

월부판매금융 financing for sales by installment payment

월차계산서 monthly statement

월차대차대조표 monthly balance sheet

월차비례배분방식 monthly prorata fraction system

월차손익계산서 monthly income statement

월차시산표 monthly trial balance

월차체감약관 monthly diminishing clause

월차총평균법 monthly average method

월할계산 accounting by month

웨이브이론 Wave Theory

웨이브포스팅 wave posting

웨이스트서큐레이션 waste circulation

웨지 wedge

웨지포메이션 wedge formation

위기레이트 crisis rate

위로금 consolation money

위문금 present of money in token of sympathy

위반 breach

위반하다 contravention

위반행위 misconduct

위법행위 illegal; wrong

위상 topology

위생요인 hygiene factor

위성방송 direct broadcasting

위성시장 satellite market

위성통신 satellite communication

위스키세 whisky tax

위약금 cancel money; forfeit; penalty

위약금액 penal sum

위약손실보상준비금 default loss compensation reserve; reserve for compensation for default loss

위약이자 penal interest

위원회 committee

위원회결 panel decision

위임기업동맹 blind pool
위임장 letter of attorney; power of attorney; stockpower; warrant of attorney; warrant
위임장근유 proxy solicitation
위임장쟁탈전 proxy fight
위임장투표 proxy vote
위임통지 notice of abandonment
위임통치국 mandatory
위임하다 delegate
위장분실 false missing
위장자금 laundered money
위조 counterfeit
위조담보약관 forgery insuring clause
위조보험 forgery insurance
위조수표 forged check
위조어음 forged bill
위조죄 crimen falsi
위조주 bogus stock
위조주권 forged stock
위조지폐 forged note; green goods
위조카드 counterfeit card
위증자 straw man
위치결정 positioning
위치매체 position media
위크오더 week order
위크폼 weak form
위클리리저벌 weekly reversal
위탁거래 agency transaction
위탁계약 consignment contract
위탁계약서 commission of authority
위탁금 money in trust; trust money
위탁금착복 defalcation
위탁매매 consignment sales and purchases
위탁매매인 commission; commission agent
위탁매입 buying on commission
위탁무역 trade on commission
위탁보증금율 margin requirements
위탁수수료 brokerage commission; commission on consignment; consignment fee
위탁업무수수료 entrusted business commission
위탁연구 sponsored research
위탁인 consignor
위탁증거금 consignment guarantee money
위탁증거금; 차금; 중간이윤 margin
위탁판매 best-efforts selling; consignment sale; sale on commission; selling on a consignment basis
위탁판매계약 consignment sales contract
위탁판매미수입금 account due on consignment-out
위탁판매수수료 commission to consignee
위탁판매수입 import on consignment
위탁판매수출 export on consignment
위탁판매적송품 consignment
위탁품 consignment goods; trial consignments
위탁품송장 consignment invoice
위헌의 unconstitutional
위험 hazard; jeopardy; peril
위험기간 duration of risk
위험노출 risk exposure
위험발생률 frequency of risk
위험변동 change of risk
위험보험료식 보험 risk premium insurance
위험부담인수 assumption of risk
위험부담정지약관 while clause
위험분산 diffusion of risks
위험비율분석방식 analytic system
위험선택 selection of risk
위험선호자 risk lover
위험약관 peril clause
위험의 종류 class of risk
위험자본리스크 risk capital
위험자산 risk assets
위험자산 믹스 risky assets mix
위험자산비율 risk asset ratio
위험전가현상 risky shift phenomenon
위험점 peril point
위험준비금 contingency fund
위험체증의 원리 principle of increasing risk

위험한정효과 effect of limiting risk
위험회피 risk aversion
위험회피; 리스크헤지 risk hedge
유가약인(有價約因) valuable consideration
유가증권 negotiable securities; securities
유가증권거래세 securities transfer tax
유가증권거래세법 securities transaction tax law
유가증권계정 securities account
유가증권계출서 registration statement
유가증권관리신탁 securities administration trust
유가증권기입장 securities register
유가증권담보대부금 loan secured by securities
유가증권매각기입장 investment sold register
유가증권매각손 loss on securities
유가증권매입 securities purchase
유가증권매입기입장 investment purchased register
유가증권매출집금 collection of securities by purchase
유가증권명세표 schedule of securities
유가증권보고서 financial report
유가증권분류 classification of securities
유가증권손익 security income and expense
유가증권신탁 securities in trust
유가증권양도 transfer of securities
유가증권양도소득 income from transfer of securities
유가증권원장 investment ledger; securities ledger
유가증권위조보험 forged securities policy
유가증권을 법정평가하는 방법 statutory valuation method of securities
유가증권의 범위 scope of securities
유가증권이자 interest on securities
유가증권이전세 tax for transfer of securities
유가증권인수업법 securities underwriting business law
유가증권준비 securities reserve

유가증권취득가액 acquisition cost of securities
유가증권평가 appraisal securities
유가증권평가방법 appraisement method of securities
유가증권평가익 gains from appreciation of securities
유가하락 collapse in oil prices
유급휴가 compensated absence; vacation with pay
유급휴가회계 accounting for compensated absences
유기 dereliction
유기적 성장 organic growth
유기적인 자본구성 organic composition of capital
유기체모델 organismic model
유년 natural infancy
유니버설뱅킹 universal banking
유니버설생명보험 universal life policy
유니온숍 union shop
유닛당 순자산가치 net asset value per unit
유닛로드 unit load
유닛링크보험 unit linked life insurance
유닛오프어카운트채 unit of account bond
유도심문 leading questions
유동담보 floating charge
유동담보를 결정함 crystallization
유동리엔 floating lien
유동부분 liquid part
유동부채 current liabilities; floating liability
유동비율 current ratio; liquid ratio; working capital ratio
유동성 liquidity
유동성 배열 current-first order
유동성 배열법 current arrangement
유동성 격차 liquidity differential
유동성 관리 liquidity management
유동성 동기로 인한 매매 liquidity-motivated transactions
유동성 딜레마 liquidity dilemma

ㅅ
ㅇ

유동성 리스크 liquidity risk
유동성 배열법 order of liquidity
유동성 부족 liquidity scarcity
유동성 분산 liquidity diversification
유동성 비율 liquidity ratio
유동성 상장주 liquidity-driven issue
유동성 선호이론 liquidity preference theory
유동성 예금 liquid deposit
유동성의 함정(계략) liquidity trap
유동성 준비금 liquid reserve
유동성 지향 상장 liquidity-driven market
유동성 창출 liquidity creation
유동성 포지션 liquidity position
유동성 프리미엄 liquidity premium
유동성 효과 liquidity effect
유동자본 circulating capital; floating capital;
  liquid capita
유동자산 circulating assets; current assets;
  floating assets; liquid assets
유동자산가설 liquid-asset hypothesis
유동자산회전기간 current-asset cycle
유동주 floating stock
유동증권; 포괄보험증권 floater
유동지수 liquidity index
유동채무 floating debt
유러금융시장 Eurocurrency banking market
유러기업어음 Eurocommercial paper
유러노트퍼실리티 Euronote facility
유러달러 Eurodollar
유러달러선물옵션 Eurodollar futures option
유러달러예금 Eurodollar deposit
유러달러예금금리선물 Eurodollar depositary
  interest futures
유러달러자금시장 Eurodollar market
유러달러정기예금 Eurodollar time deposit
유러대부시장 Eurocredit market
유러라인 Euroline
유러마크선물 Euromark futures
유러머니 Euromoney
유러시장 Euromarket
유러신디케이트론 Eurosyndicate loan

유러엔 Euroyen
유러엔금리 Euroyen interest rate
유러엔시장 Euroyen market
유러엔채발행 Euroyen bond issue
유러채 Eurobond
유러채시장 Eurobond market
유러통화시장 Eurocurrency market
유러통화신디케이트론시장 Eurocurrency
  syndicated loan market
유러트랙 Eurotrack
유러펀드채 Europound bond
유러피언옵션 European option
유럽경제공동체 European Economic
  Community
유럽경제위원회 Economic Commission for
  Europe
유럽경제지역 European Economic Area
유럽경제협력기구 Organization for European
  Economic Cooperation
유럽계산단위 European unit of account
유럽공동체 European Communities
유럽방식 European term
유럽석탄철강공동체 European Coal and Steel
  Community
유럽시장의 어음교환소 Euroclear
유럽식 복리이율 annual compounding
유럽안보협력회의 Conference on Security
  and Cooperation in Europe
유럽연합 European Union
유럽예탁증권 European Depositary Receipts
유럽예탁증서 Curacao Depositary Receipts
유럽원자력공동체 European Atomic Energy
  Community
유럽의회 European Parliament
유럽자유무역연합 European Free Trade
  Association
유럽주식예탁증서 Continental Depositary
  Receipts
유럽중앙은행 European Central Bank
유럽지불동맹 European Payment Union
유럽타입 European type

유럽통화기금 European Monetary Fund
유럽통화단위 European Currency Unit
유럽통화제도 European Monetary System
유럽통화협력기금 European Monetary
  Cooperation Fund
유럽통화협정 European Monetary Agreement

유럽투자신탁기관 European Investment Trust
유럽투자은행 European Investment Bank
유럽회의 Council of Europe
유로금리 interest rate on the Eurocurreney
  market
유료방송 subscription television
유루사항 casus omissus
유류분(遺留分) legally secured portion of
  succession
유리발행 interest bearing issuance
유리자부채 liability with interest
유리한 투자 high grade investment
유망객결정 qualifying activity
유발투자 induced investment
유배주 dividend-paying stock
유보공제액 allowance for undistributed profits
유보금 retention money
유보금액 undistributed profits
유보사항 reservation; saving clause
유보소득에 대한 세 tax on undistributed
  profits
유보수익률 accumulated earning tax
유보이익 retained surplus
유보조건 under reserve
유보주식 reserved common stock
유복한 deep pocket
유사 analogy
유사물제작 imitation
유사품 similar goods
유사한 투자매체 similar investment media
유산 legacy
유산관리 administration estate
유산관리소송 administration suit
유산관리인 administrator of bequest

유산분할 partition of the estate
유산상속 inheritance of bequest; succession
  of property
유산세 legacy duty
유산소득 estate income
유산수취인 legatee
유산에 관계된 기초공제 basic deduction for
  bequest
유산회계 estate accounting
유상계약 onerous contract
유상소지인 holder for value
유상신탁 trust for value
유상증자 paid-in capital increase
유상취득 acquisition for value
유선방송 cable television
유세상각 taxable depreciation
유아거치보험 child's deferred insurance
유아보험 children's insurance
유어즈(팔았을 때) yours
유언 testament
유언부 유산관리인 administrator cum
  testamento annexo
UHF ultra high frequency
유의수준 level of significance; significance
  level
유의차 significant difference
유인 inducement; invitation
유인적인 방해물 attractive nuisance
유입 influx
유자격 eligible
유자격자 good and lawful men
유저액티브 user-active
유전스 usance
유전스레이트 usance rate
유전적인 알고리즘 genetic algorithm
유족급부금 benefits for survivor; survivor
  benefit
유족연금 survivor annuity
유죄 culpability; guilty
유죄가 확정된 자 malefactor
유죄결정 conviction

유죄답변(절차) plea of guilty
유죄선고 condemnation
유죄판결기록 record of conviction
유증(부동산의) devise
유증자(遺贈者) devisor
유지 maintenance
유지가격 support price
유지가능한 균형상장 sustainable equilibrium exchange rate
유지관리비용 administrative and maintenance expenses
유지광고 retentive advertising
유지비 cost of maintenance; maintenance cost; upkeep
유지비; 계약유지비 maintenance expense
유지자금 maintenance funds
유지준비금 maintenance reserve
유지증거금 maintenance margins; margin money
유지하다 sustain
유진사(有診査)보험 medicalinsurance
유책성 delictum
유체동산 chose in possession
유체상속부동산 corporeal hereditament
유치하다 distrain
유통 negotiation
유통경로 channel of distribution; distribution channel
유통경로선택 distribution channel selection
유통광고 trade advertising
유통기관을 분산화함 institutional decentralization
유통기구 distribution structure
유통로지스틱스 distribution logistics
유통문제 liquid stock
유통믹스 distribution mix
유통비분석 distribution cost analysis
유통성이 없는 nonnegotiable
유통세 circulation tax
유통속도 velocity of circulation
유통시장 secondary market; trading market

유통시장에서의 채권딜링 secondary bond dealing
유통시장조작 operation in the secondary market
유통업계 distribution industry
유통증권 negotiable instrument; traded securities
유통탄력성 elasticity of distribution
유통혁명 distribution revolution
유통화폐 current money
유틸리티소비 utility consumption
유한내용연수자산 limited-life assets
유한불입 limited premium payment
유한성 finiteness
유한연금 limited annuity
유한차분 finite difference
유한책임 limited liability
유한책임보증회사 company limited by guarantee
유한책임조합 limited partnership
유한책임회사 limited company
유한회사 limited private company
유행예측 fashion forecasting
유행주기 cycle of fashion
유형고정자산 tangible fixed assets; tangible property
유형고정자산명세표 schedule of tangible fixed assets
유형고정자산에서 공제함 deduction from property
유형공급 visible supply
유형론 typology
유형상각자산 tangible depreciable property
유형손실 tangible loss
유형자산 tangible assets
유형자산가치 tangible value
유효경쟁 effective competition; workable competition
유효기간 effective life
유효기한 term of validity
유효성 measurement of attitude

유효성측정 measurement of effectiveness

유효수요 effective demand

유효수요의 원리 principle of effective demand

유효통계 efficient statistics

유효프론티어 efficient frontier

유효한 good; valid

유휴건물 unused buildings

유휴설비 idle equipment; idle plant; spare plant capacity; surplus equipment

유휴시설 idle facilities

유휴자산 idle assets

유휴자산 idle properties

유휴토지 unused land

유흥음식세 amusement and restaurant tax

육상운송비 overland freight

윤리 ethics

윤리규정 code of ethics

윤리에 반하는 거래 bond washing

윤택한 경제 affluent economy

융자 loan

융자규제 loan restrictions; regulation of lending

융자신청 loan application

융자실행 extension of loan

융자잔고 balance of loans; outstanding balance

융자준칙 financing regulation

융자한도 loan limit

융통 accommodation

융통어음 accommodation bill; kite

융통어음발행인 accommodation maker

융합과정 fusion process

은닉동기 ulterior motive

은닉한 적립금 hidden reserve

은밀오퍼 confidential operation

은본위제 silver standard

은사법(恩赦法) act of grace

은선(隱線)처리 hidden line elimination

은행 POS bank point-of-sales

은행간상장 inter-bank rate

은행간예금 inter-bank deposit

은행간예금금리 interest rate on inter-bank deposit

은행간의 inter-bank

은행거래약정서 banking transaction contract

은행거래일 banking day

은행거래정지 disposition by suspension of bank credit

은행거래정지처분 suspension of banking transaction

은행검사 bank examination

은행계신용카드 bank credit card

은행계좌 bank account

은행공황 bank crisis

은행권 bank note

은행단 banking syndicate; syndicate of banks

은행딜러 bank dealer

은행법 bank act

은행보증 bank guarantee

은행부기 bank bookkeeping

은행수표 bank check; cashier's check; official check

은행신용장 banker's credit

은행어음 bank bill

은행업무 banking business

은행예금 bank deposit; cash in bank; deposit due to bank

은행예금잔고 balance at the bank; bank balance

은행예금잔고증명서 certificate of bank balances

은행위조보증증권 bankers forgery bond

은행유동성 bank liquidity; liquidity of the banking system

은행을 통한 증권금융 security credit by banks

은행의 어베이러빌러티 availability of bank

은행이율 bank rate

은행이자 bank interest

은행인수어음 banker's acceptances

은행인수어음할인 discount on banker's acceptances

은행자동납부시스템 bank's automatic accounts transfer system

은행조사 audit on bank account

은행조회 bank reference

은행주의 banking principle

은행주주회사 bank holding company

은행준비 bank reserve

은행증권간의 담장논쟁 issue of the wall between banking and security business

은행차입 loan from banks; owing to bank

은행차입금 bank loans payable; notes payable to banks

은행포괄보증 banker's blanket bond

은행풀딜링 bank full dealing

은행할인료 bank discount rate

은행할인방법 bank discount method

은행휴업일 bank holiday

은혜로서 ex gratia

은환 silver exchange

~을 제외하고는 except for

음량 amplitude

음성순응 negative adaptation

음성응답시스템 voice recognition & response system

음성인식 voice recognition

음원편집소프트 wave editing soft

응낙 acknowledgment of order

응능원칙 ability to pay principle

응답시간 answering time

응모가격 subscription price

응모금액 amount subscribed

응모자이율 subscriber's yield

응모자이익 yield to subscriber

응소 appearance

응소보험 defense insurance

응소주장 defensive allegation

응용조사 applied research

응용프로그램 application program

응익부담원칙 benefit principle

의견거절 disclaims

의견거절보고서(재무제표에 대한 감사의견 중 하나) disclaim report

의견광고 idea advertising

의견조사 opinion survey

의결권 voting right

의결권부 사채 bond with voting right

의결권불통일행사 diverse exercise of voting right

의결권신탁 voting trust

의결권신탁증서 voting trust certificate

의결권이 없는 주 nonvoting stock

의결권주식 voting stock

의뢰반송 requested return

의료과실 medical malpractice

의료과실; 부당행위 malpractice

의료급부채무 health care obligation

의료법인 medical corporation

의료보조금 medical assistance

의료보험 insurance of medical expenses

의료비 medical expenses

의료비공제 deduction for medical expenses; medical credit; medical expenses deduction

의료비담보 medical payment coverage

의료비보험 medical expense insurance

의료비지불보험 medical payments insurance

의료사정 medical underwriting

의료손해배상책임 medical professional liability

의료수리학 medico-actuarial science

의료신고약관 medical treatment clause

의무위반 breach of duty

의무재보험 obligatory reinsurance

의미가 명백하게 불명료함 patent ambiguity

의미론 semantics

의미분별법 semantic differential

의미분별법의 기준 semantic differential scale

의사 intention

의사감염 spurious contagion

의사결정 decision making

의사결정단위 decision making unit

의사결정지원시스템 decision support system

의사결정후의 불협조 post-decision

dissonance

의사록 minutes

의사상관 spurious correlation

의사와 행위 animus et factum

의사일치 aggregatio mentium

의사진단서 medical certificate

의손금 alms

의식주의 비용 clothing and shelter expenses

의인화이론 personification theory

의장 designs; speaker

의장권 design right; registered design

의장등록 registration of design

의장료 design fee

의장법 design law

의제인도 constructive delivery

의제자본 fictitious capital

의제자본; 수할자본 watered capital

의제자산 fictitious assets

의제증서 notional certificate

의제퇴거 constructive eviction

의존 dependence

의존도 degree of dependence

의존효과 dependence effect

의학적인 선택 medical selection

이 경우에 한하여 pro hac vice

이관채권 transferred debt

이권 right and interest

이권양도 transfer of rights

이권획득 acquisition of concessions

이노베이터집단 innovator group

이단계 재고컨트롤시스템 two-level inventory control system

이단계오퍼 two-tier offer

이단자리스크 maverick risk

이더넷 ethernet

이동가중평균 moving weighted average method

이동계속연금 portable pension

이동장벽 mobility barrier

이동점포 mobile shop

이동체통신 group special mobile communication

이동평균 moving average; moving averages

이동평균모델 moving average model

이동평균법 moving average cost method; moving average method

이동평균수속분산 트레이딩법 moving average convergence divergence trading method

이동평균지수 moving average index

이동평균치 moving average deviations

이동형 프랜차이즈 mobile franchise

이득기회 gain opportunity

이득행렬 payoff matrix

EDGAR 시스템 electronic data gathering analysis and retrieval system

이락기간 ex-interest period

이락채권 ex-interest bond

이론가격 theoretical price

이론가치 theoretical value

이론경제학 theoretical economics

이론상의 환매수익률; **IRR** implied repo rate

이론선물가격 theoretical future price

이론적 theoretical

이론적인 가설 theoretical hypothesis

이론적인 지시 theoretical support

이론적인 환상장 theoretical rate of exchange

이류서비스 minor service

이르게 하다; 이끌다 lead

이름 name

이면계약 nongenuine agreement

이문화비교분석 cross-cultural analysis

이뮤니제이션펀드 immunization fund

이미 발행한 채권 already-issued bond

이미 이행한 executed

이미지광고 image advertising

이미지메이커 image maker

이미지보드 image board

이미지셋터 image setter

이미지전략 image strategy

이미지조사 image research

이미지프로질 image profile

이미지형식 image formation
이보증(裏保證) guarantee in favor of the primary guarantor
이부금융채 coupon bank debenture
이분법 dichotomy
이분변수 dichotomous variable
1/2 후생보험 half tax
이분질문법 dichotomous question
이불기일 coupon payment date
이븐베일스스와프 even bails swap
이사, 임원 director
이사회 board of directors; corporate board of directors
이사회결의 corporate resolution
이산(離散)시간형 discrete time
이산변수 discrete variable
이상성장모델 abnormal growth model
이상손실 unusual loss
이상손익항목 unusual profit or loss item
이상손해재보험 catastrophe reinsurance
이상손해준비금 catastrophe reserve
이상수익 abnormal returns
이상위험준비금 contingency reserve; reverse for extraordinary casualties; unsual casualty reserve; unusual risks reserve
이상적인 밸런스 idle balance
이상표준원가 ideal standard cost
이상항목 abnormal item; extra item; unusual item
이서 backing; endorsement; indorsement
이서금지 prohibition of endorsement
이서금지어음 nonnegotiable bill
이서금지이서 nonnegotiable endorsement
이서된 endorsed
이서보증 guarantee by endorsement
이서수수료 endorsement fee
이서양도 endorsement for transfer; transfer of endorsed note
이서양도어음 note endorsed; notes endorsed for payment
이서어음 endorsed bill; endorsed note; indorsed note; notes and bills endorsed
이서연속 succession of endorsement
이서인 endorsers; indoser
이서채권 endorsed bond
이송데포 transfer depot
이송명령 certiorari
이송신청기록 record on removal
이송영장청구소장 bill of certiorari
이순위보험금수취인 secondary beneficiary
24시간거래시장 round-the-clock market
EC공동플로팅 EC joint floating system
이업종간경쟁 intertype competition
이연 deferred delivery
이연계약 carrying-over contract
이연계정 deferred account; deferred item
이연대변항목 deferred debit; deterred credit
이연법인세채무 deferred income tax liability
이연보수비용 deferred compensation
이연부채 deferred liabilities
이연불입채권 deferred payment note
이연비용 deferred charge; deferred charges; deferred expenses
이연비용계정 deferred charge account
이연상각 deferred depreciation
이연소득세채무 estimated future income taxes
이연손실 loss carryback
이연수선비 deferred repairs
이연수익 deferred income; deferred revenue; income received but unearned
이연연금 deferred annuity
이연이자표 extended coupon
이연자산 deferred assets; preoperating cost and similar deferrals
이연자산상각특례 exception to amortization of deferred charge
이연지출 deferred expenditure
이연채권 deferred bond
이연판매수수료 back-end load
이연하는, 연기하는 noncallable
이용가능자산 available assets

이용가능채권 available bond
이용도 availability
이용원가 utilized cost
이원배치 two-way layout
이월 carried forward; carry forward
이월가액 carrying value
이월결손금 net loss carried forward
이월계산표 post-closing trial balance
이월기장 opening entry
이월보전차압 advance preservative seizure
이월사용 carryover of expense
이월손익 profit and loss carried forward
이월이익잉여금 net earned surplus forwarded
이월이자; 재산보유비용 carrying charge
이월자산상각 amortization of deferred assets
이월재해손실 casualty losses carried over
이월지분 carried interest
이월평균단가불출법 month-end average
    method
이월하다 bring forward
이위계약 nonconcurrent policies
이위성(異位性) nonconcurrency
이유개시명령 rule to show cause
이윤극대화 profit maximization
이윤동기 profit motive
이윤분배신탁 profit-sharing trust
이윤원리형 투자함수 investment function of
    profit principle type
이윤인플레이션 profit inflation
이윤증권 profit-sharing securities
이율 earnings yield
이율곡선리스크 yield curve risk
이율곡선평준화 flattening of the yield curve
이율보증계약 guaranteed interest contract
이율비 yield rate
이율입찰 yield auction
이의 demurrer to evidence; objection
이의결정 decision on request for
    reinvestigation
이의신청 adverse claim; protestation
이의심리청 reinvestigation organization

이의제기 request for reinvestigation
이익 income; investment return; profit
이익 및 수수료담보양식 profit and
    commissions form
이익감소 profit slide
이익개선 pick-up of yield
이익개선스위치 yield improvement switch
이익격차 difference in yield; yield
    differential; yield spread
이익계정 profit account
이익계획 profit planning
이익곡선 profit curve
이익관리 profit control; profit management
이익구매 buying on an yield basis
이익구조 yield structure
이익금 대 배당비율 ratio of earnings to
    dividends
이익누적형 투신 contractual accumulation
    plan
이익도표 profit chart; profit control chart
이익률 margin ratios; profit ratio
이익률저하 slimmer profit margins
이익반환 profit commission
이익방정식 profit equation
이익배당 distribution of profits
이익배당부 연금 participating premium;
    participating annuity
이익배당세 tax on dividend
이익배당주 participating stock
이익배당준비금 bonus reserve
이익보험 loss of profits insurance; profit
    insurance
이익보험증권 policy proof of interest
이익분배(제) profit-sharing
이익분배계획 bonus scheme
이익분배사채 profit-sharing bond
이익분배제도 profit-sharing system
이익분배채 income share note
이익성장률 profit growth rate
이익수수료 contingent commission
이익수준 yield standard

이익신장 profit growth
이익실현 income realization
이익에 반하는 공술 declaration against interest
이익여잉금계산서 statement of retained earnings
이익요인 yield factor
이익을 계상하다 record a profit
이익을 더하다, 가격을 인상하다 mark up
이익을 재투자함 plowing-back
이익의 시계열변동 time series behavior of earnings
이익의 질 quality of earnings
이익이 같이 변동함 co-movement of earnings
이익잉여금 accumulated earnings; accumulated surplus; dividend declared; earned surplus; earnings retained in business; reinvested earnings; retained earnings
이익잉여금계산금 earned surplus statement
이익잉여금으로 대체함 addition to retained earnings
이익적립금을 자본편입함 capitalization of accumulated earnings
이익준비금 earned surplus reserve
이익참가사채 participating bond
이익책임 profit responsibility
이익처분 appropriation of profit; distribution of net profit
이익처분계정 appropriation account
이익처분부문 appropriation section
이익처분에 따른 사외유출액 amount paid out lo the outside distribution of net profit
이익평준화 income leveling; leveling of income
이익표 yield book
이익할당 profit quota
이익함수 profit function
이익회수 repatriation
이입(移入) import for manufacturing

이자금융채 interest-bearing bank debenture
이자기산일 dated date
이자단위 minimum denomination on which interest is calculated
이자락 ex-interest
이자력 force of interest
이자배당 dividend on interest
이자법 interest method
이자부 interest bearing
이자부 어음 interest bill
이자부 최고한도 maximum limit for interest rate
이자부담 interest burden
이자부담배율 times-interest earned; times-interest earned ratio
이자부부채 interest-bearing debt
이자부증권 interest-bearing security
이자부채 interest-bearing bond
이자부채권 active bond
이자비용 interest cost; interest cover
이자세 interest tax
이자소득 interest income
이자소득으로 귀속됨 real obtainer of interest income
이자에 대한 이자 interest on interest
이자율변화 interest rate change
이자율체계 system of interest rates
이자인상 interest rate raise
이자일괄불 이자부금융채 debenture with lump-sum payment at maturity
이자적립 accumulations
이자제한법 law of a maximum interest rate; usury law
이자지불 coupon payment; interest payment
이자지불방법 interest payment method
이자클레임 interest claims
이자평가이론 interest rate parity theory; interestrate parity theory
이자표 coupon; cuttings
이자표가 떨어진 coupon off
이자표가 붙은 coupon on

이자표부 cum coupon
이전 alienation; removal; remove
이전가격세제 transfer pricing taxation
이전가격조작 transfer pricing
이전가능한 alienable
이전경비 transfer expenditure
이전등기 registration of transfer
이전료 expenses incurred for having the user
    remove
이전소득 transfer income
이전의 preceding
이전의 자유 freedom of movement
이전지출 transfer payment
이전효과 transfer effect
이중가격 double price
이중가격표시 dual pricing
이중경제 dual economy
이중경제구조 economic dualism
이중계산 double counting
이중계약주의 duplex system
이중계정거래 dual trading
이중과세 double taxation; duplicate taxation
이중과세방지조약 convention for the
    avoidance of double taxation
이중구조 dual structure
이중구조시장 two tier market
이중금리정책 dual interest policy
이중급부배제 nonduplication of benefits
이중만기 double dated
이중면제채 double exemption bond
이중목적 dual purpose
이중바닥 double bottom
이중보증의 double barreled
이중부채 double liability
이중분배 double distribution
이중상장 dual listing
이중성 duality
이중세율제 double tariff
이중옵션 dual option
이중용량 dual capacity
이중운임제 dual rate system

이중은행제도 dual banking system
이중의 위험 double jeopardy
이중이익의 double dipping
이중이자 double account interests
이중차압 double attachment; double seizure
이중천장 double peak
이중추출법 double sampling
이중탈퇴잔존표 double decremental table
이중통화기준 dual currency
이중통화기준채 dual currency bond
이중환시장 dual exchange market
이질수요 heterogeneous demand
이질시장 heterogeneous market
이질적인 경쟁 heterogeneous competition
이질적인 과점 heterogeneous oligopoly
이차계획서 quadratic programing
이차납세의무 secondary tax liability
이차데이터 secondary data
이차동인 secondary drive
이차보이콧 secondary boycott
이차보험 excess insurance
이차부동산이전행위 secondary conveyance
이차부채 secondary liability; secondary rally
이차분매 secondary distribution
이차비용함수 quadratic cost function
이차사정비 unallocated claim expense
이차산업 secondary industry
이차손실함수 quadratic loss function
이차수요함수 quadratic demand function
이차온라인 second generation on-line system
이차익 interest surplus
이차자극 secondary stimulus
이차재원에서 급여를 지급함 salary from
    secondary source
이차저당 second mortgage
이차저당금융 secondary financing
이차적인 증거 secondary evidence
이차적인요구 secondary needs
이차집단 secondary group
이차차압 second-distress
이차초과액특약 second surplus treaty

이차트렌드 secondary trend
이출(移出) export to an overseas territory
이출과세 taxation on shipment
이퀄라이저 equalizer
이타주의 altruistic
이탈 departure
이폭 profit margin
이표락 ex-coupon
이표채; 이자부채권 coupon bond
이항계수 binomial coefficient
이항목방식 two-item form
이항분포모델 binomial model
이항전개 binomial expansion
이해가 충돌함 conflict of interest
이해관계 concern
이해관계가 없는 disinterested
이해관계가 없는 사람 disinterested party
이해관계가 없는 증인 disinterested witness
이해관계자 interested party; stakeholder
이행보증 performance guarantee
이행보증보험 performance bond insurance
이행보증증권 performance bond
이행불능 impossibility of performance
이행증거금 performance guarantee deposit
익금불산입 exclusion from gross revenue
익금산입 inclusion in gross revenue
익금처분 distribution of surplus
익명광고 blind advertisement
익명의 blind
익명입찰 blind bidding
익명조합 anony mous association; dormant partnership; secret partnership
익명참가 silent participation
익명참가베이스 silent base
익명참가자 silent partner
익스텐더블채권 extendible debt security
익스텔카드 extel card
익스포저 exposure
익영업일인도 regular settlement
익월물 overmonth loan
익월인도 over-the-month delivery; value next month

익월일부조건 proximo terms
익일물레포 overnight repo
익일반제 overnight
익일불대부 overnight money
익일인도 overnight delivery; value tomorrow
익일자금화 자금 next day fund
익일차입, 삼일후 반제 tomorrow-next
인가장 corporate charter
인가조합 approved society
인간공학 human engineering
인간관계 human relations
인간의 생명가치 human life value
인감 seal impression
인감조회 verification of a seal impression
인감증명서 certificate of seal impression
인건비 employment cost; personal expenses
인건비율 ratio of personnel expenses
인격특성 personality trait
인계 assume
인계부채 assumed liability
인계자산을 과대평가함 overestimation of inherited assets
인공생명 artificial life
인공지능 artificial intelligence
인공환경 artificial environment
인과관계 causal relationship; causality
인과분석 causal analysis
인과패스분석 causal path analysis
인구구성 population composition
인구동태통계 vital statistics
인구밀도 population density
인구통계 demographic statistics
인구통계적인 요인 demographic factors
인근의 adjacent
인기50문제 nifty fifty
인기가 높을 때 팔고 낮을 때 삼 trade against the trend
인기가 떨어진 물건 wall flower
인기주 active stock; popular stock
인기증권 hot issue

인더스트리얼다이나믹스 industrial dynamics
인덱스옵션 index option
인덱스채 index linked bond
인덱스채권 index bond
인덱스파티시페이션 index participation
인덱스펀드 index fund
인덴처수탁인 indenture trustee
인도 delivery
인도가격 delivered price; delivery price
인도감시 monitoring of delivery
인도결제 delivery settlement
인도기준 delivery basis
인도리스크 settlement risk
인도불이행 nondelivery
인도일 settlement day
인도장소 place of delivery
인도재보험 cede back
인도적격상표 deliverable issue
인도조건 terms of delivery
인도최적채권 most deliverable bond
인도필 delivered
인도하다 bring over
인두세 capitation tax; head money; head tax; poll tax
인디케이션방식 indication method
인명계정 personal account
인명부 name list; roll; roster
인명원장 personal ledger
인물평가법 personality inventory
인바스켓방법 in-basket method
인베스터즈릴레이션즈 investors relations
인벤토리리세션 inventory recession
인보이스방식 invoice method
인사감사 personnel audit
인사고과 employee evaluation; performance rating
인사관리 personnel management
인사부 personnel division
인사이더 insider
인사이더거래 insider trading
인사이동 personnel reshuffle

인사전략 personnel strategy
인서트편집 insert editing
인세 royalty on a book
인소싱 in-sourcing
인쇄매체 print media
인쇄물 printed matter
인쇄물을 철사로 엮는 방법 side stitching
인쇄판 machine plate
인쇄프로세스컬러 cyan magenta yellow black
인수 honor
인수간사단 management group
인수거절 dishonor
인수계약서 underwriting agreement
인수계정 accounts to receive
인수계정 대 재고자산비율 ratio of receivable to inventories
인수계정보험 accounts receivable insurance
인수계정회전율 turnover of receivables
인수과세 taxation at time of receipt from bonded area
인수금지물건 prohibited risks
인수단 syndicate; underwriting group
인수도 document against acceptance
인수된 어음 수취어음 acceptance receivable
인수매출 sale on an underwriting basis
인수모집수수료 gross spread
인수방식 acceptance system
인수불 payment against acceptance
인수사절 declination
인수수수료 acceptance commission; underwriting commission
인수슬립 acceptance slip
인수어음 trade acceptances payable
인수업무 business of underwriting; underwriting; underwriting business
인수업자 underwriter
인수업자간계약 agreement among underwriters
인수연도별 계산 policy year basis
인수인 acceptor

인수전문보험회사 distress carrier
인수조건부 신용공여 acceptance credit
인수증여 presentation for acceptance
인수통지 acceptance notice
인수필 자본금 capital stock subscribed
인수필 환어음 bill accepted
인수하다 underwrite
인수한도 acceptance line
인수한도액 limit of cover
인수한도표 line guide
인수회사 underwriting company; underwriting firm
인수후 상장 street price
인스토어머천다이징 instore merchandising
인식 knowledge
인식론적인 기준 epistemological criteria
인식종료 derecognition
인식할 수 있는 identifiable assets
인신의 자유 personal liberty
인앤드풋딜러 in-and-put dealer
인원계획 manpower plan
인자부하행렬 factor loadings matrix
인자분석 factor analysis
인재개발 human resources development
인재모집광고 placement advertisement
인재스카우트담당자 head hunter
인적 in gross
인적 약관 personal covenant
인적과세 personal taxation
인적과세제외 personal exclusion from taxation
인적담보 personal security
인적미디어 personal media
인적배상책임담보 bodily injury liability cover
인적상속재산 persona hereditament
인적소송 personal action
인적자원회계 human resources accounting
인적재산 effects; goods and chattels
인적판결 personal judgment
인적회계 manpower accounting

인접경험 adjacent experience
인접하다 abut
인정사업연도 constructive taxable year
인정상여 constructive bonus
인정생명보험사회(일본)인정생명보험사회 Chartered Life Underwriters in Japan
인정수입 constructive receipt
인정장치 certified equipment
인증 authentication
인증기관 certification body
인증등본 attested copy; certified copy; exemplification
인증마크 certification market
인증하다; 제시하다 adduce
인증행위 authentic act
인지 filiation; public acknowledgment; stamp
인지과학 cognitive science
인지납부 tax payment by stamp
인지된 가치 perceived value
인지된 리스크 perceived risk
인지명령 order of filiation
인지불협화음 recognitive dissonance
인지세 documentary stamp tax; stamp duty
인지수입 stamp revenue
인지자의 수익 neighborhood benefits
인지적인 판단 cognitive judgment
인질 hostage
인출 close of the session
인출플랜 withdrawal plan
인컴게인; 배당소득 income gain
인컴인헨서 income enhancer
인컴펀드 income fund
인코텀스 incoterms
인크리먼트카드 increment card
인터내셔널포트폴리오 international portfolio
인터넷 Internet
인터레스트스키밍 interest skimming
인터뱅크 상장 interbank rate
인터뱅크 환거래 inter-bank exchange transaction
인터뱅크론 interbank loan

인터뱅크장 inter-bank market
인텔리전트네트워크 intelligent network
인텔리전트빌딩 intelligent building
인텔샛; 국제상업통신위성기구 International
 Telecommunication Satellite Consortium
인포머셜 informercial
인포스트럭처 infostructure
인플레감응도 inflation-sensitivity factor
인플레갭 inflation gap
인플레격차 inflation differential
인플레공급곡선 inflationary supply curve
인플레기대 inflationary expectation
인플레머니 inflationary money supply
인플레수요곡선 inflationary demand curve
인플레억제 control of inflation; controlling
 inflation
인플레예비비 price contingency
인플레율 rate of inflation
인플레율이 상승함 pick-up of inflation rate
인플레이션 inflation
인플레이션헤징 hedging against inflation
인플레헤지주 stock for inflation hedging
인플레회계 inflation accounting
인핸스드그래픽어댑터; **EGA** enhanced
 graphics adapter
~일 현재 as at
일견하여 first blush
일계매매 day trading; daylight trading
일계표 blotter; daily account; daily trial
 balance
일관생산 integrated production; process
 production
일관성 consistency
일관수송 through transportation
일관회계 throughout accounting
일괄거래 package deal
일괄계약 contract in bulk
일괄구입 basket purchase; lump-sum
 purchase
일괄담보보험계약 block policy
일괄등록제도 block registration system

일괄매매 sale by bulk
일괄매매주문 all-or-none order
일괄매출 sale in gross
일괄매출; 블록오퍼 block offer
일괄반제리스크 crisis at maturity
일괄비례배분방식 proportional method
일괄상환 shelf redemption
일괄완제 pay-off
일괄운송 aggregated shipment
일괄원가 bunched cost
일괄전불 up front
일괄주문 blanket order; bulk order
일괄증권 master policy
일괄지불 lump-sum payment; single lump
 sum credit; single payment
일괄파일 batch file
일년 이상의 채권을 발행해서 확보한 차입금
 funded debt
일년기준 one year rule
일년당 per annum
일년이 안 되는 해 fractional year
일대비교법 semantic differential method
일드커브 yield curve
일드커브스와프 yield curve swap
일람 sight
일람불 payable at sight
일람불상장 sight selling rate
일람불신용장 sight letter of credit
일람불약속어음 note at sight; sight note
일람불어음 at sight bill; demand bill; draft at
 sight; presentation bill; sight draft
일람불어음; 송금수표 demand draft
일람불어음매입률 at sight buying rate
일람불환상장 sight rate
일람불환어음 sight bill
일람후 정기불환어음 time draft
일람후 지불 days after sight
일렬; 정렬; 배열 alignment
일류사채 prime corporate bonds
일류은행인수어음 prime bankers acceptance
일률적 uniform

일물일가(一物一價)의 법칙 law of indifference

일미금융협의 U.S. Japan financial talks

일미포괄협의 U.S. Japan framework talks

일반가격 prevailing price

일반간접비 general indirect cost; general overhead

일반감사 general audit

일반감세 general tax reduction

일반경비 general expenses

일반경비율 ratio of general expenses to current income

일반경쟁입찰 open bid; open tendering

일반고정자산자금 general fixed-assets fund

일반공채 general-obligation bonds

일반공채자금 general binded-debt fund

일반관리비 administrative expense; general and administrative expenses

일반관리비 및 판매비 general administrative and selling expenses

일반관리비예산 administrative expenses budget; administrative expenses variance; general administrative expenses budget

일반교서 state of the union message

일반담보계약 general security agreement

일반대차대조표 general balance sheet

일반대출 conventional loan

일반목적재무제표 general-purpose financial statements

일반무역조건 general terms and conditions of trade

일반문서 jacket

일반문언 general words

일반물가수준 general price level

일반물가수준회계 general price-level accounting

일반배상책임보험 general liability insurance

일반사업 general business

일반사업채 general corporate bond

일반손익 general corporate revenues and expenses

일반손해배상책임담보 public liability coverage

일반시장 general market

일반영업활동비 general operating expenses

일반예금 ordinary deposit

일반운송업; 공중전기통신사업자 common carrier

일반임금 prevailing wage; genera fund

일반자동차보험 basic automobile policy

일반재산세 general property tax

일반재원채 general obligation bond

일반적으로 공정타당하다고 인정하는 회계 기준 generally accepted accounting principle

일반적인 사회사 ordinary private company

일반적인 지불수단 general means of payment

일반정부부문 general government section

일반조건서 general conditions and terms of the contract

일반주택지 분양계획 general building scheme

일반차입결정 General Agreement to Borrow

일반채권자 unsecured creditor

일반투자가 individual investor

일반항목 common counts

일반현금 general cash

일반협정 general agreement

일반화물 genera cargo

일반회계 general account

일반회계세출 general account expenditure

일반회계원칙 general accounting principles

일반횡선수표 general crossed check

일방적인 거래 unilateral transaction

일방적인 기록 unilateral record

일방적인 상황설명 earmuff problem

일방적인 재보험 nonreciprocal reinsurance

일본손해보험요율산정회 Fire and Marine Insurance Rating Association of Japan

일본은행계정 accounts of the Bank of Japan

일본은행권발행세 Bank of Japan note issue tax

일본은행법 Bank of Japan Act

일부 moiety

일부보험 under insurance; underinsurance

일부불입채권 partly paid bond

일부상장 first section market

일부양도 partial assignment

일부위탁 partial abandonment

일부이행 part performance

일부인도 partial delivery

일부인수 partial acceptance

일부준비제도 partial reserve system

일부증액반제 incidental increase payment

일부지급 partial payment; payment in part; payment on account

일순위 보험금수취인 primary beneficiary

일시귀휴 temporary leave from work

일시금 money paid temporarily; single sum

일시대부금 temporary loan

일시불거치연금 single premium deferred annuities

일시불보험료 single premium

일시불연금 lump-sum pension

일시불유가증권 nonamortizable securities

일시불입 payment in lump sum

일시불종신보험 single premium

일시불형 bullet

일시사용 temporary use

일시소득 occasional income

일시소득특별공제 occasional income deduction; special deduction for occasional income

일시이직 temporary layoff

일시입체 temporary advance

일시적인 transitory

일시적인 가격설정 provisional rating

일시적인 반등 brief rally; short-lined rally; temporary rally

일시적인 자산대부 temporary loan on property

일시적인 호황 temporary boom

일시지불 single payment annuity

일시차입금 flooring debt; temporary borrowing

일시차입어음 deficiency bill

일시투자 temporary investment

일용잡화, 식료품 convenience goods

일은신용 Bank of Japan credit

일인당 per capita

일인당 국민총생산 per capita gross national product

일인당 상여 bonus paid per employee

일인당 세율 per capita rate

일인회사 one-man company

일일계약 one day contract

일일고용노무자건강보험 daily workers insurance

일일당 per diem; per-diem allowance

일일잔고 daily balance

일일차트 daily chart

일임신탁 discretionary trust

일임주문 discretionary order

일정 기일이 있는 bearing date

일정가격차에 따른 조합주문 contingent order

일정기한지불 single-order term

일정세율 fixed tax rate

일정한 연속복리 constant continuously compounded

일정형 모델 constant model

일주간지불 weekly payment

일주당 배당금 dividend per share

일주당 수익성장률 earnings growth ratio per share

일주당 수치 per share data

일주당 순익 earning per share

일주당 순자산 net asset worth per share; net asset per share

일주당 이익 profit per share

일주주주 one share shareholder

일중독 workaholism

일직수당 day duty allowance

일차계정 primary account

일차데이터 primary data
일차부채 primary liability
일차분매 primary distributions
일차산업 primary industry
일차산품 primary goods
일차산품생산국기구 organizations of primary commodity producers
일차산품수출 primary industry product export
일차손해보험 first risk policy
일차자극 primary stimuli
일차자본 primary capital
일차적인 부동산이동행위 primary advance
일차준비자산 primary reserve assets
일차체감약관 daily diminishing clause
일차초과액특약 first surplus treaty
일차평가 initial par value
일치 accordance; consensus
일치계열 coincident series
일치시키다 match
일치지수 coincident indicator
일품당 매가 selling price per unit
일할반환보험료 daily pro-rata return of premium
일회불대부 single payment loan
일회성 고객 one shot customer
일회용 제품 throwaway product
임검 official inspection
임계위험 criticality hazard
임계질량 critical mass
임계치 critical point
임금 salaries and wages
임금격차 wage disparity
임금계정 labor account
임금공제 payroll deduction
임금급료지불부 pay-roll register
임금단위 wage unit
임금동결 pay pause; pay-freeze; wage freeze
임금물가 가이드라인 wage-price guideline
임금물가통제 wage-price control
임금상승률 rate of wage increase
임금생활자 wage earner

임금세 payroll tax
임금소득 wage income
임금수준 wage level
임금원장 wages ledger
임금인상 wage increase
임금인플레이션 wage-push inflation
임금차이 wage variance
임금체계 wage structure
임금컷 wage cut
임금투쟁 wage-hike drive
임금하청대금지불보증증권 labor & material payment bond
임금협정 wage contract
임대가격 rental value
임대료 house-rent income; rental
임대료 및 사용료수입 rents and royalties
임대료수입 rent income
임대법 house-rent law
임대보증증권 lease bond
임대업 rental service
임대인 lessor
임대차계약보증증권 lease contract bond
임료 ancient rent
임률차이 labor rate variance
임률표준 labor rate standard
임무완료 functus officio
임상요구 request for wage increase
임시결의 extraordinary resolution
임시계정 temporary account
임시금리조정법 Temporary Money Rates Adjustment Law
임시금지명령 temporary injunction
임시급여협정 annual bonus agreement
임시비 contingent outlay; emergency funds; extra expenditure; extraordinary expenses
임시비용보험 extra expense insurance; increase in cost of working insurance
임시생계비보험 additional living expense insurance
임시세리사 temporary tax accountan
임시소득 extraordinary income; temporary

income
임시손익 unusual gains or losses
임시손익항목 nonrecurrent item
임시수선비 extraordinary repairs
임시수입 perquisite
임시의 ad hoc; ad interim
임시의; 중간의 interim
임시이익 nonrecurring profit
임시자산손실 unexpected property loss
임시지출 casual expenses
임신출산보험 maternity insurance
임원급료 officer's salary
임원배상책임보험 directors and officers liability insurance
임원보수 compensation paid to directors; director's salaries and remuneration; executive salaries; officer's compensation
임원보장을 위한 옵션 executive compensation option
임원상여 bonus paid to director
임원상여금 officer's bonus
임원채무면제 cancellation of debts of directors
임원퇴직금 officers retiring allowance
임원퇴직급여금 director's retirement allowance
임율 wage rate
임의감사 voluntary audit
임의규정 adoptive provisions
임의급여 ex gratia payment
임의납세지 voluntary place of tax payment
임의로 ex proprio motu
임의법 adoptive act
임의보험 voluntary insurance
임의비용 discretionary expenses
임의상각 voluntary depreciation
임의상각법 voluntary depreciation method
임의상환 optional redemption
임의상환이익 yield to call
임의상환조항 call provision
임의상환채권 callable bond

임의의; 약인없이 voluntary
임의인도 free payment
임의재보험 facultative reinsurance
임의재보험협정 facultative reinsurance agreement
임의재판보증증권 optional court bond
임의정리 voluntary liquidation
임의조합 voluntary partnership
임의준비금 voluntary reserve
임의진술 gratis dictum
임의출두 gratis appearance
임의출자재보험 semi-facultative reinsurance
임의편입액 voluntary additions
임의해산 voluntary dissolution; voluntary winding
임의해약 optional cancellation
임의형 계속투자플랜 voluntary accumulation plan
임점검사 field examinations
임차권 right of lease
임차권; 리스 lease
임차권보험 leasehold interest insurance
임차권이권 working interest
임차료지불능력 rent-paying capacity
임차부동산 leasehold estate
임차수수료 rental agents' commissions
임차인 lessee
임차지 leased land
임팩트론 impact loan
임팩트프린터 impact printer
임퓨테이션방식 imputation method
임플라이드선도금리 implied forward rates
입고 warehousing
입국 entrance to korea
입국세 alien tax; landing tax
입금 money received
입금예정의 공백을 메우기 위해 받는 융자 bridge finance; interim loan
입금예측액 prospective cash receipts
입금전표 paying in slip; receipt slip; receive slip

입금취소 charge back
입금통지 advice of credit
입금표 credit slip
입막음돈, 무마비 hush-money
입법기관제정법 legislative act
입법취지 mens legislatoris
입원비보험 hospital expense insurance
입으로 전해지는 소문 word of mouth
입장가액 entry value
입장세 tax on admission
입장세법 admission tax law
입장자수 admissions
입증책임 burden of proof; onus of proof
입증할 수 있는 채권 provable debt
입지정책 location policy
입찰 bidding
입찰; 매긴 값 bid
입찰공고 advertisement for bid
입찰발행 issue by tender
입찰보증보험 bit guarantee insurance
입찰보증증권 bid bond
입찰서 form of bid
입찰약관 tender clause
입찰인수; 견적사양서 tender
입찰자 bidder
입찰자에 대한 지시서 instruction to bidders
입찰증권 tender security
입체경비 reimbursed expenses
입체금 advance money
입체지불 charges forward
입퇴료 compensation for eviction
입항비용 expenses of entering port
입항세 harbor dues; port dues
입회 attendance

입회금 entrance fee; initiation fee
입회시간 market hours; session period
입회심사 examination of entrance
    qualification
입회장 arena
입회장상표 floor issue
입회장에서 거래할 수 있는 회원 physical
    access member
입회정지 suspension of transactions
입회죄종가격(거래소에서의)입회죄종가격
    closing quotation
입회지 commons
잉여가치 surplus value
잉여금 surplus; surplus funds
잉여금거래 surplus transaction
잉여금결합계산서 statement of income and
    retained earnings
잉여금계산서 statement of surplus; surplus
    statement
잉여금계정 surplus account
잉여금구분 surplus section
잉여금구분의 원칙 principle of surplus section
잉여금부과 surplus charge
잉여금분석 surplus analysis
잉여금수정 surplus adjustment
잉여금조정 adjustment of surplus
잉여금조정서 reconciliation of surplus
잉여금처분계산서 surplus appropriation
    statement
잉여익금 surplus profit
잉여인슈런스 surplus insurance
잉여적립금 surplus reserves
잉크젯프린터 ink jet printer

ㅈ

자가매체 house media
자가배달; 자가인도 alongside delivery
자가보험 private insurance; self-insurance
자가보험기금 self-insurance fund
자가보험제도 self-insurance plan
자가보험준비금 reserve for self-insurance;
 self-insurance reserve
자가보험취급기관 association captive
자가브랜드; 프라이베이트브랜드 private
 brand
자가소비 self-consumption
자가영업소득 self-employment income
자가용 자동차보험 private automobile policy
자가용자동차종합보험 special automobile
 policy
자가운용 internal investment management
자격기준 qualification criteria
자격법 qualification laws
자격을 빼앗다 disqualify
자격이 있는; 관할권이 있는 competent
자격제도 special status system
자고자산 inventory assets
자국 nostro
자국내 on-shore
자국통화 domestic currency; home currency
자국통화유통 rate in home currency
자국환매입외국환 home currency bill bought
자극된 수유 stimulated demand
자극판매 stimulatory marketing
자극하다 boosting
자금 중의 자금 fund of funds

자금결제 fund settlement
자금계정 fund account
자금공급 supply of investible funds
자금과부족 financial surplus or deficit
자금관련스와프 fund swap
자금대차대조표 fund balance sheet
자금대체서비스 fund transfer service
자금부족 financial deficit; fund shortage;
 funding; shortage of funds
자금부채 fund obligation
자금사용 use of funds
자금상환업무 capital redemption
자금세정 money laundering
자금수요 demand for fund
자금수지표 statement of cash flow
자금순환 money flow
자금순환계정 flow of fund account
자금순환분석 flow of funds analysis
자금순환표 money-flow tables
자금운영 fund management
자금운용부 trust fund bureau
자금운용수단 fund management method
자금운용표 application of funds statement;
 cash flow statement; fund statement;
 statement of source and application of funds
자금원 source of funds
자금의 장래흐름 future cash flows
자금이 딸림 tightness of money
자금이 크게 팽창된 overfunded
자금이동 movement of funds; transfer of fund
자금이전 fund transfer

자금인출 draw down
자금잉여금 fund surplus
자금재조달 refinancing; refunding
자금조달 financing; funding; raising of funds
자금조달력 fund raising capacity
자금조달방법 financing method
자금조달업무 fund raising business
자금조달코스트 cost of raising funds; fund cost
자금조작 exchange funds operation
자금조정거래 exchange fund cover
자금조정법 financing adjustment law; financing regulation law
자금조표 statement of cash receipts and disbursement
자금포지션 fund position
자금풀법 pool of fund approach
자금화 자금 good value
자금회계 fund accounting
자금회전율 turnover of funds
자금효율 leverage
자금흡수력 fund absorption
자기개념 self-concept
자기계정 own account
자기계정매매 proprietary trading
자기계정매매익 investment profit
자기고유의 sui generis
자기금융비율 self-finance ratio
자기매매 dealing; transaction on a dealer basis
자기부인 voluntary adjustment
자기사정 one's own convenience
자기생산에 관련된 고정자산 self-produced fixed assets
자기시고 self-assessment; self-return
자기신고납부제도 self-assessment system
자기신고제 self-return system
자기실현 self-actualization
자기앞수표 self-addressed check
자기에게 이익이 되는 공술 self-serving declaration

자기융자 financing from brokers' own capital
자기의견 personal opinion
자기자본 equity capital; net worth equity capital; own capital; owned capital
자기자본규제 capital requirement
자기자본대용 trading on equity
자기자본부가 equity at book value
자기자본비율 capital ratio; equity ratio; owner's equity to total assets; ratio of net worth to total capital; self-owned capital ratio
자기자본비율규제 capital adequacy requirements
자기자본성장률 equity growth rate
자기자본시가 equity at market value
자기자본이익률 earnings on; net profit to net worth; percentage of profits available on net worth
자기자본합계 total net worth
자기자본회전율 turnovers of net worth
자기자신의 pro se
자기잠식현상 cannibalization
자기정산의 self-liquidating
자기제조에 관련된 재고자산 self-produced inventories
자기주 treasury stock
자기주식 common stock for treasury
자기파산 voluntary bankruptcy
자기회귀모델 autoregressive model
자동가치증가보험약관 automatic increased value clause
자동결제 automatic settlement
자동결제기구 automated clearinghouse
자동계속정기예금 automatic renewal time deposit
자동계속제도 automatic renewal system
자동고객계정대체 automated customer account transfer
자동대체계좌 automatic transfer account
자동대체서비스 automatic transfer service
자동성 automaticity

자동안정장치 built-in stabilizer
자동예금수납기 automated teller machine
자동예약서비스 automated reservation service
자동인가방식 automatic approval system
자동정지 automatic stay
자동증액소아보험 jumping juvenile
자동증액연금 automatic increasing annuity
자동집금(集金)서비스 automatic collection service
자동차론 저당증서 certificate of automobile receivables
자동차배상책임보험 motor third party insurance
자동차보험 automobile insurance; motor insurance
자동차보험요율산정회(일본)자동차보험요율산정회 Automobile Insurance Rating Association of Japan
자동차세 auto tax; automobile tax
자동차손해배상책임보험심의회 Compulsory Automobile Liability Insurance Council
자동차손해배상책임보험 automobile liability insurance
자동차손해배상책임보험증명서 automobile liability insurance certificate
자동차수리비지수 automobile repair costs index
자동차승객보험 motor vehicle passenger insurance
자동차연맹 Automobile Association
자동차운전자 손해배상책임보험; 드라이버보험 automobile drivers' liability insurance
자동차종합보험 package automobile policy
자동차중량세 automobile tonnage tax
자동차차량보험 motor hull insurance
자동차취득세 automobile acquisition tax
자동차판매금융 automobile sales finance
자동차판매대수 auto sales
자동차포괄손해배상책임보험 automobile comprehensive liability policy

자동치하락 automatic markdown
자력보증 financial guarantee
자력으로 되찾음 recaption
자력집행권 self-enforcement
자립성장 self-maintaining growth
자매출판물 sister publications
자매회사 sister company
자문위원회 advisory committee
자발적 항목 autonomous item
자발적이 아닌 involuntary
자발적인 실업 voluntary unemployment
자발적인 저축 voluntary saving
자발적인 조직 voluntary association
자백 confession
자본 capital
자본 대 산출고비율 capital-output ratio
자본가 capitalist
자본가계급 capitalist bracket
자본가동률 capital working rate
자본감모준비 capital consumption allowance
자본거래 capital transaction
자본거래자유화 liberalization of capital transactions
자본거출 capital contribution
자본경영분리 separation between capital and administration
자본계수 capital coefficient; capital account; capital balance; capital stock account; stock account
자본계정지출 expenditure on capital accounts
자본고정비율 net worth to fixed capital
자본고정자산비율 worth and fixed assets ratio
자본공급국 capital supplier nation
자본과세 capital levy
자본구성 capital composition; capital structure; formal capitalization of reserves
자본구성비율 percentage of capital structure
자본금 stock capitalization
자본금구성 잉여금 capitalized surplus
자본금명세표 schedule of capital

ㅈ
ㅊ
ㅋ

자본금합계 total capital
자본금현재고 outstanding capital stock
자본도피 capital flight
자본등식 capital formula
자본배당 dividend from capital
자본부담비율 capital and liabilities ratio
자본부채 capital liabilities
자본부채비율 net worth to debts; worth debts ratio
자본비용 capital cost
자본생산성 capital productivity; productivity of capital
자본설비 capital equipment
자본설정표 capital-reconciliation statement
자본세 capital duty; capital stock tax; capital tax
자본소득 capital income
자본소비 capital consumption
자본소비를 조정함 capital consumption adjustment
자본수요 demand for capital
자본수입 capital import; capital receipt
자본수정 adjustment of capital; capital adjustment
자본수지 capital account balance
자본수출 capital export
자본수출국 country having deficit in cap transaction
자본스톡조정 capital stock adjustment
자본스톡조정원리 capital stock adjustment principle
자본시장 capital market
자본시장선 capital market line
자본예산 capital budget
자본유입 capital inflow
자본유지 maintenance of capital
자본유출 capital outflow
자본의 최저한도 minimum surplus
자본이윤 capital profit
자본이익률 profit ratio of capital; ratio of profit to capital

자본이자 capital interest
자본이자세 capital interest tax
자본이전 capital transfer
자본이전수단 medium of capital transfer
자본자산 capital assets
자본자산가격모델 capital asset pricing model
자본자유화 capital liberalization
자본장비율 capital equipment ratio
자본재 capital goods
자본절약을 위한 기술진보 capital saving technical progress
자본주계정 proprietary account; stockholder's
자본주의 capitalism
자본준비금 additional paid-in capital; capital in excess of par or stated value; capital reserve; capital surplus; capital surplus reserve
자본지출 capital disposition; capital expenditure; capital outlay
자본지출로 처리하는 개선 capital improvement
자본집약성이 낮은 산업 low capital intensive industry
자본집약적인 상품 capital-intensive merchandise
자본참가 capital participation; equity participation
자본축적 accumulation of capital
자본출자하다 take a capital stake in
자본코스트 cost of capital
자본투자 capital spending
자본편입 capitalization
자본한계효율표 schedule of the marginal efficiency of capital
자본형성 capital formation
자본형성; 자본수정 recapitalization
자본형성계정 capital formation account
자본환원율 capitalization rate
자본회수분석 payback analysis
자본회전율 capital turnover; turnover of capital; turnover rate of capital; turnover

ratio of capital

자사배송시스템 private delivery system

자사수요 company demand

자사제품 in-house product

자사주 company's own stock; corporation's own stock

자사주저가격구입권 incentive stock option

자사카드 own-named cards; proper card

자산 assets

자산가치 asset value

자산감가상각 depreciation on property

자산감정 appraisal of assets

자산갱신률 ratio of replacement

자산거래 transaction in assets

자산격차 assets differentials

자산결제 asset settlement

자산계획 estate planning

자산과 부채의 미스매치 mismatch between assets and liabilities

자산과 지분 assets and equities

자산교환 exchange of property

자산구성비율 percentage of each classification of assets to total assets

자산담보율 asset coverage

자산담보의 left-hand

자산담보증권 asset backed securities

자산대치 replacement of property

자산매각 asset sales

자산매입 asset acquisition

자산보유 holding of assets

자산부채종합관리 asset and liability management

자산부채증감법 net worth method

자산분배법 asset allocation technique

자산상실비 loss on property destroyed

자산상태 asset position

자산선택 portfolio selection

자산선택이론 theory of portfolio selection

자산선호 asset preference

자산세 tax on property

자산세그먼트 asset pool segment

자산소득 asset income; income from assets

자산소득의 세대합산과세 family taxation of assets income

자산소유 possession of property

자산소유비용 cost of carry

자산손실 loss on assets

자산양도 transfer of assets; transfer of property

자산양도익 gains from the transfer of property

자산운용자 money manager

자산운용투자 portfolio investment

자산을 개량함 improvement of the property

자산의 소실 extinguishment of property

자산이체 asset reshuffling

자산임대 lease of property

자산재평가 asset revaluation

자산재평가법 assets revaluation law

자산재평가세 asset revaluation tax; tax on the write-up

자산주 income stock

자산준비금 asset reserves

자산처분 disposition of assets

자산취득 acquirement of properties

자산취득원가 cost of assets

자산평가 valuation of assets

자산평가론 theory of asset valuation

자산평가손 loss on property revaluation

자산평가익 profit from valuation of assets

자산평가준비금 asset valuation reserve

자산폐기손 loss on property abandoned

자산할당방법 assets share method

자산화 단위 capitalization unit

자산화폐 assets money

자산활용 asset utilization

자산활용율 asset-utilization ratios

자산회계 asset accounting

자산회전율 asset turnover ratio; assets turnover

자산효과 assets effect

자서 sign manual

자선 philanthropy

ㅈ ㅊ ㅋ

자선기부금 charities and donations
자세히 조사함 detailed check; due diligence
자손사고보험 self-sustained personal accident
　insurance
자신에 대한 증거 self-regarding evidence
자신에게 불리한 증거 self-disserving
　evidence
자연경계 natural boundary
자연권 natural rights
자연발생적 분류 natural classification
자연발화 spontaneous combustion
자연법 law of nature; natural law
자연보험료 natural premium
자연사 death from natural causes
자연실업률 natural rate of unemployment
자연언어체계 natural language system
자연영업연도 natural business year
자연이자율 natural rate of interest
자연인 natural person
자연자본 natural capital
자연적 지지 natural support
자연적인 자유 natural liberty
자연적인 추정 natural presumption
자연증수 automatic increase in tax revenue
자연증식(이자)계정 accrual account
자연증식계정 accrual item; accrued account
자연증식자산 accrued assets
자연채무 moral obligation
자연회귀 return to nature
자영 self-management
자영업자 individual proprietor
자영업자 퇴직연금 Keogh Plan
자영의 self-employed
자원 resources
자원개발 tapping of resources
자원배분 resource allocation
자원재이용전략 recycle strategy
자유가격 free-price
자유경제 free economy
자유금리 deregulated interest rate
자유금리상품 deregulated interest rate

　product
자유기업제도 free enterprise system
자유도 degree of freedom
자유무역지대 free trade zone
자유반제시스템 free payment system
자유변동상장제 free floating exchange rates
　system
자유보유토지의 allodial
자유오퍼 free offer
자유요율 free rate
자유원계정 free won account
자유원예금 free won deposit
자유잉여금 free surplus
자유재량 discretion
자유주 free share
자유준비 free reserves
자유토지보유권 freehold
자유형상모델링 free form modeling
자유형상변형법 free form deformation
자유화규약 code of liberalization
자율반등 autonomously strong; technical
　rebound
자율성 autonomy
자익자본이익률 return on loll§.term liabilities
　plus equity capital
자재부 materials department
자재사용곡선 materials usage curve
자재소요량계획 material requirement
　program
자재요구계획 materials requirements
　planning
자주검사 self-inspection
자주결정 autonomic decision
자주관세 autonomous tariff
자주규제 self-regulation; self-restraint
자주규제계획 voluntary restraint program
자주규제금리 self-restraint interest
자주규제기관 self-regulatory organization;
　self-restraint agency
자주납부 voluntary tax payment
자주점유 hostile possession; occupancy

자체, 글꼴 letter form
자치 home rule
자필서명한 onomastic
자필증서 chirograph; holograph
자행유전스 own usance
자행인수 own bill
자형 계정 skeleton form account T
자회사 daughter company; offshoot; subsidiary; subsidiary company
자회사대부금 loan to subsidiary
자회사선수금 advance from controlled companies
작도법 visual curve-fitting method
작성; 발행 drawing
작성부인의 항변 nient le fait
작성자 maker
작성하다; 발행하다 draw
작업 work
작업가설 working hypothesis
작업능률 operation efficiency
작업문서 working document
작업비 operation expenses
작업손실 loss of work
작업시간 working hours
작업시간단축 working hour curtailment
작업시간차이 labor time variance
작업연구 work study
작업일수 working days
작업장 workshop
작업전표 job slip
작업조건 working condition
작업지도서 job order
작업지시서 work instruction
작업표 job ticket
작업표 production card
작은 가게 slightly firmer
작은 반대명제 sub-contrary
잔고 amount outstanding; remainder
잔고계정 balance account
잔고부족 insufficient funds
잔고시산표 trial balance of balances

잔고식 balance form
잔고장 balance book
잔고조정식 reconciling type
잔고조회 inquiry for the balances
잔무정리 winding-up of pending affairs
잔상 after image lag
잔액인수; 스탠드바이인수 standby agreement
잔업 overtime duties; overtime working
잔업수당 overtime allowance
잔업수당계정 account in arrears
잔여, 재방송할증요금 residual
잔여기간 time to expiration
잔여배분 residual share
잔여부분 residue
잔여순이익 residual net income
잔여원가 residual cost
잔여이익 residual profits
잔여재산 residual property; residuary estate
잔여재산분배 distribution of residual property
잔여재산여분 share of the residual property
잔여지분 residual equity
잔여지출 residuary outlay
잔여청구권 residual claim
잔존가격 residual value
잔존가액 scrap value
잔존계정 old account
잔존기간 remaining period; time to maturity
잔존내용연수 remaining useful life
잔존물 remnant
잔존물대위 subrogation arising out of salvage
잔존보험금액 sum insured left
잔존수입제한 residual quantitative import restriction
잔존원본 outstanding balances; outstanding principal
잔존율 residual ratio
잔지(殘地)보상금 compensation for residual land
잔차수익률 residual return
잔차표준편차 residual standard deviation

잔채 balances
잔채방식 charge on the declining balances
잔품 goods left
잔품; 팔다 남은 물건 frozen stock
잘라버림 write-down
잠재가격 shadow price
잠재고객 potential customer
잠재변수 latent variable
잠재수요 latent demand; potential demand
잠재실업 latent unemployment
잠재워런트 latent warrant
잠재의식광고 subliminal advertising
잠재이익 profit potential
잠재적인 가해 potential injury
잠재적인 경쟁 potential competition
잠재적인 존재 potential existence
잠재적인 콜옵션 latent call option
잠정세율 provisional tariff; rate of temporary duty; temporary tariff rate
잠정예산 provisional budget; tentative budget
잠정적 temporary
잠정적인 효력을 지니다 de bone esse
잠정청산인 provisional liquidator
잠정합의 tentative agreement
잡거빌딩 omnibus building
잡계정 sundry account
잡담 small talk
잡비 general merchandise; miscellaneous expenses; petty expenses; unclassified expenses
잡비내역장 petty expense analysis book
잡소득 miscellaneous income
잡손 casualty loss; miscellaneous losses
잡손공제 casualty loss deduction; deduction for casualty losses
잡손실을 이월공제함 carryover of casualty loss
잡손익 petty loss and profit
잡수익 miscellaneous revenue; other income; other revenues
잡수입 miscellaneous receipts; sundry income

잡익 miscellaneous gains
잡자산 miscellaneous assets
잡종보증증권 miscellaneous bond
잡종세 miscellaneous local taxes
잡화 sundry goods
장거리이동에 따른 재산처분 delivery of substitute property
장기공사를 인도함 delivery of long-term contract work
장기구입 long-term buying
장기국채 long-term government bond
장기균형 long-run equilibrium
장기금리 long-term interest rate
장기금융 long-term finance
장기금융시장 long-term money market
장기대부금 long-term loan receivable
장기보유전략 buy and hold strategy
장기부채 캐시플로비율 cash flow ratio to long-term liabilities
장기부채반제액 current maturities of long-term debt
장기부채순고정자산 net tangible asset ratio to long-term debt
장기부채자기자본비율 equity capital ratio to long-term liabilities
장기부채자기자본율 equity capital ratio to long-term capital
장기사업 long-term business
장기선도거래 long-dated forwards
장기신용 long-term credit
장기신용금융기관 financial institutions for long-term credit
장기양도소득 long-term capital gains
장기어음 long-dated bill; long-term bill
장기연기채권 long-term suspended claims
장기외화유통채권 long-term accounts receivable foreign currency
장기외화유통채무 long-term accounts payable in foreign currency
장기이율 long term yield
장기임금협정 long-term wage agreement

장기임대계약예금 deposits on long-term leases
장기임대차계약 long term lease
장기자금 long-term fund
장기자본 long-term capital
장기자본거래 long-term capital transaction
장기자본수지 long-term capital balance
장기적인 경제성장 secular economic growth
장기종합보험 long-term comprehensive insurance
장기지불능력 long-term solvency
장기차입금 long-term borrowing; long-term loan payable
장기차입반제액 reductions in long-term debt
장기차입에서의 자금증가 proceeds from long-term debt
장기채 long-term bond
장기채무 long-term debt; noncurrent liabilities
장기채무증가 long-term debt assumed
장기채차환예정증권 bond anticipation notes
장기청부공사 long-term contract
장기투자 long-term investment
장기파동 long waves
장기프라임레이트 long-term prime rate
장기환 long exchange
장기환예약 long-term forward exchange agreement
장내 inside the room
장내교통 store traffic
장내방송 storecasting
장내방송장치 public address
장래가치 future value
장래권 executory interest
장래근무수당 future service pension
장래근무연금 future service benefits
장래법 prospective method
장래의 고유리스크 future specific risk
장래의 근속실적 future service credits
장래이자율 forward interest rate
장려 incentive

장려효과 incentive effect
장르 genre
장문식 보고서 long-form report
장문식감사보고서 detailed audit report
장부 accountbook; book
장부가격 book value
장부가격감소 decrease in book value
장부계 book-keeper
장부관리 run the book
장부기입 book entry; booking
장부기재가격 stated value
장부를 마감하다 close
장부방식 account method
장부서류를 정리하고 보존함 maintenance of books and records
장부열람 access to books
장부외자산 asset out of books; nonconcealed assets
장부외채무 liabilities off the book
장부원가 recorded cost
장부위조 cooking of a book
장부잔고 book balance
장부재고 book inventory
장부정리 adjustment of accounts
장부화폐 book money
장소에 어울리지 않는 사람 outsider
장애인공제 deduction for physically handicapped person
장애자공제 credit for handicapped person; exemption for handicapped person; physically handicapped person allowance
장외거래 curb dealings; outside dealing; over-the-counter transaction; trading on the over-the-counter market
장외거래시장 third market
장외거래점 bucket shop
장외등록기업 OTC company
장외매매고 volume of over-the-counter transaction
장외시세 quotation of over-the-counter issue
장외시장 curb market; off-board market;

over-the-counter market
장외옵션 over-the-counter option
장외주 over-the-counter stock
장외중매인 street broker
장외증권 unlisted securities
장외통화옵션 over-the-counter currency
　option
장중기금리 long and medium-term interest
　rate
장치, 설비 device
장표관리 forms control
장해보상 disablement benefit
재(財) goods
재개발 redevelopment
재건 reorganization
재건계획 reorganization scheme
재건계획결정 decision of a reorganization
　scheme
재결서 written decision
재고; 현재의 수량 amount on hand goods in
　stock
재고금융 inventory financing
재고단위 inventory unit
재고량 volume of inventories
재고를 줄임 destocking
재고모델 inventory model
재고변동 inventory change
재고보충 replenishment of stock
재고손 inventory loss
재고순환 inventory cycles
재고율 inventory shipments ratio;
　inventory-sales ratio; stock-to-sales ratio
재고자산 inventory; inventory capital
재고자산계산법 inventory method
재고자산보관 storage of inventories
재고자산의 범위 composition of inventory
재고자산의 시가 market value of inventory
재고자산이익 inventory profit
재고자산증감 inventory variation
재고자산취득가액 acquisition cost of
　inventory

재고자산평가 inventory valuation
재고자산평가방법 cost flow assumption;
　inventory valuation method
재고자산평가준비금 inventory reserve;
　inventory valuation reserves
재고자산평가하락 decline in prices of
　inventories
재고자산회계 accounting for inventories
재고자산회전율 inventory turnover
재고정리 inventory control
재고정리자산감사 inventory audit
재고정리자산매상률 sales to inventories
재고정리자산회전일수 number of days' sales
　in inventories
재고조사법 retail inventory method
재고조정 inventory adjustment
재고조회 checking inventory
재고증명서 inventory certificate
재고채권 bond inventory
재고투자 inventory investment
재고평가액 inventory value
재고평가조정 inventory valuation adjustment
재고표 inventory sheet; inventory tag;
재고품 clearance goods; stock ill the
　inventory
재고품대장; 주식대장 stock book
재고품을 싸게 처분함 close-out
재고회전율 stock turnover
재구성비율을 인하하다 reduce holding ratio
재구축 restructuring
재단; 창설 foundation
재단저당 foundation collateral
재단채권 superior obligation
재담보설정 rehypothecation
재대부(再貸付) further advance
재량대출 discretionary loan
재량행위 discretional act
재료 raw material
재료; 팩터; 요인 factor
재료가격차이 material price variance
재료관리 material control

재료구입고 materials purchased
재료구입장 stores purchase book
재료분개장 materials distribution sheet
재료비 material cost
재료비차액 materials variance
재료사양서 materials specification
재료수량차이 material quantity variance
재료예산 material cost budget; materials budget
재료원장 materials ledger
재료재고 materials inventory
재료표준가격 materials price standard
재료표준소비량 standard quantity of materials consumed
재무 financial affairs
재무감사 financial audit
재무개황 financial review
재무건전성 financial strength
재무계획 financial planning
재무고문 financial advisor
재무관리 financial management
재무국 local finance bureau
재무내용 financial condition
재무담당임원 chief financial officer
재무대리인 fiscal agent
재무대리인계약 fiscal agent agreement
재무레버리지 financial leverage
재무레버리지비율 financial leverage ratio
재무면의 증익효과 financial leverage effect
재무면의 증익효과도 degree of financial leverage
재무밸런스 financial balance
재무보고회계 financial reporting accounting
재무부 Department of Treasury
재무부 단기어음 cash management bill
재무부령 Finance Ministry Ordinance
재무부원안 budget draft by Ministry of Finance
재무부장 treasurer
재무부장관 Chancellor of the Exchequer
재무부장기증권 Treasury Bond

재무부중기저축채권 Treasury Savings Notes
재무부중기증권 Treasury Note
재무부증권 Finance Ministry note
재무부증권; 재무부단기증권 Treasury Bill
재무부증권발행 재무부발행증권 Treasury Bill issued
재무부증권시장 treasury securities market
재무부증권이율 treasury yield
재무부채무증서 Treasury Certificate of Indebtedness
재무부투자채권 Treasury Bonds Investment Series
재무분석 financial analysis
재무비율 financial ratio
재무상의 배려 financial considerations
재무상의 슬랙 financial slack
재무수익 financial revenue
재무제표 financial statements
재무제표각주 notes to financial statement
재무제표감사 financial statement audit
재무제표규칙 regulations of financial statements
재무제표부속명세표 schedules of financial statements
재무제표분석 financial statement analysis; statement analysis
재무제표적요표 abstract of financial statements
재무제표준칙 rules for the preparation of financial statements
재무제한조항 restrictive financial covenant
재무처리 management of property
재무체질 financial structure
재무코스트 financial cost
재무평가 financial appraisal
재무활동 financing activities
재무회계 financial accounting
재무회계기준심의회 Financial Accounting Standards Board
재무회계기준자문위원회 Financial Accounting Standards Advisory Council

재물손괴 property damage
재발방지 avoidance of recurrence
재배부원가 redistributed cost
재벌 financial clique
재보험 reinsurance
재보험계약 reinsurance agreement
재보험계약명세서 bordereau
재보험금 reinsurance recovery; reinsurance premium
재보험반려금 reinsurance return
재보험보고서 reinsurance bordereau
재보험수수료 reinsurance commission
재보험요율 reinsurance premium rate
재보험자 ceding reinsurer
재보험조항 reinsurance clause
재보험중매인 reinsurance broker
재보험지불액 burning ratio
재보험특약 continuous reinsurance cover; reinsurance treaty
재보험특약기간 종료후의 잔존책임 run-off
재보험특약서 treaty wording
재보험풀 pooling arrangement; reinsurance pool
재분류 reclassification
재산 belongings; estate; property
재산검사 inspection of property
재산관리명령 receiving order
재산관리보증 conservator bond
재산관리상의 태만 improvidence
재산구 property ward
재산권 property right
재산권수용권 eminent domain
재산목록 general inventory; list of property
재산반환영장 amoveas manus
재산부동산 hereditaments
재산분여 distribution of property
재산생명보험 property life insurance
재산소득 property income
재산양도 conveyance of estate
재산에 부속하는 권리 appurtenance
재산원장 property ledger

재산을 무상으로 사용함 gratuitous use of property
재산의 우선순위를 결정함 marshaling assets
재산이전금지법 disabling statutes
재산인도 cession
재산조사 audit on property
재산증가 accretion
재산차압 levy of attachment
재산처분능력 disposing capacity
재산평가 appraisement; extent
재산평가익 income from appreciation of assets
재생산 reproduction
재생산; 재가공 rework
재생산원가 cost of reproduction; reproduction cost
재생산표식 scheme of reproduction
재생원재료 reclaimed materials
재송정정방식 request repeat system
재수정기입 readjusting entry
재심 new trial
재심리 rehearing
재심리신청 motion for new trial
재심리신청서 bill of advocation
재원 financial resources; source of revenue; ways and means
재인도 second deliverance
재일외은 foreign banks in Japan
재재보험특액 retrocession treaty
재전환 reconversion
재정 award
재정가격결정이론 arbitrate pricing theory
재정개혁 fiscal reform
재정거래 arbitrage business; arbitrage operation; arbitrage transaction
재정거래자 arbitrageur
재정경직화 fiscal inflexibility
재정규모 scale of central and local public finance
재정금융정책 fiscal and monetary policy
재정기회 arbitrage opportunity
재정긴축정책 tight fiscal policy

재정력지수 index of financial condition
재정마진 arbitrage margin
재정목표 fiscal target
재정민주주의 financial democracy
재정방식 pension financing method
재정법 finance law; public finance law
재정상 긴급처분 emergent financial
　disposition
재정상태 financial position; financial
　standing; financial status
재정상태변동표 statement of changes in
　financial position
재정수지 fiscal balance
재정예견 fiscal outlook
재정인플레이션 fiscal inflation
재정적자 budget deficit; deficit of fiscal
　balance
재정정책 fiscal policy
재정제도심의회 Finance System Council
재정제한 crunch
재정지출 fiscal expenditure
재정착각 fiscal illusion
재정투융자 fiscal investment and loan;
　treasury investment and loan
재정투자 fiscal investment
재정팽창억제 fiscal drug
재정포지션 arbitrage position
재정핍박 fiscal tightness
재정환율 arbitrated rate of exchange
재조달가치 prevailing value
재조달비용보험 replacement cost coverage
재조정 realignment
재조정교섭 realignment negotiation
재직기한 length of service; tenure of office;
　term of office
재직접심문 redirect examination
재취득가격 current replacement cost
재취득리스크 replacement risk
재측정 remeasurement
재택간호서비스 at-home nursing service
재테크 financial engineering

재투자 reinvestment
재투자리스크 reinvestment risk
재투자이율 reinvestment rate
재판 adjudication; resale
재판(再版)구입 buying for resale
재판가격 resale price
재판가격유지 resale price maintenance
재판매가격기준법 resale price method
재판매업자 reseller
재판비용 judicial costs
재판상의 자유 judicial confession
재판상의 협정 judicial convention
재판소 curia
재판소규칙 rules of court
재판소법 judicature acts
재판에 따른 입법 judicial legislation
재판외의 extra-judicial
재판을 받을 권리 access to courts
재판을 속행함 continuance
재판절차 legal procedure
재판청구권 right of access to courts
재판할 수 있는 권한 high justice
재평가 reappraisement; reassessment;
　rebalance
재평가; 재검토 reappraisal
재평가익 revaluation profit
재평가잉여금 appreciation surplus;
　revaluation surplus; surplus from
　revaluation
재평가적립금 appraisal surplus; revaluation
　surplus reserve
재평가차액 revaluation excess
재할인 rediscount
재할인금리 rediscount rate
재할인정책 rediscount policy
재해 casualty; casus major
재해 및 보증보험회사협회 Association of
　Casualty and Surety Companies
재해보장 accident compensation; casualty
　insurance
재해보험회사해외협회 Accident Offices'

Association

재해준비금 reserve for accidents

재형저축 worker's property accumulation savings

재화(載貨)적성 cargoworthiness

재확인 double check

쟁점; 발행 issue

쟁점기록 demurrer book

쟁점사항 matter in issue

쟁점에 달한 at issue

쟁점주의 limitation on issue principle

저가격 lower in quotation

저가격시장 lower end of the market

저가법 lower-of-cost-or-market method

저가재 lower order goods

저가주 fancy stocks

저가주 【영】; 값싼 주식 penny stock

저감; 감소 decrement

저감하다 erode

저고도궤도 low earth orbit

저고정가격 lower closing quotation

저궤도통신망 low earth orbit communication

저금금리 interest on savings deposit

저금리론 low interest loan

저금리예상 anticipation of low interest rate

저당(담보)물 pledge

저당계약 impignorative contract

저당권; 모기지 mortgage

저당권부 사채 secured bond

저당권설정 establishment of hypothec; settlement of mortgage

저당권설정등기 register of settlement of mortgage

저당권설정약관 mortgage clause

저당권설정자 mortgage debtor; mortgagor

저당권설정자 완성보증증권 mortgagor's completion bond

저당권소멸 extinguishment of hypothec

저당권을 설정하다 hypothecate

저당권자 mortgagee

저당권집행; 포어클로저 foreclosure

저당금융회사 mortgage company

저당론 mortgage loan

저당물 pawn

저당보험 insurance on mortgagee's interest; mortgage insurance

저당부 모기지증서 collateralized mortgage obligations

저당신용조합 Mortgage Credit Association

저당신용채 mortgage credit bond; mortgage debenture

저당약관 insecurity clause

저당우선권 priority of mortgage

저당은행 mortgage bank

저당을 되찾음 redemption of pledge

저당이 될 수 있는 동산 mortgageable chattels

저당자산 pledged assets

저당잡힘 impignoration

저당재산을 되찾다 redeem

저당증권 mortgage securities

저당증권보험 mortgage guarantee insurance

저당증서류 mortgage documents

저당차입금 mortgage payable

저맥락 low context

저배주 low-dividend stock

저비용전략 low-cost strategy

저사망율 light mortality

저성장 low growth

저소득국 low income countries

저속상장 stagnant market

저스트인타임 방식 just-in-time system

저액면주식 low-par issue

저액양도 transfer at low price

저온멸균 pasteurization

저온유통조직 cold chain

저위주 low grade stocks; lower-priced stock

저작권 copyright

저작권사용료 royalty of the copyright

저장경비 storage costs

저장원재료 materials in storage

저장품 inventories of merchandise and

supplies; stocks; stored goods
저장품관리 storage management
저조업도원가 idle capacity cost
저지 arrestment
저지가격 keep-out price
저축계정 saving account
저축대부기관 savings and loan association
저축동향조사 family saving survey
저축률 savings ratio
저축성향 propensity to savings
저축예금 savings deposit
저축은행 savings bank
저축은행생명보험 savings bank life insurance
저축채권 savings bond and debenture
저축함수 saving function
저탄(貯炭) coal stock
저투입지속형의 low input sustainable
저하시키다 deteriorate
저하율 decreasing rate
저항선 resistance line
적게 관여하는 형태의 구매 low-involvement purchases
적격담보 eligible security
적격성 eligibility
적격성확인프로세스 qualification process
적격인 qualified
적격인도 good delivery
적격조건 eligibility requirements
적격퇴직연금 approved retirement annuity; approved superannuation fund; qualified pension plan
적격퇴직연금계약 approved pension contract; qualified pension contract
적격퇴직연금적립금 approved pension funds; qualified pension funds
적격퇴직연금제도 qualified pension system
적격투자 eligible investment
적격투자가 accredited investor
적극신탁 active trust
적극예산 expansionary budget
적극재산 positive property

적극재정, 팽창재정 positive financial policy
적극적 훼손 voluntary waste
적극적인 딜러 active dealer
적극적인 매입 active buying
적극적인 운용 active bond management; active management; aggressive portfolio
적극적인 조정정책 positive adjustment policies
적극적인 항변 affirmative defense
적극적인 확인 positive confirmation
적극조건 positive condition
적극투자이론 active investment management theory
적기 apt time
적당한 가격의 modestly-priced
적대적인 매수를 고려하는 주식취득자 raider
적립금 accumulated fund; reserve; reserve fund
적립금반려 surplus reserves transferred to income
적립금반환 reversal of surplus
적립금편입 additions to reserves
적립방식 funding method
적립방식연금 balance sheet reserve system annuity
적립보험 savings-type insurance
적립이월 provision for surplus
적립자산 accumulated assets
적립정기예금 installment time deposit
적립한도액 allowed limit of accumulation
적법계약 legal contract
적법성담보 warranty of legality
적법의 lawful; legal
적법절차 due process of law
적법한 통지 legal notice
적선하증권 red B/L
적성검사 aptitude test
적성상하한계수익률 optimal threshold return
적성정도 fit
적송인 shipper
적송품 shipment

ㅈ
ㅊ
ㅋ

적송품선수금 advances received on consignment out

적요 abridgment

적용면제 dispensation

적용법 applicable statutory useful life

적용법정내용연수 applicable useful life

적용순서 order of application

적용원가 applied cost

적용제외 contracted out

적용제외증권 exempted securities

적용하는 정당한 이유 justifiable reason to apply

적용할 수 있는 applicable

적은 주 scarce stock

적응수준 adaptation level

적응전략 adaptive strategy

적응행동 adaptive behavior

적자 deficit; red figure

적자경영 loss making operations

적자국채 deficit-covering bond

적자금융 deficit-covering finance; finance for deficit

적자보전 covering of a deficit; filing up of a deficit; making up of a deficit

적자생존 survival of the fittest

적자예산 unbalanced budget

적자융자 deficit financing; financing for deficit-covering

적자잔고 red herring

적자잔액 red-balance

적자재정 deficit finance

적자전락 turn to red figures

적재목록 manifest

적재비용 loading charges

적재적소 right person in a right position

적재한 선박의 이름을 알지 못함 vessel unknown

적절정보 relevant information

적절하게 성장하는 growing at a moderate speed

적정 fair

적정교환비 social and entertainment expenses provided in lump sum

적정베이시스 equilibrium basis

적정비용 cost of conformity

적정성장률 warranted rate of growth

적정외화준비고 optimum foreign exchange reserves

적정유동성 adequate liquidity

적정임금 fair wage

적채기준 issue standards

적취비율 trade sharing

적하가격신고서 valuation form

적하매각위탁계약 accomenda

적하처분기간 induciae

적합범위 relevant range

적합성 conformity

적합하지 않은 ineligible

전(前)판결 former adjudication

전가성이론 shiftability theory

전가하다 pass on

전개를 기다림 waiting for further development

전광정보판 broad tape

전구성원이 공유함 tenancy in common

전국광고 general advertising

전국기업단기경제관측 short-term economic survey of all businesses

전국브랜드 national brand

전국손해보험대리업협회(일본)전국손해보험대리업협회 All Japan Fire & Marine Insurance Agency Association

전국시가지 가격지수 indices of urban land prices

전국은행계정 banking accounts of all banks

전국은행신탁계정 trust accounts of all banks

전권 plenipotentiary

전기 previous term

전기가스세 electricity and gas tax

전기간평균 career average

전기세 electricity tax

전기손익수정 prior period adjustment

전기수정항목 correction of prior periods
전기통신사업 telecommunication business
전기하다 post
전날 종가보다 싼 거래 downtick
전년 preceding year; previous year
전년대비변화율 year-to-year percentage change
전년도 preceding fiscal year
전년도손익수정항목 prior year adjustment items
전년동기 corresponding period of last year
전달 과정에서 발생한 차이 errors in posting
전달자; 발신기 communicator
전당포 pawn-shop
전대제도 putting-out system
전대하다 sublet
전도금 advanced money; down payment
전도자금 imprest cash
전략 strategy
전략개발 strategy development
전략경영 strategic management
전략광고 strategic advertisement
전략분석 strategy analysis
전략분야 strategic field
전략사업단위 strategic business unit
전략성과 strategic performance
전략우위제 strategic advantage
전략적 교두보 strategic beachhead
전략적인 경쟁 strategic competition
전략적인 의사결정 strategic decision
전략적인 제휴; 전략동맹 strategic alliance
전략적인 집단 strategic group
전략정보시스템 strategic information system
전략형성 strategy formulation
전력가스주 utilities stock
전력비 electric power expense; power expense
전력채 utilities bond
전망 near time prospect
전매 public monopoly
전매 환매를 마치고 거래관계를 청산함(신용

거래나 선물거래에서) 전매 환매를 마치고 거래관계를 청산함 evening up
전매과세 monopoly assessment; taxation on government monopoly
전매납부금 state monopoly payment
전매이익 monopoly profit
전매장 sellers over
전문가 professionals
전문상품취급업자 special product firm
전문스텝 specialist staff
전문업계지 vertical publication
전문적으로 artificially
전문적인 상장 professional's market
전문적인 증권회사 boutique
전문점 specialty store
전문지 professional publication
전문직과실책임보험 malpractice insurance
전문직업인배상책임보험 professional liability insurance
전문화; 특화 specialization
전미(全美)선물협회 National Futures Association
전미(全美)정보기반 national information structure
전미담보특약 all status endorsement
전미증권분석가연합회 Financial Analysts Federation
전미증권업협회 분쟁처리규칙 Code of Procedure for Handling Trade Practice Complain
전반검사 general survey
전반자산 general corporate assets
전반적인 경기회복수준보다 회복이 더딘 경제분야 laggard
전반적인 시황 undertone
전방수직통합 forward vertical integration
전방차분 forward difference
전방통합 forward integration
전보험종목인수기구 all lines organization
전보험종목인수회사 all lines insurer
전부보험 full value insurance; insurance to

value

전부원가 absorption cost; full cost; total cost

전부원가계산 absorption costing; full costing; total costing

전부차압 grand distress

전불(前仏) 전불사망보험금 accelerated benefits

전불금 imprest

전불금반환보증 refundment guarantee

전불금반환보증증권 refund bond

전불보험료 insurance prepaid

전불분담금 advance call

전불식 할부판매금융 finance for prepaid installment sales

전불여비 travel advances

전불임금 advance wages

전불지대 forehand rent

전사업연도 preceding taxable year; prior taxable year

전상관 total correlation

전세보증금; 거래보증금 deposit with landlord

전속관할권 exclusive jurisdiction

전속시장 captive market

전속외무원제도 career agency system

전속중개자 tied-agent

전손 total loss

전손 및 구조비담보 free from all averages but to cover salvage charges

전손만의 담보 total loss only

전수(前受)수익 income in advance

전수익금 unearned revenue

전술계획 tactical planning

전술적인 자산배분 tactical asset allocation

전술한 사항 premises

전신거래환 reverse telegraphic transfer

전신매상장 telegraphic transfer buying rate; telegraphic transfer selling rate

전신송금 cable transfer; electronic fund transfer; wire transfer

전신신용장 cable credit

전신환 telegraphic transfer

전액보험 full insurance

전액불입 fully paid-up payment in full

전액영수서 receipt in full

전액정화준비제도 total reserve system

전액지불 full payment

전액지불필 주식 full-paid capital stock

전액출자한 자회사 fully owned subsidiary

전용 exclusive use

전용의 single purpose

전용주택 exclusive-occupation house

전원일치 nemine contradicente; unanimous

전원일치로 una voce

전위컴퓨터 front end computer

전위프로세서 front end processor

전위험담보 against all risks

전일부 antedated

전일부로 하다 predate

전일부수표 antedated check

전일종가 last close

전일종치 previous close

전자금융 electronic banking

전자도서관 electronic library

전자매체 electronic media

전자메일 electronic mail

전자북 electronic book

전자산합동방식 portfolio method

전자주문전달시스템 electronic order transfer system

전자출판 electronic publishing

전자파일링시스템 electronic Filing system

전자화폐 electronic money

전장(前場) morning session

전장입회 first board

전쟁약관 war clause

전쟁위험 war perils

전쟁행위 act of war

전적 change in employment

전제적인 preemptory

전차인 undertenant

전체론 holism

전통시장 traditional market

전통적인 경로 traditional channel

전통적인 마케팅경로 conventional marketing channel

전통적인 상품시장 conventional commodity market

전표 chit; ticket; voucher

전표대조 vouching

전표식 부기 slip bookkeeping

전표식회계법 slip system of accounting

전표제도 slip system

전표지불제도 chit system

전화가입권 right of telephone; telephone subscription right

전화로 거래를 권유함 cold call

전화요금 telephone rates

전화주문 order by telephone

전화확인 verification by telephone

전환 디스카운트 conversion discount

전환가격 conversion price

전환가격방식 conversion price formula

전환가격을 넘는 금액 premium over conversion value

전환가치 conversion value

전환모기지 convertible mortgage

전환부대리인 standing agent

전환비율 conversion parity; conversion ratio

전환사채 convertible bond; mezzanine money

전환우선주 convertible preferred stock

전환점 turning point

전환조건 conversion conditions

전환주식 convertible stock

전환증권 convertible securities

전환청구기간 conversion period

전환특전 privilege of conversion

전환프리미엄 conversion premium

전회규칙 front-foot rule

전후방통합 forward-backward integration

절대고정자본 absolute fixed capital

절대명령 rule absolute

절대빈도 absolute frequency

절대소득가설 absolute income hypothesis

절대양도 absolute conveyance

절대우위 absolute advantage

절대원가 absolute cost

절대적인 면책위험 risk absolutely excluded

절대전손 absolute total loss

절대주의 absolutism

절대치 absolute value

절대확산모델 amortizing diffusion model

절도의사 animus furandi

절도행위 act of stealing

절상; 재평가; 평가절상 revaluation

절세 tax saving

절세거래 tax oriented transaction

절점 node

절차 routing

절차감사 procedural audit

절차법 adjective law

절차서류 documented procedure

절차중지신청자 caveat

절충방식 compromise method

절하 devaluation

절호의 매장 attractive trading opportunity

젊은 층 지향 youth orientation

점수기록제 point scoring

점수법 point system

점수사정법 numerical rating method

점유 demesne; possession; seisin

점유권 monopoly

점유기간 occupancy terms

점유를 수반하지 않는 권리 mere jus

점유소송 possessory action

점유자 occupant

점유채무자 debtor in possession

점유침탈 disseisin

점유통합 unity of seisin

점유하다 perception

점유하지 않은 not possessed

점유한 seized

점진적인 국유화 creeping nationalization

점진적인 진부화 progressive obsolescence

점추정 point estimate

ㅈ
ㅊ
ㅋ

점포감사 store audit
점포근대화 store modernization
점포배열 store arrangement
점포선고 store preference
점포종합보험 storekeepers' comprehensive insurance
점포포화상태 store saturation
점포휴업보험 store business interruption insurance
점프과정 jump process
접근용이성 accessibility of store
접대비 amusement expenses
접수로 인한 손실 expropriation loss
접수총액 handle
정격치 rated value
정관 articles
정관변경 amendment of articles of corporation
정관세칙 by-laws
정규가 아닌 상장 back door listing
정규가 아닌 판매 back-door selling
정규감사절차 normal auditing procedures
정규곡선의 범위 area of normal curve
정규단체보험 true group insurance
정규부기의 원칙 principle of orderly system of bookkeeping
정규분포 normal distribution
정규분할불보험료 true installment premium
정규절차 normal procedure
정규확률분포 normal probability distribution
정규확립분포곡선 normal probability curve
정기간행물 periodicals
정기감사 periodic audit
정기거래 periodical transaction; time bargains; time transaction
정기대부 time loan
정기보험 term insurance
정기생명보험계약 term policy
정기생명연금 temporary annuity
정기수익 periodical return
정기실지재고 periodic actual inventory
정기연금 term annuity

정기예금 fixed deposit; installment savings; term deposits; time deposit
정기예금계정 time deposit account
정기예금금리 interest rate on time deposit
정기예금담보대출금리 interest rate on loans secured by time deposit
정기예금증서 certificate of time deposit; time deposit certificate
정기재고조사 periodic inventory
정기적금 periodical deposits
정기콜시장 period call market
정당방위 self-defense
정당성 validity
정당점유신청 avowry
정당하다고 인정하다 validate
정당한 권한이 있는 기관 legal organ
정당한 보상 just compensation
정당한 지대(地代) rent reasonably fixed
정당행위 justifiable act
정당화 justification
정량모델 quantitative model
정량분석 quantitative analysis
정량인인 시장분석 quantitative market analysis
정량적인 애셋앨로케이션 quantitative asset allocation
정량적인 어프로치 quantitative approach
정령(政令) government ordinance
정리; 해결 strengthening
정리기입 adjustment entry
정리사채 adjustment bond
정리후 시산표 adjusted trial balance
정밀도 precision
정밀조사상품 search goods
정박료 groundage
정박세 anchorage
정번상품 regular assortment
정보가전 information home electronics
정보가치 information value
정보공개 information disclosure
정보공개전의 증권거래 gun jumping

정보누설 tip
정보동기로 인한 거래자
　information-motivated trader
정보동기에 따른 매매 information-motivated
　transaction
정보벤더 information vendors
정보시스템 information system
정보시스템사업 information system business
정보원 source of information
정보원효과 source effects
정보입력 information input
정보제공자 common informer; information
　provider
정보제공자; 정보제공기업 content provider
정보지수 information ratio
정보처리설비 information processing facility
정보출력 information output
정보혁명 information revolution
정보화사회 information society
정보효용 information utility
정부간 무역 government to government trade
정부개발원조 Official
　Development-Assistance
정부거래 government transaction
정부경상여잉 government current surplus
정부계 기간채권 bond issued by government
　related agency
정부계 기관 government agency
정부계 기관증권 securities issued by
　government related agency
정부계 기관채권 government agency bond
정부계정 government account
정부관계예금 government related deposit
정부구입 government purchases
정부규제 regulation by government
정부금융기관 government financial agency
정부기관증권 government agency securities
정부기관증권담보증권 agency backed
　securities
정부기관채 agency note
정부기업 government enterprise

정부단기증권 finance bill; short-term
　government securities
정부무역 government trade
정부보증채 government guaranteed bond;
　government obligation
정부브로커 government broker
정부이전수지 government transfers
정부저당금고 Government National
　Mortgage Association
정부저축 government saving
정부증권 government securities
정부증권상환 redemption of government
　securities
정부지출 government expenditure
정부지폐 government note
정부차관 government credit
정부채무 national government debts
정부통화 currency note
정산 settlement of debt
정산표 work sheet
정산표방식 worksheet method
정상배부율 normal burden rate
정상상각 normal depreciation
정상상업순환 normal operating cycle
정상상태 stationary state
정상원가 normal cost
정상이윤 normal profit
정상이익 normal return
정상잔고 normal balances
정상재고 running stock
정상재고고 normal stock
정상표준원가 normal standard cost
정상환상장 normal rate of exchange
정서가 불안정한; 걱정하는 hung up
정성기준 qualitative criteria
정성분석 qualitative analysis
정수계획법 integer programming
정시감사 regular audit
정시불 payment at regular fixed times
정시불사용료 royalty to be paid every fixed
　time

ㅈ
ㅊ
ㅋ

정시상환 redemption at fixed date; scheduled repayment

정식계약 formal contract

정식본권 definitive bond

정식편입액 formula additions

정신적인 충격 nervous shock

정액감가상각법 straight-line depreciation

정액공제면책율 flat deductible

정액과세 fixed amount taxation

정액법 constant dollar plan; fixed amount method; fixed installment method

정액보수실비지불계약 cost plus fixed fee contract

정액상각 fixed installment

정액연금 fixed annuity

정액전도자금 imprest fund

정액전도제 imprest system

정액지대 rents of assize

정액지불변동이부채 level pay floating rate note

정액책임보증증권 fixed penalty bond

정액청부계약 lump-sum contract

정오조항 noon clause

정위치 fixed position

정율감가상각법 declining balance depreciation; fixed percentage depreciation

정율법 declining balance method; fixed percentage on unexpired cost method; fixed-percentage on declining balance method; method of fixed percentage on cost

정율보수 fixed fee

정율상각 diminishing balance depreciation

정율상각법 percentage on diminishing value plan

정의 definition

정정 reformation; revision

정정매출 corrective selling

정정상장 corrective market

정족수를 채우지 못했다고 인정하여 유회하다 count out

정지 suspension

정지명령 cease orders

정지시효 suspension of prescription

정지조건 condition precedent

정지조건부 옵션 knock-out option

정책수단을 할당함 policy assignment

정책적인 감가상각 policy depreciation

정책포지션 policy state

정책협조 policy coordination

정체산업 stagnant industry

정치단체 political corporation

정치리스크 political risk

정치범죄 political crime

정치안정지수 political system stability index

정치적인 관직 political office

정치적인 권리 political rights

정치적인 혼란 political turmoil

정크본드 junk bond

정탄성 분산모델 constant elasticity of variance model

정태리스크 static risk

정태분석 static analysis

정태비율 static ratio

정태시장 static market

정태통계 static statistics

정학모델 static model

정학승수 static multiplier

정형무역조건 trade terms

정형적으로 규정된 약관 conditional sales agreement

정형화이외거래기간 odd date

정화(正貨) specie money

정화의; 특정의 ill specie

정화준비(正貨準備) specie reserve

정확도 degree of accuracy

정황증거 circumstantial evidence

정회원 fellow

정회원 regular member

제 1권 first exchange

제 1심관할권 original jurisdiction

제 1차온라인 first generation on-line system

제 2 지방은행 member bank of the Second

Association of Regional Banks
제 3구역 third sect
제 3세계 각국 third world countries
제 3섹터 quasi-public corporation
제 3자 강제배상책임보험 compulsory third party liability insurance
제 3자의 권원 outstanding title
제 3채무자 garnishee
제거 scrapping
제거가액 retirement price
제거단위 retirement unit
제거법 relief method
제거비 retirement cost
제거비용 removal expenses
제거손실 loss on retirement of fixed assets
제거자산 scrapped property
제거하다 subduct
제거회계 retirement accounting
제경비 oncost; overhead
제너럴모기지 general mortgage
제너럴모기지사채 general mortgage bond
제너럴스태프 general staff
제너럴크레딧 general credit
제너릭시장 generic market
제도광고 institutional advertising
제도분석 institutional analysis
제도적인 저축 institutionalized saving
제도학파 institutional school
제로발주모델 zero-order model
제로베타포트폴리오 zero-beta portfolio
제로섬게임 zero-sum game
제로코스트옵션 zero cost option
제로코스트옵션거래 zero-cost option trading
제로코스트칼라 zero-cost collar
제로쿠폰채 zero-coupon bond
제로쿠폰커브 zero-coupon curve
제로펄스틱 zero-plus tick
제명회원 lame duck
제목; 머리말 caption
제본 book binding
제삼자 stranger; third party

제삼자배상책임보험 third party liability insurance
제삼자배상특약보험 third party liability cover
제삼자법적배상책임보험 third party legal liability insurance
제삼자이의신청소송보증증권 third party claimant bond
제삼자지불약관 loss payable clause
제삼자할당 allocation of new shares to a third party
제삼자할당주 stock allotted to third persons
제시기간 time of presentation
제시지연 late presentation
제시하지 않는 특약수표 memorandum-check
제안제도 suggestion scheme
제안하다 move; propound
제외; 면책 exclusion
제외사항 exception
제외위험 excepted risks
제외하고 net of
제외한; 면책으로 하다 exclude
J 커브효과 J curve effect
JPEG 이미지 파일 Joint Photographic Expert Group
제일순위 저당권부사채 first mortgage bond
제일심 first instance
제일심재판소 court of first instance
제일우선주 prior preferred stock
제일우선주식 first preferred stock
제일저당 first mortgage
제작중인 물건 goods in process; stock in process
제작중인 물건원장 goods in process ledger
제작중인 물건의 원장 work in process ledger
제잡비 sundry expenses
제재관세 punitive tariff
제정법 statute
제정조항 enacting clause
제조간접비 factory expenses; factory overhead; manufacturing burden; production cost

제조간접비배부 overhead allocation
제조간접비배부계정 applied manufacturing expenses account
제조간접비예산 manufacturing expenses budget
제조간접비원장 manufacturing expenses ledger
제조경비 manufacturing expenses; production expenses
제조공정 manufacturing process
제조과세 manufacturing taxation
제조능률차이 production efficiency variance
제조물책임 product liability
제조물책임보험 product liability insurance
제조보고서 production statement
제조부문 manufacturing department; production department
제조부문비 producing departments cost
제조부문이 없는 개발메이커 fabless
제조비 on cost
제조비예산 cost of production budget
제조설비 production equipment
제조예산 production budget
제조원가 cost of manufactured goods; fabricating cost; output cost
제조원가계산 manufacturing cost accounting
제조원가보고서 factory cost report; manufacturing statement; statement of production cost
제조자리스크 manufacturer's risks
제조지도서 manufacture order; production order; work order
제조허가 manufacturing license
제지; 억제 restraint
제출; 신청 offer; presentment
제출연기 extension of time to file
제특성 qualifying dimensions
제판동맹 manufacturing-retailer alliance
제표 tabulation
제품 manufactured goods; product
제품가격 product price

제품개량 product improvement
제품계정 finished products account
제품계획 product planning
제품공간 product space
제품구비 product assortment
제품구비불일치 discrepancy of assortment
제품군 product family
제품다양화 product diversification
제품동기 product motive
제품라이프사이클 product life cycle
제품만족 product satisfactions
제품믹스 product mix
제품별 원가계산 cost accounting by product; product cost accounting
제품보증 product warranties
제품보증준비금 reserve for guarantee far completed work
제품분류 product classification
제품삭제 product deletion
제품성숙 product maturity
제품소지액 finished products on hand
제품속성곡선 product attribute curve
제품수입 manufactured imports
제품원가 cost of finished goods; cost of product
제품이미지 product image
제품재고액 finished products inventory
제품조사 product research
제품증식효과 product proliferation
제품차별화 product differentiation
제품카테고리 product category
제품통계 production statistics
제품특성 product attribute
제품포지셔닝 product positioning
제품포트폴리오 product portfolio
제품포트폴리오매니지먼트 product portfolio management
제품품질 product quality
제품회수 product recall
제한납세의무 limited tax liability
제한납세의무자 taxpayer with limited tax

liability

제한법화 limited legal tender

제한부 계정 restricted account

제한부 부동산권 estate upon limitation

제한부 잉여금 restricted surplus

제한부동산권 base free

제한세율 limited tax rate

제한외발행세 tax on excess issue

제한외발행주식 overissue

제한요인 limitational factor

제한적인 교환성 limited convertibility

제한적인 면책특권 qualified privilege

제한적인 보증 limited guarantee

제한적인 보험 limited policies

제한적인 재산권 qualified property

제한조치 sanction

제한주 restricted share

제휴 collaboration

제휴론 affiliated loan; tie-up loan

제휴자사카드 private label card

제휴카드 co-branded card

조건 condition; terms and conditions

조건; 단서 proviso

조건; 준비금 provision

조건개요서 term sheet

조건교섭 negotiation on terms and conditions

조건부 conditional; with a proviso

조건부 계약 conditional contract

조건부 국고보조금 conditional subsidy from the national treasury

조건부 날인증서 escrow

조건부 매매 conditional sales

조건부 부동산권 estate upon condition

조건부 분포 conditional distribution

조건부 승인 conditional approval

조건부 유동성 conditional liquidity

조건부 융자 conditional loan; tied loan

조건부 인수 conditional acceptance

조건부 회귀분석 conditional regression analysis

조건인수 qualified acceptance

조기경보시스템 early warning system

조기반제 early repayment

조기사망 premature death

조기상환 early redemption; prematurity redemption

조기상환; 콜 call

조기상환리스크 prepayment risk

조기상환예상 prepayment projection

조기상환옵션 early redemption option

조기완제 full repayment before maturity

조달가격 acquisition cost price

조달금리 borrowing rate

조달비 procurement cost

조달코스트 funding cost

조례 municipal by-laws; municipal law; ordinance; ordinance by local government

조립공업 assembly industry

조립공정 assembly process

조립명령서 assembly order; assembly production order

조립보험 erection insurance

조립부문 assembly department

조립순위표 assembly order sheet

조립원가계산 assembly cost system

조미료 sweetener

조별법 group method

조별상각 group depreciation

조별원가 class cost

조별원가계산 class cost system

조사 examination by reference

조사기회 research opportunity

조사목적 research objectives

조사비 research expenditure

조사선입견 survey bias

조사수법 research method

조사자료 materials for investigation

조사후 소득 income after tax audit

조상상환이익 yield-to-call

조서 process verbal

조성과실 contributory negligence

조성금 grant in aid

조세 tax
조세 및 인지수입 tax and stamp revenues
조세감면 reduction or exemption of tax
조세공채계정 treasury tax and loan account
조세구조 tax structure
조세국가 tax state
조세귀착 tax incidence
조세를 전가함 shifting of tax burden
조세범 tax criminal
조세부담 incidence of taxation; tax burden
조세부담경감 tax relief
조세부담율 tax burden ratio
조세부담자 ratepayer
조세사정 tax assessment
조세선취특권 tax lien
조세수금청부 farming of taxes
조세예납 prepayment of tax
조세우선권 priority of taxes
조세원칙 principle of taxation
조세의 수익자부담원칙 compensation
    principle of taxation
조세의 중립성 neutrality of taxation
조세정책 tax policy
조세조약 tax convention; tax treaty
조세준비증권 tax anticipation bill
조세징수 collection of taxes
조세채권 tax claims
조세채무관계설 theory of liabilities taxation
조세체계 system of taxation
조세특별조치 special taxation measures
조세특전 tax benefit
조세환부청구권 claim for tax refunds
조세회피 tax avoidance
조수표 set of exchange
조악화 adulteration
조약 treaty
조약의정서; 프로토콜 protocol
조언의견 advisory opinion
조언적 advisory
조업 operation; run
조업개시기념축연 celebration of the

beginning of operation
조업단축 curtailment of operation; output
    reduction; reduction of operation
조업도 operating rate; operation capacity;
    production level; rate of output
조업도; 생산고 volume
조업도지수 volume indicator
조업도차이 operation variance; utilization
    variance; volume variance
조업률 operation ratio
조업일수 operated days
조위금, 부조금 condolence money
조이율 gross margin ratio
조이익률 gross profit margin rate
조이익이 증감함 changes in gross margin
조이익총계 aggregate gross margin
조작 manipulation
조작목표 operating target
조정 conciliation; pause; reconciliation; shade
조정가능고정상장 adjustable peg system
조정가능생명보험 adjustable life policy
조정금리저당론 adjustable rate mortgage loan
조정보험 adjustable policy
조정보험료 adjusted premium; adjustment
    premium
조정세액 tax amount settled
조정소득금액 adjusted income
조정인 overman
조정인보증증권 referee bond
조정인플레이션 adjustment inflation
조정증권 adjustment securities
조정패턴 consolidation pattern
조정필 adjusted
조정하다 adjust
조정항목 adjustment item; reconciliation item
조정화재보험증권 adjustable fire policy
조정후 배당증가율 adjusted dividend increase
조정후 양도소득 adjusted capital gain
조정후 중앙은행통화스톡 adjusted central
    bank money stock
조제 compilation

조종대, 제어탁자 console
조직간 시스템 interorganizational system
조직개발 organization development
조직구매자 organizational buyer
조직구조 organizational structure
조직목표 organizational goal
조직변경 organizational change
조직적인 분석 systematic analysis
조직전략 organizational strategy
조직편제비용 setup costs
조직편제시간 setup time
조직하다 organizing
조판 composing
조합 check; partnership; reconcilement; society; tally; union
조합; 중재합의 reference
조합방식재보험 combination plan reinsurance
조합보험 combination policy
조합원 partners
조합원 선취득권 lien of partners
조합원자격유지 maintenance of membership
조합재산 partnership assets
조합정관 articles of partnership
조합증표 union label
조항 article; clause; stipulation
조회 checking; comparison
조회; 조사; 연구 enquiry
조회계정 adjustment account
조회적합률 matching ratio
조회처은행 reference bank
조회표 comparison slip
조회필 기호 check mark
존속실체 surviving entity
존속회사 surviving company
존재명제 existential proposition
존재영역 realm of being
졸업조항 graduation clause
졸업채 exit bond
종가 Final value; last price
종가(거래소의)종가(終價) closing price
종가가 전일의 종가보다 값이 낮다 close

down
종가가 전일의 종가보다 값이 높다 close up
종가보관료 ad valorem storage
종가세 ad valorem tax
종가세율 ad valorem tariff
종가지정주문 market on close
종교법인 religious corporation
종국사망표 ultimate table
종국의 final
종국판결 definitive sentence
종량보관료 specific storage
종량세 specific duty
종량세율 specific tariff
종속 dependency
종속; 하위 subordination
종속변수 dependent variable
종신건강보험 permanent health insurance
종신고용제 permanent employment system
종신보험 permanent life insurance; whole life insurance
종신보험증권 life time policy
종신연금 life annuity; perpetual annuity; straight life annuity
종신연금보험 life annuity insurance; whole life annuity
종업원 employee
종업원 겸 임원 employee-director
종업원급여수당 employees bonus and allowance
종업원복지급여제도 employee welfare benefit plan
종업원에 대한 채무 account owed to employees
종업원연금기금적립금 employees' pension fund
종업원연금제도 employee pension benefit plan
종업원예금 deposit from employees; employees' deposits
종업원의 자기사정 employees' own conveniences

ㅈ
ㅊ
ㅋ

종업원자사주구입권 qualifying stock option
종업원조합 employees union; workers union
종업원주식구입계획 employee stock purchase plan
종업원지주제도 employee stock ownership plan
종업원할인 employee discount
종이홍수 paper crisis
종장무렵 at the close of the market
종합감가상각 composite depreciation
종합개인배상책임보험 comprehensive personal liability insurance
종합거래정보시스템 composite quotation system
종합경기지수 composite index
종합계정; 요약 summary
종합계좌 multiple purpose bank account
종합고액의료비보험 comprehensive major medical insurance
종합과세 comprehensive income taxation; general taxation; taxation on aggregate income; taxation upon total income
종합내용연수 composite useful life; synthetic useful life
종합디지털방송 integrated services digital broadcasting
종합명제 synthetic propositions
종합배상책임보험 comprehensive general liability policy
종합보세지역 comprehensive bonded area
종합보험 comprehensive insurance
종합보험증권 broad form
종합보험회사 composite office
종합분개장 summary journal
종합상각자산 composite depreciation assets
종합상태 pen position
종합세율 synthesis tax rate
종합소득세 consolidated income tax
종합수지 overall balance
종합수지흑자 favorable balance of overall
종합원가계산 process cost system

종합이율 total return
종합전략 grand strategy
종합조직 integrated organization
종합주가지수 broad based stock index; composite stock price index
종합주가표 composite stock price tables
종합주식티커 consolidated stock ticker
종합증권회사 national full line firm
종합지고 overall position
종합지수 general index
종합테이프 consolidated tape
종합평가법 overall evaluation method
종합표 aggregate table
종합할증보험료 combined marine surcharges
종합효과세율 effective aggregate tax rate; overall effective tax rate
좌우양면기사광고 double truck
좌초 stranding
좌표계 coordinate system
죄수의 딜레마 prisoner's dilemma
죄악이 없는 한 dum bene se gesserit
죄의 상쇄 compensatio criminum
죄의 주체 corpus delicti
주 explanatory note
주가 market price of stock; share price; stock price
주가가 일정 수준 이하로 떨어질 때까지 지속적으로 매각함 go on selling
주가가 천정부지로 치솟음 topless
주가규제 regulation of stock price
주가동향 fluctuation of stock prices; price movement of stocks; share price performance
주가분석 stock price analysis
주가상승 rise on stock price
주가수익률 per share earning ratio
주가순자산배율 price book-value ratio
주가안정조작 operations for stabilizing the stock market price
주가정보 stock quotations
주가조작 manipulation of stock price; stock

manipulation; stock price manipulation

주가지수 share index; stock index; stock price index

주가지수선물 stock index futures

주가지수선물거래 stock price index futures trading

주가지수선물옵션 options on stock index futures

주가지수옵션거래 stock price index option transaction

주가지수재정거래 stock price index arbitrage transaction

주가트렌드 price-trend on stocks

주가하락 falling in stock price

주간사 lead manager

주거 dwelling house

주거겸용주택 combined house

주거비 housing expenses

주거수당 housing allowance

주거침입죄 house breaking

주관적인 지각 subjective perception

주관적인 확률 subjective probability

주권 certificate of share; sovereign power; sovereignty; stock certificate

주권국 sovereign

주권대부 stock loan

주권대체기관 depositary trust company

주권리스크 sovereign risk

주권명의변경 transfer of a share-certificate

주권명의변경정지 transfer books closed

주권명의변경정지해제 transfer books open

주권양도위임장 stock power

주권양도증 stock receipt

주권이 있는 주식 certificated share

주권제권판결 judgment of exclusion on shareholders rights

주금불입명령 balance order

주기 cycle

주내보험자의 소화가 안되는 보험 surplus line

주내지점설치 state branching

주도권; 헤게모니 hegemony

주도보험자 leading underwriter

주도주 leaders

주력부문 core business division

주력은행 major relationship bank

주류 alcoholic beverage

주류심의회 council on alcoholic beverages

주류판매세 ale-silver

주름지게 접기 accordion fold

주말효과 weekend effect

주면허조직 state-chartered association

주목할 만한 noteworthy

주문 operative clause

주문부거래 order book trading

주문빈도 order frequency

주문생산 production upon order

주문의 불균형 imbalance of orders

주문이 쇄도함 rush order

주문잔액 backlog of orders

주문중개업자 introducing firm

주문집행 execution of order

주문집행확인서 exchange ticket

주문회송 order turnaround

주민세 inhabitant tax; residents tax

주법은행 state bank

주법인세 state franchise tax

주변시장 fringe market

주보험국 state insurance department

주부족 scarcity of stock

주사(走査) scan

주사무소; 본사 main office

주사선 scanning line

주석 annotation; chief; head

주석서 institutes

주성분분석 principal component analysis

주세 liquor tax

주소득세 state income tax

주소득자 main income earner

주순환 major cycles

주식 share

주식; 재고 stock

주식; 형평법; 지분 equity
주식거래 stock dealing
주식거래소 stock exchange
주식거래소공보 stock exchange daily official list
주식거래소대부 stock exchange loan
주식거래소회원권 stock exchange seat
주식거래소휴일 stock exchange holiday
주식거래실적 actual results of recent stock transactions
주식거래원 broker agent
주식결제연기이식 contango
주식계정 share account
주식공개매부 tender offer
주식공개매입 takeover bid
주식공개화 going public
주식공황 stock exchange panic; stock-market crash
주식구입계획 stock purchase plan
주식구입권부 equity kicker
주식구입선택권 stock option plan
주식담보금융 stock collateral loan
주식대장 stock ledger
주식딜러 equity securities dealer
주식리스크추정 stock risk estimation
주식매각손실준비금 securities transaction loss reserve
주식매각익 profit from sales of stocks
주식매수; 주식구입에 의한 매수; 주식취득 stock acquisition
주식매수권증서 option warrants
주식매입선택권; 스톡옵션 stock option
주식매입옵션 stock purchase option
주식매취권부 사채 bond with stock purchase warrant
주식매취청구권 appraisal rights of shareholder
주식명 stock name
주식모집개시 subscription book open
주식모집마감 subscription book closed
주식발행비용 cost of issuing stocks

주식배당 dividend on stock; stock dividend
주식병합 consolidation of stocks; reverse split of stocks
주식보관인 custodian
주식보상제도 stock compensation plan
주식보유율 holding ratio for a company's stock; share holding ratio
주식분류 classification of shares
주식분포 distribution of stocks
주식분할 share split-up; split-ups of stocks
주식분해 stock split-up
주식불입잉여금 paid-in capital in excess of par; premium on capital stock
주식브로커 share broker
주식비율 interlocking stockholding; stock rating
주식상각 retirement of shares
주식상장표시판 ticker
주식선물거래 stock futures transaction
주식소각 cancellation of shares
주식소유와 관련있는 배당 dividend from stocks owned
주식스와프 stock swap
주식시장 stock market
주식시장의 변동 stock market fluctuation
주식신용거래 stock dealing on credit
주식신용거래나 상품선물거래에서 성립된 판매주문 writing
주식신청금 application money for stock
주식신청서 subscription blank
주식심볼 stock symbol
주식액면 par
주식약어 stock abbreviation
주식양도 assignment of stock
주식양도제한 restriction on transfer of shares
주식어음계정 share draft account
주식워런트 equity warrant
주식원장 stock register
주식위험프리미엄 equity risk premium
주식을 시가발행함 increase in capital at the market price

주식을 통한 자금조달 equity financing

주식응모 stock subscription; subscription for shares

주식의 종류 classes of stocks

주식이율 stock yield

주식인수계정 subscription's receivable account

주식자금조달 financing for stocks

주식자본 share capital

주식제정거래 stock arbitrage

주식중매인 stock broker

주식지분 equity stake

주식지분가치 stock equity value

주식채 equity note

주식청산소 stock exchange clearing house

주식취득 acquisition of stock

주식취득신고 exchange offer

주식투기 speculation in stocks; stock speculation

주식투자 equity investment; investment in stocks; stock investment

주식투자가 equity investor

주식투자신탁 stock investment trust

주식편입률 equity weighting

주식평가 stock valuation

주식평가개요 stock valuation summary

주식할당 allotment of sharps

주식할당증서 share allotment certificate

주식할당통지 share allotment letter

주식합병 share consolidation; share split-down

주식환매 stock buyback

주식환매계획 stock repurchase plan

주식회사 company limited; company limited by shares; joint stock company

주식회사설립증서 deed of incorporation

주신신청서 application form for stock

주심문 examination in chief

주요 substantive

주요가공품 primary processed goods

주요거래 main customer

주요거래처 key account

주요계정 main account

주요기업단기경제관측 short-term economic survey of principal enterprises

주요딜러 responsible and recognized dealer

주요부분 staling part

주요사고 major casualties

주요사실 fact in issue; ultimate fact

주요산업 major industry

주요수입화물요율협정 Major Import Agreement

주요원인 efficient cause; key factor

주요원재료 main materials

주요이용자 primary user

주요인 prime factor

주요장부 head book; main books; principal books

주요제조지도서 principal production order

주요주주 major stockholders

주요트렌드 major trend

주요한 원재료 major raw materials

주원인 proximate cause

주의 diligence; prudence

주의의무 duty of care

주의환기 nudge

주임감사원 lead auditor

주임변호인 leading counsel

주임회계사 accountant in charge; in-charge accountant

주장 allegation

주장의 요점 points

주장하다 allege

주재감사인 resident auditor

주재원사무소 liaison office; representative office

주정보증증권 alcohol bond

주정부증권 state government securities

주정부채권 state government bond and debenture

주제(州際)통상 interstate commerce

주제(州際)통상위원회 Interstate Commerce

Commission

주제품 major product; prime product; principal products

주조가격 mint price

주조세 brewery-tax

주주 shareholder; stockholder

주주결의 shareholder resolution

주주권 shareholder's right; stockholder's right

주주명부 list of shareholders; shareholder's list

주주명부상의 주주 holder of record; shareholders of record

주주안정공작 stable stockholder

주주에 의한 임의청산 member's voluntary winding-up

주주우선배정 privileged allocation of issuance to stockholders

주주원장 shareholders ledger

주주자본 owner's capital; shareholder's equity

주주자본이익률 return on equity capital

주주지분 shareholder's interest; stock equity

주주지분계산서 statement of stockholders' equity

주주총회 general meeting of shareholders; meeting of shareholders; shareholder's meeting

주주총회결의 decision of a general meeting of stockholders

주주총회소집통지 proxy statement

주주할당 allotment to shareholders; issues to shareholders; rights offering

주주행동주의 shareholder activism

주지불 principal paying

주지불대리인 principal paying agent

주차결산 weekly accounting

주택건축착공수 housing starts

주택금융 housing loan

주택금융회사 housing loan corporation

주택모기지 home mortgage

주택물건 dwelling risk

주택손해배상책임보험 residence liability

policy

주택신용 housing credit

주택용 토지 land for residence

주택저당세액공제 mortgage credit

주택저축공제 deduction for housing savings; housing savings tax credit

주택종합보험 all risks dwelling house insurance; comprehensive dwelling policy; householders' comprehensive insurance

주택착공허가건수 housing permits

주택투자 residential investment

주택화재보험 fire insurance on dwelling houses

준강제저축 quasi-compulsory saving

준거법(準據法) applicable law; proper law; governing law

준거법(準據法)조항 governing clause

준거행동 reference behavior

준계약 implied contract; quasi-contract

준고정비 semi-fixed cost

준금반언(準禁反言) quasi-estoppel

준금치산자 quasi-incompetent person

준대물소송 action quasi in rem

준변동비 semi-variable charge

준변동비항목 semi-variable expenses

준변동원가 semi-variable cost

준보통주 common stock equivalents

준보험 quasi-insurance

준불법행위 quasi-delict

준비금계정 provision account; reserve account

준비금의 타당성 reserve adequacy

준비금이월 addition to reserve

준비금투자 reserve investments

준비서면 brief

준비서면; 소송 case

준비시간 make-ready time

준비예금제도 reserve deposit requirement system

준비율조작 reserve requirement operation

준비은행 reserve bank

준비잉여금 reserved surplus
준비자산 reserve assets
준비제도 reserve system
준비통화 reserve currency
준비포지션 reserve position
준비필 재산 property reserved
준사법권력 quasi-judicial power
준소비대차 quasi-loan for consumption
준수 compliance
준언어 paralanguage
준인플레이션 semi-inflation
준주식 quasi-equity
준중재인 quasi-arbitrator
준지역권 quasi-easement
준체인 quasi-chain
준톤티식 배당 semi-Tontine dividend
준통화 near money; quasi-currency
준화폐 quasi money
준확정신고 quasi-final return
준회원 quasi-member
중가산금 heavy additional charge imposed
중가산세 heavy additional tax; heavy penalty tax
중간값 mean price
중간결산 interim closing; semi-annual closing of accounts
중간계산서 interim statement
중간계정 interim account
중간래그 intermediate lag
중간매상 interim sales
중간발행 issue at intermediate price
중간배당 interim dividend
중간보고 interim report
중간분담금입금청구 interim call
중간세율 intermediate tariff
중간수치 middle rate
중간시장 intermediate market
중간신고 interim tax return
중간신고서 interim return form
중간업자 middleman
중간의 interlocutory; mesne

중간이득반환청구소송 trespass for mesne profits
중간재무제표 interim financial statements
중간지불이자 interim interest payment
중간층 middle class
중간치 mean value
중간판결 interlocutory judgment
중간회의 interim meeting
중개 introducing
중개변수 intervening variable
중개업무 broking business
중개업자 broker
중개은행 intermediary bank
중개인 concession hunter
중개자 intermediary
중견주 middle-sized stock
중계증폭기 transponder
중고자산 used property
중과실 gross negligence
중국인민보험공사 People's Insurance Company of China
중국펀드 medium-term government bond fund
중급회계학 intermediate accounting
중기국채펀드 medium-term government bond fund
중기대부 medium-term loan
중기예상 intermediate term market outlook
중기유러채 Euronote
중기이자부국채 medium-term fixed rate government bond
중기전망 medium-term outlook
중기채 medium-term bond
중노동 hard labor
중단클레임 suspension of work claims
중대한 부실표현 material misrepresentation
중도재료비 material in process
중도전환계약 convertible contract
중도해약 cancellation before maturity; cancellation of a contract; mid-term cancellation

ㅈ ㅊ ㅋ

중도환금 redemption before maturity
중량용적증명서 certificate of weight and measurement
중립국선증명서 sea-letter
중립선증명서 sea brief
중립성 neutrality
중매인 floor broker; jobber
중매인의 가격차이 jobber's turn
중매행위 jobbing
중미공동시장 Central American Common Market
중복계정 overlapping account
중복되지 않은 시청자수 unduplicated audience
중복보험 double insurance; overinsuance by double insurance
중복보험약관 co-existing cover clause
중복보험의 순위주의약 American clause
중복채무 overlapping debt
중부유럽자유무역연합 Central European Free Trade Association
중상관계수 coefficient of multiple correlation
중성위험 perils not covered
중세 heavy taxation
중소기업 small-and medium-sized enterprises
중소기업근대화시책 small-and medium enterprise modernization activities
중소기업금융공고 Small Business Finance Corporation
중소기업금융기관 financial institutions for small business
중소기업사업단 Small Business Corporation
중소기업의 근대화 modernization of smaller enterprise
중심경향 central tendency
중앙사망율 central death rate
중앙시장 central market
중앙은행 central bank
중앙은행의 공정할인율상회 dealer's turn
중앙은행할인율 central bank rate
중앙의 마주보는 양면 center spread

중앙치 median
중역실, 입회장 board room
중요부문 crown jewel
중요사실 material fact
중요성 materiality
중요성 원칙 materiality principle
중요성을 평가함 evaluation of importance
중요성의 원칙 principle of materiality
중요하지 않은 쟁점 immaterial issue
중요하지 않은 증거 immaterial evidence
중요한 significant
중요한 금액 significant amount
중요한 변수 material alternation
중요한 부분 integral part
중요한 요소 important factor
중요한 자회사 significant subsidiaries
중요한 주장 material allegation
중요한 증거 material evidence
중장기파이낸스 term financing
중장기협조융자 syndicated term loan
중재 arbitration
중재; 재정거래; 차익매매 arbitrage
중재부탁합의 submission
중재비용 cost of arbitration
중재소 arbitrage house
중재업자 arbitrage trader
중재인 arbiter; arbitrator
중재인선정기관 appointing authority
중재절차 arbitration proceeding
중재조건 arbitration clause
중재조정위원회 arbitration Commission
중재판단 arbitrament
중재판단항변 arbitrament and award
중재판정부 arbitral tribunal
중전(重電)스톡 heavy electrical stocks
중죄소추 appeal of felony
중핵 core
즉결판결 summary judgment
즉매 spot sale
즉매하다 sell on the spot
즉시 또는 취소주문 fill-or-kill order

즉시 이용가능한 자금 immediately available fund

즉시개시연금 immediate annuity

즉시방면 eat inde sine die

즉시상환가능한 채권 callable debt

즉시속행 fresh pursuit

즉시에 instanter

즉시유동성 immediacy

즉시지불 재보험금 cash loss

즉일인도 cash delivery

증가담보 additional collateral

증가세 appreciation duty

증가소득세 increased income tax

증가수익 incremental return

증가운전자본 increasing working capital

증가자본 additional capital

증가토지 accommodation lands

증감대조식 self-balancing type

증감법 increase and decrease method

증개축론 home improvement loan

증거 evidence; proof; witness

증거금 more margin

증거금거래 margin transaction

증거금계정; 신용거래구좌 margin account

증거금내부규제 house margin rule

증거금부족 margin deficiency

증거금부채 margin collateral margin debt

증거금율 margin rate

증거금제도 margin money system

증거금취급업자 carrying firm

증거불충분 not proven

증거사실 evidentiary facts

증거서류 documentary evidence; evidenced document

증거서류; 첨부서류 exhibit

증거요약 summing-up

증거의 무게 weight of evidence

증권거래법 securities and exchange law

증권거래세법 securities business tax law

증권거래소 securities exchange

증권거래소 준회원 allied members

증권거래심의회 securities exchange commission

증권거래업자협회 trade associations

증권고유리스크 security-specific risk

증권규칙 securities regulations

증권금융 securities financing; securities loan; security credit

증권금융회사 securities finance company

증권납부 tax payment by securities

증권담보대부 security loan

증권담보론 secured loan on securities

증권리스크 security risk curve

증권매리 marrying transaction of securities company

증권매매익 trading profit

증권발행 flotation; securities issue

증권발행수료 policy fee

증권발행시장 primary securities market

증권보유수요 demand to hold securities

증권분석 analysis of securities

증권분석전문가 security analyst

증권선물거래 securities futures

증권시장 securities market

증권시장선 securities market line

증권업 securities business

증권업계 securities industry

증권업자의 대리인으로서 거래소에 나와 거래하는 점원 floor representative

증권외무원 registered representative

증권위탁납부 request payment by securities

증권의 특권 bell and whistle

증권이율 securities yield

증권이익곡선 security yield curve

증권인수업자수수료 underwriting contract

증권자본 securities capital

증권적용지역 policy territory

증권투자 securities investment

증권투자사업 bond investment business

증권투자상담 securities investment advisory service

증권투자신탁 investment trust on securities;

securities investment trust
증권특별계정 special account for inward
   portfolio investment
증권할당 allotment
증권행정 securities administration
증권화 securitization
증권회사 securities company
증권회사가 판매를 위해 보유한 채권
   securities inventory
증권회사딜러 securities house dealer
증명문서 attestation clause
증명서 certificate
증명증인 attested witness
증명하다 attest; prove; vouch
증배 dividend increase
증분분석 incremental analysis
증분수익률 incremental rate of return
증분원가 incremental cost
증서대부 loan on deeds
증서배당 scrip dividend
증서본문 witnessing part
증서사항 matter in deed
증서의 문면 face of instrument
증서이전이 되는 lie in grant
증설적립금 reserve for additions
증세 increased tax; tax increase
증식보험 increased value insurance
증언 testimony
증언기록 deposition
증언에 따라 by deed
증언을 증거로 보전함 perpetuating testimony
증언의무면제특권 immunity of witness
증언하다 testify
증여 donation; gift; presentation
증여세 donation tax; gift tax
증여세율 tax rate of gift tax
증여은행 presenting bank
증여잉여금 donated surplus
증여자 donor
증여재산 donated property
증여주 donated stock

증익 profit increase
증인능력이 있는 증인 competent witness
증인심문 examination of witness
증인심문위탁서 commission to examine
   witnesses
증인예비심문 precognition
증인탄핵 impeachment of witness
증자 amount added to capital; capital
   increase; increase in capital stock
증자권리락 ex-rights of capital increase
증자권리부 주식 stock cum rights
증자신주매수권 stock right
증자압박 potential oversupply produced by
   new issues
증정사망율 adjusted death rate
증지징수 tax collection by stamp
지가제도(持家制度) one's own house system
지각선택성 perceptual selectivity
지구개발 sectional development
지구규모산업 global industry
지구배율 territorial multiplier
지구외무원 home service agent
지구특약권 territorial right
지급 supply
지급개시연령 pensionable age
지급주문 immediate order
지나친 행위 overshoot
지니메이 Ginnie Mae
지니메이채 Government National Mortgage
   Association debenture
지대(地代) rent
지대(地代)부담 rent charge
지대; 조세; 연공(年貢) gavel
지대위양 transfer of land tax
지대차압보증증권 bond for distrain of rent
지대표(地代表) rent roll
지도 direction
지도금지어음 nonorder bill
지도식 또는 소지인불식 payable to order
지도식 이서 endorsement to order
지도인식 선하증권 order bill of lading

지도적인 판례 leading case
지도평결 directed verdict
지명경쟁입찰 selective bid; selective tendering
지명권 power of appointment
지명네트 designated net
지명입찰 private tender
지명채권 claim payable to a specific person
지명하다 nominate
지목(地目) classification of lan; land category
지목변환 change of category of land
지목변환계 declaration of change of land category
지방 local
지방거래소 regional exchange
지방검사 district attorney
지방공공단체 municipal corporation
지방공공단체채권펀드 municipal bond fund
지방광고매체 local media
지방교부세 local grant tax
지방교부세교부금 distribution of local allocation tax
지방국 regional station
지방도로세 local road tax
지방도시인구이동 rural-urban shift of population
지방등록소 district registry
지방법원 local court
지방분여세 local allocation tax; partial tax transfer to local government
지방비 local expenditure
지방사무소 regional office
지방세 local tax; prefectural inhabitants tax; rate payment
지방세연체금 arrears of local tax
지방시장 regional market
지방양여세 local transfer tax
지방업자 regionals
지방은행 regional bank
지방의 관습 local custom
지방자치 local autonomy

지방자치체 local authorities; local government; local public entity
지방재정 local public finance
지방증권거래소 local stock exchange
지방증진금융 soil bank
지방채 local bond; local government bond; municipal bonds; prefectural bond
지방채선물 municipal futures
지방판 regional issue
지배모델 conjunctive model
지배시장 control market
지배적인 기업 dominant firm
지배주 control stock
지배집중도 degree of concentration of control
지배회사 controlling company
지분 holdings
지분; 이해관계; 이권 interest
지분법 equity method; equity purchase accounting
지분주 shareholdings
지분주식 equity share
지분풀링 pooling of interests
지불 defrayal; disbursement
지불가능가격 acceptable price
지불거절 under protest
지불거절선언 declaration of nonpayment
지불거절수표 rejected check
지불계정기준상장 giving quotation
지불고 amount paid
지불기일연기서면 letter of license
지불기일이 도래한 payable
지불기일이 되는 fall due
지불기일이 온 보험료 premium due
지불기입장 payment book
지불기한 due date for payment; term of payment
지불능력 ability to pay; solvency
지불능력과세설 faculty theory of taxation
지불능력기준 ability to pay basis
지불능력이 있는 solvent
지불능력평가 evaluation of solvency

지불대리인 disbursing agent; paying agent
지불명령 order to pay
지불명세 payment statement
지불보증 certification of payment
지불보증은행 certifying bank
지불보증증권 payment bond
지불분개장 cash-disbursement journal
지불불능판결 decree of insolvency
지불불능행위 act of insolvency
지불불능회사 insolvent corporation
지불비금 claim reserve
지불수수료 del credere commission
지불순환 disbursement cycle
지불어음 acceptance payable; bill payable; notes and bills payable
지불어음기입장 note payable register
지불여력 margin of solvency; margins of solvency
지불워런트 대리인계약서 paying & warrant agency agreement
지불유예 grace of payment; indulgence; postponement of payment
지불유예기간 days of grace; moratorium period
지불은행 paying bank
지불인 payer
지불인도 delivery against payment; delivery versus payment
지불인수수표 certified check
지불임대료 rent payable
지불장 cash disbursement book
지불전표 debit slip
지불전표기입장 payable register; voucher payable register
지불정지 payment stop; suspension of payment
지불정지; 모라토리엄 moratorium
지불정지통지 stop-payment order
지불조건 conditions for payment; payment terms
지불조서 payment record; record of payment

지불준비계정계약 payment account agreement; proceeds account agreement
지불준비금 reserve for outstanding claims
지불준비율 reserve rate
지불준비율정책 reserve requirement policy
지불준비제도 reserve requirements system
지불증여 presentation for payment
지불증여기간 presentation period for payment
지불지 place of payment
지불지도 payment order
지불지정어음 domiciled bill
지불채무 notes and accounts payable; trade payables
지불초과 unfavorable balance
지불카드 debit card
지불통지서 note of payment
지불편의조항 facility of payment clause
지불필 계정 account paid
지불필 보험금 claim paid
지불필 수표 paid check
지불한 프로젝트비용 as spent project cost
지불항목 items of payment
지불해야 할 owing
지사제도 branch system
지상권 surface right
지상권설정 settlement of superficies
지상권자 superficiary
지상물 superficium
지상위험담보 ground coverage
지선 branch line
지소(地所) demises
지속 continuation
지속계약 continuing contract
지속계정 continuing account
지속교육 continuing education
지속기업 going concern
지속기업가치 going concern value; going value
지속보증계약 guaranteed continuous policy
지속비 continued expenses; continuing expenditure

지속사업 continuing operations
지속사업부문의 이익 income from continuing operations
지속성장 sustainable growth
지속성장률 sustainable growth rate
지속약관 continuation clause
지속재고 continuous inventory
지속적인 매매 continuous buying and selling
지속적인 예정보험계약 continuous policy
지속적인 호조 remain buoyant
지속적인 흑자 remain in surplus
지속패턴 continuation pattern
지속회계감사 continuous audit
지수 index
지수리스크 index risk
지수법 index number technique
지수보유 index holding
지수보험 index clause insurance
지수분포 exponential distribution
지수성장 exponential growth
지수신가보험 index new value insurance
지수약관 index clause
지수재정거래자 index arbitrager
지수함수 exponential function
지수화 indexation
지시 instruction
지시신탁 directory trust
지시유증 demonstrative legacy
지시적인 법률 directory statute
지시증권 order paper
지시평결을 신청함 motion for directed verdict
지식공학 knowledge engineering
지식의 보고(백과사전 등) thesaurus
지식집약산업 knowledge intensive industry
GNP 디플레이터 GNP deflator
지역간 대체 transfers between geographic areas
지역격차 regional differences
지역경쟁 local competition
지역경제 regional economy
지역계획 regional plan

지역공익신탁 community trust
지역권 easement
지역권; 노역 servitude
지역권설정 settlement of easement
지역권자 easement holder; servitude holder
지역법 local law
지역별 가격제 geographical pricing
지역분석 regional analysis
지역브랜드 regional brand
지역사회신문 community paper
지역선정 area selection
지역연관분석 interregional analysis
지역적인 가격차이 geographical price different
지역주의 regionalism
지역지향 regioncentrism
지역활동참가 community involvement
지연결제 delaying settlement
지연손해금 delinquent charge; late payment charge
지연을 위한 항변 dilatory plea
지연이자 interest arrears; interest for arrears
지위체계 status system
지입자본 brought-in capital
지적 acreage
지적부호화 intelligent encoding
지적소유권 intellectual property right
지점 branch; branch office
지점개설 opening of branch
지점상호간손실 interbranch loss
지점상호간이익 interbranch profit
지점상호계정 interbranch account
지점원장 branch ledger
지점은행제도 branch banking system
지점회계 accounting for branch office; branch accounting
지정 appointment
지정가격주문 leave order; limit order
지정거래소 designated exchange
지정계좌 designated account
지정권자 appointor

지정기부금 donation to designated organization
지정도시 designated city
지정명의인 designated nominee
지정상속분 specified portion
지정상표 designated stock
지정상품 appointed goods
지정수표 check to order
지정예금 designated deposit
지정요건 specified requirement
지정인지불어음 bill payable to order
지정입찰 approved tender
지정입찰자 approved bidder
지정통계 designated statistics
지정통화 designated currency
지정하청업자 nominated subcontractor
지조(地租) land tax
지조(地租)기준면적 carucate
지조; 토지수익에 부과하는 조세 agrarium
지조부가세 surtax on land tax
지주 landlord
지주매입협정 buy-out arrangement
지주미필배상책임보험 landlords' contingent liability policy
지주배상보험 landlords' liability policy
지주비율 ratio of shareholding
지주회사 holding company
지진보험 earthquake insurance
지진위험담보특별약관 earthquake clause
지참인 bearer
지참인불 payable to bearer
지참인지불수표 check to bearer
지참인지불식 증권 bearer instrument
지참인지불어음 bill payable to bearer
지체 delay
지체클레임 delay claims
지출 cash disbursed; expenditure; outgo; outlay; spending
지출가능자금 expendable fund
지출국민소득 national income expended
지출삭감 expenditure curtailment

지출세 expenditure tax
지출소비 outlay expiration
지출원가 outlay cost
지출율 expenditure rate
지출전표제도 voucher system
지침 guidance
지탱 support
지폐 paper currency
지표 indicator
지표가 되는 지수 reference index
지표상표 bellwether issue
지표증권 benchmark securities
지하경제 underground economy
지하자금 underground money
지하조건클레임 adverse physical conditions claims
지행계수 lagging series
지행지수 lag indicator
지형 topography
지휘명령 commanding
직간접비율 ratio of direct and indirect taxes
직거래 direct deal
직계상속인 heir of the body
직계존속 ascendants; descendant
직교, 직각 orthogonal
직교인자 orthogonal factor
직교좌표 rectangular coordinates
직권 attribution; competence; official power
직권남용죄 oppression
직근원인 immediate cause
직능급 wage according to job evaluation; wages on job evaluation
직능별 조직 functionalized organization
직무급 wages attached to a post
직무내용 job contents
직무명세 job specification
직무별 포괄보증증권 position blanket bond
직무별 포괄신용보험 position floating policy
직무상의 책임 functional responsibility
직무순회 job rotation
직무집행비용 disbursements

직무충실 job enrichment
직무평가 job evaluation
직무확대 job enlargement
직물 spot
직물거래 spot operation; spot transaction
직물위치 spot position
직별업자 trade contractor
직선법 strait-line method
직선생산 line production
직업 profession
직업감사인 professional auditor
직업별 상호보험 class mutual
직업안정소 employment service
직업재해 occupational accident
직업회계사 professional accountant
직접경비 direct expense; direct overhead
직접공격 direct attack
직접국세 direct national tax
직접금융 direct financing; direct loan
직접금융형 리스 direct financing lease
직접노동 direct labor
직접노무비 direct labor cost
직접매출페이퍼 direct issue paper
직접모집 direct placement
직접모집제도 direct writing system
직접법 direct method
직접부문 direct department
직접상각 direct method of depreciation
직접상속 immediate descent
직접세 direct tax
직접손해 proximate damage
직접심문 direct examination
직접예금 direct deposit
직접원가계산 direct costing
직접원가배부법 prime cost method
직접원인 causa causans
직접이익 current yield; direct yield
직접이해관계 direct interest
직접인식 personal knowledge
직접임금 productive wages
직접자본 direct capital

직접재료비 direct material cost
직접정산법 direct pricing
직접증거 direct evidence
직접증권 primary securities
직접참가방식단체연금계약 immediate participation guarantee contract
직접참가예탁관리계약 direct rated deposit administration contract
직접참가프로그램 direct participation program
직접투자 direct investment; direct or equity investment
직접평가 direct valuation
직접표시 direct presentation
직접환거래 direct dealing
직접환재정 direct exchange arbitrage
직책 job description
직판경로 direct channel
진공포장 vacuum packing
진단과정 diagnostic process
진동이론 oscillation theory
진부화 상각자산 obsolescent depreciable property
진부화 자산 obsolete assets; obsolete property
진부화자산상각 depreciation on obsolete assets
진사(생명보험을 계약할 때 피보험인의 건강 상태를 조사함) medical examination
진성대부법 truth in lending
진실로 정당한 권리자 really rightful person
진실성의 원칙 principle of truth
진실하며 공정함 true and fair
진입 ingress
진입장벽 advancement barrier; barriers to entry
진정준비금 true reserve
진정한 authentic
진정한 원가 bona fide cost
진정한 증명 attestation
진체이익준비금 reserve for intercompany

ㅈ
ㅊ
ㅋ

profit

질감 sizzle

질권 right of pledge

질권등기 registration of the right of pledge

질권설정 establishment of the right of pledge

질권설정계약 pignorative contract

질권설정자 pledger

질권자 pawnee

질로 도피함 flight to quality

질멜식 책임준비금 Zillmerized reserve

질문검사권 authority to inquire and inspect

질물수탁자 pledgeholder

질병급부 sickness benefit

질서있는 수출 orderly export marketing

질적실질성의 원칙 qualitative substantiality test

질적인 경제정책 qualitative economic policy

질적인 금융통제 qualitative credit control

짐을 옮겨실음 transshipment

집계계정 summary account

집계의 문제 aggregation problem

집계표 summary sheet

집권관리 centralized management

집권조직 centralized organization

집단규범 group norm

집단기능 function of group

집단내 계층분화 within-group stratification

집단면접 group interview

집단소송 class action

집단압력 group pressure

집단역학 group dynamics

집단적립제 collective accumulation

집단적용면제 block exemption

집단적합 group conformity

집단지도 collective leadership

집단행동 group behavior

집약척도 summary measure

집적과정 accumulation process

집적손해제한약관 location clause

집중도 degree of concentration

집중마케팅전략 concentrated marketing strategy

집중머천다이징 concentrated merchandising

집중배제; 분권 decentralization

집중분석 convergence analysis

집중시키는 funnel

집중적으로 거래되는 주 highly traded stock

집중전략 focus strategy

집중캠페인 saturation campaign

집중투자 concentrated investment; intensive investment

집중효과 concentration effect

집하서비스 assembly service

집합법인 corporation aggregate

집합이론 aggregate theory

집행 laps

집행관 marshal

집행관리 executive officer

집행권 executive power

집행기간 term of execution

집행기일 date of execution

집행수수료 poundage

집행연기 reprieve

집행위원회 executive committee

집행유예 probation

집행자 executor

집행재산 leviable property

집행절차 executive proceedings

집행정지 suspension of execution

집행정지명령 casset execution

집행채권자 execution creditor

집행처분 executive measure

징발 impressment

징발보상금 imprest money

징벌적인 손해배상 punitive damages

징세 tax collection

징세기구 tax collection system

징세비용 cost of tax collection

징세상의 편의 convenience of tax collection

징수 collecting tax

징수경비 collection charge

징수권 power of collection

징수권소멸시효 statute of limitations on collection
징수료 collection fee
징수명령 order for collection
징수비용 collection expenses
징수수수료 collecting commission
징수순위 precedence rule on tax collection
징수액 collected amount
징수액계산서 accounting sheet of collected amount

징수어음 collection bill
징수유예 postponement of tax collection
징수은행 collection bank
징수의무자 collecting agent
징수촉탁 entrust of collection
징수하다 collect
징역 penal servitude
징후형 행동 symptomatic behavior
짧은 광고방송 plug
찌꺼기; 토막 scrap

ㅊ

차고료 warehouse charges
차관공여 loan extension
차관반제 replacement of loan
차관수령 loan received
차금 differences
차금거래 speculating for difference;
    speculation for margin
차금결제 net settlement
차금계정 debt account
차기 next time
차기(借記)통지서 debit advice
차기결산 next closing of account
차기계정 ensuing account
차기이월고 amount carried forward
차등세율 graded tariff
차량보항 automobile physical damage
    insurance
차변 debit; debit side
차변계정 debit account; debtor account
차변메모 debit memorandum
차변승인 debit authorization
차변잔고 debit balance; debtor balance
차변표 debit note
차별가격 discriminative price
차별관세 discriminating duty
차별대우 discrimination
차별세율 discriminative tariff
차별요율 differential rate
차별이득 differential payoff
차별해서는 안되며 not unfairly discriminatory

차별화 differentiation
차별화전략 differentiation strategy
차세대사진필름 new print film
차순위보험금수취인 contingent beneficiary
차압 attachment; distress; seizure
차압금지채권 exemptions
차압대상재산 property subject to seizure
차압명령 order for attachment of property
차압명장 warrant of attachment
차압물건 attached goods; seized goods
차압물건매각 distress sale
차압물인도 transfer of seized goods
차압서 document of seizure
차압선착순주의 principle of priority to first
    seizure
차압유예 suspension of seizure
차압인 distrainor; seizor
차압재산환가 conversion into cash of seized
    property
차압조서 record of seizure
차압지소등기 register of cancellation of
    attachment
차압통지서 notice of seizure; seizure note
차압해제 release of seizure
차압해제청구보증증권 release of libel bond
차액 difference; gap
차액수입 takeout
차액식 remainder type
차액원가 differential cost
차용개념 adopted concept

차원 dimension
차원성 dimensionality
차이 discrepancy; variance
차입금 borrowed money; borrowing; debt
　loan; loan payable
차입금계정 borrowing account
차입금금리 interest rate on borrowing
차입금이자 interest on borrowed
차입반제보증 guarantee of repayment
차입보증금 guaranty money deposited
차입수요 borrowing demand
차입예약 standby arrangement
차입유가증권 borrowed securities; pledged
　security; securities borrowed
차입으로 자금을 조달함 debt finance
차입이자를 자산계상함 capitalization of
　interest cost
차입자본 borrowed capital; loan capital
차입잔고를 일괄지불함 balloon payment
차입주식 borrowed share
차입주잔주, 차주잔고 short interest
차입초과 overborrowing
차입코스트 borrowing cost
차입필요액 borrowing requirements
차입한도액 debt ceiling
차주(借主)잔고 balance of stock loans
차지권 lease tenant right
차지권; 대차권 tenant right
차지권가격 fair leasehold value
차지권설정 establishing a lease;
　establishment of leasehold; settlement of
　leasehold
차지권을 부여하는 계약 leasehold
차지권의 기간이 경과함 lapse of the leasehold
차지권자 leaseholder
차지권취득원가 acquisition cost of leasehold
차지인 lease-holder; tenant
차지증 lease of land
차지커플디바이스 charge coupled device
차터파티 **B/L** charter party B/L
차트 chart; chat

차트분석 chart reading
차트패턴 chart pattern
차티스트 chartist
차환발행 conversion issue; refinancing issue;
차환정책 funding policy
차환증권 refunding securities
차환채 refinancing bond
착복 misappropriation
착불 freight collect
착선 arrival
착실한 신장 steady rise
착오 mistake
착지거래 transaction with delayed settlement
착취 exploitation
착하 arrival of shipment
찬반투표 yeas and nays
참가 participation
참가방식 participation method
참가시장 entry market
참가우선주 participation preferred stock
참가우선주식 participating preferred stock
참가융자 participation loan
참가은행 participation bank
참가인수 act of honor
참가자 participant
참가증권 participation certificate
참가지불 payment supra
참가집단 participation group
참가차압 participation in seizure
참고기간 reference period
참고상장권 reference range; reference zone
참고상장시장 indicated market
참고수치 proforma amount
창고금융 warehouse financing
창고료 warehouse fee
창공법; 부정증권거래금지법 blue sky law
창구 window
창구지도 window guidance
창립 creation; organization
창립사무소 organization office
창립위원 organization committee

ㅈ
ㅊ
ㅋ

창립자 founder; organizer
창립준비비 preopening expenses
창립총회 inaugural meeting; organization meeting
창업비 formation expenses; initial expenses; promotion expenses
창업비상각 amortization of initial expenses
창업자이익 founder's profit
채광권 placer claim patent; ancient lights
채굴권 mining concession; mining rights
채굴료 diggings
채굴면허 ore-leave
채굴예정연수 estimated mining period
채권 active debt; bond; bond and debenture; debenture
채권; 청구 claim
채권가격 bond price; dollar price
채권계정 bond account; debentures account
채권계출 filing of claims
채권구입 bond purchase
채권국 creditor country
채권권리자 bond creditor
채권기일 redemption of bond
채권담보 finance receivables as collateral; security for obligation
채권대체결제제도 book-entry system for bond
채권등급을 매김 bond rating
채권딜러 bond dealer
채권발행 bond issue; issuance of bond
채권발행은행 bond issuing bank
채권발행차입금 bonded debt
채권법 law of obligations
채권변제 liquidation of claim; settlement of claim
채권보유 bond holding
채권보전 preservative attachment
채권보전화재보험 fire-insurance for mortgagee interest
채권브로커 bond broker
채권상각특별계정 special bad debts reserve
채권상각특별계정제거 liquidation of special bad debts

채권상승액 bond premium
채권상응이율 equivalent bond yield
채권선물 bond futures
채권선물옵션 bond futures option
채권선택옵션 bond selection option
채권수요 bond demand
채권순위 order of credit
채권스와프 bond swap; swap of bond
채권시장 bond market
채권시장균형 bond market equilibrium
채권신탁증서 bond trust indenture
채권양도 assignment of claim; cession of an obligation
채권에 대한 데디케이트포트폴리오 dedicated bond portfolio
채권옵션 bond option
채권을 대량발행함 large-scale bond issue
채권을 뒤로 미룸 long-term postponement of credit
채권응모 bond subscription
채권의 등급을 매김 bond credit rating; rating of bond
채권의 임의상환조항 bond call provision
채권의 표면이자율 coupon rate
채권이연계정 unamortized discount on debenture accounts
채권이율 bond return; bond yield
채권이익 yield on bond
채권인수 bond underwriting
채권입체거래 bond switching
채권자 creditor; obligee
채권자구제수속 receivership
채권자대위권 subrogation right of obligee
채권자에 의한 임의청산 creditor's voluntary winding-up
채권자회의 creditor's meeting
채권장외옵션 bond option at over-the-counter
채권절차 process of garnishment
채권주식조합 bond-stock mixes
채권차압 foreign attachment

채권차압인 garnisher

채권차압통지 garnishment

채권차환 bond refunding

채권채무 debts and credits

채권채무계약 receivable and payable contract

채권펀드 bond fund

채권평균만기 duration of bond

채권할인 bond discount

채권확정판결 judgment of definite liabilities

채권환산이율 bond-equivalent yield

채권회수 collection of claim; debt collection; recovery of credits

채널라인 channel line

채도 chroma; saturation

채무 indebtedness; obligation

채무; 부채 debt

채무; 책임 liability

채무가 있는 stand in debt

채무계약해제 defeasance

채무공제 deduction of liabilities

채무국 debtor country

채무레버레지 debt leverage

채무매입계약 note purchase agreement

채무면제 acquittal; debt relief; discharge of debts; forgiveness of debt; release from debts; waiver of obligation

채무면제익 gains from forgiveness of debt; income from discharge of indebtedness

채무반제 debt retirement

채무반제비율 debt service ratio

채무변제충당; 보험계약자의 사실고지; 신청요항 application

채무보증 guaranty of liabilities

채무부담날인채무증서 single bill

채무불이행 default of obligation

채무불이행 예측지표 predictors of default

채무불이행 프리미엄 default risk premium

채무불이행리스크 default risk

채무삭감 debt reduction

채무상환; 정액상각 amortization

채무상환계획 amortization schedule

채무상환적립금 surplus appropriated for redemption fund

채무소멸 expiration of obligation

채무수단 debt instrument

채무스와프 liability swap

채무승낙 cognovit actionern

채무완제 acquittance

채무의 상호성 mutuality of obligation

채무의 채권화 debt bond swap

채무인계 succession of liabilities

채무인수 assumption; debt assumption

채무일괄조정 debt pooling

채무자 debtor; obligor

채무자 및 파산재단 debtor and estate

채무자보증증권 debtor's bond

채무자예금 debtor's deposit

채무자의 반제(返濟)불능 insolvency of debtors

채무정리 arrangement

채무정리계획 scheme of arrangement

채무정리증서 deed of arrangement

채무조정 adjustment of debts

채무증권 bill of credit; debt securities

채무증서 bill of debt; certificate of indebtedness; evidences of indebtedness

채무초과 insolvency; liabilities exceeding assets

채산라인 profitable line of business

채산수준 break-even line

채산주 income share

채용곡선 adoption curve

채용단계 adoption process

채용모델 adoption model

채용시간 time of adoption

책상조사 office audit

책임 accountability

책임능력 doli capax

책임단위 accountability unit

책임무능력 doli incapax

책임보유리스크 current risks

책임원가계산 responsibility costing

ㅈ
ㅊ
ㅋ

책임자 accountable person
책임준비금 liability reserve; policy reserve
책임준비금증가액 inside build-up
책임한도액 total maximum liability
책임할당 assignment of responsibility
책임회계 responsibility accounting
처분 disposal; disposition
처분가격 disposal price
처분가치 disposal value; salvage value
처분매출 selling out
처분비용 cost of disposal
처분수입 proceeds from disposals
처분제한증서 backbond
처분청산계산서 statement of realization and liquidation
처분필 이익잉여금 appropriated earned surplus
처음부터 ab initio
처짐, 늘어짐 sag
척도법 scale method
천연가스파이프라인 natural gas pipeline
천이확률행렬 transition matrix
천재자금 natural disaster relief loans
천정권 vicinity of the upper limit
철거자산 removed assets
철도수송 rail transportation
철도채 railroad bonds
철사로 박는 제본방식 saddle stitching
철수 evacuation; withdrawals
철수; 반환 repossession
철수장벽 divestiture barrier; exit barrier
철수지체 delay of evacuation
철회 revocation
철회의사 animus revocandi
철회할 수 없는 irrevocable
첨단기술 emerging technology
첨단업계 emerging industry
첨부광고 stuffer
첨부서류 accompanying document; appendix; attached document
첫 도중산환일 first call date

첫 이자지불일 first coupon date
청구 request
청구권 right of claim
청구권보험 claim right insurance
청구명세서 bill of particulars
청구불이행 nonclaim
청구서 invoice book
청구서; 법안 bill
청구액 amount billed; amount claimed
청구원인분할 splining a cause of action
청구지체손해 belated claims
청구취지신청 prayer
청구한 즉시 on call
청년중역 junior director
청부계약 construction contracts
청부공사 contract work
청부공사미수금 contract work account receivable
청부모집; 잔액인수발행 standby underwriting
청부인 independent contract
청부제도 contract system; contract work system
청산 clearing; settlement; settling
청산가격 clearing price
청산가치 break-up value; liquidation value
청산거래 clearing contract; clearing transaction
청산계정 liquidation accounts; settled account
청산기관 clearing agency; clearing organization
청산기능 clearing function
청산대차대조표 liquidation balance sheet
청산명령 winding-up order
청산배당 liquidating dividend; liquidation dividend
청산사무 liquidation affairs; liquidation matter
청산사무소 liquidation office
청산서 statement of liquidations
청산소득 income at liquidation; liquidation income

청산소득세 liquidation tax
청산손익 liquidation profit and loss
청산수속 liquidation proceedings
청산우선권 liquidation preference
청산인 liquidating partner; liquidator
청산잉여금 surplus at liquidation
청산절차 clearing procedure
청산절차중인 법인 corporation under liquidation
청산중인 법인 corporation in the course of liquidation
청산치 liquidation price
청산하다 settle
청산협정 clearing agreement
청산확정신고 liquidation final return
청산확정신고서 Final return of liquidation
청산회사 clearing corporation; liquidated company
청산회원 clearing member
청색신고 blue form return
청색신고법인 corporation filing a blue return
청색신고승인을 취소함 cancellation of approval of filing a blue return
청색신고자 taxpayer filing a blue return
청색신고제도 blue return system; system of blue return
청색신고특별공제 special deduction for blue return
청원 petition
청원권 right of petition
체감원가 degressive cost
체감원가법 diminishing balance method
체감잔고법 reducing balance method
체감정기보험 decreasing term insurance
체결; 이행 execution
체납 arrears; delinquency; tax delinquency
체납독촉수수료 charge for demand for tax in arrears
체납세 back tax; delinquent tax
체납임차금 back rent
체납자 delinquent taxpayer

체납처분 disposition for failure to pay
체선료; 하차유치료 demurrage
체인뱅킹 chain banking
체인브레이크 chain break
체인지오버 change over
체증비 progressive cost
체증연금 increasing annuity
체증정기보험 increasing term life insurance
체증종신보험 increasing whole life insurance
체크개런티카드 check guarantee card
체포 apprehension
체포보고서 cepi corpus
체화금융 financing for carrying unsold inventories
체화금융 stockpile financing
체화융자 loan for carrying unsold inventory
초감 first check
초고화질텔레비전 ultra definition television
초과공급 excess supply
초과공동해손 excess general average
초과대부 overdrawn
초과대출 overdrawing
초과대출계정 overdrawn account
초과매매 overtrading
초과매출 overselling
초과매출의 oversold
초과발행이자 overdraft interest
초과배부 overabsorption
초과보험 overinsurance
초과사망율 excess mortality
초과사용시간 overused hours
초과상각 depreciation in excess of the limit; excessive depreciation deduction
초과세율 tax rate higher than standard
초과소득 excess income
초과손해액 excess of loss
초과손해액특약재보험 excess of loss treaty reinsurance
초과손해율보험 stop loss cover
초과손해율재보험 excess of loss ratio reinsurance

ㅈㅊㅋ

초과손해재보험 excess of loss reinsurance; spread toss reinsurance; stop loss reinsurance

초과수요 excess demand

초과액 excess line

초과액재보험 excess line reinsurance; excess reinsurance

초과액특약재보험 surplus treaty reinsurance

초과이윤 excess profitability; excess profits; excess profits tax

초과이윤공제 excess profits credit

초과인출경제 overdraft economy

초과준비 excess reserves

초과증거금 excess margin

초과지불 excess disbursement; excess payment

초과차압 excessive seizure

초과책임담보약관 excess liabilities clause

초국적기업 transnational corporation

초기단계전략 take-off strategy

초기반제모기지론 early ownership mortgage loan

초기상각 initial depreciation

초기설정 initial establishment

초기증거금율 initial margin requirement

초기채용자 early adopters

초기추종자 early majority

초기측정 initial measurements

초기투입자금 seed money

초년도수수료 first year commission

초년도수익 annates

초년정기식 책임준비금 full preliminary term reserve

초벌인쇄 preprint

초본 abstract; abstract of register

초연도특별상각 initial special depreciation

초인플레이션 hyper inflation

초일류은행 prime name bank

초장기국채 ultra long-term national bond

초저가격광고상품 nailed down

초토작전 scorched earth defense

초회금 amount of the first payment

초회준비금 initial reserve

촉성법 forcing methods

촉진세제 special incentive measures

촉진자; 운송업자 forwarder

촉진클레임 acceleration claims

촉탁서 rogatory letters

촌수 degree of consanguinity

총거래 gross transaction

총계 aggregate; grand total; total sum

총계로 all totaled

총계의 combined

총계정원장 general ledger

총계정원장계정 general ledger account

총공급량 aggregate supply

총공급함수 aggregate supply function

총과실 gross loss

총괄경영층 general management

총괄운임 lump-sum freight

총괄조항 omnibus clause

총노말포트폴리오 aggregate normal

총대리인 universal agent

총대리점 general agent

총대리점제도 general agency system

총매상고 gross sales; total sales

총매상원가 gross cost of merchandise sold

총매입계약 total buying contract

총매출계약 total selling contract

총무처; 사무국 secretariat

총반응곡선 aggregate response curve

총발행제주식수 total stocks issued

총발행필주식수 whole issued stock

총보상한도액 aggregate limit

총부채자기자본율 equity capital ratio to total debt

총비용곡선 total cost curve

총상품매매차익 gross merchandise margin

총생산고 total turnover

총선거 general election

총소득 gross income

총소득금액 total net income

총손품가액 arrived damaged value
총수요 gross demand
총수익 gross earnings; gross gain; gross revenue; total earnings
총수익률 total rate of return
총수입 total receipts
총시장가액 total market value
총시장델타치 total market delta
총시청자 total audience
총액 gross amount; sum
총액베이스 gross base
총액예산주의 principle of gross budget accounting
총액주의 gross amount principle
총액티브리스크 aggregate active risk
총영업이폭 gross operating spread
총예금 total deposit
총운용포트폴리오 aggregate managed portfolio
총원가 gross cost
총이익 gross profit; gross profit method
총이익률 gross profit percentage
총이익분석 gross profit analysis
총이익테스트 gross profit test
총익금 gross profits
총익률 gross profit ratio
총인수액누적조사카드 aggregate liability index
총자본 gross capital; total liabilities and net worth
총자본수익률 profit rate of total liabilities and net worth; total capital profit ratio
총자본회전율 turnover of total capital
총자산 gross assets; total assets
총자산매상률 sales to total assets
총자산수익률 return on assets
총자산이익률 return on total assets
총자산회전율 total asset turnover ratio
총장기자금 total capitalization
총장부가격 gross book value
총재 governor; president

총정품가액 gross sound value
총준비 total reserves
총지출 gross expenditure
총지출접근방법 absorption approach
총출자금액 all amounts invested in capital
총칙 genera provisions
총통화공급고 total money supply
총투자 gross investment
총평균 aggregate average
총평균법 periodic average method; progressive average inventory method
총화법지수 index number by aggregative method
총회의 결정 decision of the general meeting
최고가격에 도달하다 reaching the top price
최고가입찰자 top bidder
최고경영책임자 chief executive officer
최고급부금; 자본액 capital sum
최고발행액제한제도 maximum limit system
최고법원 Supreme Court
최고보유액 maximum retention
최고서 notification
최고손해액 maximum probable loss
최고시세에 달하다 hitting the ceiling
최고액 ceiling price
최고업무책임자 chief operating officer
최고최저세율제 maximum and minimum tariff system
최대선의 utmost good faith
최대세력계획 maximum effort plan
최대수요 maximum demand
최대운전재고량 maximum operating stock
최대재고량 maximum inventory
최대최소척도 maximin criterion
최대피영향국 most seriously affected countries
최대화 maximization
최량증거 best evidence
최빈치, 최빈값 mode
최선노력원칙 best-efforts basis
최소공간분석 smallest space analysis

ㅈ
ㅊ
ㅋ

최소변동단위 minimum fluctuation unit
최소부채 minimum liability
최소비용원칙 minimum cost principle
최소세력의 원리 principle of least effort
최소이윤 minimum profit
최소제곱법 least-squares method
최소치 minimum value
최소한계비용 minimum marginal cost
최신의 state of the art
최염가저당 cheapest-to-deliver
최우선인수권 right of first refusal
최저가격 knockdown price
최저가격라인 opening price point
최저거래단위 round lot
최저경매가격 upset price
최저과세 minimum tax
최저대출비율 minimum lending rate
최저리스지불액 minimum lease payment
최저면세소득 minimum exempt income
최저목표수익률 hurdle rate
최저보증부 종신연금 guaranteed minimum life annuity
최저보험료 minimum premium
최저수급연령 minimum age requirement
최저수준까지 하락하다 hit the bottom
최저시세까지 내려감 bottoming out
최저시세로 떨어짐 touching the bottom
최저요율 minimum rate
최저운임 minimum freight
최저유동성비율 minimum liquidity ratio
최저의 희생 minimum sacrifice
최저의무기간 minimum service requirement
최저이율 minimum rate of interest
최저이폭 minimum margin
최저임금 minimum wage
최저임금제도 minimum wage system
최저자본금제도 minimum capital system
최저재고 minimum inventory; minimum stock
최저적립기준 minimum funding standard
최저점 descending tops

최저주문량 minimum quantity
최저증거금율 minimum margin requirement
최저지불액 minimum payment
최저한도지불의무액 fixed amount minimum payment
최적관세이론 theory of optimum tariff
최적광고비 optimum advertisement cost
최적규모 optimal scale; option seller
최적네트워크 optimum network
최적분배 optimum distribution
최적생산량 optimum output
최적성장률 optimum rate of growth
최적성장모델 optimal growth model
최적이자율 optimum rate of interest
최적자원배분 optimum allocation of resources
최적재고량 optimum inventory
최적전략지수 optimal strategy index
최적정보 optimal information
최적조건 optimal condition
최적조업도 optimal operating ratio; optimum rate of operations
최적통화지역 optimum currency
최적폴리시믹스 optimal policy mix
최적화 optimization
최종거래일 final transaction date; last trading day
최종검증 final verification
최종구입원가법 last cost method; last purchase method; method of price of last purchase
최종구입원가법 most recent purchase method
최종급료형 final pay type
최종기입부 book of final entry
최종목적 ultimate objectives
최종목표 policy objective
최종분담금 final call
최종분위기(거래소의)최종분위기 closing tone
최종상속인 last heir
최종생산물 final products
최종생존자연금 last survivor annuity

최종설립취지서 final prospectus
최종소비자 ultimate consumer
최종수요 final demand
최종수요자 end-user
최종수익률 final rate of return
최종수익자 final beneficiary
최종이익 Final yield
최종잔고방식 final balance method
최종적으로 확정한 재무제표 finally settled financial statements
최종투자가 retail investor
최종투자이익 Final yield on investment
최종회의 closing meeting
최초인도 initial delivery
최초취득자 first purchaser
최혜국대우 most favored nation treatment
최혜국조항 most favored nation clause
최혜재보험자약관 most favored reinsurer clause
최후의 대주(貸主) last resort lender
최후조건설 theory of ultimate cause
추가 및 생략 additions and omissions
추가가격인상 additional markup
추가기입 post-entry
추가마크업 add-on markup
추가문서 addenda
추가보증 additional security
추가보험료 additional premium
추가분담금 additional call
추가비용 accruing costs; additional charge; additional expenses; extra cost
추가비용약관 additional expenses clause
추가사례금 refresher
추가설정 additional establishment; additional issue
추가소유 adding to holdings
추가수익 remargin
추가요금 add-on charge
추가위험 extra risk
추가이익 additional margin
추가이해관계자 additional interest

추가조항 additional conditions; codicil
추가증거금 maintenance call; margin call
추가지불 pay-up
추가출자 additional investment
추가특별예금제도 supplementary special deposits scheme
추가할인 added discount
추계 estimate
추계과세 taxation by estimate
추계를 통한 갱정 determination by estimate
추단(推斷) implication
추량차이 physical variance
추론엔진 inference engine
추리 inference
추문 scandalous matter
추방 banishment; relegation
추세 trend
추세분석 trend analysis
추수(追隨)가격 imitative price
추수(追隨)보험자 following underwriter
추이모델 transition model
추이율 passing ratio
추이확률 transition probability
추적가능원가 traceable cost
추정 presumption
추정량차이 quantity variance
추정상속인 heir presumptive
추정신탁; 복귀신탁 resulting trust
추정악의 constructive notice
추정의 constructive; putative
추정증거 presumptive evidence
추정치표준오차 standard error of estimate
추징처분 punishment on penalty tax
추천광고 testimonial advertising
추천주 recommended stock
추첨상환 redemption by lottery
추측통계학 stochastics
축소재생산 reproduction on a diminishing scale
축소하다 narrow
축적교환 stored and forward switching

ㅈ
ㅊ
ㅋ

춘투 spring offensive
출금전표 disbursement slip; payment slip
출납부 account book; cash-book
출납소 treasury
출납전표 cash slips
출산급부 maternity benefit
출산율 birth rate
출생률 fertility rate
출생지법원 forum origins
출소기한 limitation of actions
출신주 home state
출원권 application right
출원권취득 acquisition of the application right
출입국관리령 Emigration and Immigration Central Order
출입금지 off limit
출자 capital subscription; investment; subscription
출자계약 equity instruments
출자금 equity fund; investment in capital
출자법 law of subscription
출자사원 partner
출자액 amount invested
출자의무자 contributories
출자자 equity participant; financier; investor; lessor owner
출자증권 subscription certificate
출자할당액 quota
출장여비 traveling expenses for business
출장총대리점 gripsack general agent
출재(出再)수수료 ceding commission
출재(出再)회사 ceding company
출재보험자 cedent
출재한도액 limit of cession
출정영장 habeas corpus
출판권 publishing right
출판물광고 publising advertising
출판법 press law; publishing law
출판비 publishing cost
출판의 자유 freedom of the press
출항수수료 clearance fee

충당금 money appropriated; money earmarked
충당순위 priority order of application
충돌 collision
충동구매 impulse buying; impulse goods
충동구매상품 impunity
충분한 보상 full compensation
충분한 보호 adequate protection
충성선서 affidatio
충성의무 allegiance
취급비 handling expenses
취급설명서 user instruction
취급수수료 lifting charges
취득 acquisition
취득; 근접 accession
취득가격 acquisition value
취득시 환산표 translation method at historical rates
취득시효 acquisitive prescription; adverse possession; positive prescription; prescription
취득원가 historical cost; original cost
취득원가기준 historical cost basis
취득원가법 acquisition cost method; original cost method
취득원가조정 acquisition cost adjustment
취득원가주의 명목가치회계 historical cost/nominal dollar accounting
취득원가주의 안정가치회계 historical cost/constant dollar accounting
취득원가주의 재무제표 historical-cost financial statements
취득원가주의회계 current cost accounting
취득일 이전의 유보이익 preacquisition profit
취득잉여금 acquired surplus
취득자산 property
취득잔고비례법 cost depletion method
취득재산 acquest
취리히의 난쟁이; 스위스금융계의 실력자 gnomes of Zurich
취소 repeal

취소가능신용장 revocable letter of credit

취소권 annulment right

취소불능신용장 irrevocable letter of credit

취소소송 revocation suit

취소주문 cancel order

취소하다 annul; countermand; revoke; set aside

취소할 때까지 유효한 주문 good-until-canceled orders

취소할 수 없는 허가 irrevocable license

취소할 수 있는 권원 defeasible title

취약산업 thin industry

취약성 sign of fragility

취업규제 work rules

취업불능소득보상보험 disability income insurance

취업중의 사고 accident at work

취조 interrogation

취직촉진수당 allowance for promotion of employment

취하 discontinuance

측량 surveying

측정계약 measurement contract

측정관리 measurement control

측정효율 efficiency of measuring

치과치료보험 dental insurance

치료비보험 physician's expense insurance

치안문란행위 disorderly conduct

치외법권 extraterritoriality

치킨마켓 chicken market

치폭제한 restriction of price range

칙령으로 허가된 회계사 chartered accountant

친권자 persons in parental authority

친족 family member

친회사 parent company

친회사보증부 parent guaranteed

침몰 sinking

침묵 mute; silence

침식률 erosion rate

침투가격 penetration price

침투가격전략 penetration price strategy

침하; 후퇴 dip

침해 transgression

침해소송 trespass

침해자 trespasser

ㅈ ㅊ ㅋ

ㅋ

카드갱신 card renewal
카드결제 pay by card
카드도난보험 credit card burglary insurance
카드론 card loan
카드범죄 card criminal fraud
카드시스템 card system
카드식 기장법 card system of bookkeeping
카드식별코드 card discrimination code
카드위조 card counterfeiting
카드유효기한 expiration date of the credit card
카드재발행 card replacement
카드표준화 card standardization
카드회사 card issuer
카드회원 card member
카라일생명표 Carlisle Mortality Table
카르텔 cartel
카르텔관세 cartel tariffs
카리브공동체 공동시장 Caribbean Community and Common Market
카버거래 커버거래 exchange cover
카오스 chaos
카테고리킬러 category killer
카테고리폭 category width
카펜터식 재보험 Carpenter cover
칵테일스와프; 복합스와프 cocktail swap
칼라 collar
칼라스와프 collared swap
칼럼수 column number
칼럼폭 column measure

캐나다달러장기국채 Canadian'dollar long-term bond
캐드 computer aided design
캐리인컴 carry income
캐비넷오퍼 cabinet offer
캐시마켓 cash market
캐시매니지먼트서비스 cash management service
캐시매칭 cash-matching
캐시매칭기술 cash-matching techniques
캐시플로 cash flow; price cashflow ratio
캐시플로 대 유동부채 cash flow to current liabilities
캐시플로계약 cash forward contract
캐시플로리턴 cash flow return
캐시플로부담배율 cash flow coverage ratio
캐시플로비율 cash flow ratio
캐시플로예측 cash flow projection
캐시플로이율 cash flow interest
캐시플로해석 interpretation of cash flows
캐피탈게인; 매매이익 capital gain
캐피탈게인과세 capital gain taxation; tax on capital; taxation on capital
캐피탈게인펀드 capital gain fund
캐피탈기어링 capital gearing
캐피탈로스 capital loss
캐피탈론 capital loan
캐피탈리스 capital lease
캐피탈리스크 capital risk
캐피탈플로 capital flow

캐핑 capping

캔슬드오더 canceled order

캔슬러블스와프 cancelable swap

캔슬카드 cancellation card

캘린더스프레드 calendar spread

캘린더스프레드거래 calendar spread transaction

캠페인광고 campaign advertising

캠페인컨셉 campaign concept

캡&플로어 cap and floor

캡; 상한 cap

캡부론 capped loan

캡부채 capped floating rate note

캡슐점포 capsule shop

캡스와프 capped swap

커런시컨버전채 currency conversion bond

커런트어섬션종신보험 current-assumption whole life insurance

커머디티스와프 commodity swap

커머디티풀 commodity pool

커머디티플로방법 commodity flow method

커먼갭 common gap

커뮤니케이션갭 communication gap

커뮤니케이션분석 communication analysis

커뮤니케이션장애 communication barrier

커뮤니케이션전략 communication strategy

커뮤니케이션채널 communication channel

커미션제 commission system

커버드옵션 covered option

커버드워런트 covered warrant

커버드콜 covered call

커버드콜옵션 covered call option

커버드포지션 covered position

커버딜링 cover dealing

커버비드 cover bid

커브를 가파르게 함 curve steepening

커스텀인덱스 custom index

커스텀퍼포먼스스탠다드 customized performance standards

컨베이어시스템 conveyer system

컨설팅세일즈 consulting sales

컨셉설명서 concept statement

컨셉테스팅 concept testing

컨소시엄뱅크 consortium bank

컨슈머릴레이션 consumer relations

컨테이너수송 containerization

컨트리익스포저 country exposure

컨퍼밍하우스 confirming house

컬러비디오신호 color video signal

컬러차트 color chart

컴워런트 cum warrant

컴팩트디스크 compact disk

컴퍼넌트신호 component signal

컴포지트시그널 composite signal

컴포지트프라이스 composite price

컴퓨서브 CompuServe

컴퓨터애니메이션 computer assisted animation

컴퓨터요원 computer personnel

컴퓨터지원협조작업 computer supported cooperation work

컴퓨터화 computerization

케인스학파 Keynesian

케인스혁명 Keynesian revolution

코레스거래금융기관 correspondent financial institution

코레스계약 correspondent agreement

코레스계정 correspondent account

코레스관계 correspondent relation

코레스은행 correspondent bank

코브-더블러스생산함수 Cobb-Douglas production function

코스모모델 comprehensive system model

코스트삭감 cost reduction

코스트트레이드오프 cost trade-off

코스트평균투자법 dollar cost averaging

코스트푸시인플레이션 cost-push inflation

코어프린지모델 core-fringe model

코어홀딩 core holding

코퍼레이트컬러 corporate color

콘글로머리트; 거대복합기업 conglomerate

콘글로머리트머천다이징 conglomerate

merchandising
콘도르스프레드거래 condor type spread
  transaction
콘드라티에프파(주기) Kondratieff wave
콘솔공채 consolidated annuities; Consols
콘솔리데이션론 consolidation loan
콘허그순환 corn hog cycle
콜러블론 callable loan
콜러블스와프 callable swap
콜러블스왑션 callable swaption
콜레이쇼 백스프레드거래 call ratio back
  spread transaction
콜레이트 call money rate; call rate
콜론; 단자; 당좌차입금 call loan
콜론이자 interest on call loans
콜머니 call money
콜머니이자 interest on call money
콜스왑션 call swaption
콜스프레드 call spread
콜시장 call market
콜어음매매시장자금 call money discount
  markets
콜어음시장 call and bill market
콜옵션 call option
콜옵션의 옵션료 call premium
콜옵션평가 valuation of call option
콜옵션평가와 배당 call option valuation and
  dividend
콜이율 per-diem rate for call loan
콤비나트 industrial complex
쿠리어서비스 courier service
쿠션채 cushion bond
쿠폰광고 coupon advertisement
쿠폰만의 통화스와프 coupon-only currency
  swap
쿠폰방식 coupon plan
쿠폰세일 coupon sale
쿠폰수입 coupon income
쿠폰스와프 coupon swap
쿠폰재투자수입 income by coupon
  re-investment

쿠폰패스 coupon pass
쿼트리포터 quote reporter
퀵링 quick ring
크라우드거래 crowd trading
크라우딩아웃; 구축 crowding out
크라우딩아웃효과; 구축효과 crowding out
  effect
크레디트트란시 credit tranche
크레디트퍼실리티; 신용편의 credit facility
크레디트히스토리 credit history
크레딧이용권 right of credit availability
크로마키 chroma key
크로스거래 cross trading
크로스디폴트 cross default
크로스디폴트조항 cross default clause
크로스레이트 cross rate
크로스마진 cross margin
크로스매매 cross
크로스섹셔널 평가법 cross-sectional
  valuation approach
크로스오더 cross order
크로스임팩트분석 cross impact analysis
크로스재정 cross arbitration
크로스집계표 cross tabulation
크로스헤지 cross hedge
크롤링페그; 단계적인 평가변동방식
  crawling peg
크롤링페그를 관리함 managed crawling peg
크리에이티브전략 creative strategy
크리티컬패스메소드 critical path method
크리티컬패스회계 critical-path accounting
크리핑인플레이션; 잠행성 인플레이션
  creeping inflation
크림스키밍 cream skimming
큰 기관투자가 large institutional investors
큰 벌이 killing
큰 변화가 없는 virtually unchanged
큰; 주요한 major
클라이언트와 서버 client and server
클러스터마케팅 cluster marketing
클러스터분석 cluster analysis

클러터포지션 clutter position
클로즈드기 closed period
클록주파수 clock frequency
클리어링펀드; 결제기금 clearing fund
클리어밴드 clear band
클리어비전방송 extended definition television
클린론; 무담보론 clean loan
클린신용장 clean letter of credit
클린오피니언 clean opinion

클린컷시스템 clean cut system
클린플로트; 자유변동시세제도 clean float
클린 **B/L** clean bill of lading
키국(局) key station
키스톤채권 keystone bond funds
킥백 kick back
킬로바이트 kilo byte
킬로비트 kilo bit
킹스턴체제 Kingston Regime

ㅈ
ㅊ
ㅋ

E

타겟발행 target issue
타겟존; 목표상장권 target zone
타기업비교 cross sectional analysis
타당성시험 validation test
타당성조사 feasibility study
타당성확인 validation
타물부속 appurtenant
타보험조항 other insurance clause
타블로이드판 tabloid size
타소불수표 out town check
타소불어음 out town bill
타소인도 out town delivery
타이밍옵션 timing option
타인자본 outside capital
타인자본회전율 turnover ratio of total liabilities
타임디케이 time decay
타임바이어스 time bias
타임스팬 time span
타임카드 time card
타임필터 time filter
타주권자 alien juris
타행인수 bill of others
타협 compromise
타회사 other account
탁상공론 armchair theory
탄력관세 elastic tariff
탄력성 낙관 elasticity optimism
탄력성 비관 elasticity pessimism
탄력성 어프로치 elasticities approach

탄력성지수 elasticity index
탄력성계수 coefficient of elasticity
탄력적인 수요 elastic demand
탄핵 impeachment
탄핵재판 court for the trial of impeachments
탄핵조항 articles of impeachment
탈공업화 사회 post-industrial society
탈선 derailment
탈세 evasion of tax; tax evasion; taxdodging
탈세방조범 accessory to tax evasion
탈세범 criminal of tax evasion
탈취 cepit
탈환, 회복 recapture
탑승자상해보험 automobile passengers' personal accident insurance
태도변용 attitude change
태도연구 attitude study
태도용이조사 attitude change research
태도조사 attitude survey
태도측정 attitude measurement; measure of value
태만 cesser
태스크방법 task method
태스크환경 task environment
태평양지역경제협력기구 Organization of Pacific Economic Cooperation
태환권발행세 tax on bank note system
태환준비 convertible reserve
태환지폐 convertible note
태환통화 convertible currency

택스리스 tax lease
택스리조트; 세금휴양소 tax resort
택스스와프 tax swap
택스컷백 tax cutback
택스파라다이스; 조세피난처 tax paradise
택스플레이션 taxflation
택스헤븐; 세금피난처 tax haven
택지개발세 land development tax
택지조성비 development cost of residential site
택트시스템 tact system
탭발행 tap; tap issue
탭빌 tap bills
탭채 bond on tap; tap stock
탭채로 발행하다 issue on a tap basis
터널 속의 뱀 snake in the tunnel
턴키계약 turn-key contract
텀론 term loan
텀페더럴펀드 term federal fund
텀페드 term fed
텅스텐라이트 tungsten light
테이크아웃론 takeout loan
테이크원즈 take-ones
테일링 tailing
테일헤지 tail hedge
테크놀로지어세스먼트 technology assessment
테크니컬트레이딩 technical trading
텍스트편집프로그램 text editor program
텐더빌 tender bill
텐더패널 tender panel
텔레마티크 telematique
텔레비전방식 television system
텔레비전회의 television conference
텔레시네변환 telecine translation
텔레컴퓨팅 telecomputing
텔레포트 teleport
텔레폰마켓 telephone market
템퍼러리본드 temporary bond
토목 civil engineering
토목공사 civil engineering works
토의보고서 issues paper

토지 land; land lot; landed property; limitation on proprietary right of land
토지 한 필 parcel
토지가격세 land-value tax
토지강제관리영장 elegit
토지개량 land improvement; land reform
토지개량비 land improvement expenses
토지개량사업 land improvement enterprise
토지건물 land and building
토지건물임차계약 lease of premises
토지경계 metes and bounds
토지과세대장 land tax register book
토지관리인 steward
토지대금양도저당 purchase-money mortgage
토지대장 land ledger; terrier
토지대장의 cadaster
토지등기 land registration
토지등기소 land registry
토지배분제도 allotment system
토지보유 land tenure
토지보유자 land-tenant
토지부담 encumbrance; land charges
토지부담의 권리자 토지부담권리자 encumbrancer
토지세제 land taxation
토지소유 land ownership
토지소유자 landed proprietor
토지수용 condemnation of land; expropriation of land; land expropriation
토지수용권 land expropriation right
토지양도승인 attornment
토지에 대한 부담 incumbrance
토지점유 possession of land; vesture
토지조성비 ground-making expenses
토지측량자 arpentator
토지평가 plottage
토지회복영장 cape
토킨펀드 tokkin
토핑아웃 topping out
톤세 tonnage due
톤세 납부서 note for payment of tonnage dues

톤틴배당 Tontine dividend
톱다운 top-down forecasting
톱다운기법 top-down technique
톱리버설데이 top-reversal
톱버티컬컴비네이션 top vertical combination
톱스트래들 top straddle
통계가정 statistical assumption
통계가정이론 statistical decision theory
통계로 altogether
통계방법 statistical technique
통계법칙 statistical laws
통계분석 statistical analysis
통계샘플링 statistical sampling
통계용어 statistical terminology
통계처리 statistical procedure
통계표준도시권 standard metropolitan statistical areas
통계학 statistics
통고처분 notification procedure
통과 passage
통과무역 transit trade
통과선하증권 through bill of lading
통관수속 customs procedures
통관용 송장 customs invoice
통괄계정 control account; controlling account
통괄국세사찰관 chief investigator
통괄국세조사관 chief examiner
통괄국세징수관 chief revenue officer
통달 directive
통산 integration
통상거래증권 seasoned issue
통상결산 general closing
통상결제 ordinary payment
통상비용 ordinary charges; regular fee
통상사용시간 normal and average use hours
통상상속인 heir general
통상손해 customary losses; ordinary tosses
통상약관 usual covenants
통상양도증서 ordinary conveyance
통상어음 ordinary bill
통상외국세액공제 ordinary foreign tax credit

통상운용 ordinary and normal recurring operations
통상이자율 ordinary interest rate
통상인도 regular delivery; regular way of delivery
통상정관 articles of association
통상조항 commerce clause
통상주의 ordinary care
통상총회 ordinary general meeting
통상해산 common liquidation
통상형 모기지론 conventional mortgage loan
통상확대법 trade expansion
통신비 communication charges
통신위성 communication satellite
통신제어장치 communication control unit
통신제어절차 communication control procedure
통신판매 mail-order
통일경리기준 uniform accounting regulations
통일브랜드 family brand
통일상사법전 Uniform Commercial Code
통일상표 blanket brand; unified brand
통일원가계산 uniform cost accounting
통일원가계산제도 uniform cost accounting system
통일전표 standardized slip
통일회계제도 uniform accounting system
통장 passbook
통장저축예금계좌 passbook savings account
통지 notice
통지보험 declaration policy
통지예금 demand deposits; deposit at notice; notice deposit; savings at call
통지은행 advising bank; notifying bank
통지전표 advice slip
통치행위 sovereign act
통합기 period of integration
통합시황정보시스템 consolidated quotation system
통행권 way
통행료 toll

통행방해 forestall

통행세 passengers tax; toll charges; travel tax; traveling tax

통화 currency

통화가치 currency value

통화가치저하 depreciation of currency

통화가치하락 currency depreciation

통화간 채무교환거래 cross currency swap

통화개혁 monetary reform

통화공급량 money supply

통화관리 monetary control; monetary management

통화금융정책 monetary and financial policy

통화단위 currency unit; monetary unit

통화당국 monetary authority

통화동맹 monetary union

통화등귀 currency appreciation

통화디플레이션 currency deflation

통화바스켓 currency basket

통화방위 protecting the currency

통화변동 currency fluctuation

통화보상 currency indemnity

통화불안 monetary instability

통화상품 currency commodity

통화선물 currency futures

통화선물가격동향 currency futures price movement

통화선물거래 currency futures trading

통화선택권 multicurrency clause

통화성 금융자산 monetary financial assets

통화성 예금 currency deposit

통화스와프 currency swap

통화스와프채 currency swap bond

통화스톡 money stock

통화승수 money multiplier

통화안정 monetary stability

통화옵션거래 currency option trading

통화위기 currency crisis

통화위험 monetary crisis

통화유통고 currency in circulation

통화인플레 currency inflation

통화재팽창 reflation

통화절상 currency upvaluation

통화절하 currency devaluation

통화조정 currency alignment

통화주의 currency principle; monetarism

통화준비 monetary reserve

통화체계 currency system

통화총량 monetary aggregate

통화침투설 trickle down

통화팽창 expansion of currency

통화협정 monetary agreement

통화환산 currency conversion

퇴거명령 eviction order

퇴거시킴 eviction

퇴장가액 exit value

퇴직금 retirement pay

퇴직금공제계약 mutual aid contract for retirement allowance

퇴직금을 일괄지급함 retirement allowance in a lump sum

퇴직금적립금 superannuation payment

퇴직금제도 retirement plan

퇴직급여 retirement allowance

퇴직급여규정 regulation of retirement allowance; retirement allowance regulations

퇴직급여예비금 accrued severance indemnities

퇴직급여이익 employees' retirement benefit

퇴직급여적립금 reserve for pension fund

퇴직급여준비금 accrued employees retirement benefit

퇴직소득 retirement income

퇴직소득공제 allowed retirement income deduction; deduction for retirement income; retirement income deduction

퇴직소득부 보험 retirement income

퇴직소득신고서 return form for retirement income

퇴직수당 severance benefit; terminal pay allowance

퇴직연금 retirement annuity; retirement

ㅌ
ㅍ
ㅎ

pension
퇴직연금과세 taxation on retirement annuity
퇴직연금부금 premium payment of a
retirement annuity
퇴직연금수취인 beneficiary of the retirement
annuity
퇴직연금업무 retirement annuity business
퇴직연금적립금 retirement annuity reserve
퇴직연령 age of retirement
퇴직일시금 retirement lump sum grants
퇴직한 종업원 retired employee
퇴직후 급부 postretirement benefit
투기 speculation
투기거래 speculation transaction; speculative
transaction
투기계정을 정리함 liquidation of speculative
accounts
투기구매; 매점매석 speculative buying
투기구입 speculator buying
투기꾼 speculative buyers; speculator
투기동기 speculative motive
투기리스크 speculative risk
투기매입 bull speculation
투기시장 speculative market
투기열 craze for speculation; speculative
enthusiasm
투기이윤 speculative gain
투기자금 speculative money
투기전 deal between speculators; speculative
dealing
투기전에서 손해를 봄 taking a bath
투기주(株) cats and dogs stock; speculative
stock
투기함 taking a flier
투매 selling off; shaking-out; slaughter sale
투매; 출혈판매 distress selling
투매; 헐값으로 팔기 sacrifice sale
투신상표 portfolio of investment trust
투영법 projective methods
투웨이마켓 two-way market
투입계수 input coefficient

투입변수 input variable
투입산출분석 input-output analysis
투입산출표 input-output table
투자가치 investment value
투자결정 investment decision
투자경기 investment boom
투자경비 investment expense
투자계정부문 investment account
투자계획 investment program
투자계획기간분석 horizon analysis
투자고문 investment advisor
투자고문법 investment advisory law
투자고문업 advisory service
투자고문업계 investment advisory industry
투자고문회사 investment management
company
투자곡선 investment curve
투자공제 investment credit
투자관리자와 고객의 관계 manager-client
relations
투자기간 investment period
투자기관경합시스템 competitive market
maker system
투자기회 investment opportunities
투자달러 investment dollar
투자대상 investment outlet
투자대상기업 investment grade corporate
투자매 investment buying
투자매니저 investment manager
투자목적확인서 investment letter
투자목표 investment objectives
투자분석 investment analysis
투자분쟁해결국제센터 International Center
for Settlement of Investment Disputes
투자선택개괄 investment selection summary
투자성과 investment result
투자성향 investment propensity; propensity to
investment
투자세액공제 investment tax credit
투자소득 investment income
투자수요 investment demand

투자수익 return on investment

투자수익율이 같음 break-even yield

투자수익을 예측함 prediction of investment return

투자승수 investment multiplier

투자승인리스트 approved investment

투자시장 investment market

투자신탁 investment fund; investment trust

투자신탁상환가격보증보험 mutual fund redemption value insurance

투자신탁위탁 management company

투자신탁위탁업무 management business of investment trust

투자신탁위탁회사 investment trust management company

투자신탁판매회사 securities investment trust sales company

투자연기 deferment of investment; postponement of investment

투자연도별 방식 investment year method

투자위원회 investment committee

투자유가증권 investment in securities; investment securities

투자유연성 investment flexibility

투자유인 inducement to invest

투자융자업계 investment and loan

투자은행 investment bank

투자은행가 merchant banker

투자은행금융기관 Investment Banking Financing Company

투자의 이중성 이중적인 투자 dual character of investment

투자이익률 return on investment ratios

투자자보호 protection of investor

투자적격 investment grade

투자적격대상 legal investment

투자전략 investment strategy

투자정보원 investment information sources

투자정책 investment policy

투자주 investment stock

투자증권 investment security

투자지출 investment expenditure

투자척도 investment criteria; measure of investment

투자철학 investment philosophy

투자카운셀러 investment counselor

투자클럽 investment club

투자통화 investment currency

투자판단을 내릴 수 없는 사람 fence sitter

투자함수 investment function

투자허가리스트 authorized investment list

투자환경 investment climate; investment environment

투자활동 investing activities

투자회사 investment company; unit investment trust company

투표 voting

투표행위 suffrage

투하자본 invested capital

트라이앵글 triangle

트라이앵글리버설패턴 triangle reversal patterns

트란시방식 tranche issue

트래킹 tracking

트랜스벡션 transvection

트랜스퍼머신 transfer machine

트랜스퍼메카니즘 transfer mechanism

트랜스퍼문제 transfer problem

트러블슈터 trouble shooter

트럼프세 playing cards tax

트레이더 trader

트레이드로직 trade logic

트레이드오프 trade-off

트레이드티켓 trade ticket

트레이딩목적유가증권 trading securities

트레이딩스탬프 trading stamp

트레이딩풀 trading pool

트레이서빌리티 traceability

트렌드라인 trend line

트렌드채널 trend channel

트렌드플라워 trend follower

트리거가격 trigger price

트리구조 tree structure
트리밍 trimming
트리티쇼핑 treaty shopping
트리플크로스오버법 triple crossover method
트리플톱 triple top
트윈카드 twin-card
특가품(싸게 파는) loss leader
특권 및 면제 privileges and immunities
특권남용 breach of privilege
특권료 option money
특권면책 privilege
특례 special tax treatment; special treatment
특매상품 basement merchandise
특매상품전략 leader merchandising
특별가격전략 premium pricing strategy
특별감사 special audit
특별감세국채 special tax reduction bond
특별검찰관 special prosecutor
특별결의 special resolution
특별결제 special payment
특별계정잔고 balance of the amount charged to special account
특별공제 special deduction
특별공채이자과세제도 special non-taxable treatment on small government bond
특별과징금 special assessment
특별교환 special exchange
특별구 special ward
특별구민세 special ward inhabitants tax
특별국세조사관 special examiner
특별국세징수관 special revenue officer
특별대부계정금리 special loan account interest rate
특별대행구매 specialist block purchases
특별매개기관 special intermediary institution
특별목적세채권 special tax bond
특별배당 bonus nausea; dividend extra; extra dividend; plum; special dividend
특별배당금보험 insurance with bonus
특별배당주 bonus stock
특별보도방송 special event

특별비 special expenses
특별비용 particular charges; special charges
특별상각 accelerated depreciation; extraordinary depreciation; special initial depreciation; special depreciation
특별상각률 ratio of special depreciation deduction
특상각부족액 shortage of special depreciation
특별상각준비금 reserve for special depreciation; special depreciation reserve
특별상각한도액 maximum special depreciation allowance
특별소득세 special income tax
특별손실 extraordinary loss
특별손익 extraordinary profit and loss; special profit and loss
특별손익전 이익 earnings before extraordinary items
특별손익항목 extraordinary items
특별손해 special damages
특별수선비 special repair expenses
특별수수료 overriding commission
특별시 county borough
특별약관 special clause
특별예금제도 special deposit scheme
특별요율적용; 편차 deviation
특별위험 special risks
특별은행계정업자 special bank account firm
특별이익 extraordinary gain
특별인출권 Special Drawing Rights
특별적립금 special reserve
특별적립잉여금 assigned surplus; special surplus fund
특별조건서 special conditions of the contract
특별증거금요건 special margin
특별지방교부세 special local grant tax
특별지방소비세 special local consumption tax
특별징수 special collection
특별징수의무자 special collecting agent
특별참가자 special participant
특별채 special bond

특별청산 special clearance
특별청산승인 approval of special liquidation
특별청산지수 special quotation
특별토지보유세 special landholding tax
특별톤세 special tonnage due
특별편익설 special benefit theory of taxation
특별한 감가상각방법 special methods of computing depreciation
특별한 경제적 이익 special economic benefit
특별한 상각방법 special depreciation method
특별한 평가법 special valuation method
특별항목 special item
특별회계 special account
특설서비스장소 accommodation area
특성선 characteristic line
특손(特損) special loss
특수공정 special process
특수관계인 associated person
특수매체 specific media
특수법인 juridical person in a public law
특수분개장 special journal
특수비율 salient ratio
특수생산요소이론 specific productive factors
특수수익 peculiar benefits
특수용도면세 nontaxable-goods for special use
특수원가조사 special cost studies
특수회사 special corporation
특약리베이트 loyalty rebate
특약이 없는 계약 open contract
특약일결제거래 special day delivery transaction
특약재보험 treaty reinsurance
특약재보험예금 premium deposit
특약조항; 약인 covenant
특약판매 franchise selling; selective selling
특유재산 separate property
특정경쟁상대 specific foe
특정관심층출판 special interest publishing
특정금전신탁 specified money in trust
특정기간인도 broken term

특정기부금 specified donation
특정담보 fixed charge; specific charge
특정목적재무제표 special-purpose financial statement
특정보험계약 specific policy
특정사업의 용지매수 land purchase for specified business
특정설비폐기세액공제 scrapping of equipment tax credit
특정수입고 restricted receipts
특정용도면제 tax exemption for specific use
특정위험 named peril
특정의료법인 specified medical corporation
특정의료법인의 특별세율 reduced tax rate on specified medical corporation
특정이자 specified interest
특정이해집단 special interest group
특정이행 special performance; specific performance
특정자산 specified assets
특정재원채 industrial revenue bond; limited obligation bond; revenue bond
특정전문투자신탁 specialized fund
특정제조지도서 special production order
특정주 specified stock
특정증을 대상으로 한 매체 class media
특정지역 포트폴리오 regional portfolio
특정지역지점설치 limited branching
특정질병보장보험 specified disease insurance
특정퇴직금공제단체 mutual aid organization for specific retirement allowance
특정현물출자 specified investment in kind
특정현물출자증권 securities acquired by the specified investment in kind
특정횡선수표 special crossed check
특주의 tailor made
특징 characteristics
특허권 patent; patent right
특허권교환 cross license
특허권교환계약 cross license contract
특허권사용료 royalties received for use of

patents
특허권수여자 patentor
특허권자 patentee
특허권침해 infringement of patent; patent
　infringement
특허료 patent fee
특허법 patent law
특허변리사 patent attorney
특허보유지 charter-land
특허부여 enfranchisement
특허세 franchise tax
특허에 대한 일부포기각서
　memorandum of alteration
특허유효기간 patent period

특허자격 patentability
특허증 letters patent
특허출원중 patent applied for; patent pending
특허품 patented article
특혜관세 preferential duty; preferential tariff
특혜적인 preferential
TED 스프레드 Treasury Euro-dollar spread
T자형 계정 T form account
티저광고 teaser advertising
티켓판매금융 ticket sale finance
틱 tick
틱테스트룰 tick-test rule
틸포비드 till-forbid

ㅍ

파견사원 detached employees
파괴처분 destructive disposition
파급경로 transmission mechanism
파급권 recourse right
파급급여 back pay
파급불배당금 back dividend
파급수정 catch-up adjustments
파급효과 knock-on effect; multiplied effect; repercussion effect; spread effect
파급효과클레임 impact claims
파는 값 selling price
파는 권리 selling right
파는 자의 시장 sellers' market
파는 쪽 bargainor; seller
파동조정 rolling readjustment
파동함수 wave function
파라메트릭디자인 parametric design
파라메트릭테스트 parametric test
파레토 상수 pareto's constant
파렴치죄 infamous crime
파리동맹 Paris Union
파리클럽 Paris Club
파면책채권 undischargeable claim
파벌 clique
파산 bankruptcy
파산감사관 comptroller in bankruptcy
파산고지 bankruptcy notice
파산관리 administration in bankruptcy in bankruptcy; case administration
파산관재인 administrator in bankruptcy; bankruptcy administrator; receiver; receiver in bankruptcy; syndic; trustee in bankruptcy
파산규칙 bankruptcy rules
파산명령 adjudication order
파산법 bankrupt law; bankruptcy law
파산법원 bankruptcy court
파산선고 adjudication of bankruptcy; declaration of bankruptcy
파산신립채권자보증증권 bond of petitioning creditors
파산신청 petition in bankruptcy
파산심리인 referee in bankruptcy
파산예기 contemplation of bankruptcy
파산우선지불 preferential payment in bankruptcy
파산원인 cause of bankruptcy
파산자 bankrupt; insolvent debtor
파산자 재산차압명령 warrant in bankruptcy
파산재단 bankrupt's estate
파산재판소 court of bankruptcy
파산절차 bankruptcy proceedings
파산채권 claim in bankruptcy
파산채무자 bankruptcy debtor
파산청산인 accountant in bankruptcy
파산취소 discharge in bankruptcy
파산하다 fail
파산행위 act of bankruptcy
파생거래 derivative transaction
파생상품 contingent claim; derivative product
파생소득 derived income

파생소송 derivative suit
파생예금 derivative deposit
파생적인 contingent
파생증권 derivative security
파생취득 derivative income
파생패스스루증권시장 derivative pass-through securities market
파손 breakage
파쉐계산식 Paasche formula
파업을 깨뜨리는 사람 scab
파울B/L foul B/L
파이낸셜뉴스지수옵션 Financial News index option
파이낸스리스 finance lease
파이버 투 더 홈방식 fiber to the home
파이카(활자 크기의 한 종류) pica
파인더 finder
파일드 par yield
파일럿마케팅 pilot marketing
파일럿플랜트 pilot plant
파일링 filing
파일압축 file compression
파일앨로케이션테이블 file allocation table
파탄기업 failing company
파트너샤프트 partner shaft
파트타임으로 근무하는 사람 part-timer
파포워드 par forward
파형 waveform
팍스아메리카나 Pax Americana
판결 decree; judgment
판결기록 judgment record
판결등록 entry of judgment
판결부활 revival of judgment
판결승인 confession of judgment
판결신청 motion for judgment
판결언도 rendition of judgment
판결언도를 위한 출정명령 capias ad audiendum judicium
판결에 따라 by judgment
판결을 파기함 reversal of judgment
판결저지 arrest of judgment

판결적요 syllabus
판결채권이 상쇄됨 judgment set-off
판결채권자 Judgment creditor
판결채무자 judgment debtor
판권등록 registration of copyright
판권침해 infringement of copyright
판례법 case law
판례집 law reports
판로 sales network
판매 sale
판매가; 입찰가격 bid price
판매가액약관 selling price clause
판매가와 원가의 차액 maintained markup
판매간접비 selling overhead
판매경로 marketing channel
판매계약 selling agreement
판매금액 sales amount
판매금융 sales finance
판매금융회사 sales finance company
판매기간 subscription period
판매기회 sales opportunity
판매단 selling group
판매단계약서 selling group agreement
판매력 sales force
판매리스 sales-type leases
판매목표액 sales targets
판매방법 sales method
판매보증증권 sale bond
판매비 distribution cost; marketing cost; selling expenses
판매비용 selling charges
판매비차이 selling expense variance
판매성과 sales performance
판매수량 quantity sold
판매수수료 load; sales commission; selling concession
판매순환 selling cycle
판매시점정보관리 point of sales
판매업자일괄보험 commercial block policy; mercantile block insurance
판매오파 selling offer

판매용 상품 goods for sale

판매용 토지 real estate held for sale

판매운임 freight out

판매원 salesman

판매원가 cost of sales

판매원관리 sales force management

판매원모집 sales-force recruitment

판매원성과분석 sales force performance analysis

판매원전도금 advance made to salesmen

판매자 vendor

판매자구조 seller structure

판매자독점 seller's monopoly

판매자회사 sales subsidiary

판매장부표 sales record

판매적성품질 good merchantable quality

판매촉진 sales promotion

판매촉진비 sales promotion expense

판매콘셉트 selling concept

판매할당 dollar sales volume quota; sales quota

판매할인 sales discount

판매협정 marketing agreement

판매환 selling exchange

판매활동지수 sales activity index

판매회계 sales accounting

판사 judge; justice

판사실 judge's chambers

판정 divasa; enactment

판정의 기초가 되는 주주 basic stockholder

팔다 offer for sale

팔다남은 unsold

팔레트화 palletization

패널조사 panel research

패니메이; 저당증권 Fannie Mae

패드 fade

패럴렐마켓 parallel market

패리티가치 parity value

패리티계산 parity account

패리티그리드 parity-grid

패리티지수 parity index

패리티직선 parity line

패스스루증권 pass-through securities

패스스루증권 청산시장 cash immediate market

패스워드 password

패자의 게임 losers game

패클러공식 Fackler's formula

패키지딜 package-deal contract

패키지리스 package lease

패키지폴리시 package policy

패킷교환 packet switching

패킷통신 packet communication

패턴변수 pattern variable

팩맨디펜스 Pac-man defense

팩터리스크 factor risk

팩터베타 factor beta

팩터수수료 factorage

팩토리프리셋 factory preset

팩트북 fact book

팬라인 fan line

팬이론 Fan theory

퍼 발행 issue at par

퍼블릭도메인소프트웨어 public domain software

퍼블릭억셉턴스 public acceptance

퍼센티지리스 percentage lease

퍼스널리티체계 personality system

퍼스트디맨드본드 first demand bond

퍼실리테이션오더 facilitation order

퍼지이론 fuzzy theory

퍼포먼스비례보수체계 performance-based fee system

퍼포먼스증거금 performance margin

퍼포먼스측정 performance measurement

퍼포먼스특성 performance attribution

퍼포먼스펀드 performance fund

펀드 대 미달러율 cable

펀드매니저 fund manager

펀드멘털분석 fundamental analysis

펀드멘털즈악화 fundamentals deterioration

펀드베타수치를 비교함 comparison of beta

values of funds
펀드블록 pound bloc
펀드앤드트러스트 fund and trust
펀드위기 pound crisis
펄스코드변조 pulse code modulation
펄하버파일 pearl harbor file
펌뱅킹 firm banking
페넌트 pennant
페르시아만협력회의 Gulf Cooperation Council
페이다운 paydown
페이드아웃 fade out
페이드아웃방식 fade-out formula
페이드인 fade in
페이먼트인카인드 우선주 payment-in-kind preferred stock
페이스루채권 pay-through bond
페이오프 payoff
페이오프다이어그램 pay-off diagram
페이오프패턴 payoff pattern
페이즈시프터 phase shifter
페이지설명언어 page description language
페이텔레비전 pay television
페이퍼리스트레이딩 paperless trading
페이퍼뷰 pay per view
페이퍼컴퍼니 paper company; shell corporation
편도 one way
편도헤지 one sided hedge
편무계약 unilateral contract
편의 convenience
편의수익 convenience yield
편의일괄등록 convenience shelf registration
편의치적선 flag of convenience vessel
편익공작물 accommodation works
편익관세 beneficial duty
편입률 weighting
편탄력성 partial elasticity
편평비변환 aspect ratio translation
평가 parity; reputation
평가가격 estimated value

평가가치 assessed valuation
평가감후 가격 written-down value
평가계정 valuation account
평가과목 valuation item
평가기관 rating agency
평가기준 appraisal standard; numeraire; valuation basis; valuation standards
평가모델 valuation modeling
평가방법변경 change in valuation method
평가방법변동 change of valuation method
평가방법을 선택함 selection of valuation method
평가법 appraisal method
평가성준비금 valuation reserve
평가손 appraisal loss; valuation loss
평가손익 appraisal profit or loss
평가시기 term for evaluation
평가액 amount assessed; appraisal value; valuation
평가원칙 principle of valuation; valuation principle
평가이상 above par
평가익 appraisal profit; profit accured from valuation; valuation profit
평가익의 익금불산입 exclusion of profit accrued from valuation profit
평가인 appraiser
평가증가 write-up
평가차액 variance of the estimate
평가특성 valuation characteristics
평가하기 어려운 매매 scale trading
평가하다 value
평결 verdict
평결에 따른 판결 judgment on the verdict
평균가격가중지수 price weighted index
평균개인세율 personal average tax rate
평균결제 settlement of balance
평균고장간격 mean time between failures
평균곡선 mean curve
평균과세 average taxation
평균금리캡 average interest rate cap

평균발행잔고 average balance outstanding
평균배당률 average rate of dividend
평균법인세율 corporate average tax rate
평균변동율 average volatility
평균보험금액 mean sum insured
평균보험료 average premium
평균보험료방식 average premium system
평균부채기간 average maturity of debts
평균상환연한 average term to maturity
평균생산기간 average period of production
평균세율 average tax rate
평균소득 average income
평균손해가액 average cost of claims
평균수복시간 mean time to repair
평균수익 average earnings
평균시가법 average current cost method
평균신장률 average growth rate
평균실제노동시간 actuarial hours
평균여명 average future lifetime; expectation of life
평균연불보험료 equal annual premium
평균요율 average rate
평균원가 average cost
평균원가법 average cost method
평균이율 average yield
평균이익가산율 average markup percentage
평균자본연령 vintage
평균잔존연수 average life
평균잔존연한이익 yield for average life
평균재고 average inventory
평균재귀 mean reverting
평균절대오차 mean absolute error
평균절대편차 average absolute deviation; mean absolute deviation
평균제곱오차 mean squared error
평균주가 stock price average
평균주가채용문제 issue used in the average
평균주가채용주 stock used in the average
평균지불기일 equaled time of payment
평균차 mean difference
평균투자수익 average return on investment

평균편차 mean deviation
평균표준보수월액 average index monthly earnings
평균품질 fair average quality
평균회귀 mean reversion
평균회귀과정 mean reverting process
평균회수기간 average collection
평년도 full year
평생 동안의 권리 life-interest
평생교육 life-long education
평시봉쇄 pacific blockade
평온한 점유 peaceable possession
평의회 council
평정가산법 summated rating
평준보험료 level premium
평준보험료식 보험 level premium insurance
평준상장 parity quotation
평준순보험료 level net premium
평준순보험료식 책임준비금 net level premium reserve
평준화준비금 equalization reserve
평행거래 parallel transaction
평행기채 parallel issue
평행수입 parallel import
평행시장 parallel money market
평행이동 parallel shift
평형개입 central bank intervention
평형날인계약서 deed poll
평형부기 position bookkeeping
평형으로 회귀함 return to equilibrium
평형준비금 equalization fund
평활정수 smoothing constant smorgasbord plan
폐기물 mortality; waste
폐기법 retirement method
폐쇄매각 private sale
폐쇄시장 closed market
폐쇄식 closed-end type
폐쇄식 담보 closed-end mortgage
폐쇄식 담보부사채 closed-end mortgage bond

ㅌ
ㅍ
ㅎ

폐쇄식 신탁 closed-end trust
폐쇄형 듀얼펀드 closed-end dual fund
폐쇄형 채널 exclusive channel
폐쇄형 펀드 closed-end fund
폐쇄회로시스템 closed-circuit system
폐업 discontinuance of business
폐잔설비 discarded equipment; retired
   equipment; scrap equipment
폐정 rising of the court
폐정기; 법정을 닫는 시기 out of term
폐지 abolition; abrogation
폐지부문 discontinued operations
폐지부문의 이익 income from discontinued
   operations
폐회 prorogation
포고 edict
포괄가격계약 blanket pricing agreement
포괄곡선 envelope curve
포괄급부 unallocated benefit
포괄담보설정방식 blanket system
포괄마케팅시스템 comprehensive marketing
   system
포괄보험계약 blanket policy; umbrella cover
포괄보험증서 open policy
포괄손익계산서 all-inclusive income
   statement
포괄예정보험 open insurance
포괄예정보험계약 floating policy
포괄유증 universal legacy
포괄재산 floating property
포괄저당권 blanket mortgage
포괄저당권부 채권 blanket bond
포괄적인 comprehensive
포괄적인 권한 general authority
포괄적인 전략 generic strategy
포괄조항 blanket clause
포괄주의 all-inclusive basis
포괄주의이익개념 all-inclusive income
   concept
포괄통상법안 comprehensive trade bill
포나인 four nine

포렉스클럽 forex club
포뮬러타이밍 formula timing
포뮬러투자 formula investing
포뮬러펀드 formula fund
포뮬러플랜 formula plan
포스트스크립트그래픽 postscript graphic
포워드캘린더 forward calendar
포이즌필 poison pills
포인트앤드피규어법 point and figure method
포장명세서 packing list
포장비 packing; packing and wrapping
   expenses; packing charge
포지셔닝분석 positioning analysis
포지션감마 position gamma
포지션델타 position delta
포지션매매 position trading
포지션지도 position instruction
포지션트레이더 position trader
포지티브정보 positive credit file
포지티브캐리어 positive carry
포지필름 positive Film
포토다이오드 photo diode
포트폴리오 business portfolio; world market
   portfolio
포트폴리오가격결정법 portfolio pricing
   methodology
포트폴리오관리 portfolio management
포트폴리오리스크모델 portfolio risk model
포트폴리오모니터링 portfolio monitoring
포트폴리오믹스 portfolio mix
포트폴리오밸런스어프로치 portfolio balance
   approach
포트폴리오보험료 portfolio premium
포트폴리오분석 portfolio analysis
포트폴리오뷰 portfolio view
포트폴리오수법 portfolio approach
포트폴리오수정 portfolio revision
포트폴리오양도 cession of portfolio
포트폴리오엔지니어 portfolio engineers
포트폴리오의 미경과부분을 일괄인양함
   withdrawal of portfolio

포트폴리오의 수익패턴 pattern of portfolio return

포트폴리오의 특성선 portfolio characteristic line

포트폴리오재보험 portfolio reinsurance

포트폴리오재편 portfolio restructuring

포트폴리오최적화 portfolio optimization

포합의 tie-in

포합판매 tie-in sale

포획나포부담보조항 free from capture and seizure clause

폭락 collapse; sharp drop

폭포이론 cascade process

폰트 font

폴리시믹스 policy mix

폴리시어셋믹스 policy asset mix

폴리시어셋앨로케이션 policy asset allocation

폴리크로닉 polychronic

표류믹스 drifting mix

표면금리 nominal interest rate; nominal rate

표면모델 surface model

표면상의 권원 color of title

표면상의 대리 apparent agency

표면상의 직권 color of office

표면예금 nominal gross deposit

표면이율 nominal coupon

표면적인 커뮤니케이션 surface communication

표명 representation

표본검사 blind check

표본분산 sample variance

표본설비 sample error

표본정밀도 samples accuracy

표본조사 sampling survey

표본추출오차 sampling error

표본추출정밀도 sampling precision

표본평균치 sample means

표색계 color system

표시를 통한 매매 sale by description

표시부채 stated liabilities

표시원가 scheduled cost

표시작업 representation work

표식원장 tabular ledger

표적집단 target group

표정급부 allocated benefit

표준 benchmark; criteria

표준 이상으로; 경상수지계산의 above the line

표준 EPS normalized EPS

표준가격권 benchmark rate

표준견본 representative sample

표준금리 standard interest rate

표준기계시간 standard machine time

표준노무비 standard labor cost

표준득점 standard score

표준바스킷 standard currency basket system

표준배부율 standard burden rate

표준보험약관 standard policy conditions

표준부품 standard part

표준산업분류 standard industrial classification

표준생산량 standard-run quantity

표준서식 standard documentation

표준세율 standard tax rate

표준손료 standard depletion expenses

표준오차 standard error

표준원가 standard cost

표준원가계산 standard cost accounting

표준은달러 standard silver dollar

표준이익 standard profit

표준인구 standard population

표준일 standard date

표준재료비 standard material cost

표준재무제표 standardized financial statements

표준저당권자 지불약관 union mortgage clause

표준적인 변화 normative change

표준정규분포 standard-normal distribution

표준제조간접비 standard manufacturing expense

표준주 barometer stock; standard stocks

표준체 average risk; standard lives
표준치 standard values
표준크로스디폴트조항 standard cross default provision
표준품매매 sale on standard
표준하체 substandard
표준하체보험계약 insurance of substandard lives
표준화 standardization
표준화 볼라틸리티 standardized volatility
표현의 자유 freedom of expression
푸쉬풀 push pull
푸쉬회선 push phone telephone line
푸터블스와프 puttable swap
푸터블스왑션 puttable swaption
푸터블채권 puttable bond
풀계산 pool account
풀뱅킹서비스 full-banking service
풀재보험 pool reinsurance
풀전략 pull strategy
풀조작 pool operation
풀코스트원칙 full cost principle
풀쿠폰본드 full coupon bond
풀특약 pool treaty
풀헤지 full hedge
품의 request for decision
품절 all gone; all sold; outright sales
품절코스트 underage cost
품질감시 quality surveillance
품질개선 quality improvement
품질관련코스트 quality related cost
품질관리 quality control
품질기록 quality record
품질로스 quality loss
품질루프 quality loop
품질목표 quality objective
품질방침 quality policy
품질변수 quality variable
품질설명 quality description
품질시스템 quality system
품질의식 quality awareness

품질이 같은 of like grade and quality
품질코스트법 quality cost approach
품질효과 quality effect
풋 put
풋가격선 put-value line
풋내기의 lay
풋다이어그램 put diagram
풋레이쇼백스프레딩 put ratio back spread trading
풋보유자 put holder
풋스왑션 put swaption
풋옵션 put option
풋콜비율 put-call ratio
풋콜인도 option delivery
풋콜조합옵션 option combination
풍수해보험 wind storm and flood insurance
퓨어캡 pure cap
프라이머리딜러 primary dealer
프라이베이트리스크 private risk
프라이베이트패스스루 private passthrough
프라이스리더 price leader
프라이스메이커 price maker
프라이스필터 price filter
프라임레이트 prime interest rate; short-term prime rate
프래그머티즘 pragmatism
프랙탈 fractal
프랜차이즈가맹점 franchised retail store
프런트엔드피 front-end fee
프런팅 fronting
프런팅비즈니스 fronting business
프레디맥 Freddie Mac
프레비드계약 prebid agreement
프레임릴레이 frame relay
프레임수 변환 frame translation
프레임에디팅 frame editing
프레페이드카드 prepaid card
프로그래밍방식 programming method
프로그램공급업자 program supplier
프로그램매각 program trading
프로그램매매 exchange for physical program

프로그램보증준비금 reserve for electronic computer programs
프로그램예산 program budgeting
프로그램학습 programed instruction
프로덕션론 production loan
프로덕트사이클론 product cycle theory
프로모션믹스 promotion mix
프로모션용구 promotools
프로모션전략 promotional strategy
프로비저널섬; PS단가 provisional sum
프로세스관리특성 process variable
프로세스변경 process modification
프로세스이노베이션 process innovation
프로세스제품 processed material
프로세스컬러 process color
프로젝트시뮬레이터 project simulator
프로젝트파이낸스 project finance
프로텍티브풋 거래 protective put trading
프로포절레터 proposal letter
프로포절방식 proposal method
프로핏센터 profit center
프리미엄; 환전 agio
프리미엄발행 premium issue
프리미엄시가방식 premium quotation system
프리미엄환원 returning of premium
프리파이낸셜펀드 free financial fund
프리플로시스템 free flow system
프린지뱅킹 fringe banking
플라스틱머니; 신용카드 plastic money
플라워본드 flower bond
플라자합의 Plaza accord
플라즈마디스플레이 plasma display
플라토성향 plateauing
플랜가입자 plan beneficiaries
플랫거브 flat curve
플랫론 flat loan
플랫마켓 flat market
플랫폼 platform
플러스틱 plus-tick
플레인딜 plain deal
플레인바닐라 plain vanilla

플레징 pledging
플렉서블타임 flexible time
플렉서블포워드거래 flexible forward contract
플렉스폼 flexform
플로어드스와프 floored swap
플로어트레이더; 룸트레이더 floor trader
플로차트 flow chart
플로터스와프 super floater swap
플로팅베이시스 floating basis
플리트계약자 fleet insured
플립오버조항 flip-over clause
플립플롭채권 flip-flop
피감사자 auditee
피고 defendant
피고보증증권 defendant bond
피고인 accused
피공소인 respondent
피난 parking
피드백 feedback
피드백정보 feedback information
피라미딩과정 pyramiding process
피메일 feemail
피발송은행 receiving bank
피보나치수열 Fibonacci sequence
피보험기 covered quarter
피보험위험 insured peril; risk covered
피보험이익 insurable interest
피보험자 assured; insured
피상소인 appellee
피설득성 persuasibility
피셔효과 Fisher effect
PCM 방송 pulse code modulation broadcasting
POP; 구매시점 point of purchase
피이서인 endorsee
퍼트 (PERT) program evaluation and review technique
피임명자 appointee
피지배회사 controlled company
피케팅 picketing
피코초 pico second
피크업본드 pickup bond

피통괄계정 controlled account
피트 pit
피트리포터 pit reporter
피프 pip
피플미터 people meter
피합병법인 corporation amalgamated
피합병회사 predecessor company; transferor
　　corporation
피해자산 damaged property
피해자직접청구 direct claim of claimant
픽토그램; 그림도표 pictogram
필기시험 written examination
필라델피아플랜 Philadelphia plan
필름감도 film sensitivity
필립스곡선 Phillips curve

필수가구 necessary household furniture
필수조건 essential condition; mandatory
　　clause; sine qua non
필요가산이익 mark-on required
필요경비 necessary expense
필요당사자 necessary party
필요물 estovers
필요성원칙 principle of need
필요요건 requisite
필요자본계수 required capital coefficient
필요조건 causa sine qua non; needs test
필요증거금법 margin required method
필요한 세무수속 necessary tax procedure
필요한 증거서류 necessary evidence
　　documents

ㅎ

하강 descending; drop; fall; moving downward

하강곡선 descending curve

하강국면 downswing phase; downward phase of the business cycle

하강기조 down trend

하강선 downhill course

하급법원 base courts

하급판사 magistrate

하도지시서 delivery order

하드디스크 hard disk

하드랜딩 hard landing

하락 downfall; setback

하락기조상장 falling market

하락삼각형 descending triangle; descending triangle pattern

하락시세 bear market

하락전환패턴 bearish reversal patterns

하락촉진 big push in the downward move

하락하다 decline

하루의 일부 fraction of a day

하루이자 daily rate

하루중 고저치 intra-day high and low

하리키리스와프 harakiri swap

하반기 latter half; second half of the year

하부문자 inferior character

하우스빌 house bill

하우스에이전시 house agency

하우징리뉴얼프로그램 housing renewal program

하위목적 subobjective

하위문화 subculture

하위사채 subordinated bond; subordinated debenture

하위성 무담보사채 subordinated unsecured debenture

하위열후 junior subordinated

하위전략 substrategy

하위주 subordinated stock

하위증권 junior issue

하위채권 subordinated debt

하위채권자 subordinated creditor

하위페이먼트인카인드채 subordinated payment-in-kind bond

하이리스크하이리턴 high-risk high-return

하이에세이모델 high assay model

하이쿠폰 high-coupon bond

하이테크상품개발자 rocket scientist

하이테크주식 high-tech stock

하이파워드머니 high powered money

하이프네이션 hyphenation

하인(荷印) shipping marks

하자가 없는 자격 bad standing

하자가 있는 권원 defective title

하자담보문서 defendemus

하자보수보증증권 maintenance bond

하적료 stowage

하조비용, 옮겨쌓기비용 shifting charge

하주위험부담 owner's risk

하청 subcontract

하청공장 subcontract factory
하청선불금 advance to subcontractor
하청업자 subcontractor
하청으로 돌리 hive off
하청하다; 연금적용제외 contracting out
하치지시선 support line
하한; 입회장 floor
하한금리 floor rate
하한상장 lower limit rate; lower price
하향수정 downward revision
하향수정된 faded
하향수정하다 make a downward revision
하향제한스트래들 bottom straddle
하향탄력성 downside potential
학교구 school district
학교법인 incorporated school
학부장 dean
학생종합보험 student comprehensive insurance
학습곡선 learning curve
학자보험 educational endowment
학제 interdisciplinary
한 쌍 비교법 paired comparison
한가한 시간 idle time
한계 threshold
한계가치 marginal value
한계가치곡선 marginal value curve
한계공제제도 marginal deduction system
한계단위원가 marginal unit cost
한계대부선 revolving line of credit
한계분석 marginal analysis
한계비용 cost at the margin; marginal cost
한계비용곡선 marginal cost curve
한계비율 marginal ratio
한계생산 marginal production
한계생산비 marginal cost of production
한계생산성 marginal productivity
한계세율 marginal tax rate
한계소비성향 marginal propensity to consume
한계손익계산 marginal income statement

한계수익 marginal returns
한계수익률 marginal rate of return
한계수입 marginal revenue
한계수입성향 marginal propensity to import
한계수치 limit deviation
한계순적합도 marginal net suitability
한계신용 marginal credit
한계예대율 marginal loan-deposit ratio
한계요소 marginal factor
한계원가계산 marginal costing
한계원리 marginal principle
한계이론 marginal theory
한계이익 marginal balance; marginal profit
한계이익도표 profit volume graph
한계이익률 marginal profit ratio
한계자본계수 marginal capital coefficient
한계자본지출 marginal capital expenditure
한계저축성향 marginal propensity to save
한계정 transfer account
한계조건 marginal condition
한계효과 marginal effect
한계효용 marginal utility
한계효율 marginal efficiency
한도를 넘은 차용 outstanding debt
한산 thin
한산시장 inactive market; narrow market
한산한; 활발하지 않은 inactive
한월(限月) contract month; delivery month
한은(韓銀)인수 underwriting by the Bank of Korea
한정감사 limited audit
한정감사보고서 qualified audit certificate
한정된 special
한정매출 restrict sales
한정보고서 qualified report
한정사항; 적격성; 면책사항 qualification
한정상속 qualified acceptance heritage; qualified acceptance of inheritance; qualified inheritance
한정요인 limiting factor
한정의견 qualified opinion

한정이서 qualified endorsement
한정적인 판로 limited distribution
한정적인 판로정책 restricted distribution
 policy
한정조항; 부작위약관 restrictive covenant
한정준비금 qualifying reserve
한쪽 당사자(계약의)한쪽 당사자
 counterparty
할당서 allotment letter
할당예산원장 allotment ledger
할당장 letter of allotment
할당재보험 reinsurance by quota
할당적립방식 allocated funding instrument
할당증 allotment certificate
할당추출법 quota sampling
할당표준 quota sample
할부 installment
할부가격 face of note; total payment of
 installments
할부구매 installment purchase
할부구입알선 third party sales credit
할부기준 installment basis; installment method
할부매상미실현익 unrealized gross profit on
 installment sales
할부미수입금 installments receivable
할부수수료 charge for installment payment
할부외상금 installment receivable
할부운송임 freight pro-rata
할부채권 installment credit
할부카드 multiple payment credit card
할부판매 time sales
할부판매법 installment plan
할부판매전용어음 special bills for installment
 sales credit
할인 discounting
할인가격 haggling price
할인계수 discount factor
할인구조 discount structure
할인국채 discount government bond
할인금융채 discount bank debenture
할인력 force of discount

할인발행 discount issue
할인보증계정 per contra noted discounted
 account
할인상사 discount house
할인수수료 discount commission
할인수익 discounted cash flow
할인수취계정 account receivable discounted
할인시장 discount market
할인액기간 대응할부 accrual of discount
할인어음 discounted bill; note received
 discounted; notes and bills discounted; sold
 bill
할인어음계정 bill discounted account
할인어음기입장 discount register
할인어음원장 discount ledger
할인율 discount charge; discount rate
할인율의 리스크구조 risk structure of
 discount rate
할인은행 discount bank
할인이익 discount yield
할인일수 days to run
할인적격어음 eligible bill
할인정책 discount policy
할인주 bargain stock
할인지방채 compound interest bonds
할인창구 discount window
할인채 discount bond
할인채상환익 profit on redemption of
 discount bond
할인함수 discount function
할인효과 effect of discount
할증보험료 extra premium
할증상각 additional depreciation deduction;
 extra depreciation
할증운임 additional freight
할증임금 extra wage
핥다; 빨아먹다 suck
함구령 gag order
함리스워런트채 harmless warrant
합격기준 acceptance criteria
합계 sum total; total

합계시산표 trial balance of totals
합계잔고시산표 trial balance of totals and balances
합계하다 foot
합동 combine; trust joint
합동공모채계정 pooled publicly traded bond account
합동보통주계정 pooled common stock account
합동부동산계정 pooled real property account
합동사모(私募)채계정 pooled private placement bond account
합동사채 joint bond
합동수익기금 pooled income fund
합동운영펀드 commingled fund
합동운용신탁 joint trust
합동운용펀드 managed fund
합동운용형 펀드 collective investment fund
합리원칙 rule of reason
합리적인 동기부여 rational motivation
합리적인 의문 reasonable doubt
합리적인 평가 rational valuation
합리화 rationalization
합명회사 unlimited partnership
합법적인 절차 legal process
합변사업 Joint venture
합병 amalgamation; joint investment
합병; 매수 merger and acquisition
합병; 혼동 merger
합병계약서 contract of merger
합병교부금 delivered money due to merger
합병교부주식 delivered stock due to merger
합병법인 transferee corporation
합병사업연도 accounting period in case of merger; taxable year of merger
합병손익계산서 combined income statement
합병으로 소멸한 회사 corporation ceased to exist after merger
합병을 위한 주주총회 capital meeting for merger
합병잉여금 amalgamation surplus

합병절차 amalgamation procedures
합병조건 merger terms
합병차익 profit form amalgamation; profit from consolidation; profit from merger; surplus from merged company
합병촉진세액공제 promoting mergers tax credit
합병확정신고 filing final return of merger
합병확정신고서 final return of merger
합산 aggregation
합산과세 unitary taxation
합성고무 synthetic rubber
합성자산 synthetic assets
합성포지션 synthetic position
합성현물재정거래 synthetic cash arbitrage transaction
합유 joint right
합유부동산권 joint tenancy
합유채권 joint obligation
합의관할재판소 agreement jurisdictional court
합의를 위한 사실기재서 case reserved
합의사건 agreed case
합의사실기재서 statement of facts
합의사실진술서 agreed statement of facts
합의에 따른 국제분업 international agreed specialization
합의하여 사건을 위탁함 reference on consent
합의확인서 letter of intent
핫머니시장 hot money market
항, 단락 paragraph
항공기배상자력법 aircraft financial responsibility act
항공기연료세 aviation fuel tax
항공기책임보험 aircraft liability insurance
항공기체보험 aircraft hull insurance; aviation hull insurance
항공로 airway
항공보험협회 Associated Aviation Underwriters
항공보험회사협회 Aviation Insurance

Offices' Association
항공상해보험 aircraft passenger insurance
항공수송 aerial transport
항공요금 air fare
항공운송보험 air transport insurance;
　air-borne cargo insurance; aviation cargo
　insurance
항공운임 airway freight
항공책임보험 aircraft third party liability
　insurance
항공화물운송업자 air carrier
항공화물운송장 air waybill
항구적인 변경 permanent change
항구적인 시설 permanent establishment;
　permanent facility
항만료 port charges
항만세 in-port duty
항목 heading; item
항목; 총계 count
항목특성치 item parameter
항변 defense
항상 운영함 day-to-day management
항상단가 standing cost
항상비용 standing charge
항상상태 steady state
항상상품 staple items
항상소득 permanent income
항상손해액분포 constant claims amount
　distribution
항상위험 constant risk
항상제수(恒常除數) constant divisor
항소취의서 bill of exceptions
항해보험 voyage policy
항해사업 marine adventure
항해에 견디는 seaworthy
항행(航行)방해죄 obstruction of navigation
항행가능한 navigable
해결하다 strengthen
해고수당 allowance for dismissal without
　notice in advance
해고통지 dismissal notice

해난 marine casualty
해난보고서 marine protest
해당사실없음 nient comprise
해당의 concerned
해독; 해독하다 decode
해로운 태만 malign neglect
해머링마켓; 값을 몹시 깎는 시장 hammering
　the market
해방 emancipation
해방담보 open mortgage
해방형 채널 extensive channel
해사검사인 marine surveyor
해사고용감독관 shipping commissioners
해사법 maritime law
해사법규 sea law
해사사건보증증권 admiralty bond
해사선취특권 maritime lien
해사의 maritime
해사재판소 admiralty court; Court of;
　maritime court Admiralty
해사저당 maritime hypothecation
해사협회 maritime association
해산 dissolution; winding up
해산가치 breakup value
해산에 따른 청산소득 liquidation income
　from dissolution
해상 및 운송보험 marine and transport
　insurance
해상고유의 위험 perils of the sea
해상대물운송계약 affreightment contract
해상도; 결의 resolution
해상보험 marine insurance
해상보험계정 marine insurance account
해상보험조항 marine clause
해상보험증권 marine insurance
해상운송계약 affreightment
해상위험 dangers of navigation; marine
　perils; maritime perils; sea peril
해석 construction
해석전손(全損); 추정전손(全損) constructive
　total loss

해석조항 interpretation clause

해소하다 liquidation by compromise

해손정산인 average adjuster

해손정산인보험 Association of Average Adjusters

해약 cancellation; rescission

해약공제 surrender charge

해약권 right of cancellation

해약금 cancellation money

해약기일 canceling date

해약률 surrender ratio

해약반려금 return premium for cancellation; surrender value

해약반환금 cancellation return; cash surrender value

해약예고 notice to quit

해약옵션채권 liquid yield option note

해약익(解約益) surrender profit; gain from forfeiture

해약조항 surrender provisions

해약청구 cancellation request

해약할 수 없는 noncancellable

해약할 수 없는 보험계약 noncancellable insurance

해양의 자유 freedom of the sea

해외거래 overseas transaction

해외계정거래 external transactions account

해외관계회사 overseas affiliated firm

해외근무수당 foreign service allowance

해외금리 interest rate abroad; overseas interest rate

해외법정준비금 overseas legal reserves

해외부채 overseas liabilities

해외사업 foreign operations; overseas business

해외사업법인 overseas undertaking corporation

해외상장 quotation on overseas markets; rate in overseas market

해외생산능력 overseas production capacity

해외생산비율 overseas production ratio

해외여행비 overseas traveling expense

해외여행상해보험 overseas travel accident insurance

해외여행질병보험 overseas travel sickness insurance

해외원조 development assistance

해외원천소득 foreign source income

해외자산 overseas assets

해외전보수신인 cable address

해외주요시장 overseas major market

해외지역별 foreign geographic areas

해외직접투자 foreign direct investment

해외투자 foreign investment; investment abroad; investment overseas

해외투자보고서 overseas investment report

해외투자손실준비금 overseas investment loss reserve; reserve for overseas investment loss

해운 marine transportation; maritime traffic; shipping

해운수입 shipping receipts

해운시장 shipping market

해제권소멸 extinguishment of the right of rescission

해제조건부 매매 sale and return

해제조항 defeasance clause

해제하다 defease

해체; 분쇄 demolition

해체비 demolition expenses

해협 narrow seas

핵심시장 core market

핵심역량 core competence

핵심주 core stock

핵점포 magnet store

행간 line space

행간기입 interlineation

행내교환 in-house exchange

행동과학 behavior science

행동규범 norms of behavior

행동기준 behavior criteria

행동수정 behavioral modification

행동우선이론 behavior-primacy theory

행동이론 behavioral theory

행동적인 어프로치 behavior approach

행렬승수 matrix multiplier

행방이 정해지지 않은 idle money

행사가격 exercise price

행사명의대리인 custodian's agent

행사하다; 발행하다 utter

행사하지 않음 nonuser

행상인 badger

행위 feasance

행위; 제정법 act

행위능력 legal capacity

행위세 act tax

행위에 바탕을 둔 ex facto

행위이론 theory of action

행위지 venue

행정개혁 administrative reform; reform of the
administrative structure

행정구제 administrative remedy

행정권 administrative power

행정명령 administrative order

행정법 administrative law

행정불복심사법 administrative appellate law

행정소송 administrative litigation

행정입법 administrative

행정재량 administrative discretion

행정쟁소 administrative dispute

행정지도 administrative guidance

행정직원 administrative officer

행정처분 administrative disposition

행정해석 administrative interpretation

행정행위 administrative act

허가 license

허가, 인가 grant

허브 hub

허용변동폭내 개입 intramarginal intervention

허용손해율 permissible loss ratio

허용오차 permissible error

허용원가 allowed cost

허용자산 admitted assets

허용차; 공차 tolerance

허용하다 allow; suffer

허용한도 tolerance limit

허용한도액 allowable maximum amount

허용할 수 없는 inadmissible

허위신고 false return

허위진술 false statement

허위표시 false representation

헌법상의 권리 constitutional right

헌터보험 hunters' insurance

헐레이션 halation

험프드커브 humped curve

헤드마운트디스플레이 head mount display

헤드앤드숄더 head and shoulder

헤비유저 heavy users

헤어컷 hair cut

헤이그의정서 Hague Protocol

헤저 hedger

헤지 hedge

헤지거래 hedge trading; hedge transaction

헤지계산대행서 hedge account representation
letter

헤지기능 hedging function

헤지비율 hedge ratio

헤지수단 means for hedging

헤지스킴 hedging scheme

헤지조작 hedge operation

헤지채 hedged bond

헤지코스트 hedging cost

헤지펀드 hedge fund

헤징; 연계매매 hedging

헬로효과 hello effect

헬오어하이워터조항 hell or high water clause

혁신; 갱정 innovation

혁신적인 경쟁 innovative competition

혁신적인 효율 innovative efficiency

현가법 present value method

현가율 present value rate

현가표 table of present value

현금 ready money

현금 및 예금통화 currency and demand

deposits
현금가격 cash price
현금감사 cash audit
현금거래 cash take; dealing for money
현금결제 cash settlement
현금계산서 cash statement
현금과부족계정 cash over and short account
현금구매 cash purchase
현금구입 bought for cash
현금기록 cash records
현금대부 cash loan
현금매매 cash sale
현금매상장 cash buying rate; cash selling rate
현금반송 cash remittance
현금배당 cash dividend
현금배당결의액 cash dividend declared
현금부채 cash liabilities
현금분개장 cash journal
현금비율 cash ratio
현금상태 cash position
현금상환 cash redemption
현금선지급 cash advance
현금송장 cash letters
현금수납장 cash receipt book; cash receipt journal
현금수령 cash receipt
현금수입 cash earnings; cash income; money income
현금에 부착함 suction to cash
현금예금 cash and deposits with banks; cash deposit
현금예금계정 cash and deposits banks accounts
현금유동부채비율 cash to current liabilities ratio
현금자산 cash assets
현금자산가치 cash asset value
현금잔고 cash balance
현금주문 cash with order
현금주의 cash basis
현금주의회계 cash basis accounting

현금준비 reserve cash
현금준비고 cash reserves
현금지불 cash and carry; cash disbursement; cash payment; pay down; payment by cash
현금지불거래 cash and carry trade
현금지불기 cash dispenser
현금지불방식 cash and carry system
현금지불비용 out-of-pocket cost
현금지불장 cash payment journal; disbursement book; paid cash book
현금지출 cash outlays
현금지출비 out-of-pocket expense
현금출납계 cashier; teller
현금출납과 cashier's department
현금출납장 cash book
현금출자 investment in money
현금통화 cash currency
현금판매 sale for cash
현금판매를 전문으로 하는 재고업자 cash and carry wholesaler
현금할인 cash discount
현금항목 cash items
현금화 cashing
현금화; 청산 liquidation
현금화하다 liquidate
현금환가가치 actual cash value
현금회수 cash flow-back
현대포트폴리오이론 modern portfolio theory
현명한 투자가 smart money
현물가격 spot price
현물급여 truck system; wage in kind
현물납부 payment of tax in kind; tax payment in kind
현물보상 replacement in kind
현물상장 spot quotation; spot rate
현물상장; 직물환상장 spot exchange rate
현물선도거래 cash forward transaction
현물수도 actual delivery
현물시장 spot market
현물옵션 cash option
현물인도 actual delivery of stock sold; spot

delivery
현물증권 underlining security
현물지급 allowance in kind
현물출자 investment in kind
현물출자를 과대평가함 overestimation of
  investment in kind
현물출자취득주 stock acquired by the
  investment in kind
현물환 spot exchange
현상 status quo
현상분석 present data analysis
현시선호 revealed preference
현실거래 actual receipt of stock purchased
현실성장율 actual rate of growth
현실인도 physical delivery
현실전손 actual total loss
현실점유 possession in deed
현실표준원가 actually expected standard cost
현예금 cash equivalent
현예금회전율 sales to cash
현장감사 field inspection; site audit
현장감사인 field inspector
현장인도가격 loco price
현재 소유한 vested in possession
현재가격 present price; spot value
현재가치 current value; present value; present
  worth
현재가치로 환원하다; 디스카운트 discount
현재고 amount on hand
현재근무연금 current service pension
현재수량, 재고 amount in hand
현재시장 actual market
현재연령 attained age
현재원가 current cost
현재유효한 보험 current insurance
현재유효한 연금 current annuity
현재의 주가수준 current level of stock price
현재종업원 active employee
현재품 stock in hand
현저하게 unreasonably
현저하게 낮은 가격 remarkably low price

현주 spot share
현지생산공장 local production factory
현지일관생산 full-scale local production
현지조달율 local content ratio
현지지향 polycentrism
현지통화 local currency
현직자기금 active life fund
현품주문 order stock; unfilled orders
현학적인 전문용어 buzz word
현행시장가액 current market value
현행이자율 current interest rate
현행절도죄 open theft
현행프리미엄 current premium value
현회계연도 current fiscal year
혈연 blood relationship
혈연상속인 natural heirs
혈통이 탁해짐 corruption of blood
혐의 suspicion
협동조합 cooperative association; cooperative
  society
협박 threat
협박, 긴축 tightening
협약 pact
협의 conference
협의사항 agenda
협의인수 negotiated underwriting
협정가격 contract price; price agreed upon;
  stipulated price
협정관세 conventional tariff
협정무손상가액 conventional undamaged
  value
협정무역 trade by agreement
협정보험가액 agreed insured value; policy
  valuation
협정서; (조합의)규약; 정관(회사의)
  memorandum
협정손해율; 준비금 allowance
협정요율 tariff by agreement
협정임금 contractual wage
협정전손 arranged total loss; compromised
  total loss

협조가격하락 coordinated cut
협조개입 concerted intervention; coordinated intervention
협회 association
협회단체보험 association group insurance
협회약관 Institute clauses
협회화물약관 Institute cargo clauses
형법 crown law
형사법규 penal statute
형사상급재판소 court of justiciary
형사상의 penal
형사소송 criminal action; penal action
형사소송절차 criminal proceedings
형사제일심 court of general sessions
형상모델 geometric model
형식 form
형식모델 formal model
형식적인 formal
형집행정지 stay of execution
형태 shape
형평법상의 모기지 equitable mortgage
호가 bid and offer; nominal price quotation
호가 스프레드 bid-offer spread
호경기시대 prosperous days
호성적 되돌림 good result return
호이율 good yield
호재 favorable factor; favorable news; good news
호재료 strong incentive
호적 census register; family-register
호전 upturn
호전개가 되다 perform well
호주달러유러채 down under bond
호출장 summons
호혜관세 reciprocal duties
호환성 interchangeability
호황 boom
호황시장 active market
혹이 있는 humped
혼동 confusion
혼례시장 bridal market

혼성의; 엇갈린 mixed
혼인상의 주소 matrimonial domicile
혼인상태 matrimony
혼인전의 ante-nuptial
혼재배송시스템 consolidated delivery system
혼합 hybrid
혼합거래 mixed transaction
혼합경제 mixed economy
혼합계약 mixed contract
혼합계정 mixed account
혼합보험 mixed insurance; mixed policy
혼합불법방해 mixed nuisance
혼합소송 mixed action
혼합신탁 hybrid trust
혼합잉여금 mixed surplus
혼합자산 mixed assets
혼합재고정리 mixed inventory
혼합재산 mixed property
혼합주식 hybrid stocks
혼합준비금 mixed reserve
혼합증여 mixed gift
혼합차이 mixed variance
혼합캡 hybrid cap
혼합투자계정 commingled investment account
혼합형 hybrid model
홀드포인트 hold point
홀로그래피 holography
홀로그램 hologram
홀세일뱅크 wholesale bank
홀소트카드 hole sort card
홈메이드인플레 home made inflation
홈뱅킹 home banking
홈에퀴티론 home equity loan
화면 1인치당 도트수 dots per inch
화물 freight
화물관리인 supercargo
화물손해검사 cargo damage survey
화물손해방지위원회 Cargo Loss Prevention Committee
화물수입 freight earnings; goods earnings

화물운임 freight rates; freight tariff
화물적재능력 cargo capacity
화물해상보험 cargo insurance; marine cargo insurance
화물해상보험증권 marine cargo policy
화석연료 fossil fuel
화소 pixel
화의 bankruptcy and composition; composition
화의법 composition law
화재보험 fire damage; fire insurance
화재보험금 fire insurance proceeds
화재보험료 fire insurance premium
화재보험약관 fire clause
화재보험증권 fire insurance policy
화재상호보험 fire mutual insurance
화재손실 fire loss
화재손실미결산계정 fire loss suspense account
화재손해 fire company
화재위험 fire peril
화폐가치변동회계 accounting for changing prices
화폐가치일정공준 stable dollar assumption
화폐개량설 quantity theory of money
화폐베일이론 money-veil theory
화폐분석 monetary analysis
화폐성장모델 monetary growth model
화폐수요 demand for money
화폐수요함수 demand function for money
화폐의 구매력 purchasing power of money
화폐의 대외가치 external purchasing power of money
화폐이자율 monetary interest rate
화폐자본유지 maintenance of financial capital
화폐제도 monetary system
화폐환각 money illusion
화폐환상 monetary illusion
화해 concord
화해양도인 deforciant
화환신용장 documentary credit

화환어음 documentary bill
확대경제 expansive economy
확대되는 격차 widening gap
확대상장변동 wider margin
확대신용공여제도 extended fund facility
확대 EC enlarged European Communities
확률곡선 probability curve
확률론적 모델 probabilistic model
확률론적 브랜드선택 probabilistic brand choice
확률론적 선호모델 probabilistic model of preference
확률모델 stochastic model
확률방법 stochastic method
확률변동 random variable
확률분석 probability distribution
확률에 따른 특성선 probabilistic characteristic lines
확률이 높은 probable
확률적 예측 probabilistic forecasting
확률표본 probability sample
확률프로세스 stochastic process
확률함수 probability mass function
확률해석 stochastic calculus
확산 proliferation
확산변환모델 displaced diffusion model
확신적인 입증 convincing proof
확실성 자산 certain assets
확실히 하다 ensure
확실히 회수할 수 있는 good and collectible
확실히 회수할 수 있는 자금 good debt
확약 affirmation
확약; 전액인수 firm commitment
확약가격 firm quote
확약증언자 affirmant
확인 confirmation; homologation
확인결정 declaratory decree
확인약속 assertory covenant
확인은행 confirming bank
확인장 confirmation letter
확인지불 pay on application

ㅌ
ㅍ
ㅎ

확인청구 confirmation request
확인테스트 authorization test
확인통지서 confirmation note
확인필 신용장 confirmed letter of credit
확인하다 declaratory
확인해야 할 곳 referable name
확장 extension
확장급부 extended benefit
확장담보이서 additional extended coverage endorsement
확장담보특약 extended coverage
확장마케팅개념 broadened marketing concept
확장모드 expand mode
확장슬롯 extended slot
확장제품 augmented product
확정 lock-in
확정가격 firm price
확정가격제시 firm offer
확정거출형 연금플랜 defined contribution plan
확정결산 definite settlement of accounts
확정계약 firm contract
확정계정 account rendered; account stated; liquidated account
확정권리 vested interest
확정급부채무 vested benefit obligation
확정급부형 연금플랜 defined benefit plan
확정된 손실 hit
확정매호수치 firm bid
확정모델 deterministic model
확정배당 guaranteed dividend
확정보르드로 definite bordereau
확정보험료 definite premium
확정보험증권 definite policy; definitive policy
확정부채 direct liabilities
확정손해배상액 limited damages
확정손해배상청구통지서 final notice of claim
확정신 final declaration
확정신고 final return; final tax return
확정신고에 따른 납부 final payment

확정신고에 따른 환급 refund by final return
확정신탁 fixed trust
확정연금 annuity; annuity certain
확정연금종가 amount of annuity certain
확정이부채 fixed coupon bond
확정이익 fixed gain
확정이자 fixed interest
확정이자부 증권 fixed interest security
확정이자부 증권 벤치마크 fixed-income benchmark
확정이자부 채권 fixed interest-bearing bond; fixed-rate bond
확정이자부 타겟 fixed-income target
확정일 return day
확정일부 date proved by notary; fixed date
확정일불 payable on a fixed date
확정일인도 fixed date delivery
확정일지불보험 fixed term policies
확정일지불어음 bill payable at a fixed date
확정잉여금 established surplus
확정자본금 stated capital
확정잔여권 vested remainder
확정주문 firm order
확정차액 fixed difference
확정채무 fixed obligations; liquidated debt
확정통지 definite declaration
확정한 결산 final settlement of accounts
환; 거래소 exchange
환가 encashment; realization
환가능계정 transferable account
환가불능자산 unrealizable assets
환가처분 conversion into cash; tax sale
환개입 exchange intervention
환거래 exchange dealing; transfer transactions
환거래소 bourse
환결제 exchange settlement
환결제청산 exchange clearing
환경난민 environmental refugee
환경변수 environmental variable
환경변화 environmental change
환경오염배상책임보험 environmental

impairment liability insurance
환경진단 environmental diagnosis
환경파괴 destruction of environment
환경평가 environment assessment
환관리 exchange control
환구입 buying exchange
환금성 상품 cashability goods
환금성이 높은 available
환금판매 realization sales
환급된 조세 tax refunded
환급수료 return commission
환기입 transfer entry
환끝환산차금 inter-office exchange
　adjustment account
환당좌대 export account
환당좌대이자 interest on overdrafts for export
　bills
환당좌대출 overdrafts for export bills
환덤핑 exchange dumping
환동향 currency movement
환딜러 exchange cambiste; exchange dealer
환류 channeling back; reflow
환리스크 exchange risk
환매가; 재취득가격 repurchase price
환매결제 short covering
환매권 rights of repurchase
환매를 조건으로 매각함 sales under
　agreement to repurchase
환매리 exchange marry
환매리이익 exchange marriage profit
환매의무 repurchase obligation
환매입 bill bought
환매조건부 거래 repurchase agreement
환매조건부 매각어음 discount on bills sold
　on condition of repurchase
환매조건부 매출오퍼레이션 selling operation
　under repurchase agreement
환매청구권 repurchase
환매출 bill sold
환번호 transfer number
환변동 exchange fluctuation

환변동보험 exchange risk insurance
환변동폭 width of currency movements
환보유고 position
환보유고조정조작 exchange risk cover
환부가산금 interest on refund
환부금 refund; repayment money
환부금의 익금불산입 exclusion of refund
　from gross revenue
환부금지불통지서 notification of payment of
　refund
환부금충당 appropriation of refund
환부금충당통지서 notification of
　appropriation of refund
환부법인세 refunded corporation tax
환부세 refund tax
환부청구 claim for a refund
환부청구권시효 statute of limitations on
　refund claim
환불 reimbursement
환불세 tax rebate
환불세급부 drawback allowance
환브로커 exchange broker
환산 change; commutation
환산계수테이블 table of price factors
환송명령 mandate on remission
환수급안정성 stability of the foreign
　exchange market
환수수료 charges for remittance
환승 switch
환심리설 psychological theory of exchange
환안정기금 exchange stabilization fund
환어음 draft bill of exchange
환어음; 어음 draft
환어음을 증여함 presentment of bill of
　exchange
환업무 exchange business
환예약 exchange contract; exchange
　reservation
환원; 이익 return
환원장 transfer ledger
환위험 transfer risk

환율 exchange rate
환율문언 exchange clause
환은행 exchange bank
환은행이 환보유고를 조정하기 위해 다른 은
　행과 조건이 일치할 때 하는 거래
　exchange cover rate
환이익 transfer profit
환인수율 accepting rate of exchange
환자금조정거래 exchange fund cover or
　operation
환자유화 liberalization of exchange control
환재정 arbitration of exchange
환재정거래 exchange arbitrage; exchange
　arbitrage transaction
환저금계좌 transfer savings account
환전상 money changer
환전표 transfer slip
환조작 exchange manipulation; exchange
　operation
환조정의 소득효과 income effect of exchange
　adjustments
환지고(持高) exchange position
환지처분 substitution of land lot
환차손 exchange loss; foreign currency
　translation gain or loss
환차손익 exchange loss and profit
환차익 exchange gain; exchange profit
환청산협정 exchange clearing agreement
환투기 exchange speculation
환평가 exchange parity
환평형계정 exchange equalization account
환평형기금 exchange equalization fund
환평형조작 exchange equalization operation
환프리미엄 exchange premium
환헤지 currency hedging
환환산수정 effect of exchange rate changes
환환산조정 translation adjustments
환환산차손익 exchange gain or loss
활계정 working account
활기를 잃다 languish
활동계정 active account

활동범위구조 orbital structure
활동영역 domain
활동율 activity rates
활동회계 activity accounting
활자 type
활황 gather steam
활황시장 brisk market
황금률 golden rule
황금분할 golden section
회계감사 accountant's inspection; auditing
회계감사업무 accountancy service
회계거래 accounting transactions
회계검사관 controller
회계검사원 Board of Audit; General
　Accounting Office
회계공준 accounting postulate
회계과 accounting division; accounting
　section
회계관리 accounting control
회계규정 accounting regulation
회계기 tabulating machine
회계기간 fiscal period
회계기록 accounting records
회계기준 accounting standards
회계단위 accounting unit
회계단일원칙 principle of unified accounting
회계담당자 accountable officer
회계등식 accounting identity
회계매뉴얼 accounting manual
회계방침 accounting policy
회계베타수치 accounting beta value
회계보고 accounting report
회계사 accountant
회계사무소 accounting firm
회계사무처리 accounting data process
회계사배상책임보험 accountant liability
　policy
회계사보 junior accountant
회계사보조 assistant certified public
　accountant
회계사사무소 accountant's office

회계사상 accountable condition
회계사업 accounting profession
회계사책임 accountant's responsibility
회계실무 accounting practice
회계실체 accounting entity
회계연구공보 Accounting Research Bulletin
회계연도 accounting year; financial year; fiscal year
회계연도를 공준함 postulate of accounting period
회계연속통첩 Accounting Series Release
회계용어 accounting terminology
회계워런트 accountable warrant
회계원칙 accounting convention; accounting principle
회계원칙변경 changes in accounting principles
회계원칙심의회 Accounting Principles Board
회계이익 accounting earnings
회계자기자본이익률 accounting ratio of profits to net worth
회계장부 accounting book; financial books
회계장표 set of accounts
회계절차 accounting procedures
회계절차위원회 Committee on Accounting Procedure
회계제도 accounting system
회계조직 accounting information system; accounting organization; system of accounts
회계주임 chief accountant
회계주임, 경리담당자 paymaster
회계증거 accounting evidence
회계직능 accounting function
회계처리 accounting treatment
회계통칙 accounting rules
회계평가 accounting valuation
회계학 accountancy
회귀계수 regression coefficient
회귀기대 regressive expectations
회귀모델 regression model

회귀방정식 regression equation
회귀분석 regression analysis
회귀분석법 regression analysis method
회귀상관 regression correlation
회귀식 regression
회기 session
회답률 response rate
회답오차 response error
회복할 수 없는 침해 irreparable injury
회비 club dues; membership fee
회사 incorporated company
회사간계정 intercompany account
회사간이익 intercompany profit
회사간제거 intercompany elimination
회사갱생 corporate reorganization; reorganization of corporation
회사갱생법 company rehabilitation law; corporation reorganization law
회사갱생절차관재인 equity receiver
회사기록을 검사함 inspection of corporate record
회사대리인 company representative
회사등기소 registrar of companies
회사레포트 corporation report
회사명의의 회원 membership in the capacity of a corporation
회사법 company law
회사분할 corporate separation; partition of corporation
회사상호간 대차소법 elimination of intercompany indebtedness
회사상호간 이익소법 elimination of intercompany profits
회사상호간 지분소법 elimination of intercompany ownership
회사상호간손실 intercompany loss
회사설립등기 registration of incorporation
회사설립면허 certificate of incorporation
회사설립수속 incorporation procedures
회사설립전 이익 profit prior to incorporation
회사설립취지서 prospectus of promotion

ㅌ
ㅍ
ㅎ

회사설립허가서 charter provision
회사의 신용을 유지하기 위한 배당 fictitious dividend
회사정관 articles of incorporation
회사조직 company organization
회사중역 corporate executive
회사청산요구 bust-up proposal
회사특권 corporate franchise
회사행위 corporate action
회상법 recall method
회수 collection; recall
회수; 회복 recovery
회수가능가치 recovery value
회수가능원가 recovery cost
회수가능지출 recovery expenditure
회수가능한 collectible; recoverable
회수규제 regulation of debt collection
회수기간 collection period; pay-back period; payback period
회수기술 collection management technique
회수기준 collection basis
회수기한도래기준 due date coming basis
회수된 원가 absorbed cost
회수불능 frozen credit
회수불능원가 irrecoverable cost; sunk cost
회수순환 collection cycle
회수업무 collection practices
회수업자 collection agency; debt collector
회수에 문제가 있는 대부 substandard loan
회수율 percentage of debt collection
회원권 seat
회원명부 list of members
회원비즈니스 membership business
회원사의 대리요율신청 agency filing
회원제 점포 closed door membership store
회원회사 member firm; member organization
회의비 convention expense
회전기간 turnover period
회전무역 revolving trade
회전신용장 revolving letter of credit
회전신용장; 리볼빙크레딧 revolving credit

회전어음 endorsed bills exchanged between two parties
회전율 rate of turnover; turnover rate; turnover ratio; turnover ratios
회전자금 revolving fund
회피 abstention
회피가능원가 avoidable cost; escapable cost
회피불가능원가 unavoidable cost
회피불능비 inescapable cost
회피하다 evade
횡단데이터 cross-sectional data
횡단분석 cross-sectional analysis; horizontal organization
횡령 embezzlement
횡령; 환산 conversion
횡선수표 crossed check
효과 effect
효과가 높은 high-leveraged
효과음 sound effects
효과파급 relation
효력발생문언 operative words
효력이 없는 법률행위 void transaction
효력이 없는 쿠폰 invalid coupon
효용곡선 utility curve
효용을 창조함 creation of utility
효용이론 utility theory
효용최대화 utility maximization
효용함수 utility function
효율성 operational efficiency
효율적인 규모 efficient-scale facility
효율적인 시장 efficient market
효율적인 시장 가설 efficient market hypothesis
효율적인 포트폴리오 efficient portfolio
효익세분화 benefit segmentation
후견 guardianship
후견선출매가환원법 LIFO adaptation of retail method
후견인 conservator; curator; guardian ad litem
후견인보증증권 committee bond
후계자 successor

후기 latter half of the year
후기배당 dividend for the second half
후발발전도상국 least less developed countries
후발사상 subsequent events
후방수직통합 backward vertical integration
후방유통경로 backward channel
후방차이근사치 backward difference
후방통합 backward integration
후배주 deferred share
후불; 연납 deferred payment
후비용 after cost
후생경제학 welfare economics
후생연금 welfare pension
후생연금보험 welfare pension insurance
후순위담보 junior security
후순위저당 junior mortgage
후순위저당우선 tacking
후순위채권 junior bond
후순위채권자 junior creditor
후일부의 dating backward
후일불신용장 deferred payment credit
후임유산관리인 administrator de bonis non
후입선출기준 last-in first-out basis
후입선출법준비금 LIFO reserve
후장 afternoon session
후진국 backward countries
후천적인 수요 acquired needs
후퇴 pulling-back
후퇴하다 back away
훈계; 권고 admonition
훈련계획 training program

훈련비 training expenses
훼손수표 mutilated check
휘도 luminance
휘도신호 luminance signal
휘발유세 gasoline tax
휴가수당 vacation pay
휴먼어세스먼트 human assessment
휴먼인터페이스 human interface
휴면구좌 sleeping account
휴면회원 sleeping member
휴식하다; 잔여 rest
휴지계정 dormant account
휴지잔고 dormant balance
휴항환불보험료 lay-up refund
흑백논리 disjunctive allegation
흑자 positive figure
흑자재정 surplus finance
흡수된 회사 absorbed corporation
흡수합병 consolidation take-over; purchase
　　acquisition
흥미 appetite
흥행권 playright
희귀주 rare stock
희망적; 낙관적 bullish
희박화 방지조항 anti-dilution clause
희석필 fully diluted
희석화 dilution
희소자원 scarce resources
희소통화조항 scarce currency clause
히스토그램법 histogram method

최신 약어

A

AAA American Arbitration Association
미국중재협회

AACM Afro-Asian Common Market
아시아·아프리카 공동시장

AAE affirmative action employer 차별 철폐
고용자

AALL American Association of Law
Libraries 미국법률도서관협회

AALS Association of American Law Schools
미국로스쿨협회

AAR against all risks 전위험담보

AASB American Association of Small
Business 미국중소기업협회

AB able-bodied seaman 숙련선원

ABA American Bankers Associatio
미국은행협회

ABA American Bar Association
미국변호사회

ABC atomic, biological and chemical weapon
화생방병기

ABU Asian-Pacific Broadcasting Union
아시아태평양 방송연합

ABWR advanced boiling water reactor
신형비등수형 경수원자로

A.C. ante Christum 서력기원전

a/c account 계정과목계좌계정

AC Advertising Council 공공광고기구

AC alternating current 교류

ACAP Association of Consumers Affairs
Professionals 소비자관련전문가회의

ACAT Automated Customer Account
Transfer Service 고객계정 자동대체
서비스

ACC Administrative Committee on
Coordination 국제연합행정조정위원회

ACC All Japan Radio TV Commercial
Council 전 일본 라디오·텔레비전 CM 협
의회

ACCU Asian Culture Center of UNESCO

유네스코아시아문화센터

ACE Amex Commodity Exchange 아멕스
상품거래소

ACH Automated Clearinghouse
자동결제기구

ACLU American Civil Liberties Union
미국시민자유인권협회

ACM Andean Common Market 안데스 공동
시장

ACRR American Council on Race Relations
미국인종문제협의회

ACRS Accelerated Cost Recovery System
가속상각제도

ACU Asian Clearing Union 아시아청산동맹

ACU Asian Currency Unit 아시아통화단위

ACUS Administrative Conference of the
United States 합중국행정협의회

AD automatic depositor 자동예금기

ADA Americans With Disabilities Act
장애인차별금지법

ADB African Development Bank
미국개발은행

ADB Asian Development Bank
아시아개발은행

ADF African Development Fund
아프리카개발기금

ADF Asian Development Fund
아시아개발기금

ADI Agency for International Development
국제개발공사

ADR American Depositary Receipt
미국예금증권

A.E. and P. Ambassador Extraordinary and
Plenipotentiary 특명전권대사

AEC Atomic Energy Commission
원자력 위원회

AELE Americans for Effective Law
Enforcement 실효적인 법집행을 위한
미국인의 모임

부
록

AEROSAT aeronautical satellite 항공위성

AESJ Atomic Energy Society of Japan 일본원자력학회

A.F. advance freight 전불운임

AFA automatic fund allocation 외화 자금 자동할당제

AFDC Aid to Families with Dependent Children 아동부양급부

AFL American Federation of Labor 미국노동총동맹

AFL-CIO American Federation of Labor and Congress of Industrial Organizations 미국 노동총동맹산별회의

AFP Agence France-Presse 프랑스통신사

AFTA ASEAN Free Trade Area 아세안자유무역권

AG Attorney General 법무장관

AG Aktiengesellschaft 주식회사

AGV automatic guided vehicle 무인반송차

AI artificial intelligence 인공지능

AI artificial insemination 인공수정

AIBD Association of International Dealers 국제채권딜러협회

AICPA American Institute of Certified Public Accountants 미국공인회계사협회

AID Agency for International Development 국제개발청

AIPLA American Intellectual Property Law Association 미국공인회계사협회

A.J. associate justice/judge 배석재판관

a.k.a. also known as 별칭, 통칭

ALGOL Algorithmic Language 알고리즘 언어

ALI American Law Institute 미국법률협회

AU Administrative Law Judge 행정법심판관

ALM asset-liability management 자산부채종 합관리

ALTA American Land Title Association 미국토지거래협회

AM amplitude modulation 진폭변조

AMA American Medical Association 미국의학회

AMA American Management Association 미국경영자협회

AMeDAS Automated Meteorological Data Acquisition System 지역기상관측시스템

AMEX American Stock Exchange 미국증권 거래소

AMT alternative minimum tax 선택적인 최저 세액

Amtrak American Track 미국철도여객수송 공사

AMU Arab Maghreb Union 아랍·마그레브 연합

ANS American Nuclear Society 미국원자력 학회

ANS Asian News Service 아시아통신사

ANSA Agenzia Nazionale Stampa Associata 이탈리아공동통신사

ANSI American National Standards Institute 미국규격협회

ANZUS Australia, New Zealand and the United States Treaty 태평양안전보장조약

A.P additional premium 추가보험료

AP advise and pay 통지지불

AP Associated Press 미국연합통신사

APA Administrative Procedure Act 행정수속법

APA American Pharmaceutical Association 미국약학회

APB Accounting Principles Board 회계원칙심의회

APCA Air Pollution Control Association 대기오염방지협회

APEC Asia Pacific Economic Cooperation 아시아태평양경제협력회의

API American Petroleum Instisute 아시아석유협회

APR annual percentage rate 연리(年利) 퍼센테이지

APT automatic picture transmission 자동 화상 송신장치

APWR advanced pressurized water reactor
신형가압수형 원자로

AQ achievement quotient 성취지수

ARAMCO Arabian-American Oil Company
아라비안·아메리칸석유회사

ARB Accounting Research Bulletin
회계연구공보

ARIMA autoregressive integrated moving
average model 자기회귀화분이동평균모델

ARM adjustable rate mortgage 조정 금리 모
기지

ARMA autoregressive moving average model
자기회귀이동평균모델

ARP adjustable rate preferred stock
변동 배당율 우선주

AS account sales 매상계산서

AS at sight 일람불

ASA American Standards Association
미국규격협회

ASA American Statistical Association
미국통계협회

asap as soon as possible 가능한 한 빨리

ASCAP American Society of Composers,

Authors and Publishers 미국작곡가·작사가
·출판자협회

ASCII American Standard Code for
Information Interchange 아스키

ASEAN Association of South-Hast Asian
Nations 동남아시아국가연합

ATF advanced tactical fighter 신형전술전투
기

ATLA Association of Trial Lawyers of
America 미국사실심변호사협회

ATM automated teller machine
현금자동입출금기

ATM asynchronous transfer mode switching
system 광대역 ISDN용 교환기

ATS automatic transfer service account
자동대체계좌

ATS automatic train stopper
자동 열차 정지장치

ATT American Telephone & Telegraph
Company 미국전신전화회사

AWACS airborne warning and control system
공중경계관제시스템

B

BA Banker's acceptance 은행인수어음

BASIC Beginner's All-Purpose Symbolic
Instruction Code 베이직 언어

B&B bed and breakfast 아침식사가 딸린 숙박

BBC British Broadcasting Corporation
영국방송협회

B/C. bill for collection 서력기원전

B/C bill for collection 대금수금어음

BCD binary-coded decimal 2진화 10진법

BDR Bearer Depositary Receipts
무기명 예탁 증권

B/E bill of exchange 환어음

BEI Banque Europeenne d'Investissement
유럽투자은행

Benelux Belgium, the Netherlands,

Luxemburg 벨기에·네덜란드·룩셈부르크 3
국의 경제연맹

BETRO British Export Trade Research
Organization 영국무역진흥회

BFOQ bona fide occupational qualification
진정한 직업요건

BFP bone fide purchaser 선의매수인

BIAC Business and Industry Advisory
Committee 경제산업자문위원회

BIE Bureau International des Expositions
만국박람회 국제사무국

BIGI Bond Investors Guaranty Insurance
Company 지방채보증회사

BIOS basic input output system 기본입출력
시스템

부록

BIS Bank for International Settlements
국제결제은행

B-ISDN broadband 광대역 ISDN

B/L bill of lading 선하증권

B.M. bachelor of medicine 의학사

BNC broadband communications network
광대역통신망

BNOC British National Oil Corporation
영국국영석유공사

BO brought over 이월

BOE Bank of England 잉글랜드은행

BOJ Bank of Japan 일본은행

BP bills payable 지불어음

BP British Petroleum 영국석유공사

bps bits per second 1초 동안 전송할 수 있는
비트의 수

Bq becquerel 베크렐 방사능의 단위

BR bills receivable 수금환어음

B.S. bachelor of science 이과학사

BS balance sheet 대차대조표

BS broadcasting satellite 방송위성

BSI British Standards Institution
영국규격협회

BSI British standard time 영국 표준시

BT British Telecommunications Corporation
브리티시텔레콤사(社)

BTA British Tourist Authority 영국관광청

BTN Brussels Tariff Nomenclature 브뤼셀관
세품목분류표

BTS broadcasting technical standard
방송기술규격

BTV business television 비즈니스텔레비전

B.W. black and white 흑백

BWC Biological Weapons Convention
생물병기조약

BWR boiling water reactor 비등수형 원자로

C

C/A credit account 외상거래계정

C/A current account 당좌예금

CA chronological age 역연령생활연령

CA corporate art 커퍼레이트아트

Ca. Resp. capias ad respondendum 응소를 위
한 구인영장

Ca. Sa. capias ad satisfaciendum 변제를 위한
구금영장

ca. circa 대략

CAA Clean Air Acts 대기정화법

CAAC Civil Aviation Administration of
China 중국민간항공총국

CAB cable box 공동구

CAB Central African Bank 중앙아프리카은행

CAB Civil Aviation Bureau 운수성항공국

CACM Central American Common Market
중미공동시장

CAD computer-aided design 컴퓨터지원설계

CAE computer-aided education 컴퓨터 지원
교육

CAE computer-aided engineering
컴퓨터 지원 엔지니어링

CAES Computer Assisted Execution System
상장주식매매주문용 자동집행시스템

CAES Computer-Assisted Excution System
자동거래집행시스템

CAFEA Commission on Asian and Far
Eastern Affairs 극동아시아문제위원회

CAFTA Central America Free Trade
Association 중미자유무역연합

CAJ Cofederation of ASEAN Journalists
아세안 · 저널리스트연맹

CAL computer-assisted learning 컴퓨터 지원
학습

CALS continues acquisition life-cycle support
칼스생산 · 조달통합지원

CAM computer-aided manufacturing
컴퓨터 지원 제조

CAP Common Agricultural Policy
공통농업정책

CAPM capital asset pricing model
금융 자산 가격 모델

Capcom Capsule Communicator 우주선의 교
신담당자

CAPS convertible adjustable preferred stock
전환조정가능 우선주

CAPTAIN Character and Pattern Telephone
Access Information Network 캡틴

CARD Campaign against Racial
Discrimination 인종차별철폐운동

CARE Cooperative for American Relief to
Everywhere 해외구제물자발송협회

CARICOM Caribbean Community
카리브공동체

CARP controlled adjustable rate preferred
stock 보증부 변동배당우선주

CASE computer-assisted software
engineering 케이스

CASL CAS language 캐슬

CAT city air terminal 시티 에어 터미널 도심
공항터미널

CAT clear-air turbulence 청천 난류, 맑은 하
늘에서 발생하는 난기류

CAT computerized axial tomography
컴퓨터화 체축 단층사진

CAT credit authorization terminal
신용정보조회단말기

CATS certificate of accrual on treasury
securities 제로쿠폰재무성증권

CATV cable television 유선텔레비전

c.a.v. curia advisari vult 비(非) 즉시언도판결

CB convertible bond 전환사채

CB character brand 캐릭터 · 브랜드

CB chemical and biological 생물화학

CBC Canadian Broadcasting Corporation
캐나다방송협회

CBF cancer breaking factor 암파괴인자

CBI certificate of beneficial interest
부분수익증권

CBI Caribbean Basin Initiative 카리브해
원조 구상

CBI Confederation of British Industry
영국산업연맹

CBO Congressional Budget Office
의회예산국

CBOE Chicago Board of Options Exchange
시카고옵션거래소

CBS Columbia Broadcasting System CBS

CBT Chicago Board of Trade 시카고 상품 거
래소

CC circuit court 순회재판소

CC chamber of commerce 상업회의소

CC commercial card 커머셜카드

cc cubic centimeter 세제곱센티미터

CCC Commodity Credit Corporation
상품금융공사

CCC Customs Cooperation Council
관세협력이사회

CCD Conference of Committee on
Disarmament 군축위원회회의

CCI Chamber of Commerce and Industry
상공회의소

CCIS coaxial cable information system
동축 케이블 정보시스템

CCP Chinese Communist Party 중국공산당

CCR Commission on Civil Rights
공민권위원회

CCTV closed-circuit television 폐쇄회로
텔레비전

CD certificate of deposit 양도가능 정기예금
증서

CD cash dispenser 현금자동지급기

CD coference on disarmament 군축회의

CDA Camp David Accord 캠프 데이비드
합의

CDMA code division multiple access
부호분할다원접속

CDR Continental Depositary Receipts
컨티넨탈 예탁증권

CDR Curacao Depositary Receipts
컨티넨탈 예탁증서

CDS central data system 중앙데이터시스템

부록

CDV compact disk video 컴팩트디스크
비디오
CE Council of Europe 유럽회의
CEA Council of Economic Advisers
경제자문위원회
CEC Commission of European Community
유럽공동체위원회
CED Committee of Economic Development
미국경제개발위원회
CEDEL Cetrale de Livraison de Valeurs
Mobilieres 세델유러채집중예탁 · 집중결제
기관
CEO chief executive officer 최고경영책임자
CEPT Conference of European Post and
Telecommunication 전기통신주관청회의
CERCLA Comprehensive Environmental
Response, Compensation, and Liability
Act 환경에 관한 포괄적인 대응, 보상, 책
임법
CERDS Charter of Economic Rights and
Duties among States 국가간 경제권리의무
헌장
GET common external tariff 대외공통관세
C.F. conversion factor 변환계수
C&F cost and freight 본선도가격에 운임을 더
한 가격
CF cash flow 캐시플로
CF common fund for commodities 일차산품
공통기금
cf. confer 비교하여라
CFA certified financial analyst 공인 재무
분석가
CFF compensatory financing facility
수출수입보상금융제도
C.F.& I. cost, freight and insurance
운임보험료 포함
CFIS credit & finance information system
크레디트 앤드 파이낸스 인포메이션 시스템
CFO chief financial officer 재무담당임원
CFR Code of Federal Regulations
연방행정명령집

CFR Council on Foreign Relations
외교문제평의회
CFTC Commodity Futures Trading
Commission 미국상품선물거래위원회
CG computer graphics 컴퓨터그래픽스
CG consul general 총영사
CGT capital gains tax 자본이득세
CHIPS Clearing House Inter-Bank Payment
System 뉴욕 어음 교환소의 은행 간 결제 시
스템
C&1 cost and insurance 보험료 포함
CI corporate identity 기업이미지통합전략
CI Certificate of Indebtedness 재무성
단기채권
CI composite index 경기종합지수
CIA Central Intelligence Agency
중앙정보국
CIB compound interest bonds 복리 할인
지방채
CICA Canadian Institute of Chartered
Accountants 캐나다공인회계사협회
CICT Commission on International
Commodity Trade 국제상품무역위원회
CIEC Conference on International Economic
Cooperation 국제경제협력회의
GIF cost, insurance and freight 보험료, 운임
포함 가격
CIFCI cost, insurance. freight, commissions
and interest and interest
보험료, 운임, 수수료, 이자 포함가격
CIFE cost, insurance, freight and exchange
보험료, 운임, 환비용 포함가격
CIM computer-integrated manufacturing
CIM
CIO chief information officer 정보담당임원
CIO Congress of Industrial Organization
산업별노동조합회의
CIS Commonwealth of Independent States 독
립국가연합
CITES Convention on International Trade in
Endangered Species 워싱턴 조약

CITO Charter International Trade Organization 국제무역헌장하바나헌장

C.J. chief justice/judge 수석판사

CL carlord lot 차량을 전세 내어 실은 화물

CME Chicago Mercantile Exchange 시카고상업거래소

CMO collateralized mortgage obligations 모기지담보증권

CMS cash management service 캐시 매니지먼트 서비스

CMTA Clearing Member Trade Agreement 청산회원간거래협정

CNA Central News Agency 중앙통신사

CNC computerized numerical control 컴퓨터 수치 제어

CNN Cable News Netwotk 케이블 뉴스 네트워크

c/o care of 기부

COBOL Common Business Oriented Language 코볼

COCOM Coordinating Committee for Export Control 코콤

C.O.D. cash/collect on delivery 현물 상환 방식

COMECON Council for Mutual Economic Assistance 공산권경제상호원조협의회

COMEX Commodity Exchange 뉴욕 상품 거래소

Comsat Communications Satellite (미국의)통신위성회사 컴샛사(社)

COO chief operating officer 최고업무집행책임자

COSTI Committee on Scientific and Technical Information 연방과학기술정보위원회

COUGERS Certificate on Government Receipt 쿠거

CP commercial paper 기업어음

CP counterpurchase 대응구매

CPA certified public accountant 공인회계사

CPI consumer price index 소비자물가지수

CPM critical path method 크리티컬패스방법

CPS consumer price survey 소비자물가조사

CPSA Consumer Product Safety Act 소비자제품안전법

CPSC Consumer Product Safety Commission 소비자제품안전위원회

CPV cetral processing unit 중앙처리장치

CQS Consolidated Quotation Service 종합시황정보시스템

CR consumers' research 소비자조사

CRD Central Registration Depository 중앙등록예탁기관

CRS Congressional Research Service 국회조사부

CRT cathode-ray tube CRT

CS communication satellite 통신위성

CS customer satisfaction 고객만족도

CSA conditional sales agreement 조건부 판매 계약

CSCE Conference on Security and Cooperation in Europe 유럽안전보장협력회의

CSIS Center for Strategic and International Studies 전략국제연구센터

CSM climate system monitoring 기후감시

CSM customer satisfaction measurement 고객만족도

CSPI corporate service price index 기업서비스가격지수

C/T cable transfer 전신환

C.T.A. administrator cum testamento annexe 유언부 유산관리인

CTD Committee on Trade and Development 무역개발위원회

CTL constructive total loss 추정전손

CTOL conventional take-off and landing 통상이착륙기

CTS computerized typesetting system 전산사식컴퓨터조판

부록

CULCON Japan-United States Conference on Cultural and Educational Interchange 일미문화교육교류회의

CUSIP Committee on Uniform Securities Identification Procedures 통일증권식별수속위원회

CVCF constant voltag 6 and constant frequency unit 정전압 정주파 전원장치

CVS computer-controlled vehicle system 고속무인조종차량

CWA Clear Water Acts 수질정화법

D

D/A document against acceptance 인수인도

D/A deposit account 예금계좌

DA district attorney 지방검찰관

DAE Dynamic Asian Economies 다이내믹 아시아 경제군

DAF Department of Air Force 공군성

DARTS Dutch auction rate transferable securities 더치입찰방식 배당률조정가능증권

DATES Daily Adjustable Tax Exempt Securities 이동평균금리면제지방채

DB due bill 유가증권인도표

D.B.A. doing business ~의 영업명의로

D.B.N. administrator de bonis non 후임유산관리인

DBS direct broadcasting by satellite 직접위성방송

DD direct dealing 직접환거래

DD direct debit 공과금대리납부

DD Oil direct-deal crude Oil DD 원유

DDX digital data exchange 디지털 데이터 교환망

DEA Designated Examining Authority 지명감사기관

DEA Drug Enforcement Administration 연방마약단속국

DEB debenture 채권

DHC district heating and cooling 지역열공급

DHHA Department of Health and Human Services 보험복지부

DHUD Department of Housing and Urban Development 주택도시개발부

DI diffusion index 경기동향지수

DI discomfort index 불쾌지수

DIDC Depository Institutions Deregulation Committee 예금기관 디레귤레이션위원회

DIN Deutsche Industrie-Norm 독일공업규격

DINGO Discounted Investment in Negotiated Government Obligations 양도성정부채권에 대한 할인투자

DISC domestic international sales corporation 국제판매회사

DJ. district judge 지방법원의 판사

DJIA Dow Jones Industrial Average 다우존스 공업평균지수

DLF Development Loan Fund 개발차관기금

D.M. doctor of medicine 의학박사

d.n.e. discretion not exercised 재량권을 행사하지 않음

DOD Department of Defense 국방부

DOE Department of Energy 에너지부

D&OI directors and officers liability insurance 회사임원배상책임보험

DOL Department of Labor 노동부

DOS/A Disk Operating System j4.o/V DOS/V

DOT Department of Transportation 운수부

DOT Department of the Treasury 재무부

DOT designated order turnaround 도트시스템

D/P document against payment 지불인도

DP dynamic programming 동적 계획법

DPI Disabled Persons International 장애자 인터내셔널

DR depositary receipts 예탁증권
DR debetor 빌리는 사람 차변
DRAM dynamic random access memory
디램
DRG Diagnostic Related Groups 정액의료지
불제도
DRS Depositary Receipts of Singapore
싱가폴예탁증권
DS depositary shares 예탁주식
DSCS Defense Satellite Communications
System 국방위성통신망

DSR debt service ratio 채무반제비율
DTP desktop publishing 데스크탑 퍼블리싱
D.U.I. driving under the influence of alcohol
음주운전
DVE digital video effect 디지털비디오효과
DVI digital video interactive media
디지털비디오 인터랙티브 미디어
D.W.I. dying without issue 직계존속이 없는
상태에서 사망함
D.W.I. driving under intoxicated 취한 상태에
서 운전함

E

EAC East African Community
동아프리카공동체
EAEC East Asia Economic Caucus
동아시아경제협력체
EAJS European Association of Japanese
Studies 유럽일본연구협회
EB electronic banking 일렉트로닉뱅킹
EBIC European Banks' International
Corporation 유럽국제은행
EBRD European Bank for Reconstruction and
Development 유럽부흥개발은행
EBU European Broadcasting Union
유럽방송연맹
EC European Community 유럽공동체
EGA Economic Commission for Africa
국제연합아프리카경제위원회
ECAFE Economic Commission for Africa
and the Far East 국제연합극동아시아경제
위원회
ECB European Central Bank 유럽중앙은행
ECE Economic Commission for Europe
유럽경제위원회
ECLA Economic Commission for Latin
America 라틴아메리카경제위원회
ECM European Common Market
유럽공동시장
ECO Economic Cooperation Organization

경제협력기구
ECOR International Engineering Committee
on Oceanic Resources
해양자원기술위원회
ECOSOC Economic and Social Council
경제사회이사회
ECOWAS Economic Community of West
African States 서아프리카제국경제공동체
ECR electronic cash register 전자 금전
등록기
ECU European Currency Unit 유럽통화단위
EDC European Defense Community
유럽방위공동체
EDF European Development Fund
유럽개발기금
EDGAR electronic data gathering analysis &
retrieval system 에드가
EDP electronic data processing
컴퓨터 데이터 처리
EDR European Depositary Receipts
유럽예탁증권
EDRC Economic and Development Review
Committee Review Committee
경제개발검토위원회
EDTV extended definition television
클리어비전
EEA European Economic Area 유럽경제영역

EEC European Economic Community
유럽경제공동체

EECO European Economic Cooperation
Organization 유럽경제협력기구

EEOC Equal Employment Opportunity
Commission 평등고용기회위원회

EFP exchange for physical program
프로그램매매

EFTA European Free Trade Association
구주자유무역연합

EIA environment impact assessment
환경영향평가

EIB European Investment Bank 유럽투자은행

EIB export-import bank 수출입은행

ELDO European Launcher Development
Organization 유럽우주로켓개발기구

ELINT electronic intelligence 전자정보

ELSEC electronic security 전자보전

EMA European Monetary Agreement
유럽통화협정

EMCF European Monetary Cooperation Fund
유럽통화협력기금

EMF European Monetary Fund 유럽통화기금

EMIF Emerging Markets Investment Fund
이머징마켓투자펀드

EMS European Monetary System
유럽통화제도

EMU Economic and Monetary Union
경제통화동맹

ENA Ecole nationale d'administration
국립행정학원

E&OE errors and omissions excepted
오차와 탈루를 제외하고

E.O.M. end of month 월말

EOS earth observation system 지구관측시스템

EPA Environmental Protection Agency
환경보호청

EPA Economic Planning Agency 경제기획청

EPS earnings per share 일주당이익

ER emergency room 응급실

ERA Equal Rights Amendment 성차별금지

수정조항

ERD escrow receipt depository program
에스크로보관증서예탁제도

ERIC Educational Resources Information
Center 교육정보자료센터

ERISA Employee Retirement Income Security
Act
에리사 종업원 퇴직 소득보장법

ERM Exchange Rate Mechanism
환율조정장치

ESA Employment Standards Administration
노동기준국

ESCAP Economic and Social Commission for
Asia and the Pacific
아시아태평양경제사회위원회

ESCB European System of Central Banks
유럽중앙은행제도

ESOP employee stock ownership plan
종업원지주제도

ESPRIT European Strategic Programme for
Research and Development in Information
Technology
유럽정보기술연구개발전략계획

ETA Employment and Training Administration
고용훈련국

ETA estimated time of arrival 도착예정시간

ETD estimated time of departure
출발예정 시간

ETR easy growth treasury receipts
재무부 간이증권수령증서

ETUC European Trade Union Confederation
유럽노동조합연맹

EU European Union 유럽연합

EURATOM European Atomic Energy
Community 유럽원자력공동체

EURCO European Composite Unit
유럽복합단위

EUREKA European Research Coordination
Agency 유럽첨단기술공동연구기구

EURIT European Investment Trust
유럽투자신탁기관

Euroapace Committee for European
  Aerospace 유럽우주산업연합회
EV exposure value 노출수치
EWS Engineering Work Station 엔지니어링

F

FAA Federal Aviation Administration
  연방 항공국
f.a.c. fast as can 가급적 신속하게
FAI Federation aeronautique internationale
  국제항공연맹
FAR Federal Acquisition Regulations
  연방조달규칙
FAR Federal Aviation Regulations
  연방항공규칙
FAS free alongside ship 선측도
FASB Financial Accounting Standard Board
  재무회계기준심의회
FB financing bill 금융어음
FB finance bill 정부단기증권
FB firm banking 팜뱅킹
FBE foreign bill of exchange 외국환어음
FBI Federal Bureau of Investigation
  연방조사국
FBR fast-breeder reactor salaam 고속증식로
FC franchise chain 프랜차이즈체인
FCA Farm Credit Administration 농업신용국
FCBP foreign currency bills payable
  외화지불어음
FCC Federal Communications Commission
  연방통신위원회
FCCJ Foreign Correspondents' Club of Japan
  재일(在日)외국특파원협회
FCI Federal correctional institution
  연방교정시설
FCIC Federal Crop Insurance Corporation
  연방농산물보험공사
FCO foreign currency option 외국통화옵션
FCOP foreign currency option participant
  외국통화옵션참가자
FDA Food and Drug Administration

워크스테이션
ex-d ex-dividend 배당락
EXIM Export-Import Bank of USA
  미국수출입은행

식품의약품국
FDIC Federal Deposit Insurance Corporation
  연방예금보험공사
FEC Federal Election Commission
  연방선거위원회
FECA Federal Employees' Compensation Act
  연방피고용자화재보장법
Fed Federal Reserve Board
  연방준비제도이사회
Fed Federal Reserve Bank 연방준비은행
Fed.R.Civ.p. Federal Rules of Civil Procedure
  연방민사소송규칙
Fed.R.Crim.P. Federal Rules of Criminal
  Procedure 연방형사소송규칙
FEMA Federal Emergency Management
  Agency 연방긴급관리청
FEP front-end processor
  프론트 엔드 프로세서
FEPC Federation of Electric Power
  Companies 전기사업연합회
FERA Federal Employers' Liability Act
  연방고용자책임법
FFB Federal Financing Bank 연방금융은행
F.G.A. free from general average
  공동해손부담보
FHA Federal Housing Administration
  연방주택국
FHFB Federal Housing Finance Board
  연방주택금융위원회
FHL Federal Home Loan Mortgage
  Corporation 연방주택대부저당공사
FHLB Federal Home Loan Bank 연방주택대
  부은행제도
FHLMC Federal Home Loan Mortgage
  Corporation 연방주택금융저당공사

부록

fi. fa fieri facias 강제집행영장
FIA Futures Industry Association
  미국선물거래업자협회
FICA Federal Insurance Contribution
  Association 연방보험거출금협회
FIDB Federal Intermediate Credit Bank
  연방중개신용은행
FIFO first-in, first-out 선입선출법
FIGS Future Income Growth Securities
  피그스
FINOP financial and operation principal
  재무 및 업무책임자
FIO free in and out 적재, 양륙하주부담
FIP Fixed-income Security Options Permit
  고정금리증권옵션인가
FIR flight information region 비행정보구
FIT failure unit 고장률 단위
FIW free into wagons 화차인도
FLB Federal Land Bank 연방농지은행
FLRA Federal Labor Relations Authority
  연방노동관계원
FLSA Fair Labor Standard Act 공정 노동 기
  준법
FM frequency modulation 주파수 변조
FMC Federal Maritime Commission
  연방해운위원회
FMC flexible manufacturing cell 플렉시블 생
  산 셀
FMS flexible manufacturing system
  플렉시블 생산 시스템
FMV fair market value 공정시장가격
FNMA Federal National Mortgage
  Association 파니메이연방저당금고
fo. folio 2절판
FOB free on board 본선인도
FOC free of charge 무료
FOCUS financial & operation combined

uniform single report 재무·업무 통일 단일
  보고서
FOIA Freedom of Information Act
  정보자유법
FOMC Federal Open Market Commission 연
  방공개시장위원회
FOQ free on quay 부두인도
FOR free on rail 화차인도
FORTRAN formula translation 포트란
FP floating policy 예정보험계약
FP financial planner 금융자산관리사
FPA free from particular average
  단독 해손부 담보
FPR Federal Procurement Regulation
  연방조달규칙
FRA Federal Railroad Administration
  연방철도국
FRA forward rate agreement 금리선도취인
FR&CC free of riots and civil commotions
  폭동·내란면책
FRCD floating rate certificate of deposit
  변동금리 CD
FRD Federal Rules Decisions 연방소송규칙
  판례집
FRN floating rate note 변동이부채
FRS Fellow of the Royal Society 학사원회원
FRS Federal Reserve System 연방준비제도
FSF first sinking fund date 첫 감채기금상환일
FSLIC Federal Savings and Loan Insurance
  Corporation 연방저축금융보험공사
FTC Fedeal Trade Commission
  연방상업위원회
FTC Fair Trade Commission 공정거래위원회
FTCA Federal Ton Claims Act 연방불법행위
  청구권
FY fiscal year 회계연도

G

GA general average 공동해손
GAAP Generally Accepted Accounting

Principle 일반적으로 공정타당하다고 인정
된 회계원칙

GAAS Generally Accepted Auditing Standard 일반적으로 공정 타당하다고 인정된 감사 기준

GAB General Agreement to Borrow 일반차입결정

Gal gal 가속도단위

GAO General Accounting Office 회계검사원

GATT General Agreement on Tariffs and Trade 가트관세와 무역에 관한 일반협정

GBC German Bearer Certificate 독일무기명증서

GCC Gulf Cooperation Council 페르시아만협력회의

GCF greatest common factor 최소공배수

GCM greatest common measure 최대공배수

GCOil government-to-government crude oil 정부간거래원유

GDE gross domestic expenditure 국내총지출

GDP gross domestic product 국내총생산

GE grant element 그랜트엘리먼트

GEM Growing Equity Mortgage 젬

GES Gold Exchange of Singapore 싱가폴금거래소

GFTU General Federation of Trade Unions 노동조합총연합

GHG greenhouse gases 온실효과가스

GHQ general headquarters 총사령부

GIT guaranteed insurance trust 보증부 보험 신탁

GLC Greater London Council 런던수도권회의

GmbH Gesellschaft mit beschrankter Haftung 유한책임회사

GMP Good Manufacturing Practice 의약품적정제조기준

GN global negotiations 국제연합포괄교섭

GND gross national demand 국민총수요

GNE gross national expenditure 국민총지출

GNI gross national income 국민총소득

GNMA Government National Mortgate Association 정부저당금고

GNP gross national product 국민총생산

GNS gross national supply 국민총공급

GNW gross national welfare 국민총복지

GPO Government Printing Office 정부인쇄국

GRP gross rating 종합시청률

GSA General Services Administration 일반조달국

G7 Group of Seven 선진 7개 국가

GTC good 'til cancelled 굿틸캔슬드

GUI graphical user interface 그래픽을 통한 사용자 중심의 인터페이스

H

HB House Bill 하원법안

HC House of Commons 하원

HDTV high-definition television 하이비전

HE human engineering 인간공학

hi-fi high fidelity 하이파이

HITS High-income Trust Securities 고액 신탁 증권

HIV human immunodeficiency virus 인간면역 부전바이러스

HKDR Hong Kong Depositary Receipts 홍콩 예탁증서

HMO health maintenance organization 보건기관

HOLC Home Owners' Loan Corporation 주택소유자자금대부회사

HOW house owners warranty 주택하자담보보증

HPR holding period return 보유기간수익률

HR House of Representative 하원

HSST high-speed surface transport 초고속지표수송기

HST Hubble Space Telescope 허블우주망원경

HST hypersonic transport 극초음속여객기
H.T. hoc titulo ~의 표제 아래에서
HUD Department of Housing and Urban
Development 주택도시개발부
HWR heavy water reactor 중수로

I

IAA International Academy of Astronautics
국제우주여행학회
IAEA International Atomic Energy Agency
국제원자력기구
IAS International Accounting Standards
국제회계기준
IASC International Accounting Standards
Committee 국제회계기준위원회
IATA International Air Transport Association
국제항공운송협회
ib. ibidem 같은 장소에, 같은 책에
IBF International Banking Facility
국제은행업무
IBI international bank for investment
국제투자은행
IBI International Broadcasting Institute
국제방송협회
IBJ Industrial Bank of Japan 일본흥업은행
IBRD International Bank for Reconstruction
and Development
국제부흥개발은행
ICA International Coffee Agreement
국제커피협정
ICA International Commodity Agreement
국제상품협정
ICAC International Cotton Advisory
Committee 국제면화자문위원회
ICAO International Civil Aviation
Organization 국제민간항공기관
ICBM intercontinental ballistic missile
대륙간탄도탄
ICC Interstate Commerce Commission
주제통상위원회
ICC International Chamber of Commerce
국제상업회의소

ICCA International Cocoa Agreement
국제코코아협정
ICJ International Commission of Jurists
국제법률가위원회
ICJ International Court of Jurists
국제사법재판소
ICO International Coffee Organization
국제커피기관
ICPO International Criminal Police
Organization 국제형사경찰기구
ICRC International Committee of the Red
Cross 적십자국제위원회
ICSID International Center for Settlement of
Investment Disputes
투자분쟁조정국제센터
ICU intensive care unit 집중치료실
ID industrial design 공업디자인
IDA International Development Association
국제개발협회
IDB Industrial Development Bond
산업개발채권
IDB Inter-American Development Bank
미주개발은행
IDCA International Development
Cooperation Agency 국제개발협력국
IDE Institute of Developing Economies
아시아경제연구소
IDL international date line 날짜변경선
IDR International Depositary Receipts
국제예탁증서
IDS institutional delivery system 대체 결제시
스템
IE industrial engineering 산업공학
IEA International Energy Agency
국제에너지기관

IEC International Electrotechnical Commission 국제전기표준회의

IF index fund 인덱스펀드

IFAD International Fund for Agricultural Development 국제농업개발기금

IFC International Finance Corporation 국제금융공사

IFJ International Federation of Journalists 국제저널리스트연맹

IFR instrument night rules 계기비행방식

IFTU International Federation of Trade Unions 국제노동조합연맹

IGO Intergovernmental Organization 정부간국제조직

IIF Institute of International Finance 국제금융협회

ILO International Labour Organization 국제노동기관

IMF International Monetary Fund 국제통화기금

IMF International Metalworkers Federation 국제금속노동조합연맹

IMM International Monetary Market 국제통화시장

IMO International Maritime Organization 국제해사기관

IMP interplanetary monitoring platform 행성간공간관측위성

INGO International Non-Governmental Organization 비정부간국제조직

INMARSAT International Maritime Satellite Organization 인말새트 국제해사위성기구

INS Immigration and Naturalization Service 입국귀화국

INS infomation network system 고도 정보 통신 시스템

Intelpost Intelsat Post 국제전자우편

INTELSAT International Telecommunication Satellite Organization 인텔새트 국제전기통신위성기구

I/O input/output 입출력

IOC International Olympic Committee 국제올림픽위원회

IOCU International Organization of Consumer's Unions 국제소비자기구

IOSCO International Organization of Securities Commissions 국제증권거래위원회기구

IOSCO International Organization of Securities Commissions 증권감독자국제기구

IOU I owe you 차용문서

IP industrial policy 산업정책

IP information provider 정보제공자

IPA international phonetica alphabet 국제음성기호

IPA International Publishers Association 국제출판연합

IPC International Property Committee 지적소유권위원회

IPO initial public offering 주식공개

IPPF International Planned Parenthood Federation 국제가족계획연맹

IPPRI International Peace Policy Research Institute 국제평화정책연구소

IFS Institute for Policy Science 정책과학연구소

IPTC International Press Telecommunications Committee 국제신문통신위원회

IPU Inter-Parliamentary Union 국제의회연맹

IQ import quota 수입할당

IQ intelligence quotient 지능지수

IR investors relation 인베스터스 릴레이션

IR information retrieval 정보검색

IRA Individual Retirement Accounts 개인퇴직연금계정

IRA Irish Republican Army 아일랜드공화국군

IRAN individual retirement annuity 개인퇴직연금

IRB individual retirement bond
개인퇴직연금채권
IRB Industrial Revenue Bond
면세지방특정재원채
IRB International Resources Bank
국제자원은행
IRBM intermediate range ballistic missile
중거리탄도탄
IRC Internal Revenue Code 내국세입법전
IRO interest-rate option 금리 옵션
IRR internal rate of return 내부수익률
IRS Internal Revenue Service 내국세입청
ISA International Sugar Agreement
국제설탕협정
ISAM indexed sequential access method
아이샘
ISCC International Securities Clearing
Corporation 국제결제기관
ISDA International Swap Dealers Association
국제스왑딜러협회
ISDB integrated services digital broadcasting
종합디지털방송
ISDN integrated services digital network
디지털종합서비스망
ISO International Sugar Organization
국제설탕기관
ISO International Standardization
Organization 국제표준화기구
ISSA International Social Security
Association 국제사회보장협회
ISSC International Social Science Council 국
제사회과학협의회
ISU International Space University
국제우주대학
ISY International Space Year 국제우주년
ITC International Trade Commission
국제무역위원회
ITFL International Task Force on Literacy 국

제교육운동협의회
ITM in the money 인더머니
ITO International Trade Organization
국제무역기구
ITS Inter-market Trading System
시장 간 거래시스템
ITT International Telephone and Telegraph
Corp. 미국국제전신전화회사
ITU International Telecommunication Union
국제전기통신연합
ITV industrial television 공업용 텔레비전
IU international unit 국제단위
IUCN International Union for Conservation of
Nature and Natural Resources
국제자연보호연맹
IULA International Union of Local Authorities
국제지방자치체연합
IVA intervehicular activity 우주선 선내 활동
IWA International Wheat Agreement
국제소맥협정
IWC International Wheat Council
국제소맥이사회
IWC International Whaling Commission
국제포경위원회
IWRA International Water Resources
Association 국제수자원협회
IWW Industrial Workers of the World
세계산업노동자동맹
IWY International Women's Year
세계 부인의 해
IYC International Year of the Child
세계 어린이의 해
IYDP International Year of Disabled Persons
세계 장애인의 해
IYP International Year of Peace
세계 평화의 해
JAA Japan Aeronautic Association
일본항공협회

J

JAIDO Japan International Development
Organization 일본국제협력기구

JAIWR Japan Association of International
Women's Rights 일본국제여성지위협회

JAPIC Japan Project Industry Council
일본프로젝트산업협의회

JAPIO Japan Patent Information Organization
일본특허정보기구

JAS Japan Astronautical Society
일본우주여행협회

JC Japan Junior Chamber 일본청년회의소

JCA Japan Consumer Association
일본소비자협회

JCAE Joint Committee on Atomic Energy
양원원자력위원회

JCI Junior Chamber International
국제청년회의소

JCS Joint Chiefs of Staff 통합참모본부

JD juris doctor 법학박사

JDB Japan Development Bank
일본개발은행

JDR Japanese Depositary Receipts
일본예탁증권

JETRO Japan External Trade Organization
일본무역진흥회

JFK John F. Kennedy 케네디국제공항

JIBICO Japan International Bank and
Investment Co. 일본국제투자은행

JICA Japan International Cooperation Agency
국제협력사업단

JICST Japan Information Center of Science
and Technology 일본과학기술정보센터

JIM Japan Institute of Metals 일본금속학회

JIS Japanese Industrial Standard
일본공업규격

JMA Japan Medical Association 일본의사회

j.n.o.v. judgment non obstante verdicto
평결을 무시한 판결

JOCV Japan Overseas Cooperation
Volunteers 일본청년해외협력대

JOM Japan Offshore Market 도쿄 오프쇼 어
마켓

JP justice of the piece 치안판사

JPEG Joint Photographic Expert Group
이미지 파일 포맷의 한 종류

JRA Japan Racing Association
일본중앙경마회

JRC Japan Red Cross Society
일본적십자사

JSA Japan Scientists' Association
일본과학자회의

JSA Japan Shipowners' Association
일본선주협회

JSA Japan Standards Association
일본규격협회

JSC Japan Science Council 일본학술회의

JSDA Japan Securities Dealers' Association
일본증권업협회

JSF Japan Special Fund 일본특별기금

JSIA Justice System Improvement Act
사법제도개선법

JST Japan Standard Time 일본 표준시

JTU Japan Teachers' Union 일교조

JUSEC Japan-U.S. Economic Council
일미경제협의회

JV joint venture 공동기업체

JWA Japan Weather Association
일본기상협회

K

kB kilobyte 킬로바이트

KCBT Kansas City Board of Trade
캔자스시티 상품거래소

KD knocked down 녹다운

KE knowledge engineering 지식공학

KGB Komitet Gosudarstvennoi ue
Bezopasnosti 구소련국가보안위원회

KID key industry duty 기간산업보호관세

KKK ku klux klan 백인우월주의비밀결사

KWIC key word in context 문맥 내의 색인

L

L.S. locus sigilli 날인개소
L/C letter of credit 신용장
LACM Latin America Common Market
  라틴아메리카공동시장
LAFTA Latin American Free Trade
  Association 라틴아메리카자유무역연합
LAN Local Area Network 기업 내 고속정보
  통신망
LBO leveraged buyout 레버리지드 바이아웃
  차입매수거래
LCA low-cost automation 간이자동화
LCD liquid crystal display 액정디스플레이
LD laser disk 레이저디스크
LD learning disabilities 학습장애
LDC least developed countries
  후발개발도상국
LDP Liberal Democratic Party 자유민주당
LDR London Depositary Receipts
  런던예탁증서
LEAA Law Enforcement Assistance Act
  법집행원조법
LEAA Law Enforcement Assistance Agency
  법집행원조국
LEO low earth orbit 저지구 궤도
LHWCA Longshore and Harbor Workers'
  Compensation Act 항만노동자재해보상법
LIBOR London Inter-Bank Offered Rate
  런던은행간거래금리

LIC low-intensity conflict 저강도분쟁
LIFFE London International Financial Futures
  Exchange 런던국제금융선물거래소
LIFO last-in, first-out 후입선출법
LISP list processor 리스프
L,L language laboratory LL 교실
LM lunar module 달착륙선
LME London Metal Exchange 런던국제금융
  선물거래소
LMG liquefied methane gas 액화메탄가스
LNG liquefied natural gas 액화천연가스
logo logotype 로고
LORAN long range navigation 로란
LP line printer 라인프린터
LP linear programming 선형계획법
LPG liquefied petroleum gas 액화석유가스
LRBM long-range ballistic missile
  장거리 탄도탄
LSAT Law School Admission Test 로스쿨
  입학공통테스트
LSE London Stock Exchange
  런던증권거래소
LSI large scale integration 대규모 집적회로
LSS life-support system 생명유지장치
LST local standard time 지방표준시
LTCB Long-Term Credit Bank of JAPAN
  일본장기신용은행
LWR light water reactor 경수로

M

M.A. Master of Arts 문학수사
M&A merger and acquision 합병·매수
MA Maritime Administration 해운국
MA mental age 정신연령
MACDTM moving average
  convergence/divergence trading method

  이동평균수속/분산트레이딩법
MACE Mid-America Commodity Exchange
  중미상품거래소
MACRS modified accelerated cost recovery
  system 수정가속원가회수법
MARC machine readable catalog 마크

MARS manned astronautical research station
유인우주조사스테이션

MAS Monetary Agency of Singapore
싱가폴통화청

MATV master antenna television
공동수신방식

MAVR modulating amplifier by variable
reactance 가변유도저항변조증폭장치

MBA master of business administrarion
경영학석사

MBB mortgate backed bond 모기지담보채권

MBCS Municipal Bond Comparison System
지방채비교시스템

MBDA Minority Business Development
Administration 마이너리티기업개발국

MBO management buyout 자사주매점

MBO management by objectives 목표관리

MBS mortgage backed security
모기지담보증권

MBSCC Mortgage Bond Securities Clearing
Corporation 부동산저당증권결제회사

MC marginal cost 한계비용

MC master of ceremonies 사회자

MC Member of Congress 국회의원

MCA Mortgage Credit Association
저당신용조합

MCA Management Coordination Agency
총무청

MCC mortgage credit certificates 주택저당세
액공제담보

MCCA Mercado Comun Centroamericano 중
미공동시장

MD mini disk 미니디스크

MDC more developed country 중진국

MDS multipoint distribution system 다지점
분배시스템

MeV million electron volts 메브

MF medium frequency 중주파

MFN most favored nation 최혜국

M16 Military Intelligence, section six
영국첩보 제6부영국의 대외첩보기관

MIGA Multilateral Investment Guarantee
Agency 다수국간투자보증기관

MIP monthly investment plan
월부식 적립투자법

MIP most important person 최중요인물

MIPS million instructions per second
컴퓨터의 성능지표

MIT Massachusetts Institute of Technology
매사추세츠공과대학

MITI Ministry of International Trade and
Industry 통상산업부

MLD median lethal dose 반수치사량

MLR minimum lending rate
최저대출금리제도

MMA money market account
자유금리예금계정

MMC money market certificate
시장금리연동형예금

MMDA money market deposit accounts
단기금융시장예금계정

MMF money market fund
단기금융상품투자신탁

MMF money management fund
단기공사채투자신탁

MMI money market index 단기금융시장지수

MMI major market index 메이저마켓지수

MMP money market preferred
머니마켓 우선주

MMU memory management unit
메모리 관리기구

m.o. modus operandi 범행

MO magneto-optical 광자기

MODEM modulator/demodulator 모뎀

MOF Ministry of Finance 재무부

MOF multiple-option facilities
멀티플 옵션 퍼실러티

MOR middle of the road 중도파

MOSS market-oriented sector-service
시장분야별 개별협의

MOT Ministry of Transport 운수부

부
록

MPD Metropolitan Police Department
경찰청

MPEG moving pictures expert group 엠펙

mph miles per hour 시속마일

MPT modern portfolio theory
현대 포트폴리오 이론

MPU micro processing unit 마이크로프로세서

MRBM medium range ballistic missile
중거리탄도탄

MROM mask read only memory 마스크 ROM

M.s. master of science 이학석사

ins. manuscript 원고

MS-DOS microsoft disk operating system
MS사에서 개발한 컴퓨터 운영체제

MSA Maritime Safety Agency 해상보안청

MSB mutual savings bank 상호저축은행

MSC Manned Spacecraft Center
유인우주선센터

MSHA Mine Safety and Health
Administration 광산보안위성국

MSPD Merit System Protection Board
성과급제 보호위원회

MSR missile site rader
미사일·사이트·레이더

MSS manned space station 유인우주정거장

MSY maximum sustainable yield 최대지속생
산량

MT magnetic tape 자기테이프

MTO Multilateral Trade Organization
다국간무역기구

MTTR mean time to repair 평균수복시간

MUSE multiple sub-nyquist sampling
encoding 뮤즈방식

MVP most valuable player 최우수선수

MYBF mean time between failures
고장과 고장 사이의 평균시간

N

n nano 나노

n/a not applicable 적용하지 않음

NAA National Association of Accountants
전미회계사협회

NAACP National Association for the
Advancement of Colored People of Colored
People
유색인종지위향상전국협회

NAB National Association of Broadcasters
전미방송연맹

NAC National Advisory Council on
International Monetary and Financial
Problems
국제통화금융·정책국가자문위원회

NACC North Atlantic Cooperation Council
북대서양협력평의회

NAFTA North American Free Trade
Agreement 북미자유무역협정

NAIRU non-accelerating inflation rate of
unemployment 비인플레가속적 실업률

NAR National Association of Realtors
전국부동산업자협회

NASA National Aeronautics and Space
Administration 미국항공우주국

NASAA North American Securities
Administrators Association
북미증권행정관협회

NASD National Association of Securities
Dealers 전미증권업협회

NASDA National Space Development
Agency of Japan 일본우주개발사업단

NASDAQ National Association of Securities
Dealers Automated Quotations System
나스닥

NAT North Atlantic Treaty 북대서양조약

NATO North Atlantic Treaty Organization
북대서양조약기구

NAV net asset value 순자산가치

N,B. nota bene 주의하라

NB national brand 내셔널브랜드

NBC National Broadcasting Company
　NBC 방송

n/c no change　변경사항 없음

NC numerical control　수치제어

NCD nimine contra dicente　전회일치

NCD negotiable certificate of deposit
　양도가능정기예금증서

NCNA New China News Agency　신화통신

NCR no carbon required　탄소불필요

NDT nondestructive testing　비파괴검사

NEA nonrate earnings assets　비금리자산

NECS Newly Export-oriented Countries
　신흥수출지향국

n.e.i. non est in ventus　소재불명

nem. com. nemine contradicente　전회일치

nem. dis. nemine dissentiente　전회일치

NEPA National Environment Policy Act
　연방환경정책법

NFA National Futures Association
　전국선물협회

NGL natural gas liquid　액화천연가스

NGO Non-Government Organization
　비정부조직

NGRI not guilty by reason of insanity
　심신상실을 이유로 무죄

NHTSA National Highway Traffic Safety
　Administration　전국고속도로교통안전국

NI national income　국민소득

NIC net interest cost　순금리비용

NICs newly industrializing countries
　신흥공업국

NIEO New International Economic Order
　신국제경제질서

NIEs newly industrializing economies
　신흥공업경제지역

NIF note issuance facility　증권발행보증

NIFO next-in, first-out　차입선출법

NII National Information Infrastructure
　전미정보기반

N'ISDN narrow ISDN
　협대역 종합정보통신망

NIT negative income tax　역소득세

NKA now known as　현재명칭

n.l. non liquet　진위불명

NLF National Liberation Front
　민족해방전선

NLRA National Labor Relations Act
　연방노동관계법

NLRB National Labor Relations Board
　연방노동관계국

nm nautical mile　해리

NMS National Market System
　전미시장 시스템

NNF net national expenditure　국민순지출

NNP net national product　국민순생산

NNSS navy navigational satellite system
　항해위성시스템

NNW net national wel fare　국민복지지표

no. nombre　논블페이지번호

n.o.c. not otherwise classified　기타

n.o.p. not otherwise provided　특약이 없는 한

NOPEC non-OPEC petroleum exporting
　coutries
　OPEC에 소속되지 않은 석유수출국

NOx nitrogen oxides　질소산화물

NP notary public　공증인

NPE National Partnership Exchange
　전미파트너십거래시장

NPL non-rate paying liability　비금리부채

NPT Nuclear Nonproliferation Treaty
　핵확산방지조약

NR noise reduction　소음제거방법

NRO nonresident-owned investment
　corporation　비거주자투자회사

NSC National Security Council
　국가안전보장회의

NSC Nuclear Safety Commission
　원자력안전위원회

NSCC National Securities Clearing
　Corporation　미국증권거래소 결제기관

NSI new social indicators　국민생활지표

부록

NSTA National Security Traders' Association
전미증권거래자협회
NT National Trust 내셔널트러스트문화보호
협회
NTB non-tariff barrier 비관세장벽
NTM non-tariff measures 비관세 조치
NTSB National Transportation Safety Board
국가운수안전위원회
NTSC National Television System Committee
전미텔레비전방식위원회
NYBOR New York Inter-Bank Offered Rate

뉴욕은행간거래금리
NYCE New York Cotton Exchange
뉴욕면화거래소
NYCE New York Cash Exchange
뉴욕현금교환네트워크
NYFE New York Futures Exchange
뉴욕선물거래소
NYMEX New York Mercantile Exchange
뉴욕상품거래소
NYSE New York Stock Exchange
뉴욕증권거래소

O

O ozone 오존
O/A on account 일부불입
O/A on or about …경
OADA Overseas Agricultural Development
Association 해외농업개발협회
OAEC Organization for Asian for Asian
Economic Cooperation
아시아경제협력기구
OAPEC Organization of Arab Petroleum
Exporting Countries 아랍석유수출국기구
OAS Organization of American State
미주기구
OASDI old age, survivors' and disability
insurance 노인, 유족, 신체장애자를 위한
국가보험
ob. obiit 그는 죽었다
OBV on balance volume 거래량균형지표
OCA Olympic Council of Asia
아시아올림픽평의회
OCI overall commodity index 종합국제상품
지수
OCP optional calling plan 선택통화요금
OCR optical character reader
광학식문자판독장치
OD organization development 조직개발
ODA Official Development Assistance
정부개발원조
ODR official discount rate 공정률

ODR ordinary shares 보통주식
OECD Organization for Economic
Cooperation and Development
경제협력개발기구
OECF Overseas Economic Cooperation Fund
해외경제협력기금
OEEC Organization for European Economic
Cooperation 유럽경제협력기구
OEM original equipment manufacturing
OEM; 상대선브랜드생산
Off-JT off-the-job training 직장외 훈련
OGL open general license 포괄수입허가제
OHP overhead project 오버헤드프로젝터
OHV overhead valve 오버헤드밸브
OJT on-the job training 직무교육
OMA orderly marketing agreement
시장질서유지협정
OMB Office of Management and Budget
행정관리예산국
OMR optical mark reader 광학마크판독
O.P. out of print 절판
op-ed opposite editorial page
사설란의 양 페이지
OP Art Optical Art 시각적 미술
OPEC Organization of Petroleum Exporting
Countries 석유수출국기구
OPI option performance index
옵션 퍼포먼스 지수

OPM option pricing model
옵션가격결정모델
ORP ordinary, reasonable and prudent man
통상인의
OS official statement 공식선언서
OS operating system 운영체제

P

PA particular average 단독해손
PA public acceptance 퍼블릭액셉턴스
PA public address 장내확성장치
PAC Pan-American Congress 전미회의
PAC Political Action Committee
정치활동위원회
PACS principal appreciation conversion
securities 원본증가전환형 증권
PAL phase alternation line
팔TV 방송표준의 한 종류
PAM pulse amplitude modulation
펄스진폭변조
PAP positive adjustment policies
적극적 조정정책
PASCAL Program applique a la selection et a
la compilation automatique de la litterature
파스칼, 컴퓨터 프로그래밍 언어의 일종
PBEC Pacific Basin Economic. Council
태평양경제위원회
PBGC Pension Benefit Guaranty Corporation
연금급부보증공사
PBR price bookvalue ratio 주가순자산배율
PBS Public Broadcasting Service
비영리공공방송조직
PBX private branch exchange 구내교환기
PC personal computer 개인용 컴퓨터
PC politically correct 차별 없는
pc persec 퍼섹(천문단위)
PCE personal consumption expenditure
개인소비지출
PCF Parti Communiste Francais
프랑스공산당

OST Office of Science and Technology
과학기술국
OTB option tender bonds 옵션변동금리채
OTC over-the-counter 장외
OTM out of the money 상금이 없는
OUI operation under influence 음주운전

PCI Partito Comunista Italiano
이탈리아 공산당
PCU Permanent Court of International Justice
상설국제사법재판소
PCM pulse code modulation 펄스부호변조
PCN personal communication network
개인통신망
PCT Patent Cooperation Treaty
특허 협력조약
PD public domain 공공재산
PDS public domain software
저작권이 소멸된 소프트웨어
PDS Partei Demokratischen Sozialismus
민주사회주의당
PEACE Pacific Economic and Cultural
Enclave 태평양경제문화권
PEG Pacific Economic Community
태평양경제공동체
PECC Pacific Economic Cooperation
Conference 태평양경제협력회의
PEFCO Private Export Funding Corporation
수출촉진금융회사
PEP Program Execution Processing
프로그램매매집행처리
PER price earnings ratio 주가수익률
PERT program evaluation and review
technique 퍼트
P&F point and figure 포인트 · 앤드 · 피규어
pH Potenz H 페하수소이온농도
ph.D. doctor of philosophy 박사학위
PHS personal handyphone system 휴대전화
PI portfolio insurance 자산보증

부록

PICA Private Investment Company for Asia
아시아민간투자회사

PIPS participating incentive preferred stock
의결권부 우선주

PKO peace keeping operations
국제연합평화유지활동

P&L protection and immunity
선주책임상호보험

P&L profit and loss statement 손익계산서

PL pamphlet law 법률 속보

PL product liability 제조물 책임

PL public law 일반 법률

PLA Palestine Liberation Army
팔레스타인해방군

PLATO Programmed Logic for Automatic
Teaching Operations 플래토

PLC Public Limited Company
공개유한책임회사

PLI people's life indicators 신국민생활지수

PLO Palestine Liberation Organization
팔레스타인해방기구

PLSS portable life support system
휴대용 생명유지장치

PM phase modulation 위상변조

PNC Palestine National Council
팔레스타인민족평의회

PO postal order 우편환

POD port of debarkation 양륙항

POP point-of-production 생산현장

POP point-of-purchase 포프구매시점

POS point-of-sale 포스판매시점정보관리

Q~R

Q.E.D. quod erat demonstrandum 증명되기
도 하고

q.h. quaque hora 1시간마다

QC quality control 품질관리

QCD quantum chromodynamics 양자크로모
역학

QE quick estimation 국민경제계산속보

pp parcel post 소포우편

pp post paid 우편요금선불의

pp propria persona 본인에 의한

PPI policy proof insurance 명예보험증권

PPI producer price index 생산자물가지수

PPM product portfolio management
제품 포트폴리오 관리

PPM pulse phase modulation 펄스위상변조

ppp Polluters Pay Principle
공해발생자비용부담원칙

ppp purchasing power parity 구매력평가

PR public relations 홍보활동

PRP proper return port 복귀항

ps post script 추신

PS public statute 일반제정법

PSE Philadelphia Stock Exchange
필라델피아증권거래소

PSI Partito Socialista Italiano
이탈리아 사회당

PSSI Peace Science Society International
국제평화과학협회

PTI pre-trial intervention
형사재판전의 사건처리

PUD Planned Unit Development
계획단위개발

PV present value 현재가치

pw present worth 현재가치

PWN pulse width modulation 펄스폭변조

PWR pressurized water reactor
가압수형 원자로

RA risk assessment 위험도평가

RAES Retail Automatic Execution System
소액거래자동집행시스템

RAM random-access memory 램

RBA representative bid and asked prices 매
매의 대표가격

R&D research and development 연구개발

RDB relational database
관계형 데이터베이스
RDC running down clause 충돌 약관
RDF Research & Development Fund
유럽지역개발기금
RECOVER remote continual vertification
상시원격감시시스템
REIT real estate investment trust
부동산투자신탁
RFP request for proposal 견적요청
RGB red, green, blue 적, 록, 청
(컬러 화상의 3원색)
RICO Racketeer Influenced and Corrupt
Organizations Act 강제청구적 부정조직단
속법
RISC reduced instruction set computer
리스크명령어축약형 컴퓨터
RMA random multiple access
임의다중동시교신
RMS root-mean-square 이승평균
ROA return on asset 총자산수익률
ROE return on equity 주주자본이익률
ROI return on investment 투자이익률
ROM read-only memory 롬
ROR rate of return 수익률
RPS retail price survey 소매물가통계조사
RS Revised Statutes 현행제정법집
RSA rate sensitive assets 금리감응자산
RSI relative strength index 상대력지수
RSL rate sensitive liability 금리감응부채
R.s.v.p. repondez s'il vous plait
답신을 주세요.

S

S.A. societe anonyme 주식회사
s.a.e. self-addressed envelope 답신용 우표를
붙인
SAR stock appreciation rights
주식평가보상제
S/B shipping application 선적신청서
SB Senate Bill 상원법안
SBA Small Business Administration
중소기업청
SBF standby facilities 스탠바이퍼실리티즈
s.c. same case 동일사건
SC Security Council 안전보장이사회
SC Supreme Court 최고재판소
SCSI small computer systems interface
스카시
SD standard deviation 표준편차
S/DB/L sight draft bill of lading attached
일람불선하증권부
SDPJ Social Democratic Party of Japan
일본사회당
SDR Special Drawing Rights 특별인출권
SE sound effect 음향효과

SE system engineer 정보처리기술자
SEA Single European Act 단일유럽의정서
SEAQ Stock Exchange Automated Quotation
런던증권거래소 시황정보시스템
Seasat sea satellite 시샛
SEC Securities and Exchange Commission
미국증권거래위원회
sec. second 초
SECAM sequentiel couleur a memoire 세캄
SECO SEC only 시코
SED Sozialistische Einheitspartei
Deutschlands 독일사회주의통일당
SEPAC Space experiments with Particle
Accelerators 인공오로라계획
SFE Sydney Futures Exchange
시드니선물거래소
SFN Swiss franc note 스위스프랑기준채권
SFX special effects 특수촬영기술
S/H.E. Sundays and holidays excepted
일요일, 휴일은 제외함
SIA Securities Industry Association
미국증권업자협회

부
록

SIA Semiconductor Industry Association
반도체공업회
SIB Securities Investment Board
증권투자위원회
SIBOR Singapore Inter-Bank Offered
Inter-Bank Offered Rate
싱가폴은행간거래금리
SICBM small intercontinental ballistic missile
소형대륙간탄도탄
SIG special interest group 시그
SII Structual Impediments Initiative
일미구조협의
SIMEX Singapore International Monetary
Exchange 싱가폴국제금융거래소
SIPC Securities Investor Protection
Corporation 증권투자자보호공사
S&L savings and loan 저축대부조합
SL session laws 회기별 법률집
SL statute laws 제정법
SMS stationary meteorological satellite
정지기상위성
SNG satellite news gathering 통신위성이용수
집시스템
SNG synthetic natural gas 대체천연가스

T

TA technology assessment 기술평가
TAB tax anticipation bill 납세국채
TAN tax anticipation note 납세지방채
TB Treasury Bill 재무부단기증권
TC U.S. Tax Court 합중국조세재판소
TC traveler's check 여행자수표
TC Memo Memorandum Decision of the U.S.
Tax Court
합중국조세재판소 메모랜덤판결
TCA Technical Cooperation Administration
국무부 기술협력국
TCP/IP transmission control protocol/interest
protocol
계산기네트워크 국제표준협회규격

SOES Small Order Execution System
소액거래처리시스템
sonar sound navigation and ranging 소나
SOx sulfur oxides 유황산화물
s.p. sine prole 무자손
s.p. same point 동일논점
s.p. same principle 동일원칙
SP security police 비밀경찰
SPC security purchase contract
증권 구입 계약
SQ special quotation 특별정산지수
ss scilicet 즉, 다시 말하면
SSA Social Security Administration
사회보장총국
SSC small savers certificate 소액예금증권
sss Selective Service System 선발징병제도
STABEX Stabilization of Export Earning
Scheme 수출소득보상제도
STAGS Sterling Transferable Accruing
Government Securities
양도가능제로쿠폰영국펀드
START Strategic Arms Reduction Talks
전략병기감축교섭

TDB Trade and Development Board UN
무역개발이사회
TEDIS Tax-Exempt Deferred Interest
Securities 면세이자지불이연증권
Tercom terrain contour matching 지형조회
TFE Toronto Futures Exchange
토론토선물거래소
three-D three-dimensional 3차원
TIBOR Tokyo Inter-Bank Offered Rate
도쿄은행간거래금리
TIGR Treasuty Investment Growth Receipt
재무부 증권제로쿠폰투자증권
TIP tax-based income policy
세제기반소득정책

TIR Transfer Initiation Request
계좌이전청구

TLO total loss only 전손만 담보험

TNC Trade Negotiation Committee
무역교섭위원회

TNC transnational corporation 다국적기업

TNF theater nuclear forces
전역(戰域) 핵탄력

TNW tactical nuclear weapons 전술핵병기

TNW theater nuclear weapons
전역(戰域) 핵병기

TOB takeover bid 주식공개매입

TOEFL Test of English as a Foreign
Language 토플

TOEIC Test of English for International
Communication 토익

TOPIX Tokyo Stock Exchange Stock Price
Index 토픽스도쿄증시주가지수

TOPS triple option preferred stock
3종 선택권부 우선주

TPO time, place, occasion TPO

TR Treasuty Receipts 재무부증권수취증서

TRIM trade-related investment measures
무역관련투자조치

TRO Temporary Restraining Order
긴급금지명령

TSCA Toxic Substance Control Act
독성물질규제법

TSCJ Telecommunications Satellite
Corporation of Japan
일본통신방송위성기구

TSE Toronto Stock Exchange
토론토증권거래소

TSE Tokyo Stock Exchange 도쿄증권거래소

TT telegraphic transfer 전신환

TTB telegraphic transfer buying rate
전신환매입상장

TTC total traffic control 열차운행시스템

TTS telegraphic transfer selling rate
전신환매출상장

TFr time temperature tolerance
허용온도시간

TUC Trades Union Congress
영국노동조합회의

TVA Tennessee Valley Authority
테네시계곡개발공사

U

UAW United Automobile Workers
전미자동차노동조합

UCC Uniform Commercial Code 통일상법전

UCC Universal Copyright Convention
국제저작권협정

UCCC Uniform Consumer Credit Code
통일소비자신용법전

UCCJA Uniform Child Custody Jurisdiction
Act 통일자감호사건관할법

UCLA University of California at Los
Angeles 캘리포니아대학 로스앤젤스교

UCMJ Uniform Code of Military Justice
군사재판통일법전

UDITPA Uniform Division of Income for
Tax Purposes Act 통일과세상소득분배법

UFO unidentified flying object
미확인비행물체

UFTA Uniform Fraudulent Transfer Act
통일사기피해양도법

UHF ultrahigh frequency UHF

UI unemployment insurance 실업보험

UICN Universal Intelligent Communication
Network 종합지적통신망

UIT unit investment trust 유닛형 투자신탁

VLSI ultra large-scale integration
초고밀도집적회로

UN United Nations 국제연합

UNA United Nations Association
국제연합회의

UNC United Nations Charter 국제연합헌장

부록

UNCDF United Nations Capital Development
Fund 국제연합자본개발기금

UNCED United Nations Conference on
Environment and Development
국제연합환경개발회의

UNCHS United Nations Center for Human
Settlements 국제연합인간거주센터

UNCIOS United Nations Commission on the
Law of the Sea 국제연합해양법회의

UNCITRAL United Nations Commission on
International Trade Law
국제연합국제상거래법위원회

UNCPUOS United Nations Committee on the
Peaceful Uses of Outer Space
국제연합대기권외평화이용위원회

UNCRD United Nations Center for Regional
Development
국제연합지역개발센터

UNCTAD United Nations Conference on
Trade and Development
국제연합무역개발회의

UNDC United Nations Disarmament
Commission 국제연합군축위원회

UNDD United Nations Development Decade
국제연합발전연대

UNDOF United Nations Disengagement
Observer Force 국제연합격리감시군

UNDP United Nations Development Program
국제연합개발계획

UNDRO United Nations Disaster Relief
Coordinator 국제연합재해구제기관

UNEDA United Nations EConomic
Development Administration
국제연합경제개발국

UNEF United Nations Emergency Forces
국연긴급군 (국제연합긴급군)

UNEP United Nations Environment Program
국연환경계획 (국제연합환경계획)

UNESCO United Nations Educational,
Scientific and Cultural Organization
국연교육과학문화기관 (국제연합교육과학문
화기구)

UNF United Nations Force 국제연합군

UNFPA United Nations Population Fund
국제연합인구기금

UNGA United Nations General Assembly
국제연합총회

UNHCR United Nations High Commissioner
for Refugees 국제연합난민고등판무관사무소

UNIC United Nations Information Center
국제연합홍보센터

UNICEF United Nations Children's Fund
국제연합아동기금

UNIDO United Nations Industrial
Development Organization
국제연합공업개발기구

UNIDR United Nations Institute for
Disarmament Research
국제연합군축연구소

UNISIST United Nations Intergovernmental
System on of Information in Science and
Technology
국제연합정부간과학기술정보시스템

UNITAR United Nations Institute for
Training and Research
국제연합훈련조사연구소

UNIX 유닉스

UNPROFOR United Nations Protection Force
국제연합보호군

UNRISD United Nations Research Institute
for Social Development
국제연합사회개발조사연구소

UNRRA United Nations Relief and
Rehabilitation Administration
국제연합구제부흥기관

UNSC United Nations Security Council
국제연합안전보장이사회

UNSF United Nations Security Forces
국제연합평화군

UNTAC United Nations Transitional
  Authority in Cambodia
  국제연합캄보디아잠정행정기구
UNTC United Nations Trusteeship Council
  국제연합신탁통치이사회
UNTDB United Nations Trade and
  Development Board
  국제연합무역개발이사회
UNTSO United Nations Truce Supervision
  Organization in Palestine
  국제연합팔레스타인휴전감시기구
UNU United Nations University
  국제연합대학교
UNV United Nations Volunteers
  국제연합봉사단

V

VAN value-added network 부가가치통신망
VAT value added tax 부가가치세
VB venture business 벤처비즈니스
vc venture capital 벤처자본
VE venditioni exponas 매각영장
VHD video high-density disk VHD방식 비디오
VHF very high frequency 초단파
VHS video home system VHS방식 비디오

W~X

WA with average 분손담보조건
WAN wide area network 광역정보통신망
WASP White Anglo-Saxon Protestant 와습
WATS Wide Area Telephone Service 와츠
W.B. waybill 승객명부화물운송장
WB World Bank 세계은행
WB bonds with warrants 워런트채
WCA Workers' Compensation Act
  노동자재해보장법
wee World Council of Churches
  세계교회협의회
WCIP World Council of Indigenous

UPA Uniform Partnership Act
  통일파트너십법
UPI United Press International UPI 통신사
UPU Universal Postal Union 만국우편연합
USC United States Code 합중국법률집
USIT Unit Stock Investment Trust
  유닛형 주식투자신탁
USTR United States Trade Representative 미
  국통상대표부
UT universal time 세계시
UTC coordinated universal time 협정세계시
UTO United Towns Organization
  자매도시단체연합
UV ultraviolet 자외선

VICS Vehicle Information Communication
  System 도로교통정보통신시스템
VIP very important person 최중요인물
VLSI very large scale integration
  초고밀도집적회로
V.S.O. very superior old VSO
V.S.O.P. very superior old pale VSOP
VTOL vertical takeoff and landing
  수직이착륙기

  Peoples 세계선주민족회의
WCL World Confederation of Labour
  국제노동조합연합
WCRP World Conference on Religion and
  Peace 세계종교육평화회의
wcs World Conservation Stratery
  세계자연보전전략
WEU Western European Union 서구동맹
WFTTJ World Federation of Trade Unions
  세계노동조합연맹
WFUNA World Federation of United Nations
  Associations 국제연합협회세계연맹

부록

WHO World Health Organization
세계보건기구
WINGS Warrants into Negotiable
Government Securities
유동성국채구입옵션
w.p. weather permiting 날씨가 허락하는 한
WRI World Resources Institute
세계자원연구소
WTI West Texas Intermediate 서부 텍사스 유

WTO World Trade Organization
세계무역기구
WWB Women's World Banking
세계여성은행
WWF Worldwide Fund for Nature
세계자연보호기금
XD ex-dividend 배당락
XR ex-rights 권리락

계약 용어

A

absolute discretion 완전한 재량으로
acceptance of extension 연장을 승인함
accompanied by 수반하는
accordingly 따라서
account for 차지하다
accrue prior to 이전에 발생하는
accumulate 누적되다
acknowledgment 확인
acquire 취득하다
act of God 불가항력
actual damages 실손
addressee shown below 하기명의 수신인
affected party 영향을 받는 당사자
agency agreement 대리점계약
agenda 사항
aggrieved party 손해당사자
agree as follows 아래와 같이 합의하다
agree to ~에 합의하다
allocate 분배하다
alphabetical order 알파벳순으로
alter 바꾸다
alteration 변경
amend 수정하다
amended agreement 수정계약
among other things 예를 들면
annually 일 년 마다
any 어떠한
any party 어떤 당사자
anything other than 이외의 것
applicable law 적용법
apply for 신청하다
apply mutatis mutandis 같은 내용의 계약을 맺고
apply to 적용하다
appoint 임명하다
appropriate 적절한
arbitration 중재
arbitration association 상사중재협회
arise from ~을 일으키다

arising out of ~발생하다
arithmetic mean 단순평균
arm's length 시장원칙에 따라
article 조
as defined in 정의된 대로
as far as ~에 관한 한
as from ~부터
as is 현상 그대로
as long as ~하는 한
as may be necessary 필요하다고 생각되는 경우에는
as of as 현재
as specified in ~로 특정되다
as the case may be ~의 경우에 따라
asset purchase agreement 자산구입계약
assigned or transferred 양도되는
assignment 양도
assume obligation 의무를 인수하다
at any time 어떠한 경우에도
at one's discretion 그 재량으로
at latest 늦어도
at least 적어도
at least prior to 적어도 ~전에
at liberty 자유로
at one's option ~의 선택으로
at one's own expense 자기비용으로
at one's risk 자기책임으로
at one's sole option 자유의지로
at the cost of ~의 부담으로
at the end of each month 매월말에
attached hereto 본계약서에 첨부한
attorney-at-law 변호사
attorney fee 변호사비용
attorney-in-fact 대리인
attributable to 기인하는
authorized representative 권한이 있는 대표자
automatically extend 자동으로 연장하는
award shall be final 재정은 최종의 것으로 하다

B

base price 기준가격
based on 바탕으로 하여
be adjudged 판단되는
be disclosed 개시되는
be fully satisfied 충분히 만족하는 것으로
be held liable for 책임이 있는
be indebted to ~에게 지불하다
be kept confidential 비밀로 하는
be liable for 에 책임이 있는
be presumed to be ~로 간주되다
be represented 입회하다
bear 부담하다
because of 때문에

become effective 유효하게 되다
beyond the control of ~의 지배가 미치지 않는
bid bond 입찰보증
bill of lading 선하증권
bind 구속하다
binding 구속력이 있는
binding upon parties 당사자를 구속하다
bona fide 성실한
both parties 양당사자
breach 위반
bushel 부셸
by and between ~에 의해
by means of ~의 수단으로

C

calendar year 역년(曆年)
carry out 수행하다
causative of 원인으로
cause this agreement to be duly executed 정
    당하게 본계약을 작성하고
cause 감쪽같이 집어내다
cease to ~을 그만두다
chief executive officer 경영최고책임자
clironological order 연대순으로
clause 조항
coextensive in scope with ~와 같은 내용의
collect 징수하다
commencing on ~부터 시작되는
commission 보수
commit a breach 위반을 범하다
commitments 약속
compensation 보수
completely 완전히
compliance with law 법률에 따라
comply with 준수하다
composition 화의
concerning 관하여
conditions precedent 전례

confer upon 주다
confirm and accept 확인하고 승인하다
conflict 상반
conform to 적합하다
conformity to the specifications 사양에 일치
    함
consecutive 연속하여
consequence 결과
consequential damages 간접손해
consideration 대가
consignee 수탁자
consignor 위탁자
consortium 컨소시엄
constitute an integral part ~와 떨어질 수 없는
    일부를 구성하다
constitute the entire agreement 유일하게 완
    전한 합의를 하다
construed by 해석되다
context 문맥
contingent fee 성공보수
contract price 계약금
contractual obligation 계약의무
contribute to 헌신하다

cooperate with 협력하다
corresponding date 동일
countersign 카운터사인
covenant 약속
create obligation 의무를 창출하다
created by 발생하다

credit 대변에 기입하다
credit note 크레디트노트
creditor 채권자
cumulative 누적적인
cure 구제

D

damages 손해배상액
damages assessed 입은 손해
date first above written 계약체결일
date hereof 계약일
date of the execution 조인일
de facto 사실상
de jure 법률상
dead weight ton 재화중량톤
debit 차변기입하다
debit note 데빗노트
deduct 공제하다
deductibles 면책액
deemed to have been received on ~에 받은
    것으로 간주하다
defective products 결함상품
define ~as ~로 정의하다
definition 정의
delay 늦다; 뒤지다
delay in completion 완성지연
delegate one's obligations 의무를 전부(轉付)
    하다

denominator 분모
described in 설명된
designate 지정하다
desire to ~하기를 원하다
desired date 바람직한 날
directly or indirectly 직간접적으로
disburse 지불하다; 대출을 실행하다
disclaim 보증을 부정하다
disclaimer 면책문서
discrepancy 차이; 상이
discrimination 차별
dispatch 파유하다
dispose of 처분하다
disputes or differences 분쟁
distributorship agreement 대리점계약
doctrine of equivalents 균등론
due on 지불기일이 오다
during—days ~일간
during the life of this agreement 본계약기간
    중에
duty 의무

E

effect insurance 보험을 부보(付保)하다
effective as of ~일에 유효하게 되다
employ 채용하다
employment agreement 고용계약
enact 제정하다
encumber this agreement 본계약을 담보로 하
    다
enforce 실행하다

engage subcontractors 하청기업을 고용하다
entered into 체결하다
entire agreement 완전합의
entitled to ~의 권리를 지닌
equal to 동등한
escrow account 에스크로계정
escrow transaction 에스크로거래
event of default 지불불능사유

every anniversary 매년 같은 날에
every month on the ~th day 매월~일
every two months 2개월마다
exceed the specifications 사양 이상의 것
exceeding 넘어; 초과하여
except as otherwise expressly stipulated 별도
   합의하는 경우를 제외하고
except that ~을 제외하고
exchange loss 환손
exclude 제외하다
exclusive jurisdiction 전담관할법원
exclusive of 제외하고

exclusive right 독점권
execute 작성하다
exercise of right 권리행사
exert one's best efforts 최선의 노력을 다하다
exhibit 부속서
existing law 기존법률
existing under the law of ~의 법률하에 존재
   하는
expected to persist 계속한다고 생각되는
export license 수출허가
express or implied 명시 또는 묵시적으로라도
extend 연장하다

F

fail to ~하지 않는
failing agreement 합의에 도달하지 못하는 경
   우에는
fee 보수
figure from the decimal point 소수점 이하의
   숫자
file a petition ill bankruptcy 파산을 신청하다
filed 배
Filed 신청된
first so meeting 최초의 그와 같은 회의
following order 다음순서
following words 다음어구
for—days ~일간
for a period of ~의 기간 사이
for further period of 다음의~사이
for the purpose of 때문에
for the time being 그때

force majeure 불가항력
foregoing 상기
formal agreement 정식계약
formal or informal 공식 혹은 비공식적으로
forward 제출하다
fraction and decimal 분수, 소수
   one and one-half 1.5
   one and one-half times 1.5배
   one-half 2분의 1
   one-third 3분의 1
   three-fifths 3분의 5
   two point zero one two three 2.0123
   zero point zero one two 0.012
free from 따르지 않는
free from defects 결함이 없는
from such date 계약일로부터
from time to time 이따금; 때때로

G

general terms 일반조건
give notice 통지하다
given conditions 여건
go into liquidation 청산절차를 시작하다
good faith 성실

governed by ~에 준거한
governing law 준거법
government approval 정부승인
grant 인가하다
guaranty 보증

H

having one's principal office ~에 본점이 있는
herein contained 본계약서에 포함되는
hereinafter called as 이하~라 칭하다

hereinafter referred to as 이하~라 칭하다
hereunder 본계약에서

I~J

if any 있다고 하면
if deemed necessary 필요하다고 여겨지는 경우에는
if deemed recommendable 바람직하다고 여겨지는 경우에는
if necessary 필요하면
if required 필요한 경우
impose hardship on 곤란한 상태에 처하다
in addition to 더해서
in connection with 관계하여
in consideration of 약인(約因)으로서
in default of being reached 합의하지 못할 경우에는
in duplicate 2부
in equity 형평하게
in excess of ~을 초과하여
in force 유효
in good faith 성실하게
in one's judgment 그 판단에서
in one's own name 본인으로서
in proportion to ~ 따라
in re ~에 대하여
in relation to 관련하여
in strict accordance with 엄밀하게
in such proportions as ~의 비율에 따라서

in the absence of ~가 없는 경우에는
in the case of ~의 경우
in the event of ~의 경우
in the manner specified in ~로 규정된 방법으로
in the same proportion 같은 비율로
in the sole discretion of ~라는 판단이 적절함
in witness whereof 상기를 증명하기 위해
in writing 서면으로
including, but not limited to ~로 한정되지 않고 제시되다
inclusive of 포함하여
incorporating 집어넣은
incur 생기다
indemnify 보상하다
indemnify and hold harmless 면책으로 하다
insofar as us ~하는 한에 있어서는
integral multiple 정수배
integral part 불가결한 부분
inter alia 예를 들면
inverse order 역순
it is expressly understood 분명히 이해되다
it reads 해석이 되다
jointly and severally 연대책임으로

L

lease 임대차
lease agreement 임대차계약
legal binding 법적 구속력
legend 범례
less 제외하고
lesser sum of the two 어느 쪽이든 적은 쪽

letter of guaranty 보증장
letter of indemnity 보상장
letter of intent 각서
liabilities 책임
licensee 라이센시
licensor 라이센서

limited to ~에 한정된
liquidated damages 예정된 손해배상액

liquidation 청산
long arm statute 역외적용

M

maintenance bond 멘터넌스본드
maintenance of good relation 양호한 관계를
  유지함
make good 수복하다
make no variation 변경하지 않는
make use of 이용하다
managing director 사장
material breach 중대한 위반
material change 중대한 변화

materially 실제로
may be entered in any court having
  jurisdiction thereof 관할법원에 판단을 요
  청할 수 있다
minimize 각서
minutes of meeting 의사록
mutual agreement 상호합의
mutual benefit 상호이익을 위해

N

negligent act 과실
neither party 어느 쪽 당사자도 ~하지 않는
next higher 다음으로 높은
no force or effect 효력을 갖지 않는
nonexclusive 비독점의
not later than ~까지는

notarize 공정하다
notify 통지하다
notwithstanding the above 상기에도 불구
  하고
null and void 무효의
numerator 분자

O

obliged to 의무가 있는
obtain approvals 허가를 취득하다
of any kind or nature 어떠한 종류 또는 본질
  의
on a ~basis ~라는 조건으로
on account of ~가 원인인
on an as-is basis 현상 그대로
on and after 이후
on behalf of 에 대신하여
on one's account 자기계정으로
on or before 이전에
on the occurrence of any event ~가 발생한

경우에는
opinion letter 변호사의견서
option 선택권
or otherwise 또 그 이외의
oral or written 구두 또는 문서로
order of priority 우선순위
other obligations or liabilities 다른 의무
otherwise 그렇지 않으면
out-of-pocket money 현금으로
outstanding order 발주필 주문
over ~ days ~ a ~일간
owner 소유자

P

pari passu 동렬로

pari evidence 구두증거

particulars 명세
party experiencing ~를 경험한 당사자
pass from~to ~로 옮기는
patentee 특허권자
penalty 벌금
perform provisions 조항을 이행하다
performance 수행
performance bond 이행보증
performance of the obligations 의무이행
pledge 담보에 넣다
power 권한
power of attorney 위임장
practicable 실제적인
preceding month 전월
premises 상술한 사항
present 참가자
prevailing 그 때의
principal 본인
principal place of business 본점의 위치
principal terms 주요조건

prior agreement 과거계약
prior commitments 과거약속
privilege 특권
privity 계약관계
pro rata ~의 비율에 따라
procedural defense 절차상의 항변
procedures 절차
proceed with ~를 진행한
proceeds 수취액
product liability 제조물책임
promptly upon ~후 즉시
proportionate 비례한
prorated amount 비율에 따른 액
prove to be ~임을 안다
provided that 단
proviso 단서
punitive damages 징벌적인 손해배상금
purchase order 발주자
pursuant to 따라서

Q~R

quarterly 3개월마다
re 관하여
reach 바로 앞에 닿다
receiver 관재인
reduce the effect 영향을 줄이다
reduced to writing 서면으로 하다
Reference is made to ~에 관하여
referred to as ~라고 간주되다
regarded as ~라고 간주되다
regarding 관하여
registered place 등기상의 장소
relevant authority 관계당국
relieve from 에서 벗어나다
remain in force 유효하다
remain liable to ~에 책임을 지다
remedy 구제하다
remit 송금하다
render 제공하다
rental 임대차

renumeration 보수
repay the loan 론을 변제하다
representations and warranties 표명과 보증
reproduce 복제하다
requirements 요건
reserve the right 권리를 보유하다
resolutions 결의
resort to legal means 법적수단에 호소하다
restore 원래로 되돌리다
retroactively 소급적으로
right of First refusal 우선권
rights granted under this agreement 본계약에
  서 인정된 권리
round down 끝수를 자르다
round off 사사오입을 하다
round up 끝수를 올리다
royalty 로얄티
run from 유효가 되다

S

save insofar 없는 한
scope of work 업무범위
semi-annually 반년마다
serve to ~을 목적으로 하다
set forth 정하다
set one's hand 서명하다
set opposite 우측에 적은
settle 정산하다
settled by arbitration 중재로 해결되다
settlement of accounts 결의
severability clause 잔여조항의 유효성에 대한
　조항
shall be amended to read as follows 이하와
　같이 수정하다
shall not 해서는 안된다
shall not be relieved of any responsibility 어
　떠한 책임에서도 벗어날 수 없다
similar to 동등한

so identified 그와 같이 특정된
sooner terminated 빨리 해약된
specifications set forth 정해진 사양서에 따라
specified in 특정되는
stamp duty 인지(印紙)
statement 명세서
statute 제정법
stipulate 말하다; 진술하다
subject to 를 조건으로 하여; 에 따라
subrogate 를 대신하여 떠맡다
succeeding day 다음날
successive term 다음기간
such as 등
supersede prior agreements 사전의 합의로 대
　신하다
supplement 보유
suspend 중단하다

T

take all steps within its power 만전의 조치를
　취하다
take effect on ~에 유효가 되다
take place 발생하다
tax exemption 면세
technical data 기술자료
term 기간
terminate 해제하다
termination 해제
terms 용어
terms and conditions 조건
territory 지역
then outstanding credits 그 때 남은 채권
then ratio 그 때의 비율

thereby 그것으로
this agreement 본계약
This agreement made and entered into 본계
　약은~에 체결되다
three consecutive terms 연속3기
time of completion 완성시간
to one's satisfaction 만족할 수 있도록
to the contrary 반대로
to the effect 그 내용의
to the extent 범위에서
to the extent possible 가능한 한
to the fullest extent 최대한
total proceeds 총대금

U

unanimous 전원일치
under this agreement 본계약

undersigned 하기서명자
unit price 단가

unless otherwise agreed 별도로 합의하지 않은 경우

unless terminated 해약되지 않는 한

unless the context otherwise requires 다른 의미가 되지 않는 한

unpaid balance 미불부분

unreasonably withheld 부당하게 거절당하지 않는

until ~days prior to ~일 전까지

until—shall be fulfilled ~가 달성되기까지

until the expiry 기한까지

up to the date 까지

upon bankruptcy 파산시기

upon mutual agreement 상호합의후 즉시

use one's best endeavors 최선의 노력을 하다

usury law 이자제한법

V

valid 유효

validity of this agreement 본 계약의 유효성

vary 변경하다

verify 확인하다

vested with 기득의; 기존의

viewed as 간주하다

violation 위반

vis major 불가항력

vouchers therefor 그것들의 증표류

W

waive the right 권리를 포기하다

waived 포기된

waiver clause 권리포기조항

waiver of sovereign immunity 국가주의면책을 포기함

warrant 보증하다

warranty 보증

weighted average 가중평균

whatsoever 어떠한

when due 지불기일이 오다

whether in writing or otherwise 또는 다른 방법에 의한

whether or not ~이든 아니든

whichever occurs later 어느 쪽이든 나중에 일어난

willing to ~을 원하는

with recourse 구상권부의

with respect to 에 관하여

withdraw 후퇴하다

withhold 보류하다; 유보하다

withholding tax 원천징수세

without any commitment 의무를 지지 않고

without limiting the foregoing 그것이 모두라고 한정할 수 없으며

without prejudice to ~를 손상하지 않고

without prejudice to any other rights 다른 어떠한 권리도 손상하지 않고

without prior notice 사전에 통지하지 않고

Without recourse 구성권이 없는

words in capital letters 대문자어구

work to be performed 수행되는 작업

written consent 서면동의

부록

멀티미디어 용어

A

A/D conversion 아날로그에서 디지털로 변환함

acceptable use policy AUP

access time 액세스 타임

accumulator 누산기

access point 액세스 포인트

acoustic coupler 음향 커플러

active method 액티브 방식

Ada Language 에이더 언어

adaptive differential PCM ADPCM

adaptive transform acoustic coding 애트랙

address space 어드레스 공간

advanced compatible television 에이시 텔레비전

advanced television 선진 텔레비전

affine transformation 아핀 변환

after recording 애프레코

agent oriented 에이전트 지향

Algol Language 알골 언어

algorithm 알고리즘

ambient light 앰비엔트 광

American National Standards Institute 미국규격협회

American Standard Code for Information

Interchange 아스키; 미국정보교환표준코드

amplitude 음량

analog to digital conversion 아날로그에서 디지털로 변환함

anigle of view 화각

aperture grille 애퍼처 그릴

aperture grille pitch 애퍼처 그릴 피치

append 데이터 추가

application 애플리케이션

application program 응용프로그램

arbiter 조정회로

archiver 아카이버

argument 인수

aspect ratio translation 아스펙트비 변환

assemble editing 어셈블 편집

assembly language 어셈블 언어

asynchronous transfer mode ATM: 비동기 전송모드

audio interchange file format 오디오 인터체인지 파일 포맷

augmentation 광대

authoring tool 오서링 툴

autonomy 자율성

auxiliary channel 여잉 채널

B

backbone 백본

backlighting 역광

basic software 기본소프트

batch processing 일괄처리

beat per minute 1분간 박수(拍數)

binary 바이너리

boundary representation 바운더리리프리젠테이션

bridge format 브릿지 포맷

broadband integrated services digital network B-ISDN

broadcaster 방송국

bulletin board system 블러틴 보드 시스템

bus 버스

byte 바이트

C

C language C언어

cable television 케이블 텔레비전

calibration 캘리브레이션

caption 캡션

carrier sense multiple access with collision detection 충돌검출형 반송파 다중액세스

cathode ray tube CRT

central processing unit CPU; 중앙처리장치

chaos 카오스

charge coupled device 차지 커플 디바이스

circuit switching 회로 교환

color chart 칼라 차트

color lookup table 칼라 룩업 테이블

color naming system 색명법

color proof 색 교정

color separation 색 분해

color temperature 색 온도

color video signal 컬러 비디오 신호

common language business oriented language COBOL언어

communication Karaoke 통신 카라오케

compact disk 콤팩트디스크

compact disk read only memory CD-Rom

complex instruction set computer CISC; 복합 명령 세트 컴퓨터

comprehensive 캠프

CompuServe 컴퓨서브

computer aided design 캐드

computer assisted software engineering CASE

computer supported cooperation work 컴퓨터 지원 협조 작업

computer tomography scanner CT스캐너

computer virus 컴퓨터 바이러스

computer worm 컴퓨터 웜

cracker 크래커

CRT projection display CRT; 투사 디스플레이

cryptography 암호

cyan magenta yellow black CMYB; 인쇄 프로세스 컬러

cyber-punk 사이버 펑크

D

datacasting 데이터방송

decode 신장

demodulation 복조

desk top music 데스크탑 뮤직

desk top publishing 데스크탑 퍼블리싱

desk top video 데스크탑 비디오

DIG color 디그 컬러

digital audio 디지털 오디오

digital audio tape 디지털 오디오 테이프

digital audio workstation 디지털 오디오 워크 스테이션

digital library 전자도서관

digital signal processor 디지털 시그널 프로세서

digital video disk DVD; 디지털 비디오 디스크

digital video interactive 디지털 비디오 인터랙 티브

disk 디스크

distance learning 원격 교육

dots per inch 1인치 당 도트의 수

dual side double density double track 2DD

dual side high double density double track 2HD

dynamic data exchange 다이내믹 데이터 교환

dynamic RAM DRAM

E

E-mail Address 이메일 주소

effect 효과

electronic book 전자북

electronic ordering system 전자발주시스템

emulator 에뮬레이터

enableware 인에이블웨어

enhanced graphics adapter 인핸스드 그래픽 어댑터

equalizer 이퀄라이저
escape sequence 에스케이프 시퀀스
ethernet 이더넷
exceptional character 외자
expert system 익스퍼트 시스템

extended architecture 확장 아키텍처
extended slot 확장 슬롯
extension board 확장 보드
extension card 확장 카드
external memory unit 외부 기억장치

F

fiber distributed data interface FDDI
file allocation table 파일 앨로케이션 테이블
file transfer protocol 파일 트랜스퍼 프로토콜
fire wall 파이어 월
firmware 펌웨어
flash memory 플래시메모리
floppy disk 플로피디스크

formula translation language 포트란 언어
fractal 프랙탈
free barrier 프리 배리어
free form deformation 자유형상변형법
free form modeling 자유형상모델링
frequency modulation FM
frequency modulation oscillator FM 음원

G

gamma correction 감마 보정
gateway 게이트웨이
general MIDI GMIDI
genetic algorithm 유전적 알고리즘
giga byte 기가바이트
giga chip 기가칩

gradation 계조
graphical user interface 사용자 편의를 위한
  그래픽 인터페이스; GUI
group special mobile communication
  이동통신
groupware 그룹웨어

H

hacker 해커
half duplex 반이중
half tone 망판(網版)
Hardware Description Language HDL언어
head mount display 헤드 마운트 디스플레이

hidden line elimination 숨김선 처리
high definition television 하이비전 텔레비전
hub 허브
hyper-media 하이퍼미디어

I

icon 아이콘
ID code 아이디코드
idea processor 아이디어 프로세서
image printer 이미지 프린터
image processing 이미지 처리
image scanner 이미지 스캐너

image setter 이미지 세터
impact printer 임팩트 프린터
in-sourcing 인소싱
indent 인덴트
index sequential file 인덱스 시퀀셜 파일
information network system INS

부록

information provider 정보 제공자
Information Superhighway 초고속 통신망,
　정보고속도로
Information Technology Promotion Agency
　정보처리진흥협회
informercial 인포머셜
infostructure 인포스트랙처
initialize 이니셜라이즈
ink jet printer 잉크젯 프린터
input 입력
insert editing 인서트 편집
intaglio 요판
integrated services digital broadcasting
　종합디지털방송
integrated services digital network ISDN

interaction 쌍방향성
interactive television 쌍방향 텔레비전
interactive video disk 쌍방향 비디오 디스크
interlace 비월주사
International Marine
　Satellite-Telecommunication Organization
　국제해사위성통신기구
International Relay chat 인터내셔널 릴레이
　차트
International Telecommunication Union
　국제전기통신연합
Internet 인터넷
interoperability 상호운용성
IP Address IP 주소
Indium Plan 이리듐 계획

J~K

Japan Network Information Center 일본 네트
　워크 인포메이션 센터
Japanese Industrial Standards JIS 규격
Joint Photographic Expert Group JPEG

（이미지압축파일의 한 종류）
kilo bit 킬로비트
kilo byte 킬로바이트

L

large scale integration LSI: 대규모집적회로
laser disk read only memory LD-ROM
line feed 개행 문자를 다음 행의 같은 위치에
　이동시키는 제어문자
line space 행간

liquid crystal display 액정 디스플레이
local area network 로컬 에어리어 네트워크
low earth orbit 저궤도
luminance 휘도

M

magnet optics disk 엠오 디스크
main frame 메인 프레임
mega byte 메가 바이트
mega drive 메가 드라이브
mega transport network 메가트랜스포트 네트
　워크
mega-industry 메가 인더스트리
memory unit 기억장치

metropolitan area network MAN
micro process unit 초소형 연산장치
million instruction per second MIPS;
　연산속도단위
mimic 모방
mini disk 미니 디스크
mobile computing 모바일 컴퓨팅
montage 몽타주

motion model 운동모델
Moving Picture Expert Group 동화상 압축의
　한 방식; MPEG
Multi Media Extension MME
multimedia PC MPC
multimedia personal computer
　멀티미디어 컴퓨터
multiple sub-nyquist sampling encoding
　뮤즈 방식
Multipurpose Internet Mail Extension
　MINE 규격
multisourcing 멀티소싱
multitask 멀티태스크
Musical Instruments Digital Interface
　MIDI 규격

N

narrowband integrated services digital
　network N-ISDN
National Information Infrastructure NII:
　전미정보기반
NetNews 넷뉴스
network control unit 망 제어장치

network security 통신망기밀보호
network service provider 네트워크 서비스
　제공업체
news on demand 뉴스 온 디맨드
non-preemptive 논 프리엠프티브
noninterlace 순차주사

O

object linking and embedding OLE
object oriented 오브젝트 지향
object oriented database 오브젝트 지향 데이
　터베이스
object space 오브젝트 공간
octet 오크텟트
off talk service 오프 토크 통신서비스
offset printing 옵셋 인쇄
on hook dial 온 후크 다이얼
open architecture 오픈 아키텍처
open document architecture 개방형 문서구조

open media framework 오픈 미디어 프레임
　워크
operating system 오퍼레이팅 시스템
optical character reader OCR
optical communication 광통신
optical fiber 광섬유
optimization 최적화
out-sourcing 아웃소싱
outline font 아웃라인 펀드
output 출력
over drive processor 오버 드라이브 프로세서

P

packet communication 패킷 통신
parabola antenna 파라볼라 안테나
Pascal Language 파스칼 언어
password 패스워드
pay per view 페이 퍼 뷰
Pentium 펜티엄
Personal Computer Memory Card

International Association PCMCIA 규격
personal digital assistant 퍼스널 디지털
　어시스턴트
personal handyphone system 간이 휴대전화
Phase Alternation by Line 펄 방식
phase shift keying 위상변조방식
pica 파이카

pixel 화소
platform 플랫폼
postscript graphic 포스트스크립트그래픽
precision adaptive sub-band coding 고정밀서
 브밴드코딩
pretty good privacy PGP

Q~R

quick ring 퀵링
Quick Time 퀵타임
random access memory RAM
random number 난수
read only memory ROM
receiving monitor 상수선택기능
recommended standard 232C RS232C
 (직렬로트)
red green blue RGB

S

safety envelop 세이프티엔벨롭
sampling frequency 샘플링 주파수
satellite communication 위성통신
satellite news gathering 새트라이트 뉴스
 개더링
satellite station 위성기지
semantic network 의미 네트워크
sensitivity 감도
server 서버
set top device 세톱 디바이스
signal to noise ratio 신호잡음비
silicon audio 실리콘 오디오
simulation theater 체감극장

T

table of contents TOC
TCP/IP TCP/IP
thin film transistor 박막 트랜지스터
three dimension 3차원

protocol 프로토콜
public address 장내방송장치
public domain software 퍼블릭 도메인 소프트
puke code modulation 펄스 코드
pulse code modulation 펄스 부호 변조

reduced instruction set computer RISK;
 명령어 축약형 컴퓨터
remote computing service 리모트 컴퓨팅
 서비스
resolution 해상도
ring topology 링 토폴로지
rotation effect 로테이션 효과
router 루터

small computer system interface SCSI;
 스카시
solid 입체의
spreadsheet program 표계산 프로그램
static RAM SRAM
structured query language SQL 언어
super bit mapping 슈퍼 빗 매핑
super-twist nematic STN; 에스티엔
 (LCD의 패널 구성 형태)
symbolic link format 링크
synchronous transfer mode 동기 전송 모드
system engineer SE

3DO 3디오
threshold 2치화상 처리
token bus system 토큰 버스 시스템
token ring 토큰링

TRON 트론
TVTI 1.5메가

type 활자

U

ultra high definition television 초고품위
   텔레비전, 초고선명 텔레비전
ultra high frequency UHF

UNIX 유닉스
UNIX to UNIX Copy UUCP
up load 업로드

V

variable length record 가변조
Vehicle Information and Communication
   System vies VLSI
very high frequency VHP
very large scale integration 초고밀도집적회
   로
video capture board 비디오 캡처보드
video journalism 비디오 저널리즘
video on demand 비디오 온 디맨드
video random access memory VRAM
video system control architecture 비디오

   컨트롤 아키텍처
video transmission service 영상 전송 서비스
videotex 비디오텍스
viewpon 뷰폰
virtual interface environment workstation 가
   상환경 워크스테이션
virtual reality 가상현실
virus 바이러스
voice recognition 음성 인식
voice synthesis 음성 합성

W~X

wide area network WAN; 광역정보통신망
wide very high frequency WVHF
wizard 워저드

World Wide Wave 월드와이드웨이브
X-MODEM X-모뎀

인터넷 용어

A

abort 어보트(명령이나 처리를 중단하여 종료함)

access 액세스

access control 액세스 접속

access number 접속 번호

access point 접속 포인트

access request 접속 요구

account 어카운트, 과금

accumulator 어큐뮬레이터; 연산기

ACK Acknowlegement (modem) 긍정응답

ACM Association of Computing Machinery 미국계산기학회

acronym 두문자어

activate 기동하다, 활동하다

actuation 조작, 작동

add 가산하다, 가하다

address email address or WEB address 어드레스, 번지

address book 어드레스 장

addressing 어드레스 지정

ADN Advanced Digital Network 어드밴스드 디지털 네트워크

ADPCM Adaptive Digital Pulse Code Modulation 적응형 작동 PCM

AFS Andrew File System 앤드류 파일 시스템

angent 에이전트

AI artificial Intelligence 인공지능

algorithm 알고리즘

alias 에이리어스, 별명, 위명

align 정렬시키다, 위치를 맞추다

allocate 할당하다

allow 허락하다, 가능하게 하다

alpha 알파(DEC사의 프로세서명)

alt 앨트(뉴스 그룹의 하나의 분야)

alter 변경하다

ampersand 앰퍼샌드

analog 아날로그

analysis 분석

anchor 앵커

angels 엔젤

annotations 주석, 코멘트

anonymous FTP internet file transfer protocol 익명 FTP

ANSI American National Standards Institute 미국규격협회

API Application Programming Interface 응용프로그램 인터페이스

append (새로운 데이터 등을) 추가함

applets 애플릿

application program 응용 프로그램

application software 응용 소프트웨어

archie 아치(아키브 파일을 검색하는 소프트)

architecture 아키텍처, 체계

archive 보관, 보존, 기록(과거의 메일 뱅크를 가리킴)

ARJ Archive Program for MS-DOS MS-DOS의 아키브 프로그램

ARP Address Resolution Protocol 어드레스 레졸루션 통신 규격

ARPANET Advanced Research Project Administration Network 미국국방성연구 네트워크

array 배열

arrow 화살, 화살표

article 뉴스기사, 논문

AS Autonomous System 동일 조직이 운영하는 네트워크

ASCII American Standard Code for Information Interchange 아스키; 미국정보 교환표준코드

ASCII file 아스키 파일

ASP Active Server Pages 액티브 서버 페이지

assembler 어셈블러

assembly language 어셈블리 언어

asynchronous 비동조의

AT commands AT 코맨트

ATM Asynchronous Transfer Mode 비동기 전환모드

attached file 첨부파일

attachment 어태치먼트, 서류 첨부
attribute 애트리뷰트, 속성
audio board 오디오보드
AUI Attachment Unit Interface
　접속기구 인터페이스
AUP Acceptable user policy
　인터넷 이용 규정, 제한폴리시
authentication 인정, 확인

B

back space 백스페이스
back up 백업, 지원
backbone 백본, 기간통신회로
backbone LAN 백본 LAN
background 백그라운드, 배경
bandwidth 밴드폭
bang 뱅
banner 배너
barcode 바코드
baseband 베이스밴드
BASIC Beginners All-purpose Symbolic
　Instruction Code 베이직, 기본어
batch file 배치 파일
baud rate 보드 속도
baudo code 보드코드
BBS Bulletin Board System 전자 게시판
Bee : blind carbon copy 블라인드 카피
BCPL programming language BCPL
　프로그램 언어의 하나
beam 빔(파일 전송)
beep 비프음
benchmark 벤치마크
BFT Binary File Transfer 바이너리파일전송
Big Blue another name for IBM Business
　Machine IBM의 애칭
binary file 이진법 파일
binary numbers 이진법 번호
BIOS Basic input/output System 기본 입출력
　시스템

auto answer 자동반답
auto dialing 자동다이얼
auto kerneling 오토커넬링
auto numbering 오토넘버링
automate 오토메이션화하다
automation 오토메이션
avoid 피하기
AZERTY keyboard AZERTY 키보드

bit Binary Digit 비트
bitmap 비트맵
blank 블랭크
bleep 신호음
blink 점멸
block 블록
body 바디, 본체
bookmark 북마크
Boolean (boolean logic) 불의 이론
boot 부트
boot strap 부트스트랩
Bot ROBOT 로봇
bounced message 바운스 메시지
bps bits per second 비트/초, 송신 속도의 단위
break 브레이크
Bridge 브리지
brightness 휘도
broadband 광주파수 대역
broadcast 브로드 캐스트
Browser 브라우저
BT British Telecom 브리티시텔레콤사
buffer 버퍼
bugs 버그
bulletin board 게시판
bus network 버스형 네트워크
Byte 8 bits 바이트
byte code 바이트 코드
byte exchange 바이트 교환
byte information 바이트 정보

C

cache 캐시
CAD 캐드, 컴퓨터원용설계
CAD/CAM 컴퓨터원용제조
calculator 계산기
call-up 호출
cancel 취소
capacity 캐퍼시티
caret mark 캐럿마크
carriage return 복귀
carrier 캐리어, 반송파
cartridge 카트리지
cascade 캐스케이드
cc carbon copy 카본카피
CC Mail CC 메일
CD (Compact Disc) 컴팩트 디스크
CD-ROM 판독전용기억장치
cell 셀
CFML (cold fusion markup language)
　콜드퓨전메이크업언어
CGI (Common gateway interface)
　커먼게이트웨이트인터페이스
character string 문자열
chart 차트, 도표
Chat 채트
checkbox 검사상
checksum 검사합계
circuit board 서킷판
Cisco vendor name 시스코사
CIX (Commercial Internet Exchange)
　커머셜인터넷익스체인지협회
click 클릭
Client 클라이언트
client server model 클라이언트 서버 모델
clipboard 클립보드
clock 클록
clone 클론
cluster controller 클러스터 컨트롤러
cold-boot 콜드부트
colon 콜론

column 자리수, 열
COM communication port 통신포트
command line 커맨드라인
comment 코맨트
commercial server 상용 서버
communications software 통신 소프트웨어
compatibility 호환성
compiler 컴파일러
complete 작업완료
compressed file 압축파일
compression 압축
CompuServe 컴퓨서브
computer 컴퓨터
computer game 컴퓨터 게임
computer language 컴퓨터 언어
configuration 구성, 환경 설정
connect 접속
connect time 접속 시간
connector 커넥터
content 컨텐트
contrast 콘트라스트
control panel 제어패널
control signal 제어신호
cookie 쿠키
copy 카피
cordless 무선
core 코어
corrupt 변화, 개악
counter 카운터
couple 커플
cpi characters per inch 인치, 카운트 수
cps chasracters per second 자(字)/초
CPU Central Processing Unit 중앙처리장치
cracker 크래커
crash 크래시
CRC (Cyclic Redundancy Check) 전송 중의
　오차를 검출함
cross post 크로스포스트
cross-over 크로스오버

CSU Channel Service Unit 채널 서비스 유닛
CTCP Client-to-client Protocol
　고객 대 고객의 프로토콜
current 커런트, 흐름
cursor 커서
CU-SeeMe Video conferencing software 인

터넷비디오회의의 소프트웨어의 하나
custom made 주문으로 만든
cut and paste 잘라 붙임
Cyberspace 사이버스페이스
cyclic redundancy check 주기용장검사

D

daisy-chain 데이지체인, 한 가지 일로 여러 일
　이 생겨남
data 데이터
data acquisition 데이터 수집
data integrity 데이터 통합
data item 데이터 항목
data processing 데이터 처리
database 데이터베이스
database management system 데이터베이스
　시스템
DCE Data Communications Equipment
　데이터통신기기
debug 벌레잡기(컴퓨터), 프로그램의 결함을
　발견해 수정하다
decipher 해독하다
decode 디코드
decoder 디코더, 해독기
decrement 감소
decription 해독
dedicated line 전용라인
delay 지연
delete 삭제
delete key 삭제 키
demo software 데모용 소프트
desktop 탁상용
desktop video 탁상용 비디오
develop 개발
device 장치
device control 장치제어
device driver 장치드라이버
DHCP Dynamic Host Communication
　Protocol 다이나믹호스트통신규약

DHTML Dynamic HTML 다이나믹 HTML
dial 다이얼
dial-up account 다이얼업 어카운트
dial-up connection 다이얼업 접속
digit 숫자, 자릿수
digital signal 디지털 신호
digital transmission 디지털 전송
digitized sound 디지털음
direct connection 직접 접속
directory 디렉토리
discussion group 토론그룹
disk 디스크
disk drive 디스크드라이브
disk error 디스크 에러
disk operating system 디스크 오퍼레이팅 시
　스템
diskette 디스켓
display 디스플레이
distribution 분배
DLL Dynamic Load Library 다이나믹로드라
　이브러리
DNS Domain Name Service 도메인명 서버
document 문헌
document processing 도큐먼트 처리
document source 도큐먼트 소스
Domain 도메인
Domain Name Server 도메인 이름 서버
DOS Disk Operating System 디스크 오퍼레
　이팅 시스템
dot address 도트 어드레스
dot file 도트파일
dot period 도트, 점

download 다운로드
downtime 다운시간
dpi dots per inch 점/인치(1인치당 도트수)
drag 드래그
driver 드라이버
drop down menu 드롭다운 메뉴
DSS Digital Signature Standard 디지털 시그
  니처 스탠다드
DSU Digital Service Unit 디지털 서비스 유닛
DTE Data Terminal Equipment 데이터 터미

널기
Dumb terminal 덤 터미널
duplex 듀플렉스, 이중의
duplicate 복제
DVD Digital Versatile Disk DVD; 디지털 비
  디오 디스크
DVORAK DVORAK 키보드
dynamic RAM 다이나믹 RAM
dynamic SQL 다이나믹 SQL
dynamic webpage 웹페이지

E

echo 에코
edit 편집
Editor 편집 프로그램
EFF 전자 프론티어 펀데이션
efficiency 효율
elapsed time 지나간 시간
electronic mail 전자 메일
electronic mall 전자 몰
electronic publishing 전자출판
electronic store 전자점
E-Mail 메일
e-mail shorthand 메일 필기
emulation 에뮬레이션
encode 부호화
encryption 암호
enter 입력
enter key 입력키

equipment 장치
erase 소거
ergonomics 인간공학
error 에러, 착오
escape 도피
ethernet 이더넷
Eudora 유도라
even 짝수
execute 실행
exclude 배제
exit 출구
expansion board 확장 보드
expansion slot 확장 슬롯
extensions 확장자
extract 추출
extranet 엑스트라넷

F

facsimile machine 팩스기
FAQ Frequently Asked questions 자주 묻는
  질문
FAX 팩스
feature 기능, 특징
fetch 패치
fiber optics 파이버 옵틱스
figure 숫자

file 파일
file compression 파일 압축
file encryption 파일 암호
file extension 파일 확장
file name 파일명
file server 파일 서버
Firewall 파이어 월
firmware 팜웨어

부록

flame 플레임
flicker 화면의 흔들림
floppy disk 플로피 디스크
flowchart 플로우 차트
folder 폴더
font 폰트
footer 풋터
footprint 풋프린트
foreground 전경
form 폼
format 포맷
formula 포뮬러공식
frame 프레임, 틀

frame relay 프레임 릴레이
Free Net 프리넷
freeware 프리웨어
FSP same as File Transfer Protocol
　　파일 전송 프로토콜
FTC Federal Trade Commission
　　연방 무역 커미션
FTP File Transfer Protocol
　　파일 전송 프로토콜
full duplex 전이중(통신)
full motion video 풀 모션 비디오
function key 기능키
FYI (for your information) 참고로서

G

GIF Graphic Interchange Format GIF(이미지
　　압축파일의 한 종류)
Giga 기가
gigabit 기가비트
gigabyte 기가바이트
glitch (기계 등의) 작은 결함
glossary (전기기구 등의) 갑작스런 고장

gopher 고퍼
gopherspace 고퍼스페이스
graph 그래프
graphics 그래픽스
GUI Graphical User Interface 그래픽을 통한
　　사용자중심의 인터페이스

H

hacker 해커
half duplex 반이중(통신)
handle 핸들
handset 전화 등의 송수화기
handshake 응답확인방식
hang 행
hard copy 하드카피
hard disk 하드디스크
hardware 하드웨어
header 헤더
helper applications 헬퍼애플리케이션
hexadecimal 16진법
hierarchy 계층
high level language 고수준언어
hits 히트

home computer 홈컴퓨터
home shopping service 통신판매서비스
homepage 홈페이지
host computer 호스트 컴퓨터
hot plugging USB or firewire interface
　　핫플러깅
hot list 핫리스트
HTML (Hyper Text Markup Language)
　　하이퍼텍스트 메이크업 언어
HTTP Hyper Text Transport Protocol
　　하이퍼텍스트 트랜스포트 규약
Hub 허브, 중심, 축
hyper link 하이퍼링크
hypermedia 하이퍼미디어
Hyper text 하이퍼텍스트

hyphenation 하이퍼네이션

I

I/O 입출력
I/O device 입출력 장치
icon 아이콘
ID 신원확인, 식별
IE MS (Internet Explorer MS)
　인터넷 익스플로러
image compression 이미지압축
imaging 결상, 이미징
IMAP (Internet Message Access protocol) 인
　터넷 메시지 접속 프로토콜
implement 실현
improve 개선
increase 증가
increment 증분
index 색인
indexing 색인부
information packet 정보패킷
Information Services Manager 정보 서비스
　매니저 시스템
information system 정보시스템
information technology 정보기술
in-house 구내
initialize 초기설정하다
ink-jet printer 잉크젯 프린터
input A/J 입력
input device 입력기
input port 입력포트
input-output (I/O) 입출력
install 인스톨, 설정
instruction 인스트럭션

instruction set 명령세트
integer 정수
interactive 대화형
interactive video 대화형 비디오
interface 인터페이스
internal modem 내부 모뎀
Internet 인터넷
internet account 인터넷 어카운트
internet backbone 인터넷 백본
internet radio 인터넷 라디오
internet society 인터넷 사회
internet telephony 인터넷 텔레폰
internetworking 인터넷워킹
**InterNIC (Internet Network Information
　Center)** 인터넷워크정보센터
interrupt 끼어들다
intranet 인트라넷
IP (Internet Protocol) 인터넷 프로토콜
IP address (IP 어드레스)
IP Faxing (IP 팩싱)
IP Telephony (IP 텔레폰)
IRC (Internet Relay Chat) 인터넷릴레이차트
ISDN (Integrated Services Digital Network)
　디지털 서비스 통합 서비스 망
**ISO (International Organization for
　Standardization)** 국제표준기구
ISP (Internet Service Provider) 인터넷서비스
　제공업자
IT (Information Technology) IT; 정보기술

J~K

Java 자바
Java Bean 자바 빈즈
Javascript 자바스크립트
job 져브

kbps 킬로바이트(매초 1킬로바이트의)
Kernel 커널
key 키
key pals 키펄스(인터넷 상의 펜팔 상대)

keyboard 키보드
keypad 키패드
key word 키워드

L

label 라벨
lap 처지다, 뒤떨어지다
LAN (Local Area Network) 구내통신네트워크
laser printer 레이저프린터
launch 런치, (새로운 제품 등의) 시장에 내다
library 라이브러리, 등록집
link 링크
linkage editor 링케이지
Liquid Crystal Display (LCD)
　액정 디스플레이

M

machine address 기계어드레스
machine language 기계어
magnetic card reader 자기 카드 판독
mail e-mail 메일
mail filter 메일 필터
mailing list 메일링 리스트
mainframe computer 대형 컴퓨터
management information system
　MIS 경영 정보 시스템
margin 마진, 여백
mass storage 대용량 기억장치
Mega million 메가
megabyte 메가바이트
megaflop 메가플롭, 수치계산능력을 나타내는
　단위
memory 메모리, 기억(장치)
menu 메뉴(선택할 수 있는 처리의 일람표)
menu-driven 메뉴에 따라 조작하는 구조인
message 메시지
meta 메타
micro 마이크로
microchip 마이크로칩

kill file 킬파일(삭제파일)
Kilobyte 킬로바이트

list 리스트
listserv 리스트서브
load 로드
load module 로드모듈
log 로그, 송신기록
logical operation 논리연산
log-in (log-on) 로그인; 컴퓨터 사용 개시
log-out (log-off) 로그아웃; 컴퓨터 사용 종료
low level language MAC Address
　MAC 어드레스

microcomputer 마이크로컴퓨터
Microsoft Internet Explorer 마이크로소프트
　인터넷익스플로러
MIDI (Musical Instrument Digital Interface)
　디지털 음악 데이터 표준 규격
MIME (Multipurpose Internet Mail
　Extension) 다목적 인터넷 전자우편 확장
MIPS Millions of instructions per Second 명
　령의 실행속도를 나타내는 단위
mirror site 미러사이트
mnemonic 니모닉; 연상기호코드
modem 모뎀
monitor 모니터, 감시
morphine 모핑
Mosaic graphical browser 모자이크
mouse 마우스
multicast 멀티캐스트
multimedia 멀티미디어
multi-user 멀티유저
multi-tasking 멀티태스킹
MX Mail Exchange 메일 교환

N

name 네임
navigation 내비게이션
Netiquette 네티켓; 인터넷 상의 예절
netizen 네티즌
Netscape 네스케이프
network 네트워크
newbie 초보자
Newsgroups 뉴스그룹
newsletter 뉴스레터
newsreader 뉴스리더

NFS (Network File System) 네트워크 파일 시스템
NIC (Network Information Center) 네트워크 정보 센터
node 노드, 절점
notebook computer 노트형 컴퓨터
NTP Network Time Protocol 네트워크 타임 프로토콜

O

object-oriented 오브젝트 지향
octal 8진법
octet 옥텟
off-line 오프라인
off-the-shelf 기성품
on-board 내장, 탑재된
on-line 온라인

online service 온라인 서비스
operating system OS; 오퍼레이팅 시스템
operator 오퍼레이터
option 옵션, 임의 선택
output 출력
output device 출력 장치
output port 출력 포트

P

packet 패킷
packet switching 패킷 스위치, 교환
paint software 페인트 소프트
palmtop 팜톱
panel 패널
parallel 병렬
parallel I/O 병렬 입출력
parity 패러티
parity bit 패러티 비트
parity check 패러티 체크
parse 파스; 구문 해석 프로그램
partition 파티션
password 패스워드
paste 붙여넣기
peer-to-peer 대등하게
pen based computer 펜식 컴퓨터

performance 퍼포먼스, 성능
peripheral 주변장치
peripheral bus 주변장치 버스
PIO 병렬 입출력
pirate 저작권 침해자, 해적판 출판자
Pixel 픽셀
planfile 플랜파일
Platform 플랫폼
plug-and-play compatibility 플러그앤플레이 호환성
plug-in 플러그인(기능 확장용 소프트웨어)
pointer 포인터(기능장치식별자)
POP post office protocol 포스트 오피스 프로토콜
Popmail 팝메일
port 포트
port number 포트번호
portable computer 휴대용 컴퓨터

post 포스트
posting 포스팅
PostScript 포스트스크립트
PPP point to print protocol 포인트 대 포인트
　프로토콜
printer 프린터
processing 처리

processor 프로세서
program 프로그램
programming 프로그래밍 언어
protocol 프로토콜
provider 프로바이더
public database 공적인 데이터베이스
public domain 공적인 도메인

Q~R

query 조회, 질문
QWERTY QWERTY 키보드
RAM Random Access 랜덤 액세스 메모리
rate 비율, 속도, 요금
raw data 미가공 데이터
readme 리드미(먼저 읽어야 할 내용)
real-radio 리얼라디오(실시간으로 웹상에서
　음성을 들음)
real-time happens in the normal perception of
　time 리얼타임, 실시간
realtime chat 실시간 차트
reboot 다시 초기화함
record 레코드, 기록
redial 재다이얼하다
refresh 복원
register 레지스터(CPU 등의 고속기억장치)

reinitialize 다시 초기화함
relevance feedback 적당한 피드백
remote terminal 원격조작
reset 리셋
restore 복원
resume 재개하다
retrieve 검색, 구슬리다
RFC request for comments 코멘트요구
RGB Red, green, blue network 적, 녹, 청(컬
　러화상의 3원색)
RISC 축소명령세트컴퓨터
robotics 로봇공학
ROM 롬(읽기전용기억장치)
root 루트
Ruby 루비

S

scan 스캔
scan rate 스캔율
scanner 스캐너
screen 화면
script 스크립트
search engine 검색엔진
segment 세그먼트(프로그램의 일부분)
sendmail 센드메일
serial 연속적인, 직렬의
Serial Server 연속서버
server 서버
service provider 서비스제공업자
shareware 쉐어웨어(무료, 소액으로 제공되는

　소프트웨어)
shield 실드
sign up 사인업
signature file 서명 파일
Silicon Valley 실리콘밸리
site 사이트, 장소, 위치
Smalltalk 잡담, 한담
smart card 스마트카드
SMTP (simple mail transfer protocol)
　간단한 메일 전송 프로토콜
Snail Mail 스네일 메일(이메일에 비해 시간이
　걸리는 기존의 보통우편)
software package 소프트패키지

source program 소스 프로그램
Spam 스팸
spell check dictionary 스펠 체크 사전
spreadsheet 스프레드 시트, 표계산 소프트
SQL (Structured query language)
　구문 쿼리언어
SSH (star network) 스타 네트워크
stylus 자동기록계기의 바늘

subnet mask 서브넷마스크
surfing 서핑
switched access 스위치식 액세스
synchronous 동기식
SYSOP system operator 시스템 오퍼레이터
system manager 시스템 매니저
systems software 시스템 소프트웨어

T

tag 태그
taskbar 태스크바
TCP/IP transmission control protocol/internet protocol
　네트워크 프로토콜의 하나
telnet 텔넷
template 템플리트
Terabyte 테라바이트
Terminal 터미널

terminal emulation 터미널 에뮬레이션
Terminal Server 터미널 서버
thread 스렛(같은 화제에 관한 일련의 투고)
time out 타임아웃(시간 경과에 따라 접속을 종료시킴)
token ring network 토큰링 네트워크
trackball 트랙볼
trunk 트렁크

U

UNIX 유닉스
upgrade 업그레이드
upload 업로드
URL universal resource locator
　유니버설(표기)

Usenet News 유즈넷 뉴스
user name 사용자 이름
user-friendly 사용하기 쉬운
utility program 유틸리티 프로그램

V

Veronica 베로니카
virtual 버츄얼
virtual reality 버츄얼리얼리티(가상현실)
virus 바이러스
virus scanner 바이러스 스캐너

virus shield 바이러스 실드
voice recognition 음성 인식
VON (Voice on the net) 넷 상의 음성
VRML (virtual reality modeling language)
　가상현실의 모델 언어

W

WAN (wide area network) 광역 통신네크워크
Watermark 워터마크
web board 웹보드

web browser 웹브라우저
web master 웹마스터
white pages 화이트페이지

부록

white board 화이트보드
whois 호이즈(넷 상의 단체개인의 정보를 검색
하는 기능)
wide band 와이드밴드
wild card 와일드카드
word processing 워드처리

X~Z

X-Modem X모뎀
X-Window X윈도우
YAHOO 야후
(인터넷 웹사이트 검색 소프트웨어의 하나)
Yellow Book 옐로북(넷 상의 홈페이지 검색

workstation 워크스테이션
World-Wide-Web 월드와이드웹
WYSIWYG what you see is what you get
본 것은 무엇이든 손에 넣는다는 제록스사가
개발한 콘셉트

소프트웨어)
Y-Modem Y모뎀
Zip 집(특수한 압축 데이터, 기억장치)
Z-Modem Z모뎀